Fodor's 06

D0051658

CROATIA & SLOVENIA

1st Edition

**Where to Stay and Eat
for All Budgets**

**Must-See Sights
and Local Secrets**

Ratings You Can Trust

Fodor's Travel Publications   New York, Toronto, London, Sydney, Auckland
www.fodors.com

FODOR'S CROATIA & SLOVENIA, 1ST EDITION

Editor: Douglas Stallings

Editorial Production: David Downing

Editorial Contributors: Mark Baker, John K. Cox, Jane Foster, Tim Gosling, Betsy Maury, Paul Olchváry, Marijana Oroz

Maps: David Lindroth, *cartographer;* Rebecca Baer and Bob Blake, *map editors*

Design: Fabrizio La Rocca, *creative director;* Guido Caroti, *art director;* Moon Sun Kim, *cover designer;* Melanie Marin, *senior picture editor*

Production/Manufacturing: Colleen Ziemba

Cover Photo (Dalmatia): SIME s.a.s./eStock Photo

SPECIAL SALES

This book is available at special discounts for bulk purchases for sales promotions or premiums. Special editions, including personalized covers, excerpts of existing books, and corporate imprints, can be created in large quantities for special needs. For more information, write to Special Markets/Premium Sales, 1745 Broadway, MD 6-2, New York, New York 10019, or e-mail specialmarkets@randomhouse.com.

AN IMPORTANT TIP & AN INVITATION

Although all prices, opening times, and other details in this book are based on information supplied to us at press time, changes occur all the time in the travel world, and Fodor's cannot accept responsibility for facts that become outdated or for inadvertent errors or omissions. So **always confirm information when it matters,** especially if you're making a detour to visit a specific place. Your experiences—positive and negative—matter to us. If we have missed or misstated something, **please write to us.** We follow up on all suggestions. Contact the Croatia & Slovenia editor at editors@fodors.com or c/o Fodor's at 1745 Broadway, New York, NY 10019.

PRINTED IN THE UNITED STATES OF AMERICA

10 9 8 7 6 5 4 3 2 1

Be a Fodor's Correspondent

Your opinion matters. It matters to us. It matters to your fellow Fodor's travelers, too. And we'd like to hear it. In fact, we *need* to hear it.

When you share your experiences and opinions, you become an active member of the Fodor's community. That means we'll not only use your feedback to make our books better, but we'll publish your names and comments whenever possible. Throughout our guides, look for "Word of Mouth," excerpts of your unvarnished feedback.

Here's how you can help improve Fodor's for all of us.

Tell us when we're right. We rely on local writers to give you an insider's perspective. But our writers and staff editors—who are the best in the business—depend on you. Your positive feedback is a vote to renew our recommendations for the next edition.

Tell us when we're wrong. We're proud that we update most of our guides every year. But we're not perfect. Things change. Hotels cut services. Museums change hours. Charming cafés lose charm. If our writer didn't quite capture the essence of a place, tell us how you'd do it differently. If any of our descriptions are inaccurate or inadequate, we'll incorporate your changes in the next edition and will correct factual errors at fodors.com *immediately.*

Tell us what to include. You probably have had fantastic travel experiences that aren't yet in Fodor's. Why not share them with a community of like-minded travelers? Maybe you chanced upon a beach or bistro or B&B that you don't want to keep to yourself. Tell us why we should include it. And share your discoveries and experiences with everyone directly at fodors.com. Your input may lead us to add a new listing or highlight a place we cover with a "Highly Recommended" star or with our highest rating, "Fodor's Choice."

Give us your opinion instantly at our feedback center at www.fodors.com/feedback. You may also e-mail editors@fodors.com with the subject line "Croatia & Slovenia Editor." Or send your nominations, comments, and complaints by mail to Croatia & Slovenia Editor, Fodor's, 1745 Broadway, New York, NY 10019.

You and travelers like you are the heart of the Fodor's community. Make our community richer by sharing your experiences. Be a Fodor's correspondent.

Happy traveling!

Tim Jarrell, Publisher

CONTENTS

CLOSEUPS

MAPS

ABOUT THIS BOOK

Our Ratings

Sometimes you find terrific travel experiences and sometimes they just find you. But usually the burden is on you to select the right combination of experiences. That's where our ratings come in.

As travelers we've all discovered a place so wonderful that its worthiness is obvious. And sometimes that place is so unique that superlatives don't do it justice: you just have to be there to know. These sights, properties, and experiences get our highest rating, Fodor's Choice, indicated by orange stars throughout this book.

Black stars highlight sights and properties we deem **Highly Recommended,** places that our writers, editors, and readers praise again and again for consistency and excellence.

By default, there's another category: any place we include in this book is by definition worth your time, unless we say otherwise. And we will.

Disagree with any of our choices? Care to nominate a place or suggest that we rate one more highly? Visit our feedback center at www.fodors.com/feedback.

Budget Well

Hotel and restaurant price categories from ¢ to **$$$$** are defined in the opening pages of each chapter. For attractions, we always give standard adult admission fees; reductions are usually available for children, students, and senior citizens. Want to pay with plastic? **AE, DC, MC, V** following restaurant and hotel listings indicate whether American Express, Diner's Club, MasterCard, and Visa are accepted.

Restaurants

Unless we state otherwise, restaurants are open for lunch and dinner daily. We mention dress only when there's a specific requirement and reservations only when they're essential or not accepted—it's always best to book ahead.

Hotels

Hotels have private bath, phone, TV, and air-conditioning and operate on the European Plan (aka EP, meaning without meals), unless we specify that they use the Continental Plan (CP, with a continental breakfast), Breakfast Plan (BP, with a full breakfast), or Modified American Plan (MAP, with breakfast and dinner) or are all-inclusive (including all meals and most activities). We always

list facilities but not whether you'll be charged an extra fee to use them, so when pricing accommodations, find out what's included.

Many Listings

★ Fodor's Choice
★ Highly recommended
⊠ Physical address
✛ Directions
🕮 Mailing address
☎ Telephone
🖷 Fax
🌐 On the Web
✉ E-mail
💶 Admission fee
🕒 Open/closed times
► Start of walk/itinerary
Ⓜ Metro stations
🚋 Credit cards

Hotels & Restaurants

🏨 Hotel
🛏 Number of rooms
⚲ Facilities
🍽 Meal plans
✕ Restaurant
🗢 Reservations
🏛 Dress code
🚭 Smoking
🍸 BYOB
✕🏨 Hotel with restaurant that warrants a visit

Outdoors

🏌 Golf
⛺ Camping

Other

☺ Family-friendly
🔢 Contact information
⇨ See also
⊠ Branch address
☞ Take note

WHAT'S WHERE

ZAGREB & ENVIRONS	Croatia's interior capital isn't the most visited in Europe for good reason: it's provincial, inconveniently located, and not chock-full of unique artistic or architectural wonders. Even the Croatians agree it lacks the stature of Vienna, Prague, or Budapest. That said, travelers will find a charming, well-kept national seat that evokes a distant Habsburg past and a pretty Upper Town lined with lively cafés and restaurants. Northwest of the city is the castle district of the Zagorje. From Zagreb, good roads lead to the coast, where Plitvice National Park—a spectacular series of 16 lakes cascading from one to the other nestled in a wild forest—is about halfway to Zadar.
SLAVONIA	The least-visited part of Croatia still has much to offer the adventurous traveler. The regional cultural center, Osijek, is filled with churches and Habsburg-era architecture. Bird-watchers may be drawn to the vast wetlands of Kopačice Rit Nature Park. And then there's Vukovar, a sobering reminder that this region is still rebuilding from the war of the early 1990s. Throughout Slavonia, you'll find more charming villages and quiet rural life than almost anywhere else in the country. Come if you want to get away from the hordes of tourists and experience a part of the country that's not often seen.
ISTRIA	The red-tiled roofs of Venetian Rovinj and the Roman amphitheater at Pula make this region feel more Italian than Croatian. A vibrant café scene and culinary delights like air-dried ham and truffles all add to *la dolce vita* of Istria. Croatia's western peninsula is well-situated, especially if you want to combine your trip with a foray into Slovenia or northern Italy. Pula and the western coast are the highlights, but a drive into the interior will reward with pretty medieval villages and vineyards.
KVARNER	Protected by mountain ranges on three sides, Kvarner enjoys a particularly mild climate. Even in winter, the weather here is rarely as cold as it is in the rest of the country. The jewel of the Kvarner is Opatija, with its yellow turn-of-the-20th-century hotels lining the main street and a long promenade along the Adriatic. Opatija in its heyday was a favorite winter getaway for the Habsburgs; today, you can still get a whiff of that faded grandeur in some of the hotel dining rooms and patios. In Rijeka, which is more an active port town and less a tourist attraction, you can get a more authentic Croatian atmosphere than in most other places on the coast. And from Rijeka, the islands of Cres, Krk, and Losinj are easily accessible by car via modern bridges.

WHAT'S
WHERE

ZADAR & NORTHERN DALMATIA	Zadar doesn't rival Split or Dubrovnik for ancient ruins, but it's a good base if you want to explore the interior and still get the feeling of the laid-back Dalmatian seaside. If you want an even quieter place, check out nearby Nin. Zadar is about midpoint on the Dalmatian coast. In its own right, Zadar has quite a few good museums and the impressive Church of St. Donat, a 9th-century Byzantine church built on the site of a Roman forum. There's good access to the 89-island Kornati archipelago from nearby Murter, as well as to the fast highway back to Zagreb.
SPLIT & CENTRAL DALMATIA	Aside from Zagreb, second-city Split has the best transport connections in Croatia. There's an international airport, train and bus stations, and (in the summer, at least) a busy ferry port. If you are looking for someplace less busy, then consider nearby Trogir. The main attraction in Split is Diocletian's over-the-top palace, which dominates the Old Town; it was built in the 4th century to house the retiring Roman emperor, who spared no expense to make it a luxurious home. You're also in a great position to set out island-hopping, either to the pretty island of Vis, the sandy beaches of Brač, or the relaxing atmosphere of Hvar.
DUBROVNIK & SOUTHERN DALMATIA	Few cities in the world impress as Dubrovnik does, with its ancient walls and towers perched above the deep, blue waters of the Adriatic. Even before you get here, it's hard to imagine the beauty of the place. Once the wealthy, semi-independent city-state of Ragusa, Dubrovnik has an interesting history as both a Roman and Slav city. It's a busy place today, so avoid the summer months if you can, when lots of day trippers clog the Old Town. If you need to escape, strike out for Korčula, which was Marco Polo's birthplace, or quiet Lopud, or even quieter Mljet, which was off-limits to tourists during the Tito years.
SLOVENIA	With dirt-cheap airfares from London, Ljubljana is a good first stop if you're looking for a gentle entry into the region on the way to Istria and Kvarner. Slovenia itself is the size of New Jersey, so Ljubljana is only a four-hour train ride from Istria's southernmost tip in Pula. The laid-back capital, gracefully situated on the Ljubljanica River, provides a good jumping-off point to explore the rest of the country: the Julian Alps and lakes to the north, or the Skočjanske or Postojnkse caves to the southwest.

QUINTESSENTIAL CROATIA & SLOVENIA

Ljubljana Tržnica

Ljubljanček begin their weekend routine with a trip to the bustling *tržnica* (Central Market) located near the Three Bridges. It's a charming European scene of old; students, families, and retired people come to buy their fresh produce, many toting traditional straw baskets and arriving by bicycle. Most people spend the balance of the morning there, buying fresh fruits and vegetables, drinking coffee or even an early schnapps with friends, and then eventually stopping for lunch in the lower level of the fish market for kalamari na žaru (grilled calamari) or local trout. The market in Ljubljana couldn't be better situated: on the leafy banks of the Ljubljanica River in an elegant structure purpose-built by local architect, Jože Plěcnik. The building, combined with some of the highest-quality seasonal produce in Central Europe, makes a Saturday trip to the market a local pleasure not to be missed.

Dalmatian Summer

For all Croatians, summer holidays mean Dalmatia. Every family has its favorite spot on the coast, and every person remembers their blissful childhood holidays on Dalmatia with the most detailed accuracy. Tales of Istrian wine, *paski sir* (goat cheese from the island of Pag), and fresh sea bass enjoyed in a simple seaside restaurant feature heavily in the national memory. Whether a holiday means a wooded campsite in a national park, a sandy beach on Brah, or a small pension on Losinj, summer holidays begin and end for Croatians on their own splendid coast. Roads, accommodations, and ferry travel along the coast have improved over the years, turning Dalmatia into an international tourist destination. After you've relaxed for a week or more, soaking up the sun Dalmatian-style, you'll ask the same question the Croatians do: Why go anywhere else?

If you want to get a sense of contemporary Croatian and Slovenian culture, and indulge in some of its pleasures, start by familiarizing yourself with the rituals of daily life. These are a few highlights—things you can take part in with relative ease.

Naturism

Like it or not, there's a long history of naturism in Croatia, and this country has been one of the most progressive in pioneering the nude resort. Naturist campsites, beaches, and even sailing charters abound in certain parts of the coast (mainly Istria), and hundreds of thousands flock here each year to enjoy some fun in the sun *au naturel*. Naturism in Croatia goes back before World War II, when a leading Viennese naturist developed a beach on the island of Rab. Since then, a thriving culture of naturism has taken root, mainly among European enthusiasts. A glossy brochure published by the Croatian National Tourist Board lists 14 naturist "camps" and "villages" and about as many officially designated "free naturist beaches" on the country's Adriatic coast. Croatians themselves don't seem to make up the bulk of the clientele at naturist resorts, but they graciously make visitors welcome.

Rakija

Get one or two Croatians together, and somebody's bound to introduce *rakija,* a distilled herbal or fruit spirit that makes up an important part of Croatian culture. All across the country business deals are sealed, friendships are cemented, and journeys are begun to the clink of a few shot glasses of the fiery schnapps. Croatians often brew rakija themselves at home, using everything from plums and pears to herbs and juniper berries. In the countryside you can often find roadside stands selling the family blend with pride. Rakija is also enjoyed in Slovenia, where it often begins a meal as an aperitif. If you're game to order one on your travels in the region, start first with the sweeter, fruitier brews (blueberry is a good choice), and then work your way up to the somewhat digestive herbals.

IF YOU LIKE . . .

Pleasures at Sea

Croatia and Slovenia offer prime opportunity to spend time by the clear blue waters of the Adriatic. Each of these unique pleasures is designed to highlight the mysteries of life by the sea. This list of favorites makes for unforgettable vacation memories.

- **Hvar Town, Central Dalmatia.** A favorite destination among the yachting fraternity, Hvar remains completely at ease with its age-old beauty: medieval stone houses are built around a natural harbor and backed by a hilltop fortress.

- **Strolling around Piran's sea wall at sunset, Istria.** It's hard to imagine a more romantic and relaxed setting: the warm sea breezes invigorate as you stroll by the charming marina with the shadow of *Trg Tartini* behind you.

- **Zlatni Rat, Bol, Central Dalmatia.** The spectacular beach on the island of Brač is the jewel of the Adriatic: white, sandy, and lapped on three sides by the gentle blue sea.

- **A walk on the Lungomare in Opatija, Kvarner.** Built in 1889, this 12-km (7½-mi) promenade along the sea leads from the fishing village of Volosko, through Opatija—passing in front of old hotels, parks, and gardens and around yacht basins—and all the way past the villages of Ičići and Ika to Lovran in the south.

- **An excursion to Mljet, Southern Dalmatia.** A long, thin island of steep, rocky slopes and dense pine forests, Mljet is one of Croatia's most remote islands. One of Croatia's few sand beaches, Saplunara, is at its southeastern tip, which remains relatively wild and untended.

Soft Adventure

National parks abound in Slovenia and Croatia, with surefire opportunities to commune with the great outdoors. In every season, there are peaks to climb, seas to dive in, and white-water rivers to conquer. The thrills are more thrilling in Slovenia. Here are some of our favorite spots for those seeking a bit of soft adventure.

- **Biking around Lake Bohinj, Slovenia.** You can enjoy some easy pedaling along tiny country roads, through dairy farms and villages right out of the 19th century, with the Julian Alps in the background.

- **Rafting on the Soča River, Slovenia.** Rafting the Soča River: A rush of adrenaline strikes you as you fly across the bracing blue and green waters that run through unspoiled national forest.

- **Diving in Kvarner Bay.** Diving in the crystal-clear waters of Kvarner Bay—particularly near the islands of Cres and Losinj—is an eye-opening experience. Just remember that the most thrilling sights below the waves are usually wrecks.

- **Hiking in Risnjak National Park, Kvarner.** The thick pine forest, meadows that are stuffed with wild flowers in the spring, and limestone peaks, crevices, and caves cover around 30 square km (18½ square mi).

Boutique Hotels

Slowly but surely local entrepreneurs in Slovenia and Croatia are renovating historic properties and opening boutique hotels. These properties are where you'll find peace and quiet (and usually good food), not to mention owners who are committed to making your stay special.

- **Villa Angelo D'Oro, Rovinj, Istria.** This enchanting hotel opened in 2001 and has already gained an excellent reputation. In a beautifully restored 16th-century building, rooms are individually furnished with antiques and quality fabrics.

- **Hotel Vestibul Palace, Split, Central Dalmatia.** Luxury and romance are combined in this small boutique hotel within the walls of Diocletian's Palace, as minimalist designer details are played off against exposed Roman stone and brickwork.

- **Pučić Palace, Dubrovnik, Southern Dalmatia.** Showing the new direction of Croatian tourism, this small luxury hotel occupies a romantic baroque palace in Dubrovnik's Old Town.

- **Dvorac Bezanec, Zagorje, Zagreb & Environs.** This lovely old manor house 15 minutes east of Veliki Tabor, is a renovated 17th-century castle complete with period furniture and authentic fittings. Enjoy the beautiful landscape of the Zagorje with old-fashioned frills.

- **Kendov Dvorec, Slovenia.** A lovingly restored villa filled with period furnishings in an idyllic rural setting. The owner will go out of her way to cater to your every need.

Roman History

The cultural and historical richness of Croatia make it a destination that satisfies even the most well-traveled visitor. All over the country, there are ruins of former civilizations and empires that give you a glimpse of the country's past. A trip to this list of favorites will enrich any vacation to Croatia.

- **Diocletian's Palace, Split.** Roman Emperor Diocletian's summer palace built in the 3rd century AD is one of the most spectacular sites in all of Croatia. It's unmissable.

- **The Arena, Pula.** Designed to accommodate 22,000 spectators, the Arena is the sixth-largest building of its type in the world (after the Colosseum in Rome and similar arenas in Verona, Catania, Capua, and Arles), and one of the best preserved.

- **Crkva sv Donata, Zadar.** Zadar's star attraction, this huge, cylindrical structure is the most monumental early Byzantine church in Croatia.

- **Eufrazijeva Basilica (St. Euphrasius Basilica), Poreč.** This is among the most perfectly preserved Christian churches in Europe and one of the most important monuments of Byzantine art on the Adriatic.

- **Katedrala Sveti Lovrijenac (Cathedral of St. Lawrence), Trogir.** A perfect example of the massiveness and power of Romanesque architecture, the most striking detail is the main portal, decorated with minutely carved stonework during the 13th century.

IF YOU LIKE . . .

Summer Nightlife

Seaside nightlife in Croatia and Slovenia generally doesn't disappoint. All over the coast people are enjoying themselves outside most evenings, sipping trendy cocktails, listening to music, or tasting the local wine. Even the smallest village on the coast is littered with outdoor cafés and bars in the summertime. If you find yourself near any of these this summer, join in the fun!

- **Dubrovnik Summer Festival, Southern Dalmatia.** The world-renowned summer festival in Dubrovnik offers quality theatrical performances and classical-music concerts with international performers, all set against the backdrop of the azure Adriatic.

- **Aquarius, Zagreb.** Having climbed out of its post-war depression, Zagreb is once again alive at night. Aquarius is the top spot for dancing 'til dawn—in the summer and all year-round.

- **Carpe Diem, Hvar, Central Dalmatia.** A harborside cocktail bar with a summer terrace is where Hvar's richest and most glamorous visitors come to see and be seen. Stop in here to see why Hvar has been labeled the next Ibiza.

- **Enigma, Jelsa, Central Dalmatia.** Tiny but stylish, Jelsa combines a White Lounge and Cocktail Garden serving champagne and cocktails with a late-night club attracting international guest DJs.

- **Ambasada Gavioli, Izola, Slovenia.** Gavioli, southwest of the Izola port in the city's industrial area, remains one of the coast's and the country's best clubs. DJs are regularly brought in from around the world to play techno, trance, funk, and fusion.

Going Native

You can find gustatory pleasures at every level in Slovenia and Croatia. Sometimes the ones to seek out are the favorites of the locals, who don't allow restaurants to rest on their laurels. Whether it's a snack at a market stall or a simple seaside restaurant, one of the great pleasures of travel is finding these popular spots. All of these are favorites for their commitment to local, seasonal food.

- **Slavonska Kuća, Osijek, Slavonia.** This small, local restaurant is about as atmospheric as can be. If you stick to the local specialties, you'll enjoy a fine introduction to Slavonian cuisine.

- **Restauracija Topli Val, Kobarid, Slovenia.** Family-run and informal, this restaurant—connected to the Hotel Hvala—serves some of the best fish in Slovenia. It's worth a special stopover if you're on your way north to Bovec and Kranjska Gora.

- **Konobe Kod Sipe, Sali, Northern Dalmatia.** This rustic favorite is known for serving some of the freshest fish dishes in town. Fishnets hanging from the ceiling's wooden beams plus an outdoor terrace shaded by grapevines add to the homey atmosphere.

- **Sirius, Losinj, Kvarner.** The national press claim that this would be a top contender for best restaurant in the country if it were open year-round, so deserved is its reputation for fresh seafood.

- **Vodnjanka Restaurant, Vodnjan, Istria** This is the place to go for the most mouthwatering homemade pastas dishes you can imagine, not least *fuži* with wild arugula and prosciutto in cream sauce—delicious.

Wining & Dining

A vacation wouldn't be a vacation if you didn't seek out some of the country's finest dining. All of the following have built their reputation on first-rate cuisine and an impressive wine list to match.

- **Adio Mare, Korčula, Southern Dalmatia.** The menu at this renowned eatery hasn't changed since it opened in 1974: traditional Dalmatian seafood and Balkan meat specialties, prepared over burning coals. Dinner here is unforgettable.

- **Enoteca Al Gastaldo, Rovinj, Istria.** Walls lined with wine bottles create a warm and intimate atmosphere in this sophisticated eatery, hidden away in the Old Town. Indulge in spaghetti with either truffles or crab or fresh fish prepared over an open fire.

- **Katunar, Krk Town, Vrbnik, Kvarner.** The wines produced on Krk Island are among the best in Croatia. The torch-lit grill is the place for dinner, but the experience is all about the wine.

- **Valsabbion, Pula, Istria.** This superb restaurant was one of the first in Croatia to specialize in what has come to be known as "slow food" and has been voted the best restaurant in Istria as well as Croatia several times. The menu changes regularly, but you can expect such delights as frogfish in vine leaves or tagliatelle with aromatic herbs and pine nuts.

- **Paviljon, Zagreb.** The Italian-inspired menu of this chic restaurant includes dishes such as tagliatelle with prosciutto and asparagus, crispy roast duck on red cabbage with figs, and oven-roasted monkfish with breadcrumbs, pine nuts, and thyme.

Natural Wonders

Croatia and Slovenia are not short on natural wonders. The unusual Karst terrain of this region has created caves and waterfalls and made a home for many species of wildlife. Many of the region's best natural areas are now protected as national parks that are accessible throughout the year.

- **Nacionalni Park Plitvička Jezera, Velika Poljana, Zagreb & Environs.** One of the first-class natural areas in Croatia, this national park has 16 cascading lakes nestled in a protected forest.

- **Skočjanske Jama, Slovenia.** The breathtaking, enormous underground cavern is so deep it looks as if it could hold the skyscrapers of Manhattan.

- **Kornati National Park, Zadar, Northern Dalmatia.** More than 100 remote islands here are privately owned. Although anything but lush today, their almost mythical beauty is ironically synonymous with their barrenness: the bone-white to ochre colors represent a striking contrast to the azure sea.

- **Brijuni Archipelago, Istria.** Designated a national park in 1983, this group of 14 islands north of Pula has long been a vacation retreat par excellence for almost 2,000 years. Yugoslav leader Marshal Josip Broz Tito brought famous guests here from the world over. Today, you can come, too.

- **Krka National Park, Central Dalmatia.** The Krka River and surrounding waterfalls compete with Plitvice for dramatic scenery. The park is home to all sorts of flora and fauna, including a wildlife sanctuary.

GREAT ITINERARIES

SLOVENIA & ISTRIA

Ljubljana makes an excellent starting point if your trip is meant to cover both countries in a week. You'll get the mountains and the seaside, city and countryside, and a first-class Roman ruin. This itinerary is best done by car, but it can be done (perhaps a bit more slowly) by train and bus.

Day 1: Ljubljana
Prešernov trg is a good place to begin a walking tour of Ljubljana. Native son Joe Plenik designed the Three Bridges, the Dragon Bridge, and the central market hall at Vodnik Square, and you get a good view of them all as they cradle the blue-green Ljubljanica river from here. Stroll through the market hall for a look at the season's best fruits and vegetables. Head into the Old Town and wander along the pretty cobblestoned streets up to the castle and admire the view over the city. Head back down and do some shopping at the stylish boutiques around Stari trg. ⇨ Ljubljana *in* Chapter 8.

Day 2: Lake Bled & Bohinj
Travel north toward Triglav National Park and stop in Radovljica at the Čebelarski Muzej (Beekeeping Museum) on the way up. Stop for an overnight in picture-perfect Lake Bled and row a boat out to the island church if the weather is nice. Spend the afternoon walking the perimeter of the lake and checking out Vila Bled, one of Tito's former residences. Next morning, explore the equally beautiful but more rustic Lake Bohinj in the Triglav National Park. ⇨ Lake Bled & Bohinj *in* Chapter 8.

Day 3: Day Trip to Kobarid & Bovec
Head back to Ljubljana via the mountainous Soča Valley and stop first in Kobarid,

the site of an award-winning World War I museum. Try to imagine that you are standing in what was once one of the bloodiest fields of battle between the Italians and Slovenes. From there move on to Bovec for an afternoon of rafting, fishing, or just admiring the clear, aquamarine waters of the Soča River. Try fresh trout with *tržaška* (garlic and parsley) sauce for lunch at any one of the homey *gostišces*. In good weather, take a hike or bike ride in the area. ⇨ Kobarid & Bovec *in* Chapter 8

Day 4: Day Trip to Skočjanske Jame & Štanjel
Southwestern Slovenia has many stalactite and stalagmite caves to choose from but our favorite is the UNESCO World Heritage site, Skočjanske Jame. The caves are set deep in the rugged karst and are fed by the river Reka, which is deep upstream, then disappears under the cave and then reappears to empty into the Adriatic north of Trieste. Take a drive and stop for lunch in Štanjel. The walled old town offers some of the prettiest views of the vineyard-dotted countryside. Head back to Ljubljana for another night. ⇨ Skočjan Jame & Štanjel *in* Chapter 8.

Day 5: Piran & Rovinj
Depart from Ljubljana and head south to the coast, stopping for lunch in Piran. Check out lovely Trg Tartini and the Church of St. George on Cathedral Hill and take in the sweeping view of the Adriatic Sea. Make a quick visit to the Maritime Museum. From here, get in the car and head to Istria. Cross the Croatian border and push on to Rovinj in the afternoon in time to

enjoy the sunset over the Brijuni islands that evening. Have dinner at a seaside restaurant, spend the night and explore the Venetian houses and Church of St. Euphemia in the morning. ➪ Piran *in* Chapter 8 and Rovinj *in* Chapter 3.

Day 6: Pula

From Rovinj head south to Pula and spend part of the day exploring the incredible Roman amphitheater. This is one of the best preserved sites in the Roman world. After walking about the Roman forum and amphitheater as well as the 6th Century Church of Mary Formosa, take a ferry to the Brijuni Islands for the afternoon and see the zoo and tropical gardens that Tito designed. Spend the night in Pula. ➪ Pula *in* Chapter 3.

Day 7: Motovun & Ljubljana

Head back to Slovenia via the Istrian interior. Drive north through Pazin and get out of the car for a quick glance at the Pazin Castle. North of Pazin, stop in the hill towns of Motovun or Grožnjan for lunch and breathtaking views. These medieval villages are in the heart of truffle country so keep your eyes open for some fresh goods to bring home. Continue north toward to Ljubljana. ➪ Motovun *in* Chapter 3 and Ljubljana *in* Chapter 8.

TIPS

❶ This itinerary is well served by bus, although you'll have to take a bit more time on the interior stops in both Slovenia (Skočjanske Jame and Štanjel) and Croatia (Motovun and Grožnjan).

❷ In July and August the main coastal artery connecting the west coast of Istria is crowded with tour buses and RVs. Consider driving in the evening between destinations.

❸ Istria's coast is rocky so don't plan a beach holiday without rubber water shoes and a roll-up cushion for under your beach towel. These items are widely available in tourist shops along the coast but they cost dearly, so bring your own.

❹ Slovenian roads are well paved and maintained. This level of efficiency comes at a price; there are frequent toll stops on all the highways throughout the country. Keep some small denominations (1,000, 500, 100 SIT notes and change) with you when driving through Slovenia.

GREAT ITINERARIES

ZAGREB, KVARNER & THE INTERIOR

Croatia's capital, Zagreb, will introduce you to the language and customs of the country quickly. It's a good base if you want to explore a combination of the seaside and the interior. Tourist offices are well equipped with information on the country's national parks, ferry schedules, and sailing charters. Guided tours and accommodations can be arranged from here. Many international airline carriers have connections to Zagreb.

Day 1: Zagreb

Zagreb can best be explored by foot. Begin at the massive Trg Jelačića and check out the statue of Ban Josip Jelačić, hero of Croatian resistance to the Austro Hungarian empire. It's an imposing figure on an imposing square. From here walk to the funicular and head to the *Gornji Grad* (Upper Town). Stroll around the castle area and visit the Croatian Historical Museum. You'll get a glimpse of Croatia's recent history, including the controversial nationalism of the 1990's. From here, head back down to the Lower Town and check out *Ilica*, Zagreb's modern high street. Spend the night here. ⇨ Zagreb *in* Chapter 1.

Day 2: Day Trip to Krumrovec & Varaždin

Strike north to Zagorje and spend the morning seeing Varaždin, Croatia's onetime capital. Along the drive you'll see rolling hills dotted with medieval castles and churches. Varaždin's attraction is its gently restored Baroque old town, but historically it played an important role as a key defensive outpost for the Habsburgs against the onslaught of marauding Turks. Don't miss the massive fortress (Stari Grad).

From here, wind back to Krumrovec, an important historical city of a modern kind. It was here that Josip Broz Tito was born and although the museum detailing his life seems out of step with Croatia today, it has an interesting collection of Partisan memorabilia. ⇨ Krumrovec & Varǎzin *in* Chapter 1.

Day 3: Risnjak National Park

From Zagreb head southwest toward Rijeka stopping off at Delnice and the Risnjak National Park, gateway to the Gorski Kotor, the unspoiled forested karst. This is a beautiful place for a nature walk to check out all kinds of protected flora and fauna. From here, proceed toward Opatija via Rijeka. ⇨ Risnjak National Park *in* Chapter 4.

Day 4 & 5: Opatija

Plan to spend a couple of relaxing days in Opatija as the highlight of this itinerary. Although the city doesn't offer much in the way of architectural or historical gems, once you see the palm trees lining the streets, you'll see this is a place for winding down, Habsburg-style. Choose one of the atmospheric, turn-of-the-century hotels for a little slice of nostalgia and settle in with a good book. Should you visit in winter, you'll find the weather downright Mediterranean. Take time to stroll along the 12-km- (7½-mi-) long promenade that faces the sea. If you get antsy for more seaside diversity, plan instead one night in Opatija and one night in Cres or Losinj. The islands—with their attractive Venetian town squares—have a different character altogether. ⇨ Opatija, Cres & Losinj *in* Chapter 4.

Day 6: Plitvice National Park

After you've been rejuvenated by a day or two by the sea, you'll be ready for a change of pace. Head southeast back toward the interior in the direction of Plitvice National Park. Plitvice is a naturally occurring water world, with cascading pools and waterfalls connecting each other. This is one of Croatia's biggest tourist sites and has been for years, so the park is well protected and organized. Consider getting a map and exploring the lakes, which cover about 300 square km (186½ square mi) on your own. The park is well marked but the guided tours only take you to the highlights. Relax in the evening when the tour buses have gone home and spend the night here at a nearby hotel. ⇨ Plitvice Lakes *in* Chapter 1.

Day 7: Zagreb

Head back toward Zagreb and find lodging in the city center. The next morning, check out the *Dolac* (market hall) in the Kaptol section of the upper town for a look at the city's fresh produce, meats, sausages, and souvenirs. Have a *burek* here and pick up some last minute trinkets to take home. Stroll back through to *Donji Grad* (Lower Town) and visit the Archaeological Museum and Strossmayer Gallery, two of the city's best attractions (*see* Zagreb *in* Chapter 1.

TIPS

❶ Consider renting a car for the trip to Krumovec and Varăzdin so that you can drive around the Zagorje. The rolling hills in this area are dotted with baroque castles, country houses, and lovely hilltop churches.

❷ The closest ferry crossing from Opatija to Cres and Losinj is at Brestova in Istria. If you plan to make your way there with your car for the day in the height of summer, count on a wait. The ferry operates in the winter as well and is much less crowded then.

❸ Don't plan to visit Plitvice National Park without good walking shoes and a rain slicker. Even on the guided tours, a walk through the forest takes you on wooden bridges and paths that can be muddy and damp. The tour can be even sloppier if you explore on your own.

❹ Since Plitvice is on the main highway from Zagreb to Zadar and further down the coast, consider seeing the park on a weekday. Traffic (even with the new highway) can be horrendous on the weekends in July and August.

GREAT ITINERARIES

SPLIT, DUBROVNIK & THE DALMATIAN COAST

Both Split and Dubrovnik have international airports so this itinerary could be reversed if you want to fly into Dubrovnik. Both cities are popular in summer so be warned: you won't be sightseeing by yourself in August. In some respects, this itinerary can be best enjoyed without a car as traffic and parking in high season are frazzling aspects of the southern Dalmatian coast. A little advance research about ferry schedules at the time of your travel (ferry and hydrofoil service is significantly reduced in the off season) can make this a pleasant, mostly seafaring itinerary. Try to start your week-long trip on a weekday (Monday to Monday, for example) instead of on the weekend so that your weekends are spent on a quiet island instead of bustling Split or Dubrovnik.

Day 1: Split
Arrive in Split and head to a hotel (which you booked months ago) or take one of the many private rooms available around town. Accommodations in Split can be surprisingly limited. Spend this first day getting your bearings and exploring the Meštrović Gallery and the Archaeological Museum, two of the city's best museums. Save the full day for Diocletian's Palace tomorrow. ⇨ Split *in* Chapter 6.

Day 2: Diocletian's Palace
Get up early and head into the *Grad,* the old town area that once encompassed Diocletian's palace. You'll need a whole day to explore the palace, but the area is best seen by foot. Sit in the open peristil and admire the imperial quarters, the Cathedral of St. Domnius and the Egyptian black sphinx. Walk through the Grad area notic-

ing all the different styles and materials used in the construction and renovation of the palace. Head out of the eastern Iron Gate to find a good spot for lunch and then continue along the *Riva* toward Marjan for a relaxing afternoon by the sea. ⇨ Split *in* Chapter 6.

Day 3: Island Hopping
Take one of the ferries or catamarans from Split to Brač, Hvar, or Vis and spend the night in an island paradise. This is the heart of Dalmatia, after all, and these islands are the stuff of glossy tourist brochures. Book your accommodations in advance in the summer months, or try to book a private room through an agency in Split. In summer, ferries, hydrofoils, and catamarans operate regularly to the islands. Rent a bike or scooter once you've landed and tour the backroads where you can find uncrowded coves and beaches. ⇨ Brač, Hvar & Vis *in* Chapter 6.

Day 4 & 5: Dubrovnik
Get back in the car or, if traveling without one, take the bus or ferry to Dubrovnik. The arrival by ferry is more dramatic because you'll see one of the prettiest fortified cities in the world as it was meant to be seen: from the sea. From this view, you can tell why Dubrovnik (formerly Ragusa) was once master of all of Dalmatia. Choose a hotel slightly outside of the city walls as the crowds flock there daily in high season. Have lunch in one of the many fish restaurants near the fish market and enjoy some Dalmatian wine. Save the sightseeing for the late afternoon, when the cruise-ship day-trippers have departed. Stroll

along the *placa* in the early evening with the locals, stopping along the way for some Italian-style ice cream. ⇨ Dubrovnik *in* Chapter 7.

Day 6: Elafiti Islands

The great thing about the Elafiti islands is that they're very close to Dubrovnik, so you can easily make a day trip out here if you're pressed for time. A trip out to one of the islands is ideal for a final wind down before the week's end. Most of the islands have no cars and are sparsely populated so it's just you and the sparkling Adriatic out there. Logun has the best overnight accommodations if you have an extra day, or for the wilderness seekers a trip to farther flung Mljet is rewarding in its forested beauty and serenity. All the islands have regular service in the summer, and hydrofoils and fast catamarans can get you there in half the time as the ferry. In winter there is limited boat service from Dubrovnik. ⇨ Elafiti Islands *in* Chapter 7.

Day 7: Split

Day 7 will most likely be a travel day, no matter if you travel by car or ferry. Have one last seafood lunch in a restaurant with a view of the sea, buy a bottle of Dalmatian wine to take home, and vow to come back next year. ⇨ Split *in* Chapter 6.

TIPS

❶ Don't take a car to the islands. Ferry reservations for cars must be made well in advance. Once you're there, it's easy enough to get around by bus or rented scooter.

❷ Be wary of *soba* (room) offers. Although many are legitimate private rooms, there are unscrupulous vendors out there hard at work in high season. Have a map ready and mark where the accommodation is. Some properties are so far away that your one or two days in Dubrovnik will be spent navigating the local bus routes rather than enjoying the city.

❸ Ask your concierge or host for local restaurant recommendations. A fair number are closed for the winter months. In high season (and especially during the Dubrovnik Summer Festival) many of the restaurants along the Prijeko aggressively market themselves to tourists and a meal here can have less than relaxing aspects (overcharging, gruff service).

WHEN TO GO

The tourist season in Slovenia and Croatia generally runs from April through October, peaking in July and August. The Dalmatian coast is busy all summer long. Early booking is essential in July and August when most of the summer festivals take place. Roads back from the coast are clogged with returning European tourists in the late-summer weekends. Spring and fall can be the best times to visit, when the heat has abated somewhat at the coast and the days are long.

The Slovenian countryside is prettiest in the fall, when the leaves are changing, although the peak season is July and August. The coastal resorts are enjoyable in June or September, when accommodations and parking are more readily available. In a good year, the ski season in Slovenia lasts from mid-December through March. Slovenian ski slopes tend to be less crowded than nearby Austrian or Italian resorts.

Climate

Croatia enjoys a long, hot summer that's usually dry. Southern Dalmatia can still be mild in October, when the first cold snap has already hit in the interior, although swimming then may be only for the brave. Wet winters are the norm for most of the country, making a trip here in January or February somewhat rainy and cold. Winters on the coast are milder but still wet. Kvarner, sheltered on three sides by mountain ranges, has a short, temperate winter and an early spring. It remains mild throughout the summer.

Slovenia's weather is similar to Croatia's although it's less wet as a rule. Ljubljana, which sits in a basin, is overcast most of the winter, but a quick drive out of town will often reveal sunshine in the rest of the country. The Julian Alps get similar weather to the Austrian Alps to the north: cold in December and January, sunny in February and March. Summer months are ideal for hiking and biking in the mountains.

The above graphs show the average daily maximum and minimum temperatures for major cities in the region.

⚡ Forecasts Weather Channel Connection ☎ 900/932-8437 95¢ per minute ⊕ www.weather.com.

ON THE
CALENDAR

	For exact dates and further information about events in Croatia, check the Croatian National Tourist Board Web site (⊕ www.croatia.hr). For dates and information about events in Slovenia, the Web site of the Slovenian Tourist Board (⊕ www.slovenia-tourism.si) has the details.
WINTER February	Rijeka stages its own **Karneval,** giving Croatia the second-biggest Carnival celebration in Europe after Venice. **Kurentovanje** in Ptuj, Slovenia, is the largest and most spectacular of numerous Carnival celebrations throughout the country. In an arcane pagan rite, men wearing sheepskin coats ring big cowbells to usher in both spring and fertility.
SPRING March	The **World Cup Ski-jump Championship** is held at Planica, Kranjska Gora, in Slovenia.
April	In alternate years Zagreb, Croatia's capital, hosts a **Biennale,** an international festival of contemporary music. It's attended by both the heavy hitters of the classical world as well as groundbreaking pioneers. Check out ⊕ www.biennale-zagreb.hr for up-to-date information.
SUMMER June	**Lent Festival** in Maribor, Slovenia, featuring music and dance events through June and July, opens with the traditional *Rafters' Baptism* on the River Drava. **Druga Godba,** a one-week festival of alternative and world music, takes place in Ljubljana.
July	The Roman Arena in Pula makes Istria a stunning venue for the five-day **Pula Film Festival.** Around the same time, the five-day **International Folklore Festival** in Zagreb attracts folklore groups from Eastern Europe and beyond, staging music and dance in traditional costume.
July and August	Practically every island and city up and down the Dalmatian coast has some kind of music festival in July and August, most taking place in a pretty church or palazzo on the Old Town square. Check with local tourist offices once you arrive for what's going on that week. Croatia's largest and most prestigious cultural event, the **Dubrovnik Summer Festival** (⊕ www.dubrovnik-festival.hr/default.asp?jezik=2.com), draws international artists and musicians and features drama, ballet, concerts, and opera, all performed on open-air stages within the city fortifications. Similarly, the **Split Summer Festival** hosts opera, theater, and dance events at open-air venues within the walls of Diocletian's Roman Palace. The **Motovun Film Festival** (⊕ www.motovunfilmfestival.com) highlights international independent films in a rustic medieval setting.

ON THE CALENDAR

	Slovenia is also abuzz throughout the summer with cultural and music festivals. The **International Jazz Festival** is held in Ljubljana in July, followed by the **International Summer Festival**, running through July and August, incorporating a range of events from classical music recitals to street theater. The **Primorski Summer Festival** of open-air theater and dance is staged in the coastal towns of Piran, Koper, Portorož, and Izola. **Piran Musical Evenings** are held in the cloisters of the Minorite Monastery in Piran, every Friday through July and August. The **Lace-making Festival** is held in Idrija in August, lasting one week.
July– September	In Porec, Croatia, the **Concert Season** in the Basilica of St. Euphrasius features eminent musicians from Croatia and abroad, with sacral and secular music from all periods played inside the magnificent 6th-century basilica.
FALL	
September	The **Kravji Bal** (Cow Ball) in Bohinj marks the end of summer and the return of Slovenian herdsmen and their cows from the mountain pastures to the valleys.
September and October	The **Varaždin Baroque Evenings** see eminent soloists and orchestras from Croatia and abroad perform baroque-music recitals in the city's most beautiful churches.
October	The **Ceremonial Grape Harvest** on October 1 marks the gathering of grapes from Slovenia's oldest vineyard, in Maribor. In Ljubljana, the **LIFFE International Film festival** plays host to independent films.
November	In Zagorje, Croatia, **Martinje (St Martin's Day)**, which is November 11, sees the blessing of the season's new wine, accompanied by a hearty goose feast and endless toasts. Slovenia, too, celebrates **St. Martin's Day** on November 11, which sees festivities throughout the country, culminating with the traditional blessing of the season's young wine.

SMART TRAVEL TIPS

The organizations listed in this section can provide information to supplement this guide; contact them for up-to-the-minute details, and consult the Essentials sections that appear in each chapter for facts that apply to the various regions of Croatia and Slovenia. Happy landings.

AIR TRAVEL

CARRIERS

There are no direct air connections between the United States and either Croatia or Slovenia, though some U.S.–based airlines offer codeshare flights through their European travel partners. Travelers from the United States must fly into a major European hub such as Amsterdam, London, Frankfurt, Budapest, Prague, Vienna, or Warsaw and then transfer to a flight to Zagreb, Split, or Dubrovnik. Connections are on national carriers (Croatia Airlines or Adria Airways) or another European-based carrier. Several European airlines offer connections to Slovenia and Croatia.

Adria Airways ☎ 020/7734-4630 in the U.K., 01/369-1010 in Slovenia ⊕ www.adria-airways.com. **Aer Lingus** ☎ 800/474-7424 in the U.S., 0845/084-4444 in the U.K. ⊕ www.flyaerlingus.com. **Air France** ☎ 800/237-2747 in the U.S, 0870/142-4343 in the U.K. ⊕ www.airfrance.com. **Alitalia** ☎ 800/223-5730 in the U.S., 0870/544-8259 in the U.K. ⊕ www.alitaliausa.com in the U.S.; www.alitalia.co.uk in the U.K. **Austrian Airlines** ☎ 800/843-0002 in the U.S., 020/7766-0300 in the U.K. ⊕ www.aua.com. **British Airways** ☎ 800/247-9297 in the U.S., 0870/850-9850 in the U.K. ⊕ www.britishairways.com. **Continental** ☎ 800/523-3273 in the U.S., 0845/607-6780 in the U.K. ⊕ www.continental.com. **Croatia Airlines** ☎ 020/8563-0022 in the U.K., 02/413-776 in Croatia ⊕ www.croatiaairlines.hr. **Czech Airlines** (CSA) ☎ 212/223-2365 in the U.S., 0870/9443-747 in the U.K. ⊕ www.csa.cz. **Delta** ☎ 800/221-1212 in the U.S., 0800/414-767 in the U.K. ⊕ www.delta.com. **KLM Royal Dutch Airlines** ☎ 800/225-2525 in the U.S., 0870/507-4074 in the U.K. ⊕ www.klm.com. **LOT Polish Airlines** ☎ 800/223-0593 in the U.S., 0870/414-0088 in the U.K. ⊕ www.lot.com. **Lufthansa** ☎ 800/645-3880 in the U.S., 0870/8377-747 in the U.K. ⊕ www.lufthansa.com. **Malév Hungarian Airlines** ☎ 212/566-9944 in the U.S., 0870/909-0577 in the U.K.

⊕ www.malev.hu. **Northwest** ☎ 800/225-2525 in the U.S., 0870/507-4074 in the U.K. ⊕ www.nwa. com. **United** ☎ 800/538-2929 in the U.S., 0845/ 844-4777 in the U.K. ⊕ www.ual.com.

EUROPE-BASED DISCOUNT AIRLINES

Traveling to Slovenia or Croatia using a combination of a major U.S. airline and a low-cost European airline is a good idea. If you are traveling to Istria or Slovenia, a budget flight to nearby Venice (2½ hours to Ljubljana by car or train) or Trieste (1½ hours to Ljubljana or Rijeka by car or train) is an option. Most of these discount airlines sell tickets only on the Internet. Just be aware that "London"-based discount airlines rarely fly from Heathrow. All these airlines have stringent baggage limits and offer few free inflight services, if any. And if you transfer from a major airline to a discounter, you may need to reclaim your bags and re-check them, so make sure you leave plenty of time between your flights.

EasyJet flies from London to Ljubljana and Venice. German Wings flies to Split and Zagreb from Cologne-Bonn and Stuttgart, and to Zagreb from Hamburg; the airline also has flights from London–Stansted to Cologne-Bonn and Stuttgart and from London–Gatwick to Hamburg. Ryan Air flies from London to Trieste and Venice. Sky Europe flies to Dubrovnik, Split, and Zadar from Bratislava or Budapest.

🚹 **EasyJet** 🕾 no phone ⊕ www.easyjet.com. **German Wings** ☎ 870/252-1250 ⊕ www.germanwings. com. **Ryanair** 🕾 090/6270-5656 in the U.K., 353/ 1-249-7791 worldwide ⊕ www.ryanair.com. **Sky Europe Airlines** 🕾 090/5722-2747 in the U.K., 421/ 4850-4850 worldwide ⊕ www.skyeurope.com.

FLYING TIMES

Flying time from London to Zagreb is 2 hours, 30 minutes; from Prague to Zagreb it is 1 hour, 30 minutes; and from Warsaw it is 1 hour, 40 minutes.

Flying time from London to Ljubljana is 1 hour, 20 minutes; from Bratislava to Dubrovnik is 1 hour, 25 minutes; from Budapest to Dubrovnik is 1 hour, 15 minutes; from London to Venice is 2 hours, 10 minutes.

TICKETS

Most domestic airline tickets are electronic; international tickets may be either electronic or paper. With an e-ticket, the only thing you receive is an e-mailed receipt citing your itinerary and reservation and ticket numbers. The greatest advantage of an e-ticket is that if you lose your receipt, you can simply print out another copy or ask the airline to do it for you at check-in. You usually pay a surcharge (usually at least $25) to get a paper ticket, if you can get one at all. The sole advantage of a paper ticket is that it may be easier to endorse over to another airline if your flight is cancelled and the airline with which you booked can't accommodate you on another flight.

Domestic air tickets in Slovenia and Croatia are best purchased through travel agents or airport offices in city locations. Airports in both countries have offices for the national airlines (Croatian Airlines in Croatia and Adria Airlines in Slovenia) but their opening hours are unreliable, and attempting to purchase a ticket at the airport may backfire. Both the national airlines have usable Web sites where e-tickets can be purchased.

BOOKING ONLINE

The best deals may or may not be on airline, hotel, or car rental Web sites. You really have to shop around. A travel wholesaler such as Hotels.com or Hotel-Club.net can be a source of good rates, as can a discounter such as Hotwire or Priceline, particularly if you can bid for your hotel room or airfare. Indeed such sites sometimes have deals that are unavailable elsewhere. They do, however, tend to work only with hotel chains (which make them limiting and just plain useless for getting hotel reservations outside of major cities) or big airlines (so that leaves out upstarts like jetBlue and Southwest, but also sometimes airlines like Air-India). Finally, with discounters and wholesalers, you must generally prepay, and everything is nonrefundable.

Booking engines like Expedia, Travelocity, and Orbitz are actually travel agents, albeit high-volume, online ones. And those airline travel packagers, such as American Airlines Vacations or Virgin Vacations—they're travel agents, too. But they may still not work with all the world's airlines and hotels.

Since all Web sites aren't created equally, it's wise to use an aggregator site, which will search through many sites and pull the best prices for airfares, hotels, and rental cars from them. Most aggregators compare the major travel-booking sites such as Expedia, Travelocity, and Orbitz; some also look at airline Web sites, though rarely the sites of smaller budget airlines. Some aggregators also compare other travel products, including complex packages—a good thing as you can sometimes get the best overall deal by booking an air-and-hotel package.

⚡ Booking Engines Cheap Tickets ⊕ www.cheaptickets.com. **Expedia** ⊕ www.expedia.com. **Hotwire** ⊕ www.hotwire.com also allows bidding. **lastminute.com** ⊕ www.lastminute.com specializes in last-minute travel. The main site is for the U.K., but there is also a link to a U.S. site. **Onetravel.com** ⊕ www.onetravel.com. **Orbitz** ⊕ www.orbitz.com. **Priceline.com** ⊕ www.priceline.com also allows bidding. **Travelocity** ⊕ www.travelocity.com.

⚡ Aggregators Kayak ⊕ www.kayak.com also looks at cruises and vacation packages. **Mobissimo** ⊕ www.mobissimo.com. **Qixo** ⊕ www.qixo.com also compares cruises, vacation packages, and even travel insurance. **Sidestep** ⊕ www.sidestep.com also compares vacation packages and lists travel deals. **Travelgrove** ⊕ www.travelgrove.com also compares cruises and vacation packages.

⚡ Airlines & Airports Airline and Airport Links.com ⊕ www.airlineandairportlinks.com has links to many of the world's airlines and airports.

⚡ Airline Security Issues Transportation Security Agency ⊕ www.tsa.gov/public has answers for almost every question that might come up.

FLYING TODAY

Flying may not be as care-free as it once was, but there are some things you can do to make your trip smoother.

Don't stand in a line if you don't have to. Buy an e-ticket, check in at an electronic kiosk, or—even better—check in on your airline's Web site before you leave home. If you don't need to check luggage, you could bypass all but the security lines.

Arrive when you need to, not before. Always ask about your airline's policy. It's usually at least an hour before domestic flights and two to three hours for international flights. But many airlines now have more stringent advance check-in requirements at some busy airports. The TSA estimates the waiting time for security at most major airports and publishes the information on its Web site.

Get to the gate. If you aren't at the gate at least 10 minutes before your flight is scheduled to take off (sometimes earlier), you won't be allowed to board.

Double-check your flight times. Do this especially if you have made your reservations far in advance. Airlines change their schedules, and alerts may not reach you.

Don't go hungry. Fewer airlines are providing free food for passengers in economy class. If you're scheduled to fly during meal times, verify if your airline offers anything to eat; even when it does, be prepared to pay.

Get the seat you want. Often, you can pick a seat when you buy your ticket on an airline's Web site. But it's not always a guarantee, particularly if the airline changes the plane after you book your ticket; check back before you leave. Avoid seats on the aisle directly across from the lavatories. Most frequent fliers say those are even worse than the back-row seats that don't recline.

Check your scheduling. Don't buy a ticket if there is less than an hour between connecting flights. Although schedules are usually padded, if anything goes wrong, you might miss your connection. Also, if you're traveling to an important function, consider departing a day early lest a delay make you miss out on the event.

Bring paper. Even when using an e-ticket, always carry a hard copy of your receipt; most airports now require a boarding pass to get past security.

Complain at the airport. If your baggage goes astray or your flight goes awry, complain before you ever leave the airport. Most carriers require that you file a claim immediately.

Beware of overbooked flights. Particularly during busy travel seasons and around holiday periods, if a flight is oversold, the gate agent will usually ask for volunteers and will offer some sort of compensation if you are willing to take a different flight. If you are bumped from a flight *involuntarily*, the airline must give you some kind of compensation if an alternate flight can't be found within one hour.

Know your rights. If your flight is delayed because of something within the airline's control (so bad weather doesn't count), then the airline has a responsibility to get you to your destination on the same day, even if they have to book you on another airline and in an upgraded class if necessary. Read your airline's Contract of Carriage; it's usually somewhere on the airline's Web site, though usually buried.

Be prepared. The Boy Scout motto is especially important if you're traveling during a stormy season. Be prepared to quickly adjust your plans by programming a few numbers into your cell: your airline, an airport hotel or two, your destination hotel, and/or your travel agent. Bring snacks, water, and sufficient diversions, and you'll be covered if you get stuck in the airport, on the Tarmac, or even in the air during turbulence.

AIRPORTS

In Croatia, most international flights arrive at Zagreb (ZAG); however, there are also many connecting flights from various European airports to Split (SPU) and Dubrovnik (DBV), and even a few to Pula, Rijeka (RJK), and Zadar (ZAD). Almost all flights into Slovenia arrive at Ljubljana (LJU).

⚠ Croatia Dubrovnik Airport ☎ 020/773-377 ⊕ www.airport-dubrovnik.hr. **Rijeka Airport** ☎ 051/842-132 ⊕ www.rijeka-airport.hr. **Split Airport** ☎ 021/203-171 ⊕ www.split-airport.hr. **Zadar Airport** ☎ 023/313-311 ⊕ www.zadar-airport.hr. **Zagreb Airport** ☎ 01/626-5222 ⊕ www.zagreb-airport.hr.
⚠ Slovenia Brnik Airport ✉ Ljubljana ☎ 04/206-1981 ⊕ www.lju-airport.si. **Maribor Airport** ☎ 02/629-1175 ⊕ www.maribor-airport.si. **Portorož Airport** ☎ 05/672-2525 ⊕ www.portoroz-airport.si.

BOAT & FERRY TRAVEL

Several companies run ferries from Italy to Croatia. The most popular route, which is offered by all ferry services, is Ancona to Split. Jadrolinija also runs services from Bari to Dubrovnik and from Ancona to Zadar. From June to September, SNAV runs a daily high-speed catamaran service between Ancona and Split. Jadrolinija and SEM are based in Rijeka and Split, respectively. Adriatica is based in Venice, and SNAV is based in Ancona.

From early March to late October the *Prince of Venice* hydrofoil makes regularly scheduled trips between Venice and Portorož. From mid-July to mid-September, the Italian firm Adriatica runs a round-trip service from Trieste, calling at Piran and stopping at several towns on the Croatian Adriatic coast.

⚠ Boat & Ferry Companies Adriatica ☎ 041/781-611 in Venice, Italy ⊕ www.adriatica.it ✉ Cankarjevo nab 7, Piran, Slovenia ☎ 05/674-6508. **Jadrolinija** ☎ 051/211-444 ⊕ www.jadrolinija.hr. **Prince of Venice** (Kompas Turizem,) ✉ Obala 41, Portorož ☎ 05/617-8000. **SEM** ☎ 021/338-292 ⊕ www.sem-marina.hr. **SNAV** ☎ 071/207-6116 in Ancona, Italy.

BUS TRAVEL

Bus travel in both Slovenia and Croatia is inexpensive and efficient. During the high season, the worst you'll have to put up with is crowded buses. Most buses heading out to tourist sites like Škojanske Jama or Plitvice National Park will be air-conditioned, but ask before you buy your ticket, especially if it's a blistering hot day. Buses from Zagreb to the coast get booked up quickly in the summer, so once you know your travel dates you should purchase your ticket. The bus is the best option if you are traveling from Zagreb to Slavonia and don't wish to rent a car.

Slovenian timetables can be found online in English; Croatian timetables can be found online, but the Web site is mostly in Croatian.

⚠ Timetables Croatia: **Autobusni kolodvor Zagreb** ⊕ www.akz.hr. Slovenia: **Avtobusna postaja Ljubljana** ⊕ www.ap-ljubljana.si.

BUSINESS HOURS

In Croatia business hours are from 8:30 to 4. Banks are open in all the main cities weekdays from 7 to 7, and on Saturday from 7 AM to 11 AM; in smaller towns, banks have shorter hours and are often closed during lunchtime. Post offices are open weekdays 7 to 7, and on Saturday from 7 to noon; in smaller towns, post offices are open shorter hours, sometimes only in the morning. During the high tourist season (June through September), post offices are generally open until 9 PM, including Saturday. In Zagreb, shops and department stores are open weekdays 8 to 8, and on Saturday from 8 to 1. Along the coast, most shops are open weekdays from 8 to 1 and 5 to 8, Saturday from 8 to 1. On the islands hours vary greatly from place to place, but usually at least one general store will be open Monday through Saturday for essentials.

In Slovenia, most banks are open weekdays from 9 to noon and 2 to 4:30, and Saturday from 9 to 11. The main museums are open Tuesday through Sunday 10 to 6. Larger shops are open Monday through Saturday from 10 to 6, whereas smaller ones may open mornings only from 10 to 2. Most stores are closed Sunday.

CAMERAS & FILM

Never pack film in checked luggage; X-ray machines used to view checked luggage are extremely powerful and will ruin your film. U.S.–airport X-ray machines will usually not harm film (whether exposed or unexposed), digital cameras, videotape, or computer disks, but film will become clouded after repeated exposure on long trips (more than 10 screenings). You can ask for a hand inspection, but your request may not be granted. Better, use a lead-lined bag to protect your film; if this results in hand-inspection, it will usually include all your hand luggage. Be prepared to turn on your camera or camcorder to prove to airport security personnel that the device is real.

The *Kodak Guide to Shooting Great Travel Pictures* (available at bookstores everywhere) is loaded with tips.
⚡ Photo Help **Kodak Information Center** ☎ 800/ 242-2424 ⊕ www.kodak.com.

VIDEOS

Due to differing television systems, VHS tapes bought in Croatia and Slovenia (which use the PAL standard) are not compatible with U.S. machines (which use the NTSC standard). DVDs bought in Croatia and Slovenia are not compatible with American DVD machines, either, since they are in different regions.

CAR RENTAL

When you reserve a car, ask about cancellation penalties, taxes, drop-off charges (if you're planning to pick up the car in one city and leave it in another), and surcharges (for being under or over a certain age, for additional drivers, or for driving over state or country borders or out of a specific radius from your point of rental). All of these things can add substantially to your costs. Request car seats and extras such as GPS when you book.

Rates are sometimes—but not always— better if you book in advance or reserve through a rental agency's Web site. There are other reasons to book ahead, though: for popular destinations, during busy times of the year, or to ensure that you get a certain type of car (vans, SUVs, exotic sports cars, or an automatic transmission).

Make sure that a confirmed reservation guarantees you a car. Agencies sometimes overbook, particularly for busy weekends and holiday periods.

Your driver's license may not be recognized outside your home country. International driving permits (IDPs), which can be used only in conjunction with a valid driver's license, translate your license into 10 languages. Permits ($10) are available from the AAA and the National Automobile Club.

Traveling by car is a good way to see Croatia and Slovenia, giving you the freedom to flee a crowded seaside beach and take refuge in the relatively unpopulated interior if the mood strikes you. In both Slovenia and Croatia, excursions to the national parks are best done by car so that you can take in all the sites, not just the ones the tour bus shows you. Highways in both countries are well-maintained and tolls frequent, so have some small change with you when on the road. The quality of interior roads varies; in Slovenia, they're better than you'd expect and in Croatia they can be surprisingly poor. The main artery along the Croatian coast—*the magistrala*—can come to a stand-still on summer weekends, so traveling between popular coastal destinations is best done on weekdays when there's less turnover in package vacations. A new highway from Zagreb to Zadar and Split was completed in 2005; there are plans to continue it down the coast to Dubrovnik. This should ease up the summer traffic considerably.

Unfortunately, rental cars in Croatia and Slovenia are expensive. Even if you rent locally, companies charge a daily and weekly rate that is generally higher than in most American cities. For an economy car (Opel Corsa or Renault Twingo) you're likely to pay upwards of $50 per day in Croatia (slightly less from local rental agencies), even more if you need an automatic transmission. Most companies are represented in the main tourist areas and airports. The easiest way to book a rental car from abroad is on the Internet.

▶ Major Agencies Alamo ☎ 800/462-5266 in the U.S. and Canada ⊕ www.alamo.com. **Avis** ☎ 800/230-4898 in the U.S., 800/272-5871 in Canada, 0870/606-0100 in the U.K. ⊕ www.avis.com. **Budget** ☎ 800/462-5266 in the U.S. and Canada, 0870/156-5656 in the U.K. ⊕ www.budget.com. **Dollar** ☎ 800/800-3665 in the U.S. and Canada, 0149/475-1600 in the U.K., where it has combined operations with Thrifty ⊕ www.dollar.com. **Hertz** ☎ 800/654-3001 in the U.S. and Canada, 0870/844-8844 in the U.K. ⊕ www.hertz.com. **National Car Rental** ☎ 800/227-7368 in the U.S. and Canada, 0870/400-4552 in the U.K. ⊕ www.nationalcar.com.

▶ Local Agencies Autorent In Slovenia ☎ 051/601-804 ⊕ www.rentacarslo.com. **Mack Car Rental** In Croatia ☎ 01/369-4555 ⊕ www.mack-concord.hr.

▶ Wholesalers Auto Europe ☎ 888/223-5555 ⊕ www.autoeurope.com. **Eurovacations** ☎ 877/471-3876 ⊕ www.eurovacations.com. **Kemwel** ☎ 877/820-0668 ⊕ www.kemwel.com.

▶ Automobile Associations U.S.: **American Automobile Association (AAA)** ⊕ www.aaa.com; most contact with the organization is through state and regional members. **National Automobile Club** ☎ 800/622-2136 ⊕ www.thenac.com; membership is open to California residents only. U.K.: **The Auto-**mobile Association (AA) ☎ 0870/600-0371 ⊕ www.theaa.com. Canada: **Canadian Automobile Association (CAA)** ☎ 613/247-0117 ⊕ www.caa.ca.

INSURANCE

Everyone who rents a car wonders about whether the insurance that the rental companies offer is worth the expense. No one—not even us—has a simple answer. This is particularly true abroad, where laws are different than at home.

If you own a car, your personal auto insurance may cover a rental to some degree, though not all policies protect you abroad; always read your policy's fine print. If you don't have auto insurance, then seriously consider buying the collision- or loss-damage waiver (CDW or LDW) from the car-rental company, which eliminates your liability for damage to the car. Some credit cards offer CDW coverage, but it's usually supplemental to your own insurance and rarely covers SUVs, minivans, luxury models, and the like. If your coverage is secondary, you may still be liable for loss-of-use costs from the car-rental company. But no credit-card insurance is valid unless you use that card for *all* transactions, from reserving to paying the final bill. All companies exclude car rental in some countries, so be sure to find out about the destination to which you are traveling.

Diner's Club offers primary CDW coverage on all rentals reserved and paid for with the card. This means that Diner's Club's company—not your own car insurance—pays in case of an accident. It *doesn't* mean your car-insurance company won't raise your rates once it discovers you had an accident.

Some countries require you to purchase CDW coverage or require car-rental companies to include it in quoted rates. Ask your rental company about issues like these in your destination. In most cases, it's cheaper to add a supplemental CDW plan to your comprehensive travel insurance policy (⇨ Trip Insurance *under* Things to Consider *in* Getting Started, *above*) than to purchase it from a rental company. That said, you don't want to pay for a supplement if you're required to buy insurance from the rental company.

In Slovenia, quoted rates will include both CDW and theft insurance. A compact car costs around €80 for 24 hours, with unlimited mileage. You'll need a credit card to rent. Agencies can be found in all major towns and at the Brnik Airport, north of Ljubljana.

In Croatia, CDW and theft insurance are not included in the base rate, so you'll have to add them if you don't have any other protection using your credit card. This hidden cost makes car rentals in Croatia expensive, so it's best to shop around. A compact car with CDW and theft insurance costs about 500 Kn for 24 hours in Croatia, with mileage 2.08 Kn per km (½ mi). Car-rental agencies can be found at airports and major tourist destinations.

REQUIREMENTS & RESTRICTIONS

In Croatia and Slovenia, an International Driver's Permit is not necessary to rent a car from a major agency; a valid driver's license is all you'll need. If you intend to drive across a border (as you must do if you drive from Dubrovnik to southern Dalmatia, stopping briefly in Bosnia-Herzegovina) ask about **restrictions on driving into other countries.** The minimum age required for renting is usually 21 or older, and some companies also have maximum ages; be sure to inquire when making your arrangements.

CAR TRAVEL

In Croatia, having a car certainly gives you greater mobility in rural areas on the mainland but causes endless complications if you plan to go island hopping. In high season, cars can wait for hours to board ferries even if you have made reservations. In addition, parking in coastal resorts is very restricted, and there are tolls on a number of highways throughout the country. Depending on where you plan to go, it might be a better idea to rent a car only on those days when you need one.

In Slovenia, traveling by car undoubtedly gives you the chance to reach remote areas of the country when and as you wish. Main roads between large towns are comparable to those in Western Europe. Highways charge a toll depending on the route and distance traveled. But you won't need a car if you plan to stay only in Ljubljana.

AUTO CLUBS

🄵 In Croatia & Slovenia Croatia: Hrvatski Autoklub ☏ 1/661-1-999 ⊕ www.hak.hr. Slovenia: **Automobile Association of Slovenia** ✉ Dunajska 128, Ljubljana ☏ 01/530-5300 ⊕ www.amzs.si.

EMERGENCY SERVICES

In case of a breakdown, your best friend is the telephone. Try contacting your rental agency or the appropriate national breakdown service.

🄵 Croatia ☏ 987. **Slovenia** (Automobile Association of Slovenia) ☏ 1987.

GASOLINE

In Croatia, gas stations are open daily from 7 to 7; from June through September, many stations are open until 10. In the bigger cities and on main international roads some stations offer 24-hour service. All pumps sell Eurosuper 95, Super 98, Normal, and Eurodiesel.

In Slovenia, gas stations on border crossings and main roads leading to larger towns are open 24 hours a day, whereas others are open Monday to Saturday from 7 AM to 8 PM.

🄵 Croatian Fuel Prices INA ⊕ www.ina.hr.

PARKING

In Croatia, the historic centers of walled medieval towns along the coast (Split, Trogir, Hvar, Korčula, and Dubrovnik) are completely closed to traffic, putting heavy pressure on the number of parking spaces outside the fortifications.

In Slovenia's major towns parking spaces are marked with a blue line and a sign denoting time restrictions. Buy a ticket, obtainable from gas stations and newsstands; write down the time you parked; and attach it to your windshield.

ROAD CONDITIONS

In Croatia, the coastal route from Rijeka to Dubrovnik is scenic but tiring; it can be notoriously slippery when wet. During winter, driving through the inland regions of Gorski Kotar and Lika is occasionally made hazardous by heavy snow. It's advisable not to take a car to the islands, but if you do decide to drive, remember that the roads are narrow, twisty, and unevenly maintained.

Road conditions in Slovenia are generally good, with well-maintained and cleared roads in all seasons. In the mountains, where snowfall can be heavy, it's best to drive with snow tires in the winter months. Make sure your rental car has these if you rent during this period.

ROAD MAPS

In Croatia try the tourist-information services or gas stations and main bookstores.

In Slovenia road maps are available from larger bookshops and gas stations throughout the country. The Slovenian Tourist Board offers a comprehensive tourist map, free of charge.

RULES OF THE ROAD

Croatians drive on the right and follow rules similar to those in other European countries. Speed limits are 50 kph (30 mph) in urban areas, 80 kph (50 mph) on main roads, and 130 kph (80 mph) on motorways. Seatbelts are compulsory. The permitted blood alcohol limit is 0.05%; drunken driving is punishable and can lead to severe fines.

Slovenes drive on the right and are obliged to keep their headlights on at all times. Speed limits are 60 kph (37 mph) in urban areas and 120 kph (74 mph) on highways. Local drivers are courteous by European standards. The permitted blood alcohol level is 0.05%; drivers caught exceeding this level can expect penalties similar to those of other European countries.

CRUISES

Several Croatian ports, including Dubrovnik, Split, Hvar, Korčula, and Zadar, are common port calls for Eastern Mediterranean cruises. Small ships cruise up and down the country's coastline. For more information on cruising in Croatia, see the essay "Sailing and Cruising Croatia's Coast" in Understanding Croatia, at the end of this book.

To learn how to plan, choose, and book a cruise-ship voyage, consult *Fodor's FYI: Plan & Enjoy Your Cruise* (available in bookstores everywhere).

⚄ Major Cruise Lines Carnival Cruise Line ☎ 305/599-2600 or 800/227-6482 ⊕ www. carnival.com. **Celebrity Cruises** ☎ 305/539-6000 or 800/437-3111 ⊕ www.celebrity.com. **Cunard Line** ☎ 661/753-1000 or 800/728-6273 ⊕ www.cunard. com. **Holland America Line** ☎ 206/281-3535 or 877/932-4259 ⊕ www.hollandamerica.com. **Norwegian Cruise Line** ☎ 305/436-4000 or 800/327-7030 ⊕ www.ncl.com. **Princess Cruises** ☎ 661/753-0000 or 800/774-6237 ⊕ www.princess.com. **Seabourn Cruise Line** ☎ 305/463-3000 or 800/929-9391 ⊕ www.seabourn.com.

⚄ Regional Cruise Lines Cruise Adriatic ☎ 052/212-955 ⊕ www.cruisecroatia.com. **Dubrovnik Travel** ☎ 020/313-555 ⊕ www.dubrovniktravel.hr. **Elite Travel** ☎ 020/358-200 ⊕ www.elite.hr. **Katarina Line** ☎ 051/272-110 ⊕ www.katarina-line.hr.

CUSTOMS & DUTIES

You're always allowed to bring goods of a certain value back into your home country without having to pay any duty or import tax. There's also a limit on the amount of tobacco and liquor you can bring back duty-free, and some countries have separate limits for perfumes; for exact figures, check with your customs department. The value of so-called "duty-free" goods are included in these amounts. When you shop abroad, save all your receipts as customs inspectors may request to see them as well as the items you have purchased. If the total value of your goods is more than the duty-free limit, then you'll have to pay a tax (most often a flat percentage) on the value of everything beyond that limit.

As with most European countries, you can import duty-free 200 cigarettes, 1 liter of spirits, and 2 liters of wine into both Croatia and Slovenia. Foreign citizens can bring personal items into the country without paying customs taxes.

⚄ Australian Customs Service ☎ 02/9213-2000 or 1300/363-263, 02/9364-7222 or 1800/020-504 quarantine-inquiry line ⊕ www.customs.gov.au. **Canada Customs & Revenue Agency** ☎ 800/461-9999 in Canada only, 204/983-3500, 506/636-5064 ⊕ www. ccra.gc.ca. **New Zealand Customs** ☎ 09/300-5399 or 0800/428-786 ⊕ www.customs.govt.nz. **HM Cus-**

toms and Excise ☎ 0845/010-9000 or 0208/929-0152 advice service, 0208/929-6731 or 0208/910-3602 complaints ⊕ www.hmce.gov.uk. **U.S. Customs and Border Protection** ⊕ www.cbp.gov.

DINING

The standard of food in Slovenia is very high, with restaurants serving fresh fish, pasta, and vegetable dishes even in the dead of winter. There's a definite preference for seasonal foods, so if you come in October you'll find mushroom dishes everywhere; in April it's hard to find a menu in the country that doesn't feature asparagus. There are regional specialties, of course, but since the country is so small you can usually find these outside of the specific region, and certainly in Ljubljana.

Food in Croatia varies by region. You'll find some very good restaurants in Zagreb and the coast and some mediocre ones in the interior. Fish is always a good bet here, with local calamari and sea bass being real treats for the visitor. Truffle season in Istria is in late October, and that delicacy can be found on virtually every Istrian menu then.

Pizza, in both Slovenia and Croatia, is available in just about every city, town, or village. This is most often served at a sit-down restaurant making it a good choice for both families and vegetarians. It's usually served one pie per person, not by the slice. In general, pizza in Slovenia and Croatia is freshly baked, thin-crusted, and delicious. There are loads of unusual toppings, like pineapple, tunafish, frozen peas, and fried eggs in addition to the classic *margherita* (plain cheese). For information on food-related health issues *see* Health *below*.

MEALS & MEALTIMES

Unless otherwise noted, the restaurants listed in this guide are open daily for lunch and dinner.

As the working day begins early here (with some offices opening as early as 7:30 AM on weekdays), you'll find cafés open early as well. Lunch is usually served between noon and 3 in restaurants, and dinner is most often served after 7 or so. In the height of the tourist season at the coast,

restaurants may stay open later (after 10) to handle the volume. *Bifes* (stand-up take-out places) are open most of the day and serve both hot and cold food. Around 4 PM in Ljubljana and Zagreb you'll notice people filling up coffee shops for an afternoon fix of caffeine and perhaps some cake.

Even most basic lodgings in Croatia and Slovenia include some kind of breakfast (*zajtrk* in Slovene; *doručak* in Croatian) in the room rate. Savor it; breakfast outside your hotel may be limited to a small melted ham and cheese sandwich (known as a *toast*) in a café. Later in the morning, you can wander into a cake shop (*slaščičarna* in Slovene; *slastičarna* in Croatian) for a coffee and slice of cake. You may also find a *burek* (savory meat- or cheese-filled pastry) for breakfast at one of the streetside vendors near high traffic areas. Lunch (*kosilo* in Slovene; *ručak* in Croatian) is the main meal for many locals; it usually includes hot food and perhaps a soup. In major cities, there are now such lighter offerings as salads and pastas; you can sometimes find a few sandwich shops. On the coast you find grilled meats available throughout the day at snack bars near the beaches. Dinner (*večerja* in Slovene; *večera* in Croatian) is usually taken in a restaurant (*restavracija* in Slovene, *restoran* in Croatian) and tends to be a bit more formal than in the United States. Meals are often started with a soup, followed by grilled meat or fish, and dessert. The exception is at the coast, where lively, outdoor casual restaurants are the norm.

PAYING

Credit cards are becoming more and more accepted, but it's a good idea to ask before you order, just in case. ATM machines are found in abundance on the Croatian coast, as well as in Zagreb and Ljubljana, so you can usually ensure that dinner goes on as planned. Tips should not be included in the bill, so scrutinize any bill that appears to add one. If service has been good, a 10% to 15% gratuity will be appreciated by the waitstaff.

RESERVATIONS & DRESS

Regardless of where you are, it's a good idea to make a reservation if you can. In some places (Hong Kong or Paris, for example), it's expected. We only mention specifically when reservations are essential (there's no other way you'll ever get a table) or when they are not accepted. For popular restaurants, book as far ahead as you can (often 30 days), and reconfirm as soon as you arrive. (Large parties should always call ahead to check the reservations policy.) We mention dress only when men are required to wear a jacket or a jacket and tie.

WINES, BEER & SPIRITS
Wine is produced in both Slovenia and Croatia and enjoyed regularly with meals. Both countries consume more than they produce, so tasting some vintages here is a good idea since you're unlikely to find them at home. White wines from the Vipava valley in Western Slovenia are on par with Italian whites from just across the border: dry, fruity, and full-bodied. Croatia produces wine in Istria and in certain regions along the coast and it, too, is quite drinkable.

Cocktails are becoming popular as an aperitif but only in trendy places catering to a stylish and perhaps foreign crowd. The traditional aperitif in this part of the world is *rakija,* a fruit or herbal spirit made in abundance in both countries. It's fairly cheap to buy and varies greatly in quality. The fruit varieties (pear, blueberry) are drinkable enough as an aperitif; the herbals are a bit rough going down. Many establishments brew their own with great pride. If you're staying in a family-run pension, trying some of the home brew is an instant ice breaker.

FOR PEOPLE WITH DISABILITIES
Provisions for travelers with disabilities in Central Europe are extremely limited; probably the best solution is to travel with a companion who can help you. Coastal areas in Croatia are rocky, and wheelchair accessibility is limited. Old towns in both Slovenia and Croatia have cobblestone streets and are easy to manage with a wheelchair. Although many hotels, especially large international chains, offer some wheelchair-accessible rooms, special facilities at museums and restaurants and

on public transportation are still difficult to find. However, in Slovenia a law was passed in 1997 requiring all public buildings and infrastructure, including hotels, to be made fully accessible to people with disabilities.

🚹 Local Resources Croatia: **Hrvatska udruga paraplegičara** (Croatian Association of Paraplegics) ⊠ Park prijateljstva 1, Zagreb ☎ 01/3831-195 ⊕ www.hupt.hr. Slovenia: **Slovenian Union of People with Mobility Impairments** ⊠ Stihova 14, Ljubljana ☎ 01/432-7138.

🚹 Resources for Travelers with Disabilities Access-Able Travel Source ⊕ www.access-able.com includes links to all kinds of resources, agencies, and companies that serve travelers with disabilities. **Access Outdoors** ⊕ www.accessoutdoors.org focuses on resources that are useful to travelers who want to be active outdoors. *Emerging Horizons* ⊕ www.emerginghorizons.com focuses on issues facing disabled travelers; the Web site posts selected articles and includes a blog, daily news, and a forum for travelers to post questions for the editors. **Gimp on the Go** ⊕ www.gimponthego.com covers a wide range of travel-related issues of interest to disabled travelers, including a searchable database of accessible sights, hotels, etc. **Society for Accessible Travel & Hospitality** ☎ 212/447-7284 ⊕ www.sath.org seeks to raise awareness of issues affecting the needs of travelers with disabilities.

🚹 Travel Agencies & Tour Operators B. Roberts Travel ☎ 800/444-6540 or 585/256-1680 ⊕ www.brobertstravel.com offers escorted tours and cruise trips for travelers with mobility issues. **CareVacations** ☎ 780/986-6404 or 877/478-7827 ⊕ www.carevacations.com, provides specialized equipment, including wheelchair and oxygen-equipment rentals, for travelers with medical needs. The company specializes in renting equipment for cruises. **Flying Wheels Travel** ☎ 507/451-5005 ⊕ www.flyingwheelstravel.com is a full-service travel agency that specializes in the needs of travelers with disabilities.

ELECTRICITY
If your electrical device requires a heavy, expensive converter to make it work overseas, our advice is to leave it at home. (A hair dryer or curling iron is cheaper in most countries than an electrical converter.) Don't use 110-volt outlets marked FOR SHAVERS ONLY for high-wattage appliances such as hair dryers. Most laptops and mo-

bile-phone chargers operate equally well on 110 and 220 volts and so require only an adapter, but check the label on your adapter carefully. Electricity in Slovenia and Croatia is 220 volts; both countries use standard, European plugs with two round prongs.

⚡ Steve Kropla's Help for World Travelers ⊕ www.kropla.com has information on electrical and telephone plugs around the world. **Walkabout Travel Gear** ⊕ www.walkabouttravelgear.com has a good discussion about electricity under "adapters."

EMBASSIES

⚡ Embassies in Croatia Australian Embassy ✉ Nova Ves 11, Zagreb ☎ 01/489-1200 ⊕ www.auembassy.hr. **Canadian Embassy** ✉ Prilaz Gjure Deželića 4, Zagreb ☎ 01/488-1200. **U.K. Embassy** ✉ Vlaška 121, Zagreb ☎ 01/600-9100 ✉ U.K. Consulate in Dubrovnik, Petilovrijenci 2, Dubrovnik ☎ 020/311-466 ✉ U.K. Consulate in Split, Obala Hrvatskog Narodnog Preporoda 10, Split ☎ 021/341-464. **U.S. Embassy** ✉ Hebrangova 2, Zagreb ☎ 01/661-2200 ⊕ www.usembassy.hr.

⚡ Embassies in Slovenia Australian Consulate ✉ Trg Republike 3/XII, Ljubljana ☎ 01/425-4252 🖶 01/426-4721. **Canadian Consulate** ✉ Dunajska 22, Ljubljana ☎ 01/430-3570 🖶 01/430-3575. **U.K. Embassy** ✉ Trg Republike 3/IV, Ljubljana ☎ 01/200-3910 🖶 01/425-0174. **U.S. Embassy** ✉ Prešernova 31, Ljubljana ☎ 01/200-5500 🖶 01/200-5555.

EMERGENCIES

⚡ Croatia Ambulance ☎ 94. **Fire Emergencies** ☎ 93. **Police Emergencies** ☎ 92.

⚡ Slovenia Ambulance and Fire ☎ 112. **Automobile Association of Slovenia** (AMZS) ☎ 987 for 24-hour emergency roadside assistance. **Police** ☎ 113.

FAMILY TRAVEL

Travel in Slovenia and Croatia is generally safe for families with children; both countries have low crime rates and greet children warmly. However, while you'll find playgrounds in nearly every city, there isn't a lot of special attention paid to the needs of children. It's hit or miss as to whether you'll find a high chair in a restaurant, and very few have child-specific menus. Diaper-changing stations are virtually nonexistent in public places. Swimming pools at thermal spas seldom have lifeguards, so

children need to be closely watched by parents. The beaches at the coast can be rocky and unsuitable for small children. However, some malls have indoor creches, where children can be left for an hour or so under supervised care.

DOCUMENTATION

When a child is traveling with only one parent (or with someone other than a parent), it's always wise to send along a notarized letter giving the child permission to travel. Some airlines will not allow minor children to board without such a letter, though the exact requirements vary by destination.

DISCOUNTS & DEALS

Discounts for children (varying in age) are widely available in Slovenia and Croatia. Expect to pay less for your kids to enter museums, caves, thermal baths, and even some hotels. Sights and attractions that are especially appealing to children are indicated by a rubber-duckie icon (🦆) in the margin.

⚡ Family Travel Resources *Family Adventure* ⊕ www.familyadventuretravel.com is primarily devoted to locating travel companies to help you plan your family trip, but there is also an archive of articles from the magazine on all kinds of subjects, from African safaris to trips in U.S. national parks. **Family Fun** ⊕ familyfun.go.com has a section devoted to travel. **Family Travel Files** ⊕ www.thefamilytravelfiles.com has a lot of destination-specific articles on popular destinations for family travel as well as some general advice. The Web site sends out a free bimonthly newsletter to subscribers. **Family Travel Forum** ⊕ www.familytravelforum.com has general information, but you can also join the club to get discounts and access to additional feature stories and resources; a booking engine links to Expedia. *Outside* ⊕ www.outsidemag.com publishes a special issue every year on family adventure travel; articles from that issue are archived and available on the Web site. **Smarter Travel** ⊕ www.smartertravel.com, a Web site that is mostly a resource for travel deals, also has a section called "Family Traveler" with useful articles. **Travel With Your Kids** ⊕ www.travelwithyourkids.com is a Web site geared primarily to parents who are looking for advice on family travel abroad.

GAY & LESBIAN TRAVEL

Although the level of tolerance toward gay men and lesbians varies, the region is generally conservative; strongly Catholic countries are the least accepting. In Croatia, although homosexuality is generally tolerated, open displays of affection can meet with hostile reactions especially in the less urban parts of the country. In Slovenia, homosexuality is widely tolerated. Gays and lesbians are united in several associations and clubs, with the main center at the student-run nightclub K4. K4 has a gay night every Sunday from 10 PM to 4 AM.

🔁 **Useful Web Sites Croatia** ⊕ www.gay-croatia. com. **Slovenia (K4,)** ✉ Kersnikova 4, Ljubljana ☎ 01/131-7010 ⊕ www.klubk4.org.

🔁 **Resources for Gay & Lesbian Travelers International Gay & Lesbian Travel Association** ⊕ www.iglta.org is a trade organization of travel companies and establishments that serve the gay and lesbian community. The Web site allows you to search for a member travel agency or tour operator. **Now, Voyager** ☎ 415/626-1169 or 800/255-6951 ⊕ www.nowvoyager.com is a full-service travel agency in San Francisco that caters specifically to gay men and lesbians. **Orbitz** ⊕ www. orbitz.com, though a mainstream online travel agency, sends out a periodic e-newsletter with special deals that might appeal to gay men and lesbians; a sub-site in the "Deals" section focuses on gay and lesbian travel. *Out Traveler* ⊕ www. outtraveler.com is the Web site of a glossy monthly travel magazine for gay men and lesbians. **Planetout.com** ⊕ www.planetout.com/travel is a gay-oriented Web site that has a fairly extensive travel section (formerly the *Out and About* travel newsletter) that includes profiles of popular destinations around the world (fee to access) that are sometimes good, sometimes mediocre. **Purple Roofs** ⊕ www.purpleroofs.com allows gay-owned and gay-friendly lodging establishments to post free listings; the site also accepts paid advertising. **Skylink Travel** ☎ 707/546-9888 or 800/225-5759 ⊕ www.skylinktravel.com, in Santa Rosa, California, caters specifically to women and lesbians; it is a division of Flying Dutchman Travel. **Travelocity** ☎ 800/510-7054 ⊕ www.travelocity.com, a mainstream online travel agent, has a sub-site devoted to gay and lesbian travel (look for the "Need Ideas?" box on the homepage).

HEALTH

Water is safe for drinking throughout Croatia. EU countries have reciprocal health-care agreements with Croatia, entitling those nationals to medical consultation for a basic minimum fee. Citizens from outside the EU have to pay in accordance with listed prices. Most doctors speak some English.

Drinking water is safe in Slovenia as well, although there is a national preference for bottled mineral water in restaurants. Slovenia has reciprocal health-care agreements with the rest of the EU, but citizens from outside the Euro zone will have to pay doctor's and hospital fees directly. In Ljubljana, the private Barsos Clinic deals primarily with expatriate patients.

DIVERS' ALERT

Do not fly within 24 hours of scuba diving.

🔁 **Health Warnings National Centers for Disease Control & Prevention** (CDC,) ☎ 877/394-8747 international travelers' health line ⊕ www.cdc.gov/ travel. **World Health Organization** (WHO) ⊕ www. who.int.

HOLIDAYS

In Croatia, national holidays include the following: January 1 (New Year's Day); January 6 (Epiphany); Easter Sunday and Monday; May 1 (May Day); Corpus Christi (40 days after Easter); June 22 (Anti-fascist Day); August 5 (National Thanksgiving Day); August 15 (Assumption), October 8 (Independence Day), November 1 (All Saints' Day), December 25 and 26 (Christmas).

In Slovenia, national holidays include the following: January 1 and 2 (New Year's Day); February 8 (Prešeren Day, Slovene cultural day); Easter Sunday and Monday (usually March or April); April 27 (National Resistance Day); May 1 and 2 (Labor Day); June 25 (Slovenia National Day); August 15 (Assumption); October 31 (Reformation Day); November 1 (All Saints' Day); December 25; December 26 (Christmas).

INSURANCE

What kind of coverage do you honestly need? Do you even need to buy trip insurance at all? Take a deep breath and read on. Comprehensive travel policies typically cover trip-cancellation and interruption, letting you cancel or cut your trip short because of a personal emergency, illness, or, in some cases, acts of terrorism in your destination. Such policies also cover evacuation and medical care. Some also cover you for trip delays because of bad weather or mechanical problems as well as for lost or delayed baggage. Another type of coverage to look for is financial default—that is, when your trip is disrupted because a tour operator, airline, or cruise line goes out of business. Generally you must buy this when you book your trip or shortly thereafter, and it's only available to you if your operator isn't on a list of excluded companies. We believe that comprehensive trip insurance is especially valuable if you are booking a very expensive or complicated trip (particularly to an isolated region) or if you are booking far in advance. Who knows what could happen six months down the road? But whether or not you get insurance has more to do with how comfortable you are assuming all that risk yourself.

If you're going abroad, consider buying medical-only coverage at the very least. Neither Medicare nor some private insurance carriers cover medical expenses anywhere outside of the United States besides Mexico and Canada (including time aboard a cruise ship, even if it leaves from a U.S. port). Medical-only policies typically reimburse you for medical care (excluding that related to pre-existing conditions) and hospitalization abroad and provide for evacuation. However, you will still have to pay the bills and await reimbursement from the insurer.

Expect comprehensive travel insurance policies to cost about 4% to 7% of the total price of your trip (it's more like 12% if you're over age 70). A medical-only policy may or may not be cheaper than a comprehensive policy. Always read the fine print of your policy to make sure that you are covered for the risks that are of the most concern to you. Compare several policies to make sure you're getting the best price and range of coverage available.

🔃 Insurance Comparison Sites **Insure My Trip. com** ⊕ www.insuremytrip.com. **Square Mouth.com** ⊕ www.quotetravelinsurance.com.

🔃 Comprehensive Travel Insurers **Access America** ☏ 866/807-3982 ⊕ www.accessamerica.com. **CSA Travel Protection** ☏ 800/873-9855 ⊕ www. csatravelprotection.com. **HTH Worldwide** ☏ 610/ 254-8700 or 888/243-2358 ⊕ www.hthworldwide. com. **Travelex Insurance** ☏ 888/457-4602 ⊕ www.travelex-insurance.com. **Travel Guard International** ☏ 715/345-0505 or 800/826-4919 in the U.S. ⊕ www.travelguard.com. **Travel Insured International** ☏ 800/243-3174 ⊕ www. travelinsured.com.

🔃 Medical-Only Insurers **Wallach & Company** ☏ 800/237-6615 or 504/687-3166 ⊕ www.wallach. com. **International Medical Group** ▤ 800/628 4664 in the U.S., 44/01444-465577 in the U.K. ⊕ www.imglobal.com. **International SOS** ⊕ www.internationalsos.com.

INTERNET

Internet cafés are a common sight along the coast in Croatia and in Zagreb. In Slovenia, Ljubljana has an abundance of Internet cafés, but they are much harder to find in the countryside. Wireless connections are being pitched as the new thing, with modern hotels like the Domina Grand Media in Ljubljana using their connectivity as a major selling point in brochures. Wireless service varies from place to place: some hotels and cafés offer it for free, although usually there's an hourly fee—anywhere from 40 Kn to 60 Kn in Croatia—to use your laptop in most places. Internet cafés charge about the same hourly rate. In Zagreb, there are a handful of Internet cafés along Preradovićeva ulica.

🔃 Cybercafes ⊕ www.cybercafes.com lists over 4,000 Internet cafés worldwide.

LANGUAGE

Croatia's official language is Croatian, a Slavic language that uses the Latin alphabet. In Istria signs are posted in both Croatian and Italian, and many towns and villages have two names (one Croatian, one Italian), which can be confusing. Throughout the country, English is widely spoken by people working in tourism, though German and Italian are probably more widely spoken.

In Slovenia, the chief language is Slovene. In the east signs are posted in Slovene and Hungarian; on the Adriatic coast both Slovene and Italian are officially used. English, German, and Italian are spoken in many places. In Slovene the words for street (*ulica*) and drive (*cesta*) are abbreviated to *ul* and *c*. *Nabrežje* (abbreviated to *nab*) means "embankment." The word for square is *trg*.

LODGING

If your experience of Slovenia and Croatia is limited to Zagreb and Ljubljana, you may be pleasantly surprised by hotel standards, which in most cases are as high as Western Europe. Many properties are new or recently renovated, so most rooms are equipped with modern amenities like computer connections and cable TV.

Outside major cities, hotels and inns are a bit more hit or miss. Sometimes countryside hotels can be rustic but chic, sometimes they can be downright grim with 30-year-old bathroom fixtures. Checking out a property's Web site will usually give you some idea. Sadly, you'll still find huge, impersonal Yugoslav-era concrete boxes in both Slovenia and Croatia, although most have been renovated thoroughly on the inside. In Croatia, a room in a private home will almost always be the cheapest option; acceptable rooms are fairly easy to find.

In Ljubljana and Zagreb, expect to pay high prices for hotels, on par with that of Western Europe. Ljubljana can be unreasonably expensive in the summer months, mostly due to lack of beds. Reservations are vital if you plan to visit the capitals, Piran, Istria, Dalmatia, or Plitvice National Park during the summer season. Elsewhere in the Croatian and Slovenian countryside, reservations can be made a day or two in advance.

The lodgings we list are the cream of the crop in each price category. We always list the facilities that are available, but we don't specify whether they cost extra; when pricing accommodations, always ask

what's included and what costs extra. Properties are assigned price categories based on the range from their least-expensive standard double room at high season (excluding holidays) to the most expensive. Properties marked ✕⊞ are lodging establishments whose restaurants warrant a special trip.

Assume that hotels operate on the **European Plan** (EP, with no meals) unless we specify that they use the **Breakfast Plan** (BP, with a full breakfast), **Modified American Plan** (MAP, with breakfast and dinner), or the **Full American Plan** (FAP, with all meals).

⿻ Online Lodging Resources Hotelbook.com ⊕ www.hotelbook.com focuses primarily on independent hotels worldwide and is brought to you by the same folks that operate the aggregator site Kayak.com. **Hotels.com** ☎ 214/369-1246, 800/246-8357 in U.S. ⊕ www.hotels.com is a big wholesaler (now owned by Expedia) that offers rooms in hotels all over the world. **Hotel Club** ⊕ www.hotelclub.net is good for major cities worldwide. **Quikbook** ⊕ www.quikbook.com. **Travel.com** ⊕ www.travel.com.

APARTMENT & VILLA RENTALS

In Croatia, villa rentals are becoming more popular, particularly in Istria, where some pretty medieval stone houses have been converted into high-end rental properties. Apartment rentals of mixed quality are common all over the coast. It's always best to see photos before renting a property for a week or longer. Aside from apartment rentals in Kranjska Gora, the country's major ski destination, there are few villa rentals in Slovenia.

⿻ International Agencies At Home Abroad ☎ 212/421-9165 ⊕ www.athomeabroadinc.com. **Barclay International Group** ☎ 516/364-0064 or 800/845-6636 ⊕ www.barclayweb.com. **Drawbridge to Europe** ☎ 541/482-7778 or 888/268-1148 ⊕ www.drawbridgetoeurope.com. **Homes Away** ☎ 416/920-1873 or 800/374-6637 ⊕ www.homesaway.com. **Hometours International** ☎ 865/690-8484 or 866/367-4668 ⊕ thor.he.net/~hometour/. **Interhome** ☎ 305/940-2299 or 800/882-6864 ⊕ www.interhome.us. **Suzanne B. Cohen & Associates** ☎ 207/622-0743 ⊕ www.villaeurope.com. **Vacation Home Rentals Worldwide** ☎ 201/767-9393 or 800/633-3284 ⊕ www.vhrww.com. **Villanet** ☎ 206/417-

3444 or 800/964-1891 ⊕ www.rentavilla.com. **Villas & Apartments Abroad** ☎ 212/213-6435 ⊕ www. vaanyc.com. **Villas of Distinction** ☎ 707/778-1800 or 800/289-0900 ⊕ www.villasofdistinction.com. **Villas International** ☎ 415/499-9490 or 800/221-2260 ⊕ www.villasintl.com. **Wimco** ☎ 800/449-1553 ⊕ www.wimco.com.

⚿ **Croatia Specialists Adriatica.net** ✉ Slavonska av 26/9, Zagreb ☎ 01/241-5611 ⊕ www.adriatica. net, a Web-based agent, rents villas as well as converted lighthouses in Croatia. **Broker** ✉ Split ☎ 021/547-004 ⊕ www.croatia-tourism.com. **Vintage Travel** ⊕ www.vintagetravel.co.uk, a U.K.-based company, specializes in Croatian villa rentals, particularly in Istria.

⚿ **Slovenia specialists Kranjska Gora Tourism office** ☎ 04/588-5020 ⊕ www.kranjska-gora.si rents condos and villas in the Slovenian ski area.

HOME EXCHANGES

With a direct home exchange, you stay in someone else's home while they stay in yours. Some home-exchange programs also deal with vacation homes, so you're not actually staying in someone's full-time residence, just their vacant weekend place.

⚿ **Exchange Clubs HomeLink International** ☎ 813/975-9825 or 800/638-3841 ⊕ www. homelink.org; $110 yearly for a listing, online access, and catalog; $70 without catalog. **Home Exchange. com** ☎ 800/877-8723 ⊕ www.homeexchange.com charges; $49.95 yearly for a one-year online listing; this is a Web-based company with no catalog. **Intervac U.S.** ☎ 800/756-4663 ⊕ www.intervacus. com; $125 yearly for a listing, online access, and a catalog; $65 without catalog.

HOSTELS

Hostels offer barebones lodging at low, low prices—often in shared dorm rooms with shared baths—to people of all ages, though the primary market is young travelers, especially students. Most hostels serve breakfast; dinner and/or shared cooking facilities may also be available. In some hostels, you aren't allowed to be in your room during the day, and there may be a curfew at night. Nevertheless, hostels provide a sense of community, with public rooms where travelers often gather to share stories. Many hostels are affiliated with Hostelling International (HI), an umbrella group of hostel associations with

some 4,500 member properties in more than 70 countries. Other hostels are completely independent and may be nothing more than a really cheap hotel.

Membership in any HI association, open to travelers of all ages, allows you to stay in HI-affiliated hostels at member rates. One-year membership is about $28 for adults; hostels charge about $10–$30 per night. Members have priority if the hostel is full; they're also eligible for discounts around the world, even on rail and bus travel in some countries.

Youth hostels can be found in both Slovenia and Croatia, and generally, they're clean and well-located in the main sightseeing areas. In Slovenia, most are private youth hostels, so the prices tend to be fairly high, and there's a decided paucity of hostel accommodations in Ljubljana. In Croatia, there's a mix of private and international properties.

⚿ **Organizations Hostelling International** ☎ 1707/324-170 in the U.K. ⊕ www.hihostels.com. **Hostelling International–USA** ☎ 301/495-1240 ⊕ www.hiusa.org. **Hostelling International–Canada** ☎ 800/663-5777 ⊕ www.hihostels.ca. **YHA England & Wales** ☎ 0870/770-8868 or 1629/592-700 for customer service, 0870/770-6113 or 1629/592-708 for reservations ⊕ www.yha.org.uk. **YHA Australia** ⊕ www.yha.com.au. **YHA New Zealand** ☎ 03/379-9970 or 0800/278-299 ⊕ www. yha.org.nz.

⚿ **Local Contacts Croatian YHA** ✉ Dežmanova 9, Zagreb ☎ 01/4847-472 ⊕ www.hfhs.hr.

MAIL & SHIPPING

From Croatia, airmail letters and postcards take about five days to reach other European countries and two weeks to get to Australia, Canada, and the United States. To send a post card costs 3.50 Kn to Europe, 5 Kn to the United States. A letter costs 5 Kn to Europe, 6.50 Kn to the United States.

From Slovenia, airmail postage to the United States is SIT 221 for a letter, SIT 83 for a postcard. Post offices are open weekdays 8 to 6 and Saturday 8 to noon. Stamps are also sold at hotels, newsstands, and kiosks.

MONEY MATTERS

Costs for goods and services are on a par with those of Western Europe. Notable exceptions are public transportation, alcohol, and cigarettes, all of which are cheaper in both Croatia and Slovenia. Groceries can be expensive at shops by the coast, so if you've rented an apartment for a week or more, consider buying some staples at one of the hypermarkets on your way out of Zagreb.

The Croatian currency is called the kuna (Kn), which is made up of 100 lipa. The kuna is not yet fully convertible, so you cannot buy the currency outside of Croatia or exchange it once outside the country.

The monetary unit in Slovenia is the Slovenian tolar (SIT). One Slovenian tolar is divided into 100 stotin. Additionally, most hotels in both Slovenia and Croatia are priced in euros (€).

Prices throughout this guide are given for adults. Substantially reduced fees are almost always available for children, students, and senior citizens. For information on taxes, *see* Taxes, *below.*

ATMS

In Croatia, ATMs are now found throughout the country, even on the islands. In Slovenia, ATMs are less prevalent in small towns and villages, although there are quite a few in Ljubljana.

CREDIT CARDS

Major credit cards are accepted in most hotels, and some shops and restaurants. Throughout this guide, the following abbreviations are used: **AE,** American Express; **DC,** Diners Club; **MC,** MasterCard; and **V,** Visa.

CURRENCY EXCHANGE

For the most favorable rates, change money through banks. Although ATM transaction fees may be higher abroad than at home, ATM rates are excellent because they are based on wholesale rates offered only by major banks. You won't do as well as at exchange booths in airports or rail and bus stations, in hotels, in restaurants, or in stores.

In Slovenia, you can exchange money and traveler's checks in a *banka* (bank) or

mjenjačnica (exchange office). Rates for changing currency and traveler's checks are usually about the same.

TRAVELER'S CHECKS

Traveler's checks are not necessary to travel anymore, particularly in countries like Slovenia and Croatia, where theft is unusual, ATMs are readily available, and credit cards are widely accepted. The main advantage of traveler's checks is that they are replaceable, so if they are lost or stolen, your whole vacation can be quickly recovered. In most cases replacement is guaranteed within 24 hours. When traveling in the countryside, cash is usually the best bet, especially when attempting to book a private room or get a meal at a simple restaurant.

PACKING

Packing for a trip to Croatia depends very much on the season. In summertime, you'll need little more than a swimsuit, towel, rubber water shoes, and light summer clothing for casual dining, especially if you'll spend most of your time at the coast. Don't forget that the coast is rocky, and old cities like Split, Trogir, and Dubrovnik have cobblestone streets, so if you bring your stiletto heels, pack a pair of comfortable back-up shoes as well, in case you stumble on your first night out. If you'll be in Zagreb and dining out or attending a concert, a sports coat and tie is a good bet for men, and some kind of skirt for women, as Croatians tend to be fairly polished when they dine out. At other times of year, it's a good idea to bring an umbrella and light raincoat, as the country is wet from November to March.

Packing for Slovenia depends on where you'll be for most of the vacation. Ljubljana is fairly smart but low-key, so anything stylish will do for the city's restaurants; it's not necessary to wear a sports coat or skirt. If you plan to be in the mountains (Bovec or Kranjska Gora), the look here is more sporty and outdoorsy; there are plenty of diners wearing hiking books at restaurants. The coast as well is quite casual, although Portorož casinos can be pretty swanky. In either Croatia or Slovenia, bring comfortable walking shoes in order to explore caves, lakes, and castles. Sneakers are the telltale sign of a foreign tourist everywhere, so if you're an independent traveler who wants to blend in, consider another comfort option.

Hotels in both Slovenia and Croatia are generally well-equipped. However, washcloths are rare in hotels, so if you need one for a relaxing vacation, better pack your own. A swimsuit is good item to toss in your suitcase at any time of the year. Both Slovenia and Croatia have a number of clean, well-maintained thermal spas that are open all year long.

PACKING & LUGGAGE TIPS

The following tips are the result of our collective wisdom and experience through many trips all over the United States and the rest of the world. However, we don't presume to understand your needs. If you insist on carrying two 26-inch suitcases with you to Venice, then so be it. This list is meant to be a help, not a prescription:

Pack carefully. Never pack something in your checked luggage if you absolutely cannot do without it (prescription medication or that $1000 digital SLR camera, for example).

Be prepared to do it yourself. Unless you are going on a guided tour or a cruise, bring luggage that you can carry yourself. You can't always count on finding porters these days.

Don't take too much stuff. Travel with clothing that can be mixed and matched. Expect to wear most everything more than once, and for those things that can't be reworn, plan on doing a bit of laundry in your hotel room, or if you don't want to do that, then budget to pay for laundry along the way.

Stack 'em and roll 'em. Stack and then roll your clothes when you pack them; they'll wrinkle less.

Lock it up. Although you can't normally lock your luggage when traveling domestically in the United States, several companies now sell TSA-approved locks that can be unlocked by all security personnel in case your bags need to be opened and inspected. Alternatively, you can use a simple plastic cable tie, which you can buy at any hardware store in bundles.

Keep your carry-on small. Carry-on limitations can be more stringent outside of the United States, particularly for domestic and budget flights. Always check with your air carrier to see what the limit is for all the flights that you're on.

Watch the weight. Checked baggage limits are getting more stringent everywhere. In the United States, you may be charged extra if your bag weighs more than 50 pounds—all the more reason to pack light. Outside of the United States, some airlines don't allow you to check a bag that weighs more than 70 pounds, and sometimes the weight-limit is closer to 66 pounds or even less.

Tag it. Always put tags on your luggage with some kind of contact information; you can use your business address if you don't want people to know your home address. Put the same information (and a copy of your travel itinerary) inside your luggage, too.

Insure it. Airlines are only liable for $2,500 per person for bags in the United States, and on international carriers, the liability limit is around $635 per bag. If your stuff is worth more than that, then consider buying excess-value insurance.

Report problems immediately. If you discover that something is missing from your bag or that it is damaged, file a written claim with your airline (do it before you leave the airport if you can). The same advice applies if your bag doesn't arrive. If your bag was opened for security reasons in the United States and something is missing, file a claim with the TSA.

PASSPORTS & VISAS

We're always surprised at how few Americans have passports—only 25% at this writing, though the number is expected to grow in coming years, when it becomes impossible to re-enter the United States from trips to neighboring Canada or Mexico without one. Remember this: a passport verifies both your identity and nationality—a great reason to have one.

U.S. passports are valid for 10 years. The cost to apply for one is $97 for adults, $82 for children under 16; renewals are $67, and you can renew with as little as one year of validity left. Allow six weeks to process the paperwork for either a new or renewed passport. For an expediting fee of $60, you can reduce the time to about two weeks. If your trip is less than two weeks away, you can get a passport even more rapidly by going to a passport office with the necessary documentation. Private expediters can get things done in as little as 48 hours but charge hefty fees for their services. Children under 14 must appear in person to apply for or renew a passport; both parents must accompany the child (or send a notarized statement with their permission) and provide proof of their relationship to the child.

Australian, Canadian, U.S., and U.K. citizens do not need visas to enter either Croatia or Slovenia for a typical vacation visit.

SAFETY

Croatia and Slovenia are both relatively safe by Western standards (Slovenia claims to have one of the lowest crime rates in Europe), and there are no particular local scams that visitors should be aware of. Violent crime is rare. Be on guard for pickpockets in crowded markets, and don't wander alone down dark streets at night.

In Croatia the exceptional danger from land mines has been greatly reduced by government programs; however, care should be taken when in East Slavonia, the former area of conflict; all deserted and unreconstructed areas should be considered still potentially hazardous. Nevertheless, even in this region the main roads are guaranteed to be safe.

GOVERNMENT ADVISORIES

As different countries have different world views, look at travel advisories from a range of governments to get more of a sense of what's going on out there. And be sure to parse the language carefully. For example, a warning to "avoid all travel" carries more weight than one urging you to "avoid nonessential travel," and both are much stronger than a plea to "exercise

caution." A U.S. government travel warning is more permanent (though not necessarily more serious) than a so-called public announcement, which carries an expiration date.

🖪 **General Information & Warnings U.S. Department of State** ⊕ www.travel.state.gov. **Consular Affairs Bureau of Canada** ☎ 800/267-6788 or 613/944-6788 ⊕ www.voyage.gc.ca. **U.K. Foreign & Commonwealth Office** ☎ 0870/606-0290 ⊕ www.fco.gov.uk/travel. **Australian Department of Foreign Affairs & Trade** ☎ 300/139-281 travel advice ⊕ www.dfat.gov.au. **New Zealand Ministry of Foreign Affairs & Trade** ☎ 04/439-8000 ⊕ www.mft.govt.nz.

SENIOR-CITIZEN TRAVEL

Seniors are often entitled to discounted admission to attractions, cheaper tickets to arts events and movie theaters, discounted travel, hotels, and sometimes even special menus at chain restaurants. It never hurts to ask. Membership in organizations such as the AARP (open to all Americans 50 and older for a $12.50 annual fee) comes with myriad discounts on travel packages, hotels, airfares, and car rentals.

🖪 **Travel Resources for Seniors Elderhostel** ☎ 877/426-8056, 978/323-4141 international callers, 877/426-2167 TTY ⊕ www.elderhostel.org offers educational programs at universities and colleges in the United States and abroad for people over 55. **Eldertreks** ☎ 800/741-7956 ⊕ www.eldertreks.com is a Canadian company that specializes in soft adventure travel for people over 50, including some trips in the United States and Canada. **Grand Circle Travel** ☎ 800/959-0405 ⊕ www.gct.com organizes guided trips for groups of travelers age 50 and up. These trips are sold directly through the company; they are not available through travel agents. **Grand Travel** ☎ 800/247-7651 ⊕ www.grandtrvl.com specializes in educational trips that include grandparents and their grandchildren. **Interhostel** ☎ 603/862-1147 or 800/733-9753 ⊕ www.learn.unh.edu is a program from the University of New Hampshire that offers learning vacations in countries all over the world. **Saga Holidays** ☎ 0800/096-0089 to request a brochure, 44/130-377-1190 ⊕ www.saga.co.uk is a British company that specializes in group travel for those over 50; it's a part of a company offering many different products and services for the 50-plus group in the United Kingdom. **Vantage Deluxe World Travel**

☎ 800/322-6677 ⊕ www.vantagetravel.com operates guided tours and cruises for 50-plus travelers.
Tours cover both domestic and foreign destinations.

STUDENTS IN CROATIA & SLOVENIA

Full-time students can purchase an International Student Identity Card; if you're
not a full-time student but are still under
26, consider the International Youth Identity Card. Many hotels, attractions, and
museums offer significant discounts to
holders of either card. Both cards cost
$22, and if purchased in the United States,
both cards include basic accident and
health insurance while you travel abroad.
For information on hostels, *see* Hostels *in*
Finding a Place to Stay, *below.*

🛈 **Travel Resources for Students STA Travel**
☎ 800/784-4040 in the U.S., 888/427-5639 in
Canada, 0870/1-600-599 in the U.K. ⊕ www.
statravel.com is the world's largest travel agency fo-
cused on travel for students and young people. It
has offices on most major college campuses. STA
sells the International Student Identity Card (for full-
time students) and International Youth Identity Card
(for non-students). **Travel Cuts** ☎ 800/592-2887 in
the U.S., 416/979-2406 or 866/246-9762 in Canada
⊕ www.travelcuts.com, based in Canada, is owned
by the Canadian Federation of Students, and specializes in arranging travel for students and young
people, offering many exclusive fares and travel
products. Travel Cuts sells the International Student
Identity Card (for full-time students) and International Youth Identity Card (for non-students).

TAXES

In Croatia, foreigners who spend over 500
Kn in one store on a single day can reclaim
PDV (tax) return upon leaving the country. To do this, you need to present the receipts and the goods bought at the *carina*
(customs) desk at the airport, ferry port,
or border crossing on your way out of
the country.

In Slovenia, any visitor who buys goods
worth more than SIT 19,000 at any one
store is entitled to a refund of taxes.
When you make a purchase ask for a Request for VAT Refund form, *Zahtevek za
vracilo DDV.* A customs officer will cer-
tify the form when you leave the country.
To obtain the refund, go to the Kompas

MTS office at the border crossing point or
the airport. Exporting historic artifacts is
forbidden.

TELEPHONES

In both Slovenia and Croatia, you can
make calls from the *pošta* (post office),
where you enter a kiosk and pay when
you have finished, or from a public telephone booth on the street, where magnetic phone cards are necessary. Phone
cards can be purchased at the post office
or newsstands.

AREA & COUNTRY CODES

Area and country codes are as follows:
Croatia (385), Dubrovnik (20), Split (21),
Zagreb (1); Slovenia (386), Ljubljana (1).

When dialing a number from abroad, drop
the initial 0 from the local area code.

INTERNATIONAL CALLS

To make an international call in Croatia,
dial "00," then the appropriate country
code (Australia 61; Canada 1; United
States 1; and United Kingdom 44).

🛈 **Croatia International Directory Assistance**
☎ 902. **Slovenia International Directory Assistance** ☎ 989.

LONG-DISTANCE SERVICES

AT&T, MCI, and Sprint access codes
make calling long distance relatively convenient, but you may find the local access
number blocked in many hotel rooms.
First ask the hotel operator to connect
you. If the hotel operator balks, ask for
an international operator, or dial the international operator yourself. One way to
improve your odds of getting connected
to your long-distance carrier is to travel
with more than one company's calling
card (a hotel may block Sprint, for example, but not MCI). If all else fails, call
from a pay phone.

🛈 **Access Codes AT&T Direct** ☎ 0800/220-111 in
Croatia, 800/435-0812 in Slovenia ⊕ www.att.com.
MCI WorldPhone ☎ 0800/220-112 in Croatia,
080-8808 in Slovenia ⊕ www.mci.com. **Sprint International Access** ☎ 0800/220-113 in Croatia,
800/877-4646 in Slovenia ⊕ www.sprint.com.

LOCAL CALLS

To make a local call in Croatia, dial the
area code (if you are not already in that

area) followed by the number you wish to reach.

In Slovenia, pay phones take magnetic telephone cards, available from post offices and kiosks. Lower rates apply from 10 PM to 7 AM and all day Sunday.

⁊ Local Directory Assistance ☎ 988.

MOBILE PHONES

If you have a multiband phone (some countries use different frequencies than what's used in the United States) and your service provider uses the world-standard GSM network (as do T-Mobile, Cingular, and Verizon), you can probably use your phone abroad. Roaming fees can steep, though: 99¢ a minute is considered reasonable. And overseas, you normally pay the toll charges for incoming calls. It's almost always cheaper to send a text message than to make a call since text messages have a very low set fee (often less than 5¢).

If you just want to make local calls, consider buying a new SIM card (note that your provider may have to unlock your phone for you to use a different SIM card) and a prepaid service plan in the destination. You'll then have a local number and can make local calls at local rates. If your trip is extensive you could also simply buy a new cell phone in your destination as the initial cost will be offset over time.

If you travel internationally frequently, save one of your old mobile phones or buy a cheap one on the Internet; ask your cell phone company to unlock it for you, and take it with you as a travel phone, buying a new SIM card with pay-as-you-go service in each destination.

In Slovenia, Mobitel, the biggest mobile-phone provider, has roaming contracts with several overseas cellular-phone companies. Check the company's Web site to see if you can use your service with a prepaid phone card for calling in Slovenia. T-Mobile now owns Hrvatska Telekom and has contracts with other T-Mobile worldwide providers. Check the company's Web site for local roaming rates.

⁊ Cellular Abroad ☎ 800/287-3020 or 310/829-6878 ⊕ www.cellularabroad.com rents cell phones

and sells country-specific SIM cards as well as mobile phones that are usable in many different countries. **Hrvatska Telekom** ⊕ www.tportal.hr. **Mobitel** ⊕ www.mobitel.si. **Planet Fone** ☎ 888/988-4777 ⊕ www.planetfone.com rents cell phones, but the calling rates are fairly expensive per minute.

TIME

Croatia and Slovenia are on Central European Time (CET), one hour ahead of Greenwich Mean Time and six hours ahead of the Eastern time zone of the United States.

TIPPING

In Croatia, when eating out, if you have enjoyed your meal and are satisfied with the service, it is customary to leave a 10% to 15% tip. It is not usual to tip in cafés or bars. Maids and taxi drivers are not usually tipped. Tour guides do receive a tip, especially if they are particularly good.

In Slovenia, tax is already included in listed prices. Tips are not included in bills, however, and a 10% tip is customary. If the service is especially good, tip 15%.

TOURS & PACKAGES

GUIDED TOURS

Guided tours are a good option when you don't want to do it all yourself. You'll travel along with a group (sometimes large, sometimes small), stay in hotels that have been pre-booked for you, eat with your fellow group-members (sometimes included in the price of your tour, sometimes not), and travel on a schedule. But not all guided tours are a "If This is Tuesday, It Must Be Belgium" kind of experience. A knowledgable guide can take you places and show you things that you might never have discovered on your own, and you may be pushed to see more than you would have otherwise. Tours aren't for everyone, but when you're going to a place where making travel arrangements is difficult or time-consuming (particularly when you don't speak the language of the destination), they can be a god-send. Whenever you book a guided tour, make sure that you understand what is included and what isn't. A "land-only" tour includes all your travel (by bus, in most cases) in the destination, but it may not include flights to the destination or even flights that you are required to take as a part of the tour. In most cases, the prices you see in a tour brochure won't include fees and taxes, so make sure you understand all the extras before you sign on the dotted line. And remember that you'll be expected to tip your guide at the end of the tour, so don't forget to budget for tips; guides will want to be tipped cash.

🔢 Tour-Operator Recommendations American Society of Travel Agents (⇨ Travel Agencies, *below*). **National Tour Association** (NTA,) ✉ 546 E. Main St., Lexington, KY 40508 ☎ 859/226-4444 or 800/682-8886 ⊕ www.ntaonline.com. **United States Tour Operators Association** (USTOA,) ✉ 275 Madison Ave., Suite 2014, New York, NY 10016 ☎ 212/599-6599 or 800/468-7862 🖷 212/599-6744 ⊕ www.ustoa.com.
🔢 Super-Deluxe Abercrombie & Kent ☎ 800/554-7016 ⊕ www.abercrombiekent.com.
🔢 Deluxe Brendan Vacations ☎ 800/421-8446 🖷 818/772-6492 ⊕ www.brendanvacations.com. **Globus** ☎ 866/276-1241 ⊕ www.cosmos.com. **Overseas Adventure Travel** ☎ 800/493-6824 ⊕ www.oattravel.com. **Tauck Tours** ☎ 800/788-7885 🖷 203/221-6866 ⊕ www.tauck.com.

SPECIAL-INTEREST TOURS
🔢 Food & Wine Tours Adriatic Holidays ✉ 1 Victor St., Oxford OX2 6BT U.K. ☎ 0186/551-6577 ⊕ www. adriaticholidaysonline.com. **My Croatia Ltd.** ✉ 80 Bulmershe Rd., Reading R61 5RJ U.K. ☎ 0870/7622-842 ⊕ www.mycroatia.co.uk.
🔢 Bicycling & Hiking Backroads ☎ 800/462-2848 ⊕ www.backroads.com. **Butterfield & Robinson** ✉ 70 Bond St., Toronto, Ontario M5B 1X3 ☎ 800/678-1147 ⊕ www.butterfield.com.
🔢 Yachting & Sailing Adriatic Holidays ✉ 1 Victor St., Oxford OX2 6BT U.K. ☎ 0186/551-6577 ⊕ www.adriaticholidaysonline.com. **The Moorings** ☎ 800/952-8420 ⊕ www.themoorings.com. **Sail Croatia** ✉ 963 Fulham Rd., London, SW6 5JJ U.K. ☎ 020/8459-8787 ⊕ www.sailcroatia.com. **Sailing Holidays Ltd.** ✉ 105 Mt. Pleasant Rd., London, NW10 3EH U.K. ☎ 020/8459-8787 ⊕ www. sailingholidays.com. **Sunsail** ⊕ www.sunsail. com. **Unique World Cruises** ☎ 800/669-0757 ⊕ www.uniqueworldcruises.com.
🔢 History & Art Smithsonian Study Tours and Seminars ☎ 202/357-4700 ⊕ smithsonianjourneys. org.

PACKAGES
Packages *are not* guided tours. Packages combine airfare, hotel accommodations, and perhaps a rental car or other extras (theater tickets, guided excursions, boat trips, reserved entry to popular museums, transit passes), but they let you do your own thing. During busy periods, packages may be your only option because flights and rooms may be otherwise sold out. Packages will definitely save you time. They can also save you money, particularly in peak seasons, but—and this is a really big "but"—you should price each part of the package separately to be sure. And be aware that prices advertised on Web sites and in newspapers rarely include service charges or taxes, which can up your costs by hundreds of dollars.

Some packages and cruises are sold only through travel agents. Don't always assume that you can get the best deal by booking everything yourself.

Each year consumers are stranded or lose their money when packagers—even large ones with excellent reputations—go out of business. How can you protect yourself? First, always pay with a credit card; if you have a problem, your credit-card company may help you resolve it. Second, buy trip insurance that covers default. Third, choose a company that belongs to the United States Tour Operators Association, whose members must set aside funds ($1 million) to cover defaults. Finally choose a company that also participates in the Tour Operator Program of the American Society of Travel Agents (ASTA), which will act as mediator in any disputes. You can also check on the tour operator's reputation among travelers by posting an inquiry on one of the Fodors.com forums.

Croatia is a popular European package-tour destination with loads of tours heading there every week throughout the summer season. Packages including flights booked from the United States are less common, and you may have to look long and hard to find one. If a package is what you're looking for, you can combine a low-cost flight to the United Kingdom with one of the following tours and in the end make out fairly well on price. The following companies have package tours originating in the United Kingdom.

Packagers Bond Tours ⊠ 2 Upper High St., Epsom, Surrey KT17 4QJ U.K. ☎ 01372/745-300 ⊕ www.bondtours.com. **Simply Travel** ☎ 0870/166-4979 ⊕ www.simply-travel.co.uk. **Tapestry Holidays** ☎ 020/8235-7800 ⊕ www.tapestryholidays.com.

TRAIN TRAVEL

In Croatia, Zagreb is connected to Rijeka and Split by rail, but there is no line south of Split to Dubrovnik. International services run from Zagreb to the European cities of Ljubljana, Budapest, Belgrade, Vienna, Munich, Berlin, and Venice.

In Slovenia, daily trains link Ljubljana with Austria, Italy, Hungary, and Croatia. Many are overnight trains with sleeping compartments. The internal rail network is limited, but trains are cheap and efficient.

RAIL PASSES

The "Zone D" Interail pass is valid for Croatia for EU residents, but Eurail is not.

TRAVEL AGENTS

If you use an agent—brick-and-mortar or virtual—you'll pay a fee for the service. And know that the service you get from some online agents isn't comprehensive. For example Expedia or Travelocity don't search for prices on budget airlines like JetBlue, Southwest, or small foreign carriers. That said, some agents (online or not) *do* have access to fares that are difficult to find otherwise, and the savings can more than make up for any surcharge.

A knowledgeable brick-and-mortar travel agent can be a godsend if you are booking a cruise, a package trip that's not available to you directly, an air pass, or a complicated itinerary including several overseas flights. What's moretravel agents that specialize in a destination may have access to deals that are unavailable elsewhere, and they may know about things such as charter flights

that aren't publicized in the mainstream press. Agents who specialize in types of travelers (seniors, gays and lesbians, nudists) or types of trips (cruises, luxury travel, safaris) can also be invaluable.

A top-notch agent planning your trip to Russia will make sure you get the correct visa application and complete it on time; the agent booking your cruise may get you a cabin upgrade or arrange to have bottle of champagne chilling in your cabin when you embark. And complain about the surcharges all you like, but when things don't work out the way you'd hoped, it's nice to have an agent to put things right.

Remember that Expedia, Travelocity, and Orbitz are travel agents, not just booking engines. To resolve any problems with a reservation made through these companies, contact them first.

Agent Resources American Society of Travel Agents ☎ 703/739-2782 ⊕ www.travelsense.org. **Association of British Travel Agents** ☎ 020/7307-1907 for agent referrals ⊕ www.abta.com. **Association of Canadian Travel Agencies** ☎ 613/237-3657 ⊕ www.acta.ca. **Australian Federation of Travel Agents** ☎ 02/9264-3299 or 1300/363-416 ⊕ www.afta.com.au. **Travel Agents' Association of New Zealand** ☎ 04/499-0104 ⊕ www.taanz.org.nz.

VISITOR INFORMATION

Before You Leave Croatian Tourist Board ⊠ 350 5th Ave., Suite 4003, New York, 10118 ☎ 212/829-4416 ⊠ 2 The Lanchesters, 162-164 Fulham Palace Rd., London W6 9ER U.K. ☎ 44/208-563-7979. **Slovenian Tourist Office** ⊠ 2929 E. Commercial Blvd., Suite 201, Fort Lauderdale, FL 33308 ☎ 954/491-0112 ⊕ www.slovenia-tourism.si ⊠ South Marlands, Itchingfield, Horsham, West Sussex RH13 0NN U.K. ☎ 0870/225-5305. **In Croatia Croatian Tourist Board** ⊠ Iblerov trg 10/4, Zagreb, 10000 ☎ 01/455-6455 ⊕ www.croatia.hr. **In Slovenia Slovenian Tourist Board** ⊠ Dunajska 156, Ljubljana, 1000 ☎ 01/189-1840 🖷 01/189-1841 ⊕ www.slovenia-tourism.si.

Zagreb & Environs

1

By Paul
Olchváry

CROATIA HAS SUCCESSFULLY REEMERGED as a tourist destination in recent years, and much of its success has to do with the country's spectacular Adriatic coast—beautiful medieval towns, crystal clear azure waters, and, of course, well-developed tourist resorts. However, it is all too easy to overlook the fact that much of the country's natural beauty and cultural heritage is rooted in places well inland from the sea. Unless you arrive overland from Slovenia, by boat from Italy, or by one of the few air routes that deliver you straight to the coast, chances are that your first encounter with Croatia will be Zagreb. Instead of high-tailing it to Dalmatia or Istria, stay a couple days; stay a week, if you can. You'll be in for a pleasant surprise and will go home with a fuller, more satisfying appreciation of what this alluring country is all about.

Above all, there is Croatia's quietly lovely capital. With its historic center situated on the northern bank of the Sava River, Zagreb has the walkability of Prague with spacious, friendly public spaces, grand Austro-Hungarian architecture, and a rich array of churches and museums.

With the exception of the vast plains of Slavonia that stretch to the east (and which are covered in Chapter 2), the rest of the inland region, with Zagreb as its approximate center, can be divided into two parts, north and south of Zagreb. To the north is the hilly, castle-rich Zagorje region and, just a tram and cable-car ride from the city center, the hiking trails and ski slopes of Sljeme. South is the relatively busy route to the coast that includes Karlovac, an important regional center, as well as Croatia's most visited national park, Plitvice Lakes; a second route southeast of the capital goes along the less traveled banks of the Sava River to Lonjsko Polje, a marshy, less frequented region that is nonetheless worth exploring for its natural beauty, a well-preserved 16th-century fortress, and historical reminders of Croatia's role in World War II.

Exploring Zagreb & Environs

About the Restaurants

This isn't the seacoast, so you'll certainly find more in the way of roasted meats accompanied by heavy side dishes such as *zagorski štrukli* (baked cheese dumplings), with walnut-, jam-, and/or sweet curd-cheese–filled *palačinke* (crêpes) prominent among the desserts on nearly every menu. Balkan-style grilled meats such as *ćevapčići* (grilled spicy cubes of minced meat, often served with raw onions) are much in evidence and, as elsewhere, lower in price than more elaborate main courses. The influence of Slavonia to the east and Hungary to the north is evident in the form of paprika-rich (and salt-rich) dishes, whether *fiš paprikas* (made from fish and also called *riblji paprikas*) or various goulashes; likewise, spiced sausages and salamis add further zest. Some restaurants, particularly in Zagreb, and especially those owned and operated by folks from Dalmatia, do excel in fresh seafood straight from the Adriatic. But when it comes to fish, you are likely to find as much or more in the way of freshwater options such as carp, pike, and pike-perch. As on the coast, many restaurants serve pasta dishes and pizzas

To explore Croatia's interior, begin with Zagreb and work your way outward from there. If you have just a day or two, stick to the capital, but the more time you have beyond that, the more you will want to explore. If you're headed to the coast, anyway, you'll pass by Plitvice Lakes National Park; keep that natural wonder on your radar screen for a daytime visit at the very least.

If you have 3 days

Stick to **Zagreb,** with a side trip to its immediate environs. As compact as it is compared to other regional capitals such as Budapest, Croatia's capital nonetheless invites long strolls and more than a fleeting look into at least a few of its museums and parks. This alone can take three days; but you can probably cover most key sights without feeling rushed in two days, leaving a bit of time to spare for a half-day excursion to **Samobor,** for example, or into the hills north of the capital. Renting a car will allow you to cover more of the castles and towns of the **Medvednica hills** and the Zagorje region, but even if you have only one full day at your disposal, you can take in a couple of such nearby sites by bus.

If you have 5 days

Start as above, devoting at least two or, better yet, two-and-a-half days to Zagreb, with a half-day excursion to the Medvednice hills on the third day. Visit a castle or two in the Zagorje, such as **Veliki Tabor,** on the fourth day, and spend the night either in the nearby countryside or else in **Varaždin** before making your way back for a fond farewell to Zagreb on the fifth.

If you have 7 days

Do all of the above, but take in both a castle in the Zagorje and an afternoon and evening in Varaždin; throw in a one-night visit to **Plitvice Lakes National Park,** with a daytime stopover in Karlovac on the way. This one-week option will work well if, for example, you wish to spend the second (or first) week on the Adriatic coast.

as budget alternatives, but you'll find noticeably fewer restaurants focusing on Italian-style fare; which is not surprising given that this region's history (and cuisine) was more bound up in centuries past with Austria and Hungary, for example, than with Italy.

As for prices, expect to shell out about the same in Zagreb for a main course at a good restaurant as you would on the coast. If you head to Varaždin or a smaller town, however, prices will drop noticeably, if not quite dramatically. As elsewhere in Croatia, you can always pick up a *burek* (a cheese- or meat-filled pastry) at a bakery for a quick, on-the-go, decidedly budget, decidedly greasy little meal.

WHAT IT COSTS in Croatian Kuna (Kn)				
$$$$	**$$$**	**$$**	**$**	**¢**
RESTAURANTS over 80	60–80	35–60	20–35	under 20

Restaurant prices are per person for a main course at dinner.

About the Hotels

It's a fact of life that Zagreb doesn't get the same sort of tourist traffic as the coast, so the region's major hotels have gone to great lengths since the end of the Yugoslav war to cater to business travelers. Although this trend has yielded a spate of impressive renovations (some still ongoing or planned as of this writing), it has also driven prices up considerably. Rates of €100 or (much) more for a double room are not at all uncommon in central Zagreb's largest hotels, though a 10- to 20-minute walk or short tram ride from downtown will bring you to comfortable, modern pensions for considerably less. You have to go to smaller towns or to the countryside to get cheaper options, though some private rooms and agrotourism-style accommodations (where the owners often don't speak English, and you don't get such frills as cable TV and AC) are quite inexpensive indeed.

WHAT IT COSTS in euros (€) and Croatian kuna (Kn)				
	$$$$	**$$$**	**$$**	**$**	**¢**
IN EUROS	over € 225	€175–€225	€125–€175	€75–€125	under €75
IN KUNA	over 1,650	1,300–1,650	925–1,300	550–925	under 550

Hotel prices are for two people in a double room in high season, excluding taxes and service charges.

Timing

Although Zagreb and environs is well worth a visit at any time of year, the capital really comes alive in fair weather, which essentially means anytime between early May and mid-September. The sole drawback of a trip to Zagreb during the warmer months is that the temptation to spend more time on the coast will mean much less time acquainting yourself with the cultural and natural wealth of this part of inland Croatia. You will be greeted by a more peaceful ambience and a less pricier hotel scene in Zagreb if you can plan your visit for May through early June, or September through early October. Unless you're in town to do business, avoid visiting during the one-week Zagreb Trade Fair in mid-September, when rooms are harder to come by and may be up to 20% pricier.

ZAGREB

The capital of Croatia, Zagreb, has a population of roughly one million and is situated at the extreme edge of the Pannonian Plain, between the north bank of the Sava River and the southern slopes of Mount Medvednica. Its early years are shrouded in mystery, though there are indications of a neolithic settlement on this site. The Romans are said to have established a municipality of sorts that was destroyed around AD 600, when Croatian tribes moved in.

Like so many other notable European cities, Zagreb started out as a strategic crossroads along an international river route, which was followed much later by north–south and east–west passage by road and then rail.

Walking in Zagreb
Zagreb—a pedestrian-friendly, and just plain friendly city—is a sheer pleasure, what with its rich array of attractive parks and squares as well as its museums and churches. At its center is its spacious main square, Trg Bana Jelačića, whose fine examples of Viennese Secessionist architecture are delightful, and whose constant flow of people- and tram-traffic is invigorating. Nearby is Tkalčićeva, the main, bustling pedestrian avenue in the old quarter. Among several churches of note, Crkva Svetog Marka leaves a striking impression with its brilliant, multicolored tile roof. And parks such as Trg Zrinjskog, with its fountains and majestic plane trees, and lovely Maksimir Park on the outskirts of downtown soothe the soul.

1

Natural Beauty
Plitvice Lakes National Park is not to be missed. This UNESCO World Heritage Site is Croatia's most-visited park, for good reason. Even if sharing the trail with throngs of other tourists (especially in mid-summer) is not your idea of a peaceful escape to nature, the sixteen crystal-clear lakes connected by numerous waterfalls and cascades that comprise this natural wonder will leave you in awe. Besides, it's right on the way to the Dalmatian coast, midway between Zagreb and Zadar.

Zagorje Castles & Villages
Centuries of onslaughts by foes such as the Ottomans have left the forested hills to the north of Zagreb that extend to the Slovenian border ornamented by more than a few lovely fortresses, from the 15th century Veliki Tabor to the neo-Gothic, 19th-century Trakošćan. A one- or two-day drive through this area will also reveal some charming villages, including Kumrovec, the birthplace of the late leader of the former Yugoslavia, Josep Broz Tito.

Cuisine
Here you get the best of both worlds. In Zagreb in particular, there are not only plenty of fine restaurants offering the best of Central European meaty fare—from spicy, Balkan-style dishes to paprika-rich cuisine and sausages more characteristic of Slavonia to the east and Hungary to the north—but also some excellent places to get that fresh tuna, scampi, and octopus salad even this far from the coast, thanks in part to natives of Dalmatia who have opened a number of top-notch seafood restaurants in recent years.

For much of its history the city also served as a bastion on a defensive frontier, pounded for half a millennium by thundering hordes of invaders, among them Hungarians, Mongols, and Turks.

From the late Middle Ages until the 19th century, Zagreb was composed of two adjoining—but separate—towns on the high ground (Gornji Grad): one town was secular, the other religious. In 1242, the secular town, named Gradec (Fortress), was burned to the ground in a wave of destruction by the Tartars, after which it locked itself up behind protective walls and towers. It is from this time that the real Zagreb (meaning Behind the Hill) began to evolve; it was accorded the status of a free royal city in the same year by the Hungarian–Croatian king Bela IV. In the 15th century, the ecclesiastical center, named Kaptol (Chapter House), also enclosed itself in defensive walls in response to the threat of a Turkish invasion.

When Zagreb became the capital of Croatia in 1557, the country's parliament began meeting alternately in Gradec and at the Bishop's Palace in Kaptol. When Kaptol and Gradec were finally put under a single city administration in 1850, urban development accelerated. The railway reached Zagreb in 1862, linking the city to Vienna, Trieste, and the Adriatic. It was at this time that Donji Grad (Lower Town) came into being. Lying between Gornji Grad and the main train station, it was designed to accommodate new public buildings—the National Theater, the university, and various museums. Built in grandiose style and interspersed by wide, tree-lined boulevards, parks, and gardens, it makes a fitting monument to the Habsburg era.

The Tito years brought a period of increasing industrialization coupled with urban expansion, as the new high-rise residential suburb of Novi Zagreb was constructed south of the Sava. In 1991, the city escaped the war of independence relatively unscathed, but for an attempted rocket attack on the Croatian Parliament building in Gradec. Zagreb did, however, suffer severe economic hardship as the country's industries collapsed, post-Communist corruption set in, and an influx of refugees—mainly Croats from Herzegovina—arrived in search of a better life.

Since 2000, public morale has picked up considerably: trendy street cafés are thriving, numerous smart new stores have opened, and the public gardens are once again carefully tended. However, underlying this apparent affluence, unemployment remains a lingering problem. The prospect of European Union membership for Croatia at some point in the not too distant future holds out the promise of continued economic vitality.

Exploring Zagreb

The city is clearly divided into two distinct districts: **Gornji Grad** (Upper Town) and **Donji Grad** (Lower Town). Although hilltop Gornji Grad is made up of winding cobbled streets and terra-cotta rooftops sheltering the cathedral and the Croatian Parliament building, Donji Grad is where you'll find the city's most important 19th-century cultural institutions, including the National Theater, the university, and a number of museums, all in an organized grid.

Numbers in the text correspond to numbers in the margin and on the Zagreb map.

Gornji Grad (Upper Town)

The romantic hilltop area of Gornji Grad dates back to medieval times and is undoubtedly the loveliest part of Zagreb.

a good
walk

Begin your walk from the main square, **Trg Bana Jelačića ❶**, a vast paved area flanked by busy cafés. Traffic-free—except for the constant coming and going of some half-dozen tram lines—this is the focal point of the city's pedestrian activity. From here, wide steps lead up to **Dolac ❷**, the central market, also known as the "Belly of Zagreb." From Dolac, take a narrow side street to the right to arrive in front of the **Katedrala Svetog Stjepana ❸**, where a gilded statue of the Virgin, protected by four angels, stands on a high stone column. From the cathedral, Kaptol's main wide street (also Kaptol) runs uphill past tile-roofed antique houses. Take the first turn left; then turn right to pass through a doorway into a walled public garden and descend a short flight of steps to arrive on **Tkalčićeva ❹**. Turn left and walk down Tkalčićeva; then turn right into a narrow passage known as Krvavi Most (Bloody Bridge), the scene of bloody armed combat between the warring factions of Gradec and Kaptol during the Middle Ages. This brings you to Radićeva, where you should turn right and walk uphill; then take the first left, at Trg Brače Hrvatskog Zmaja (dominated by an equestrian statue), onto Kamenita, to arrive at the delightful **Kamenita Vrata ❺**.

Follow Kamenita to Markov trg, dominated by much-photographed **Crkva Svetog Marka ❻**. The building on the east of the square is the Hrvatski Sabor. Leave Markov trg by Mletačka, diagonally across the square from where you entered, which brings you to the **Meštrović Atelier ❼**, displaying a fine collection of works by Ivan Meštrović, Croatia's most prominent 20th-century sculptor. Continue to the end of Mletačka; then turn right onto Demetrova to reach Opatička, home to the **Muzej Grada Zagreba ❽**. Now retrace your steps to Markov trg, cross the square, and take Ćirilometodska to arrive at the **Hrvatski Muzej Naivne Umjetnosti ❾** for an introduction to Croatian naive art.

East of where Ćirilometodska ends is **Crkva Svete Katerine ❿**, considered by many to be Croatia's most beautiful baroque church. Close by, **Kula Lotršćak ⓫** offers a dramatic panorama across the city to Novi Zagreb on the far side of the River Sava, whereas below the tower Strossmayer Šetalište (Strossmayer Promenade) follows the line of Gradec's former south-facing wall and affords more stunning rooftop views. At the foot of the tower stands a *uspinjaca* (funicular railway), dating back to 1891 and connecting Gornji Grad to Ilica, Zagreb's main shopping street. Either ride down or take the steps; then turn left on Ilica to return to Trg Bana Jelačića, the original starting point.

TIMING   This tour is best done in the morning, when stalls at the open-air market are heaving with a colorful array of fruits and vegetables and you are more likely to find the church doors open. Then again, if you want a taste of what Zagreb's nightlife is all about—be prepared for the crowds on Tkalčićeva in particular—start out in mid- or late-afternoon and continue strolling until after the sun sets.

WHAT TO SEE   **Crkva Svete Katerine** (St. Catherine's Church). Built for the Jesuit order
★ ❿   between 1620 and 1632, this church was modeled on Giacomo da Vignola's Il Gesù in Rome. Inside, the vaults are decorated with pink and white stucco and 18th-century illusionist paintings, and the altars are

Exploring ▶

Arheološki Muzej **18**
Botanički Vrt **16**
Crkva Svete Katerine . . . **10**
Crkva Svetog Marka **6**
Dolac **2**
Hrvatski Muzej
Naivne Umjetnosti **9**
Hrvatsko Narodno
Kazalište **12**

Kamenita Vrata **5**
Katedrala Marijina
uznesenja i svetog
Stjepana **3**
Kula Lotrščak **11**
Meštrovič Atelier **7**
Muzej Grada Zagreba . . . **8**
Muzej Mimara **14**
Muzej za Umjetnost
i Obrt **13**

Strossmayerova Galerija . . . **17**
Starih Majstora **15**
Tehnički Muzej **4**
Tkalčičeva **1**
Trg Bana Jelačiča **1**

Restaurants ▶

Atlanta Caffè
Restaurant **3**
Baltazar **1**

Biban **9**
Dubravkin Put **5**
Gostionica Purger **11**
Konoba Antica **4**
Medvedgrad Pivnica **22**
Paviljon **16**
Pizzeria 2 . . . . **2**
Pod Gričkim Topom **7**
Stari Fijaker **6**

Hotels

Arcotel Allegra **20**
Best Western
Premier Hotel Astoria . . . **18**
Hotel Central **17**
Hotel Dubrovnik **10**
Hotel Sliško **21**
Palace Hotel Zagreb **14**
Pansion Jägerhorn **8**
Regent Esplanade **15**

Sheraton Zagreb **19**
Villa Tina **12**
Westin Zagreb **13**

KEY

1 *Exploring Sights*
① *Hotels & Restaurants*

the work of Francesco Robba and 17th-century Croatian artists. ⊠ *Katerinin trg, Gornji Grad* ▣ *Free* ☉ *Daily 8–8.*

★ ❻ **Crkva Svetog Marka** (St. Mark's Church). The original building was erected in the 13th century and was once the parish church of Gradec. The baroque bell tower was added in the 17th century, while the steeply pitched roof—decorated in brilliant, multicolored tiles arranged to depict the coats of arms of Zagreb on the right and the Kingdom of Croatia, Dalmatia, and Slavonia on the left—was added during reconstruction in the 19th century. ⊠ *Markov trg, Gornji Grad* ▣ *Free* ☉ *Daily 8–8.*

❷ **Dolac** (Market). Farmers from the surrounding countryside set up their stalls here daily, though the market is at its busiest on Friday and Saturday mornings. On the upper level, brightly colored umbrellas shade fresh fruit and vegetables on an open-air piazza, while dairy products and meats are sold in an indoor market below. ⊠ *Trg Bana Jelačića, Gornji Grad* ☉ *Weekdays 7–4, weekends 7–noon.*

❾ **Hrvatski Muzej Naivne Umjetnosti** (Croatian Museum of Naive Art). This unusual school of painting dates back to the 1930s and features more than 1,600 works of untutored peasant artists, primarily from the village of Hlebine in Slavonia. Canvases by the highly esteemed Ivan Generalić dominate here, though there are also paintings, drawings, sculptures, and prints by other noted members of the movement, plus a section devoted to foreigners working along similar lines. ⊠ *Ćirilometodska 3, Gornji Grad* ☎ *01/485–1911* ⊕ *www.hmnu.org* ▣ *10 Kn* ☉ *Tues.–Fri. 10–6, weekends 10–1.*

❺ **Kamenita Vrata** (Stone Gate). The original 13th-century city walls had four gates, of which only Kamenita Vrata remains. Deep inside the dark passageway, locals stop to pray before a small shrine adorned with flickering candles. In 1731 a devastating fire consumed all the wooden elements of the gate, except for a painting of the Virgin and Child, which was found in the ashes, remarkably undamaged. Kamenita Vrata has since become a pilgrimage site, as can be seen from the numerous stone plaques saying *hvala* (thank you). ⊠ *Kamenita, Gornji Grad.*

❸ **Katedrala Marijina uznesenja i Svetog Stjepana** (Cathedral of the Assumption of the Blessed Virgin and St. Stephen). Built on the site of a former 12th-century cathedral destroyed by the Tartars in 1242, the present structure was constructed between the 13th and 16th centuries. The neo-Gothic facade was added by architect Herman Bolle following the earthquake of 1880, its twin steeples being the identifying feature of the city's skyline. Behind the impressive main altar are crypts of Zagreb's archbishops and of Croatian national heroes. The interior is otherwise relatively bare, the main point of interest being the north wall, which bears an inscription of the Ten Commandments in 12th-century Glagolitic script. ⊠ *Kaptol 31, Gornji Grad* ▣ *Free* ☉ *Daily 8–8.*

⓫ **Kula Lotršćak** (Lotršćak Tower). Formerly the entrance to the fortified medieval Gradec, Kula Lotršćak now houses a multilevel gallery with occasional exhibits of contemporary art. Each day at noon, a small cannon is fired from the top of the tower in memory of the times when it was used to warn of the possibility of an Ottoman attack. You can climb the tower partway via a spiral wooden staircase for a look into the gallery rooms (which occupy several floors) or all the way to the observation deck up top for splendid views of Zagreb and environs. ⊠ *Strossmayer Šetalište, Gornji Grad* ☎ *01/485–1926* ⊠ *Observation deck 10 Kn; gallery free* ⊙ *Tues.–Sun. 11–8.*

★ ❼ **Meštrović Atelier** (Meštrović Atelier). This 17th-century building, with its interior courtyard, served as home and studio to Ivan Meštrović from 1922 until his emigration to the United States in 1942. The building was extensively remodeled according to plans devised by the artist and was turned into a memorial museum with a permanent exhibition of his sculptures and drawings after his death in 1962. (There is a larger collection of his works in the Meštrović Gallery in Split.) ⊠ *Mletačka 8, Gornji Grad* ☎ *01/485–1123* ⊠ *20 Kn* ⊙ *Tues.–Fri. 10–6, weekends 10–2.*

❽ **Muzej Grada Zagreba** (Zagreb City Museum). Well worth a visit for anyone interested in urban design, this museum traces the city's most important historical, economic, political, social, and cultural events from medieval times up to the present day. Exhibits include detailed scale models of how the city has evolved, as well as sections devoted to the old trade guilds, domestic life, and sacral art. ⊠ *Opatička 20, Gornji Grad* ☎ *01/485–1361 or 01/485–1362* ⊕ *www.mdc.hr/mgz* ⊠ *20 Kn; free guided tours at 11 AM weekends* ⊙ *Tues.–Fri. 10–6, weekends 10–1.*

❹ **Tkalčićeva.** This street was once a channel forming the boundary between Kaptol and Gradec, then known as Potok (the brook). Today it is a pretty pedestrian zone lined with 19th-century town houses, many of which have been converted into popular café-bars at street level. ⊠ *Tkalčićeva north of Krvavi Most, Gornji Grad.*

need a break? For morning coffee or an early evening aperitif, stop at **Sunčani Sat** (⊠ Tkalčićeva 27, Gornji Grad). Take a comfy wicker chair on the open-air summer terrace and enjoy watching the comings and goings of Zagreb café life. In the evening this space transforms, as with so many others along Tkalčićeva, into a trendy, crowded watering hole.

❶ **Trg Bana Jelačića** (Ban Jelačić Square). Buildings lining the square date from 1827 onward and include several fine examples of Viennese Secessionist architecture. The centerpiece is an equestrian statue of Ban Jelačić, the first Croatian viceroy, erected in 1866. After World War II the Communist government ordered the dismantling and removal of the statue, but it was put back in place in 1991. ⊠ *Between Ilica to the west, Praška to the south, and Jurišićeva to the east, Gornji Grad.*

need a break? If you are looking for a quick and inexpensive lunch, consider the groundbreaking **Pingvin Sandwich Bar** (⊠ Nikola Tesla 7, Gornji Grad), an extremely popular stand just a couple minutes' walk from Trg Bana Jelačića where you can get all sorts of sandwiches. Pictures out front will help you decipher the Croatian words for their various sandwiches.

Donji Grad (Lower Town)

Donji Grad came into being during the late 19th century. The urban plan, which follows a grid pattern, was drawn up by Milan Lenuci and combines a succession of squares and parks laid out in a "U" shape (known as the Green Horseshoe), all overlooked by the city's main public buildings and cultural institutions.

a good walk

Leave Trg Bana Jelačića, which is right on the border between the upper and lower town, on Gajeva Street, passing the Hotel Dubrovnik; then turn right onto Bogovićeva to arrive at Preradovićev trg, better known to locals as Cvijetni trg (Flower Square) in tribute to the flower sellers who used to set up their stalls here. At the far right corner of the square stands the Orthodox church, still attended by Zagreb's now depleted Serb community. Leave the square by Preradovićeva (i.e., toward the left from the point where you entered), and then take the first right onto Masarykova, a moderately bustling shopping street, to reach the vast green Trg Maršala Tita, the first of a series of three squares that make up one side of Lenuci's so-called Green Horseshoe. The dominant building here is the monumental neo-baroque **Hrvatsko Narodno Kazalište ⑫**. Close by, on the western side of the square, the **Muzej za Umjetnost i Obrt ⑬** displays an impressive collection devoted to Croatian arts and crafts. The next square, Mažuranića trg, is on the far side of the Hrvatsko Narodno Kazalište, but there's not much there of great interest aside from some trees; but if you continue south a bit to the right, down busy Savska cesta, Roosevelt trg will be on your right once you cross the next intersection. There you will find the renowned **Muzej Mimara ⑭**. South from here, farther down Savska cesta, lies the **Tehnički Muzej ⑮**.

Assuming you've gone the extra couple blocks to the Tehnički Muzej, retrace your steps a little way up Savska cesta, and then take the second street on the right, Vodnikova, which becomes Mihanovićeva and runs between the south side of Marulićev trg and the **Botanički Vrt ⑯**, a carefully tended garden offering respite from the bustle of city life. Proceed along Mihanovićeva to arrive at Tomislavov trg, overlooked by the *glavni kolodvor* (main railway station) and presided over by an equestrian statue of King Tomislav, the first king of the medieval state of Croatia. At the north end of the square stands the Umjetnički Paviljon, a 19th-century domed structure hosting temporary exhibitions. You are now on the second series of three adjoining squares that complete the Green Horseshoe. Continue to Strossmayerov trg, home to the impressive **Strossmayerova Galerija Starih Majstora ⑰**, where you can view a fine collection of Old Master paintings. Overlooking the majestic plane trees, flowerbeds, and fountains of the next square, Trg Zrinjskog, stands the **Arheološki Muzej ⑱**. Complete the walk by returning to Trg Bana Jelačića, the original starting point of the tour, via Praška.

TIMING This walk can be done in either the morning or the afternoon, but if you plan to visit some of the museums listed, you should check opening times (which vary from day to day) before setting out.

WHAT TO SEE **Arheološki Muzej** (Archaeological Museum). Museum exhibits focus on
⑱ prehistoric times to the Tartar invasion. Pride of place is given to the
Vučedol Dove, a three-legged ceramic vessel in the form of a bird, dating back to the 4th millennium BC, and a piece of linen bearing the longest
known text in ancient Etruscan writing. The courtyard features a collection of stone relics from Roman times. ⊠ *Trg N. Zrinjskog 19, Donji
Grad* ☎*01/487–3101* ⊕*www.amz.hr* ⊠*20 Kn* ☉ *Tues.–Fri. 10–5, weekends 10–1.*

⑯ **Botanički Vrt** (Botanical Garden). Founded in 1889 as research grounds
for the faculty of botany at Zagreb University, the garden includes an
arboretum with English-style landscaping, a small artificial lake, and an
ornamental Japanese bridge. ⊠ *Marulićeva trg 9a, Donji Grad* ⊠ *Free*
☉ *Mon. and Tues. 9–2:30, Wed.–Sun. 9–6.*

⑫ **Hrvatsko Narodno Kazalište** (Croatian National Theater). The building
dates from 1895, designed by the Viennese firm Hellmer and Fellner as
part of the preparations for a state visit by Emperor Franz Josef. In front
of the theater, set deep in a round concrete basin, is Meštrović's little,
eerily lifelike sculpture *Zdenac Života* (*Fountain of Life*), from 1912,
which depicts four naked couples writhing uncomfortably in each other's
arms around a small pool of water while one lone, likewise naked gen-
tleman stares meditatively into the pool. The only way to see the inside
of the theater is to attend a performance. ⊠ *Trg Maršala Tita 15, Donji
Grad* ☎ *01/482–6920 or 01/482–8550* ⊕ *www.hnk.hr.*

⑭ **Muzej Mimara** (Mimara Museum). In a huge gray building that's dull
compared to some of those nearby, this vast private collection, including paintings, sculpture, ceramics, textiles, and rugs, was donated by
Ante Topić-Mimara (1898–1987), a Croatian who spent many years
abroad where he made his fortune, supposedly as a merchant. On display are canvases attributed to such Old Masters as Raphael, Rembrandt,
and Rubens, as well as more modern works by the likes of Manet, Degas,
and Renoir, and ancient artifacts including Egyptian glassware and Chinese porcelain. ⊠ *Rooseveltov trg 4, Donji Grad* ☎ *01/482–8100*
⊠ *20 Kn* ☉ *Tues., Wed., Fri., and Sat. 10–5, Thurs. 10–7, Sun. 10–2.*

⑬ **Muzej za Umjetnost i Obrt** (Arts & Crafts Museum). Designed in 1888
by Herman Bolle, the architect responsible for the Katedrala Marijina
uznesenja i Svetog Stjepana facade, this pleasant museum traces the development of the applied arts from the baroque period up to the 20th
century. Exhibits are displayed in chronological order, and although furniture design predominates, there are also sections devoted to sacral art,
clocks, and clothing. ⊠ *Trg Maršala Tita 10, Donji Grad* ☎ *01/482–
1111* ⊕ *www.muo.hr* ⊠ *20 Kn* ☉ *Tues.–Sat. 10–7, Sun. 10–2.*

⑰ **Strossmayerova Galerija Starih Majstora** (Strossmayer Gallery of Old
Masters). Now under the custody of the Croatian Academy of Sciences
and Arts, this impressive gallery was founded in 1884 by Bishop Strossmayer and later expanded to include many private donations. Works
by Venetian Renaissance and baroque artists such as Bellini and Carpaccio predominate, but there are also masterpieces by Dutch painters
Brueghel and Van Dyck, as well as a delightful Mary Magdalene by El

Greco. ✉ *Trg Zrinjskog 11, Donji Grad* ☎ *01/481–3344* ⊕ *www.*
mdc.hr/strossmayer 🎟 *10 Kn* ⏱ *Tues. 10–1 and 5–7, Wed.–Sun. 10–1.*

need a break?

The green expanse of Strossmayerov trg with its carefully tended
flower beds makes an ideal stopping place for weary feet. At the terrace
of the Viennese-style café of the **Palace Hotel** (✉ Strossmayerov trg
10), you can sip a cappuccino on a vine-enveloped sidewalk terrace
across from this leafy square, while sampling from a range of tempting
cakes and pastries.

🐾 **⑮** **Tehnički Muzej** (Technical Museum). It may be in a drab box of a building, but this museum is guaranteed to appeal to children and civil en-
gineers alike; try to see it in the afternoon on a weekday or in the late
morning on the weekend, when a series of guided visits are offered. The
highlight here is the demonstration of some of Nikola Tesla's inventions,
which takes place weekdays at 3:30 and weekends at 11:30, but there's
also the tour of a lifelike reconstruction of a coal mine at 3 on weekdays and 11 on weekends, and a planetarium visit at 4 on weekdays,
noon on weekends. That's not to mention all the various engines on display, as well as a fascinating historical exhibit of firefighting equipment
including trucks, ladders, and hoses aplenty. ✉ *Savska c 18, Donji
Grad* ☎ *01/484–4050* ⊕ *www.mdc.hr/tehnicki* 🎟 *Museum 20 Kn,
planetarium 10 Kn extra* ⏱ *Tues.–Fri. 9–5, weekends 9–1.*

off the beaten path

MAKSIMIR PARK – For a peaceful stroll in southeastern Europe's
oldest landscaped, English-style park, hop on a tram and go visit
Maksimir Park. A short ride east of the center of Zagreb (10 minutes
on tram 11 or 12 from Trg Bana Jelačića or 15 minutes on tram 4 or
7 from the train station), this 18-hectare (44½-acre) expanse of vine-
covered forests and several artificial lakes was a groundbreaker when
it opened back in 1794. After getting off the tram, you walk forward
a bit and enter on the left, through a prominent gate opposite the
city's main soccer stadium, aptly named Stadion Maksimir. A long,
wide promenade flanked by benches leads from here to Bellevue
Pavilion (1843), perched atop a small hill and featuring a café.

ZOOLOŠKI VRT ZAGREB – To your right along the way are some
small lakes and, beyond, the city's modest zoo, where admission is 20
Kn; it's open daily from 9 AM to 7 PM (last tickets sold at 6). To your
left is a playground.

Where to Eat

For budget fare, go up the steps from the main square, Trg Bana Jelačića,
and just off the right before you reach the top is a row of bistros where
you can get everything from *bureks* (a savory cheese- or meat-filled pastry) to simple pizzas to Balkan-style grilled meats for around half what
you'd pay at a modestly priced restaurant. And do remember, though
Zagreb is not exactly overflowing with budget sandwich shops, traditional bakeries have long fulfilled that role for locals; at such places, which

FUNNY FELIX

SREĆKO PUNTARIĆ CELEBRATED his 30th anniversary in 2005—and much of Croatia knew about it. The event in downtown Zagreb celebrated his distinguished reputation as Croatia's best-loved cartoonist. Popularly known by the alias "Felix" (also the name of his cartoon), this fifty-something, amiable fellow with a boyish face has published 27 books on themes ranging from a history of animals (heavy on dog and cat cartoons) to "computers in the stone age." He has won numerous international awards, and his cartoon in the national newspaper Večernji brings a smile to tens of thousands of his compatriots each day.

Among the cartoonists who have most inspired Felix is America's Gary Larson, of Far Side fame. "There has been no great cartoonist internationally since Larson," he laments, explaining that rampant consumerism in recent years has been much to the detriment of individual creativity. Indeed, Felix's cartoons are vaguely reminiscent of Larson's, what with their simply rendered figures whose faces are grossly out of proportion (Felix specializes in long snouts), and their often absurd situations that are funny even to those who cannot read the Croatian text. (Of course, you might well end up with a different reading of the situation than someone who can attach the words to the pictures.)

Felix does much of his work in what he calls his "cartoon gallery," the Felix Fun Factory. This quiet little shop-cum-workshop, a short tram ride from Zagreb's main square, is indeed one of Europe's few cartoon galleries. Here Felix not only works, but he, his wife, and his son sell postcards, posters, books, and mugs featuring his cartoons—limited edition products that can be had nowhere else. Felix has, to date, resisted the idea of selling his work to dealers, as he doesn't like the idea of his cartoons being commercialized. He likes the idea that they are available in only one place. Although a Felix Web site is in the works at this writing, you'll still be able to buy cartoons and merchandise only in the shop, in person.

Felix began cartooning in 1975 as a student, when, he explains, he undertook "a frontal assault" on a publication by churning out one cartoon after another. His rush of inspiration earned the publication's respect and gained some broader recognition for his work. But cartoons remained a hobby as Felix began a seven-year career as a mechanical engineer. From there, he became the advertising designer for a Zagreb-based chocolate company. Eventually, as the books and honors piled up, he quit that job to pursue his passion full-time. "Here in the shop," he says without a trace of vanity, "sometimes I feel like one of those solitary old masters, pursuing his art in isolation from the world."

To get to the Felix Fun Factory and perhaps meet Felix yourself (he generally mans the shop during the second, 4 to 7 shift), take tram 11 or 12 six stops east of Trg Bana Jelačića, almost as far as Maksimir Park, walk back a few yards, and take the first left onto Harambašićeva. The gallery, at no. 10, will soon be on your right. It's open weekdays from 10 to 1 and 4 to 7. You can call the gallery at ☎ 01/231–4915.

are on practically every street corner, you can pick up a burek for as little as 10 Kn a piece.

$$$$
Fodor's Choice
★

✕ **Paviljon.** This chic restaurant—with its round, colonnaded dining room and grand piano—occupies the ground floor of the charming 19th-century Art Pavilion, which faces the train station from across a wide, green mall. The Italian-inspired menu includes dishes such as tagliatelle with prosciutto and asparagus, crispy roast duck on red cabbage with figs, and oven-roasted monkfish with bread crumbs, pine nuts, and thyme. The wine list is equally impressive, with a choice of Croatian, Italian, and French vintages. ✉ *Tomislavov trg 22, Donji Grad* ☎ *01/481–3066* ▤ *AE, DC, MC, V* ⊘ *Closed Sun.*

$$$–$$$$
Fodor's Choice
★

✕ **Dubravkin Put.** Nestled in a verdant dale in Tuškanac Park, a 15-minute walk from the center in a low-rise building that might be mistaken for a ranch-style house, this prestigious fish restaurant specializes in dishes from the Dubrovnik area, with the house favorites including *buzara* (stew prepared with shellfish and scampi and/or fish) and sea bass filets in saffron and scampi sauce as well as appetizers like avocado with scampi, not to mention a few meat delicacies. The dining room is light and airy, with candlelit tables, a wooden floor, palmlike little trees, and colorful abstract art. Throughout summer there's outdoor seating on a spacious, leafy terrace. Reservations are recommended, but only on weekdays, oddly enough, as the Dubravkin Put is a popular venue for business dinners. ✉ *Dubravkin put 2, Gornji Grad* ☎ *01/483–4970* ▤ *AE, DC, MC, V.*

★ $$$–$$$$

✕ **Pod Gričkim Topom.** This cozy, endearingly rustic yet elegant restaurant, built into a stone wall on the hillside up a modest flight of steps from the Pansion Jägerhorn, on Ilica, and close to the funicular station in Gornji Grad, affords stunning views over the city rooftops. Dalmatian cooking predominates, with dishes such as *Jadanske lignje na žaru* (grilled Adriatic squid) and *crni rižoto od sipe* (cuttlefish-ink risotto) appreciated by locals and visitors alike. ✉ *Zakmardijeve stube 5, Gornji Grad* ☎ *01/483–3607* ▤ *AE, DC, MC, V.*

★ $$–$$$$

✕ **Gostionica Purger.** A flashing neon sign out front seems to suggest you are passing by a diner. Not so. Wildly popular with locals but with a faded, elegant air, this is the sort of restaurant that reminds you of what Zagreb must have been like before the Communists. The food is top-notch, and with animated conversations all around you (at snugly fitting tables—but then this is part of the appeal) and bright yellow walls adorned with historical sketches of Zagreb, this is one fine restaurant. The menu includes everything from goulash with white-wine sauce, on the low end of the price scale, to *domaće krvavice* (black pudding) at the middle, to suckling pig on the spit at the top. ✉ *Petrinjska 33, Donji Grad* ☎ *01/481–0713 or 01/481–8631* ▤ *AE, DC, MC, V* ⊘ *Closed Sun.*

★ $$–$$$$

✕ **Konoba Antica.** One of Zagreb's most precious dining secrets, this irresistibly cozy, convivial little cellar serves the freshest seafood in town. The secret of owners Zoran Petanjek and Ivan Brekalo is to simply let the seafood's natural flavors speak for themselves. You might begin with tuna carpaccio (raw tuna with a few drops of olive oil, lemon juice, and arugula), or try creamy, vegetable-rich conger eel soup. For a main course, try oven-baked octopus with potatoes or *gregada*, an eclectic blend of seafood boiled with a mix of vegetables—which is the house specialty. For dessert, there's nothing as sinfully heavenly as "*rozata* from Dubrovnik," a custard with a crusty layer of caramelized sugar on top. ⊠ *Kaptol 27, Gornji Grad* ☎ *01/481–2187, 098/268–8806, or 091/ 728–9438* ▤ *AE, DC, MC, V* ☉ *Closed Sun. and 3 wks in mid-July.*

$$–$$$ ✕ **Atlanta Caffè Restaurant.** One of the first restaurants to open among the myriad thriving cafés that line Tkalčićeva, Atlanta boasts a stylish interior with warm terra-cotta walls hung with enormous gilt-framed mirrors. You might begin with the risotto with arugula and prosciutto, followed by steak with truffles, rounded off with tiramisu. ⊠ *Tkalčićeva 65, Gornji Grad* ☎ *01/481–3848* ▤ *AE, DC, MC, V.*

★ $$–$$$ ✕ **Baltazar.** Situated deep in a courtyard a 10-minute walk uphill beyond the cathedral, Baltazar is best known for classic Balkan dishes such as *ražnjići* (pork on the spit), *čevapčići* (spiced, ground-meat kebabs), and *zapečeni grah* (oven-baked beans). Inside it's sparkling elegance; the courtyard has a spacious, covered, carnation-fringed terrace. ⊠ *Nova Ves 4, Gornji Grad* ☎ *01/466–6999* ▤ *AE, DC, MC, V* ☉ *Closed Sun.*

$$–$$$ ✕ **Stari Fijaker.** An old-fashioned restaurant with vaulted ceilings, wood-paneled walls, and crisp white table linens, Stari Fijaker lies just off Ilica, a five-minute walk from the main square on a cobblestone side street. The menu features carefully presented traditional Croatian dishes such as *zagorskajuha* (Zagorje-style potato soup with ham and mushrooms), *pečena teletina* (roast veal), *punjene paprike* (stuffed peppers), and even ostrich steak. ⊠ *Mesnička 6, Donji Grad* ☎ *01/483–3829* ▤ *AE, DC, MC, V.*

★ $–$$$ ✕ **Boban.** Close to Hotel Dubrovnik, Boban is both a street-level bar and a restaurant specializing in pasta dishes in a large vaulted cellar space below. The owner, Zvonimir Boban, was captain of the Croatian national football team during the 1998 World Cup. This place is extremely popular with locals, so be prepared to line up for a table since reservations are not accepted. ⊠ *Gajeva 9, Donji Grad* ☎ *01/481–1549* ▤ *AE, DC, MC, V.*

$–$$$ ✕ **Medvedgrad Pivnica.** Best known for its excellent beers, which are brewed on the premises, Medvedgrad also serves up generous portions of roast meats, goulash, and beans and sausage, accompanied by a range of salads. The location is close to the Cibona stadium. To get here, take either Tram 4 from the train station or Tram 17 from the main square. ⊠ *Savska 56, Donji Grad* ☎ *01/617–7110* ▤ *AE, DC, MC, V.*

$–$$ ✕ **Pizzeria 2.** The wooden tables and vaulted ceilings here give you that oh-so-pleasant cellar feel even though you're on the ground floor of Zagreb's leading pizzeria-cum-pasta joint, popular with the young crowd looking for a budget meal. The location is near the start of Nova Ves, just beyond Tkalčićeva. ⊠ *Nova Ves 2, Gornji Grad* ☎ *01/466–8888* ▤ *AE, DC, MC, V.*

Where to Stay

Zagreb offers a good choice of large, expensive hotels well geared to the needs of business travelers. This may be in part because tourists tend to frequent the coast, whereas the corporate crowd can at least get more work done in the city than at the seaside. In any event, in the past couple of years several of the capital's major hotels have come under new ownership and been given complete makeovers, generally of a sparkling, if somewhat standard, sort guaranteed to appeal to those seeking mid- to upper-range accommodations. The establishments listed here are quite central and reasonably priced for what they offer.

$$$$
Fodor'sChoice
★

Regent Esplanade. This beautiful hotel, diagonally across from the train station, was built in 1925 for travelers on the original *Orient Express.* A thorough renovation completed in 2004 has only enhanced its lux- ury and elegance. Spacious, high-ceilinged rooms have marble bathrooms stocked with Trussardi toiletries. Classical music plays in the hallways. From its immaculate, Habsburg-era lobby to its dining room replete with huge, resplendent chandeliers; from its domed ballroom to its spacious outdoor terrace with a sweeping views, the Esplanade may be a sym- bol of an era gone by, but it remains as adored as ever by business trav- elers and tourists alike. This is not to mention that it is yards away from the large, underground mall, the Importanne Centar. ⊠ *Mihanovićeva 1, Donji Grad, 10000* ☎ *01/456–6666 or 01/456–6600* 🖷 *01/456–6050 or 01/456–6020* ⊕ *www.regenthotels.com* 🛏 *209 rooms, 12 suites* ♨ *2 restaurants, room service, some in-room safes, in-room data ports, minibars, cable TV, massage, sauna, health club, casino, business cen- ter, Internet, convention center, meeting rooms, ballroom* ⊟ *AE, DC, MC, V* ⊘ *BP.*

$$$$
Sheraton Zagreb. High standards make this modern, six-story hotel, on a small side street but just a 10-minute walk from the city center, a relative bargain. The main draw for tourists will be the relative luxuri- ous look and feel; at least you can see what you're paying for here, which isn't always the case when you're down on the coast. Rooms are fur- nished in classical style with en-suite marble bathrooms. Behind the glass facade are excellent sports, business, and entertainment facilities. ⊠ *Kneza Borne 2, Donji Grad, 10000* ☎ *01/455–3535* 🖷 *01/455–3035* ⊕ *www.starwoodhotels.com* 🛏 *312 rooms, 11 suites* ♨ *2 restaurants, room service, in-room data ports, some kitchenettes, minibars, some re- frigerators, cable TV with movies, indoor pool, gym, sauna, bar, piano bar, casino, nightclub, babysitting, Internet, business services, conven- tion center, meeting rooms, car rental, some pets allowed* ⊟ *AE, DC, MC, V* ⊘ *BP.*

$$$$
Westin Zagreb. After a complete renovation in 2005, this colossal 17- story modern structure between the Mimara Museum and the Botani- cal Garden—previously the Opera Zagreb—still looks homely on the outside, but on the inside it's a sparkling, five-star affair. Rooms are bright, spacious, and clean, if a bit uninspiring; the signature "Heavenly Beds" are exceptionally comfy. Note that in addition to its 22 suites, the Westin also offers 19 "guest offices," comprising a complete office (in- cluding a separate powder room) that adjoins the bedroom (which has its own full bath). Sports and business facilities are first-rate, and a hotel limousine is available for transfers to and from the airport. ⊠ *Kršnjavoga 1, Donji Grad, 10000* ☎ *01/489–2000* 🖷 *01/489–2001* ⊕ *www. starwoodhotels.com* 🛏 *377 rooms, 22 suites* ♨ *2 restaurants, room ser- vice, in-room data ports, minibars, cable TV with movies, in-room safes, indoor pool, gym, hair salon, massage, sauna, bar, laundry ser-*

vice, lounge, business services, meeting rooms, car rental ▤ *AE, DC, MC, V* ⑪ *BP.*

★ **$$$** ▦ **Arcotel Allegra.** Zagreb's first trendy boutique hotel opened in 2003. Design is the word here. Everything—from bedspreads and pillowcases, which picture the faces of such luminaries as Verdi, Kafka, Frida Kahlo, and Einstein, to the soft, synthetic leather armchairs and "mobile tables" in each room, to the deep-blue carpeting that features a map of the world (Zagreb highlighted by a red dot)—is intended to soothe or inspire. All this compliments of Austrian artist, designer, and architect Harald Schreiber. In the Executive rooms (a small supplement to the standard), you get free newspapers, slippers, bathrobes, and chocolates. The hotel's likewise stylish restaurant is probably the only place in town where you can get such fare as "freshly seared Adriatic Cajun tuna with wasabi dressing and green salad." ✉ *Branimirova 29, Donji Grad, 10000* ☎ *01/469–6000* 🖷 *01/469–6096* ⊕ *www.arcotel.at* ⇘ *151 rooms* ⚘ *Restaurant, café, minibars, in-room safes, cable TV, DVD players, in-room data ports* ▤ *AE, DC, MC, V* ⑪ *BP.*

★ **$$$** ▦ **Palace Hotel Zagreb.** Built in 1891 as the Schlessinger Palace and converted in 1907 to become the city's first hotel, the Palace Hotel offers romantic, old-fashioned comfort but few extras. The spacious rooms have something of their original art-nouveau look, with somber, golden hues predominating. Overlooking a green square between the train station and the city center—and only a 5-minute walk from either—it's best known by locals for the street-level, Viennese-style café. ✉ *Strossmayerov trg 10, Donji Grad, 10000* ☎ *01/481–4611 or 01/489–9600* 🖷 *01/481–1358 or 01/481–1357* ⊕ *www.palace.hr* ⇘ *123 rooms, 5 suites* ⚘ *Restaurant, café, room service, in-room data ports, minibars, in-room safes, cable TV, casino, laundry service, meeting rooms* ▤ *AE, DC, MC, V* ⑪ *BP.*

$$–$$$ ▦ **Best Western Premier Hotel Astoria.** The Hotel Astoria reopened with a new name and a luxurious new look in March 2005 after a six-month makeover. Less than 5 minutes by foot from the train station and 10 minutes from downtown, it offers bright, modern rooms with the silky bedspreads and partly marble bathrooms that meet the requirements of its Premier category. It may be Zagreb's first hotel in which the shutters roll up automatically when you enter your room—do remember that before tearing your clothes off in a fit of passion. The standard (double) rooms are on the small side; the executive rooms, which have king-size beds, are more spacious but also quite a bit more expensive. ✉ *Petrinjska 71, Donji Grad, 10000* ☎ *01/480–8900 or 01/480–8910* 🖷 *01/480–8908 or 01/481–7053* ⊕ *www.bestwestern.com* ⇘ *100 rooms, 2 suites* ⚘ *Restaurant, café, room service, in-room data ports, minibars, in-room safes, cable TV, meeting rooms* ▤ *AE, DC, MC, V* ⑪ *BP.*

★ **$$** ▦ **Hotel Dubrovnik.** Claiming the most central location in the city, just off Trg Bana Jelačića, Hotel Dubrovnik has been popular with business travelers and tourists alike since opening back in 1929. The garish mirrored-glass facade conceals the results of a thorough 2002 renovation: bright, modern, beige-curtained rooms that are a tad tight on space. Beyond its other amenities, the hotel is also home to one of Zagreb's most popular hangouts, the Cafe Dubrovnik, which has a great view of the main square. ⊠ *Gajeva 1, Donji Grad, 10000* ☎ *01/486–3555* 🖶 *01/ 486–3550* ⊕ *www.hotel-dubrovnik.hr* ⤴ *266 rooms, 8 suites* ᵭ *Restaurant, café, room service, in-room data ports, minibars, some refrigerators, in-room safes, cable TV, bar, business services, meeting rooms, parking (fee)* ⊟ *AE, DC, MC, V* ⦿| *BP.*

$ 🖽 **Hotel Central.** On the opposite side of the train station from the Regent Esplanade—and in one boring, concrete block of a building—the Central is convenient rather than quaint. The spacious rooms, which still sparkle from a renovation in 2001, are simply furnished in shades of blue, and the staff are friendly and efficient. ⊠ *Branimirova 3, Donji Grad, 10000* ☎ *01/484–1122 or 01/484–0555* 🖶 *01/484–1304* ⊕ *www. hotel-central.hr* ⤴ *76 rooms, 3 suites* ᵭ *Bar, casino, some in-room data ports, some minibars, cable TV, laundry service, meeting room, car rental* ⊟ *AE, DC, MC, V* ⦿| *BP.*

$ 🖽 **Pansion Jägerhorn** At the far end of a shop-filled courtyard off Zagreb's busiest shopping street, a minute's walk from Trg Bana Jelačića, this friendly pension-cum-restaurant occupies the building where Zagreb's first restaurant opened back in 1827. Rooms are spacious and bright, with skylights, floral bedspreads (but hard mattresses), and walls adorned with soothing watercolors. You enter through the popular restaurant, which features not only its very own artificial waterfall but is highly regarded for its wild-game dishes, as you might guess from the stuffed deer, birds, and so forth all over the walls alongside World War II–era menus. ⊠ *Ilica 14, Donji Grad, 10000* ☎ *01/483–3877 or 01/ 483–0161* 🖶 *01/483–3573* ⊕ *www.hotel-pansion-jaegerhorn.hr* ⤴ *11 rooms, 2 apartments* ᵭ *Restaurant, café, minibars, cable TV, free parking* ⊟ *AE, DC, MC, V* ⦿| *BP.*

$ 🖽 **Villa Tina.** This delightful family-run hotel is out of the center, on a peaceful side street close to Maksimir Park. Each room is individually and tastefully furnished; you're likely to find such extras as fresh fruit and flowers. There's a good restaurant with a summer garden and a beautiful indoor pool. ⊠ *Bukovačka c 213, Donji Grad, 10000* ☎ *01/244– 5138* 🖶 *01/244–5204* ⊕ *www.vilatina.com* ⤴ *25 rooms* ᵭ *Restaurant, minibars, cable TV, indoor pool, sauna* ⊟ *AE, DC, MC, V* ⦿| *BP.*

¢ 🖽 **Hotel Sliško.** This small, friendly hotel is just a 5-minute walk from the bus station and a 15-minute walk from the center. Rooms are smart and functional, and there's a bar and breakfast room. It's normally fully booked during trade fairs (and rates are 20% more then), so check for dates well in advance. Cash payments yield a 10% discount. ⊠ *Bunićeva 7, Donji Grad, 10000* ☎ *01/619–4210 or 01/618–4777* 🖶 *01/619– 4223* ⊕ *www.slisko.hr* ⤴ *15 rooms, 3 apartments* ᵭ *Restaurant, bar, cable TV* ⊟ *AE, DC, MC, V* ⦿| *BP.*

Nightlife & the Arts

Climbing full-steam ahead out of the economic depression caused by the war, Zagreb now has a lively entertainment scene. Bars, clubs, and cinemas are predominantly frequented by the city's student population, whereas the concert hall and theater remain the domain of the older generation. For information about what's on, pick up a free copy of either the monthly *Events and Performances,* published by the city tourist board.

Nightlife

BARS & NIGHTCLUBS **BP Jazz Club** (✉ Teslina 7, Donji Grad ☎ 01/481–4444 ⊕ www.bpclub. hr), the capital's top venue for live jazz, is a smoky basement bar. **Bulldog** (✉ Bogovićeva 6, Donji Grad ☎ 01/481–7393) is a popular split-level café-cum-pub with a large summer terrace. **Old Pharmacy** (✉ Andrije Hebranga 11a, Donji Grad ☎ 01/455–4367), a peaceful pub with CNN on television and a selection of English-language newspapers, also has a non-smoking side room. **Oliver Twist Pub** (✉ Tkalčićeva 60, Gornji Grad ☎ 01/481–2206) is definitely not a bleak house. This is *the* place to be after dark on Tkalčićeva. Although in good weather practically all the (mostly young) patrons are seated out front, inside is an immaculate English-style pub whose walls, on the upper floor, are each adorned with memorabilia associated with different Dickens novels. **Pivnica Medvedgrad** (✉ Savska 56, Donji Grad ☎ 01/617–7110) is a beer hall and microbrewery serving the best ale in town. **Tantra** (✉ Gajeva 2, Donji Grad ☎ 01/487–2544), until recently a popular restaurant, is now a popular place to kick back, drink, and chat in soft tones while watching the crowds on Trg Bana Jelačića below. Pillow-equipped white divans and wicker-backed lounge chairs provide an unbeatable view of Zagreb's main square. To get here, pass through the narrow arcade between the bookshops yards away from the square and go up the spiral wooden staircase that's to the left just before a small giftshop.

DISCOS **Aquarius** (✉ Aleja mira, Jarun ☎ 01/364–0231 ⊕ www.aquarius.hr) is Zagreb's top club for dancing, especially for disco and techno music. It overlooks the beach at *Malo jezero,* the smaller of the two interconnected lakes comprising Lake Jarun, 4 km (2½ mi) from the city center. **Saloon** (✉ Tuškanac 1a, Gornji Grad ☎ 01/483–4903) is the city's most glamorous club, where you can rub shoulders with the stars and dance not only to commercial as well as Croatian techno but also, once a week, to classic rock.

The Arts

ARTS FESTIVALS For one week in mid-September, the **World Theatre Festival** brings to Zagreb theater companies from all over Europe—if not exactly the world— for one or more performances each evening at various theatrical venues about town. For the best of concerts in the park, keep your eye out for the free **Promenade Concerts** by Croatian chamber orchestras, brass bands, and choirs once a week from around mid-August to mid-October at the music pavilion set amid the lovely plane trees and fountains of Zrinjevac Park, on Zrinskog trg. Adding color to this series are 19th-century-costume contests and displays, an antiques market, a play area and programs for children, rides in horse-drawn carriages, and even souvenir stands.

FILM **Broadway Tkalča** (✉ Nova Ves 17, Gornji Grad ☎ 01/466–7686) is Croatia's first multiplex cinema, in the Centar Kaptol shopping complex, behind the cathedral. Most foreign films (including those from the United States) are shown in their original language with Croatian subtitles.

MAJOR VENUES The **Hrvatsko Narodno Kazalište** (Croatian National Theater; ✉ Trg Maršala Tita 15, Donji Grad ☎ 01/482–8532 ⊕ www.hnk.hr), a beautiful 19th-century building, hosts classical and contemporary dramas, opera, and ballet performances. **Komedija** (✉ Kaptol 9, Gornji Grad ☎ 01/481–4566 ⊕ www.komedija.hr) is a small theater specializing in operettas and Croatian musicals, close to the cathedral. **Koncertna Dvorana Vatroslav Lisinski** (Vatroslav Lisinski Concert Hall; ✉ Stjepana Radića 4, Donji Grad ☎ 01/612–1166 ⊕ www.lisinski.hr), a large, modern complex with two auditoriums, is Zagreb's top venue for orchestral- and classical-music concerts.

Shopping

The number of Croats who take shopping buses to Italy and Austria suggests that Zagreb, for all its other attractions, still has a limited selection of affordable, high-quality clothing, household goods, and other such products for sale. However, a walk down the bustling Ilica or other nearby shopping streets will always reveal new stores full of high fashion. Meanwhile, Frankopanska is turning into something of a fashion avenue, with labels like Lacoste and Cacharel and the British design duo Gharari Štrok. Don't pass up the chance to stroll through the beautiful Oktogon shopping arcade, whose long, bright yellow, spacious hall and lovely glass ceilings dating to 1901—with elaborate, wrought-iron gates at each end, and culminating in an octagonal ceiling dome with floral motifs—connects Ilica 5 with Trg Petra Preradovića and offers more than a few high-class shops along the way.

Shopping Centers & Markets

Surprisingly, it's easy to miss the capital's largest shopping mall, the **Importanne Centar** (✉ Mihanovicéva ul, Donji Grad), since it's completely underground and not well marked on the street level. Look for the escalators leading down, and once you're inside, good luck finding your way back out. Behind the Cathedral is the **Centar Kaptol** (✉ Nova Ves 11, Gornji Grad), whose stores include Marks & Spencer, Kenzo, and Max & Co. For an authentic Croatian shopping experience, visit the **Dolac open-air market** (✉ Trg Bana Jelačića, Gornji Grad), where besides fresh fruit and vegetables there are also a number of arts-and-crafts stalls. It's open weekdays 7 to 4 and weekends until noon.

Specialty Stores

Ties may not be the most original of gifts, but they are uniquely Croatian. During the 17th century, Croatian mercenaries who fought in France sported narrow, silk neck scarfs, which soon became known to the French as *cravat* (from the Croatian *hrvat*). At **Croata** (✉ Ilica 5 [within the Oktogon arcade], Donji Grad ☎ 01/481–2726 ⊕ www.croata.hr ✉ Kaptol 13, Gornji Grad) you can buy "original Croatian ties" in presentation boxes, accompanied by a brief history of the tie. **Croatia Records** (✉ Bogoviceva 5, Donji Grad) has a good selection of Croatian and international pop and rock music. **Natura Croatica** (✉ Preradovićeva 8, Donji Grad ☎ 01/485–5076) offers all manner of Croatian delicacies that use only natural ingredients, from brandies and liqueurs to jams, olive oils, cheeses, truffles, soaps, wild-game jerkies, and pâtés. Housed in a tastefully arranged, vaulted brick cellar, **Vinoteka Bornstein** (✉ Kaptol 19, Gornji Grad ☎ 01/481–2363) stocks a wide range of quality Croatian wines, olive oils, and truffle products.

THE ZAGREB CARD

At 26 venues about town—including tourist-information offices, several major hotels, and youth hostels—you can pick up one of the best deals in town. The Zagreb Card, which costs 90 Kn, not only covers 72 hours (from the date and time stamped on the card) of public transport but also offers you discounts of up to 50% at more than 30 museums and galleries as well as the zoo, similar savings on parking and car rental, and 20% discounts at many shops, restaurants, theaters, and concert halls. Considering the cost of similar cards in other European capitals, this can be counted a true bargain.

EXCURSIONS NORTH OF ZAGREB

A favorite excursion to the outskirts of Zagreb is to the heights of Sljeme and its observatory. And then there is the peaceful spa town of Stubičke Toplice and, a bit further to the northeast, the Catholic pilgrimage site of Maria Bistrica. Further to the north, beyond the Medvednica Hills, lies a pastoral region known as Zagorje. The scenery is calm and enchanting: red-brick villages, such as Kumrovec, are animated with ducks and chickens, and the hillsides are inlaid with vineyards and orchards. Medieval hilltop castles, including Veliki Tabor and Dvor Trakoščan, survey the surrounding valleys. To the northeast of Zagreb is the charming baroque town of Varaždin. Although Sljeme and Stubličke Toplice are reasonably easy to get to from the capital by bus, having a car at your disposal for a day or two will give you a chance to cover more ground efficiently (e.g., without having to return to Zagreb to board yet another bus).

Numbers in the margins refer to numbers on the Excursions from Zagreb map.

Sljeme

⑲ *5 km (3 mi) north of Zagreb by tram and cable car.*

A favorite excursion to the outskirts of Zagreb is to the heights of Sljeme, the peak of **Mt. Medvednica**, at 1,035 meters (3,363 feet). You can reach it taking Tram 14 (direction Mihaljevac), all the way to the terminal stop, where you should change to Tram 15 (direction Dolje), also to its terminal stop. From there a cable car operates hourly for the 20-minute journey to the top of the mountain for breathtaking views over the surrounding countryside. It's an ideal place for picnicking, but you may wish to save your appetite for dinner at one of the excellent restaurants on the road home. ⊠ *Dolje* 🚡 *Cable car 17 Kn* ⊗ *Daily 8–8.*

Where to Eat

$$$ ✕ **Stari Puntijar.** On the road between Zagreb and Sljeme, Stari Puntijar is renowned for game and traditional 19th-century Zagreb dishes such as *podolac* (ox medallions in cream and saffron), *orehnjaca* (walnut loaf), and *makovnjaca* (poppy-seed cake). The wine list is excellent. ✉ *Gračanka c 65, Medveščak, Zagreb* ☎ *01/467–5500* 🗖 *AE, DC, MC, V.*

Stubičke Toplice

⑳ *37 km (23 mi) north of Zagreb.*

Established in 1805 on the foundations of a Roman-era thermal bath and expanded into a full-fledged complex in 1930, this peaceful spa at the northern edge of the Medvednica hills is where the capital's residents go to soak away those nerves and ailments in temps ranging from 45°C to 65°C (113°F to 149°F). Set at the edge of a large park replete with tall spruce trees, the **Matija Gubec** hotel is the place to go to give it a try yourself—though you needn't stay overnight at this complex of six beige, concrete, interconnected ranch-house-like buildings. After paying a small admission fee, you get access to the complex's eight outdoor pools as well as the hotel's indoor pool, sauna, and fitness facility. The rooms (€72) are decent, with cable TV and phones but otherwise have no frills and no air-conditioning. If you are looking for a bite to eat, Restaurant Bilikum, across the street from the hotel, is a good choice. ✉ *Viktora Šipeka 31, Stubičke Toplice* ☎ *049/282–501* ⊕ *www.hotel-mgubec.com* 🗖 *45 Kn (40 Kn after 3 PM); sauna only 20 Kn for 20 minutes* ⊘ *Weekdays 7 AM–10 PM, weekends 7 AM–midnight.*

Marija Bistrice

㉑ *17 km (11 mi) east of Stičke Toplice, 40 km (25 mi) northeast of Zagreb.*

Other than its famous pilgrimage site, there's not much of interest in Marija Bistrice. Definitely do this as a day-trip, unless you want to spend a night in nearby Stubičke Toplice.

Croatia's preeminent religious pilgrimage site, the **Hodočasnička Crkva Marije Bistricvkve** (Pilgrimage Church of St. Mary of Bistrica) is home to the Blessed Virgin of Bistrica, a black, wooden, 15th-century Gothic statue of the Holy Mother associated with miraculous powers (having survived not only the Turkish invasion but a subsequent fire) and set in the main altar. The church, which was proclaimed a Croatian shrine by the nation's parliament in 1715, was rebuilt in neo-Renaissance style in the late 19th century by Hermann Bollé, who also designed the Zagreb cathedral; the shrine complex adjacent to the church was enlarged in time for a 1998 visit by Pope John Paul II, who was in town to beatify Alojzije Stepincac, who became Archbishop of Zagreb in 1937 but was jailed and later placed under house arrest in post-war, Tito-led Yugoslavia. Behind the church is a huge amphitheater that was built for the pope's visit, and from there you can climb up *Kalvarija* (Calvary Hill) to the stations of the cross, ornamented with sculptures by Croatian artists. ⊠ *Trg Ivana Pavla II, Marija Bistrice* ☎ *049/469–156 or 049/468–350* 🎫 *Free* ⊙ *Daily 7:30 AM–6 PM.*

> **need a break?**
>
> If your pilgrimage leaves you famished in a bodily sense, a sure bet for well-prepared grilled meats and seafood is **Purga** (⊠ Grančarska 45b, Zlatar Bistrica ☎ 049/461–949 ▤ AE, DC, MC, V) a roadside restaurant 6 km (4 mi) north of Marija Bistrica, which has pleasantly rustic decor with wooden tables and charming seat cushions with an embroidered look, as well as moderate prices.

Kumrovec

★ ㉒ *40 km (25 mi) northwest of Zagreb.*

The former Yugoslavia's late president Josip Broz Tito was born here in 1892, and his childhood home has been turned into a small memorial museum. In the courtyard of his birthplace stands an imposing bronze likeness of him by Antun Augustinčić. The old quarter of Kumrovec, known as **Kumrovec Staro Selo** (Kumrovec Old Village), is an open-air museum with beautifully restored thatched cottages and wooden farm buildings, orchards, and a stream giving a lifelike reconstruction of 19th-century rural life. On weekends craftsmen, including a blacksmith, a candlemaker, and others, demonstrate their skills. ⊠ *Kumrovec* ☎ *049/ 553–107* ⊕ *www.mdc.hr/kumrovec* 🎫 *20 Kn* ⊙ *Apr.–Sept., daily 9–7; Oct.–Mar., daily 9–4.*

Veliki Tabor

★ ㉓ *15 km (9 mi) north of Kumrovec.*

On a lofty hilltop stands the massive fortress of Veliki Tabor. The main pentagonal core of the building dates back to the 12th century, whereas the side towers were added in the 15th century as protection against the Turks. The colonnaded galleries of the interior cast sublime shadows in moonlight. Nine buses daily will get you here from Zagreb's main bus station in 2½ hours for 69 Kn one-way; but after getting off you have a 3-km (2-mi) walk still ahead of you. Hence, as true more generally of site-hopping in the Zagorje region, a rental car may come in handy. ⊠ *Desinić* ☎ *049/343–052* ⊕ *www.veliki-tabor.hr* 🎫 *20 Kn* ⊙ *Daily 10–6.*

Where to Eat

★ **$$–$$$** ✕ **Grešna Gorica.** Visiting this rustic tavern is like stepping into a friend's home. That said, your friend's home is unlikely to have a stuffed fawn and a pair of *kuna* (martens, the national currency's namesake) on the wall (this monetary history of kuna dates from the days when the fur of this large, weasel-like creature was in fact a currency). All produce used here is supplied by local farmers, and the menu features typical Zagorje dishes, including *zagorski štrukli* (baked cheese dumplings) and *pura s mlincima* (turkey with savory pastries). The garden affords sublime views down onto Veliki Tabor fortress. ⊠ *Desinić* ☎ *049/ 343–001* ▤ *No credit cards.*

Where to Stay

$ ⊞ **Dvorac Bežanec.** There's a lovely old manor house waiting for you—
Fodor'sChoice a 15-minute drive east of Veliki Tabor—where you can have your spa-
★ cious room with period furniture and breakfast, too, for under €100 a
night. Owned by various barons since Count Keglević built it in the 17th
century, Bežanec castle got a new lease on life as a luxury hotel in 1990.
Part of its charm is its authenticity, and the furnishings, while in tip-
top, dust-free shape, actually feel like the real, 17th-century McCoys.
Splendid works by various Croatian artists, including a whole series of
superb naive paintings by Slauko Stolmik, line the halls. With advance
notice, the hotel will pick up guests who arrive by bus in Veliki Tabor.
Any activity, from hot-air balloon rides and horseback riding instruction to tennis and archery, can be yours, too, for reasonable fees. Sure,
there's no air-conditioning—but was there any in the 18th century? ⊠ *Valentinovo, 49218 Pregrada* ☎ *049/376–800* 📠 *049/376–810*
⊕ *www.bezanec.hr* 🛏 *20 rooms, 5 suites* ⚒ *Restaurant, minibars,
cable TV, tennis court, massage, sauna, billiards, meeting room; no a/c*
🝙 *AE, DC, MC, V* ⊗⊙ *BP.*

¢ ⊞ **Trska.** Exactly 2 km (1¼ mi) beyond the side road leading to the Grešna
Gorica restaurant (*see* Where to Eat, *above*)—turning left at the sign to
Pregrada, that is—is an "agroturizm" sign pointing left. Turn here and
drive less than 1 km (½ mi) up a steep hill to the Ptičar family farmhouse, where the sounds of mules braying and cocks crowing will con-
vince you that you're truly in the countryside—for a steal. No, English
isn't spoken here, but that's not necessarily a barrier to essential communication and a scrumptious meal followed by a peaceful night of sleep
far away from it all, with a stunning view of the countryside below. It's
an excellent budget option if you're adventurous and in the area. ⊠ *Tro-
vec Desinićki, Desinić* ☎ *No phone* 🛏 *8 rooms* ⚒ *No TV, no a/c*
🝙 *No credit cards* ⊗⊙ *BP.*

Krapina

🌕 **㉔** *20 km (12½ mi) east of Veliki Tabor, 66 km (41 mi) north of Zagreb.*

Zagorje's quaint administrative and cultural center is on the tourism radar
screen primarily as home of *krapinski čovjek* (Krapina man)—no, not
the town's one male inhabitant but a Neanderthal of a sort, whose bones
were discovered on a hillside a short walk from the town center in 1899,
in what was a settlement of these early humanlike creatures 30,000 to
40,000 years ago. Indeed, this may be one of the few places in the world
today where you can meet up with a family of such hominids and even
a fearsome bear in the woods—that is, with life-size statues of Neanderthals going about their daily business (wielding clubs, throwing
rocks, tending fire), at the spot where the discovery was made. Displays
at the **Museum of Evolution,** which is near the location of the actual discovery, provide insight into who these early Neanderthals were and how
they lived, and more broadly into the region's geology and history.
⊠ *Šetalište V Sluge* ☎ *049/371–491* 🎟 *15 Kn* ⊙ *Apr.–Oct., Tues.–Sun.
9–5; Nov.–Mar., Tues.–Sun. 8–3.*

Trakošćan

★ ㉕ *41 km (25½ mi) west of Varaždin, 36 km (22½ mi) northeast of Veliki Tabor.*

Fodor'sChoice
★
Perched resplendently several hundred feet above the parking lot where the tour buses come and go, the romantic white hilltop **Dvor Trakošćan** (Trakošćan Castle) is set amid beautifully landscaped grounds, overlooking a small lake. Croatia's most visited castle took on its present neo-Gothic appearance during the 19th century, though there has been a building here since the 13th century. Inside, the wood-paneled rooms are filled with period furnishings and family portraits, giving you some idea of how the wealthy local aristocracy once lived. A restaurant, café, and souvenir shop occupy an uninspiring, Ministry of Culture–owned building at the foot of the hill. ⊠ *Trakošćan* ☎ *042/796–281 or 042/796–422* ⊕ *www.trakoscan.net* ✉ *20 Kn* ☉ *Apr.–Sept., daily 9–6; Oct.–Mar., daily 9–4.*

Varaždin

㉖ *70 km (48 mi) northeast of Zagreb.*

Situated on a plain near the River Drava, Varaždin is the most harmonious and beautifully preserved baroque town in this corner of the continent. A vibrant commercial and cultural center, especially in the 18th century, Varaždin is richly adorned by extraordinary churches and the baroque palaces of the aristocratic families that once lived here. It was Croatia's capital from 1756 until a devastating fire in 1776 prompted a move to Zagreb. First mentioned under the name Garestin in a document by the Hungarian-Croatian king Bela III from 1181, it was declared a free royal town by King Andrew II of Hungary's Arpad dynasty in 1209 and went on to become an important economic, social, administrative, and military center. Near the heart of the city, in a park surrounded by grassy ramparts, the well-preserved castle is the main attraction. A short walk from the castle, on the outskirts of town, is one of Europe's loveliest cemeteries, with immense hedges trimmed and shaped around ornate memorials.

What to See

Fodor'sChoice
★
Today a historic museum, Varaždin's main attraction is the impressive **Stari Grad** (Castle), which assumed its present form in the 16th century as a state-of-the-art defense fortification against the Turks, complete with moats, dikes, and bastions with low, round defense towers connected by galleries with openings for firearms. In the ensuing centuries it was often reconstructed by the families that owned it; for more than three centuries, until its 1925 purchase by the city, it belonged to the Erdödy clan. From the 12th century up until 1925, the castle served as the seat of the county prefect. You enter through the 16th-century tower gatehouse, which has a wooden drawbridge, to arrive in the internal courtyard with three levels of open-arched galleries. Indoors, there's an extensive display of antique furniture, with pieces laid out in chronological order and each room representing a specific period. ⊠ *Stross-*

VARAŽDIN'S GUITAR GREAT

IT'S NOT BY CHANCE that Varaždin's distinguished string instrument maker Vladimir Šimunov Proskurnjak, whose studio is in the heart of downtown, at Krančevićeva 5, specializes in guitars. This particular instrument holds a special place in the hearts of the classical-music lovers of Varaždin. Indeed, there was a time when the guitar was among the most popular instruments in Croatia and elsewhere in Europe and earned the respect of the great music critics of the day. That time, in Croatia, peaked in the first half of the nineteenth century. The nation's greatest guitarist of the era, and one of the continent's best, was Varaždin's own Ivan Padovec.

Born in 1800, Ivan was often ill as a child and extremely nearsighted. To make matters worse, at the age of 10 he was left half-blind when a stone thrown at him by another boy hit his left eye. Since his physical limitations meant he could not become a priest, as his parents had hoped, Padovec trained to become a teacher. However, he chose quite another path.

By the age of 19 Ivan Padovec had not only taught himself to play the guitar, he was indeed able to support himself by giving lessons to friends. Before long he decided to devote his life to music. Within five years, Padovec had a reputation not only as a virtuoso guitarist but also as a talented composer. By 1827, he was giving concerts from Zagreb and Varaždin to Zadar, Rijeka, and Trieste, and before long he'd earned the respect of even the court in Vienna. While living in the Austrian capital from 1829 to 1837, Padovec gave concerts throughout Europe, though weakening eyesight eventually forced a return to his native Varaždin. After a concert in Zagreb in 1840, one critic wrote, "[Padovec] showed that even on such an instrument it was possible to play tenderly and skillfully, thus surpassing everyone else." In addition to writing more than 200 compositions, he authored an influential book on guitar instruction and invented a 10-string guitar.

Completely blind by 1848, Padovec retreated to his sister's house in Varaždin, unable to compose or teach. In 1871, he gave his final performance at the city theater. A life of music reaped little financial compensation for Padovec, and he died in poverty on November 4, 1873. Appropriately, Varaždin's tourist office is located in the house where he was born, at Ivana Padovca 3.

mayerovo Šetalište 7 ☎ 042/210–399 ⊕ *www.varazdin.hr* ✉ *15 Kn* ⊙ *Oct.–Apr., Tues.–Fri. 10–3, weekends 10–1.*

need a break? For a bite of Varaždin's specialty baked good, a *klipić* (a salted, finger-shaped bread), stop by at one of the bakeries at the city's open-air **food market** (✉ Trg Bana Jelačića), which is open Monday through Saturday from 7 AM to 2 PM.

Consecrated to Varaždin's patron saint in 1761 on the site of an older church, the **Župna Crkva Sv. Nikole** (Parish Church of St. Nicholas) is a baroque structure that is more attractive on the outside than the inside. Note the red-tiled, conical steeple and the fake yet imposing white columns built into the facade. ✉ *Trg slobode 11.*

The **Uršulinska Crkva Rođenja Isusovog** (Ursuline Church of the Birth of Christ), a single-nave, pale-pink baroque church, was consecrated in 1712 by the Ursuline sisters, who came to Varaždin from Bratislava nine years earlier at the invitation of the Draškovic family. Its charming, strikingly slender tower was added in 1726. ⊠ *Uršulinska 3.*

Consecrated in 1650 on the site of a medieval predecessor, the pale yellow **Franjevačka Crkva** (Franciscan Church) has the highest tower in Varaždin, at almost 55 meters (180 feet). Right out front is a statue of 10th-century Croatian bishop Grgur Ninski, who is memorialized in a feverish pose; this is a replica of the original, which is in Split. ⊠ *Franjevački trg 8.*

Housed in the Herzer Palace, which is among many of Varaždin's architectural attractions that were under renovation as of this writing, the ⓒ **Entomološka Zbirka** (Entomological Collection) museum holds in store a fascinating presentation of some 1,000 different insects. ⊠ *Franjevački trg 6* ☏ *042/210–474* ⊡ *20 Kn* ◷ *Tues.–Fri. 10–5, weekends 10–1.*

The 16th-century **Lisakova kula** (Lisak Tower) is the only part of Varaždin's northern town wall that has been preserved. The wall formed part of the onetime city fortress, but most of it was razed in the early 19th century. Unfortunately, you can't enter the tower. ⊠ *Trg Bana Jelačića.*

The **Galerija Starih i Novih Majstora** (Gallery of Old and Modern Masters) is housed in the striking, 18th-century rococo Palača Sermage (Sermage Palace)—characterized by cinnamon-colored, black-framed geometric medallions decorating its facade and an impressive wrought-iron terrace. The museum has a rich array of traditional paintings by Croatian and other European artists. ⊠ *Trg M. Stančića 3* ☏ *042/214–172* ⊡ *20 Kn* ◷ *Tues.–Fri. 10–5, weekends 10–1.*

Gradska Vijećnica (City Hall), one of Europe's oldest city halls, is still in use. This imposing, flamingo-pink landmark has been the seat of Varaždin's public administration since December 14, 1523. Restored after a fire in 1776, it received a thorough external makeover in 1793. Stop by on a Saturday morning between 11 and noon (April through October) to watch the changing of the guard, a 250-year tradition that lives on.

Built in 1773 and thoroughly re-landscaped in 1905 by Hermann Haller, a tailor who revolutionized traditional notions of what graveyards should look like, Varaždin's **Gradsko Groblje** (Town Cemetery) is as pleasant a place for a restful stroll as it may be, when the time comes, to be laid to rest. Replete with flowerbeds and rows of tall, coniferous hedges and linden trees flanking ornate memorials and laid out in geometric patterns, the cemetery sublimely manifests Haller's conviction that each plot should be a "serene, hidden place only hinting at its true purpose, with no clue as to whether its occupant is rich or poor, since all are tended equally, surrounded by every kind of flower . . . producing perfect harmony for the visitor." You can get there by walking about five minutes east of the Castle along Hallerova aleja. ⊠ *Hercega* ◷ *8 AM–7 PM.*

Where to Eat

★ **$$–$$$** ✕ **Restoran Zlatna Guska.** In a lovely, vaulted brick cellar, the Golden Goose Restaurant makes a good stopping-off point for a quick lunch or a relaxed dinner over a bottle of local wine. Here you'll find not only a whole array of soups hard to get elsewhere, such as cream of nettle, but an impressive salad bar and vegetarian fare such as fried cauliflower in mushroom sauce with sesame seeds. They also serve plenty of seafood and meat. The wood-covered menu has helpful photos of imaginatively named main dishes—"Last Meal of Inquisition Victims" (a soup, actually), "Daggers of Count Brandenburg" (skewered meat with pasta and vegetables), and "Countess Juliana Draškovic's Flower" (a pair of crêpes filled with fruit and topped with powdered sugar and whipped cream)—itself almost worth the trip. ⊠ *J. Habdelića 4* ☎ *042/213–393* ⊟ *AE, MC, V.*

$–$$ ✕ **Gostionica Grenadir.** Fish is king in this elegant, spacious, red-carpeted cellar restaurant near Trg M. Stančića. Well-prepared dishes include sea bass and trout, but also a good selection of meats and poultry. ⊠ *Kranjčevićeva 12* ☎ *042/211–131* ⊟ *AE, DC, MC, V.*

★ **$** ✕ **Pizzeria Domenico.** This little gem of a place is hidden away at the end of a cobblestone alleyway off one of Varaždin's main squares. With red-checkered tablecloths and a spacious, airy inner room—with little windows that look out onto a peaceful courtyard on the other side—it's a justifiably popular place for pizza. ⊠ *Trg Slobode 7* ☎ *042/212–017* ⊟ *AE, DC, MC, V.*

Where to Stay

Your choices are rather limited in Varaždin, as far as hotels go, but prices are refreshingly lower than in Zagreb. The town has only one large hotel, the characterless Hotel Turist. **T-Tours Agency** (⊠ Gundulićeva 2 ☎ 042/210–989) can book a private room for you. Though it will most likely than not be in a high-rise apartment building that looks and feels dreary but is at least close to the center, it will cost less (around 190 Kn for two people, 130 Kn for one) than even the most modestly priced pension.

¢ 🏨 **Pension Garestin.** Just down the road from the Pension Maltar and a bit further from the town center, this pension has been set up in an elegant, onetime single-family house. The 13 simply furnished, modern rooms in this small hotel are along one hallway. There's also a spacious but smoky restaurant, whose green- and gold-hued, glittery ambience is a bit overwhelming. ⊠ *Zagrebačka 34, 42000* ☎ *042/214–314* ⊕ *www.gastrocom.hr* ⊅ *13 rooms* ⌂ *Restaurant, bar, cable TV, mini-bars, free parking* ⊟ *AE, DC, MC, V* ⧖ *BP.*

¢ 🏨 **Pension Maltar.** A short walk from the town center, this small pension has clean, no-frills, but spacious rooms that are not quite sparkling but are still quite acceptable for a short stay. Rooms with double (French) beds are the same price as those with twins, and many rooms include a couch, too. The café is rather smoky, by the way. ⊠ *F. Prešernova ul 1, 42000* ☎ *042/311–100* 🖶 *042/211–190* ⊅ *11 rooms* ⌂ *Café, cable TV, free parking* ⊟ *AE, DC, MC, V* ⧖ *BP.*

Nightlife & the Arts

For three weeks from mid-September to early October, the **Varaždin Baroque Evenings** take the form of classical-music concerts in various churches, palaces, and other venues throughout town. This is one of the most important cultural events in north Croatia. For 10 days from late August to early September, the **Špancirfest** (translated in tourist brochures as "Street Walkers' Festival"), on various squares in the center of town, features a colorful array of free, open-air theatrical and acrobatic performances, live music from classical to rock, traditional and modern dance, arts-and-crafts exhibits, and more.

Pub Zlatni Lampas (⌂ Trg Bana Jelačića 3 ☎ 042/214–615), right on the main square, is an English-style pub popular in particular with the young crowd that comes here to indulge not only in beer and inexpensive pizza (not to mention sausages and smoked tongue) but also loud, hip tunes, and perhaps a game of darts.

SOUTH OF ZAGREB TOWARD THE COAST

Numbers in the margins refer to numbers on the Excursions from Zagreb map.

Samobor

㉗ *20 km (12½ mi) west of Zagreb.*

That Samobor has been one of the capital's top weekend haunts since before the turn of the 20th century without really being on the way to anything else in Croatia testifies to its abounding cultural and natural charms. Close to the Slovenian border, this picturesque medieval town on the eastern slopes of the lushly forested *Samoborsko Gorje* was chartered by the Hungarian-Croatian king Bela IV in 1242. The town and environs are popular with hikers, trails leading into the hillside right from the center of town. Perched there, a 30-minute walk from town— and visible in all its sublimity from the main square—are the ruins of a 13th-century castle. And what would a visit to Samobor be without a stroll along Gradna, the peaceful stream that runs through town?

After an energetic hike, you may wish to fortify yourself with a glass of locally made *bermet*, a vermouthlike drink whose secret recipe was apparently brought here by French forces during their occupation of 1809 to 1813.

By far, Samobor's most famous event is its carnival, the *Samobor fašnik* (⊕ www.fasnik.com), which draws many thousands of visitors to town for several days beginning the weekend before Lent to catch the dazzling sight of its float-equipped parades and masked revelers.

The rectangular main square is called **Trg Krajla Tomislava**. Its largely baroque look is positively lovely, all the more so because some building facades show a bit or more of art-nouveau influence. In particular, the pharmacy building at no. 11 has two angels presiding, appropriately, on top. Also overlooking the square is a 17th-century parish church.

May 2003 saw Croatia's first private museum open in a quiet street just above Trg Krajla Tomislava. **Museum Marton** was created to house a private collection of furniture, paintings, glass- and metalware, porcelain, and clocks previously on loan to the Zagreb Museum of Arts & Crafts. ⊠ *Jurjevska 7* ☎ *01/336–4160* ⊕ *www.muzej-marton.hr* ⊠ *15 Kn* ☉ *Weekends 10–1 and 3–6.*

> **need a break?**
>
> If you need a dose of sugar to perk you up, try some *samoborska kremšnita,* a mouthwatering block of vanilla custard between layers of flaky pastry that, served warm, can be tasted at its best at the otherwise small and smoky café **U Prolazu** (⊠ Trg Krajla Tomislava 6).

In the lovely, streamside park by the square is the **Samobor Museum,** which tells the story of the town's past. ⊠ *Livadićeva 7* ☎ *01/336–1014* ⊠ *5 Kn* ☉ *Tues.–Fri. 8–3; weekends 9–1.*

Where to Eat

★ **$$–$$$** ✕ **Pri Saroj Vuri.** Small yet ever so cozy, its walls decorated with old clocks (as per its name in Croatian) and by paintings by noted Croatian artists, this lovely old villa a few minutes' walk from the main square is the best place in town to try such meaty fare as *teleća koljenica* (knuckle of veal) and *češnjovke* (smoked sausage cooked in sour cabbage). Unfortunately, the latter is available only late in the year, after the hogs are butchered and the sausage smoked. Round off with a glass of bermet, served with lemon and ice. ⊠ *Giznik 2* ☎ *01/336–0548* ▤ *AE, DC, MC, V.*

Where to Stay

¢ 🏨 **Hotel Livadic.** If you want to spend more than a half-day in Samobor, you could do much worse than this elegant and pleasant hotel right on the main square. Although the rooms vary in size, they're all spacious, and the pine floors impart a soothing scent while the silky bedspreads and golden-framed mirrors help yield a luxurious historical ambience. Some rooms have showers only. A health club and air-conditioning in all rooms are both in the planning stages at this writing. Downstairs is a splendid and spacious, if smoky, café. ⊠ *Trg Krajla Tomislava 1, 10430* ☎ *01/336–5850 or 01/336–5851* ▤ *01/332–5588* ⊕ *www.hotel-livadic.hr* ⇆ *23 rooms* ⌂ *Minibars, cable TV; no a/c in some rooms* ▤ *AE, MC, V* ❏ *BP.*

Karlovac

㉘ *40 km (25 mi) south of Zagreb.*

Many tourists have tasted the beer, but few have visited the city. Karlovac is, however, much more than just home to one of Croatia's most popular brews, Karlovačko. Founded all at once on July 13, 1579, by the Austrians as a fortress intended to ward off the Turks, Karlovac is today that big dot on the map between Zagreb and the coast that visitors to the country more often than not pass by. Well, anyone intrigued by the question of how a onetime fortress—still much in evidence—can develop into an urban center will want to stop here for at least a half-day and, perhaps, spend a night on the way to or from the coast.

Once you pass through the city's industrial-looking suburbs, there is a redolent historical center awaiting you, one rendered that much more atmospheric because it is wedged between two of Croatia's most important rivers, the Kupa and the Korana. The city's Renaissance-era urban nucleus is popularly known as the *Zvijezda* (Star), since its military planners were moved to shape it as a six-pointed star—as evident from the surrounding moat, which is today a pleasant, if sunken, green space that is even home to a basketball court. Eventually, this center's military nature gave way to civilian life, and it took on the baroque look more evident today. Though the town walls were razed in the 19th century, their shape is still discernible.

At the center of this old part of town, which you access over any of several bridges over the moat, is the main square, **Trg Bana Josip Jelačić,** one side of which, alas, features a great big empty building with some missing windows. At the center of this otherwise largely barren square is an old well dating to 1869; long filled in, it is ornamented with allegorical imagery.

Where to Eat

$$–$$$ ✗ **Ribarska kuča Mirnah.** Off on its own, overlooking the quietly flowing Korana River on the edge of the town center, this restaurant, which has a terrace for outdoor dining, makes the best of the view. The seafood here—whether squid, octopus, sea bass, or freshwater varieties such as carp, pike-perch, catfish, pike, or trout—is abundant and excellent. Round off your meal with a jam- or walnut-filled palačinke and reflect on what went through the mind of whoever designed the funky, hectagonal tubing of the ceiling lights. ⊠ *Rakovačko šetalište* ☎ *047/654–172* ▭ *AE, DC, MC, V.*

$$ ✗ **Restoran Kerempuh.** Cozy and friendly, with hip music that's just a bit too loud, the Kerempuh is on a side street a few minutes' walk from the historic center. The offerings include decent meat and poultry (including grilled rabbit) and a few odd fish dishes at rustic wooden tables and benches. ⊠ *V. Nazora 4* ☎ *042/614–366* ▭ *AE, DC, MC, V.*

Where to Stay

★ $ ▦ **Hotel Korana Srakovčić.** Deep within a tree-shaded park a few minutes' walk from the Old Town and overlooking a peaceful stretch of its namesake, the Korana River, this luxury hotel opened in 2003. It's a completely new structure, a re-creation of the 19th-century Park Hotel that had long fallen into disrepair. Catering mostly to businesspeople, it has bright, modern, somewhat bland rooms with maroon spreads. Its main restaurant, the Dobra, offers excellent fare and has a terrace with a soothing river view. You'll pay less for a room without a balcony. ⊠ *Perivoj Josipa Vrbanića 8, 47000* ☎ *047/609–090* ▤ *047/609–091* ⊕ *www.hotelkorana.hr* ⇆ *20 rooms, 3 suites* ⚫ *2 restaurants, cable TV, minibars, in-room safes, Wi-Fi, indoor pool, hot tub, sauna, massage, bar, meeting rooms, parking* ▭ *AE, DC, MC, V* ❏ *BP.*

¢ ▦ **Hotel Carlstadt.** At the center of Karlovac's business district a couple minutes' walk from the Old Town, the Carlstadt—the town's original name under Austrian rule—offers simply furnished, modern rooms. Though somewhat cramped, they are otherwise fine, considering the rel-

BLOODY EASTER

IT'S CALLED "BLOODY EASTER" *for a good reason. Sunday, April 2, 1991, has gone down in Croatian history as the day Croatia suffered its first casualties—and its first fatality—in its war of independence with the former Yugoslavia. And the unlikely setting was none other than one of Europe's most visited natural wonders, Plitvice Lakes National Park.*

Two days earlier, Croatian Ministry of Interior commando units—under the direction of General Josip Lucić, later to become head of the Croatian Armed Forces—were dispatched to Plitvice to restore order after the region had been occupied by Serbs led by Milan Martić, who aimed to annex the park to Serbian Krajina. The commandos were ambushed en route, near the group of hotels at Entrance 2. One member of the team, Josip Jović, was killed and seven of his comrades were wounded. As recorded in the annals of Croatian history, nine of the "terrorists" were arrested, and order was restored. For a time.

The region, which had long been home to many Serbs, was occupied by Serb forces for the next four years. The national park actually became a military encampment, and soldiers threatened to blow up the fragile travertine dams separating the lakes. UNESCO sent missions to prevent war from wreaking such havoc on a natural wonder. In the end, with the exception of the park's red-deer population, which fell dramatically during the occupation—the park's natural beauty pulled through intact. Only the human infrastructure was damaged, including the hotels. By 1999, four years after Croatian forces reoccupied the park and painstakingly cleared the area of mines, the last of the three hotels reopened, and the park was fully back in business.

Today, a memorial in the park marks the life and death of Josip Jović, the first fatality in what was to be a long and bloody war.

---

atively affordable price. ☒ *Av Vraniczanya 1, 47000* ☎ *047/611–111* ⊕ *www.carlstadt.hr* ⇆ *37 rooms* ⚘ *Restaurant, cable TV, minibars, in-room data ports, bar, parking* ⊟ *AE, DC, MC, V* ⏺ *BP.*

Nacionalni Park Plitvička Jezera

㉙ *128 km (79 mi) southwest of Zagreb*

Fodor'sChoice
★
Triple America's five Great Lakes, shrink them each to manageable size (i.e., 217 hectares, or 536 acres, in all), give them a good cleaning, envelop them with a dense, green forest, and link not just two but all of them with a pint-sized Niagara Falls, including one whose 78-meter (254-foot) height leaves you in awe all the same. The result? **Nacionalni Park Plitvička Jezera** (Plitvice Lakes National Park), a UNESCO World Heritage Site and Croatia's top inland natural wonder. And it's not even out of the way. The park is right on the main highway (E71) from Zagreb to Split, but it's certainly worth the three-hour trip from the capital regardless.

This 8,000-acre park is home to 16 beautiful, emerald lakes connected by a series of cascading waterfalls, stretching 8 km (5 mi) through a valley flanked by high, forested hills home to deer, bears, wolves, wild boar, and lots of trout (but no fishing!). Thousands of years of sedimentation of calcium, magnesium carbonate, algae, and moss have yielded the natural barriers between the lakes; and since the process is ongoing, new barriers, curtains, stalactites, channels, and cascades are constantly forming and the existing ones changing. The deposited sedimentation, or tufa, also coats the beds and edges of the lakes, yielding their sparkling, azure look. Today, a series of wooden bridges and waterside paths leads through the park. The only downside: as lovely as it is, all of Europe wants to see it, so the trails can get crowded from June through September. (That said, there's not a bit of litter along the way—a testament either to respectful visitors or to a conscientious park staff, or both.) No camping, no bushwhacking, no picking plants. This is a place to visit, for a day or two, but not to touch. It is, however, well worth the 80 Kn entrance fee.

There are two entrances, aptly named Entrance 1 and Entrance 2. The hotels are near Entrance 2, but Entrance 1 is typically the start of most one-day excursions, if only because it's within a 20-minute walk of Veliki slap, the big waterfall (78 meters [256 feet] high). Hiking the entire loop that winds its way around the lakes takes six to eight hours, so you may opt for one of three other options the park suggests, ranging from two to four hours and all involving a combination of hiking and being ferried across the larger of the park's lakes by national-park service boats.

There's a café at Entrance 1, but avoid it for anything but coffee, as the sandwiches and strudels leave much to be desired; however, the heavenly strudels you can buy for the same price from one of the ladies at nearby stands (where great big blocks of cheese are also on sale) leave nothing whatsoever to be desired. At the boat landing near Entrance 2, by the way, you can rent gorgeous wooden rowboats for 50 Kn per hour. ⊠ *Velika Poljana* ☎ *053/751–014 or 053/751–015* ⊕ *www.np-plitvicka-jezera.hr* ⊠ *80 Kn (95 Kn July and Aug.) for a one-day pass, 95 Kn (125 Kn July and Aug.) for a two-day pass* ☉ *May–Sept., daily 8–7; Oct.–Apr., daily 9–4.*

Where to Eat

Although there's a restaurant near the hotels at Entrance 2, it has the same uninspiring look and feel as the hotels, and few people flock to it. You're much better off heading over to the excellent restaurant at Entrance 1—unless of course the food store near Entrance 2 provides you enough in the way of staples for all the hiking you'll be up to.

$$–$$$$ ✗ **Restoran Lička Kuća.** With unadorned log walls, white-curtained windows, lively Croatian folk music playing, and an open kitchen (with an open hearth) at the center of its spacious room, this is exactly what a restaurant in a great national park should be. Fill up on hearty *lička juha* (a creamy soup of lamb, vegetables, and eggs), followed by boiled lamb with vegetables, suckling pig, or a peasant platter (a wide array of meats—from beef to turkey, pork chops to sausage and bacon). Meat and poultry are the focus, here; grilled trout is the only fish on the menu. Finish off with an apple (or cheese) strudel. The place is buzzing with tourists, but it's the only decent restaurant for miles around. ⊠ *Across from Entrance 1, Velika Poljana* ☎ *053/751–024* ☰ *AE, MC, V.*

Where to Stay

None of the park's state-run, Communist-era hotels is much to write home about—and they were damaged extensively by Serb forces during the early 1990s. However, the main advantage of staying in a park hotel is that you'll be right in the center of all the hiking action. The hotels are particularly convenient if you arrive without your own car.

As an alternative, there are lots of private rooms in the immediate vicinity where doubles go for around 220 Kn, a bargain compared to the hotels. In the one-road village of Rastovača, just off the main road a few hundred yards north of Entrance 1 (where the bus stops), practically every single house you pass has rooms for rent—generally bright, clean, modern rooms in newish-looking houses. You can also get a private room in Jezerce, just south of Entrance 2. The National Park office will provide addresses and help with bookings in July and August and will provide contacts the rest of the year. A bit further afield, the village of Rakovica, 12 km (7½ mi) north of the park, usually has more vacancies in high season. The tourist office in Rakovica (☎ 047/784–450) can help with bookings.

$ ▦ **Hotel Jezero.** Yards away from two other, lower priced, fewer-frills hotels (the Plitvice and the Bellevue), this long, three-story, wood-paneled building looks almost like a U.S.–style motel. The rooms are simply furnished and a bit worn, but clean, and offer cheap plastic chairs on the unappealing terraces (not all rooms have terraces). It's not a great value but quite all right for a one-night stay. Some rooms have only showers; all have a somewhat smoky scent. ⊠ *Near Entrance 2, Velika Poljana* ☎ *053/751–015* 🖷 *053/751–013* ⊕ *www.np-plitvicka-jezera.hr* ⇱ *229 rooms* ♿ *Restaurant, cable TV, minibars, hair salon, hot tub, sauna, massage, bar* ☰ *AE, DC, MC, V* ⫴ *BP.*

LONJSKO POLJE

An excursion southeast of Zagreb to the Lonjsko Polje region along the Sava River will bring you to an area that is rarely seen by most visitors. Along Croatia's extensive border with Bosnia Herzegovina are two sights of pronounced historical interest and one with special appeal to lovers of big birds, along with plenty of pretty wooden architecture in and around the sleepy villages along the way.

Sisak

③⓪ *75 km (47 mi) southeast of Zagreb via the Autocesta Expressway.*

The unassuming little town of Sisak was the site of one of the more important battles in Croatia's history.

A bit to the south of the town center—3 km (2 mi) to be exact—lies a once-mighty **Sisak Fortress**—with one prominent bastion at each point of its famously triangular form—that has a hugely significant past. It was here, on June 22, 1593, that the Habsburgs, in the company of Croats and Slovenes, pulled off a monumental victory over the fearsome Ottoman Turks, a triumph that figured prominently in halting the Turks' advance toward Zagreb and further into Western Europe. Today the locals celebrate the victory over the Turks with their annual **Knightly Tournament** on a weekend in early June. A whole lot of folks in medieval garb will entertain you with archery and equestrian contests, not to mention balloon rides, souvenirs, and plenty of food and drink. Check with the Sisak tourist-information office for details on this free event.

Čigoć

31 *28 km (17½ mi) southeast of Sisak.*

The charming village of Čigoć is officially known as the "European Village of Storks" because it draws so many of the migrating birds each spring, and a testament is its annual Stork Festival in late June. That said, people live here, too, as attested to by the wooden, thatched-roof houses that are likewise a sight to behold. But several hundred of the birds while away much of the summer here before most embark on the long journey to southern Africa.

The **Čigoć Information Center** (✉ Čigoć 26 ☎ 044/715–115), which is on the main road that runs through the village center, can tell you all you need to know about storks and the Stork Festival, as can the Sisak tourist office.

Jasenovac

32 *35 km (22 mi) southeast of Čigoć.*

Where the Sava marks Croatia's remaining long stretch of east–west border with Bosnia until it arrives in Serbia more than 150 km (94 mi) away, is Jasenovac, the site of Croatia's most notorious World War II labor camps. Current estimates are that somewhere between 56,000 and 97,000 people—mostly Serbs, it is believed, along with Jews, Gypsies, and Croatian antifascists—perished at this string of five camps on the banks of the Sava River between 1941 and 1945 from exhaustion, illness, cold weather, and murder. Though the camp was razed after the war, a memorial park was eventually established at the site, along with a **museum** featuring photographs and other documentation of what happened. At this writing, the museum is closed, but a new permanent exhibition is expected to open by summer 2006. ✉ *Braæe Radiæ 147* ☎ *044/ 672–033* ⊕ *www.jusp-jasenovac.hr* ✑ *Free* ☉ *Weekdays 7–3.*

In addition to the labor-camp memorial, Jasenovac is home to the headquarters of **Lonjsko Polje Nature Park** (✉ Trg Krajla Petra Svačića ☎ 044/ 672–080), which provides park maps and other information on where to go and what to see.

ZAGREB & ENVIRONS ESSENTIALS

AIR TRAVEL

There are no direct flights between the United States and Zagreb. However, the national carrier, Croatia Airlines, flies to Zagreb from Amsterdam, Brussels, Frankfurt, London, Paris, and Vienna, where connections can be made to and from U.S. flights, and major European carriers also have flights to Zagreb from their European bases. Zagreb is also a destination from most carriers in other Eastern and Central European countries. Croatia Airlines operates at least two flights daily to Split (45 mins) and three flights daily to Dubrovnik (55 mins). Through summer, there is also daily service to Prague (1 hr, 30 mins) and flights several times a week to Warsaw (1 hr, 40 mins).

CARRIERS ☎ **Airlines & Contacts Adria** ☎ 01/481–0011. **Air France** ☎ 01/483–7100. **Alitalia** ☎ 01/480–5555. **Austrian Airlines** ☎ 01/626–5900. **British Airways** ☎ 01/456–2506. **Croatia Airlines** ☎ 01/481–9633. **CSA** ☎ 01/487–3301. **Delta Airlines** ☎ 01/487–8760. **KLM–Northwest** ☎ 01/487–8600. **LOT** ☎ 01/480–5555. **Lufthansa** ☎ 01/487–3123 or 060/505–505 **Malev** ☎ 01/483–6935.

AIRPORTS & TRANSFERS

Zagreb Airport (ZAG) is in Pleso, 17 km (10 mi) southeast of the city. ☎ **Zagreb Pleso Airport** ☎ 01/626–5222 general information, 01/456–2229 lost and found ⊕ www.zagreb-airport.hr.

AIRPORT   A regular shuttle bus runs from the airport to the main bus station every
TRANSFERS   30 minutes from 7 AM to 8 PM and from the main bus station to the airport from 6 AM to 7:30 PM. A one-way ticket costs 25 Kn, and the trip takes 25 minutes. By taxi, expect to pay 150 Kn to 200 Kn to make the same journey; the trip will be slightly faster, about 20 minutes. ☎ **Airport bus** ☎ 01/615–7992.

BUS TRAVEL

Frequent regular coach service to destinations all over mainland Croatia departs from the capital. The traveling time is 6 hours from Zagreb to Split and 10½ hours from Zagreb to Dubrovnik. There are also daily international bus lines to Slovenia (Ljubljana), Hungary (Barcs and Nagykanisza), Yugoslavia (Belgrade), Austria (Graz), Germany (Munich, Stuttgart, Frankfurt, Dortmund, Cologne, and Dusseldorf), and Switzerland (Zurich). Timetable information is available from the main bus station, a 20-minute walk from the center.

About 10 buses run daily between Zagreb and Karlovac in just under an hour and for a one-way fare of 28 Kn.

Samobor is a 50-minute bus ride from Zagreb; buses between Zagreb and Sambor run every 30 minutes or so weekdays, roughly every hour on weekends; the fare is 20 Kn each way, and Samobor's little bus station is about 100 yards north of the main square.

Most buses between Zagreb and Split will stop at both entrances of Plitvice Lakes National Park; the fare is usually 60 Kn to 70 Kn one-way by bus between Zagreb and Plitvice.

A small handful of buses daily go on from Sisak on narrow, two-lane roads, to the charming village of Čigoć.

🚌 **Zagreb Bus Station** ✉ Av M Držića, Donji Grad, Zagreb ☎ 060/313-333 ⊕ www. akz.hr.

BUS & TRAM TRAVEL WITHIN ZAGREB

An extensive network of city buses and trams—in the center of town, almost exclusively trams—runs both during the day (4 AM–11:45 PM) and at night (11:35 PM to 3:45 AM). Tickets cost 6.50 Kn if you buy them from a newspaper kiosk, or 8 Kn from the driver. A full-day ticket (18 Kn) available at some kiosks is valid until 4 AM the next morning. As an alternative, for 90 Kn you can buy the Zagreb Card, which covers public transport within the city limits for three days and offers substantial discounts at various museums and other cultural venues. After you board the bus or tram, you must validate your ticket with a time stamp; tickets are good for 1½ hours and are transferable in the same direction. If you are caught without a valid ticket, you will be fined 150 Kn payable on the spot.

🚌 **ZET** (Zagreb Transport Authority) ☎ 01/660-0442 ⊕ www.zet.hr.

CAR RENTALS

Prices vary, and you might pay less if you rent from a local company that's not part of an international chain; it's best to shop around. A small car (e.g., Opel Corsa or Fiat Uno) costs at least 400 Kn per day or 2,100 Kn per week. A slightly larger car (e.g., Opel Astra or Fiat Punto) costs more like 550 Kn per day or 2,700 Kn per week. A large car (e.g., Opal Astra Automatic) costs closer to 800 Kn per day or 4,200 Kn per week; automatic transmission is rarely available on smaller cars. These prices include CDW (collision damage waiver) and TP (theft protection) but not PAI (personal accident insurance) and allow for unlimited mileage. If you drive one-way (say, from Zagreb to Dubrovnik), there is an additional drop-off charge, but it depends on the type of car and the number of days you are renting.

🚗 **AE** ✉ Kršnjavoga 13, next to the Westin Zagreb hotel, Donji Grad, Zagreb ☎ 01/483-6025 or 01/483-6026. **Avis** ✉ Sheraton Zagreb, Kneza Borne 2, Donji Grad, Zagreb ☎ 062/222-226 ⊕ www.avis.com.hr ✉ Zagreb Airport, Pleso ☎ 01/626-5840. **Budget** ✉ Praška 5, Donji Grad, Zagreb ☎ 01/480-5687 ⊕ www.budget.hr ✉ Zagreb Airport, Pleso ☎ 01/626-5854. **Dollar Rent A Car & Thrifty Car Rental** ✉ Sub Rosa, Donji Grad, Zagreb ☎ 01/483-6466 or 021/399-000 ⊕ www.subrosa.hr ✉ Zagreb Airport, Pleso ☎ 01/626-5333. **Europcar** ✉ Pierottijeva 5, Donji Grad, Zagreb ☎ 01/483-6045 or 091/430-3046 ⊕ www.europcar.com ✉ Zagreb Airport, Pleso ☎ 01/626-5333. **Hertz** ✉ Mažuranićev trg 2, Donji Grad, Zagreb ☎ 01/484-7222 or (central reservations line) 062/727-277 ⊕ www.hertz.hr ✉ Zagreb Airport, Pleso ☎ 01/456-2635. **National** ✉ Westin Zagreb, Kršnjavoja 1, Donji Grad, Zagreb ☎ 0800/443-322, 01/481-1764, or 483-8232 ⊕ www.nationalcar.hr ✉ Zagreb Airport, Pleso ☎ 0800/443-322 or 01/621-5924. **Sixt** ✉ Roosevelt trg 4, Donji Grad, Zagreb ☎ 01/482-8385 ⊕ www.e-sixt.com ✉ Zagreb Airport, Pleso ☎ 01/621-9900.

CAR TRAVEL

While staying in the capital you are certainly better off without a car, though if you wish to visit the nearby hills of Zagorje, a vehicle is helpful unless you want to be riding to a different attraction by bus each day (as the various places there are connected by bus to Zagreb but not to each other). So do consider a car rental of at least one or two days if it fits your budget. When it comes to moving on, you will find that Rijeka in the Kvarner region to the west is well-connected to Zagreb by both train and bus, as are Split in Dalmatia to the south. However, a car makes your travel plans more flexible.

EMERGENCIES

🚩 Ambulance **Ambulance** ☎ 94.
🚩 Doctors & Dentists **Hitno Ponoč** (Ponoč Hospital) ✉ Draškovićeva 19, Donji Grad, Zagreb ☎ 01/461-0011.
🚩 Fire **Fire Emergencies** ☎ 93.
🚩 Pharmacies **Zagreb 24-hour Pharmacy** ✉ Trg Bana J. Jelačića 2, Donji Grad, Zagreb ☎ 01/481-6159 ✉ Ilica 301, Donji Grad, Zagreb ☎ 01/375-0321. **Talan** ✉ Trg Slobode 1, Varaždin ☎ 042/200-550.
🚩 Police **Police Emergencies** ☎ 92.

INTERNET

At Charlie's Internet Cafe, which is just yards from Trg Bana Jelačića, you can surf the Web for 4 Kn for 15 minutes and 0.25 Kn for every additional minute. Hidden in a courtyard a few blocks away, in a one-time apartment, is the Sublink Internet Centar, where it's 0.245 Kn per minute, which adds up to 14.70 Kn per hour.
🚩 **Charlie's Internet Cafe** ✉ Gajeva 4a, Donji Grad, Zagreb ☎ 01/488-0233. **Sublink Internet Centar** ✉ Teslina 12, Donji Grad, Zagreb ☎ 01/481-1329.

MAIL & SHIPPING

Zagreb's Central Post Office is one block east of Trg Bana Jelačića.
🚩 **Main Post Office** ✉ Jurišićeva 13, Donji Grad, Zagreb ☎ 01/481-1090.

TAXIS

You can find taxi ranks in front of the bus and train stations, near the main square, and in front of the larger hotels. It is also possible to order a radio taxi. All drivers are bound by law to run a meter, which should start at 25 Kn and increase by 7 Kn per kilometer. Each piece of luggage incurs a further 5 Kn. The night tariff operates from 10 PM to 5 AM and implies a 20% markup; the same tariff applies to Sunday and holidays.
🚩 **Radio Taxi** ☎ 01/668-2505 or 01/668-2558 ⊕ www.radio-taksi-zagreb.hr.

TOURS

The tourist-information center closest to the Zagreb train station organizes amusing and informative guided tours of the city.
🚩 **Zagreb Tourist Information** ✉ Trg Nikole Šubića Zrinskoga 14, Donji Grad, Zagreb ☎ 01/492-1645.

TRAIN TRAVEL

Zagreb's main train station lies in Donji Grad, a 10-minute walk from the center. There are daily international lines to and from Budapest (Hungary), Belgrade (Yugoslavia), Munich (Germany), Vienna (Austria), and Venice (Italy).

From Zagreb, there are four trains daily to Split in Dalmatia (8 hrs) and five trains daily to Rijeka in Kvarner (3½ hrs). The easiest way to get to Varaždin from Zagreb is by rail, with 15 trains daily. Travel time is about 2½ hours and costs 50 Kn each way. About 10 trains run daily between Zagreb and Karlovac (with a like number of buses), in just under an hour and for a one-way fare of 28 Kn. If you don't have wheels, your best bet reaching Sisak is by rail, with 15 trains daily from Zagreb that take just over an hour.

🚆 **Zagreb Train Station** ✉ Trg Kralja Tomislava, Donji Grad, Zagreb ☎ 060/333–444 domestic train information, 01/481–1892 international train information ⊕ www.hznet.hr.

VISITOR INFORMATION

Zagreb's main tourist-information center overlooks the main square, Trg Bana Jelačića. It's open weekdays 8:30 AM to 8 PM, Saturday 9 to 5, and Sunday 10 to 2. A smaller office is a tad closer to the train station and open weekdays 9 to 5.

🚆 **Jasenovac Tourist Information** ✉ Trg Petra Svačića 3, Jasenovac ☎ 044/672–490. **Karlovac Tourist Information** ✉ Ul Petra Zrinskog 3, Karlovac ☎ 047/615–115 ⊕ www.karlovac-touristinfo.hr. **Kumrovec Tourist Information** ✉ C Lijepe naše 6a, Kumrovec ☎ 049/502–044 ⊕ www.kumrovec.hr. **Marija Bistrica Tourist Information** ✉ Zagrebacka, Marija Bistrice ☎ 049/468–380 ⊕ www.marija-bistrica.hr. **Plitvice Lakes National Park Tourist Information** ✉ Plitvička jezera, at Entrance 1, Velika Poljana ☎ 053/776–798 ⊕ www.np-plitvicka-jezera.hr. **Samobor Tourist Information** ✉ Trg Krajla Tomislava 5, Samobor ☎ 01/336–004 ⊕ www.samobor.hr. **Sisak Tourist Information** ✉ Rimska, Sisak ☎ 044/522–655 ⊕ www.sisakturist.com. **Stubičke Toplice Tourist Information** ✉ Viktora Šipeka 24, Stubičke Toplice ☎ 042/282–727 or 042/210–985 ⊕ www.tourism-varazdin.hr. **Varaždin Tourist Information** ✉ Ivana Padovca 3, Varaždin ☎ 042/210–987 or 042/210–985 ⊕ www.tourism-varazdin.hr. **Zagreb Tourist Information** ✉ Trg Bana Jelačića 11, Donji Grad, Zagreb ☎ 01/481–4051 or 01/481–4052 ⊕ www.zagreb-touristinfo.hr ✉ Trg Nikole Šubića Zrinskog 14, Donji Grad, Zagreb ☎ 01/492–1645.

Slavonia

WORD OF MOUTH

"Some of the most interesting places in Croatia are the Caffè (Coffee) bars . . . .. These are bars that also serve coffee, cocoa, sodas, etc. They are enjoyed by kids as well as adults, and sometimes families come in to spend some time together. Many have chairs by the windows or outside for people-watching. They really are friendly places."

—alyssamma

"A sobe is a room in a private home. Many Croatians rent out rooms in their houses . . . the signs will say 'Sobe,' 'Zimmer,' or 'Room.' You ask them the particulars and the price and take it from there. If it doesn't turn you on, just say 'no' and walk away."

—nukesafe

By Paul
Olchváry

A COUNTRY'S BREADBASKET is, of course, often flat, and so it is also a place visitors tend to pass through rather than go to (or never pass through in the first place). Regrettably, it can also be a place where wars rage most intensely. All this is true of Slavonia, the sweeping agricultural plain of eastern Croatia. Long a vital transport route (not least, between Zagreb and Belgrade), Slavonia today is still recovering from the aftermath of the Yugoslav war of the early 1990s, which left much of it economically and psychologically devastated—most famously, the once lovely baroque town of Vukovar, whose siege and utter destruction in 1991 brought home to TV viewers around the world that the former Yugoslavia was indeed at war, and earned Croatia international sympathy in the process. Despite some remaining hurdles, however, not only has the region made great strides since peace settled in, but it is also replete with attractive towns and charming villages whose rural surroundings—from cornfields and sunflower fields to vineyards—have a certain appealing flavor that can only be called "Slavonian."

Slavonia has been inhabited since ancient times, and the Romans had a settlement called Mursa on the outskirts of present-day Osijek. Though its flatness is broken in places—by the Papuk Hills and around the celebrated wine region of Ilok in far eastern Slavonia—the region's largely lowland terrain has seen it inhabited and traversed through the ages by more ethnicities than practically any other region of Croatia. It has been home to Croats, Serbs, Hungarians, Germans, Turks, and others. Though settled by Slavic tribes in the 7th century and later an integral part of the Hungarian-Croat kingdom, Slavonia experienced a sea change of culture with Sultan Sülejman the Magnificent's march toward Hungary and Austria in 1526. For almost 150 years much of the region became an Ottoman stronghold. Osijek flourished not as part of Christian Europe, but rather as a full-fledged, mosque-filled Turkish town.

The Turkish retreat in the late 17th century brought with it a new era of Austrian influence, with Osijek, now with a vastly different look, still the region's economic, administrative, and cultural capital. Though damaged in the Yugoslav war, Osijek pulled through in much better shape than Vukovar, and since the late 1990s it has made impressive headway in re-establishing itself as an appealing center of regional culture. North of Osijek is the Baranja, a marshy, particularly fertile corner of northeastern Slavonia that straddles the gentle, vineyard-rich hills of southern Hungary to the north. North of the Drava River—which veers southeast after a long east-west course along the Hungarian-Croatian border before feeding into the Danube—is Kopačice Rit Nature Park, whose vast wetlands play host to a multitude of birds and other wildlife.

Slavonia is rich in ecclesiastical attractions, from Osijek's Župna Crkva Sv. Petra i Pavla to the twin-steepled, red-brick Katedrala in Dakovo, about 40 minutes to the southwest. To Osijek's southeast is Vukovar, where recovery—architecturally, at any rate—is today more characteristic of its urban scene than are bombed-out buildings (which, however, are also still there for anyone to see first-hand). Imposing palaces, once owned by aristocratic families, include the Pejačević Palace in Našice,

If you have 3 days	Spend two days in **Osijek** with a short visit either to nearby **Kopački Rit Nature Park,** or—if a spa stirs your fancy more than a bird sanctuary—a morning or afternoon of soaking in the thermal saline water at **Bizovac.** If time allows, drop by **Dakovo,** which is only a bit further away but whose cathedral is well worth a look.

If you have 5 days	Begin with the above, by all means include **Dakovo** on your agenda as well as a half-day visit to **Vukovar.** If **Kopački Rit** soothes you, you may want to spend more time there, opting for a longer excursion and perhaps a stroll around the village of **Kopač** and a meal at its excellent Zelena Žaba restaurant.

one of the first towns in western Slavonia that you pass through by train if you're on your way eastward toward Osijek.

Exploring Slavonia

About the Restaurants

With paprika-rich Hungary not far away, you'll often see dishes characterized by an unmistakable, bright-red zest. As in Vienna and Budapest, vegetables are typically prepared in a flour-thickened sauce. Though far from the Adriatic, Slavonia counts fish among its staples—namely, freshwater varieties including carp, pike, catfish, and pike-perch. You'll often find the scrumptious, spicy-hot, paprika-flavored fish stew known as *riblji paprikaš* or *fiš paprikaš*. Meat is also a key part of the dining picture. Regular menu staples include *čobanac,* a stew of pork and another type of meat, bathed in paprika sauce and served with spaetzle; chicken paprikash; *sarma* (pork-stuffed cabbage leaves); pork-stuffed paprika; and, last but not least, paprika-flavored sausages and blood sausages. As for wines, look for dry whites, in particular those from Ilok, such as fraševina, riesling, and traminac. And then there is the ubiquitous *rakija* (fruit brandy).

Dining out is somewhat less expensive than in Zagreb and on the Adriatic coast, with substantial main courses from around 30 Kn to 40 Kn.

WHAT IT COSTS in Croatian Kuna (Kn)					
	$$$$	$$$	$$	$	¢
RESTAURANTS	over 80	60–80	35–60	20–35	under 20

Restaurant prices are per person for a main course at dinner.

About the Hotels

Although business travelers have been streaming into Osijek in larger numbers in recent years, tourists have been few. Thus, Osijek offers a small selection of hotels plus a couple of smaller, pension-style accommodations with practically no private rooms. At least everything available is in the heart of town and costs less than comparable accommodations in Zagreb or on the coast. When traveling outside of Osijek, bear in mind that, unlike more tourist-trodden reaches of the country, such frills as air-conditioning and cable TV are not necessarily given. The region is, after all, still recovering from war, and renovations are proceeding at a slower pace.

WHAT IT COSTS in euros (€) and Croatian wkuna (Kn)					
	$$$$	$$$	$$	$	¢
IN EUROS	over € 225	€175–€225	€125–€175	€75–€125	under €75
IN KUNA	over 1,650	1,300–1,650	925–1,300	550–925	under 550

Hotel prices are for two people in a double room in high season, excluding taxes and service charges.

Timing

Slavonia can get hot in summer, and there's no sea to cool off in, so you may want to save this region for spring, late summer, or early fall. Indeed, given that hundreds of thousands of birds gather at the Kopački Rit Nature Park in April, May, and early June and again around September and into October, a visit during such a time would be optimal. The last weekend of September sees one of the region's largest annual cultural events, the *Dakovački vezovi* (Dakovo Embroidery) festival. Of course, regardless of when you come to Croatia, a couple of days in Slavonia are always worthwhile.

Numbers in the margins correspond to numbers on the Slavonia map.

OSIJEK

❶ *280 km (175 mi) east of Zagreb.*

Far from where sea-spirited tourists typically tread—and surrounded on all sides by cornfields—Osijek is an often overlooked treasure trove of cultural and architectural attractions. Although it came out of the Yugoslav war the worse for wear, a revival has been going on here ever since. Eastern Croatia's largest city (pop. 115,000) and the economic, administrative, and cultural capital of Slavonia, it rests on the south bank of the Drava River, 22 km (14 mi) west of that river's confluence with the Danube, a short drive from the Hungarian border to the north and the Republic of Serbia and Montenegro to the east.

Osijek is, in a sense, three towns in one. By the mid-12th century it was a prosperous market town in the Hungarian-Croatian kingdom, occupying the area of present-day **Trvđa**, which functions today as more of a cloistered and somewhat sleepy historical and cultural center. After more than 150 years of Ottoman occupation in the 16th and 17th centuries, Osijek was a flowering Turkish town, mosques and all. At 11 AM on September 26, 1687, that era ended, with the flight of the last Turkish soldier. (As a continuing legacy of this watershed event, the church bells of Osijek undertake a celebratory ringing each and every

2

Strolling Around Osijek
Set in its somewhat sleepy splendor on the south bank of the Drava river, Slavonia's economic, administrative, and cultural capital is especially pleasant to explore on foot. The magnificent, neo-Gothic Župna Crkva Sv. Petra i Pavla is the main attraction in Gornji Grad, and a 15-minute walk or short tram ride away—past a lovely, spacious park, Perivoj Krajla Tomislava—is the historic, baroque district of Trvda.

Bird-Watching
Embracing more than 30,000 hectares (74,100 acres) just north of the Drava, where that fast river flows eastward into the Danube, this vast natural area is covered with immense reed beds as well as willow, poplar, and oak forests and crisscrossed by ridges, ponds, shallow lakes, and marshes. More than 285 bird species can be spotted here. The park plays host to several endangered species, including the white-tailed sea eagle, the black stork, and the European otter.

Seeing the Vukovar Renewal
Though more of an experience than a pleasure, perhaps, this once lovely baroque town on the Danube offers the chance to see for yourself—rather than just on TV—the destruction wrought by war. More of a pleasure, actually, is noticing how Vukovar has begun to make itself lovely again. In the years since 1991—when the city came under siege and thousands of its inhabitants died or went missing—great headway has been made to rebuild the city as faithfully as possible. At the same time, vital new public spaces are beginning to blossom.

Dakovo's Cathedral
Dakovo's influential 19th-century bishop, Josip Juraj Strossmayer, commissioned this magnificent structure, which was designed by architect Frederick Schmidt. The structure towers outside and is beautifully decorated inside. If you're a fan of churches, this is one you won't want to miss.

Friday at 11 AM.) Osijek henceforth became a military garrison under the Austrians, who turned it into a walled fortress in the late 17th century. The **Gornji Grad** (Upper Town) was developed by the Austrians during this period; today, it's the city's commercial and administrative center. A few years later the **Donji Grad** (Lower Town) rose to the east on the site of the ancient Roman settlement Mursa; today, it's relatively residential.

The view north across the Drava is bucolic. Across from Gornji Grad, for example, you'll see not a suburb but a striking expanse of countryside—cornfields, cottonwood groves, and the like. The region remained undeveloped because it was relatively low and marshy; more recently, the Yugoslav War turned it into a battleground, and it is still littered with land mines, whose ongoing removal is vital to the nation's continuing economic development (*see* Close-Up: "Off Limits").

A BRIDGE IS BORN

WHEN SULTAN SÜLEJMAN THE MAGNIFICENT decided in autumn of 1525 to attack Hungary, Osijek's fate was settled Emissaries from Osijek, aiming to save their town, met the Ottomans on August 8, 1526, to hand over the town keys. Less than two weeks later, an Ottoman army crossed into Osijek over a pontoon bridge across the Drava. From this point on, Osijek became a key element in the Ottoman's movement north toward Buda and east, toward Vienna. Indeed, far from suffering devastation, the town thrived.

Many an Ottoman war campaign proceeded through Osijek on its way west. However, there was the lingering problem of getting a mammoth army across the Drava and the swamps to the north. The answer: a bridge such as the world had never seen.

With the labor of 25,000 people, Sülejman's Bridge—all 8 km (5 mi) of it—was completed on July 19, 1566. Not only did it span the Drava; it also worked its way in gentle curves across that river's tributaries and across marshes to the town of Darda to the north. The bridge became known as a world wonder; it was depicted and written about by painters and other travelers who came here from afar. Thanks to Sülejman's Bridge, Osijek's strategic and commercial importance as a vital link in the communication route between Constantinople and Budapest blossomed all the more. Osijek, whose inhabitants at the time comprised mostly Turkish settlers and a smaller number of locals who'd converted to Islam, developed rapidly as the most important town in Turkish Slavonia.

Not until the defeat of the Ottoman army by Vienna in 1683 did the Turkish grip on the region begin to weaken. The following year, with the area under attack, Sülejman's Bridge was partly burned. But before long the Turks restored it. But after the last Turkish solider left Osijek in 1687, ongoing wars sealed its fate: it was eventually destroyed beyond repair. Today it lives on only in the history books and in paintings, one of which is on display at Osijek's Muzej Slovonije (Museum of Slavonia).

Exploring Osijek

Discounting the sky-high Hotel Osijek, which opened in 2004 overlooking the Drava—several blocks away, thankfully—the majestic, red-brick, neo-Gothic, single-naved **Župna Crkva Sv. Petra i Pavla** (Parish Church of Saints Peter and Paul) is the highlight of Osijek's downtown skyline. At 90 meters (292 feet), its steeple is indeed the second-highest in Croatia. Built between 1894 and 1898 on the site of a former church of the same name by the architects Franz Langenberg of Germany and Robert Jordan of Austria, and on the initiative of the famous Dakovo-based bishop Josip Juraj Strossmayer, it has no less than five Gothic altars and an unusually frescoed ceiling replete with individual praying figures human and divine. ⊠ *Trg Ante Starčevića, Gornji Grad* ☉ *Daily 8–8.*

Chief among the architectural highlights on Trvđa's main square, **Trg Svetog Trojstrva** (Holy Trinity Square), is the plague pillar at its center. The zavjetni stup svetog trojstva (Votive Pillar of the Holy Trinity) is one of Osijek's finest baroque monuments. Erected in 1729–1730 by the widow of General Maksimilijan Petraš, who died of the plague in 1728, it has an elaborate pinnacle and four pedestals at its base bearing the statues of various saints, including St. Sebastian. Overlooking the northwest side of the square is the yellow Zgrada Glavne straže (Building of the Main Guard), built in 1729 with the observation post jutting out of its roof and capped by a Venetian-Moorish dome. On the square's western side is the grand zgrada glavne komande (High Command Building), erected originally as a single-story building between 1724 and 1726 on the order of Prince Eugene of Savoy with a Renaissance facade and a dual-columned, baroque entrance; a second floor was added in 1765.

The **Muzej Slovonije** (Museum of Slavonia), Slavonia's oldest museum, was established in 1877 and moved to this location on the eastern side of Trg Svetog Trojstrva in 1946. Although most of the myriad objects on display have disappointingly little context—with hardly any explanatory text even in Croatian and nothing at all in other languages— one exception is a second-floor room that has a great deal of English-language text elucidating its display of colorful ceramics and glass from the old Franciscan monastery. A walk through the various themed rooms on the two floors nonetheless offers a worthwhile glimpse into the region's history from ancient times to the present day. You're likely to spy a little bit of everything, from stuffed animals to old coins, from pottery to swords and halberds, from a collection of 16th- to 19th-century locks and keys to timepieces and typewriters. Last but not least, there's a room full of moving photographs from the most recent Yugoslav war. The courtyard features a sarcophagus and other sculptural fragments from Mursa, the Roman settlement that was situated in present-day Donji Grad. Should you find the front door locked during open hours, press the buzzer and someone will probably let you in. ⊠ *Trg Svetog Trojstrva 6, Trvđa* ☎ *031/122–505 or 031/120–959* ⊕ *www. mdc.hr/osijek* 🖾 *13 Kn* ☉ *Tues.–Sun. 10–1.*

Near the site of the onetime Kasim-Pasha Mosque, the mustard-yellow **Župna Crkva Sveta Mihovila** (St. Michael's Parish Church) has a single nave with two bulb-topped bell towers on each side of its facade. It was built by the Jesuits over 30 years beginning in 1725. In accord with the late baroque style in fashion in continental Croatia at the time, the interior displays a conspicuous absence of paintings. Unfortunately, it's often closed except during services and weddings. ⊠ *Trg Jurja Križanića, Trvđa* ☉ *Open only during services.*

One of Osijek's most soothing spots, the **Perivoj Krajla Tomislava** (King Tomislav Gardens) is a spacious, forested oasis along the Drava that was laid out in the 18th century. It separates historic Trvđa from Gornji Grad, the more bustling, commercial heart of town. Today the park is home to playgrounds, a tennis court, and a rowing club.

The building that has housed the **Zgrada Hrvatskoga Narodnog Kazališta** (Croatian National Theater) since 1907 is an imposing ochre structure whose Venetian-Moorish style renders it the most striking of a string of classical facades along Županijska ulica. Not open for tours, the theater can only be seen if you take in a performance. ⊠ *Županijska ul 9, Gornji Grad* ☎ *031/220–700.*

need a break? With cool ceiling lights, comfy black vinyl chairs, and a spacious terrace out front, the **Mala Kavana** (⊠ Trg Marina Drzića) is a pleasant place to kick back and have a coffee or some other drink before continuing on your way.

Where to Eat

$$–$$$$ ✕ **Restoran Müller.** This is one of Osijek's finest restaurants, where not
Fodor's Choice only regional specialties but also coastal as well as continental cuisine
★ are prepared and served with great care and complemented by the finest wines. Whether you're up for *šageti fruti di Mare, fiš paprikaš, čobanac,* or beef Wellington, you will leave this elegant and intimately lit room as pleased as a plumb. The mustachioed owner, Želko Kolar, a dapper gentleman who talks proudly of the large wine cellar downstairs, makes it a matter of policy that only he and his son deal with guests. At the time of this writing, the only foreign-language menu was in German. ⊠ *Trg Jurja Križanića 9, Trvđa* ☎ *031/204–270* ▤ *AE, DC, MC, V.*

$$–$$$ ✕ **Restaurant Laguna Croatica.** With an arched brick ceiling above you and Tiffany-style windows, the cellar dining room of this restaurant a few minutes west of downtown is an awfully pleasant place to indulge in a hearty meat or freshwater fish dish—whether *ćevapčići* (grilled spicy cubes of minced meat, often served with raw onions), grilled turkey, beef, or breaded carp. You might try the Slavonian steak—grilled veal shank stuffed with ham and cheese—and wash it down with a glass of plavac mali wine. ⊠ *Dubrovačka 13, Gornji Grad* ☎ *031/369–203* ▤ *AE, DC, MC, V.*

$–$$ ✕ **Slavonska Kuća.** Just a couple blocks from Trvđa's main square, the
Fodor's Choice one small room is about as atmospheric as can be, with the rustic
★ wooden benches complemented by walls adorned with, among other things, a giant catfish and a net not nearly large enough to hold it in. Folksy Croatian background music lulls your senses as you delight in such regional fare as *riblji paprikaš* (elsewhere called *fiš paprikas*) and *perkelt* (meat in paprika sauce). For dessert, try the *palačinke* (crêpes). The menu is in Croatian only. ⊠ *Kamila Firingera 26, Trvđa* ☎ *031/208–277* ▤ *AE, DC, MC, V.*

Where to Stay

If you'd prefer to save money by staying in a private room rather than a hotel, and don't mind being 6 km (4 mi) north of town, in the village of Bilje, the friendly folks at **OK Tours** (⊠ Trg Slobode 8, Osijek ☎ 031/212–815) will arrange this for you. Figure on at least 160 Kn per person. Getting to Bilje is straightforward: there are around 10 buses daily, roughly once an hour until around 10:20 PM, so this option won't allow much of a nightlife in Osijek unless you have a car at your disposal. At 13 Kn one-way (payable to the driver), at least the price of the ticket is inexpensive.

★ **$$** ▦ **Hotel Osijek.** Thank goodness this skyline-dominating, thoroughly modern and thoroughly bluish, steel-and-glass edifice was not built any closer to the cathedral. Reopened under new ownership in 2004 after extensive renovation, the Hotel Osijek is the city's one hotel that offers both largeness and luxury. The double rooms come in two types: the classic, a bit on the small side and with showers only; and the deluxe, more of a suite, with a full bath and an outer room with its own bathroom. The fitness room, on the top floor, affords a great view of the town and river below. The hotel restaurant, Zimska Luka, in an airy room overlooking the Drava, is one of Osijek's most distinguished places to savor not only regional specialties but wild game and a broad selection of international cuisine. ☒ *Šamačka 4, Gornji Grad 31000* ☎ *031/230–333* 🖷 *031/230–444* ⊕ *www.hotelosijek.hr* ⬦ *140 rooms, 7 suites* ♨ *Restaurant, café, in-room safes, minibars, in-room data ports, cable TV, gym, hot tub, sauna, hair salon, bar, meeting rooms, free parking* ▤ *AE, DC, MC, V* ¶⊙¶ *BP.*

$$ ▦ **Hotel Waldinger.** Opened in 2004 in a 19th-century art-nouveau build-
Fodor'sChoice ing on one of central Osijek's main thoroughfares, the Waldinger—
★ named after famous local painter Adolf Waldinger—offers luxury on par with the Hotel Osijek, but on a smaller, cosier scale and with a period look and feel. Standard doubles have a jetted tub in the bathroom, whereas the suite's jetted tub is right in the bedroom. Also well worth noting: in a bucolic backyard next door, complete with a little pond, is an older, one-story pension, with seven bright, spacious, minibar- and air-conditioning-equipped rooms with tall, period curtains; further removed from the moderate bustle of the city, they go for just for 440 Kn. ☒ *Županijska 8, Gornji Grad 31000* ☎ *031/250–450* 🖷 *031/250–453* ⊕ *www.waldinger.hr* ⬦ *15 rooms, 1 suite* ♨ *Restaurant, café, in-room hot tub, in-room safes, in-room data ports, cable TV, minibars, gym, hot tub, sauna, meeting room, free parking* ▤ *AE, DC, MC, V* ¶⊙¶ *BP.*

¢ ▦ **Central Hotel.** With its red-carpeted spiral staircase and wrought-iron railing, Osijek's first hotel, which opened in 1889, is still alive and well today, even if a thorough renovation to spruce things up is yet to come. The elegant rooms include armchairs with pretty, floral upholstery. Request a large double (with a king-size or French bed) and a view of the main square for no extra cost; most of the doubles are a bit smaller, with twin beds. The entrance is off an arcade on Trg Ante Starčevića, near the towering Parish Church of Saints Peter and Paul. Across the arcade is the hotel's Viennese-style café, replete with red-velvet chairs. ☒ *Trg Ante Starčevića 6, Gornji Grad 31000* ☎ *031/283–399* 🖷 *031/ 283–891* ⊕ *www.hotel-central-os.hr* ⬦ *39 rooms* ♨ *Restaurant, in-room safes, cable TV, minibars; no a/c* ▤ *AE, DC, MC, V* ¶⊙¶ *BP.*

Nightlife & the Arts

Nightlife
Though one of Osijek's most popular dance clubs is in the heart of quiet, historic Trvđa, most of the city's nightlife is east of the Hotel Osijek on Šetalište Kardinal Franje Šepera—the promenade along the city harbor (Zimska Luka) in Gornji Grad. In fair weather, you can easily lose yourself in crowds of nighttime revelers.

Right next door to the Slavonska Kuča restaurant, the aptly named **Club Sound** (✉ Kamila Firingera 24, Trvđa ☎ 031/201–057) is an inviting place to dance the night away, with a mix of R&B, pop, and commercial hits. Theme parties are often held on Friday, Saturday, and Tuesday nights in the cool back room equipped with flashing lights. Right on the Old Town's main square, the walls of the ever popular **St. Patrick's Pub** (✉ Kuhačeva 15, south side of Trg Svetog Trojstva, Trvđa ☎ 031/205–202) is a paean to all things English, including Jack the Ripper, but the prevailing interior-decorating theme is soccer.

The Arts

The **Zgrada Hrvatskoga Narodnog Kazališta** (Croatian National Theater) (✉ Županijska ul 9, Gornji Grad ☎ 031/220–700) is Osijek's venue for a fairly broad array of Croatian and international plays from September through May. The **Children's Theater** (✉ Trg bana J. Jelačića 19, Gornji Grad ☎ 031/501–485) is the place to go for a good puppet show.

Shopping

Although Osijek has few quality opportunities, bustling Županijska, leading up to Trg Ante Starčevića, is the best stretch of street in town to see what's for sale. **Rukotvorine** (✉ Županijska 15, Gornji Grad ☎ 031/212–217) has a rich array of top-notch Slavonian embroidery and handicrafts in its small store across the street from the Hotel Waldinger. If you haven't yet acquired your all-original Croatian silk tie in Zagreb at one of the capital's attractive boutiques in the same chain, you can do so at **Croata** (✉ Županijska 2, Gornji Grad ☎ 031/200–260).

BIZOVAC

★ ❷ *18 km (11 mi) west of Osijek.*

Rising up out of the Slavonian plains 2 km (1.3 mi) outside the pretty little town of Bizovac is a vast, weirdly modern building complex with an unmistakably sci-fi look to it. Lavishly ornamented with an intricate network of pipes along part of its exterior, this is **Bizovačke toplice**, Slavonia's largest spa, which sprang up here in 1990—a year before war visited the region. Inside are Europe's only thermal salt-springs, which issue from a depth of almost 2,000 meters with a salinity approaching that of the Adriatic. Exceptionally rich in minerals and up to 96°C at its source, this water can be yours within the aptly named **Aquapolis Water City,** which consists of four indoor and two outdoor pools containing thermal water and three other pools for just plain swimming or fun. Though frequent trains make the 20-minute trip between Osijek and Bizovac, the 25-minute walk from the railway station over rural roads can hardly compete with the convenience of a 30-minute bus trip that drops you off at the hospital right across the road from the spa. ✉ *Sunčana 39* ☎ *031/685–100* ⊕ *www.bizovacke-toplice.hr* 🎟 *20 Kn* ☉ *Mon.–Thurs. 8–8, Fri.–Sun. 8–8 and 9–midnight.*

Where to Stay & Eat

You could choose to spend the night—for just 227 Kn for a no-frills, simply furnished double room (including breakfast) at Aquapolis Water City's **Termia Hotel.**

$–$$　✕ **Nacionalni Restaurant.** Technically separate from the hotel but accessible via a convoluted route from the reception desk, the restaurant is the one fine-dining venue in the Aquapolis Water City complex. With main courses ranging from simple pastas to scrumptious pike-perch, catfish, carp, or pork-rich house specialties, this brick-walled cellar restaurant is the spa's best bet for a good meal. ✉ *Sunčana 39* ☎ *031/685–252* 🖃 *AE, MC, V.*

KOPAČKI RIT NATURE PARK

★ ❸ *10 km (6 mi) northeast of Osijek.*

More than 80% of the historical wetlands along the Danube have been lost since the late 19th century. One of the largest remaining areas is now preserved in Kopački Rit Nature Park, a place of serene beauty that makes for a deeply satisfying visit whether or not you're partial to birds. Embracing more than 30,000 hectares (74,100 acres) immediately north of the Drava, where the fast river flows eastward into the Danube, the park is covered with immense reed beds as well as willow, poplar, and oak forests and crisscrossed by ridges, ponds, shallow lakes, and marshes. Its exact aquatic contours vary a tad each year, depending on the degree to which the Danube backs up under pressure from the Drava and floods over the area.

More than 285 bird species, 400 varieties plants, and dozens of species of butterflies, mammals, and fish live in Kopački Rit. A vital spawning ground for Danube river fish, the park is also a breeding area for numerous endangered species—including the white-tailed sea eagle, the black stork, and the European otter. Egrets, herons, and cormorants are abundant, as are red deer, roe deer, and wild boar. In winter, Kopački Rit plays host to thousands of migrating geese and ducks. Although efforts have been underway since 1999 to make Kopački Rit a full-fledged national park, the going has been slow on this front—in no small part because the necessary restrictions on hunting in such a game-rich area make the issue politically sensitive. The best times of year to visit are during spring and autumn bird migrations, when there are often several hundred thousand birds in the park. Should you come in warm weather, be prepared to be feasted on by mosquitoes.

Although the park administration building is in Bilje, the information office at the park entrance in Kopač serves visitors. A short nature trail leads to the landing where boat excursions set out daily into the marshy heart of the park along a channel to Kopačevo Jezero, the largest lake. English-language excursions are available if there is sufficient demand. Although you can walk or drive right past the visitor's center into the park for free, by paying the admission you get a one-hour boat ride fol-

OFF LIMITS

WHEN A YOUNG HUNGARIAN WENT HANG GLIDING in July 2005 and drifted unwittingly over the Croatian border, he landed in a field north of Osijek, brushed himself off, and was preparing to walk out when a local woman yelled, "No!" The man—who had landed in the middle of a minefield—had to stay put until a helicopter plucked him out.

Croatia is littered with mines left over from the 1990s Yugoslav war. Out of some two million such devices, it is believed that as many as 250,000 are still out there. Between 1998 and early 2005, almost 260 people have fallen victim to leftover mines, 99 of whom have died. Mines have also inflicted great harm to wildlife, including in such protected natural areas as Kopački Rit Nature Park, near Osijek, and Plitvice Lakes National Park, between Zagreb and the Dalmatian coast. Twelve of the country's 21 counties, including several in Slavonia, still have minefields. Some estimates place as many as 52,000 mines in Osječko-Baranjska County alone, putting 5% of its land off-limits to people and to development. Nearly 60% of the contaminated land is forest, but 27% is arable. Almost half of the county's 42 municipalities are affected.

Croatia's government established the Croatian Mine Action Centre (CROMAC) in 1998 to coordinate the removal of these mines and aims to de-mine its territory by 2010.

Before venturing off a road or path into field or forest, check for the skull-and-crossbones signs that warn of minefields. Even in the absence of signs, ask qualified locals whether an area is safe. For more information, visit the Web site of the Croatian Mine Action Centre at www.hcr.hr.

---

lowed by a guided walk of at least one hour along a dyke to the park's northern reaches.

In 1991, Kopački Rit became a no-man's-land along the front line of the Yugoslav war. For the next six years the natural area and the human communities around it were ravaged, not least by thousands of land mines, which have not only brought great danger to humans but have drastically reduced populations of large mammals such as deer and wild boar. Though major de-mining efforts have been underway since Croatia's reintegration of the Baranja region in 1997, about one-tenth of the surface area of Kopački Rit is still inaccessible due to minefields (*see* Close-Up: "Off Limits").

A prized hunting and fishing area for centuries—and in particular during the Austro-Hungarian Empire—Kopački Rit also has a rich cultural-historical heritage. **Dvorac Tikveš** (⊠ 15 km [9 mi] north of Bilje), a historic villa with a rich history dating back to the Austro-Hungarian monarchy, also served as a hunting lodge for Yugoslav leader Josep Broz Tito. The complex includes a restaurant and research laboratories for visiting scientists. Since 2005, the park has been offering horse-drawn carriage rides here for groups of up to 16 people, for 600 Kn.

Getting to Kopacki Rit from Osijek is simple if you have a car at your disposal—just follow the signs once you're in Bilje. If you go by bus, however, be prepared to follow the signs on foot for some 4 km (2½ mi) along rural roads after the bus drops you off in Bilje. ⊠ *Information Center near Kopaceva* ☎ *031/752–321 or 031/752–320* ⊕ *www.kopacki-rit.com* ✉ *60 Kn Apr., May, Sept. and Oct.; 40 Kn June–Aug. and Nov.–Mar.* ⊙ *May–Sept., daily 8–5, Oct.–Apr., daily 8–4.*

Where to Eat

★ **$$** ✗ **Zelena Žaba.** Also known locally by its Hungarian name, *Zöld Béka,* the Green Frog restaurant is an absolutely delightful village restaurant, with a quiet, willow-fringed marsh behind the building that you can look out upon from the back room. Its hunting-cum-fishing theme is expressed in the form of rifles, antlers, an oar, and fishnets on the walls. Try house specialties such as *žabliji kraci* (frogs' legs) and *riblji perkelt* (fish in a thick paprika sauce), not to mention other favorites such as roast pike. For dessert, there's nothing like *palačinke* filled with walnuts or jam. ⊠ *Ribarska ul 3, Kopač* ☎ *031/752–212* ⊟ *AE, DC, MC, V.*

$–$$ ✗ **Restoran Kod Varge.** On Bilje's main road a few hundred yards before the major intersection (if you're coming from Osijek and going toward Kopački Rit), this charming restaurant offers such hearty regional fare as *ribli paprikaš,* a spicy-hot paprika-flavored fish stew that is rather salty, too. If you're not troubled by the discordant but somehow appealing blend of folksy Croatian music in the background, not to mention a TV in the corner of the room that plays whatever happens to be on, you'll enjoy your meal here. ⊠ *Ul Kralja Zvonimira 37a, Bilje* ☎ *031/750–120 or 031/750–031* ⊟ *AE, DC, MC, V.*

VUKOVAR

❹ *35 km (22 mi) southeast of Osijek.*

Tourists don't exactly flock to this once-lovely baroque city that was reduced to rubble in 1991 in one of the most notorious events of the Yugoslav war. On May 2, 1991, 12 Croatian policemen were ambushed and killed in the suburb of Borovo. By September, Croat refugees had fled from outlying areas to the city center, which came under siege by the JNA (Yugoslav People's Army). After weeks of heavy bombardment that left the city in ruins, Vukovar fell on November 18. Of the thousands of Croatian residents who were captured—many had fled to the hospital, where they were awaiting the arrival of the Red Cross—a substantial number wound up in a mass grave outside the village of Ovčara, 7 km (4.4 mi) to the southeast. All told, some 2,000 Croatians perished in the siege of Vukovar, with roughly the same number still reported as missing. As of this writing, two Serbs were on trial in the Hague for allegedly carrying out the massacre of those who'd fled to the city hospital.

Vukovar was named after the ancient Vučedol culture that inhabited a site 5 km (3 mi) downstream along the Danube from the present-day city some 5,000 years ago. The area near the present-day town was later the site of a Roman settlement, and by the 11th century, a community existed at the town's present location; this settlement became the seat of Vukovo County in the 13th century. After Turkish rule (1526–1687), almost all of Vukovar and environs was bought by the counts of Eltz, a German family that strongly influenced the development of the town for the next two centuries and whose palace, severely damaged in the 1991 siege, is home to the local museum.

In a poignant reminder of what happened here not long ago, the visitor cannot help but notice a steady, somber stream of pedestrian traffic to one of present-day Vukovar's most conspicuous sites: a tall, simple concrete cross situated at the tip of a narrow causeway overlooking the Danube. While this war memorial honors all victims on both sides, with inscriptions in both cyrillic and Roman letters, within eyeshot of here is another conspicuous sight that presumably does not win the hearts of local Serbs—a bust of the late Croatian leader Franjo Tuđman on a square bearing his name.

Vukovar is as much the scene of urban renewal as it is of destruction. A steady influx of European Union reconstruction funds has been changing the face of the city; Vukovar may very well be Croatia's only town with an *ulica Europske Unije* (European Union Street). Although at least half of all structures are damaged to some degree, new houses and ongoing construction are much in evidence; and you have the sense that most of those heavily damaged buildings that *are* still standing are there precisely because their reconstruction is planned at some point. As a walk around the town center in later afternoon or early evening will amply show, public life is again taking shape here, and new public spaces are gaining vitality and purpose—even if the underlying tensions between the town's Serbian and Croatian residents remain.

Housed in the 18th-century Dvorac Eltz, which was severely damaged in the siege of Vukovar, the **Gradski Muzej Vukovar** (Vukovar Town Museum) has been back in business since 2001—since the signing of an agreement for the return of its collection, which was expropriated by the Serbs in 1991. ⊠ *Županijska 2* ☎ *032/441–270* 💳 *10 Kn* ⊙ *Mon.–Sat. 10–3.*

Vukovar's main ecclesiastical attraction, on a hill a bit to the southeast of the town center, is the 18th-century **Franjevački Samostan** (Franciscan Monastery), which was pieced back together again after being ravaged in the war. ⊠ *Samostanska ulica* ☎ *032/441–381.*

need a break? Yards away from the pedestrian bridge and across from the Velepromet supermarket, the hip little café-cum-bar **Caffe El Maritimo** (⊠ Trg Matije Gupca 21 ☎ No phone) is an inviting place either for a daytime coffee or an evening beer. Its opening in May 2005 suggests that Vukovar's social scene is beginning to blossom anew after the ruin wrought by war.

Where to Eat

$–$$ ✕ **Vrške.** Wildly popular with locals, this apricot-color restaurant with a charming farmhouse look rests on an islet that is reached by a pedestrian bridge behind the Hotel Lav. Its spacious, thatched-roof terrace overlooks the Danube, and beside it is a pavilion where live music is played; the interior features reed walls and wood-beamed ceilings. Carp, catfish, pike-perch, and other freshwater fish are the favorites here, whether grilled, fried, or in a thick, vegetable-rich sauce; they are typically complemented by French fries. You can get a huge, four-person bowl of paprika-rich *riblji paprikaš* (fish stew). Combine this with some Ilok wine and a *palačinke s marmeladom* (jam-filled crêpe). ⊠ *Parobrodska 3* ☎ *032/441–788* 🗖 *AE, DC, MC, V.*

Where to Stay

$ 🏨 **Hotel Lav.** Strange as it may seem to have a luxury hotel pop up in the middle of Vukovar, that's just what happened in 2005 when the Hotel Lav—a sparkling white building with a glass front—reopened its doors after a complete reconstruction, primarily with business travelers in mind. With bright yellow, silky bedspreads and an unmistakably modern look, the spacious rooms are nonetheless decorated with pictures of the "old" Vukovar; the suites include jetted tubs. The huge, bombed-out building next door used to be Vukovar's main shopping center, and it is slated for eventual reconstruction. ⊠ *J. J. Strossmayera 18, across from the tourist-information office, 32000* ☎ *032/445–100* 🗗 *032/445–110* ⊕ *www.hotel-lav.hr* 🛏 *39 rooms, 4 suites* ⟐ *Restaurant, café, in-room safes, minibars, cable TV, in-room dataports, gym, meeting rooms* 🗖 *AE, DC, MC, V* ⫼⊙⫽ *BP.*

¢ 🏨 **Dunav Hotel.** Vukovar's sole budget alternative to the Hotel Lav, the worn-looking Dunav has no frills, but it is an acceptable—if somber—place to stay. The rooms on the fifth floor have relatively new bathrooms and are just 30 Kn more than the rooms on the first four floors, which are more worn looking. The top two floors are empty. Ask for a room with a river view. ⊠ *Trg Republike 1, 32000* ☎ *032/441–285* 🗗 *032/441–762* 🛏 *58 rooms* ⟐ *Restaurant, bar; no room TVs, no A/C* 🗖 *AE, DC, MC, V* ⫼⊙⫽ *BP.*

ĐAKOVO

❺ *38 km (24 mi) southeast of Osijek.*

Đakovo is a peaceful little town, where the din of bicycles and the dribbling of basketballs on a Sunday afternoon outdoes the roar of cars. The relatively bustling pedestrian main street is ulica Hrv. Velikana, whose far end has a little parish church that was built rather cleverly from a former 16th-century mosque. The best time to be in town—though a difficult time to book a room on short notice—is the last weekend in September, during the annual *Đakovački Vezovi* (Đakovo Embroidery Festival), which sees a whole array of song-and-dance performances, an all-around party atmosphere, and, above all, a folklore show replete with traditional embroidered costumes, folk dancing, and folk singing—and even a show by the famous Lipizzaner horses, who train in town.

Fodor's Choice
★

In Đakovo's town center is the majestic red-brick, neo-Gothic **Đakovačka Katedrala** (Đakovo Cathedral), which was commissioned by the Bishop of Đakovo, Josip Juraj Strossmayer (1815–1905), and designed by architect Frederick Schmidt. Consecrated in 1882 after two decades of construction, the three-nave structure is distinguished by two steeples towering to 84 meters (274 feet), by beehivelike cones on either side of the entrance, and by a pinnacled cupola. The inside walls feature colorful biblical scenes—some representing the life of St. Peter, the cathedral's patron saint—painted over 12 years by the father and son team of Alexander and Ljudevit Seitz. The striking blue ceiling is dotted with gold stars; and the floor is paved with impressive red, yellow, and black checkered tile. ⊠ *Trg Strossmayera* ☎ *031/811–784* ☉ *Daily 8–noon and 3–6.*

Just north of the cathedral is the **Spomen-muzej Biskupa Josipa Jurja Strossmayera** (Strossmayer Museum) (⊠ Luke Botića 2 ☎ No phone 🖾 5 Kn ☉ Tues.–Fri. 8–7, Sat. 8–2), which presents the life of the influential bishop by displaying some of his effects and writings.

Close to the train station, a 10-minute walk from the cathedral and the town center if you follow ulica Matije Gupca but still very much in town, you will notice the unmistakable smell of horse. That is because you are approaching the **Lipizzaner stud farm,** where several dozen of these prized white horses are trained. Although there are generally no scheduled events here except during the Đakovo Embroidery Festival, you will probably be allowed in to take a glimpse of the horses while training if you stop by in the morning. ⊠ *Augusta Šenoe 45* ☎ *031/813–286.*

Where to Eat

$–$$$ ✕**Gradski Podrum.** The Đakovo Lion's Club meets under the vaulted brick ceiling of this cellar restaurant once a month, amid several fine paintings and two not-so-fine, tacky ones. The menu, which focuses on grilled, Balkan-style meats as well as poultry and a scrumptious variety of *palačinke* filled with jam, walnuts, chocolate sauce, or sweet curd-cheese, is only in Croatian and in German. ⊠ *Ulica Hrv. Velikana 9* ☎ *031/813–199* ▤ *AE, DC, MC, V.*

Where to Stay

¢ ▦ **Croatia-Tourist.** Đakovo does not have much in the way of accommodation, but this homey if uninspiringly named hotel offers a handful of bright, comfy rooms, some of which are fancier than others. All have delightful white closets built into the walls on each side of the bed, but there is otherwise a dearth of frills (such as cable TV or air-conditioning). The hotel's spacious restaurant is among the best in town, with a decent range of fish and meat specialties, as well as fried frogs' legs and even fried brains. For dessert, try a walnut-filled *palačinke* topped off with chocolate sauce. ⊠ *P. Preradovića 25, 31400* ☎ *031/813–391* 🖷 *031/814–063* 🖙 *8 rooms* 🖔 *Restaurant, pizzeria, in-room safes; no room TVs, no a/c* ▤ *AE, DC, MC, V* ⦿ *BP.*

SLAVONIA ESSENTIALS

BUS TRAVEL
Numerous daily buses connect Osijek and the rest of Slavonia, including Vukovar and Đakovo. However, a train may get you where you're going faster or at a more convenient time, so it's a good idea to check at the railway station next door before hopping on board the bus. Timetables are posted in the Osijek Bus Station. Around 10 buses daily (on weekends; more buses weekdays) make the 45-minute trip between Osijek and Vukovar, for 28 Kn one-way. You can get to Đakovo from Osijek in about 40 minutes by bus for about 20 Kn one-way. The bus station is closer to the town center than the train station.

🚍 **Osijek Bus Station** ✉ Bartula Kašića, by trg L. Ružičke, Osijek ☎ 060/334-4466. **Vukovar Bus Station** ✉ Olajnica, Vukovar ☎ 032/441-829 or 060/337-799.

CAR RENTALS
You certainly don't need a car to get around Slavonia unless you are inclined to depart substantially from the beaten path. However, if you want to visit several destinations in just one or two days, having a car at your disposal will save you trips back to Osijek each time you want to go somewhere else. You can rent a small car from for about 350 Kn per day, including taxes, insurance, and umlimited mileage.

🚗 **Budget** ✉ Kapucinska 39, Osijek ☎ 053/1211-500. **Hertz** ✉ Gundulićeva 32, Osijek ☎ 031/200-422.

EMERGENCIES
🚑 **Ambulance Ambulance** ☎ 94.
🚑 **Doctors & Dentists Hitno Pomoć** (First Aid) ✉ Huttlerova, Osijek ☎ 031/506-920. **Dežurna Stomatološka Služba** (On-Call Dental Service,) ✉ Dom zdravlja, Osijek ☎ 031/225-300.
🚑 **Fire Fire Emergencies** ☎ 93.
🚑 **Pharmacies Osijek 24-hr Pharmacy** ✉ Trg A. Starčevića 7, Osijek ☎ 031/205-722. **Vukovar 24-hr Pharmacy** ✉ Trg A. Starčevića 7 ☎ 031/205-722.
🚑 **Police Police Emergencies** ☎ 92.

INTERNET
One of Slavonia's few Internet cafés—and Osijek's only one as of this writing—is the aptly named VIP Internet Caffe. It's more a bar, actually, with a spacious terrace out front and a handful of computers just inside that you can use for 14 Kn/hour.
🌐 **VIP Internet Caffe** ✉ L. Jägera, Osijek ☎ 031/212-313.

POST OFFICE
📮 **Osijek Post Office** ✉ K. A. Stepinca 17, Osijek ☎ 031/253-868.

PUBLIC TRANSPORTATION IN OSIJEK
Although it is certainly possible to walk everywhere in Osijek, hopping aboard one of the trams that wind their way around the city and giving the driver either 7 Kn for a one-way ticket, or 18 Kn for a day-pass, will save you lots of time—not least because of the spacious park between the two main parts of town. To get between Gornji Grad and Trvđa,

take Tram no. 1; to get between the train station and Gornji Grad, it's Tram no. 2. If you are caught without a valid ticket, by the way, you will be fined 150 Kn, payable on the spot.

TRAIN TRAVEL

Six trains run daily between Zagreb and Osijek (107 Kn one-way), one of these being an express, three-hour run with only three stops before the final destination; most take four to five hours with lots of stops at towns along the way. The route cuts right through the heart of the Slavonian plain, giving you a real sense of appreciation for the sweeping vistas of Croatia's breadbasket.

You can get to Dakovo from Osijek in about 40 minutes by one of several trains daily for roughly 20 Kn one-way. The Dakovo train station is 1 km (½ mi) east of the center, at the opposite end of Kralja Tomislava. 🚂 **Osijek Train Station** ✉ Trg L. Ružičke, Osijek ☎ 060/333-444.

VISITOR INFORMATION

🚂 In addition to the local offices below, the Web sites of the tourist boards responsible for **Osijek-Baranja County** ⊕ www.tzosbarzup.hr and **Vukovar-Srijem County** ⊕ www.tzvsz.hr have information on towns within their purview without individual sites. **Bizovac Tourist Information** ✉ Krajla Tomislava 138, Bizovac ☎ 031/675-770. **Bilje Tourist Information** ✉ Krajla Zvonimira 1b, Bilje ☎ 031/751-480 ⊕ www.tzo-bilje.hr. **Dakovo Tourist Information** ✉ Krajla Tomislava 3, Dakovo ☎ 031/812-319 or 031/822-376 ⊕ www.tz-djakovo.hr. **Osijek Tourist Information** ✉ Županijska 2, Osijek ☎ 031/203-755 ⊕ www.osijek.hr. **Vukovar Tourist Information** ✉ J. J. Strossmayera 15, Vukovar ☎ 032/442-889.

Istria

3

"I would not miss Pula in Croatia. The old village is from 310 AD and [was built] by the Romans. The people are lovely and aim to please. Don't forget to try the local pivo."

—snookss

"Rovinj is, for me, the most beautiful place in Istria, and I would definitively recommend it. It is a good base for exploring Istria's coast but also the countryside, which is lovely and filled with beautiful small towns."

—Jonas

"Another place to consider in Istria is Porec; we spent several days there before going to Rovinj, [and it is] also very Italian with good restaurants. "

—aeiger

By Paul
Olchváry

THE WORD CONJURES SOMETHING MAGICAL as it rolls off the tongue: *Istria*. Beyond sounding poetic, however, the name of this region of Croatia is derived from the name of the Illyrian people who occupied this region well before the Romans first arrived in the 3rd century BC—namely, the Histrians, whose chief architectural legacy comprised numerous hilltop fortresses. Situated in the northwest corner of Croatia bordering Slovenia, the triangular-shaped Istrian peninsula looks rather like a bunch of grapes—and, given its strong viticultural heritage, some might say this is not a coincidence.

Much of Europe's history has passed through Istria for more than a thousand years, not least the history associated with three great civilizations—the Roman, the Germanic, and the Slavic. Centuries of Venetian rule later reinforced by years of Italian occupation between the world wars have left a sizable Italian minority here, and Italian influence is apparent in the architecture, the cuisine, and the local dialect. Here, even the effects of the concrete-box style of Communist-era architecture seem relatively minimal compared to the overall sense of a much deeper past suggested by the rich mix of architectural styles—from a whole array of well-preserved Roman ruins to early Christian churches, Byzantine mosaics, and Romanesque basilicas; from breathtakingly well-preserved medieval towns, towers, and town walls to baroque palaces and Austro-Hungarian fortifications.

The region's principal city and port, Pula, is on the tip of the peninsula and is best known for its remarkably preserved 1,900-year-old Roman amphitheater and Forum as well as the Triumphal Arch of the Sergians. Close by, the beautifully nurtured island retreat of Brijuni National Park can be visited in a day. Towns along the west coast have an unmistakable Venetian flavor left by more than 500 years of Venetian occupation (1238–1797). Poreč and Rovinj, Croatia's two most popular seaside resorts, are both endowed with graceful campanili, loggias, and reliefs of the winged lion of St. Mark, patron saint of Venice. Although the effects of package tourism have long encroached—to varying degrees—on the immediate outskirts of various towns, most notably Poreč among Istria's largest coastal destinations, Rovinj, though likewise brimming with tourists in high season, retains more of its ravishing historic beauty and redolence than almost any other town on the Adriatic.

A side trip to the romantic hill towns of Motovun and Grožnjan will prove unforgettable, whether as a brief excursion from the sea in the warmer months or as a more substantial autumn journey. This inland area is particularly rich in truffles and mushrooms, and from mid-September to late October these local delicacies are celebrated with a series of gastronomic festivals.

Exploring Istria

About the Restaurants

Alongside Istria's plethora of touristy restaurants, placed one after another quayside and otherwise, an increasing number of exceptional dining establishments have arisen in recent years that likewise serve seafood specialties, pastas (e.g., fuži), truffle dishes, and Istrian appetizers such as prosciutto, often served with cheese-stuffed olives—and, to a lesser extent so far from the eastern reaches of Croatia but by no means to be discounted, such spicy, meaty fare as *čevapčići* (spiced, ground-meat kebabs). Also keep your eyes peeled for such traditional favorites as *supa,* which consists mostly of red wine poured into a *bukaleta* (usually an earthenware jug), with a bit of sugar, olive oil, pepper, and some warm, toasted bread mixed in.

Dining can be costly relative to much of inland Croatia and other, less visited reaches of Eastern Europe, with average prices for main courses starting around 40 Kn to 50 Kn (for pasta dishes or pizza) and moving up the scale to around 60 Kn for grilled mackerel and 80 Kn or even twice as much for other seafood specialties (many of which are priced by the kilogram, depending on the weight of the cut of fish you're served) and certain beef dishes. You can always save money by patronizing pizzerias, of which there are some fine ones in every large town. Or else, if you don't mind filling up on carbohydrates laden with oil, you can buy a *burek* (a curd-cheese or meat-filled pastry) in a bakery for around 10 Kn apiece.

WHAT IT COSTS in Croatian Kuna (Kn)				
$$$$	$$$	$$	$	¢
RESTAURANTS over 80	60–80	35–60	20–35	under 20

Restaurant prices are per person for a main course at dinner.

About the Hotels

In Istria, as in most other reaches of the Croatian coast, it's basically a question of whether to stay at the big, relatively faceless resort hotels on beaches, with a whole host of supplemental services and activities available or smaller, often family-run establishments within (or at least closer to) the Old Towns that have been appearing increasingly in recent years. We recommend the latter where possible, though in high season rooms fill up fast, so unless you reserve well in advance you will have to go with what's available. To avoid unwelcome surprises when reviewing your bill, bear in mind that many accommodations impose a surcharge—usually 20%—for stays under three nights, since they cater primarily to tourists from neighboring countries who spend a week or two.

As a budget alternative to staying in a hotel, various tourist agencies can help you book a room for around 250 Kn or more for two people, though prices may edge upward later in the day, when it is presumed that tourists are more desperate.

WHAT IT COSTS in euros (€) and Croatian kuna (Kn)				
$$$$	$$$	$$	$	¢
IN EUROS over € 225	€175–€225	€125–€175	€75–€125	under €75
IN KUNA over 1,650	1,300–1,650	925–1,300	550–925	under 550

Hotel prices are for two people in a double room in high season, excluding taxes and service charges.

3

If you have
3 days

There is so much to see in Istria that three days is a must, though it may seem like a rush if that's all the time you have. Start in Pula, as suggested below, if you are coming from Zagreb; if from the north (from Slovenia or Italy), start with Rovinj instead. Either way, by all means do visit Rovinj. If you are interested in Istria's ecclesiastical heritage, you may want to prioritize Poreč over Pula; if Roman ruins are more your thing, by all means focus on Pula, whose architecture also gives you more of a sense of Istria's Austro-Hungarian past.

On the first day, start off in **Pula.** Visit the Arena and at least take a stroll to the Forum. By all means spend the night here. A short drive or bus ride toward the Verudella or Stoja resort area gets you to eminently swimmable, if rocky, stretches of shoreline. The next morning, head off to **Rovinj.** Visit the the 18th-century baroque Crkva Sv Eufemije, and just revel in strolling about the most beautiful town on the Istrian coast. On the third day, spend some more time in or around Rovinj, whether strolling the Old Town or taking a dip in the sea. If you're up to it, particularly if you have a car, move on to **Poreč** to see the Eufrazijeva Basilica.

If you have
5 days

Spend your first day as above, but consider adding an excursion from Pula to **Vodnjan** or **Brijuni National Park,** depending on whether you're more interested in Vodnjan's countryside, medieval atmosphere, mummies, and food, or in Brijuni's natural splendors and luxurious, seaside ambience. Move on to **Rovinj** by the evening of Day 2 or the morning of Day 3, spending at least a full day or more there. On Day 4, it's on to **Poreč.** Perhaps go inland and spend the night in **Motovun.** On Day 5, if you're driving, take a look at **Grožnjan** as well before heading back. If you're getting around by bus, it's time to head back to a major town on the coast. Indeed, why not spend a few more hours in Rovinj or Pula before bidding adieu to Istria?

If you have
7 days

Spend your first five days as above, but be sure to supplement your time in Rovinj, Pula, and Porec with a lunch in **Labin** on the east coast of Istria; if you're driving from Zagreb do it on the way to the more important towns; if you're driving through the countryside that takes you through both **Motovun** and **Grožnjan,** spend a night in or near Motovun. Before going inland, you may want to pay a visit to Vrsar and the Limski kanal or, instead, Baradine Cave. If you have a car, you can do so as you go inland or on your way back to the coast; if traveling by bus, you can get to these places most easily by a group excursion from Poreč or Rovinj. You may want to visit **Novi-grad,** too, especially if you're driving, but save Umag for a 10-day trip. Spend Day 6 in Grožnjan then go back to Porec or, better yet, Rovinj for the night. On Day 7, proceed to **Pula,** with a stop in **Labin** if you haven't been there yet and will be going further east. Perhaps spend your final night in Labin as well.

Timing

If you are partial to sun and the idea of swimming in the warm, blue–green waters of the Adriatic, and you don't mind crowds and a bit of extra expense, by all means visit Istria in late spring or summer. Otherwise, this tourism-trampled region might be best saved for earlier in the spring or for late September or early October; indeed, doing so might save you 15% to 20% on lodging.

Numbers in the margins correspond to numbers on the Istria map.

PULA

292 km (182½ mi) southwest of Zagreb.

Today an industrial port town and Istria's chief administrative center, as well as a major tourist destination where a good number of locals also live (82,000 by last count), Pula became a Roman colony in the 1st century BC. This came about a century after the decisive defeat by the Romans, in 177 BC, of the nearby Histrian stronghold of Nesactium, prompting the Histrian king Epulon to plunge a sword into his chest lest he fall into the hands of the victors, who indeed conquered all of Istria. Remains from Pula's ancient past have survived up to the present day: as you drive in on the coastal route toward its choice setting on a bay near the southern tip of the Istrian peninsula, the monumental Roman amphitheater blocks out the sky on your left. Under Venetian rule (1331–1797), Pula was architecturally neglected, even substantially dismantled. Many structures from the Roman era were pulled down, and stones and columns were carted off across the sea to Italy to be used for new buildings there. Pula's second great period of development took place in the late 19th century, under the Habsburgs, when it served as the chief base for the Imperial Austro-Hungarian Navy. Today it's as much working city as tourist town, where Roman ruins and Austro-Hungarian architecture serve as backdrop for the bustle of everyday life amid a bit of Communist-era soot and socialist realism, too. James Joyce lived here for a short time, in 1904–05, before fleeing what he dismissed as a cultural backwater for Trieste. What's more, there are some outstanding restaurants and a number of pleasant family-run hotels, not to mention the nearby resort area of Verudela, where seaside tourism thrives in all its soothing, sunny sameness.

Exploring Pula

Pula's compact commercial and administrative center is situated on a small, semicircular protrusion of land in the Puljski Zaljev (Bay of Pula), which faces west into the Adriatic. Several ringlike streets radiate inward from the port, culminating in the small, fortress-capped hill at the center of this semicircle. Most of the cultural and historical sites are along this web of streets to the south, west, and north of the hill, with the huge Roman amphitheater on the northeastern fringes of this zone (accessible via Giardini and then Istarska ulica, on the landward side of the hill, a couple blocks in from the bay); the bus station is another few minutes' walk from there. Meanwhile, a long walk (or a

3

Rovinj Rovinj is itself a complete pleasure. Istria's star attraction occupies a fantastic setting, with centuries-old red-roofed houses clustered around the hill of a former island, and is crowned by the monumental baroque Crkva Sv Eufemije (Church of St. Euphemia). It's a ravishing place that draws artists, writers, musicians, and actors. Throughout the summer, the winding cobbled streets are crowded with vacationers from all reaches of Europe.

Pula's Architecture A visit to Istria without a look at the magnificent Roman Arena—the sixth largest structure of its type in the world—and Pula's Forum would be almost beside the point. You needn't go to Italy to revel in what the Romans left behind. Pula, which like other major towns on the coast was in Venetian hands for centuries, also served for decades as the Austro-Hungarian Empire's chief naval base. As Istria's largest city and chief administrative center, it saw a spate of relatively bland, concrete-box-style construction during the Communist era as part of Yugoslavia. However, Pula—as much as any other place in the peninsula—displays a richly layered architectural heritage unique to Istria.

Churches From Poreč's magnificent Eufrazijeva Basilica—among the most perfectly preserved Christian churches in Europe and one of the most important monuments of Byzantine art on the Adriatic—to Rovinj's Crkva Sv Eufemije, to Pula's Katedrala svete Marije, Istria has a wealth of religious sites that are among the most important not only in the Mediterranean but the world. Through them, you also gain a special appreciation for the rich span of the region's history, from Roman times through Venetian rule and beyond.

Hill Towns Instead of searching for imaginary castles from *The Lord of the Rings* in the wilds of New Zealand, you can visit such magical, strikingly preserved, onetime fortress towns as Motovun and Grožnan.

Food & Wine In that order, Istria is the home of one of the Adriatic's most alluring gastronomic traditions. Here you can have not only a whole host of dishes complemented by the much sought-after truffle, but also such Istrian specialties as sheep's cheese, prosciutto, and *supa* to boot, and also such meaty-spicy fare as *čevapčići*.

---

short drive) south of the city center are suburbs that culminate with the Verudella and Stoja peninsulas, home to bustling tourist resorts, beaches, and some excellent restaurants.

Numbers in the text correspond to numbers in the margin and on the Pula map.

What to See

Aquarium Pula. Pula's newest attraction opened in 2004 on the ground floor of the onetime Austro-Hungarian fortress in the resort complex of Verudela a few kilometers from the city center. The aquarium was

originally Croatia's first sea turtle rescue center, which opened two years earlier. Its five rooms offer a colorful look at hundreds of sea creatures from the Adriatic's underwater world, and include a "touching pool" that allows you to touch a dogfish, turtle, sea urchin, crab, or sea squirt during limited periods of time. There are also exhibits of fishermen's traditional equipment and of underwater photography, and children's playgroups are regularly organized on the terrace out front. For an extra fee, a three-hour boat tour on nearby waters offers an educational program on the ins and outs of oceanography. ⊠ *Verudela* ☎ *052/381–402* ⊕ *www.aquariumpula-istra.hr* 🖅 *20 Kn, boat tour 200 Kn* ⊙ *May–Sept., daily 9–9; Oct.–Apr., weekends 11–5.*

❷ Archaeological Museum of Istria & the Twin Gates. On passing through or past the 2nd-century gates, whose paired arches account for the name Porta Gemina (Twin Gates), you will find yourself amid a potpourri of Roman ruins on the shaded grounds of Pula's most intriguing museum, home to around 300,000 artifacts from prehistoric, Roman, and medieval times. ⊠ *Carrarina 3* ☎ *052/218–603* 🖅 *20 Kn* ⊙ *May–Sept., Mon.–Sat. 9–8, Sun. 10–3; Oct.–Apr., weekdays 9–2.*

❶ Arena (Roman Amphitheater). Designed to accommodate 22,000 spectators, Pula's arena is the sixth-largest building of its type in the world (after the Colosseum in Rome and similar arenas in Verona, Catania, Capua, and Arles). Construction was completed in the 1st century AD under the reign of Emperor Vespasian, and the Romans staged gladiator games here until such bloodthirsty sports were forbidden during the 5th century. During the 16th century, the Venetians planned to move the Arena stone by stone to Venice, where it was to be reconstructed in its original form. The plan failed, and it has remained more or less intact, except for the original tiers of stone seats and numerous columns that were hauled away for other buildings. Today it is used for summer concerts (by musicians including Sting, James Brown, and Jose Carreras), opera performances, and the annual film festival in late July. The underground halls house a museum with large wooden oil presses and amphorae. ⊠ *Amfiteaterska ul* 🖅 *20 Kn* ⊙ *May–Sept., daily 8–9; Oct.–Apr., daily 9–5.*

Fodor'sChoice ★

> off the beaten path

CITY CEMETERY – For a peaceful and reflective stroll where few tourists tread, but without leaving the heart of Pula, walk over to the traffic circle just to the east of the Arena, where Flavijevska ulica meets ulica 43 Istarske Divizije. Take the latter road to the left, and then the first road to your left. After a 5-minute walk uphill you will arrive at Pula's hushed city cemetery, whose long rows flanked by tall cypresses, graves adorned with pictures of the departed, and view of Pula and the harbor below add up to a sublime and poignant atmosphere. From the cemetery, you can also see the nearby ruins of a centuries-old, albeit little-visited fortress (full of loose brickwork that makes for a risky walk if you opt to enter); a hiking trail will take you into a lovely pine forest just beyond the cemetery.

❹ Crkvica Marije od Trstika (Chapel of St. Mary of Formosa). In a green space between Sigirijeva ulica and the port, this now humble looking stone structure was once part of a magnificent basilica built in the sixth century by Bishop Maximilian of Istria, during the reign of the Byzantine emperor Justinian. Fragments of the luxurious mosaics that once adorned it can be seen at the Archaeological Museum of Istria. Although the chapel itself is usually closed to visitors, it's occasionally used as a gallery space, which will give you a chance to take a peek at the interior. ⊠ *Between Sigirijeva ul and Flaciusova ul (left off Sigirijeva ul two blocks before the Forum).*

❺ **Floor mosaic.** The central scene of this large and lovely mosaic—which otherwise features geometric patterns and plants aplenty—is of the punishment of Dirce, who, as per the Greek legend, lies under the enraged bull to whose horns she is about to be fastened. Unearthed after World War II bombing, the mosaic, which was once part of a Roman house, can be viewed for free by looking down through a grating beside an uninspiring apartment building, a stone's throw from the Chapel of St. Mary of Formosa. ⊠ *Between Sigirijeva ul and Flaciusova ul (left off Sigirijeva ul two blocks before the Forum).*

❻ **Forum.** Still Pula's most important public meeting place after 2,000 years, the ancient Roman forum is today a spacious paved piazza ringed with cafés. There were once three temples here, of which only one re-

A WRECK OF A VACATION

ON AUGUST 14, 1908, THE BARON GAUTSCH, a passenger ferry owned by Austria's royal family, was on its way from Kotor to Trieste when it collided with an undersea mine and sank 12½ km (8 mi) from Rovinj, claiming 240 lives.

One person's tragedy often becomes—years, decades, or centuries later—another's vacation. This certainly holds true as regards the longstanding tradition of diving to shipwrecks, of which Istria's coastal waters hold several good examples. Almost 100 years later, the 85-meter long, 12-meter wide Baron Gautsch is considered one of the most beautiful dive sites in the world. With its upper deck at a depth of 28 meters, its lower deck at 36 meters, and its bottom at 42 meters, the site—now home to plenty of flora and fauna, including a whole lot of lobsters—caters to advanced divers while stirring the imaginations of many others.

From shipwrecks to caves and cliffs to coral reefs, Croatia has more than 85 officially registered dive sites. There are around a dozen other shipwrecks off the Istrian coast that make for popular dives. Near Novigrad lies the Corleanus, a suspected British spy ship that sank in 1945 after hitting a mine. And then there are the war ships Dezza, Rossarol, and Flamingo, as well as the ships Draga, Varese, Tihany, Rimorchiatore, Istra, Relitto Nuovo, Josephine, and John Gilmoure. Of course, Croatia's waters abound in shipwrecks well beyond Istria. For example, the waters off Krk Island are the resting place of the Peltasis, sunk in 1968

after smashing into rocks during a storm. At a depth of 7 to 32 meters, the ship is accessible to divers of all abilities.

Diving in Croatia is permitted to those in possession of a valid diving license issued by the Hrvatski ronilacki savez (Croatian Diving Association), which is good for one year and can be purchased for 100 Kn at authorized diving centers and clubs all along the coast. This permit allows you to dive only under the supervision of a diving center instructor. To dive alone, you must take this permit to a local Harbor Master's Office and pay a hefty 2,400 Kn. Permits are issued to those who hold a license or certificate from an internationally recognized diving school—including but not limited to the BSAC (British Sub-Aqua Club), CMAS (Confédération Mondiale des Activités Subaquatiques), and IANTD (International Association of Nitrox and Technical Divers).

Although diving in Istria is possible year-round, optimal sea temperatures are to be enjoyed from May to November. Locations must be marked by orange or red buoys or flags (and, at night, fitted with a yellow or white light visible from 300 meters); the maximum allowable diving depth, when using a compressed-air cylinder, is 40 meters. Diving is prohibited in protected areas, including Brijuni National Park and Krka National Park.

Dive centers can be found in all the major destinations in Istria, including Poreč and Rovinj.

---

mains. The perfectly preserved **Augustov Hram** (Temple of Augustus; ⊡ 4 Kn ☉ Mon.–Fri. 9–8:30, Sat. 2:30–8:30) was built in the 1st century AD on the north side of the square. Next to it stands the **Gradska Palača** (Town Hall), which was erected during the 13th century using part of the Roman Temple of Diana as the back wall. The Renaissance arcade was added later.

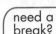 **need a break?** Stop at the chic but unpretentious **Café Galerija Cvajner** (⊠ Forum 2) for morning coffee or an evening aperitif. Inside, contemporary art and minimalist furniture play off against frescoes uncovered during restoration, and outdoor tables offer great views onto the Forum square.

❽ Kaštel (Fortress). Whether from the Cathedral or elsewhere along Kandlerova ulica, a walk up the hill will lead you within minutes to the 17th-century Venetian fortress, the Kaštel, that towers over Pula's city center and houses the **Historical Museum of Istria**. Though the museum has a somewhat lackluster collection, including scale-model ships as well as Habsburg-era relics, it does carry the value-added benefit of allowing you to wander around its ramparts. But simply walking around its perimeter also ensures fine views of the city's shipyard below and, if you look to the north, the steeple of Vodjnan's church 12 km (7½ mi) away. ⊠ *Kaštel, off Kandlerova ul* ☎ *052/211–740 or 052/211–566* ✆ *12 Kn* ☉ *May–Sept., weekdays 8–7, Oct.–Apr., weekdays 9–5.*

❼ Katedrala svete Marije (Cathedral of the Assumption of the Blessed Virgin Mary). Built originally in the 4th century by the town's defense walls and facing the sea, Pula's star ecclesiastical attraction—more often called simply St. Mary's Cathedral—was transformed in the second half of the 5th century into a three-nave basilica. Extensive reconstruction that began in the 18th century was completed in 1924, with the adjacent campanile constructed in the 19th century from stones taken from the Arena. Note that the Roman-era mosaic on the floor of the central nave bears a 5th-century donor's inscription. ⊠ *Kandlerova ul* ☎ *No phone* ✆ *5 Kn* ☉ *Daily 9:30–7.*

❾ Roman Theater. If you make your way down from the Fortress along the eastern slope of the hill, toward the Archaeological Museum and the Twin Gates, you will pass right through the redolent ruins of the 2nd-century Roman Theater, a quiet, sublime spot to rest and reflect. ⊠ *Fortress Hill.*

❸ Triumphal Arch of the Sergians. Built by Salvia Postuma Sergia in 30 BC as a monument to three members of her family who excelled in battle and otherwise, this striking monument features some elaborate reliefs that inspired even Michelangelo to draw it during a 16th-century visit to Pula. The surrounding city gate and walls were removed in the 19th century to allow the city's expansion beyond the Old Town. ⊠ *Trg Portarata, between Giardini and ul Sergijevaca.*

need a break? For a lively and aromatic atmosphere in which to have a shot of espresso, buy a banana, or just wander about gazing at food stands, do check out Pula's market square, **Narodni trg.** On one side of its stately, two-story market building—whose iron-and-glass construction was state-of-the-art when it opened to great fanfare in 1903—you'll find fruit and vegetable stands, and on the other side, cafés; on the inside is a fish market (downstairs), and fast-food eateries (second floor).

Where to Eat

$$$$ ✕⌂ **Valsabbion.** This superb restaurant and hotel is 3 km (2 mi) from
Fodor'sChoice the city center, overlooking the sea. It was one of the first restaurants
★ in Croatia to specialize in what has come to be known as "slow food"
(the owner prefers the term "creative cuisine"). Many consider it the
best restaurant in Istria, if not all of Croatia. The menu changes regularly depending on available produce, but you can expect goodies such
as frogfish in vine leaves or tagliatelle with aromatic herbs and pine nuts.
The lavender *semifreddo*—vanilla ice cream, pine nuts, and warm fig
sauce complemented by two long, delicate sticks of dark chocolate, all
served artistically on several plates arranged on a large mirror—is simply divine. For all its unimpeachable elegance, the interior also feels open
and friendly. The small hotel is likewise top-notch, with 10 rooms (at
around €100) furnished in pine with cheerful colored linens, fresh fruit,
and flowers. There's a small swimming pool on the top floor and a range
of beauty treatments and aerobics courses. ⊠ *Pješčana uvala IX/26, 52100*
☎🖷 *052/218–033* ⊕ *www.valsabbion.net* ⌂ *Reservations essential*
🖃 *AE, DC, MC, V.*

★ **$$$–$$$$** ✕ **Vela Nera.** In hot competition with Valsabbion—only a few hundred
yards away—Vela Nera is likewise located 3 km (2 mi) from the city
center, just above a yacht marina. Favorite dishes include pasta with lob-
ster and truffles, fish baked in a salt crust, and an ever-changing range
of creative seafood specialties. The quality of the wines matches that of
the cuisine, and the spacious, light-filled dining room makes for a pleas-
ant atmosphere in which to savor it all. ⊠ *Pješčana uvala* ☎ *052/219–*
209 ⌂ *Reservations essential* 🖃 *AE, DC, MC, V.*

$$ ✕ **Jupiter.** In a quiet street a couple blocks' walk above the Forum, this
is Pula's premier place for budget, Italian-style fare. Try any of its 18
types of pizza as you sip a glass of house red wine at one of the rustic
wooden tables on the rear terrace. There's a cozy little table in a nook
on your way up the stairs. ⊠ *Castrapola 38* ☎ *052/214–333 or 052/*
222–002 🖃 *AE, DC, MC, V.*

Where to Stay

One reliable bet for private rooms is **Kompas Travel** (⊠ Starih Statuta 4,
52100 ☎ 052/212–511 🖷 052/211–592), which also has offices in
Rovinj and Poreč as well as other towns in Istria and elsewhere in Croatia, and which, like other similar agencies, also offers daytime excursions to Istria's top, out-of-the-way exploring sites.

$ ⌂ **Hotel Omir.** A block from the newer Hotel Galija and likewise close
to Giardini, this small hotel offers rooms that, though cramped, have
vestibules that compensate. The dark hues are a touch somber. ⊠ *S. Do-*
bricheva ul 6, 52100 ☎ *052/210–614 or 052/218–186* ☎🖷 *052/213–*
944 🛏 *19 rooms* ⌂ *Restaurant, cable TV, minibars, pets allowed; no*
a/c in some rooms 🖃 *AE, DC, MC, V* ⍾⊙⍾ *BP.*

★ **$** ⌂ **Hotel & Restaurant Scaletta.** Ideally situated close to the Arena, this
small, family-run hotel occupies a tastefully refurbished old town house.
The interior is decorated in cheerful yellows and greens, with simple mod-

ern furniture and spanking-fresh bathrooms. The restaurant offers a small but select menu with exquisite dishes such as filet mignon in bread crumbs with dates and croquettes, and the Scaletta Pavilion, across the road, serves pizza, grilled meats, and fish dishes. ⊠ *Flavijevska 26, 52100* ☎ *052/541–599 or 052/541–025* 🖷 *052/540–285* ⊕ *www.hotel-scaletta. com* ⏚ *12 rooms* ⏁ *Restaurant, pizzeria, in-room safes, cable TV, minibars* ▭ *AE, DC, MC, V* ◥◯◤ *BP.*

¢–$ ⊞ **Hotel Guest House Riviera.** Between the train station and the Arena but also close to the sea, this slightly run-down hotel was opened in 1906, when Pula was the main port of Austria-Hungary and some 60% of the city's inhabitants were associated with the imperial military machine. In 1944, the inside was gutted by fire, and though it was renovated in 1956, the result has a rather uninspiring, Communist-era air. The grandiose yellow exterior conceals basic but reasonably comfortable rooms (the mattresses are a tad hard, and you can almost feel their springs) and a restaurant. ⊠ *Splitska 1, 52100* ☎ *052/211–166* 🖷 *052/219–117* ⊕ *www.arenaturist.hr* ⏚ *67 rooms* ⏁ *Restaurant, bar, some pets allowed* ▭ *AE, MC, V* ◥◯◤ *BP.*

¢ ⊞ **Hotel Galija.** Expanded from a restaurant into a hotel in 2002, this family-run establishment is centrally located in a bright yellow building on a quiet street just two blocks from Giardini and the Sergian Gate. The rooms are bright, spacious, and clean; nine are in the main building, with another seven plus five suites in a building right across the street. ⊠ *Epulonova 3, 52100* ☎ *052/383–802* 🖷 *052/383–804* ⊕ *www. hotel-galija-pula.com* ⏚ *16 rooms, 6 suites* ⏁ *Restaurant, pizzeria, in-room safes, cable TV, minibars, sauna* ▭ *AE, DC, MC, V* ◥◯◤ *BP.*

Nightlife & the Arts

Bars & Clubs

Club life in Pula tends to begin in early April and continue through late October or early November. Pubs are open year-round.

With an intimate rustic atmosphere marked by low lighting and wooden booths with cushioned seats, the **Bounty Pub** (⊠ Veronska 8, near Narodni trg ☎ 052/218–088) is a comfy place for a beer or, if you prefer, a coffee. The seating outside is on a stylish wooden platform. Just outside Pula in the resort area of Verudela (follow the signs once you're there), **Disco Club Oasis** (⊠ Verudela ☎ 052/218–603 or 052/218–609) is *the* place to go to dance it up on weekends from April through early November. Conveniently located in the city center, with posters announcing its various musical events ubiquitous about town, **Club Uljanik**

★ (⊠ Jura Dobrile ul 2 ☎ 052/217–117) is an exceedingly popular counter-culture haven with "DJ nights" all year and live music on its spacious terrace.

Arts Festivals

Being the most prominent place in town, the Arena hosts a fair share of the city's core art events. The decades-old annual **Pula Film Festival** (⊕ www.pulafilmfestival.hr) around the third week of July before the Motovun Film Festival (*see* Nightlife & the Arts *in* Motovun) features both Croatian and, in recent years, an increasing number of international works. The **Histria Festival** (⊕ www.histriafestival.com) an annual summer music festival that runs from June through August, has all types of performances, from opera and ballet to popular music concerts that draw famous stars such as Sting, who has been here several times.

Sports & the Outdoors

Unlike some smaller towns further up the coast, such as Rovinj, downtown Pula is a bit too much of a port and industrial center to allow for a dip in the sea in between visits to cultural attractions. Now for the good news: the **beaches** aren't far away. A short drive or bus ride to the Verudela or Stoja resort areas, each around 4 km (2½ mi) south of downtown along the coast, will provide the clear water (and rocky shores) Croatia has in no short supply. You might also try the long stretch of relatively isolated beach between the two, on the Lungomare. If you have a car or a bicycle, this lovely little stretch of undeveloped coast is close to town and popular with locals as well as tourists. Head south about 2 km (1½ mi) along the main road out of Pula and follow the signs to the right toward Stoja, a resort-cum-camping area. Once there, proceed left and then back north along the pine-fringed coastal road Lungomare as it makes its way to the Verudela resort area.

If you have a car at your disposal, drive 10 km (6¼ mi) southwest of central Pula to the Premantura peninsula. The relatively remote shoreline there, at the very southern tip of Istria, is even more scenic, punctuated by cliffs and caves, and the crowds are mercifully thinner.

Shopping

Pula is no shopping mecca, but it does have a handful of stores with quality goods from Istria and other Croatian delicacies, wines, crafts, and more. On Monday evenings in July (from 8 to midnight) and August (from 7 to midnight), the Forum hosts an open-air fair of Istrian handicrafts. A walk through the Triumphal Gate of the Sergians onto bustling Sergijevaca ulica will reveal much of what the city has available, shopping-wise; the stores listed below are on the fringe of this central business zone.

Aromatica (⊠ Laginjina 4, just beyond Garibaldi ☎ No phone) is the place to browse for a whole array of natural—fennel, rosemary, pine, and sage—"Adriatic" oils, bath salts, perfumes, and soaps. **Saxa** (⊠ Kandlerova 28, across from the Cathedral of the Assumption of the Virgin Mary ☎ 052/212–063) is yet another spot to get those Istrian wines, olive oils, honey, and, yes, truffles. As suggested by its name, **Zigante Tartufi** (⊠ Smareglina 7 ☎ 052/214–855) has everything truffle-related (or that might complement truffles on the table) that you can imagine, from a golf-ball sized box of minced truffles (black or white) to sheep cheese with truffles, as well as olive oil, honey, and herb-flavored brandies. This outlet is part of a family-owned chain throughout Istria (others are in Umag, Grožnjan, and Novigrad).

VODJNAN

★ ⓫ *12 km (7½ mi) north of Pula.*

Vodjnan may look a bit run-down at first glance, but there are three good reasons to come here: its saintly mummies; its quiet, narrow, centuries-old streets populated by a higher percentage of Italian speakers than you'll find almost anywhere else in Istria; and the Vodjnanka Restaurant's scrumptious fare. There are 10 buses daily between Pula and Vodjnan, at 12 Kn each way, payable directly to the driver.

From the tourist office on the main square, stroll down ulica Castello ꩜ to **Crkva svetog Blaža** (St. Blaise's Church), an 18th-century structure built in the style of Palladio that not only has the highest campanile in all of Istria but is also the unlikely home of the mummies or mummified body parts of six saints impressively preserved without embalming. Though some see divine intervention behind their state of preservation, the degree to which these saints are really intact—they are definitely chipping away at the edges, it must be said—is open to question. Among the best preserved of the saints are St. Nicoloza of Koper and Leon Bembo the Blessed. Nicoloza, whose relatively elastic skin and overall postmortem presentableness has given her the distinction of being among the best preserved human bodies in Europe, was born in Istria in the 15th century and developed a reputation for holiness as a nun in Venice and elsewhere; she's the one with the garland of flowers still on her head. Leon Bembo the Blessed was a 12th-century Venetian priest who was tortured to the point of disfigurement in religious riots while ambassador to Syria and spent his final years back in Venice in monastic contemplation. And then there is St. Sebastian, a Roman officer-turned-Christian who was whipped and strangled around AD 288 in Rome after initially surviving torture by arrows. The head, spinal column, neck muscles, and related parts of this very famous saint are on display here. As for St. Barbara, from 3rd-century Nicomeda (in present-day Turkey), only her leg remains; she so disagreed with her father's pagan, slave-keeping lifestyle that he personally killed her with a sword, though legend has it that he was then promptly struck by lightning and turned to ashes. Admittance to the mummy room, behind the main altar, includes an English-language recording that sums up the saints' lives and roads to mummihood. ✉ *Župni ured Sv Blaža* ☎ *052/511–420* ⊠ *38 Kn for both mummies and museum, 28 Kn for just one* ⊙ *July–Sept., daily 9–7; Oct.–June only when you can find someone to take your money and let you in.*

Where to Eat

★ **$$$** ✕ **Vodjnanka.** This restaurant is the place to go for the most mouthwatering homemade-pasta dishes you can imagine, not least *fuži* with wild arugula and prosciutto in cream sauce, which is simply unforgettable. The outer of two small rooms features bizarre but fantastic wall art by sculptor/painter Lilia Batel: 3-D reliefs with sponge-based puppets caricaturing real locals as they gaze out their windows, sit at the bar, and so on. The inner room, with its six tables and framed family-style photographs, is positively homey. Though there's no English-language menu, navigating the Italian and German menus isn't at all hard, and the staff, including the friendly owner, Svjetlana Celija, can help you in English. In the summer, be sure to make a reservation for dinner. ⊠ *Istarska, right across from where the Pula bus lets you off and about where you board for the return trip* ☎ *052/511–435* ⊟ *AE, MC, V.*

$–$$ ✕ **Pansion-Restaurant San Rocco.** For a good budget meal—pizza in particular—this is your best bet in Vodjnan. The pension is in the heart of town, a few blocks from the main square. You can also stay in one of the eight clean but no-frills rooms. ⊠ *Sv Rocco 15* ☎ *052/511–011* ⊟ *No credit cards.*

NACIONALNI PARK BRIJUNI

12   *Ferry from Fažana, which is 15 km (9 mi) northwest of Pula.*

Fodor's Choice
★

When Austrian industrialist Paul Kupelwieser set off for Brijuni by boat from Fažana in 1885 with a bottle of wine, roast chicken, bread, and peaches (and a couple of brawny locals to row him and his son there), the archipelago had long been a haven for the Austro-Hungarian military and for malaria. Kupelwieser was to change all that. In 1893, he bought the 14 islands and islets, eradicated the disease with the help of doctors, and fashioned parks from Mediterranean scrub. Thus arose a vacation retreat par excellence—not for rich Romans, as had been the case here 17 centuries earlier, but for fin-de-siècle Viennese and other European high-society sorts. Archduke Franz Ferdinand summered here, as did such literary lights as Thomas Mann and Arthur Schnitzler; James Joyce came here to celebrate his 23rd birthday. Two world wars ensued, however, and the islands' fate faded as they changed hands—coming under Italian rule and, later, Yugoslavian. From 1949 to 1979, the largest island, Veliki Brijuni, was the official summer residence of Marshal Josip Broz Tito, Yugoslavia's "president for life." Here he retreated to work, rest, and pursue his hobbies. World leaders, film and opera stars, artists, and writers were his frequent guests; and it was here that, together with Nasser of Egypt and Nehru of India, Tito forged the Brioni Declaration uniting the so-called nonaligned nations (countries adhering to neither NATO nor the Warsaw Pact). The archipelago was designated a national park in 1983 and opened to the public.

These days, **Fažana** itself seems to exist mainly as a low-key access point to Brijuni, but it too has a rich past. The archipelago's development in the late 19th century yielded a spate of construction in Fažana, including several hotels, a toffee factory, a liquor plant, a fish-processing facility, and a shipyard. Today, Fažana seems to offer little more than the usual collection of touristy restaurants along its small harbor; since tourists tend to pass through on their way to Brijuni, however, the town is at least refreshingly quiet compared to some other tourist-traveled spots along Istria's west coast. Its main cultural attractions—all just a short walk from the harbor—are the 15th-century **Church of Saints Kosmas and Damian,** whose bell may be in need of oiling, as it sounds like a fork striking a plate; and the smaller but older 14th-century **Church of**

Our Lady of Mount Carmel, which you enter through an atmospheric loggia and whose ceiling features several layers of fascinating 15th-century, Renaissance frescoes.

But you are presumably here to visit the archipelago. Before doing so, call or e-mail the Brijuni National Park office in Fažana at least one day in advance to make a reservation; you can also do so in person, but especially in mid-summer, there is a substantial risk that there won't be space. (Though various private tourist agencies in Fažana and Pula offer excursions, they do not generally measure up, either cost-wise or quality-wise, to making your arrangements directly with the National Park. Indeed, some of the tourist agencies simply reserve you a spot on the "official" tour, adding their own commission when doing so.) To get here, take the National Park ferry from Fažana, which takes about 15 minutes. The entire tour of the park takes about four hours.

Your first view of the park is of a low-lying island with a dense canopy of evergreens over blue waters. Ashore on Veli Brijun, the largest island, a **tourist train** takes you past villas in the seaside forest and relics from the Roman and Byzantine eras. The network of roads on this 6½-km- (4-mi-) long island was laid down by the Romans, and stretches of original Roman stonework remain. Rows of cypresses shade herds of deer, and peacocks strut along pathways. The train stops at the **Safari Park**, a piece of Africa transplanted to the Adriatic, its zebras, antelopes, llamas, and elephants all gifts from visitors from faraway lands. In the **museum**, an archaeological exhibition traces life on Brijuni through the centuries and a photography exhibition, "Tito on Brijuni," focuses on Tito and his guests.

Those who have made the rounds of Kupelwieser's golf course—the oldest golf course in Croatia—report that it is more a historic experience than anything else, since it looks much the same as it did when built in 1923, with "natural," sandy tees and deer grazing where there is grass; it's blessed by an absence of fertilizers. Even if isn't quite up to snuff by modern golfing standards, how often do you find a course that allows you to take a dip in the sea between holes? ⊠ *Brijunska 10, Fažana* ☎ *052/ 525–883 or 052/525–882* ⊕ *www.brijuni.hr* 🖃 *180 Kn* ☼ *Apr.–Oct., eight tours daily; Nov.–Mar., four tours daily; reservations required.*

Where to Stay

You can save money by booking a room in Fažana and taking a day trip to the islands. **Stefani Trade** (⊠ Župni trg 3, Fažana 🖦🖦 052/521–910 ☎098/980–7820), an accommodations and travel agency in Fažana, can help you arrange a place to stay, not to mention tours around the region.

★ **$$** 🖪 **Neptun-Istria Hotel.** The most luxurious of three hotels adjacent to each other on Veli Brijun has bright, spacious rooms. The rates include unlimited passages on the National Park boats between the islands and the mainland. But you must leave your bikes, boats, and pets on the mainland. A daily surcharge for a room with a sea view is 100 Kn, and secure parking in Fažana is 60 Kn per day. ⊠ *Javna Ustanova Nacionalni*

Park Brijuni, 52214 ☎ *052/525–807* 🖷 *052/521–367* ⊕ *www.brijuni. hr* 🛏 *88 rooms* ⚒ *Restaurant, room service, cable TV, in-room safes, minibars* ⊟ *AE, DC, MC, V* ❮⊙❯ *BP.*

ROVINJ

Fodor'sChoice
★

35 km (22 mi) northwest of Pula.

It is hard to imagine how Rovinj could be more beautiful than it is. In a fantastic setting, with centuries-old red-roofed houses clustered around the hill of a former island, Istria's cultural mecca is crowned by the monumental baroque Crkva Sv Eufemije (Church of St. Euphemia), which has a typical Venetian bell tower topped by a gleaming bronze figure of St. Euphemia. Far below, a wide harbor crowded with pleasure boats is rimmed with bright awnings and colorful café umbrellas. Artists, writers, musicians, and actors have long gravitated to this ravishing place to carve out apartments in historic houses. Throughout the summer, the winding cobbled streets are crowded with vacationers from all reaches of Europe who are more often than not staying in nearby resort developments. South of the harbor lies the beautiful landscaped park of Zlatni Rt, planted with avenues of cedars, oaks, and cypresses and offering numerous secluded coves for bathing.

Exploring Rovinj

Practically all of Rovinj's key cultural and commercial attractions are packed into the compact, onetime island and present-day peninsula that juts like the tip of a hitchhiker's thumb westward into the sea. The main square, Trg M. Tita, is at the southern juncture of this little peninsula with the mainland; from there, you can either cut straight up the center of the peninsula (i.e., west) along Grisia toward the cathedral or walk around the outer edge of the peninsula, or you can go south along the harbor to some fine restaurants and the beaches of Zlatni Rt beyond.

Numbers in the text correspond to numbers in the margin and on the Rovinj map.

What to See

🐾 ⑯ **Akvarij** (Aquarium). The Rovinj aquarium displays tanks of Adriatic marine fauna and flora. It opened in 1891, making it one of the oldest institutions of its type in Europe. It's housed within the Ruđer Bošković Institute's Center for Maritime Research. ⊠ *Obala Giordana Paliage 5* ☎ *052/804–712* 🎟 *10 Kn* ⊙ *May–Sept., daily 9–9; Oct.–Apr., by appointment only.*

⑮ **Church of St. Tommaso** Today a public art gallery, this small, bright yellow church dates to the Middle Ages but was rebuilt in 1722. It's on your way back down the hill from the main cathedral, and right after you pass by it, you will pass under a lovely, arched hall some 50 feet long, its ceiling replete with wooden beams. Be careful here, as signs warn of loose brickwork above. ⊠ *Begovita ul via del Monte* 🎟 *Free* ⊙ *Tues.–Sun. 6–10.*

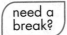

The Adriatic may not be quite as warm as the Caribbean, but at the **Havana Club** (✉ Obala Alda Negria)—a spacious, tropical-themed cocktail bar-cum-café right on the harbor—you can sip a piña colada or, if you dare, a Sex on the Beach (vodka, peach and melon juices, plus "sex mix"). There are also nonalcoholic cocktails, including, of course, Safe Sex on the Beach, as well as iced tea and coffee. Kick back and relax in a wicker chair under one of five huge, bamboo umbrellas while listening to reggae. That's not to mention the Cuban cigars you can puff for anywhere between 34 Kn and 228 Kn. Ah, the life!

⓮ Crkva Sv Eufemije (Church of St. Euphemia). Inside the 18th-century baroque church, the remains of Rovinj's patron saint are said to lie within a 6th-century sarcophagus. Born near Constantinople, Euphemia was martyred in her youth, on September 16 in AD 304, under the reign of Emperor Diocletian. The marble sarcophagus containing her remains mysteriously vanished in AD 800 when it was at risk of destruction by iconoclasts—and, legend has it, it somehow floated out to sea and washed up in faraway Rovinj! (Note the wall engraving just to the right of the entrance of St. Euphemia holding Rovinj in her arms.) Not surprisingly, Euphemia has long been among the most popular names in Istria for girls, and on September 16 of each year, many people gather to pray by her tomb. In the church, there's a great big mural on the wall in the sarcophagus room portraying Euphemia being picked at by two lions who, legend has it, didn't eat her, after all; she ended up being tied to a killer wheel. As at other churches in Croatia, a sign at the entrance makes it clear that no short-shorts or miniskirts (or dogs, or ice-cream cones, or lit cigarettes) are allowed inside. Judging from the scanty dress of some folks streaming inside in the summer heat, such rules can be bent, but you won't be let up the campanile unless you abide. ⊠ *Grisia* 🗏 *Church and sarcophagus room free, campanile 10 Kn* ☉ *Daily 10–noon and 4–7.*

⑬ Trg M. Tita. Standing on the Old Town's main square, you can't help but notice the **Balbi Arch,** which at one time was the gate to Rovinj's fish market. Notice the Venetian lion on one side and the Turkish head on the other. At the top, between the two Balbi coats of arms, is a Latin epigraph that used to be on a neighboring building and refers to the 1680 construction of the public granary. Also quite prominent on the square is the city's pinkish-orange **watch tower,** whose base houses the tourist office. Although it looks Venetian, the tower was erected in 1907. That said, the winged-lion relief on one side is indeed from the 16th century.

off the beaten path

DVIVIGRAD – When its residents abandoned Dvivigrad suddenly in the mid-17th-century—fleeing the combined misfortune of plague and attacks by Uskok raiders—and established nearby Kanfanar, surely they didn't foresee that more than three centuries later tourists would delight in what they left behind. In any case, if exploring ruins is your (or your child's) thing, this is the place for you. Along an isolated road 23 km (14 mi) east of Rovinj, outside the sleepy town of Kanfanar (a short detour if you're headed north toward Poreč, Motovun, or Goržnjan), this huge maze of dirt paths surrounded by high stone walls makes for an adventuresome, imagination-stirring walk. Indeed, just enough restoration has been done to let your imagination "reconstruct" the rest: some of the walls, which rise to around 20 feet (with signs warning of loose brickwork) are vine-covered, and much of the place is overgrown with vegetation. Nor is there a single explanatory sign, in any language. All this combines to give you the sense that you are discovering this eerie ghost town of a fortress city, even if a few other tourists are also wandering about. The battlements are impressively intact, and toward the center of the fortress you will find the remains of Crkva uznesenja (St. Sophia's Church), replete with depressions in the ground that contained the crypts of very important persons. To get here, take the main road east out of Rovinj toward Kanfanar, 23 km (14 mi) away. Just before you cross the railroad tracks and enter Kanfanar, you'll see a sign pointing to Dvivigrad, which is to your left; from the sign the ruins are about 4 km (2½ mi) down an isolated, scrub-lined road.

Where to Eat

$$$$ ✕ **Enoteca Al Gastaldo.** Walls lined with wine bottles and tables lit by
Fodor'sChoice candles create a warm and intimate atmosphere in this sophisticated eatery,
★ hidden away in the Old Town a couple of blocks back from the harbor.

Indulge in spaghetti with either truffles or crab, fresh fish prepared over an open fire, and a colorful rocket (arugula) and radicchio salad. Round off with a glass of local *rakija.* ⊠ *Iza Kasarne 14* ☎ *052/814–109 or 098/224–707* ▭ *No credit cards.*

$$–$$$ ✕ **Amfora.** Right on the harbor near the Old Town, with helpful photos of menu items outside, this elegant, spacious, light-filled, and air-conditioned restaurant is a sure bet for grilled fish specialties such as *bakalar* (oven-baked cod in salt crust), meat dishes including (of course) steak in truffle sauce, and soups, salads, and pizzas. Blue tones and damask chairs combine with a waterfall to give that extra special touch. ⊠ *Obala Alda Rismonda 33* ☎ *052/816–663 or 091/205–0034* ▭ *AE, DC, MC, V.*

$$–$$$ ✕ **Kantinon.** Wine cellar or steakhouse? That is the question. Regardless of the answer, the food and milieu are equally pleasant. Red-checkered curtains, stone floors, long wooden tables, and high vaulted ceilings befitting a wine-cellar restaurant combine scrumptiously with standard but good grilled fish and such meat specialties as veal in artichoke sauce. ⊠ *Obala V. Nazora 6* ☎ *052/811–970* ▭ *AE, DC, MC, V.*

$$–$$$ ✕ **Pizzeria Da Sergio.** With 40-plus varieties of pies and pasta dishes, there's plenty to choose from at this conveniently located venue along the narrow road leading up to the main cathedral. Inside it's pleasantly cool, even on a hot day. One of four ornamental plates on the wall to your right as you enter reads, in Hungarian, LONG LIVE THE GIRLS OF TRANSYLVANIA! A gift from one of Croatia's many Hungarian visitors, perhaps? ⊠ *Grisia 11, on the way up to the main cathedral* ☎ *052/816–949* ▭ *AE, DC, MC, V.*

$$–$$$ ✕ **Veli Jože.** This popular *konoba* lies close to the seafront, at the foot of the Old Town. Specialties include *bakalar na bijelo* (dried cod in white wine with onion and potatoes), *fuži* (pasta) with goulash, and roast lamb with potatoes. The house wine is excellent, but the rock music doesn't quite match the traditional decor that includes antlers, old photos, and the like. ⊠ *Sv Križa 1* ☎ *052/816–337* ▭ *AE, DC, MC, V.*

Where to Stay

One reliable bet for private rooms is **Kompas Travel** (⊠ Obala M. Tita 5, Rovinj 52210 ☎ 052/813–211 ☎ 052/813–478), which has offices in Pula and Poreč, as well as other towns in Istria and elsewhere in Croatia. Like other similar agencies, the company can also arrange daytime excursions to Istria's out-of-the-way exploring sites.

$$$ ▦ **Villa Angelo d'Oro.** This enchanting hotel opened in 2001 and has already gained an excellent reputation. In a beautifully restored 16th-century building, rooms are individually furnished with antiques and quality fabrics. Breakfast is served on a glorious roof terrace, and there's a high-class restaurant on the ground floor. Alas, the hotel boat and yacht, which had been at the guests' disposal, were destroyed in a fire in 2004. It's in the heart of the Old Town, one block in from the seafront. ⊠ *V Švalbe 38–42, 52210* ☎ *052/840–502* ☎ *052/840–112* ⊕ *www.rovinj.at* ⤴ *22 rooms, 1 suite* ↳ *Restaurant, room service, minibars, cable TV, hot tub, sauna* ▭ *AE, DC, MC, V* ¶◎¶ *BP.*

FodorśChoice
★

★ **$$** ⊡ **Hotel Adriatic.** Founded in 1912, this harborside hotel is the oldest (still-functioning) one in town, and its attractive, Habsburg-era facade shows its age. A comprehensive renovation in the late 1980s yielded bright, clean, and fairly spacious rooms with soft blue hues. Not only do the harbor-side rooms offer a spectacular, soothing view of the sea but also an oh-so-pleasant Adriatic aroma. The service is friendly, but as at many a hotel in Croatia's resort areas, there is a 20% surcharge for stays of less than four nights. ✉ *P. Budicin, 52210* ☎ *0800–8858 toll-free within Croatia, 052/815–088* 🖷 *052/813–573* ⊕ *www.maistra.hr* ⤴*27 rooms* 🍴 *2 restaurants, café, cable TV, in-room safes, minibars* ▤ *AE, DC, MC, V* ⦿ *BP.*

$ ⊡ **Hotel Rovinj.** Located on the tip of the peninsula, below the Church of St. Euphemia, this white, modern hotel is constructed in a series a terraces looking out to sea. Facilities are minimal and rooms are spare, but the views are wonderful—and they ought to be, since rooms with a view go for a €20 premium. ✉ *Svetog Križa 59, 52210* ☎ *052/811–288* 🖷 *052/840–757* ✐ *hotel-rovinj@pu.t-com.hr* ⤴ *13 rooms* 🍴 *Restaurant, pizzeria, bar, cable TV, minibars* ▤ *AE, MC, V* ⦿ *BP.*

Nightlife & the Arts

Every few days from late July to early September at 9 PM the Church of St. Euphemia and other major churches in Rovinj play host to classical-music recitals and concerts as part of the city's **Summer Festival.**

Situated in a residential district a 15-minute walk southeast of the town center, the **Monvi** (✉ Luje Adamovića ☎ 052/545–117), with a spacious outdoor terrace in summer, is the most popular place in Rovinj to dance the night away, in part because it is, as of this writing, reportedly the only place to do so. The musical focus is house. To get here, follow Mattea Benussia from the bus station to Fontana Fontana, which then becomes Zagrebačka, and then go slightly right after a block onto Luje Adamovića.

Puntulina Wine & Cocktail Bar (✉ Sv Križ 38) may have a hard time deciding what it is, but take the steps down to its terrace, where you can enjoy a glass of Istrian or other Croatian wine—all in a pleasant atmosphere yards from the sea, with light pop music setting the tone. And, yes, you can take a few more steps down if you wish, to the rocks, and take a dip before or after being served—for this is where Rovinj's free, public swimming area begins. It's not especially a "night" spot, so you may wish to confine your wine-sipping to daylight hours.

Will it be on the rocks? Yes? Then it'll be either the setting or a cocktail at the **Valentino** (✉ Santa Croce 28 ☎ 052/830–683), situated idyllically on the rocks across from Katarina Island, with the sea illuminated by the club's theatrical lighting. When the weather turns foul, the crowds squeeze into the small, altarlike interior. It's closed from November through March.

The **Zanzibar** (✉ P. Budicina ☎ 052/813–206) might not be the place to let it all hang out, but it is trendy—even tropical—and a bit upscale. It's also closed from November through March.

Sports & the Outdoors

As elsewhere along the coast, the Rovinj area has its share of places to dive, and several diving centers to go along with them—most of which will take you by boat for supervised dives to shipwrecks and other fascinating spots, not least the famous wreck of the *Baron Gautsch*, an Austrian passenger ferry that sank in 1908 just 13 km (8 mi) from Rovinj. *See* A Wreck of a Vacation box, *below,* for more information on the *Baron Gautsch.* **Diver Sport Center** (☒ T.N. Villas Rubin ☎ 052/816–648 ⊕ www.diver.hr) offers three- to four-hour boat trips with supervised dives for between €20 and €35 (equipment rental 30 Kn more) as well as courses ranging from a three-day program for beginners to various advanced, specialized courses for much more. **Scuba-Rovinj** (☒ Braće Brajković ☎ 052/813–290 or 098/219–203 ⊕ www.scuba.hr), has the same sort of dive programs as Diver Sport Center for similar prices.

Shopping

Rovinj is worth visiting for its beauty, not its boutiques. The souvenir market is nothing to write home about, but there are at least a couple of shops with fine Istrian and/or Croatian products worth checking out. Between the main square and the souvenir market, **Istria Terra Magica** (☒ Giuseppea 7 ☎ No phone) advertises itself as an "authentic Istrian shop," and its quality selection of wines, olive oils, vases, and framed, glass-encased sailing ships does seem to stand out among the many more tacky souvenir shops in town. **Art Studio** (☒ Grisia 48, on your left on the way up the hill soon before the main cathedral ☎ 098/274–665) is one cliché of a name, to be sure, but one gem of a little shop. Zagreb jewelrymaker (and documentary filmmaker) Radovan Sredić spends his summers here selling lovely jewelry that he creates by hand from rare, natural materials, mostly from Asia.

en route   Getting to Poreč is easier straight from Pula than from Rovinj, as you simply take the main inland highway north for 42 km (26 mi) and then follow the signs before turning west onto the secondary road that leads you another 13 km (8 mi) to Poreč—a 60- to 90-minute drive in all, depending on the traffic and how much pressure you apply to that pedal. If you go from Rovinj, you must skirt the Limski kanal.

POREČ

❶ *55 km (34 mi) northwest of Pula.*

A chic, bustling little city founded as a Roman castrum (fort) in the 2nd century BC and swarming with tourists more than 2,000 years later, Poreč may not be quite as lovely as Rovinj—nor does it enjoy the benefits of a hilltop panorama—but it is nonetheless a pretty sea of red-tile roofs on a peninsula jutting out to sea. Within the historic center, the network of streets still follows the original urban layout. Dekumanova, the Roman *decumanus* (the main traverse street), has maintained its character as the principal thoroughfare. Today, it is a worn flagstone passage lined with Romanesque and Gothic mansions and patrician palaces, some of which now house cafés and restaurants. Close by lies the magnificent UNESCO-listed Eufrazijeva Basilica (St. Euphrasius Basilica), Istria's prime ecclesiastical attraction and one of the coast's major artistic showpieces. Although the town itself is small, Poreč has an ample capacity for overnight stays, thanks to the vast hotel complexes of Plava and Zelena Laguna, situated along the pine-rimmed shoreline, an unappealingly short distance from the center.

Although you can cover the main sights in two or three hours, Poreč surely merits a one-night stay, or more if you figure in a day-trip to a nearby attraction such as the Baradine Cave or the Limski kanal.

What to See

You may want to begin exploring Poreč at the helpful **Tourist Information Center Poreč,** which not only supplies a detailed brochure-cum-map and offers 15 minutes of free Internet access, but is also just yards away from the main square. ⊠ *Zagrebačka 9* ☎ *52/451–293 or 52/451–458* ⊙ *Apr.–Oct., daily 8 AM–10 PM, Nov.–Mar., weekdays 8 AM–3 PM.*

Fodor'sChoice
★
The magnificent **Eufrazijeva Basilica** (St. Euphrasius Basilica) is among the most perfectly preserved early Christian churches in Europe and one of the most important monuments of Byzantine art on the Adriatic. It was built by Bishop Euphrasius in the middle of the 6th century and consists of a delightful atrium, a church decorated with stunning mosaics, an octagonal baptistery, a 16th-century bell tower you can climb (for a modest fee), and a 17th-century Bishop's Palace whose foundations date to the 5th century and whose basement contains an exhibit of stone monuments and of mosaics previously on the basilica floor. The church interior is dominated by Biblical mosaics above, behind, and around the main apse. In the apsidal semidome, the Virgin holding the Christ child is seated in a celestial sphere on a golden throne, flanked by angels in flowing white robes. On the right side there are three martyrs, the patrons of Poreč; the mosaic on the left shows Bishop Euphrasius holding a model of the church, slightly askew. High above the main apse, just below the beamed ceiling, Christ holds an open book in his hands while apostles approach on both sides. Other luminous, shimmeringly intense mosaics portray further ecclesiastical themes. ⊠ *Eufrazijeva* 🖾 *Basilica free; bell tower 10 Kn; Bishop's Palace 10 Kn* ⊙ *Basilica daily 7–7; bell tower daily 7–6:30; Bishop's Palace daily 7–6:30.*

Trg Marafor. This square toward the tip of the peninsula was the site of Poreč's Roman forum, whose original stonework is visible in spots amid the present-day pavement. Beside it is a park containing the ruins of Roman temples dedicated to the gods Mars and Neptune.

need a break?
Do not be deterred by the cannon facing you as you enter this 15th-century tower that now houses the **Torre Rotonda caffé bar** (⊠ Narodni trg 3a ☎ 052/98–255–731). Climb up a spiral staircase to a second floor replete with several intimate nooks, or go one more flight to the roof for an unbeatable view of Poreč and its harbor. Sip that coffee or drink at a fake-marble-top table while light pop music plays in the background.

☪ Since its opening in 2005, crowds have been flocking to **Aquarium Poreč**, which is just yards from the main square, Trg Slobode. Come if you'd like to catch a glimpse of the underwater world of some 40 species from sea horses to sea urchins, from small sharks to arm's-length octopi and foot-long crabs. ⊠ *F. Glavinića 4* ☎ *052/428–720* ⊕ *www.aquarium-porec.com* ⊠ *Apr.–Oct., 25 Kn; Nov.–Mar., 15 Kn* ☉ *Apr.–Oct. 9–9, Nov.–Mar. 10–5.*

On the main pedestrian thoroughfare through town, between the aquarium and the basilica, is Istria's oldest museum, the **Zavičajni muzej** (Regional Museum), which opened in 1884 in the 18th-century baroque Sinčić Palace. Presenting the history of Poreč and environs from ancient times through the 20th century, it features 2,000 exhibits, with highlights that include Roman tombstones, mosaics, and other archaeological fragments from antiquity, 16th-century portraits, and exhibits of baroque furniture; there's also a wonderful historical library with first editions of Diderot's 18th-century encyclopedia. ⊠ *Decumanus 9* ☎ *052/431–585* ⊠ *10 Kn* ☉ *July and Aug., daily 10–1 and 5–8; Sept.–June, daily 10–1.*

Outside of Town

☪ Far from sun and sea though it may be, the **Baradine Cave** has long been one of the Poreč area's top natural attractions. About 8 km (5 mi) northeast of town, near Nova Vas, this wonderful world of five limestone halls includes not only miniature transparent crabs and insects but, of course, stalactites, stalagmites, and dripstone formations—from "curtains" 10 yards long to "statues" resembling the Virgin Mary, the Leaning Tower of Pisa, and the body of the 13th-century shepherdess Milka, who supposedly lost her way down here while looking for her lover Gabriel (who met the same fate). One of the halls includes a hatch some 70 yards deep that leads to underground lakes. Groups leave every half-hour on a 40-minute guided tour. You can also partake in either a brief round of "speleoclimbing" that allows you to try out caving techniques with equipment and under the watchful eye of a professional spelunker; or a more involved, 5-hour "speleo-adventure" that gives you even more technical training (plus a certificate at the end) as you explore various other caves nearby. Those without car transport may wish to contact one of the various private agencies in Poreč and other nearby towns that offer excursions to Baradine Cave. ⊠ *Nova Vas* ☎ *098/224–350* ⊕ *www.baredine.com* ⊠ *Cave tour 25 Kn, speleoclimbing 40 Kn, speleo-adventure 350 Kn* ☉ *July and Aug., daily 9:30–6:30; May, June, and Sept., daily 10–5; Apr. and Oct., daily 10–4; Nov.–Mar., by appointment or occasionally on Sun. and holidays.*

There's even a bit of Norwegian-style fjord in Croatia. The **Limski kanal** is a 13-km (8-mi) long karst canyon, whose emerald green waters are flanked by forested valley walls that rise gradually to heights of more than 300 feet inland. The canyon was formed in the last ice age, and it is Croatia's most fertile breeding area for mussels and oysters—hence, you'll find some excellent seafood restaurants in the village of Sveti Loreč (if you are passing through the town, try the Viking or the Fjord restaurants). Tours are available from both Poreč and Rovinj with various agencies and independent operators, whose stands and boats are impossible to miss. A reservation a day or two in advance can't hurt, though, particularly in mid-summer. Kompas offices in either Poreč or Rovinj can arrange tours, as can Excursions Delfin and Excursions Maris, both in Rovinj (*see* Travel Agencies *in* Istria Essentials, *below*); expect to pay approximately 80 Kn for the four-hour tour or 150 Kn for a daylong tour that includes a "fish picnic." ⊠ *Sveti Loreč.*

Although the Limski kanal is a bit closer to Rovinj (which is to the south), one advantage of approaching from Poreč (to the north) is the opportunity to visit **Vrsar**, a pretty, medieval hilltop town just 13 km (8 mi) to the south and situated near the fjord's northern juncture with the sea (and yet another place you can catch a tour of the fjord). Famous since Roman times for its high-quality stone, which helped build Venice, Vrsar is home to the 13th-century Romanesque church St. Marija Od Mora (St. Mary of the Sea), which has three naves. In his memoirs, the Venetian adventurer Casanova fondly recalled the local red wine, refošak. Just a couple of miles south, by the way, is Croatia's oldest and largest naturist resort, FKK Park Koversada (*see* Barely Vacationing box, *below*).

Where to Eat

★ **$$$$** ✕ **Sv Nikola Restaurant.** Those with a discriminating palate and a not so discriminating pocketbook should try this restaurant, opened in 2004. Service is included in the price, which is a good thing, since the price is nothing to sneeze at in this sparkling, air-conditioned venue right across from the harbor. The menu offers such delicacies as fish fillet in *malvazija-* (white-) wine sauce; meat carpaccio with truffles, Parmesan, and wild arugula; and beefsteak Decumanus (with pinenuts, goose liver pâté, and black truffles). You can set forth on this culinary adventure with a plate of raw clams and oysters from Istria's west coast or Istrian prosciutto. As good as the food may be, though, the elegant, spotless interior isn't exactly brimming with character. ⊠ *Obala maršala Tita 23* ☎ *052/451–018* ♻ *Reservations essential* ▤ *AE, DC, MC, V.*

$$-$$$$ ✕ **Dvi Murve.** Since this restaurant is in a suburb on the edge of town, you'll need to drive to it unless you're up for a long walk. The acclaimed menu includes bass baked in a salt crust: the waiter delivers the salt-encrusted catch flaming to the table, where he deftly extinguishes the fire with a white cloth, removes the salt crust, skin and all, and serves you the steaming white flesh. The garnish, Swiss chard and boiled potatoes, is included in the price, which is by the kilogram and averages out to about 200 Kn for the popular meal for two. But there are also such meat specialties as beefsteak *dvi murve* (with a cream, mushroom, and ham sauce). The interior is very traditional, such as you would find in any Istrian *konoba*; outside is a large summer terrace shaded by two mulberry trees, after which the restaurant is named. Getting here is a bit tricky: go about 2½ km (1½ mi) on the main road north toward Novigrad, then straight where a fork in the road bears left. From there, follow the signs a short distance. ⊠ *Grožnjanska 17, Vranići* ☎ *052/434–115* ▤ *AE, DC, MC, V.*

CloseUp

BARELY VACATIONING

IT'S JUST LIKE ANY OTHER CAMPGROUND on the Croatian coast. People pitch tents, sit around tables talking and sipping coffee or wine beside their RVs. There's just one difference: here, practically everyone is naked. This is Koversada, the largest naturist retreat in Croatia and, in fact, in all of Europe, with a daily capacity of some 12,000 visitors, space for some 1,700 campsites, and 215 rooms in attractive villa-like buildings— not to mention eight tennis courts, Ping Pong tables, a miniature golf course, and a supermarket (some clothing obligatory inside).

In 1961, Koversada—situated just outside the picturesque little town of Vrsar, 13 km (8 mi) south of Poreč— ushered in a new commercial craze for Croatian tourism. By some estimates, today more than 100,000 people a year stay in the country's naturist resorts, and tens of thousands more shed their clothes at less official secluded stretches of the coastline. Together, this represents roughly 15% of the country's annual tourist population. As accepting and encouraging as Croatians and their government have long been of this phenomenon, however, Croatians make up only a handful of these naturists, but they are there as well.

The history of naturism in Croatia goes back to before World War II. In 1934, a leading Viennese naturist established a naturist beach on the island of Rab, and in 1936, the authorities there famously allowed England's King Edward VIII and his lover, Mrs. Wallis Simpson, to skinny dip in the sea. Apparently the experience was a happy one for them, as the king abdicated later that year and married Simpson the following year.

A glossy brochure published by the Croatian National Tourist Board lists 14 naturist "camps" and "villages" and about as many officially designated "free naturist beaches" on the country's Adriatic coast— 14 of them in Istria, 8 in the Kvarner region, a couple in northern and central Dalmatia, and a handful around Split and Dubrovnik. Many such areas are marked with signs reading FKK—short for Freikorperkultur, a German term that translates as "Free Body Culture."

Traditions vary somewhat from place to place, of course, but at Koversada, as at most such campground-cum-resorts, the theme is family-oriented naturism. Men traveling alone are usually admitted to naturist resorts in Croatia only if they can show an International Naturist Federation (INF) card. Men traveling together are likewise well advised to carry such cards.

The camping and accommodation rates at naturist facilities are, surprisingly, not all that much more than at their clothes-minded counterparts. At Koversada, for example, you pay €6 for a campsite plus €10 per person—i.e., €26 in all for two. A room is €44 per person, breakfast and dinner included (€3 less without dinner). You can contact Koversada directly at **FKK Park Koversada** (✉ Vrsar 52540 ☎ 052/441–371 or 052/441–123 🖷 052/441–761). The owner of Koversada is **Adria Resorts** (✉ V. Nazora 6, 52210 Rovinj ☎ 052/441–222, 052/800–250 or [toll-free within Croatia] 0800–8868 🖷 052/441–122 or 052/800–215 ⊕ www.maistra.hr).

$$–$$$ ✕ **Peterokutna Kula.** A 15th-century pentagonal tower in the heart of the Old Town has been cleverly renovated to accommodate this sophisticated restaurant on a series of floors and terraces, including the roof. House specialties include spaghetti with lobster and steak with truffles. Finish your meal with a glass of *šlivovica* (plum rakija). When deciding on your tip, do remember that the waitstaff must trudge up and down all those steps all day. ⊠ *Decumanus 1* ☎ *052/451–378* ☐ *No credit cards.*

$$ ✕ **Pizzeria Nono.** Right across the street from the main tourist office (where you can check your e-mail for free), the Nono is teeming with folks saying "yes, yes!" to scrumptious budget fare from pizzas and salads to such seafood standards as grilled squid. ⊠ *Zagrebačka 4* ☎ *052/453–088* ☐ *AE, DC, MC, V.*

Where to Stay

One reliable bet for private rooms is **Kompas Travel** (⊠ Obala M. Tita 16 52440 Poreč ☎ 052/451–100 🖷 052/451–114), which also has offices in Pula and Rovinj as well as other towns in Istria and elsewhere in Croatia, and which, like other similar agencies, also offers daytime excursions to Istria's top, out-of-the-way exploring sites.

☾ **$$** 🏨 **Hotel Laguna Galijot.** This large, modern hotel sits on a small peninsula surrounded by pines in the Plava Laguna resort complex, 2 km (1 mi) south of the Old Town. Most rooms have balconies and sea views. Excellent sports facilities make this ideal for families on a longer stay and those in search of an active holiday. You'll pay extra for a room with a sea view. ⊠ *Plava Laguna, 52440* ☎ *052/451–877* 🖷 *052/452–399* ⊕ *www.plavalaguna.hr* ⤴ *103 rooms* 👌 *2 restaurants, café, mini-bars, cable TV, tennis court, pool, dive shop, boating, waterskiing, bicycles, bar, parking (fee), some pets allowed* ☐ *AE, MC, V* ☉ *Closed Oct.–Apr.* ⦀ *MAP.*

$ 🏨 **Hotel Neptun.** On the seafront promenade, where Poreč's oldest hotels are found, the Neptune was renovated in 2000 to provide smart, functional accommodations right in the center of town. Still, the rooms—most of which have a sea view—are smallish and somber-hued, and the mattresses are hard. The chic, air-conditioned restaurant includes one *big* salad bar. Stays of under three nights yield a 20% surcharge, and there's a small premium on rooms with a view. ⊠ *Obala M Tita 15, 52440* ☎ *052/400–800 or 052/408–000* 🖷 *052/451–440* ⊕ *www. riviera.hr* ⤴ *145 rooms* 👌 *Restaurant, bar, room service, minibars, cable TV; no a/c* ☐ *AE, DC, MC, V* ⦀ *MAP.*

$ 🏨 **Hotel Poreč.** Not beautiful on the outside, this hotel is well situated between the Old Town and the nearby beaches, yards from the bus station and a supermarket. It's also quite okay on the inside and has friendly service to boot. The rooms are clean and modern, if smallish, but they do have balconies; the furniture has pine veneer, and the beds are a bit wobbly. Stays of under three nights yield a 20% surcharge; an extra daily supplement gets you dinner, too. ⊠ *R. Končara 1, 52440* ☎🖷 *052/451–811* 🖷 *052/451–730* ⊕ *www.hotelporec.com* ⤴ *54 rooms* 👌 *Restaurant, bar, cable TV, minibars, in-room safes* ☐ *AE, DC, MC, V* ⦀ *BP.*

Nightlife & the Arts

Live performances of Croatian jazz can be heard once a week in July and August, usually on Wednesday evening, behind the 18th-century baroque palace housing the Zavičajni muzej (Regional Museum), at Decumanus 9. Throughout August, Poreč's annual **Street Art Festival** enlivens the Old Town's streets and squares with musical, theatrical, art, multimedia, and acrobatic events.

In the Plava Laguna resort area just south of town, **Club Plava** (✉ Plava Laguna ☎ 091/202–0399) is yet another great place to live it up once the sun sets. An open-air disco set shoreside in the pines about 1 km (½ mi) south of the center of town, on the path to the Plava Laguna resort area, the **Colonia Beach Club** (✉ Šetalište A. Štifanića ☎ 091/4430–3222) is a perennial favorite (especially after midnight) with a young, trendy, international crowd for late-night revelry with live rock and jazz provided by groups from all over Croatia and beyond.

Sports & the Outdoors

Beaches

Walk 10 minutes south of Poreč along the shore, past the marina, and you'll meet with the thoroughly swimmable, if typically rocky, pine-fringed beaches of the Plava Laguna resort area. Keep walking until you're about 5 km (3 mi) south, and you'll be right in the center of the Zelena Laguna, which, though more concrete than rock, is one of the best equipped tourist resorts on the Adriatic coast.

Every day in the summer months (from May through September), two charming little "tourist trains," tiny open-walled buses, run hourly from 9 AM to midnight between the town center and the Zelena Laguna resort, as well as the Hotel Luna to the north—costing you 20 Kn but saving you the walk and providing you a virtual rail experience in a part of Istria otherwise without. Those who prefer traversing the brief distance by sea can do so by way of a ship that runs from 8:30 AM to midnight daily, likewise May through September, between Zelena Laguna and the center, making a couple of stops at other resort areas in-between. Tickets can be purchased on board.

Diving

Divers—aspiring or advanced—may want to contact the **Starfish Diving Center** (✉ Camping Porto Sole, Vrsar, 13 km [8 mi] south of Poreč ☎ 052/442–119 or 098/334–816 ⊕ www.starfish.hr) for daily diving tours to local shipwrecks, reefs, and caves or a four-day beginners' course that yields an international diving certification.

NOVIGRAD

⑱ *15 km (9⅓ mi) northwest of Poreč.*

Imagine a mini Rovinj of sorts, not quite so well preserved, it's true, and without the hill. This is Novigrad—a pretty little peninsula town that was the seat of a bishopric for more than 1,300 years, from 520 to 1831, and, like Rovinj, was at one time an island (before being connected with the mainland in the 18th-century). With its medieval structure still impressively intact, along with its Old Town wall, it merits a substantial visit and perhaps a one-night stay as you make your way up and down the coast or before heading inland toward the hill towns of Grožnjan and Motovun.

At first glance, as you enter town on an uninspiring main road bordered by Communist-era, concrete-box apartment buildings, you might wonder if it was worth coming this far. Drive on (or let the bus take you), for you then arrive at a little gem: to your right is a pint-sized, protected harbor, the Old Town is in front of you, and to your left is a peaceful park that even has a water fountain (good news for those tired of constantly buying bottles of spring water to stave off the summer heat). The bustling, harbor-side square has one of Istria's few Middle Eastern sandwich eateries—a great place for a bite if you're on a budget. A nearby ice-cream stand is manned by enterprising, acrobatic young men who wow the crowds repeatedly by hurling scoops fifty or more feet into the air to open-mouthed colleagues who then discreetly spit them into napkins, garnering much applause (and generating long lines at said ice-cream stand).

The 13th-century **Crkva svetog Pelagija** (Church of St. Pelagius), built on a 6th-century foundation and containing some elaborate baroque artwork, stands near the tip of the peninsula with its towering late-19th-century campanile. As in Rovinj, the main church faces the sea, and the statue atop the campanile doubled as a weathervane for the benefit of sailors.

On nearby Veliki trg is Novigrad's pale-red **city hall,** topped by a watchtower and contrasting sharply with the yellow building beside it. Here and there, Gothic elements are in evidence on the medieval architecture about town (e.g., two windows on a 15th-century building at Velika ulica 33).

Where to Eat

★ $$$$ ✕ **Damir e Ormela.** Tucked away in a quiet side street, this superb (and pricey) little family-run establishment is a secret wonder you may want to share only with your fellow *gourmands* who appreciate Japanese-style raw fish specialties. Indeed, it may be the one restaurant in Istria where fish—the fresh catch of the day, that is—is brought to the table this way and served with such care. The service is elegant to a tee, and friendly to boot. Although the main reason to dine here is the raw fish, you can also delight in fried or grilled seafood and *tagliatte* (tagliatelle), not to mention some fine pastries. There's no English menu, but things are somehow clear enough, and the owners' daughter, who is often on hand, speaks English. ⊠ *Ul. Zidine 5* ☎ *052/758–134* ⌕ *Reservations essential* ▭ *AE, DC, MC, V.*

$$ ✕ **Restaurant "MD" Novigrad.** A few hundred yards before you enter Novigrad's Old Town, this exceedingly popular place, which has a very pleasant garden terrace with a stone wall and a red-tile roof, is the best spot in town to have your fill of hearty food. It's a sure bet for such meat staples as *čevapčići.* Finish off with a *palačinke* (crêpe). ⊠ *Murvi 8* ☎ *052/757–147* ▭ *AE, DC, MC, V.*

$$ ✕ **Vecchio Mulino.** The Old Mill pizzeria may look touristy—it is, after all, centrally located right by the harbor, and it is packed—but it's also good, and the raised terrace gives you the feeling of being a bit above the fray. This is the place for pizza, spaghetti, salads, *čevapčići,* and tiramisu. ⊠ *Mlinska ul 8* ☎ *052/726–300* ▭ *AE, DC, MC, V.*

Where to Stay

Though hotels are also available in a resort area southeast of town, the in-town alternatives are more attractive and quite reasonably priced by Istrian standards. For private rooms, check with the tourist agency **Rakam Trade** (⊠ Mlinska ul 45 ☎ 098/366–407 ☎🖶 052/757–047 ⊕ www.rakam-trade.hr).

$ 🏨 **Hotel Cittar.** On stepping inside the Hotel Cittar you feel not so much as if you are entering a hotel, but rather the city itself. The facade of the building is, after all, part of the city wall, with a glass-covered vestibule imaginatively separating the wall from the hotel lobby. The rooms, while smallish, are bright, modern, and clean, with pine floors and silky bedspreads; the service is friendly. ⊠ *Prolaz Venecija 1, 52466* ☎ *052/ 757–737 or 052/757–229* 🖶 *052/757–340* ⊕ *www.cittar.hr* ⤶ *40 rooms* ⚘ *Restaurant, cable TV, minibars* ▭ *AE, DC, MC, V* ⦿ *BP.*

¢ 🏨 **Torci 18.** This family-run hotel offers recently renovated, modern rooms at good rates. The hotel also has one of Novigrad's best-reputed restaurants. Just inside the city walls, it's around the block from the sea, where you can take a dip at your leisure. ⊠ *Ul Torci 43, 52466* ☎ *052/ 757–799* 🖶 *052/757–174* ⊕ *www.torci.hr* ⤶ *12 rooms* ⚘ *Restaurant, cable TV, minibars* ▭ *AE, DC, MC, V* ⦿ *BP.*

UMAG

⑲ *14 km (8¾ mi) northwest of Novigrad.*

Yet another onetime island, the peninsula town of Umag draws the fewest tourists of any of the major towns along Istria's western coast, even if it has more than its share of the usual beach resorts nearby. Perhaps it's the frustration with waiters who, while twiddling their thumbs in front of their restaurants, call out to every passing tourist, "Italiano? Deutsch? English?" and, less often, "Francais?"

And yet Umag is a nice enough place to stroll for a couple of hours if you are passing this way, even if you might not be moved to stay for the night. Although the town grew up under the rule of Rome, practically none of its ancient roots are apparent in what remains of the historic core, which dates to the Middle Ages.

A spacious main square, **Trg Slobode** (Piazza Liberta—i.e., Freedom Square) is a jarring architectural mix from the medieval to the 20th-century mundane. It's where you'll find the towering **Church of the Assumption of the Virgin Mary & St. Pelegrin,** which was reconsecrated in 1760 after extensive reconstruction to repair the 14th-century original, which suffered damage in a fierce storm in 1651. Among its main attractions is a wooden, 14th-century Venetian triptych and a 16th-century painting depicting the resurrected Christ.

Just off Trg Slobode is the town's best preserved historic street, **Riječka ulica,** where the souvenir vendors tend to congregate. The palm-lined main road leading through town from the coastal road to the square is a pleasant, comparatively modern, somewhat bustling thoroughfare. Along it you'll pass a large open square to your left that is home to both the tourist office and Istria's newest aquarium. A bit further down, the **Church of St. Roche,** a lovely little stone structure, was erected in 1514 to mark the end of a plague outbreak some years earlier.

Aquarium Umag is modeled after its counterparts in Pula and Poreč. This aquarium opened in summer 2005 to bring the nearby world of Adriatic sea life closer to home—in the form of dozens of species from seahorses to starfish, morays to rays, and corals to crabs. ⊠ *Svibnja ul 1* ☎ *052/721–041* ✉ *Apr.–Oct., 25 Kn, Nov.–Mar., 15 Kn* ☉ *Apr.–Oct., daily 9–9; Nov.–Mar., daily 10–5.*

Where to Eat

$$–$$$ ✗ **Restaurant Konoba.** With a tad more ambience than the more touristy restaurants beside it, this spot on a quiet, seaside promenade right behind the cathedral is a decent place to have your fill. The one-room, rustic interior can get sultry in mid-summer, but you can always sit outside. The fare—including standard, grilled fish dishes—is well prepared. If you order water (i.e., spring water), be sure to ask for a small bottle, unless you want a *big* one for 40 Kn. Good to bear in mind when ordering water elsewhere, too. ⊠ *Ul Pod urom 7* ☎ *052/751–423* ✉ *AE, DC, MC, V.*

MOTOVUN

㉟ *30 km (19 mi) east of Poreč.*

Fodor'sChoice
★

It is an understatement to say that a day exploring the undulating green countryside and medieval hill towns of inland Istria makes a pleasant contrast to life on the coast. Motovun, for one, is a ravishing place. The king of Istria's medieval hill towns, with a double ring of defensive walls as well as towers and gates, may even evoke a scene straight from *Lord of the Rings.* Motovun is *the* place to visit if you opt to travel inland for a day or two from the sea. A walk around the ramparts offers views across the oak forests and vineyards of the Mirna Valley, and just outside the walls stands a church built according to plans by Palladio. Unless you're a fan of fine international films or fine all-night partying, however, you might want to avoid visiting in late July, when Motovun transforms for about five days into one of Croatia's liveliest (and most crowded) destinations—for the famed **Motovun Film Festival.**

Where to Eat

$$$–$$$$ ✗ **Barbacan.** On the narrow cobblestone road you traverse into the Old Town—just before you pass through the city gate—this popular restaurant, whose rustic interior, complete with pots and pans on the walls,

CloseUp
A SCENT TO SWOON OVER

A BALL-SHAPED CANDY often coated with cocoa? (That's what Webster's says about the truffle.) Think again. Such truffles are a dime a dozen compared to the real thing—namely, the sort of record-breaking, 1,310-kilogram (2,882-pound) truffle Giancarlo Zigante unearthed on November 2, 1999, with the help of his sharp-nosed dog in the village of Livante, near Motovun. What he found was—as attested to by the 100 guests he served in an effort to promote the cause of the Istrian truffle—the most delicious fungus you are likely to find.

For one thing, truffles grow underground, in a symbiotic relationship with the roots of oaks and certain other trees. As such, they cannot readily be seen. It is their scent that gives them away—a swoon-inducing scent. Sows were once the truffle-hunter's favored companion, as truffles smell a lot like male hogs. (To be fair, the earthy aroma and pungent taste of truffles, which has also been likened to garlic, is prized by gourmands the world over.) These days, dogs are the truffle hunter's best friend.

For another thing, truffles are extremely rare. Most efforts to grow them domestically have failed, not least because you first need to grow a forest full of trees whose roots are just right for truffles. The white truffle, prized for its superior scent—the "white diamond," it's often called—sells for upwards of $1,000 a pound. This was the sort unearthed by Zigante, whose family owns a chain of truffle-oriented shops in Istria. In addition to the white truffle, Istria is also home to three sorts of black truffle, which sell for a mere $300 to $500 a pound.

In Istria, truffles have been extracted since ancient times. Even Roman emperors and Austro-Hungarian aristocrats had a taste for truffles, not least because of the aphrodisiac qualities attributed to them. Truffles were once consumed and gathered like potatoes—that's how plentiful they were. That was in the 1800s. No longer, of course. Still, their fine shavings imparting an unforgettable, earthy aroma and an irresistibly pungent, vaguely garlicy taste to pastas, salads, omelettes, beef specialties, sauces, and more.

Economics and truffle scarcity being what they are, the Istrian truffle has become a hot commodity indeed. These days, for example, much of what is sold by Italy as Italian white truffles actually comes from Croatia—not least, from the moist woods around Motovun, near the river Mirna.

If you'd like to join a truffle hunt, reserve a spot on a brief truffle-hunting excursion that departs from Livade at 5 PM daily throughout the year (assuming two or more people sign up in advance) that includes an introductory drink, 1½ hours in the woods with trained truffle-sniffing dogs, and a hearty dinner. The organizer is **Activatravel Istra** (✉ Scalierova 1, Pula ☎ 052/215–497 📠 052/211–889 💰 €60 euros per person for two people, €50 euros per person for three people, €45 euros per person for four people [maximum]). The peak season for white truffles stretches from October through December, with January to September being more amenable to black truffles.

makes you feel as if you're in an Istrian farmhouse, is the best place in town for fresh seafood (no small accomplishment so far from the sea). The menu also has delectable truffle fare, from polenta (corn porridge) with black truffles and sheep's cheese, to Istrian beef with black truffles and truffle pâté. ⊠ *Barbacan 1* ☎ *052/681–791* ▭ *AE, DC, MC, V.*

$$$ ✕ **Restaurant Enoteka & Zigante Tartufi.** This family-run restaurant-cum-truffle shop 3 km (2 mi) from Motovun is not simply a gift shop (as with other branches of the chain). Here, you can feast on such delectables as gilthead carpaccio with white truffles (gilthead being a type of sea bream) or crêpes filled with white-chocolate mousse and black truffles. The place is rustic yet elegant and, above all, captivating, what with low lighting cast by wrought-iron, streetlamp-style lights, stone walls, and wooden beams overhead. ⊠ *Livade 7, Livade* ☎ *052/664–030* ▭ *AE, DC, MC, V.*

$$–$$$ ✕ **Restaurant Mčotić.** If you love truffles, whether with pasta or steak, this is a fine place to eat. Unquestionably an acquired taste, these earthy delicacies are gathered each autumn in the nearby Mirna Valley. Mčotić has a large summer terrace and occupies one of the most prominent buildings of the new Motovun, at the main intersection just below the Old Town. ⊠ *Zadrugarska 19* ☎ *052/681–758* ▭ *AE, DC, MC, V.*

Where to Stay

$ ▦ **Hotel Kaštel.** Just outside the Motovun town walls—but nonetheless nestled in a cloistered niche atop the hill—this peaceful, old-fashioned hotel makes an ideal retreat if you prefer green hills to sea and islands. Out front there's a small garden and pretty summer terrace. For just €5 more, dinner is also included. ⊠ *Šetalište V. Nazora 7, Motovun 52424* ☎ *052/681–607 or 052/681–735* ▤ *052/681–652* ⊕ *www.hotel-kastel-motovun.hr* ⌁ *30 rooms* △ *Restaurant, café, some pets allowed* ▭ *AE, DC, MC, V* ⧀ *BP.*

en route If your travel plans bring you into the vicinity of Grožnjan—and if you've gone as far north on the coast as Novigrad or Umag, you very well might get this far—you may wish to stop off at the hilltop village of Buje first. If time allows, do drive up the hill for an hour or two in this quiet, lovely town, whose pale-yellow Church of the Madonna of Mercy is situated near a hushed little square shaded by plane trees, under which is a statue of a goat that seems to be reaching, in vain, for the leaves inches above its head.

GROŽNJAN

★ ㉑ *10 km (7 mi) east of Motovun.*

Close to Motovun and a reasonable drive from Poreč, Novigrad, or Umag, Grožnjan is also among Istria's preeminent hill towns, with a Renaissance loggia adjoining the town gate. Much visited by busloads of summer tourists, it is quite empty the rest of the year.

In 1358, after at least 250 years in existence as a walled city, Grožnjan came under Venetian rule and remained so for more than 400 years. Though most of its population left after World War II, when decades of Italian rule came to an end and it officially became part of Yugoslavia, from the mid-1960s the government encouraged artists and musicians to settle here. This explains the number of painting and sculpture galleries you will encounter in this otherwise unassuming village. During the summer, an international federation of young musicians meets for training and workshops, presenting concerts beneath the stars through July and August.

Walk straight ahead from the small parking area just outside Grožnjan and you will come to the **Crkva sveta Voida i Modesta** (Church of St. Vitus and St. Modestus). Reconstructed in baroque style from an earlier, 14th-century church, it stands on a relatively unassuming, parklike space a bit removed from the gallery scene, with panoramic views of the surrounding countryside and plateaus of Istria all the way to the sea. Conveniently, there's an ATM right beside the church.

Grožjnan may be small and out of the way, but enough tourists visit to merit yet another outlet in the Zigante family's **Enoteka & Zigante Tartufi** chain. Half of the shop sells truffles and everything truffle-related you can imagine, as well as local products from aromatic herb brandies to honey to dried boletus, whereas the other side is a sparkling, impeccably intimate wine bar. It is attached to the town's loggia, which means you can sit and sip inside or outside, as you prefer. ⊠ *Ul Gorjan 5* ☎ *052/776–099.*

> **need a break?**
>
> If you are looking for a more substantial meal in Goržjnan, visit the chic if a bit smoky **Bastia Konoba** (⊠ Trg Ferrucxcia Poiania 2 ☎ 052/776–370), which is right on the main square. You can have a full meal in style for around 140 Kn, not including wine.

For a bit of wine-tasting with Istrian prosciutto and similar hearty fare to accompany the elixir, stop by at **Vina Dešković**. The house-cum-wine cellar is on a lonely country road about 10 minutes outside Grožnjan by car. You can get not only a tasty selection of five Istrian wines—for example, malvazija among the whites and teran among the reds—but also a selection of hearty snacks from its simple menu and even a breathtaking view of the tiny village of Kostanjica several hundred yards away. Though the friendly family members here speak little English, communication need not be a barrier to a pleasant experience; you need to be able to say little more than "vino" and "prosciutto." Figure on at least 50 Kn per person for food and a glass of wine. Since finding your way there through the hills outside Grožnjan is much easier said than done, do check with the town's tourist-information office for directions here and/or to similar wine-tasting opportunities nearby. You will want to have a designated driver, by the way. ⊠ *Kostanjica 58, Kostanjica* ☎ *052/776–315, 052/776–316, or 091/516–5371.*

EASTERN ISTRIA: LABIN & RABAC

Labin is 44 km (28 mi) northeast of Pula

Few travelers take time to explore Istria's often overlooked eastern coast. Although the region's mostly mountainous terrain offers a relative dearth of large towns abounding in historical sights and easy-to-access, swimmable stretches of sea, the region does contain one notable exception: Labin.

Perched in all its compact medieval redolence atop a hill a short drive
㉒ or walk from the sea, **Labin** is Croatia's former coal-mining capital and the birthplace of Matthias Flacius Illyricus, a Reformation-era collaborator of Martin Luther. Its narrow, historic streets are well deserving of a good walk followed, if time allows, by a dip in the sea at Rabac, the relatively crowded and less inspiring complex of hotels and beaches 3 km (2 mi) away. From Labin's endearing little main square, **Titov trg**, with its 16th-century loggia and bastion, it's an easy stroll to Šetališste San Marco, a semicircular promenade with a spectacular view of the sea. Walk to the end, past a half dozen or so busts of historical luminaries, and take a sharp left up the cobblestone road.

By following the word PANORAMA spray-painted with arrows on the stone walls, you will soon reach the top of the hill, where (for 5 Kn) you can climb another 30 meters (98½ feet) up for an even better view from the town's onetime fortress, the **Fortica**. From here, Labin's relatively bustling commercial center, which seemed nonexistent a few minutes ago, comes fully into view below, as do the dry, craggy hills of inland Istria. Making your way down the other side of the hill back toward the main square, you will pass by Labin's other major attractions, not least the **Crkva rođenja blažene djevice Marije** (Church of the Birth of the Virgin Mary). With a facade featuring a 14th-century rose window and a 17th-century Venetian lion of the sort you will encounter elsewhere in Istria, the church was thoroughly renovated in 1993 to repair serious damage from mining under the Old Town in the 1960s. That said, its mix of architectural styles essentially dates from a late-16th century renovation, though its foundations may date to the 11th century—and, further back, to an earlier church built here by the Avars in AD 611.

㉓ As for **Rabac** (buses hourly from Labin for 1 Kn), your first thought on arriving may be: why come all the way to Europe for a place that looks much like a generic beach resort anywhere? Its series of huge, honeycomb-shaped, Italian-owned hotel monstrosities with names like Narcis, Casino, and Mimosa are truly the last place the writer of these lines, for one, would want to stay. But wait. Make a *right* on entering town rather than a left, then walk down the hill by road or the steps to the harbor. Once you reach the harbor, go *left* and then along the harbor-side promenade, rather than right. Doing so will reveal a side of Rabac that, although still somewhat touristy, also retains something of the idyllic—with its quiet harbor replete with small yachts, motorboats, and other pleasurecraft, not to mention dozens of tiny, harbor-side coves you can walk down into for a quick dip via short flights of concrete steps. Although you can rent a plastic beach chair, making yourself comfortable on the smooth, roundish stones isn't nearly as difficult as it sounds; and even in mid-summer, you can usually find yourself a rock to sprawl out on.

Where to Eat

$$$ ✕ **Due Fratelli.** Owned by a family that also has a fishing boat down on
Fodor'sChoice the bay, this restaurant has plenty of fresh, delicious seafood specialties
★ on offer in addition to a good selection of meat and poultry dishes. Get-
ting to this well-reputed restaurant, whose decor is pleasantly folksy and
which has a cool, shaded terrace with a lush wall of pink flowers and
grapevines out front, is easy if you're driving; keep your eyes peeled along
the winding road downhill from Labin to Rabac for the restaurant's lit-
tle sign to the left as the road curves right. If you're on foot, the walk
is a bit of a haul. ✉ *Montozi 6, Labin* ☎ *052/853–577* ⌕ *Reservations
essential* 🖃 *AE, DC, MC, V.*

$$$ ✕ **Gastionica Kvarner.** This restaurant is *the* place to eat in Labin's Old
Town, both because there isn't much else and because—if you forgive
the nonenthusiastic service—it's a lovely place to sit while you have
your fill of decent, if largely tourist-oriented, fare. The fish soup is a
rather salty but definitely fishy broth with some rice thrown in, and
the tagliatelle with truffles, although filling, doesn't really have much
in the way of truffle shavings on top. There's plenty of grilled fish,
too, along with 14 types of pizza. The seating out front should offer
a superb view of the sea, but the promenade's high concrete wall
would require you to dine while standing in order to eat and gaze at
the same time. ✉ *Šetališste San Marco, off Titot trg* ☎ *052/852–336*
🖃 *AE, DC, MC, V.*

ISTRIA ESSENTIALS

BOAT & FERRY TRAVEL

In summer, the Italian company Adriatica runs a catamaran service
from Trieste and Grado (in Italy) to Rovinj and Brijuni. In Rovinj, tickets for the catamaran are available from Eurostar Travel. The Adriatica agent in Trieste is Samer & Co.

🛈 **Adriatica** ⊕ www.adriatica.it. **Eurostar Travel** ✉ Obala P. Budičina 1, Rovinj
☎ 052/813–144. **Samer & Co.** ✉ Piazza dell'Unità d'Italia 7, Trieste, Italy ☎ 040/
6702-7211.

BUS TRAVEL

There are domestic connections all over mainland Croatia to and from
Pula, Poreč, and Rovinj, and local services between these towns and
smaller inland destinations such as Motovun and Vodjnan. International
buses offer daily connections to Italy (Trieste) and Slovenia (Ljubljana,
Koper, Piran, and Portorož). Timetables are available at all bus stations.
However, as elsewhere in Croatia, the sheer number of different companies offering bus service out of each station can be confusing; so it's
best to confirm at the information window what you might find posted
on the wall.

🛈 **Poreč Bus Station** ✉ Rade Končara 1, Poreč ☎ 052/432–153. **Pula Bus Station** ✉ Trg
1 Istarske Brigade, Pula ☎ 052/500–040. **Rovinj Bus Station** ✉ Mattea Benussia, by
trg na Lokvi, Rovinj ☎ 052/811–453.

CAR TRAVEL

While visiting Pula, Rovinj, and Poreč a car may be more of a hindrance than an asset: all three towns are served by good bus connections, and having your own vehicle only causes parking problems (not to mention the high cost of fuel). However, renting a car can make day-trips that much easier (e.g., to avoid having to wait roadside an hour or more in the summer sun for the next bus), and to visit places where bus service is sporadic, such as Grožnjan. If you are traveling from Zagreb, you can, of course, rent there, but major agencies have offices in Pula, and other towns along the coast all have one or more local agencies that generally offer better rates than the major chains without sacrificing quality of service; however, they may be less equipped than the major chains to take reservations by phone. (Some, such as Vetura and Manuel, also rent bicycles and scooters [i.e., mopeds].) Lastly, bear in mind that finding an available car on short notice in mid-summer can be tricky regardless of the agency involved.

🚘 Novigrad **Avis** ✉ S Dobrića 1, Novigrad ☎ 052/223-739.

🚘 Poreč **Avis** ✉ S Dobrića 1, Poreč ☎ 052/223-739. **Budget** ✉ Obala M. Tita, Poreč ☎ 052/451-188. **Vetura** ✉ Trg Joakima Rakovca 2, Poreč ☎ 052/434-700 📠 Zelena Laguna, Poreč ☎ 052/451-391 or 052/451-395.

🚘 Pula **Avis** ✉ S Dobrića 1, Pula ☎ 052/223-739. **Budget** ✉ ACI marina, Riva 1, Pula ☎ 052/218-252. **Hertz** ✉ Hotel Histria, Verudela, Pula ☎ 052/210-868. **Manuel** ✉ Giardini 10, Pula ☎ 052/211-858 or 098/367-637. **Vetura** ✉ Verudela, Pula ☎ 091/535-8755, 091/535-8755 for airport office.

🚘 Rabac **Vetura** ✉ Obala M. Tita, Rabac ☎ 052/872-129 or 091/557-5113.

🚘 Rovinj **Avis** ✉ S Dobrića 1, Rovinj ☎ 052/223-739. **Lucky Way** ✉ Nazorova, Rovinj ☎ 052/811-503. **Unirent** ✉ Istarska, Rovinj ☎ 098/230-302. **Vetura** ✉ Nazorova, Rovinj ☎ 052/815-209.

🚘 Umag **Interauto** ✉ Trgovačka 3, Umag 📠 052/741-483, 052/741-358, or 098/214-208. **Vetura** ✉ Trgovačka 4, Umag ☎ 052/742-700.

EMERGENCIES

🚘 Ambulance **Ambulance** ☎ 94.

🚘 Doctors & Dentists **Hitno Ponoč** (Casualty) ✉ M. Gioseffija 2, Poreč ☎ 052/431-154 📠 Zagrebačka 30, Pula ☎ 052/214-433 📠 Istarska ul, Rovinj ☎ 052/813-004.

🚘 Fire **Fire Emergencies** ☎ 93.

🚘 Pharmacies Pula: **24-hr Pharmacy** ✉ Giardini 15 ☎ 052/222-551.

Rovinj: **Main pharmacy** ✉ M. Benussi-Cio St. ☎ 052/813-589 ☉ May-Sept., weekdays 8-9, Sat. 8-4, Sun. and holidays 9-noon; contact for more info.

🚘 Police **Police Emergencies** ☎ 92.

🚘 Roadside Assistance (24 hours) **Roadside Assistance** ☎ 987.

INTERNET

As elsewhere in Croatia, Internet cafés are still few and far between, with the major towns along the Istrian coast each containing but a handful (or fewer). Expect to pay at least 10 Kn for 20 minutes, or 30 Kn per hour. The Tourist Information Office in Poreč offers 15 minutes of free Internet use, more if no one is waiting in line (*see* Visitor Information, *below*).

🚘 **Enigma Internet Center** ✉ Kandlerova 19 Pula ☎ 052/381-615. **Planet Tourist Agency** ✉ Sv Križ 1 Rovinj ☎ 052/840-494.

TRAIN TRAVEL

Istria is not connected to the rest of Croatia by rail. However, there is a line running north from Pula to Slovenia.

🚆 **Pula Train Station** ✉ Kolodvorksa, Pula ☎ 052/541-733.

Travel Agencies

Kompas–Istria can arrange private accommodations, as well as tours to the Limski kanal from either Poreč or Rovinj. Excursions Delfin also arranges tours to the Limski kanal, as do several other local companies and independent operators who happen to own boats and post flyers about their towns.

🚆 **Excursions Delfin** ✉ Zagrebačka 5, Rovinj ☎ 091/514-2169 or 091/520-5309. **Kompas–Istria** ✉ Obala M. Tita 16, Poreč ☎ 052/451-1000 ✉ Obala M. Tita 5, Rovinj ☎ 52/813-211 ✉ Starih Statuta 4, Pula ☎ 052/212-511 ✉ Gradska Vrata 11, Novigrad ☎ 052/726-383 ✉ Trgovačka 13, Umag ☎ 052/741-613.

VISITOR INFORMATION

Although the official tourist offices listed below can provide you with every bit of information imaginable, they generally leave the booking of rooms and excursions to private tourist agencies. The office in Poreč does offer 15 minutes of free Internet surfing, which may be enough for you to check your e-mail.

🚆 **Brijuni Tourist Information** ✉ Fažana ☎ 052/525-888 ⊕ www.brijuni.hr. **Grožnjan Tourist Information** ✉ Umberto Gorjan 3, Grožnjan ☎ 052/776-131. **Istria Tourist Board** ⊕ www.istra.hr. **Labin & Rabac Tourist Information** ✉ A. Negri 20, Labin ☎ 052/855-560 or 052/852-399 ⊕ www.istra.com/rabac. **Motovun Tourist Information** ✉ Šetalište V. Nazora 1, Motovun ☎ 052/681-642. **Novigrad Tourist Information** ✉ Porpolella 1, Novigrad ☎ 052/757-075 ⊕ www.istra.com/novigrad. **Poreč Tourist Information** ✉ Zagrebačka 9, Poreč ☎ 052/451-293 ⊕ www.istra.com/porec. **Pula Tourist Information** ✉ Forum 3, Pula ☎ 052/219-197 ⊕ www.pulainfo.hr. **Rovinj Tourist Information** ✉ Pino Budičin 12, Rovinj ☎ 052/811-566 ⊕ www.tzgrovinj.hr. **Umag Tourist Information** ✉ Trgovačka 6, Umag ☎ 052/741-363 ⊕ www.istra.com/umag. **Vodnjan Tourist Information** ✉ Narodni trg 3, Vodjnan ☎ 052/511-672 ⊕ www.vodnjan.hr.

Kvarner

4

By Tim Gosling **SEPARATING THE ISTRIAN PENINSULA** from Dalmatia to the south, the Kvarner Gulf is a large, deep bay, backed by mountains. Four major islands: Cres, Krk, Lošinj, and Rab, along with numerous smaller specks of land, fill the heart of the bay and can be viewed from the gentle resort towns that are strung around the coastal arc.

Life on the mainland coast exists on the narrow strip of land that skirts the bay beneath the forested slopes of the mountains, whose ascent begins, at most, just a handful of miles inland. The wild Gorski kotar mountain nature park lies in these peaks to the north and east of Rijeka. Across the narrow range sits the inland part of Primorsko-goranska županija (Primorje-Gorski Kotar county), a region of small towns and agricultural land that sits on the edge of the Pannonian Basin, through which you pass if you are traveling overland to the capital, Zagreb.

The lush, rolling hills of this coastal strip trim their way around the Adriatic from Opatija on the western shore of the gulf. Heading east, the gentle high ground descends as one approaches the apex of the arc at Rijeka, moving onto dry and dusty sea-level scrub. East of Rijeka, the Magistrala cuts into the solid rock of foothills as this most scenic of roads sets off on its trip to the southern tip of Croatia.

The errant jigsaw-piece islands offer views of the mainly Austro-Hungarian coast, or their own closely neighboring isles. Krk, entered via a short bridge from the eastern shore of the gulf region, reflects that area's arid nature more than its brethren, save some parts of Rab. That said, green and succulent patches stud the center of Krk, as well as the northern stretches of the island's coast.

The northern stretches of Cres are a twisted knot of forest peaks and rocky crags, while gentler, cultivated slopes appear toward the center. Pine forests marching down to the shores provide welcome shade in the middle of the day. On the island's southern end, hollows have filled up to make freshwater lakes that provide the island's drinking water, counter-balancing the salty sea that licks at the land just a hill crest away.

At the foot of Cres, a hop across a narrow stretch of the Adriatic brings one to Lošinj. Although it has less drama than its neighbor to the north, this lush, Mediterranean oasis owes much of its charm to the gardens and villas that were built here during the heyday of seafaring in Mali Lošinj, the Adriatic's largest island town.

As you approach from the north, the silhouette of Rab resembles the humped back of a diving sea-monster. This schizophrenic beast bears a strikingly contrasting physiology: the high north is dry and barren, almost a desert of rock and scrub; the lower southern hemisphere is lush and fertile.

Although the entire northern stretch of the Croatian coast exhibits a strong Italian influence, thanks to centuries of control from across the Adriatic, most of the mainland resorts developed during Habsburg rule. Robust and sophisticated Austro-Hungarian architecture and infrastructure predominate in these towns.

If you have **3 days**   With only three days, start off on **Krk** to enjoy a little of the rustic charm of the islands, particularly that of the beaches and the restaurants. If you crave a taste of the contemporary Croatia, cross the bridge onto the mainland and make your way around to **Rijeka,** where you can possibly dive into a cultural exhibit or two. On the final day, scoot further west for some classic seaside resorting in **Opatija.**

If you have **5 days**   With five days in the Kvarner, you can complete a circle thanks to the excellent ferry transport between the islands and the mainland. Starting from whichever point you fancy, follow the above itinerary but add a visit to the relatively wild island of **Cres** by using one of the ferries that connect it to the Opatija riviera to the west and Krk to the east. A day divided between swimming at the beaches and relaxing in a café or ice-cream parlor in Cres Town can be enhanced by a second day exploring the more remote areas of the island, taking in some of the smaller villages or the rugged north.

4

If you have **7 days**   With a full week, follow the circle suggested above, but boldly break out at the point where Krk connects to the mainland and head south to sample some of the region's only sandy beaches on the beautifully lush island of **Rab.**

In contrast, the islands tend toward the cozier, less aspirational features of Italy. Dwellings are simpler, often of stone, and set in less geometric layouts. The elder population may struggle with any language other than Italian, and that includes Croatian.

EXPLORING KVARNER

The Kvarner's principal city, Rijeka, is a somewhat dilapidated port (although the 21st century has seen it making a reasonably committed effort at a comeback), with good road and rail connections to Zagreb. Genteel Opatija was founded by the Habsburgs in the mid-19th century as Croatia's first seaside resort. The regional airport is found on the island of Krk.

About the Restaurants
Without wanting to force square pegs into round holes, there are essentially four types of restaurants in Kvarner, if not the whole of the country. Unsurprisingly, many of them fall heavily under the influence of the Italian *tricolore*. In place of faith, hope, and charity, expect white pasta, green salads, and red pizza. The many pizza and pasta spots tend to be the cheaper and more casual alternatives, often offering a nostalgic and shiny 1980s decor.

Possibly the most delightful Croatian establishment is the *konoba*. Originally, the konoba was a humble cottage or shed, where fishermen would gather after returning to shore, where the men might toast to surviving another day's trip out to sea by raising a few glasses, followed by a sample of their catch cooked to soak up the booze. These rustically styled fish restaurants have cropped up everywhere in the last few years. Especially on the islands, you'll see quite a few originals around.

Few dishes come specifically from Kvarner, but several parts of the region carry a healthy reputation for certain produce. In Rijeka try *jota*, a thick soup with sauerkraut or pickled beets with meat. *Manĕtra* is the local version of minestrone, but made only with beans instead of pasta. The Gorski kotar region serves a mean polenta made with potatoes, local cheese, blood sausage, and game. On Krk try *Krk–Šurlice*, the local version of pasta; handmade on a spindle, it's often served with wild game goulash. Cres has a fierce rivalry with the northern Dalmatian island of Pag regarding who serves the best lamb in Croatia. Calamari cooked in herbs and wine is a good bet on Lošinj.

In Kvarner, *mrkač* is the local word for octopus; it's *hobotnice* in the rest of the country. If you order white fish, either grilled (*na žaru*) or cooked in white wine (*na buzara*), you'll be charged by the kilogram, whereas squid and shrimp come in regular portions, often offered cooked in the same manner. The classic accompaniment to fish is chard (*blitva*) and potatoes (*krumpir*). Many choices will come smothered in olive oil and garlic; you'll likely be told that this is what keeps the population so healthy.

Krk and Susak are home to the most highly regarded wines from the region, with the dry white *Vrbnićka žlahtina* a strong candidate for "best." *Rakija* (fruit brandies) are, of course, the common end to a meal and the start of a long night.

WHAT IT COSTS in Croatian Kuna (Kn)				
$$$$	$$$	$$	$	¢
RESTAURANTS over 80	60–80	35–60	20–35	under 20

Restaurant prices are per person for a main course at dinner.

About the Hotels

Opatija, Krk, and Lošinj have a healthy selection of quality hotels, but outside these (relatively) major resorts, hotels become a rarer commodity. Rijeka has a grand total of three!

Much more common is renting a villa or apartment. There are multitudes of these holiday homes available across the region, and local tourist offices and many agencies can assist in booking. Expect anything from a room in a block that shares a common kitchen, to a full-blown private estate. Terraces are a standard; what you'll need to verify is whether that terrace is a simple tiled slab with metal rails to prevent you toppling off, or a beautifully appointed perch, shaded by a vine-smothered trellis and with an open grill for al fresco cooking.

If you want to save money, consider renting a room in a private home. This arrangement rarely involves food, so you'll have to get up and out in the morning for your breakfast. At major transport hubs you'll often be accosted by elderly ladies attempting to entice you to their spare room.

4

Clear Water
Given the geography of the region, it's thoroughly predictable that the stars of Kvarner are the beaches that line the Adriatic. For the most part they are covered with stone, which may not be so forgiving on the body when lying upon them, nor on the feet when traversing, but you can thank the mineral shores for the stunning aquamarine purity of the water. Diving below the gentle waves is a great attraction, as is hoisting sail to allow the wind to propel you across them.

Hiking
The wonderful climate, plentiful sunshine, and fresh sea breezes should give thanks to the the the mountains that plunge toward the waters around the whole Kvarner bay. Nature lovers will enjoy hiking here, dropping into remote villages to refuel and sample a pace of life rarely found in 21st-century Europe.

Resort Towns
Kvarner offers the visitor perhaps the greatest variety of cultural and architectural styles in Croatia. The mainland, thanks to its popularity with former rulers, features resort towns built on the grand scale of the Austrian Empire, particularly on the Opatija Riviera. Although many are somewhat faded in spots—and must compete with the "modifications" of Communist-era planners—their original intention to serve the upper-echelons of late-19th-century society from Central Europe still manages to impress.

The Quiet Islands
The islands, meanwhile, are bastions of Mediterranean culture, and Italian in particular. Aside from certain tourist-heavy locations (e. g., parts of Krk), one can still lap up the joys of rustic southern Europe, including stone cottages and peaceful village harbors, in relative authenticity.

Haggling may be a good idea, especially if it's nearing evening, but generally these can be great deals, with additional pros. Croats are a house-proud race, and the facilities are likely to be spotless. Although it's doubtful you'll find yourself in the lap of luxury, facilities are more than likely to be comfortable and cozy. Your welcome will probably be very warm, with drinks—especially strong coffee—thrust under your nose the moment you step across the threshold. On a brief tourist trip, there's no better way to get a real feel for how Croats live.

It can be close to impossible to get accommodation for less than two nights, so if you want to visit Kvarner, set aside at least that much time.

WHAT IT COSTS in euros (€) and Croatian kuna (Kn)				
$$$$	**$$$**	**$$**	**$**	**¢**
IN EUROS over € 225	€175–€225	€125–€175	€75–€125	under €75
IN KUNA over 1,650	1,300–1,650	925–1,300	550–925	under 550

Hotel prices are for two people in a double room in high season, excluding taxes and service charges.

Timing

Make no mistake, the Kvarner region gets very busy in high summer, so don't even dream of heading, for instance, to Opatija or Krk in August. Late May through early June and September are the ideal times: good weather, warm seas, and open facilities await the prompt traveler. Early May and October will offer those looking for peace just that, assuming one has booked accommodation in advance and that one can amuse oneself; before and after the high season, few tourist-related activities are on offer. After November, the area offers a bit more peace than most tourists will be seeking.

Numbers in the text correspond to numbers in the margin and on the Kvarner map.

RIJEKA

182 km (114 mi) southwest of Zagreb.

Water is the essence of Kvarner, and the region's largest city expresses this simply. Whether in Croatian or Italian (*Fiume*) the translation of the name to English is the same: *river*. Although the history of Croatia's third city goes back to the days of Imperial Rome, modern Rijeka evolved under the rule of Austria-Hungary. The historic core retains vestiges of the old Habsburg monarchy from the time when Rijeka served as the empire's outlet to the Adriatic. During the 1960s, under Yugoslavia, the suburbs expanded rapidly. Rijeka is the country's largest port, with a huge shipyard, massive dry-dock facilities, refineries, and other heavy industries offering large-scale employment. Since the break-up of Yugoslavia however, Rijeka's role as a shipping town has declined significantly. Much business shifted north to the smaller Slovene ports during the crippling wars of the 1990s, and although some has returned, the volume remains less than half that seen in 1980.

At the city's core sits Korzo, a pedestrian street of shops and cafés running parallel with the harbor and just to the south of where the land begins to rise toward the peaks of the mountains that back the bay. The high ground ensures that the suburbs stretch out to the east and the west, with little space to expand to the north. The general rule is that Rijeka is more of a transit town than a holiday destination, and it's not known for its points of interest, apart from the hilltop fortress of Trsat. However, the city is well worth investigating more thoroughly than most would have you believe.

Many visitors stay in the nearby seaside resort of Opatija, and locals will often head that way in their free time as well. That said, Rijeka is a perfectly pleasant small city (approximately 200,000 people call it home); if it did not command the wonderful bay that it does, it would also be unremarkable. This makes it one of the more authentically Croatian spots in the region in summer. Those looking to avoid the hordes could do much worse than to stay in Rijeka—albeit with very few options for accommodation—and use the excellent network of ferries to explore the rest of Kvarner.

Rijeka is the home port of Jadrolinija, the coast's major ferry company. Local ferries connect with all the Kvarner islands and will take you further afield as well. If you're planning on heading south and would rather dodge the slow and dangerous roads that head that way, then let the boat take the strain. Ferries leaving Rijeka weave through islands all the way down to Dubrovnik, stopping at most major points on the way. Sunsets, sunrises, plus a mingling of stars and shore-anchored town lights in between, help transport one further than just the few hundred kilometers to the other end of the country.

Rijeka is also the start of the Jadranska Magistrala (the coastal highway), which follows the coast south, all the way to the Montenegran border. Alternately offering startling views from on high or the illusion that one could simply reach out to disturb the crystal surface of the sea with a hand trailing from the car, this is one of the most beautiful trips in Europe. However, with sharp drop-offs, series upon series of sharp curves, numerous slow-moving trucks, and many hot-headed car drivers, it's also known by many as the most dangerous road on the continent.

Exploring Rijeka

Numbers in the text correspond to numbers in the margin and on the Rijeka map.

The *Turisticka magistrala* (Tourist Route) will guide you on foot around Rijeka's main sights, many of which are labeled with plaques. The **Kvarner Tourist Guide Association** (✉ Zrinskog ☎ 051/217–714) can provide you with an official guide.

★ ❶ **City Market.** A set of five turn-of-the-20th-century halls host the city's main market, one of the liveliest spots in Rijeka on a weekday or Saturday morning. Get here before midday to enjoy the trading in full-cry. The original constructions from the 1880s have suffered a little from later additions, but the fish market, the last to be built, is a wonderful example of art-nouveau design. The castings by well-known Venetian artist Urbano Bottasso ape the fish and crustaceans being sold below. The streets surrounding the market are filled with no-frills eateries that are good for a quick lunch. It's a good bet that their offerings will be fresh. ✉ *Verdieva.*

❼ **Crkva Uznesenja Blažene Djevice Marije i Kositoranj** (Church of St. Mary of the Assumption). Formerly the city's main church and dating back to the Middle Ages, St. Mary's is still known to locals as the "big church." However, many additions and changes now obscure much of the original architecture. The relatively recent updates have not imposed severe geometry, though: the bell tower remains leaning to one side by 40 centimeters or so. Presently undergoing renovation, the interior is stuffed with baroque stucco work. We advise examining it during the spectacle of mass. ✉ *Pavla Rittera Vitezovica 3* ☎ *051/214–177* ⊙ *Daily 8–noon and 4:30–6:30.*

❽ **Guvernerova palača** (The Governor's Palace). High on a hill, the palace affords a grand view over the harbor from all the front windows, from its gardens, and from the approach. Built in 1893 by Alajos Hauszmann, who also worked on Budapest's castle and Palace of Justice for the then-governor of Hungary, the building itself is no eyesore either. The large columned facade communicates the self-confidence of the robust Habsburg empire, as do the numerous statues placed throughout its grounds. The **Maritime & Historical Museum of the Croatian Littoral,** which investigates the Kvarner's seafaring traditions and the region's cultural heritage from both the Mediterranean and Central Europe, is housed here. You can also admire the rest of the interior while viewing a temporary exhibition in the atrium or attending a meeting or concert in the impressive Marble Hall. ✉ *Muzejski trg 1* ☎ *051/213–578* ⊕ *www.ppmhp.hr* ⊙ *Tues.–Fri. 9–8, Sat. 9–1* 🎫 *10 Kn.*

❷ **Hrvatsko narodno kazalište Ivan pl. Zajc** (Croatian National Theatre Ivan Zajc). Designed by specialist Viennese architects Fellner and Helmer, Rijeka's National Theatre introduced the city to the lightbulb in 1885. In high summer, the theater plays host to a Festival of Summer Nights held beneath wonderful ceiling paintings by Gustav Klimt and emerging from behind a stage curtain decorated by an artist from the island of

Rijeka

STARI GRAD

trg Bastihanova
Brajšina
Laginjina
Pomerio
Žrtava fašizma
Grohivca
Dolec
trg Republike
Riva
Ivana Zajca
Verdieva
Vodovodna
Franie Račkog
Boškar
Šatalište Joakima Rakocca
Trsatske stube Petra Kružića
Bulevar Oslopodenja
Šatalište I Gorana Kocač
Kužanićeva
Strassmayerova
S. Cindrića
Fiumara
Mrtvi Kanal
Riecina

Krk. However, you'll have to buy a ticket to a performance to see the inside of the theater. ⊠ *Verdijeva ulica 5a* ☎ *051/355–900.*

⑥ Katedrala sv. Vida (St. Vitus's Cathedral). Unusual in this part of the world, the church centers on a rotunda, although numerous additions and mixtures of style blunt its effect on the onlooker. Fine baroque statues are sheltered by baroque and Gothic construction. Founded by the Jesuits in 1638, the cathedral was named for Rijeka's patron saint. An 18th-century gallery was reportedly built to protect young novice monks from the tempting sights presented when the local lovelies attended services. At the main entrance you can find a cannonball in the wall, apparently sent from a British ship during the Napoleonic wars. ⊠ *Grivica 11* ☎ *051/330–897.*

⑨ Muzej grada Rijeke (The Museum of the City of Rijeka). Found in a cube-shaped building on the grounds of the Governor's Palace, the museum has eleven collections but does not have a permanent exhibit. There's always a mix of military artifacts along with cultural and scientific displays. Temporary exhibits can be interesting. ⊠ *Muzejski trg 1/1* ☎ *051/336–711* ⊙ *Weekdays 10 AM–1 PM* ⊠ *10 Kn.*

★ ⑩ Prirodoslovni muzej (Natural History Museum). Exploring the geology and biology of the region invariably involves holding a sizable chunk of marine life up to the eyes. The shark and ray display here is predictably popular, starring a brigade of stuffed sharks swimming in strict formation while suspended from the ceiling. A multimedia center based on an aquarium adds to the extensive collection of non-mammalian species, which boasts 90,000 specimens in total, but includes rocks, plants, and other less animated elements of the locality. Opened in 2005, a botanical garden contributes more exotic plants to the array from the museum's grounds. Considering the fearsome appearance of some of the more fascinating inhabitants of the museum, it may be worth considering putting off a visit here until the end of your stay on the coast, lest your imagination get the better of you while bathing off the beaches. ⊠ *Lorenzov prolaz 1* ☎ *051/553–669* ⊕ *www.prirodoslovni.com* ⊠ *10 Kn* ⊙ *Mon.–Sat. 9–7, Sun. 9–3.*

⑤ Stara Vrata/Kasnoantički kastrum 4st (The Roman Gate and Remains of the 4th-Century Roman Praetorium). Enter this patch of ground from Trg Ivana Koblera by passing through the oldest structure in the city. The enormous stone arch is partly engulfed by additions from more recent times, but it was from this site many centuries ago that the chain of mountain fortresses in the region was commanded by the Romans. These days, the Roman elite's enthusiasm for comfort is catered to with a handful of park benches amidst what is left of the ancient walls and columns. ⊠ *Trg Ivana Koblera.*

③ Sveučilišna knjižnica Rijeka (University Library). Formerly a school, the University Library now houses a permanent exhibition about the Glagolitic script. Stone tablets written in the ancient Slavic script, including the important Baška tablet from Krk, are the stars. Books, paintings, masonry, and frescoes are also present. Call in advance to view the exhibition. ⊠ *Dolac 1* ☎ *051/336–129* ✆ *Free* ☉ *Mon. and Thurs. 2–7; Tues., Wed., and Fri. 10–2.*

❹ Trg Rijecke rezolucije (Rijeka Resolution Square). The buildings housing the **municipal palace** were originally part of an Augustine monastery, and they connect to St. Jerome's Church. Named for the resolution that was drawn up here in 1905—and which contributed to the formation of Yugoslavia—-the square's lemon-meringue buildings cluster around the foot of the city **flagpole,** erected on a high base in the 16th century and featuring a likeness of the city's patron saint, St. Vitus, holding a scale model of Rijeka protectively in his hand.

⓫ Trsat (Trsat Castle). The medieval castle was built on the foundations
Fodor's Choice of a prehistoric fort. In the early 1800s, it was bought by an Austrian
★ general of Irish descent, who converted it into a kind of pre-Disneyland confection that even includes a Greek temple with Doric columns. Today it hosts a popular café, offering some stunning views of the Kvarner Bay; throughout the summer, open-air theater performances and concerts take place here. Across the street, the pilgrimage church of **Sveta Marija** (St. Mary) was constructed in 1453 to commemorate the Miracle of Trsat, when angels carrying the humble house of the Virgin Mary are said to have landed here. Although the angels later moved the house to Loreto in Italy, Trsat has remained a place of pilgrimage. The pilgrimage path up to Trsat begins in the city center, close to Titov trg, at a bridge across the Rječina. It passes through a stone gateway, then makes a long, steep climb up 538 steps. Local bus 1 will get you here, too. ⊠ *Frankopanski trg* ☎ *No phone* ✆ *10 Kn* ☉ *Apr.–Oct., Tues.–Sun. 9 AM–11 PM; Feb., Mar., Nov., and Dec., Tues.–Sun. 9 AM–3 PM.*

off the
beaten
path

KASTAV – One of the finest spots from which to peruse the splendors of the Kvarner bay is Kastav, 11 km (7 mi) northwest of Rijeka. Originally a medieval fortress comprising nine defensive towers, the hilltop village sits at 377 meters (1,237 feet) in elevation and is home to 900-some people. Without the crowds of Rijeka, you, along with city-residents that spend their leisure time here, can concentrate more properly on the quality of your relaxation. The local vintage, Kastavska Belica, is a decent white wine that is gulped merrily at Kastav Cultural Summer, a festival that celebrates the day of patron St. Helena (as featured on the coat of arms) on May 22. Having been home to wealthy and powerful clans in times past, the tiny town has many splendid—if not officially noted—buildings from throughout the ages.

Shopping

Appearance is of great importance to Croatians, and the local ladies will invariably be exhibiting style and glamour that may leave you wide-eyed. To provide a ready fashion fix, many hip little boutiques offer the latest styles in clothing and shoes that are imported from Italy for the most part. Prices are generally higher than what you'd pay in Italy, so unless you're caught short needing some posh clothes, it's better for your wallet to do your high-fashion shopping elsewhere. Concentrate instead on growing too big for the clothes you already own. The Korzo, a pedestrian strip that strides through the center of Rijeka, is the best place to go should you be unable to contain your shopping urges. Fresh local produce, fish, cheeses, olive oils, wines, and *rakijas* (fruit brandy) are the items that should be on your Kvarner shopping list.

The local City Market is on Verdieva. Although there are "professional" traders present, many of the stallholders are still locals, who bring their home-produced wares to sell. Noisy and colorful, Rijeka's central market is no exception. Locals gather here to haggle over fresh produce, swap gossip and, of course, drink coffee. Pick up a picnic lunch of cheeses, salads, fruit, and nuts here, and pop into one of the multitude of bakers to complete the feast. Although a little tricky to transport, a sample of rich local olive oil is usually a good buy as well. Smaller bottles of herb extracts and oils are a good alternative if your luggage is already tightly packed.

All things that glitter or smash easily are available at the **Mala galerija** (⊠ Užarska 25 ☎ 051/335–403 ⊕ www.mala-galerija.hr). Although not entirely exclusive to Rijeka (you'll find similar, if more ostentatious, artifacts in Venice), the *Morčić* is the figurehead of a Moor wearing a white turban and is associated with the luck that all seafarers rely on. This small shop has many items bearing the "little Moor." It's closed on Sunday.

Where to Eat

$$$–$$$$ ✕ **Kukuriku.** Here's one house in Kastav that is definitely worth a visit. Having been in the same family for over a century, this wonderful restaurant has walked off with many an award for select offerings from the inland menu of Croatia, including turkey hearts cooked in fruit brandy and lamb medallions in basil and olive oil. You are advised to wander onto the terrace, and to take the time to appreciate the chic, modern form of the dishes that still maintain traditions of taste and texture. ⊠ *Kastav 120, Kastav* ☎ *051/691* ⊟ *AE, DC, MC, V* ☾ *Closed Mon.*

★ $$$–$$$$ ✕ **Municipium.** Classic dining in a fine old house, this is Croatian cuisine, both fish and meat, at its finest. It's perhaps as upmarket as one can get in Rijeka. An extensive wine list concentrates on home produce. Perhaps without import taxes padding the produce bill, the prices could be a little more economical? ⊠ *Trg riječke rezolucije 5* ☎ *051/213–000* ⊟ *AE, DC, MC, V* ☾ *Closed Sun.*

$$–$$$$ ✕ **Feral.** This excellent seafood restaurant lies on a side road close to the main bus station. House specialties are *crni rižot* (cuttlefish-ink risotto), seafood tagliatelle, and *fuži* (fusilli) with asparagus and scampi. ⊠ *Matije Gupca 5b* ☎ *051/212–274* ⊟ *AE, DC, MC, V* ☾ *Closed Sun.*

$–$$ ✕ **Tre forze.** Fish for breakfast anyone? A fairly new, family-run restaurant down by the market is stuffed with solid wood tables and chairs and a no-nonsense approach to hearty and tasty fresh food. All homemade and respectful of the seasons, the menu is handy for a filling lunch when visiting the market or before embarking at the nearby ferry terminal. ⊠ *Verdieva 19a* ☎ *051/312–056* ☾ *No dinner Sun.*

Where to Stay

The selection of hotels in Rijeka reflects the city's status as a simple transit town. If you don't like the sound of any of these, then try asking about private rooms at the information center. At the time of this writing, this was a complete guide to Rijeka's hotel stock.

★ **$$$** ▥ **Hotel Bonavia.** In the city center, one block back from the Korzo, this modern, luxury high-rise reopened in 2000 after extensive renovations. Suitable for business travelers and tourists alike, all the comfortable rooms have specially designed furnishings and original oil paintings, lending a definite feeling of luxury. Those on the top two floors have balconies and views of Kvarner Bay. The restaurant has a sophisticated dining room with tables in the garden throughout summer. A limousine and chauffeur are at guests' disposal. ✉ *Dolac 4, 51000* ☎ *051/357–100* 🖷 *051/335–969* ⊕ *www.bonavia.hr* 🛏 *114 rooms, 7 suites* ⚘ *Restaurant, coffee shop, room service, minibars, cable TV, gym, 4 bars, in-room data ports, WiFi, convention center, car rental, parking (fee)* ▤ *AE, DC, MC, V* ⫯◎⫯ *BP.*

$ ▥ **Continental.** You won't get carried away by the luxury at this hotel that's right in the heart of the city. Although you're billeted in a grand old building with a view of the park and river, you should be in a grand old building with a view of the bay! Rooms are functional and reflect a lack of investment in the niceties, but that's just the way it went in the not-so-distant past. That said, the terrace here is a delight. ✉ *Šetalište Andrije Kačića-Miošiča 1, 51000* ☎ *051/372–008* 🖷 *051/372–009* ⊕ *www.jadran-hoteli.hr* 🛏 *38 rooms, 4 suites* ⚘ *Restaurant, coffee shop, bar* ▤ *AE, DC, MC, V* ⫯◎⫯ *CP.*

$ ▥ **Neboder.** A room in the upper portions of this white "skyscraper" offers decent views of the city and proximity to all of the city's attractions in the very center of Rijeka. Accommodation is simple, but these rooms will at least keep the rare Kvarner rains off your head. ✉ *Strossmayerova 1, 51000* ☎ *051/373–538* 🖷 *051/373–551* 🛏 *32 rooms* ⚘ *Restaurant, bar, parking (fee)* ▤ *AE, DC, MC, V* ⫯◎⫯ *CP.*

Nightlife & the Arts

For a month from toward the end of June, the annual **Rijeka's Summer Nights** festival ensures that venues, streets, and squares are filled with cultural performances. You can experience classical music and theater as well as contemporary theater and music, street theater, and musical-theatrical "happenings." In late winter, timed as for any other major festival celebrating the coming of spring, is the **Rijeka Festival,** when the streets of the city are taken over by crazy antics and costumes.

Perhaps best left for a night when you're feeling particularly energetic, **El Rio** (✉ Jadranski trg 4c ☎ 051/214–220), which plays host to Rijeka's younger crowd when they fancy a spot of karaoke or theme nights at the end of the Korzo. **Karolina,** (✉ Gat Karoline Riječke ☎ 051/330–909)An upmarket greenhouse right on the quay-side, serves cocktails and wines to the smart set as they watch the tide flow in and out of the bay. The center of alternative culture in the city, **Palach** (✉ Kružna ulica 6 ☎ 051/215–063 ⊕ www.mmc.hr) is a somewhat grotty space filled with exhibitions, performance, live music, and DJs on a regular basis. For those who might remember summer nights sitting on a terrace, drinking, dancing, chatting, and actually being able to hear what others are

★ saying, the **River Pub** (✉ Frana Supila 12 ☎ 051/213–406) is the place to make it all come back. The older crowd here suits many.

Sports & the Outdoors

Fishing

The Croatian coast is well known for its population of blue-fin tuna. You need a fishing license to hunt for any marine life using a line or gun. Prices start from 60 Kn per day. In Rijeka, licenses are available from the local office of the **Ministry of Agriculture, Forestry & Water Management** (✉ Demetrova 3 ☎ 051/214–877).

Hiking & Climbing

The mountains around Rijeka—and indeed throughout the Kvarner—are riddled with tracks with international signs. Many lovely starting spots can be reached by car. Relatively small and hospitable, close to civilization, and tucked beneath gentle skies, these mountains pose few dangers. However, if you do face an emergency, contact **Mountain Rescue Service** (☎ 92 for the local police, 985 for the information center).

★ **Ad natura** (✉ Mate Sušnja 12, Rijeka ☎ 091/590–7065) can help out if you want to do some exploring on two wheels, on foot, underground, on horseback, or above the clouds in Mount Učka Nature Park. At the **Kvarner County Mountaineering Association** (✉ Korzo 40/I ☎ 051/331–212) you can find information about routes and mountain huts for overnight tramps. But be prompt; they're only open on Tuesday and Friday evenings between 6 and 8 PM.

RISNJAK NATIONAL PARK

⑫ *37 km (23 mi) northeast of Rijeka.*

The northern outpost of the voraciously forested and karst-peaked Gorski kotar region, Veliki Risnjak is the major peak in this national park, peering over Rijeka from 1,528 meters (5,013 feet). The thick pine-forest meadows that are stuffed with wild flowers in the spring, and limestone peaks, crevices, and caves cover around 30 square-km (12 square mi).

In winter, you'll find a healthy contingent of skiers desperately trying to avoid a trip up to Austria to sample the real thing. In summer however, as the sun and the tourists beat down upon the coast, this is perhaps the best place to be. The cooling mountain air—the average temperature in these heights in July is around 12°C (53°F)—is a bonus to Risnjak's virtually deserted landscape.

You'll be free to commune with the locals, which include deer, bear, wildcat, and lynx (*ris*), from which the park takes its name. Geologic and botanical features are occasionally explained by English-language information points over which you may stumble on one of the more popular walking routes. Marked trails can occupy you for an hour's evening stroll to a full seven-day trek on the monstrous Rijeka Mountain Transversal from one side of Gorski kotar to the other. Hiking huts are strung across the peaks to accommodate such ambitious expeditions. More information regarding these multiday hiking trips is available from the Kvarner County Mountaineering Association (*see* Hiking & Climbing *in* Sports & Sports, *above*). For those of a gentler disposition, there's a month-long dandelion-picking contest in May.

The park information office is in the village of Crni lug, at the eastern entrance to the park; in the off-season, from October through April, you can pick up information at the reception desk of the Motel Risnjak (open 7 AM–10 PM). You can easily explore the gentler trails on day trips from either Rijeka or Delnice. Paths from the villages of Razloge and Kupari lead up to the source of the wild Kupa River, which can then be followed down the slopes through the "Valley of the Butterflies." ✉ *Bijela vodica 48, Crni lug* ☎ *051/836–133* ⊕ *www.risnjak.hr* 🎟 *Free* ⊘ *Park information office May–Sept., daily 9–5.*

OPATIJA

⓭ *15 km (9 mi) west of Rijeka.*

In the late 19th century, Opatija (Abbazia in Italian) was among the most elegant and fashionable resorts in Europe. Its history dates from the 1840s, when villas were built for members of minor royalty. In 1882 the start of rail service from Vienna and Budapest, along with an aggressive publicity campaign, put Abbazia on the tourist map as a spa of the first magnitude. With the high mineral content of the sea water, iodine in the air, and an annual average of 2,230 hours of sunshine, it qualified as a top-rated climatic health resort and emerged as a favorite wintering spot for Central European nobility and high society.

A hint of the formality that shrouded Opatija in its heyday still survives; the narrow pines and grand buildings remind one of the Italian lakes. This means that many visitors from all over Europe continue to head to the Opatija Riviera in the summer. At the same time, this stretch of coast has not gone unnoticed by the locals. Until recent years, the town was a weekend haunt for some younger, motorized Rijeka citizens. Thanks to these driving forces, the upmarket hotel guests still share the resort with some of the region's more upwardly mobile restaurants. However, their number is dwindling, while the town's once admirable nightlife has packed up and headed back to the cooler parts of Rijeka, leaving Opatija to wealthy and more elderly visitors from the surrounding countries. These guests seem more eager to sip the waters than wine and spirits.

The main street, ulica Maršala Tita, runs parallel to the coast for the length of town, and you can go from one end of town to the other on foot in about half an hour, passing numerous terrace cafés along the way. The best seafood restaurants are in the neighboring fishing village of Volosko, a 15-minute walk along the seafront.

The mild climate year-round and resulting subtropical vegetation, frequently sunny skies, and shelter from cold north winds provided by Mt. Učka give Opatija pleasant weather for much of the year. In summer, fresh sea breezes tend to dispel any oppressive heat, making the city an ideal seaside resort.

What to See

★ If you enjoy walking by the sea, set off along the magnificent paved, waterfront **Lungomare**. Built in 1889, this 12-km (7½-mi) path leads from the fishing village of Volosko, through Opatija—passing in front of old hotels, parks, and gardens and around yacht basins—and all the way past the villages of Ičići and Ika to Lovran in the south. In the midst you'll find the popular town beach that fronts the center of Opatija. Close to many cafés, ice-cream shops, and other essentials, the beach also has a couple of protected sections of water for safe swimming. These would be handy for kids if it wasn't for the fact that the concrete sides and underwater steps feature extremely sharp stones that can slice skin quite nastily if met with sufficient force. ⊠ *Obalno Šetalište Franza Josefa.*

The grounds of **Park Angiolina** are a wonderful spread of palm-punctuated lawns with a botanical garden. The vegetation is strikingly lush, including cacti, bamboo, and magnolia, plus neatly kept beds of colorful flowers and sweet-scented shrubs. Indeed, Opatija as a whole is a town saturated with botanical splendor. Iginio Scarpa, a Rijekan aristocrat and the first settler in Opatija, began importing exotic plants, and the tradition has survived into the present. The Camellia is the symbol of the city. ⊠ *Between Maršala Tita and the seafront* ▨ *Free* ⊙ *Tues.–Sun. sunrise–sunset.*

From gentle hiking to mountain biking, climbing and paragliding, all are available in the 160 square km of **Mount Učka Nature Park,** a series of peaks that help shelter the Liburnia Riviera (which is actually the official name for the stretch of coast centered on Opatija) and the islands from weather systems to the north. Paths toward the summit of the range start in all the resorts along the coast. A climb up to the highest peak, Vojak (1,401 meters [4,596 feet]), with a fine stone lookout tower at its summit, can be well worth it, particularly on a clear day. The view offers a cheap (but somewhat distant) tour of the islands of Kvarner Bay, the Italian Alps, and perhaps even an indistinct version of Venice. Most routes up to the heights lead through forest, so you can make the trek in summer without overheating. Along the way you'll find natural springs from which to quench your thirst, along with lakes, ponds, tumbling waterfalls (in the wetter months), impressive natural stone columns and several hundred caves. The local inhabitants include deer, wild boar and, in the northernmost sections of the park, bears. Humans have been living in these hills for centuries also, rearing cattle, farming, and working the forest; you'll come across numerous tiny villages and historic sites if you roam far enough. If you're running short of time, there are many mountain biking tracks throughout the park offering the chance to expand your lungs on the way up and test your nerve rattling back down to the coast.

Where to Eat

$$$–$$$$ ✕ **Le Mandrac.** The latest restaurant to make a splash on the coast has
Fodor'sChoice a glassed terrace for winter dining. Veering from arrogant to charm-
★ ing, self-depreciating humor in the same sentence, the service here is
certainly sure of itself. The proprietors claim that the menus (the choice
is between traditional or avant-garde) change with the seasons and their
whims. Voted the second-best restaurant in the country by a national
newspaper, this is the best example of Opatija's latest application to
join the "elite" of Europe. ✉ *Supilova obala 12, Volosko* ☎ *051/701–
357* ☱ *AE, DC, MC, V.*

$$$–$$$$ ✕ **Plavi Podrum** Although this is one of the more traditional fish restau-
rants in Volosko, don't be fooled into thinking it's not classy. The owner
was "Sommelier of the Year" twice in this young century. All the usuals
are cooked excellently here for you, but *jaja od hobotnice* ("octopus egg")
is a house special featuring squid, octopus, caviar, mustard, and fresh
spinach. The terrace is a little more relaxed than inside. ✉ *Obala Frana
Supila 12, Volosko* ☎ *051/701–223* ☱ *AE, DC, MC, V.*

$–$$$ ✕ **Istranka.** With a delightful covered terrace flanked by a twisting
tree, this small restaurant is the best option for those who are not the
greatest fans of seafood (although if that's you, what you're doing in
Kvarner is a mystery). Taking its influence from the neighboring region
of Istria, the menu concentrates more on landlubber food: hams,
cheeses, and of course, the famous Istrian truffle! ✉ *Bože Milanoviča
2, Opatija* ☎ *051/271–835.*

Where to Stay

$–$$ 🏨 **Grand Hotel Kvarner-Amalia.** The former summer residence of Euro-
pean royalty, Kvarner's oldest hotel first opened its doors to guests in
1884. More suited to sedentary tourists than business travelers, it's a
grand neoclassical-style building with peaceful gardens and a terrace overlooking the sea, close to Villa Angelina. The Crystal Ballroom is used
for the annual Miss Croatia contest. ✉ *Park Tomašica 1–4, 51410*
☎ *051/271–233* 🖨 *051/271–202* ⊕ *www.liburnia.hr* ➥ *86 rooms*
♨ *Restaurant, café, room service, minibars, outdoor pool, indoor saltwater pool, massage, sauna, beach, bar, convention center, parking (fee)*
☱ *AE, DC, MC, V* ⑩ *BP.*

$–$$ 🏨 **Millennium.** On the coastal promenade, this bright pink villa is part
old and part new. Rooms are furnished accordingly, with either Louis
XV–style antiques—with most everything heavily striped in silk—or modern designer pieces. There's a pleasant café terrace overlooking the sea,
as well as outstanding beauty, fitness, and business facilities. ✉ *Maršala
Tita 109, 51410* ☎ *051/202–000* 🖨 *051/271–812* ⊕ *www.ugohoteli.
hr* ➥ *129 rooms* ♨ *Restaurant, café, room service, minibars, indoor-
outdoor pool, gym, hot tub, massage, sauna, Turkish bath, bar, shops,
in-room data ports, business services, meeting rooms, parking (fee)*
☱ *AE, DC, MC, V.*

★ **¢–$** 🏨 **Hotel Opatija.** A prime location, elegant surroundings, and helpful ser-
vice are rare at this price level; to have them all, along with something
left over in your wallet is extraordinary. Part of the Vienna International

chain, this huge villa at the top of a park in the center of town is perfectly located. It was originally a spa and sanatorium when it was built in the late 19th century. Now, guests relax on the terrace, which with almost comfortable, post-modern sofas, is a delight. There is a €10 per-night supplement for the use of air-conditioning. ⊠ *Gortanov trg 2/1, 51410* ☎ *051/271–388* 🖷 *051/271–317* ⊕ *www.hotel-opatija.com* ❥ *216 rooms* ♨ *Restaurant, café, room service, minibars, indoor pool, hot tub, massage, sauna, bar, shops, Internet, business services, meeting rooms, parking (fee); some rooms without air conditioning* ▤ *AE, DC, MC, V.*

Nightlife & the Arts

There was a time when folk from Rijeka used Opatija as their playground; then, the town offered superb nightlife options. These days however, the big city along the coast is reclaiming its post as the cultural hotspot of the region, and Opatija has been busy transforming itself back into Central and Eastern Europe's health resort. The wealthy, older Italians and Austrians that dominate here have done little to inspire energetic evenings.

Hemingway (⊠ Zert 2 ☎ 051/711–205 ⊕ www.hemingway.hr), a Croatian chain of cocktail bars for the upwardly mobile, is spreading across the country and tends to thrust its nose in the air wherever it goes. Pack your wallet with at least one gold card if you're planning on gaining entry to "the elite" bar in this most elite of resorts. Wood is big here, and it gives a warmer feel than might be expected amongst the dressed-up clientele. The two floors offer a rainbow of cocktail choices on three terraces, including one up on the roof that spies down on the small harbor. Right ★ on the main road that winds through town along the seafront, **Monokini** (⊠ Marčala Tita 96 ☎ 051/703–888) has a shaded, street-side terrace with plenty of comfortable seating, whereas inside all is funky and modern. You'll find good music, a friendly staff, loads of computers for Internet access, good drinks and cocktails, and an atmosphere that invites locals to meet up here for a chat. A city museum is slated to fill the gorgeous pink **Villa Angiolina** (⊠ Park Angiolina 1 ☎ 051/711–124) in the botanical gardens. The neoclassic design both inside and out includes superb mosaic floors and frescos. The appeal of the building and grounds makes the local artists that display here brave souls indeed. At this writing, the gallery is open from 8 AM to 3 PM from June through September.

Sports & the Outdoors

Mount Učka Nature Park, accessible from virtually any point along the coast, offers the easiest opportunity for active exploring, including mountain-bike and hiking trails up through the forested slopes. **Ad Natura,** in nearby Rijeka, can help you explore (*see* Exploring Opatija, *above*.)

CRES

➓ *Brestova is 20 km (12 mi) south of Opatija, then a 20-minute ferry ride.*

Twisting down the entire length of the Kvarner Bay on its eastern side is Cres, whose latest claim to fame is that it is the largest of all Croatian islands. For many years, squat neighbor Krk was awarded this distinction, but recent re-calculations have rectified a long-standing error. Ferries to Cres take about 20 minutes, embarking from Brestova, which is on the mainland south of Opatija, to Porozina; another ferry goes from Valbiska on Krk to Merag, on the east side of Cres.

Cres has been known as one of the most unspoiled islands in the Adriatic for a long time. More difficult to get to than Krk or Rab, and with a wilder and more rugged geography, Cres is quite frankly a delight. Its natural stretches are punctuated with olive groves and tiny towns and villages that remain authentic for the most part. Even in the capital, Cres Town, you'll find older inhabitants that struggle to speak Croatian, having been brought up under the much stronger Italian influence.

What to See

Fodor'sChoice
★

The northern end of the island is mountainous and forested, harboring wildlife such as the rare griffin vulture. **Eco-Center Caput Insulae–Beli** is run by the organization that helps protect these (in truth, pretty ugly) beasts, as well as the environment and heritage of the island. Two small exhibitions concentrate on the biodiversity and the history of northern Cres, and the center can also give you information on bird-watching and eco-trails. ⊠ *Beli 4, Beli* ☎ *051/840–525* ⊕ *www.caput-insulae.com.*

Cres Town is found tucked into a well-protected bay, midway down the island. Set around a lovely little fishing harbor, the town is small but perfectly formed, with numerous Gothic and Renaissance churches, monasteries, and palaces. For the most part these are in the Old Town, which sits protected by winged Venetian lions atop three 16th-century gates, the only remains of a defensive wall. Developed under Venetian rule, the present-day Renaissance appearance of the town is due to a reconstruction in 1552.

The **town beach,** at Kovačine campsite, holds a Blue Flag award for cleanliness. To get there, follow the path around the harbor from the main road and keep going for at least 15 minutes along the promenade, where you'll find spots to jump into the water and the odd café or restaurant to keep you fueled. Although the seaside here is man-made, for the most part it somehow doesn't detract too much from the experience.

Across the bay from Cres, the village of **Valun** has a nice beach. The town's claim to fame is the "Valun Tablet," a gravestone that is the oldest known example of Glagolitic script. The tablet is now kept in the Parish Church, right on the waterfront. Get to Valun by car or by taking the wooden boat that sits just outside the Cres Harbor wall; it's easily spotted from the main square.

The **Alan Excursion Boat** (⊠ Cres Harbor ☎ 051/571–070) is a wooden sailing ship offering differing routes around the island's coast. A trip to Valun costs 80 Kn, with an additional 50 Kn if you'd like a meal on your journey. The ship offers regularly scheduled sailings.

One of the most tempting beaches on the island is on the western coast of Cres at the foot of a steep cliff, at the top of which is the tiny village of **Lubenice,** which offers great views out to sea and up the western coast. This picturesque collection of houses that surround the 15th-century Church of St. Anthony the Hermit has been clinging to its outcrop for around 4000 years. The hamlet is popular amongst arty-types and hosts exhibitions and music performances in the summer. From the beach below, a short walk through vineyards will bring you to Žanja Cove, which has a blue grotto, a cave at water level that enjoys brilliant blue light as strong sunlight filters through the azure water.

At the southwestern tip of Cres is the town of **Osor,** whose strategic position on the channel between the island and Lošinj ensured that wealth flowed into the town from trade ships. A tour of the town makes for a pleasant afternoon. Reflecting its former status, there's even a cathedral, and many important archaeological sites have been discovered in the vicinity.The **Osor Archaeological Collection** houses booty from throughout the ages, including artifacts from across the Roman empire. ⊠ *Gradska vijecnica* ☎ *051/237–346* ◨ *8 Kn* ☉ *Apr.–Sept., daily 10 AM–noon and 7–9 PM; Oct.–Mar. by appointment only.*

Where to Eat

★ **$$–$$$$** ✕ **Hibernica.** A nice little terrace right by the bell tower in the heart of the stone hilltop town is the perfect location for a light lunch of *pršut* (prosciutto), cheese, olives, and a glass of local wine. ⊠ *Lubenice 17, Lubenice* ☎ *051/840–422* ▭ *No credit cards* ☉ *Closed Oct.–Apr.*

$$–$$$$ ✕ **Konoba Bonifačić.** The subtitle on the road signs reads *nonina kuhinja* (granny's cooking), and you were a spoiled child indeed if your grandma turned out dishes of this standard for you. The shady garden in the heart of ancient Osor is a perfect setting in which to enjoy the typical plates of the Konoba: meat, seafood, pasta, and salads. ⊠ *Osor 64, Osor* ☎ *051/237–413* ▭ *AE, DC, V.*

$$–$$$$ ✕ **Konoba Toš.** The terrace of this little konoba celebrates the famous Valun Tablet, which was discovered just up the road. If you can't get to the real thing, then spend your time perusing the replica inscriptions in the walls here. The lamb *ispod peke,* which means it stews for hours under a metal top resembling nothing more than the lid of a garbage can, is superb, although you have to order it a day in advance. ⊠ *Valun* ☎ *051/525–084* ▭ *AE, DC, V* ☉ *Closed Oct.–Apr.*

$$–$$$$ ✕ **Riva.** The colorful square on the edge of Cres Town harbor is lined with many restaurants serving seafood, pasta, and risotto. Riva is an excellent choice, although many of the alternative options are perfectly decent also. Tables edge out onto the flagstones of the square, meaning the steady stream of strollers through the town will eye your plate with appreciative glances. A good selection of shellfish is up for grabs, including the seafood spaghetti, which is wonderful. It's a good idea to reserve a table in the evenings. ⊠ *Riva creskih kapetana 13, Cres Town* ☎ *051/571–107* ▭ *No credit cards.*

Where to Stay

Reflecting its splendid, undeveloped nature, Cres offers very few hotels, though there are plenty of apartments and guest rooms available for rent on the island. A good place to start a search for private accommodation is **Autotrans Rijeka Office Cres** (✉ Zazid 4, Cres Town ☎ 051/572–050 ⊕ www.autotrans.hr), whose Web site offers a long list of options and who will look after all details. Note that the office is only open from May through September.

$$–$$$ 🏨 **Zlatni lav.** A delightful 20-minute drive south from Cres Town, in the small, west coast resort of Martinšćica, Zlatni lav is a large, new building. Rooms look across 100 meters of land to the Adriatic. The clean lines of the interior are granted a little more character by nicely designed features such as funky modernist stairs, but keep a close eye on younger children in their vicinity. ✉ *Martinšćica 18d, Martinšćica, 51556* ☎ *051/574–020* 🖶 *051/574–034* ⊕ *www.hotel-zlatni-lav.com* ⇨ *25 rooms, 5 suites* ⚐ *Restaurant, refrigerators, cable TV, bar, parking* ☰ *AE, DC, MC, V* ⦿ *BP.*

$ 🏨 **Hotel Kimen.** Submerged in a shady pine forest just a stone's throw from the town beach and a 10-minute walk from the center, Kimen's six stories provide the only hotel accommodation in Cres Town. Built in the 1970s, Kimen is not the most glamorous hotel, but its clean, straight lines are perfectly functional. The location does much to compensate for any small annoyances, but you'll hardly need to spend any time actually at the hotel anyway. ✉ *Melin 1, Cres Town 51557* ☎ *051/571–161* 🖶 *051/571–163* ⊕ *www.hotel-kimen.com* ⇨ *212 rooms* ⚐ *Restaurant, bar, parking, pets allowed (fee); no a/c, no TV in some rooms* ☰ *AE, DC, MC, V* ⦿ *BP.*

Sports & the Outdoors

Cycling
Camp Kovačine (✉ Melin 1, Cres Town ☎ 051/573–150 ⊕ www.camp-kovacine.com) is nicely set out under shady pines and right on the main town beach. The staff can rent you bikes and boats, organize diving trips, beach volley ball, and even paragliding.

Diving
If you prefer to explore underneath the waves **Diving Cres** (✉ Cres Town ☎ 051/571–706) can be found on the town beach, about a 10-minute walk from the harbor. A single orientation dive can be tried for €5.

LOŠINJ

⑮ *Mali Losinj is 26 km (16 mi) from Cres Town.*

As you approach the southern tip of Cres, you get a taste of what might be called the "diet version" of the Mediterranean climate. By the time you arrive in Lošinj, you've got a full-blooded version on your hands. Sheltered from poor weather by the Alps and closer ranges such as the Velebit, the excellent climate prompted the creation of a health resort here in 1892.

Blink and you might miss the bridge that connects Cres to Lošinj, unless you happen to arrive when the span is raised to allow a ship through the narrow channel that splits the two islands. In fact, until Roman times the two islands were one, connected near Osor. Mother Nature's inconsiderate arrangement did much to frustrate trade ships; entire vessels would be hauled across the few feet of land that blocked the route here rather than sail around the southern tip of the Apsyrdites archipelago. Eventually, some bright spark decided to cut the present-day channel, opening the shipping lanes.

Lošinj is an elongated, low-lying island covered with a pine forest. Viewed from the hills of Cres, the slim green outline of the main island and its surrounding islets, with a backbone of hills in the middle, resembles a long frog splayed out in the water, basking in the sun and contrasting beautifully with the water.

Lošinj's past and present are very much connected to the shipping industry. The sea captains who populated the towns of Veli and Mali Lošinj, when the island reached its golden age in the 19th century, are very much responsible for bringing exotic plant life here from around the world and for building the fine villas that have made this a colorful destination for vacationers, who contribute much more to the island's economy today.

The smaller islands that make up the Apsyrdites archipelago include Unije, Susak, and Ilovik—all of which are large enough to provide some type of accommodation—and even smaller islands such as Vele and Male Srakane, Orjule, Oruda, and Sveti Petar, which can be reached by tourist boats from the resorts on Lošinj.

What to See

With 6,500 inhabitants sheltered around an inlet, **Mali Lošinj** is the largest island settlement in the Adriatic. In the 19th century, Mali and Veli Lošinj experienced a golden age, when many wealthy sea captains lived on the island. Brightening the waterfront, the mansions and villas they constructed contribute greatly to the towns' appeal. A long tradition of tourism means that you'll find a healthy selection to choose from. A number of attractive churches will catch your gaze as you wander around town. Somewhat scruffy and announcing its presence with a tall, square tower that tapers to a spike at the summit, the 15th-century **St. Martin's Church** was the original centerpiece around which the town was built. The cemetery it lords over amalgamates much of the history of the town. If you wish to dig a bit deeper, **The Church of the Little Lady** hosts many fine examples of religious art.

The sea captains of **Veli Lošinj** evidently preferred to escape their working environment during their time off, and thus built their villas away from the waterfront, surrounding themselves with exotic plants brought back from their travels. Archduke Karl Stephen built a winter residence in Veli Lošinj; it's now a sanatorium surrounded by wonderful gardens, again with a range of exotic plants, and an arboretum. It's possible to stay in the sanatorium, even for the healthy, but we can't recommend the option until some serious cash is invested in reconstructing it.

A short walk beyond the main harbor is the little fishing cove of Rovenska. Beyond, there's a pebble beach and some nice restaurants. The breakwater was established by Habsburg Archduke Maximilian. Walking in the other direction brings you to a great rocky Blue Flag beach, where water-sports equipment can be rented in the Hotel Punta complex.

The intimate harbor is the centerpiece of Veli Lošinj, at the entrance to which is the delightful **Church of St. Anthony the Hermit,** with a separate bell tower in pink and cream stone. Built on the site of a former church in 1774, the church has always had a congregation of seafarers, who have filled it with religious art and altars from spots such as Venice. ✉ *On the Veli Lošinj waterfront* 🕾 *No phone* 🕙 *June–Sept., daily 10–noon and 7–9. Mass Sun. and holidays at 10.*

Opposite the harbor, but now hidden by a row of houses, are the battlements of a defensive tower, which dates from 1455. The squat construction, known as the **Venetian Tower,** now houses an art gallery with a collection of European art from the 17th and 18th centuries, as well as displays on town history and a copy of a Greek statue of Apoxiomen, which was discovered on the sea bed in 1999. ✉ *Kaštel 2* 🕾 *051/231–173* 💳 *8 Kn* 🕙 *June–Sept., daily 10–noon and 7–9 PM.*

A community of around 150 bottle-nosed dolphins make their home just off the coast of Lošinj. Locals claim that their choice of habitat here proves how clean the waters are in the area. The nonprofit **Lošinj Marine Education Centre** will tell you all about the bottle-nosed dolphins cruising just off the coast. Excellent displays and videos take you right into their underwater world. This is fascinating stuff for kids and adults alike. You may even end up adopting your own dolphin, although you can't take it home with you. For a mere 200 Kn you'll receive a bundle of stuff such as certificates and T-shirts and, of course, that warm fuzzy feeling of doing something good for the world. The best bit is that you'll be able to visit your newfound family member in his or her natural environment every time you swing through town. (He or she will laugh at you, of course.) ✉ *Kaštel 24, Veli Lošinj* 🕾 *051/604–666.*

Where to Eat

★ **$$–$$$$** ✕ **Baracuda.** Many of the yachts that line the harbor unload their human cargo at this small restaurant that enjoys a big reputation for fresh fish dinners. Tuna carpaccio, shark on the grill, and lobster *na buzaru* (cooked with wine) are all great. The occasional land-based course, such as pork medallions with asparagus, invades the lively and leafy terrace from time to time. Baracuda's size, matched with its good name, make an early arrival or a reservation advisable. ✉ *Priko 31, Mali Lošinj* 🕾 *051/233–309* 💳 *No credit cards* 🕙 *Closed Oct.–Apr.*

$$–$$$$
Fodor'sChoice
★
✕ **Bora Bar.** To help keep you entertained and for your convenience, the collection of Austrian performing-arts professionals that run this seaside restaurant offer books to read, Internet access, modern art from local artists, and even mooring services for boats. Breakfasts are movie-themed; an "Audrey Hepburn" offers a figure-conscious bowl of muesli with fruit, yogurt, and juice, while an "Al Capone" is a fear-inducing steak on toast with a glass of red wine. For effortless cool get the "Marcello Mastroianni," an espresso and a cigarette. Great lunchtime salads

CloseUp
WHEN IT ALL GETS TOO MUCH

IF THE PACE OF LIFE ON THE MAJOR ISLANDS IS TOO HECTIC, knock your engine down to quarter-speed and head out to one of the tiny islands that pepper the seas around the coast of Lošinj. The island of **Unije** is by far the largest, managing to fit in a population of 81, although many of them are summer-only residents. The tiny town of the same name has a handful of restaurants settled around a large pebble bay, although exploring the northern coasts, by foot or by boat, should reveal many private swimming spots.

Ilovik is the southernmost island of the group. Its nickname, "island of flowers," is accurate; oleander and roses surround almost every home. Watch yachts at close quarters cutting through the channel between Ilovik and the islet of Sveti Petar, on which there was once a convent. The graveyard remains, and burial processions by fishing boat still take

place. Parzine, on the southeastern coast, has a large sandy beach.

If you're from New Jersey, you may have a good chance of being related to one of the 188 people living on **Susak** since many folk from here have settled in the Garden State. Susak, flung farther out into the sea than any of the other islands, is a very different beast. First, while the rest of the Kvarner is composed of limestone karst, Susak consists entirely of sand, so its coast is far gentler both in elevation and indentation. Not wanting to be outdone, the population retain a distinctive character and culture. Their dialect is difficult for other Croats to follow, while it's not uncommon to spot women in full folk costume. The only wheeled transport on the island are wheelbarrows.

join pasta, fish, and meat on the menu. Creative presentation is central here. ⊠ *Rovenska, Veli Lošinj* ☎ *051/867–544* ▭ *AE, MC, V* ☉ *Closed Nov.–Easter.*

$$–$$$$ ✕ **Konoba Lanterna.** From this former lighthouse, which is in a working-class district by the seashore, you'll see (and hear) boats being mended. The tiny stone building has the feel of an old pub inside, and the terrace is pleasant and down to earth. You are likely to be joining a crowd of mostly elderly gents from the locality. But who cares that the clientele isn't so glamorous when you can enjoy tasty traditional food such as baked fish, or sausages cooked in wine? ⊠ *Sveti Martin 71, Mali Lošinj* ☎ *051/233–625* ▭ *AE, DC, MC, V* ☉ *Closed Oct.–Apr.*

★ **$$–$$$$** ✕ **Sirius.** This is definitely the place to go on Lošinj if you want a classic, high-quality Croatian seafood meal. The national press claim that it would be considered one of the best eateries in the whole country if it were open year-round. The terrace, looking onto the lazy little harbor that was once Veli Lošinj's fishing harbor, has a smart nautical theme with navy tablecloths and striped seats. The dining room is patrolled by a friendly and efficient crew, and the reputation for fresh seafood is well-deserved. ⊠ *Rovenska 4, Veli Lošinj* ☎ *051/236–399* ▭ *AE, DC, MC, V* ☉ *Closed Oct.–Apr.*

Where to Stay

★ **$$$$** ⊞ **Hotel Apoksiomen.** Named after a Greek statue that was recovered from the seabed near Mali Lošinj in 1999, this renovated magnolia-shaded villa imposes itself on the seafront close to the main square in Mali Lošinj and offers a good example of how to run a small, family-run establishment. Spick and span, the inside shines almost too brightly with polished marble. Rooms are comfortable and protected from noise on the busy seafront side by double-glazed windows, though the decor may seem a bit pedestrian compared with the promise of the exterior. The staff is efficient and ever eager to please. Free parking is 100 meters from the hotel, and guests get a card that allows them to drive into the center of town. ⊠ *Riva Lošinjskih kapetana 1, Mali Lošinj 51550* ☎ *051/520–820* 🖷 *051/520–830* ⊕ *www.apoksiomen.com* ➩ *24 rooms, 1 suite* ⚐ *Minibars, in-room safes, cable TV, in-room data ports, free parking* ☰ *AE, DC, MC, V* ⊙ *Closed Oct.–Apr.* �ⵙ *BP.*

$–$$ ⊞ **Villa Favorita/Residence Villa Jelena.** This lovely, historically protected
Fodor'sChoice Austro-Hungarian villa has been beautifully renovated and furnished in
★ traditional style, with wooden floors in the restaurant and rooms. Rooms offer all almost anything you might want; those in Jelena are simpler but still excellent. Luxuriating in its own gardens, the Villa and accompanying residence are protected from the hoi polloi by impressive wrought-iron fences, literally a stone's throw from the Veli Žal beach in Sunćana Uvala, a large bay, five minutes' drive from the center of Mali Lošinj. This rocky Blue Flag beach is shaded by pine trees that bring relief on hot summer afternoons. This complex is the best on the island for those who demand proximity to a family seaside facility. The restaurant with its lovely terrace overlooks the seawater swimming pool in the gardens. ⊠ *Sunćana uvala, Mali Lošinj 51553* ☎ *051/520–640 or 051/520–641* 🖷 *051/232–853* ⊕ *www.villafavorita.hr* ➩ *8 rooms* ⚐ *Restaurant, minibars, in-room safes, cable TV, Internet, pool, massage, sauna, beach, parking* ☰ *AE, DC, MC, V* ⊙ *Closed Oct.–Apr.* ⵙ *MAP.*

$ ⊞ **Hotel Punta** Punta is a cheaper option in Veli Lošinj that still offers a Blue Flag beach and a wellness center. Attractive, colored blocks line the seashore in a style that complements the old architecture of the island surprisingly well. Best (but most expensive) are the modern apartments filled with modern furnishings that open onto large balconies. Cool blue hotel rooms are simpler (and older) but perfectly acceptable, again offering balconies and sea views for the most part. A fish restaurant is on a terrace just above the beach, and a swimming pool is nearby; the terrace becomes a disco with live music in the evening and hosts children's activities during the day. The wellness center—with full facilities—is possibly the best feature, especially given Veli Lošinj's tradition as a convalescent center. ⊠ *Veli Lošinj, 51550* ☎ *051/662–000* 🖷 *51/236–301* ⊕ *www.jadranka.hr* ➩ *181 rooms, 53 apartments* ⚐ *2 restaurants, café, some kitchens, some refrigerators, cable TV, 2 pools (1 indoor), 14 tennis courts, gym, hair salon, spa, bar, beach, dive shop, jet skiing, waterskiing, bicycles, shops, children's programs (ages 4–12), recreation room, car rental, parking* ☰ *AE, DC, MC, V* ⊙ *Closed Oct.–Apr.* ⵙ *MAP.*

Sports & the Outdoors

Biking

Sanmar Tourist Agency (✉ Priko 24, Mali Lošinj ☎ 051/238–293) rents bikes for 100 Kn per day.

Diving & Sailing

Diver Sport Center (✉ Uvala Cikat 13, Mali Lošinj ☎ 051/233–900 ⊕ www.diver.hr) offers a three-day course (three hours per day, but no certification) for €110, but an orientation dive costs a whopping €50! The same center offers two- to seven-day cruises on a wooden ship with seven air-conditioned cabins starting at €240.

Flightseeing

To put it all in perspective, from **Airport Lošinj** (✉ Privlaka, Mali Lošinj ☎ 051/235–148 ⊕ www.airportmalilosinj.hr), you can take a panoramic flight over the archipelago (15 minutes for 420 Kn), or if you're in a hurry, you can take a taxi flight to destinations across Croatia or even Italy (Rome costs €705 + VAT) or Germany (Frankfurt costs €1,344 + VAT), amongst others. Most useful of the lot may be a quick lift to spend the day on the tiny island of Unije; flights to the small island leave at 8:15 AM on Monday, Wednesday, and Friday, and cost 120 Kn per person. The airport is open from March through October.

KRK

Krk Town is 53 km (33 mi southeast of Rijeka).

It's no surprise—since Krk is one of the largest Croatian islands, hosts the regional airport, and is connected to the mainland by a bridge—that the robust island is one of the most developed in the country. The dusty edges and agricultural interior get very busy during the high season, and if you visit then, you will likely find yourself in traffic jams along the snaking routes between the resort towns. Add the sight of the oil refinery on the mainland near the bridge and the terminal for tankers near Omišalj on the northern coast of the island, and you may think twice about heading here. The sights aren't exactly what you'd call picturesque. Don't be put off so easily. Krk still offers many of the same delights found in the rest of the region: great beaches, interesting history, and pretty old towns. Although other islands may offer a slower pace, Krk compensates by offering more facilities and convenience. With numerous accommodation options and more entertainments, it may very well be the best choice for families that have easily-bored children in tow.

Exploring Krk

Numbers in the text correspond to numbers in the margin and on the Krk map.

 Krk Town. In terms of its importance and the pride of the 3,000 locals, the island's capital could perhaps even be called a city. The old city walls were built by the Liburnians around the 1st century BC, and there's an

Krk Town

KORALJA → HOTEL

Narodnog preporoda

Aloizija Stepinca

Galija

Frankopanska

Obrodak Puntarske

N.U.I. Agronkin

Dr. Dinka Vitezića

Petra Žgaljića

Veli dvor

Trg Krčkih glagoljaša

Josipa Križanića

Stjepana Radića

Vinogradska

Ivana Zajca

Ivana Zajca

Kralja Tomaslava

Ivana Mažuranića

Kralja Tomaslava

Slavka Nikolića

Citadel

Trg Kamplin

Istarska

J Strossmajera

Josipa

Trg Sv. Kvirina

Matije Gupca

St. Quiriaus Cathedral

Ribarska

Old Town Hall

Obala H.R. mornarice

Trg Bana J Jelačića

Šetalište Sv. Bernardina

Obala H.R. mornarice

Bodulka

Braće Juras

Draga Genaisa

Slavka Nikolića

Kružni Tok

inscription speaking of the dimensions of the fortifications at that time (111 feet long and 20 feet high). The present-day walls, however, date mainly to the Middle Ages. The city walls have four gates bearing plaques of Saint Quiriunus, the protector of the town.

The seafront has a pleasant green area that takes you past cafés and a fish market. The main square, **Vela Placa,** is just behind the first row of houses. There's a beach underneath the town walls with a lovely view of the town.

The **old town hall** on Vela Placa was built by the Venetians in the late 16th century. Its clock shows all 24 hours: daytime on the upper part, nighttime on the lower.

Krk Town has two well-known visual anchors. The first is the imposing **citadel** that sits on Trg Kamplin. Summer concerts, theater performances, and a jazz festival are held on the square and within the citadel walls. The bell tower of **St. Quirinus** is the other, with its angular onion dome typical of Krk.

Here's a useful tip: Streets that are thoroughfares have a straight line of stones running down the middle; those without are most likely dead ends.

need a break?   **Stanic** is a wonderful gallery choc-a-bloc with works by local artists, as well as books and souvenirs. If you're not into shopping, you can simply remain downstairs at the café–bar, or the many other watering holes around Vela Placa. ✉ *Vela Placa* ☎ *051/220–052.*

Vrbnik. Lovers of majestic views or high-diving should head to the cliff-top town on the northeast coast. Clustered on a hilltop 48 meters above a small harbor, it's a mass of confusing, winding streets. Happily, as in Krk Town, you can simply follow the lines set in the streets. The bumpy terrain means that staircases crop up around most corners. One of the oldest settlements on Krk, Vrbnik may be a little ramshackle, but it's utterly charming, That's certainly what the busloads of tourists seem to think anyway. Vrbnik's fragrance is of the vine; you'll see old barrels laying around everywhere. These might once have been filled with Žlahtina, a great white wine that some claim is the best to come from the Kvarner region. The vineyards are but a short hop from town, near the picturesque village of Dobrinj.

Biserujka Cave. North of Vrbnik, near Rudine, this cave is only one of many caverns on Krk; however, it's the only one open to the public. The stalactites, stalagmites, and calcine pillars inside are lit for your pleasure. ✉ *½ km from Rudine* ☎ *098/326–203* 🎟 *15 Kn* 🕙 *Apr., May, and Oct., daily 10 AM–3 PM; June and Sept., daily 10 AM–5 PM; July and Aug., daily 10 AM–7 PM.*

Baška. On the southern end of the island, this town has a great beach as well as the conveniences of civilization. However, this naturally means that you must sometimes fight to find a spot in season. The 2-km (1-mi) beach is fronted by houses (and hotels at the southern end), which are often painted in bright colors and adorned with interesting nooks and stairways, all lending a fun and slightly eccentric air to the town. Cute backstreets behind the houses offer a selection of thirsty cafés and ice-cream shops.

Driving into Baška, you'll pass through Jurandvor and then find yourself in Baščanska draga. While on this road, take the chance to visit the ★ **Church of St. Lucy,** which has achieved cult-like status since the discovery of the glagolithic Baška Tablet on its grounds in 1851. ⊠ *Jurandvor* ☎ *051/860–184* ⊡ *12 Kn* ⊗ *Daily.*

Stara Baška. If you're looking for a more secluded spot, head to this town that sits just above the beaches that trim a wide cove and peninsula. The road here is single track through the tiny village, so you may find yourself performing intricate maneuvers in your car should you be unlucky enough to meet the local water truck that keeps the houses supplied.

Where to Eat

In the summer, you'll be sharing tables with busloads of tourists at many of Krk's best restaurants, all of which tend to be outside the capital. However, Krk Town has many restaurants that will serve you perfectly reasonable renditions of less ambitious fare, such as fish, pasta, and pizza.

★ **\$\$–\$\$\$\$** ✕ **Katunar.** The large, modern building is surrounded by vineyards on the approach to Vrbnik, and you come here as much for the wine as the food. Wines produced around Vrbnik are considered some of the best in Croatia. You can try *Vrbnicka žlahtina* here. *Biser mora* (sea pearl) is a light, semi-sparkling white, perfect for summer drinking. *Nigra* (a brand of syrah) is a full-bodied red wine ideal for easy drinking, while *porin* is dry and sparkling. All are well-priced here, cheaper than in shops. The restaurant offers both wine and rakija tasting, including brandy made from figs, which is very sweet. There's a shop and grill restaurant outside for visitors, which is an excellent choice at night, when it is lit by flaming torches. Call ahead to arrange a tour and a gastronomic accompaniment to your boozing. ⊠ *Sv. Nedilja, Vrbnik* ☎ *051/857–393* ☰ *AE, D, MC, V.*

\$\$–\$\$\$\$ ✕ **Nada.** Considered top-notch by many islanders and Croatians who know their stuff, the tiny downstairs konoba provides an authentic Croatian atmosphere. The large restaurant upstairs has much more space, although it's still quite cozy and traditional and offers a terrace with spectacular sea views. This is a great place to try Kvarner specialties. Of course, it's extremely popular, so definitely make a reservation if you choose to wade through the tour-bus crowds. ⊠ *Glavača 22, Vrbnik* ☎ *051/857–065* ☰ *AE, D, MC, V* ⊗ *Closed Oct.–Apr.*

★ **\$\$–\$\$\$\$** ✕ **Rivica** One of the best-known restaurants in the region, Rivica has a long tradition but lacks any sense of glitz. Try the *grdobina* (monk fish, which is cooked in local wine) while you sit on the terrace shaded from the sun. Should you demand that your dinner be extra special, ask the staff to recommend what's fresh in that day. ⊠ *Ribarska obala 13, Njivice* ☎ *No phone* ☰ *AE, D, MC, V* ⊗ *Closed Oct.–Apr.*

Where to Stay

☾ $$ 🏨 **Koralj.** For long days on the beach and all conveniences on tap, the Koralj is a decent choice, though it's on the edge of Krk Town, so if you plan busy evenings you may want to find somewhere closer to the center. Perched in the trees just above a tidy beach, the rooms are on the small side, but comfortable. Apartment suites on the ground floor have their own terraces, although promises of beach access mean little when there are no stairs between your terrace and the beach. Be aware of the extras that will be tacked onto the bill (balcony, insurance, etc.). There is a lot of entertainment for the kids, a definite plus for families. ⊠ *Ul. Vlade Tomašiča, Krk Town 51500* ☎ *051/655–400* 🖷 *051/655–410* ⊕ *www.zlatni-otok.hr* ⇌ *170 rooms, 20 apartments* ⚲ *Restaurant, in-room data ports, cable TV, pool, gym, beach, bar, children's programs (ages 4–12), laundry service, business services, Internet room, meeting rooms* ▤ *AE, D, MC, V* ☉ *Closed Dec.–Feb.* ⎮◎⎮ *CP.*

$ 🏨 **The Blue House.** As the island is heavily developed, hotels on Krk tend to be big and somewhat impersonal. For a little more soul, a private apartment is the best bet. This pastel-painted house offers a choice of three apartments, all with terraces looking out to Soline Bay, famous for its healthy mud (so expect to see people smothering themselves in the stuff on the beach). Down a rutted road-cum-track amid trees that reach down toward the water, the apartments are artistically adventurous in spots with bright colors dominating the sparingly furnished (in a good way) rooms. Dobrinj is possibly the most delightful old town in the region. ⊠ *Cizici 338 b, Dobrinj, 51500* ☎ *051/853–126* ⚒ *info@cizici.com* ⇌ *3 apartments* ⚲ *Cable TV, kitchens* ▤ *No credit cards* ☉ *Closed Nov.–Apr.*

$ 🏨 **Corinthia I.** This cheaper option in the busy Baška resort area might be better suited for families. Rooms at this large complex may not offer the most charm and character—unless you're enamored of standard late-1980s style furnishings—but they keep the rain off your head; those facing the sea offer a wonderful view of austere hills plunging into aqua-marine waters. Make sure you get a room with a balcony. If you can do without air-conditioning (not ideal in July or August) and an Internet connection in your room, then staying in the other parts of the complex (Corinthia II and III) can save you around 20% per person on accommodation costs. ⊠ *Emila Geistlicha 34, Baška 51523* ☎ *051/656–111* 🖷 *051/856–584* ⊕ *www.hotelibaska.hr* ⇌ *105 rooms, 13 suites* ⚲ *Restaurant, minibars, in-room safes, cable TV, pool, bar, in-room data ports* ▤ *AE, D, MC, V* ☉ *Closed Dec.–Mar.* ⎮◎⎮ *CP.*

Nightlife

Krk Town and Baška are the places to head for relatively low-key drinks in the evening. The center of the capital and the stretch of town above the beach at Baška offer numerous bars with music and tables out under the stars. A firm family favorite, Krk is definitely not the place for cutting-edge nightlife. However, if you really can't live without getting your club fix, there are a couple of large venues offering house DJs.

Cocktail Bar Volsonis (✉ Vela Placa 8, Krk Town ☎ 051/220–052) is one of the livelier nightspots in Krk Town. It's suitably, although somewhat mysteriously, symbolized by the remains of a wonderful sacrificial altar to love-goddess Venus down in the basement. **Discoclub Crossroads** (✉ Sveti Vid, Malinska ☎ No phone) hosts such shenanigans as foam parties and other sophisticated fun as well as international DJs and live bands. **Jungle Club** (✉ Stjepana Radica, Rab Town ☎ No phone) claims to be open from 10 PM to 5 AM every day, but clubbing all night is evidently too much for the staff, who sometimes just can't be bothered.

Sports & the Outdoors

Bicycling

You can bike around the island for transportation or exercise. The best place to rent a bicycle is at the **Hotel Punat** (✉ Obala 94, Punat ☎ 051/854–024).

Diving

The most interesting sights in Kvarner Bay are usually wrecks. At **Divesport** (✉ Dunat, Kornic ☎ 051/867–303 ⊕ www.divesport.de) on the Bay of Punta, a one-day diving course sets you back €26, including all the equipment you need.

Hiking

There are many marked paths in the area around Baška. For a longer hike, consider visiting the splendid remote villages at Vela and Mala Luka; take this path as part of a group, and be aware that the section of the trail through the canyon may flood if there's rain. For some nice hikes around Baška, consider the path from Baška to Mjesec Hill (5½ km [3 mi]/2 hours). Offering spectacular views over the bay, this easy route passes by St. John's Church, where you can take a breather while you contemplate higher things. The route from Baška to Jurandvor (5 km [3 mi]/2 hours) takes you through the Baška Valley and leaves you with a visit to the Church of St. Lucy, home of the Baška tablet. The short hike between Baška and Stara Baška will give you a little exercise; a delightful stretch of small, quiet beaches are the rewards for a short hike. For more hiking information, call **Krk Tourist Office** (☎ 051/ 856–817).

Waterskiing

Always fancied spraying majestic jets of water across the aqua-marine seas, but sorting out a boat and someone to drive just seems too much trouble? Well, the answer lies with **Cable Krk** (✉ Punat ☎ 091/262–7302 ⊕ www.waterski-krk.com), on a calm bay just outside the resort of Punat, between Krk Town and Stara Baška. A large wooden pier with a bar and restaurant to entertain your companions is the gateway to a cableway, which is not much different than a drag-lift at a ski resort. The cable pulls you around a short course, with tuition on hand to help you get your sea-legs. Four circuits cost 30 Kn.

DELNICE

⑰ *45 km (28 mi)east of Rijeka.*

Delnice, which sits on the road between Rijeka and Zagreb, is itself not much to write home about. However, it makes a good base to explore the mountains of the Gorski kotar region that sits above Kvarner Bay. This is the place to head for hiking trails that swing away from civilization and other humans. It's also a convenient stopover should you not be in too much of a hurry to get back to Zagreb and your transport home. Take a day or two to swap the brilliant blue domination and ramshackle culture of the coast for the bright green mountains and hearty way of life in Gorski kotar.

Where to Eat

$$–$$$$ ✕ **Volta.** The small town of Fužine is very close to Delnice and is well-known for its pine-bordered lake. *Volta,* which means vaults, tells you exactly what to expect from this vaulted, cellar-style dining room, fronted by a conservatory. The pub-like simple interior is a cut above most of the restaurants in the Gorski Kotar, which tend to be a little old-fashioned. Try the pasta with truffles or snail risotto; the house specialty is horsemeat, from which they even produce *čevapčići* (spiced meat rolled into sausage shapes and grilled), but you don't have to go there. A long list of Croatian wines rounds things off. ⊠ *Franja Račkog 8, Fužine* ☎ *051/830–030 or 051/830–035* ☰ *AE, DC, MC, V.*

Where to Stay

$ 🏨 **Hotel Risnjak.** This modern hunting lodge is unlikely to have seen too many genuine mountain men. Still, rooms are nicely appointed, displaying the more robust character of inland Croatia despite being situated just a short hop over the mountaintops from the Adriatic. ⊠ *Lujzinska, 51300* ☎ *051/812–184* 🖶 *051/847–140* 🛏 *20 rooms* ♿ *Restaurant, bar, gym, laundry service, playground* ☰ *AE, DC, MC, V* ❏ *CP.*

Sports & the Outdoors

Hiking

Delnice is a good base for hiking around Risnjak and Gorski Kotar range, which have many marked walking and hiking paths.

Rafting & Canoeing

The Kupa River either meanders or rushes down through the mountains toward the coast. You can join expeditions organized by **Outdoor Centar Kupa** (⊠ Zrinska 13, Brod na Kupi ☎ 051/837–139 ⊕ www.foris.hr), which start out at 10 AM or 3 PM from a point near Delnice that tackle the rough or the smooth sections of the river. The company also runs canyoning trips, in case you want to omit the boat portion of the exercise.

RAB

Jablanac is 100 km (62½ mi) south of Rijeka; then take the ferry 1½ nautical mi to Mišnjak, 9 km (6 mi) from the town of Rab.

Rab presents an utterly schizophrenic landscape. When you drive southward, down the Magistrala, you see that the island resembles the humped back of a diving sea monster. Once you've mounted this beast, via a short ferry ride from Jablanac to Mišnjak, you travel along the center of its back, which is almost entirely bald to the north, letting all its hair hang out to the south. The high northern coast, which bears the brunt of the northern Bora winds, is dry, rocky, and barren. Crouching below this crusty ledge, the southern half of the island could hardly differ more, and has possibly the lushest terrain found on any Croatian island. Low, green hills dip into the seas, while the ancient Dundo forest grows so voraciously that it's almost impossible to walk in.

Exploring Rab

Numbers in the text correspond to numbers in the margin and on the Rab map.

⑱ Barbat. The first town you'll come to on the southern coast of Rab after leaving Mišnjak feels more like a collection of houses, shops, and restaurants spread across the green slopes, despite being the site of a Benedictine Abby dating back to the 11th century. Nowadays, you'll find many modern houses, surrounded by terraces and colorful gardens, offering rooms and apartments at good rates. For a short stay of a just a handful of days, this could be a good place to plant yourself. The strip of path that constitutes a promenade ambles, rather than parades, past cafés, bars, and restaurants on one side and a narrow beach facing the green hillock that is the islet of Dolin across a channel on the other. Between Barbat and the ferry port on Puderica Beach, all-night parties are usually on the bill for those with the energy.

⑲ Rab Town. Sitting on a narrow peninsula halfway up the island's southern coast, the compact, well-preserved medieval village is best known for its distinctive skyline of four elegant bell towers. Closed to traffic, the narrow cobbled streets of the old town, which are lined with Romanesque churches and patrician palaces, can be explored in an hour's leisurely stroll. The urban layout is simple: three longitudinal streets run parallel to the waterfront promenade and are linked together by steep passages traversing the hillside. The lower street is Donja ulica, the middle street Srednja ulica, and the upper street Gornji ulica.

The tallest and most beautiful of Rab's campaniles, the freestanding **Veli Zvonik** (Great Bell Tower) forms part of the former cathedral complex and dominates the southwest side of the peninsula. Built in the 12th century, it stands 85 feet high. A climb to the top offers breathtaking views over the town and sea. ⊠ *Gornja ulica* 🖅 *5 Kn* ☉ *Daily 10 AM–1 PM and 5 PM–8 PM.*

Rab Town

KEY
- **1** Exploring Sights
- **①** Hotels & Restaurants

Velebitski Kanal

Goli

Lopar **20**

Supetarska Draga

Rab **19**

Barbat **18**

Dolin

TO JABLANAC →

Paski Kanal

Pag

Kampor

TO BASKA ↑

Gradska luka

Uvala Sveta Eufemija

KALDANAC

Samostan Sv. Antuna Opata

Sveta Marija Velika

Veli zvonik

Ivana Rabjanina

Put Kaldanca

Gornana

Radnička

Samostan Sv. Andrije

Trg Slobode

Stjepana Radića

Trg Municipium Arba

Obala Kralja Petra Krešimira IV

Istarska

Slovenska

Primorska

Jadranska

Rade Končara (Gornja)

Ive Lole Ribara (Srednja)

Marka Oreškovića (Donja)

Dalmatinska

Bobotine

Velizvonik

Sv. Anton

Velika Palača Dominis Nimiva

Trg Sv. Kristofora

Šetalište Markatuna Dominisa

Osmog marta

①

KOMRČAR PARK

← TO SAMOSTAN SV. EUFEMIJA

0 ——— 1/8 mile
0 ——— 1/8 kilometer

②

③

On the edge of town, the green expanse of **Komrčar Park,** laid out in the 19th century, offers avenues lined with pine trees for gentle strolling and access down to the sea. Although the old town and its immediate surroundings are Rab's chief treasures, the city is also a gateway to the great stretches of beach that rim the towns of Kampor, Suha Punta, Lopar, and neighboring islands.

need a break? **Paradiso Gallery** (⊠ Stjepana Radiča 2 ☎ 051/777–157), tucked behind the town lodge, has a wonderful atrium brimming with stone columns and palms; it's ideal for a quick lunch or just a seat and coffee. Alternatively, peruse the gallery, or stock up on local wine.

20 Lopar. Traveling to the far end of Rab brings you to a perfectly pleasant tourist town that has a couple of interesting historical sights; however, the real draw is mainly the beaches. In high season, though, you'll be lucky to make it to the beach as you meet many cars and vacationers from nearby resorts. The search for a quieter spot can be rewarding in itself; the Lopar headland is covered with paths crossing areas of scrub and forest, where you can get to all kinds of beaches. On the east side of the peninsula is **Rajska Plaža** (Paradise Beach), with the San Marino tourist complex and the location of the first Naturist Holiday Camp, which opened in 1934. The beach is sandy, but the water is frustratingly shallow: you have to walk for what feels like many miles to get to deep water. This means it's great for kids, of course. If Lopar proves a little too busy, you can always jump onto a ferry to Baška on Krk.

Where to Eat

$$–$$$$ ✗ **Konoba Santa Maria.** Although the Medieval-palace setting may be a little much for some, it does offer spectacular seating, as you are perched in front of and upon massive wooden furniture in an old stone building in the heart of town. In the evening, the torch illuminations allow the background to take a backseat. Come for excellent meat and seafood dishes. ⊠ *Dinka Dokule 6, Rab Town* ☎ *051/724–196* ▤ *AE, DC, MC, V.*

$$–$$$ ✗ **Konoba Rab.** Tucked away in a narrow side street between Srednja ulica and Gornja ulica in Rab Town, this konoba is warm and inviting, with exposed-stone walls and rustic furniture. Barbecued fish and meat are the house specialties, along with a good choice of pastas and risottos. ⊠ *Kneza Branimira 3, Rab Town* ☎ *051/725–666* ▤ *AE, DC, MC, V.*

★ $$–$$$ ✗ **Zlatni Zlatag.** In Supertarska Draga, 10 km (6½ mi) from Rab Town, this restaurant is frequently mentioned as the best on the island. Nestled in a small bay and backed by Mediterranean woods, the restaurant and its summer terrace offer wonderful views of the sea. *Škampi i školjke Sv. Kristofor* (scampi and shells baked in béchamel sauce) is a favorite offering. The family that run "Golden Sunset"—and with the west-facing terrace, this is exactly what you'll see at the appropriate time—are well known for supporting Rab's traditional cuisine. Tradition is met with a smart and modern air-conditioned interior. ⊠ *Su-*

pertarska Draga 379, Supertarska Draga ☎ *051/775–150* ▭ *AE, DC, MC, V* ⊘ *Closed Jan.*

Where to Stay

You'll see plenty of private rooms advertised on the Internet, as well as signs on the side of the road. If you want to seek out private accommodations, perhaps the best place to start is the Web site of the tourist office in the closest main town. Costs vary wildly, but private rooms are almost always a cheaper alternative to hotels.

$ ⌸ **Hotel Imperial.** On the edge of the old town amid the greenery of Komrčar Park, this peaceful 1930s-era resort hotel has excellent sports facilities and a beach. Suffering a little from a lack of investment, the Imperial clearly displays its socialist-era past. However, the setting, an admirable villa in a richly scented forest park, just a stone's throw from the center of Rab Town, atones for many sins. Certainly not glamorous, it's functional and trying hard. Rooms are modern and comfortable, offering either seaside or parkside views. ⊠ *Palit, Rab Town 51280* ☎ *051/724–522* 🖷 *051/724–126* ⊕ *www.imperial.hr* ⇗ *134 rooms* ♨ *Restaurant, café, room service, minibars, miniature golf, 3 tennis courts, gym, sauna, beach, bar* ▭ *AE, DC, MC, V* ⊘ *Closed Jan.–Mar.* ⑩ *MAP.*

♨ **$** ⌸ **Hotel Village San Marino.** A complex of five hotels stretches across the peninsula at this family-friendly resort wrapping around the gentle Paradise Beach. The focus here is on activities, ensuring that the kids are never at a loss for something to do. Expect the appropriate crowds in high season. Rooms are on the small side, and lack many luxuries, but they offer good value all the same. ⊠ *Lopar, Lopar, 51281* ☎ *051/775–144* 🖷 *051/775–128* ⊕ *www.imperial.hr* ♨ *Restaurant, café, miniature golf, 8 tennis courts, pool, beach, basketball, soccer, volleyball, table tennis, bar, shops, disco; no room TVs* ▭ *AE, DC, MC, V* ⊘ *Closed Nov.–Mar.* ⑩ *MAP.*

Nightlife

For such a small town, Rab has a surprisingly lively nightlife, although it's certainly not extreme by any length of the imagination. Trg Municipium Arbe on the waterfront is lined with bars and can get noisy as the night progresses; they're mostly anchored by troops of waiters with some attitude as well as a habit of setting drinks on fire when they're not throwing them around. All-night house parties are found at Santos Beach Club on Puderica Beach, 2 km (1 mi) from Barbat toward the ferry terminal. Buses to Puderica leave Rab Town every hour 10 AM onwards. **Café Bar Amadeus** (⊠ Biskupa Draga 25, Rab Town ☎ No phone) is a hilariously tiny bar, short on luxury but with no lack of entertainment, stuffed as it is with local fishermen pogoing to 1980s Croatian hard rock. Those after a little glitz to show off their suntan can head to the center of Rab Town nightlife at **San Antonio** (⊠ Trg Municipium Arba 4, Rab Town ☎ 051/724–145). The club is open until 4 AM.

Sports & the Outdoors

Boating

Travel Agency Kristofor (⊠ Poslovni centar, Mali Palit, Rab Town ☏ 051/ 725–543 ⊕ www.kristofor.hr) can satisfy most of your wishes, including motor-boat rentals so you can explore the coast and use it as your own private diving board. Prices start at €89 per day.

Diving

At **Aqua Sport** (⊠ Supetarska Draga 331, Supetarska Draga ☏ 051/776– 145) a single dive costs €35, a full diving course €290. In addition, you can dive at various sites from their boat, and your nondiving companions are welcome to go along for the ride.

KVARNER ESSENTIALS

BOAT & FERRY TRAVEL

During high season (July through August), Jadrolinija ferries travel between Dubrovnik and Rijeka (journey time approximately 20 hours), stopping at Zadar, Split, Stari Grad (island of Hvar), Korčula, and Sobra (island of Mljet) en route. During the rest of the year, the service is less frequent. The fare between Dubrovnik and Rijeka is 277 Kn for a reclining seat or 956 Kn to travel in your own two-berth cabin with bathroom and TV. In good weather you'll find the rear decks of the ship smothered with passengers camping out beneath the stars, which lends the journey a special atmosphere. Cars cost 614 Kn. Round-trip tickets save 20%.

Hourly on the half-hour, ferries leave Brestova, which is south of Opatija, heading to Cres; these ferries arrive at Porozina. Ferries also leave Valibska on Krk to dock at Merag on Cres. Each brief hop across the channel sets you back 14 Kn per person, 99 Kn if you have a car.

Every day in high season, ferries leave Rijeka at 5 PM to call at Ilovik, Susak, Unije, Cres, and Mali Lošinj; the entire trip from Rijeka to Mali Lošinj takes around four hours. Meanwhile, a catamaran service heads out to Rab at 4 PM, drops into the northern-Dalmatian island of Pag, and then pulls into Mali Lošinj about two-and-a-half-hours later. Six times per day from 6 AM to 6 PM, ferries head out from Baška on Krk toward Lopar on Rab. The trip costs 35 Kn, 206 Kn for a car.

Tourist boats and water taxis offering transport on shorter stretches are also abundant at many resorts.

🚺 Jadrolinija ☏ 051/211-444 ⊕ www.jadrolinija.hr.

BUS TRAVEL

There's daily international bus service to Rijeka from Italy (Trieste), Slovenia (Ljubljana and Nova Gorica), and Germany (Dortmund, Frankfurt, Munich, and Stuttgart). You can also reach destinations all over mainland Croatia from Rijeka and Opatija. Timetable information is available from the Rijeka Bus Station.

Buses travel from Rijeka to all the major towns on the mainland and the islands at least once a day. If you're traveling independently, you'll find that buses to the various islands are roughly scheduled to tie in with ferry services.

⚡ Rijeka Bus Station ✉ Žabica 1, Rijeka ☎ 051/211-222.

CAR TRAVEL

Although local buses and ferries are an excellent, stress-free method of touring the region (buses are scheduled in tandem with the docking of ferries, so don't fear that you'll be left stranded at an empty dock), touring the Kvarner by car does offer the opportunity to nose your way around some of the smaller and more remote villages on the islands and up in the mountains. In addition, despite a poor safety record and heavy traffic in high season, there are few roads more scenic than the Magistrala. A car is also useful if you plan to leave Kvarner and head for Istria (passing through the Učka Tunnel). However, good train and bus services to Zagreb and a comfortable overnight ferry to Dalmatia mean that a vehicle is not really essential for moving on to other areas.

⚡ Car Rentals Avis ✉ Riva 22, Rijeka ☎ 051/337-917.

EMERGENCIES

⚡ Ambulance Ambulance ☎ 94.

⚡ Doctors & Dentists Hitno Ponoč (Casualty) ✉ Krešimirova 42, Rijeka ☎ 051/658-111.

⚡ Fire Fire Emergencies ☎ 93.

⚡ Pharmacies 24-hour Pharmacy ✉ Jadranski trg 1, Rijeka ☎ 051/213-101.

⚡ Police Police Emergencies ☎ 92.

INTERNET

Internet cafés are common at the resorts on both the mainland and the islands. That said, they may not contain many terminals, so you may find yourself with plenty of time to relax, sip a coffee, and enjoy the wait to spend your 20 to 30 Kn per hour.

⚡ Ecom Club ✉ Ivana Zajca 24A, Rijeka ☎ 051/333-070. **Inter Club Cont** ✉ Šetalište A. Kacica Miošica 1, Rijeka ☎ 051/371-630 ⊕ www.interclub-cont.com charges 12 Kn for 15 minutes. **Internet Krk sistemi** ✉ Šetalište sv. Bernardina 3, Krk Town ☎ 051/222-999 ⊕ www.krksistemi.hr. **Grafit Dizajn Studio** ✉ Bocac 46, Mali Lošinj ☎ 051/233-495 ⊕ www.grafit-studio.hr charges 25 Kn per hour. **VIP Internet Corner** ✉ Hotel Padova, Banjol, Rab Town ☎ 051/724-54. **Monokini** ✉ Marčala Tita 96, Opatija ☎ 051/703-888. **Turisticka agencija Croatia** ✉ Cons 10, Cres Town ☎ 051/573-053.

MAIL & SHIPPING

Opening times listed are for the main tourist season; hours will be reduced from November through April. All are closed on Sunday unless otherwise indicated.

⚡ Rijeka Post Office ✉ Korzo 13, Rijeka ☎ 051/525-515 is open Mon.-Sat. 7 AM-9 PM, Sun. 7 AM-2 PM. **Opatija Post Office** ✉ Mašala Tita 145, Opatija ☎ 051/271-512 is open weekdays 7:30 AM-9 PM, and Sat. 8 AM-noon and 6-9 PM. **Cres Post Office** ✉ Cons 3, Cres Town ☎ 051/571-155 is open Mon.-Sat. 8 AM-noon and 6-9 PM. **Krk Post Office** ✉ Bodulska, Krk Town ☎ 051/221-138 is open weekdays 7:30 AM-9 PM, Sat. 8 AM-noon and 6-9 PM. **Losinj Post Office** ✉ Vladimira Gortana 4, Mali Lošinj ☎ 051/231-263 is open weekdays 7:30 AM-9 PM, Sat. 8 AM-noon and 6-9 PM. **Rab** ✉ Palit 67, Rab Town ☎ 051/724-312 is open weekdays 7:30 AM-9 PM, Sat. 8 AM-noon and 6-9 PM.

MONEY MATTERS

On the islands, bank branches can be found in the respective capitals. ATMs are numerous and easily found in many locations, save the smallest villages.

🖪 **Hypo Alpe Adria** ⊠ Jadranski trg 3, Rijeka ☎ 051/660-444. **Privredna banka Zagreb** ⊠ Maršala Tita 136/4, Opatija ☎ 051/706-405. **Volksbank** ⊠ Riva 8, Rijeka ☎ 051/339-670.

TRAIN TRAVEL

There are five trains daily from Rijeka to Zagreb (journey time is approximately 3½ hours).

🖪 **Rijeka Train Station** ⊠ Krešimirova 5, Rijeka ☎ 051/213-333.

VISITOR INFORMATION

🖪 **Cres Tourist Information** ⊠ Cons 10, Cres Town ☎ 051/571-535 ⊕ www.tzg-cres. hr. **Krk Tourist Information** ⊠ Vela placa 1/1, Krk Town ☎ 051/222-583 ⊕ www.tz-krk.hr. **Lošinj Tourist Information** ⊠ Riva lošinjskih kapetana 29, Mali Lošinj ☎ 051/231-884 ⊕ www.tz-malilosinj.hr. **Opatija Tourist Information** ⊠ Vladimira Nazora 3, Opatija ☎ 051/271-710 ⊕ www.opatija-tourism.hr. **Rab Tourist Information** ⊠ Donja ul. 2, Rab Town ☎ 051/724-064 ⊕ www.tzg-rab.hr. **Rijeka Tourist Information** ⊠ Uzarska 14, Rijeka ☎ 051/213-145 ⊕ www.tz-rijeka.hr.

Zadar & Northern Dalmatia

5

WORD OF MOUTH

"I stayed in Zadar last year and really enjoyed it . . . St. Donat and the reliquary at Sv. Marija Benedictine monastery are a must."

—Carta_Pisana

"Kornati Islands trip is a must! It's a beautiful national park."   —Marko C.

"I have been many times on Murter . . . Sv. Andrija is a small beach and in the afternoon, the sun gets behind the pine trees. . . . You can walk along the coast all the way from Sveti Andrija to the neighboring village of Jezera. Along the way there are perfect spots for swimming and sunbathing . . . Generally, it is a much more peaceful island than Hvar or Brac."

—Jonas

By Paul
Olchváry

Where exactly does Northern Dalmatia begin? Zadar may be the region's cultural and urban capital—it is, after all, the first sizeable city you encounter in Dalmatia on your way south from Zagreb or Rijeka—but it is not where the region begins, either culturally or geographically. Look instead to the southern reaches of the Velebit mountains, where that coastal range gives way to the flat, sandy coastline of Nin and environs. When you cross the long, bright-red span of the Maslenica Bridge going south, you enter Dalmatia.

Though it's easy enough to drive on straight to Zadar, don't neglect Nin, today an unassuming little town with a well-preserved 17th-century face; however, more than 1,000 years ago—and for centuries afterward—it was one of the most important Croatian towns of all. Much of the region is not on the mainland at all but rather comprises both the Zadar archipelago (which marks the region's northern border with the open sea) and, further south, the Adriatic's largest archipelago, Kornati National Park. Further inland, only miles from the coast, is a sweeping expanse of countryside still visibly recovering from the Yugoslav war of the 1990s, where tourists rarely tread. Benkovac, the region's center, is home to an imposing 16th-century fort; nearby are the massive ruins of the ancient city of Asseria, as well as a budding effort to promote "agrotourism." Zadar itself, with its mix of Roman, Venetian, Communist-era, and modern architecture, has a bustling and beautiful historic center and is also the main point of access by ferry to the islands, which include the beautiful Telašćica Nature Park.

Exploring Northern Dalmatia

If you're driving or bussing it from Zagreb or further north along the coast (e.g., Rijeka or even Istria), it is convenient to stop at Paklenica National Park before arriving in Zadar. Or else, if you plan to go further south after Zadar toward Split and Dubrovnik and want to spend more time there, you may want to save Paklenica for your return journey if time allows. The pretty little town of Nin, meanwhile, is just a half-hour north of Zadar and most easily done as a day-trip (or even a half-day trip) from there. Though many daily ferries can take you to the Zadar archipelago, Sali (two hours from Zadar by ferry) is a good place to base yourself for a night or two if you want to explore the outer reaches and have the best access to Telašćica Nature Park. A drive or bus trip to Murter will get you within a short boat ride of the spectacular Kornati National Park.

About the Restaurants

Fresh seafood is the cuisine of choice in Northern Dalmatia, as it is elsewhere on Croatia's coast. However, fine cuisine is harder to come by than in regions long accustomed to the tourist trade. Beyond standard coastal fare, look for Dalmatian specialties including lamb from the island of Pag, prosciutto and *šokol* (smoked pork neck) from Posedarjedried, as well as sheep's cheese and peppery meat dishes from inner Dalmatia and as far afield as Bosnia. All this is not to mention Zadar's famous Maraschino liqueur—compliments of the area's uniquely zesty cherry and the Maraška company—whose facility is just across the pedestrian bridge and whose brand name graces the bottles of the best maraschino.

WHAT IT COSTS in Croatian Kuna (Kn)				
	$$$$	**$$$**	**$$**	**$**	**¢**
RESTAURANTS	over 80	60–80	35–60	20–35	under 20

Restaurant prices are per person for a main course at dinner.

About the Hotels

As elsewhere along practically every populated area of the Croatian coast, package-hotel resorts are easy to find, in particular in the Borik complex on the northern outskirts of Zadar. Top-notch pensions and intimate, elegant small hotels are in somewhat short supply, though a whole host of private rooms and apartments can be found, often for half the price of larger, more established accommodations, either through the local tourist-information office or through private travel agencies. And, as per practice in other parts of Croatia, short stays (i.e., less than three days) often mean a surcharge of around 20%.

WHAT IT COSTS in euros (€) and Croatian kuna (Kn)				
	$$$$	**$$$**	**$$**	**$**	**¢**
IN EUROS	over € 225	€175–€225	€125–€175	€75–€125	under €75
IN KUNA	over 1,650	1,300–1,650	925–1,300	550–925	under 550

Hotel prices are for two people in a double room in high season, excluding taxes and service charges.

Timing

If you don't mind crowds, mid-summer is a good time to visit Northern Dalmatia—when the Adriatic is at its optimal temperature for beach-going, and you can also delight in such events as the varied music, dance, and drama of the Zadar Summer Theatre (late June to early August), the Full Moon Festival (late July) in Zadar and environs, and Sali's annual Saljske užance, which features raucous, horn-blown "donkey music" and donkey races (early August). However, if you don't mind missing out on such mid-summer culture and crowds, late spring to early autumn (until around the end of September) is preferable—when you can relax on relatively quiet beaches and enjoy discounts of up to 20% on accommodations relative to high season prices.

Numbers in the margins correspond to numbers on the Northern Dalmatia and Zadar maps.

ZADAR

347 km (217 mi) southwest of Zagreb.

Dalmatia's onetime capital for more than 1,000 years, Zadar is all too often passed over by travelers on their way to Split or Dubrovnik. What they miss out on is a city of more than 73,000 that is remarkably lovely

5

Unless you stop at Paklenica National Park, head straight for Zadar and work outward from there, depending on how much time you have. It's easier to take day-trips to visit the closer parts of the Zadar archipelago, as well as Nin. To see the farther reaches of the archipelago, stay over in Sali. Keep Benkovac and environs in mind if you have some time to spare and might appreciate a look at the relatively tourist-free interior, including the ruins of the ancient city of Asseria.

If you have 3 days Plan on two nights in **Zadar** with excursions to the city of **Nin** and also to Ugljan Island, which is in the **Zadar archipelago.** For your final day and night, go either to **Sali** to see **Telaščica Nature Park** or, if you're hankering for mountains, spend one night in Starigrad and see **Paklevica National Park** (unless you've already stopped there on the way south or might do so on your return north).

If you have 5 days Spend your first three days as outlined in the three-day itinerary but spend the third night in Zadar. Then spend one night in Starigrad or environs to devote some quality time to Paklevica National Park and a night in Sali, too.

If you have 7 days Follow the itinerary above, adding a trip to **Murter** and perhaps inland, to Benkovac or, if you have a car, to the nearby ruins of the ancient city of Asseria (*see* CloseUp: "Benkovac, Truly Off the Beaten Path").

and lively despite—and, in some measure, because of—its tumultuous history. The Old Town, separated from the rest of the city on a peninsula some 4 km (2½ mi) long and just 500 meters (1,640 feet) wide, is bustling and beautiful: the marble pedestrian streets are replete with Roman ruins, medieval churches, palaces, museums, archives, and libraries. Parts of the new town are comparatively dreary, a testament to what a world war followed by decades of Communism, not to mention a civil war, can do to the architecture of a city that is 3,000 years old.

A settlement had already existed on the site of the present-day city for some 2,000 years when Rome finally conquered Zadar in the 1st century BC; the foundations of the forum can be seen today. Before the Romans came the Liburnians had made it a key center for trade with the Greeks and Romans for 800 years. In the 3rd century BC the Romans began to seriously pester the Liburnians but required two centuries to bring the area under their control. During the Byzantine era, Zadar became the capital of Dalmatia, and this period saw the construction of its most famous church, the 9th-century St. Donat's Basilica. It remained the region's foremost city through the ensuing centuries. The city then experienced successive onslaughts and occupations—both long and short—by the Osogoths, the Croatian-Hungarian kings, the Venetians, the Turks, the Habsburgs, the French, the Habsburgs again, and finally the Italians before becoming part of Yugoslavia and, in 1991, the independent republic of Croatia.

Northern Dalmatia

**HRVATSKA
(CROATIA)**

Adriatic Sea

Cres
Krk
Baška
TO↑
RIJEKA
Cres
Lopar
Rab
Starigrad
Žuta Lokva
Rakovica
Drežnik-Grad
Plitvice
Bihać
Otočac
Korenica
Perušić
Unije
Lošinj
Mali
Lošinj
Stara
Novalja
Pag
Gospić
Udbina
Karlobag
Medak
Bruvno
Pag
Barić-
Draga
Starigrad-
Paklenica
Rok
**Paklenica
National
Park** 18
Nin 12
Posedarje
Obrovač

Zadar
1 – 11
see detail
map

Novigrad

Dugi
Otok
Ugljan 15
Zemunik
Sukošan
Benkovac
Zadar Archipelago

Sali 13
Pašman
Filipjakov
Vrana
*Vransko
jezero*
Bribir
Skradin
**Telascica
Nature Park** 14
Pirovac
Lozovac
Kornat
Murter 16
Tijesno
Vodice
Šibenik
**Kornati
National
Park** 17
Primošten

TO
SPLIT

KEY
⊢——⊢ *Rail Lines*
🛥 *Ferry*

0   30 miles
0   30 kilometers

Zadar's Churches

Even discounting its size and the fact that 60% of the Zadar was destroyed in World War II, Zadar has an astonishing number of churches of key significance to Croatia and, more broadly, to Europe—from the Crkva sv. Donata, the country's most monumental surviving early Byzantine church, to Katedrala sv. Stošije, Dalmatia's largest basilica.

Islands

Much of Northern Dalmatia—and certainly the natural wonders associated with it—consists of huge archipelagos, from the more than 100 barren but beautiful Kornati islands in the south to the Telašćica Nature Park, the splendorous, indented bay at the southern end of the Zadar archipelago's largest island, Dugi Otok. A visit to one of these places—whether a quick ferry ride to the island of Ugljan, right across from Zadar; a day or a night or more in Sali or Murter; a more substantial excursion by boat to the heart of one or both of these parks; and/or an all-out *Robinson turizm* stay in a stone cottage on one of the Kornati islands—will prove unforgettable.

Inland Beauty

Their names may sound similar, but in fact they're some distance apart, and technically, neither one is in Northern Dalmatia. But both Paklenica National Park—with its extraordinary karst features towering over the sea at the southern end of the Velebit range—and Plitvice National Park (*see* Chapter 1, Zagreb & Environs)—that most famous of all Croatia's parks, with its crystal clear connected lakes and waterfalls, enveloped by rich forests and teeming with wildlife—are both easily accessible from Zadar.

Nin & Its Beaches

Today an unassuming little town with a 17th-century historic face, Nin was once one of the most important Dalmatian towns of all. Beyond this rich legacy, for miles around the town you will find the only major stretch of sandy beaches on this part of the Croatian coast—some of the best swimming in all of Dalmatia.

Crkva sv. Marije. It is home to numerous artifacts from Zadar's past, from prehistoric times to the first Croatian settlements. Head upstairs to move back in time. The third floor focuses on ceramics, weaponry, and other items the seafaring Liburnians brought home from Greece and Italy, whereas the second floor covers the classical period, including a model of the Forum square as it would have looked back then; a smaller exhibit addresses the development of Christianity in Northern Dalmatia and contains rare artifacts from the invasion of the Goths. On the first floor you'll find an exhibit from the early Middle Ages, taking you to the 12th century. ⊠ *Trg Opatice Čike* ☎ *023/250–340* ⊕ *www.donat. com/arh* ⊠ *10 Kn* ⊗ *Mon.–Sat. 9–1 and 6–8:30.*

⑤ **Crkva sv. Donata** (St. Donat's Church). Zadar's star attraction, this huge, **Fodor's**Choice cylindrical structure is the most monumental early Byzantine church in ★ Croatia. Originally called Church of the Holy Trinity, and probably in-

CloseUp
ZADAR'S COURT PHENOMENON

IN JUNE 2005, TEAM ZADAR beat Cibona Zagreb to win the Croatian basketball league's championship for the first time in 19 years. The city was delirious with joy. Basketball has long rivaled soccer in Croatia for sheer popularity, and in Zadar this is especially the case. Its team was among the best in the former Yugoslavia, alongside Cibona Zagreb and Split's team, then called Jugoplastika Split. To see one reason for yourself, walk south from the foot of the pedestrian bridge in the Old Town about 10 minutes along Obala Kralja Tomislava to the grassy area on your left (where the bay reaches an end) and consider the huge statue of Zadar's preeminent basketball hero as he towers even higher than the 213 centimeters (6'11") he was in real life, captured meditatively with ball in hand. His name is Krešimir Ćosić. (Appropriately, the statue is across the street from Zadar's basketball auditorium.)

Born in Zagreb but raised in Zadar, Ćosić enrolled at Brigham Young University in Utah in 1970 after leading Yugoslavia to a silver medal in basketball in 1968. His decision opened the way for other foreign players to likewise hone their skills in America on the collegiate level. In both 1972 and 1973, Ćosić—who led BYU in scoring for two years in a row—won All-America honors, the first foreign player to do so. In 1973, he achieved the added distinction of being drafted by both the NBA's Los Angeles Lakers and the ABA's Carolina Cougars—and saying "no thanks." He went back home, where he continued to shine on court. Ćosić played on three more Yugoslav Olympic teams, in 1972, 1976, and finally, 1980, when he led his team to a gold medal in Moscow. He played not only for leading Croatian teams but also for the two-time Italian champions, Virtus Bologna. With the close of his playing days he turned to coaching and led the Yugoslav team to a silver medal in the 1988 Seoul Olympics. He later became the third foreign player elected to the Basketball Hall of Fame in Springfield, Massachusetts. Eventually Ćosić stepped away from the court to serve as a diplomat for his newly independent country in Washington, D.C. He died on May 25, 1995, after a long illness, at the young age of 46.

spired by plans set forth in a book by the Byzantine emperor Constantine Porphyrogenet, *On Ruling the Empire,* centuries later it was rededicated to St. Donat, who was bishop here from 801 to 814. Legend has it that Donat, an Irishman, was the one who had it built, using stone from the adjacent Forum. The stark, round interior features a circular center surrounded by an annular passageway; a sanctuary consisting of three apses attached to the lofty mantle of the church walls, set off from the center by two columns; and a gallery reached by a circular stairway. Although the church no longer hosts services, its fine acoustics make it a regular concert venue. During the off-season (November to March), when the church is closed, someone at the Archaeological Museum next door may have a key to let you in. ✉ *Šimuna Kožičića Benje* ☎ *023/250–516* 💶 *6 Kn* ☉ *May.–Sept., 9 AM–10 PM; Apr. and Oct., 9 AM–1 PM.*

Zadar

Borik

0   1/4 mile

0   1/4 kilometer

Zadarski Kanal

Jadransko More

TO BORIK

Luka

Jazine

Foča

KEY

① Exploring Sights

① Hotels & Restaurants

2 **Crkva sv. Marije** (St. Mary's Church). Legend has it that a local noblewoman founded a Benedictine convent on this site in 1066, and the adjoining St. Mary's Church in 1091. Rebuilt in the 16th century, the church was supposed to incorporate a new, Renaissance look into the remnants of its earlier style: its rounded gables remained, continuing to express a certain Dalmatian touch; early Romanesque frescoes are still evident amid the largely baroque interior; and your eyes will discover 18th-century rococo above the original columns without being any worse for the effect. Most noteworthy for modern-day visitors, however, is the adjoining convent complex, two wings of which house one of Zadar's most treasured museums. The **Permanent Exhibition of Religious Art**, whose highlight is commonly called "The Gold and Silver of Zadar," is a remarkable collection of work from centuries past by local gold- and silversmiths (including Italians and Venetians who lived here), from reliquaries for saints and crucifixes, to vestments interwoven with gold and silver thread. ☒ *Poljana Opatice Čike* ☎ *023/211–545* ☞ *Museum 20 Kn* ☉ *Museum Mon.–Sat. 10–12:30 and 6–8, Sun. 10–1.*

9 **Crkva sv. Šimuna** (St. Simeon's Church). Built in the 5th century as a three-nave basilica, it was later reconstructed in Gothic style, and again in baroque style, though the terra-cotta and white exterior pales in comparison to some of the city's other churches. St. Simeon's Church is best known for housing the gilded silver sarcophagus of Zadar's most popular patron saint. The chest, which depicts intricately detailed scenes from St. Simeon's life and the city's history, was commissioned in 1381 by Elizabeth, wife of Croat-Hungarian King Ludwig I of Anjou, and made by Francesco De Sesto of Milan, one of Zadar's best silversmiths. As for St. Simeon, legend has it that his body wound up here while being transported from the Holy Land to Venice by a merchant who got caught in a storm, took refuge here, fell ill, and died—but not before drawing attention to the saintliness of the body he'd brought with him. Palm trees outside the church lend the site a pleasant, Mediterranean touch. ☒ *Crkva sv. Šime* ☎ *023/ 211–705* ☞ *Free* ☉ *Weekdays 8–noon and 5:30–7, Sat. 8–noon. Masses 8 AM weekdays, 8:30 AM and 10 AM weekends.*

4 **Forum.** Established in the 1st century BC by the first Emperor Augustus, the Roman Forum is, more than 2,000 years later, pretty much a wide empty space with some scattered ruins. However, since it was rediscovered in the 1930s and restored to its present condition in the 1960s, the Forum has been one of Zadar's most important public spaces. A raised area on the western flank indicates the site of a onetime temple dedicated to Jupiter, Juno, and Minerva, and if you look closely you will notice what remains of its altars that served as venues for blood sacrifices. The only surviving column was used in the Middle Ages as a "Pillar of Shame," to which wayward individuals were chained. Fragments of a second column were removed from the Forum in 1729 and put back together again near the Square of Five Wells, where the column still stands today.

7 **Franjevački samostan i Crkva sv. Franje Asiškog** (St. Francis Church & Franciscan Monastery). Dalmatia's oldest Gothic church, consecrated in 1280, is a stellar example of a so-called Gothic monastic church, characterized by a single nave with a raised shrine. Although the church underwent extensive reconstruction in the 18th century, behind the main altar is a shrine dating to 1672; inside the shrine you can see choir stalls in the floral Gothic style that date to 1394. In 1358, a peace treaty was signed in this very sacristy under which the Venetian Republic ended centuries of attack and handed Zadar over to the protection of the Croat-Hungarian kingdom. You can walk around the atmospheric inner courtyard for free, by the way, but you must pay a fee to enter the church itself. From mid-October through March or April, the church may keep irregular hours. ⊠ *Samostan sv. Frane* ☎ *023/250–468* ⊠ *10 Kn* ⊙ *May–Sept., daily 9:30–3; Oct.–Apr., daily 7–noon and 4–5.*

★ ❻ **Katedrala sv. Stošije** (St. Anastasia's Cathedral). Dalmatia's largest basilica was shaped into its magnificent Romanesque form in the 12th and 13th centuries from an earlier church; though it was damaged severely during World War II, it was later reconstructed. The front portal is adorned with striking Gothic reliefs and a dedication to the archbishop Ivan from the year 1324. The interior includes not only a high, spacious nave but also a Gothic, stone ciborium from 1332 covering the 9th-century altar; intricately carved 15th-century choir stalls by the Venetian artist Matej Morozon; and, in the sacristy, an early Christian mosaic. St. Anastasia is buried in the altar's left apse; according to legend, she was the wife of a patrician in Rome but was eventually burned at the stake. Bishop Donat of Zadar obtained the remains in 804 from Byzantine Emperor Niceforos. The late-19th-century belfry, which is separate from the main church building, offers a sweeping view to those who climb to the top for a fee, but even the 20 steps up to the ticket desk rewards you with a decent view of the square below. ⊠ *Trg Svete Stos* ☎ *023/251–708* ⊠ *Church free; belfry 10 Kn* ⊙ *Belfry weekdays 8 AM–10 PM, Sat. 8–3.*

need a break? Hidden away on a quiet square between St. Anastasia's Church and the Franciscan Monastery, **Caffe Bar No. 7** (⊠ Braće Bersa 1) is a soothing place to sit and sip (anything from coffee to beer). It also goes by the name Internet Cafe No. 7, as there are two computers in the back room that you can use (when the Internet connection isn't down) for ½ Kn per minute. The spacious, shaded terrace out front has high wicker chairs beside marble-top tables with wrought-iron legs.

⓫ **Kopneva Vrata** (The Land Gate). A walk around the walls of Zadar's Old Town is a walk around what was, once, the largest city-fortress in the Venetian Republic. One of the finest Venetian-era monuments in Dalmatia, the Land Gate was built in 1543 by the small Foša harbor as the main entrance to the city. It takes the form of a triumphal arch, with a large, central passage for vehicles and two side entrances for pedestrians, and is decorated with reliefs of St. Chrysogonus (Zadar's main patron saint) on his horse, and the Shield of St. Mark (the coat of arms of the Venetian Republic).

❶ **Narodni trg** (People's Square). One of the Old Town's two main public spaces, the ever bustling Narodni trg is home of the Gradska Straža (City Sentinel), which was designed by a Venetian architect in late-Renaissance style with a large, central clock tower. The sentinel's stone barrier and railing, complete with holes for cannons, were added later. This impressive tower once housed the ethnographic section of the National Museum and is today a venue for various regular cultural exhibits.

❽ **Sea Organ.** In 2004, Zadar was provided with a round-the-clock tourist
Fodor'sChoice attraction unlike any other in the world (as of this writing). Compris-
★ ing 35 pipes under the quay stretching along a 70-meter (230-foot) stretch of Zadar's atmospheric Riva promenade, the Sea Organ yields a never-ending (and ever free) concert that delights one and all. Designed by architect Nikola Bašić with the help of other experts, the organ's sound resembles a whale song, but it is in fact the sea itself. It's hard not to be in awe as the sound of the sea undulates in rhythm and volume with the waves. ⊠ *Obala kralja Petra Krešimira IV, toward the end of the western tip of the peninsula.*

❿ **Square of Five Wells.** The square is the site of a large cistern built by the Venetians in the 1570s to help Zadar endure sieges by the Turks. The cistern itself has five wells that still look quite serviceable even though they have long been sealed shut. Much later, in 1829, Baron Franz Ludwig von Welden, a passionate botanist, established a park above an adjacent pentagonal bastion that was also built to keep the Turks at bay.

Where to Eat

★ $$$–$$$$ ✕ **Restoran Kornat.** Just outside the city walls on the tip of the peninsula, the Kornat represents fine dining at its best, even if the space is a tad dull despite (or because of) all the sparkling elegance. On the ground floor of an ochre, four-story concrete-box building, the restaurant serves original, first-rate cuisine, including delightful lamb with rosemary in red-wine sauce and a monkfish filet with truffle sauce. Desserts include melon with champagne. There's also an elegant wine list, from the best of Croatian elixirs to the smoothest shiraz. ⊠ *Liburnska obala 6* ☎ *023/254–501* ▱ *AE, DC, MC, V.*

$$–$$$$ ✕ **Foša.** The main reason to eat at the Foša, whose name includes the tag "Riblji [Fish] restaurant," is the choice setting just outside the city walls a stone's throw from the Kopneva Vrata. Although the decidedly deep-green and blue interior may be overpowering, the outdoor terrace, which overlooks quiet little Foša harbor, is a must. Whether you opt for a budget meal of spaghetti with mussels or something pricier, such as grilled squid, scampi, or boiled scallops, chances are that your palate will be pleased, too. ⊠ *Kralja Dimitra Zvibimira 2* ☎ *023/314–421* ▱ *MC, V.*

$$–$$$$ ✕ **Niko.** Just across from a public beach and near the Borik resort com-
Fodor'sChoice plex, this distinguished restaurant has been serving up a delicious array
★ of seafood, beef, veal, pork, and pasta dishes since 1963. You can choose between such lower-end fare as spaghetti with scampi or more expensive delights like scampi on the skewer. That's not to mention the mouthwatering banana splits. Upstairs are 11 pricey rooms, at €120 for a double with breakfast. ⊠ *Obala Kneza Domagoja 9* ☎ *023/337–880* ▱ *AE, DC, MC, V.*

$$–$$$ ✕ **Konoba Skoblar.** Near the Square of Five Wells, this restaurant, with its spacious outdoor terrace shaded by two huge plane trees, is a lovely

NEW WAVE MUSIC, REALLY

IN 2005, ZADAR WAS ENDOWED with a round-the-clock art installation unlike any other in the world. The first of a series of planned seaside projects aimed at enhancing Zadar's allure as a port of call for cruises, the Sea Organ has quickly become one of the city's key public (and tourist) attractions. It's visited by as many or more people as visit the city's venerable churches. Comprising 35 polyethylene pipes of varying lengths, diameters, and tilts under the quay along a 70-meter (230-foot) stretch of Zadar's already atmospheric Riva promenade, it yields a never-ending (and ever free) concert that delights and soothes one and all, of all ages.

Designed by architect Nikola Bašić with the help of a craftsman from Murter and organ builders from Zagreb, this one-of-a-kind pipe organ sounds a bit like a whale's hushed cooing, but it is in fact the sea itself. Each pipe ends in a whistle that churns out five tones in seven chords, through openings on the quayside above it. This explains all those people—many of whom might otherwise not be inclined to attend manmade concerts—bending down to place their ears against the concrete, positively entranced. Even when the sea seems otherwise still, the music plays. This is a continuous concert produced by nature itself, in unrepeatable variations. It's hard not to be in awe as the sound of the sea undulates in rhythm and volume with the waves—just wait and listen after a big boat goes by! After a while, sitting there on the simple, elegant stone steps that have been built on the quayside to allow you to savor the experience, you may find yourself wondering why there isn't a sea organ in every city in the world that enjoys the benefit of a coast.

place to have a meal, whether you opt for grilled or boiled squid or scampi, veal in lemon sauce, or just an simple seafood salad consisting of anything from marinated anchovies to marinated salmon. As an added plus, during the dog days of summer on the Adriatic, the interior is air-conditioned. ⊠ *Trg Petra Zoranića* ☎ *023/213–236* ▤ *AE, DC, MC, V.*

$$–$$$ ✗ **Trattoria Canzona Pizzeria.** This delightful and popular restaurant is hidden away in the Old Town's atmospheric Varoš district. Here you can choose between more than 20 delicious pizzas as well as a host of pasta dishes, or else go for shark in white-wine sauce, leaving room for tiramisu at the end. The interior is a seamless blend of rustic and hip, the brick walls of the inner room adorned with fake windows that give the space an open, airy feel. And "integral flour"—an option for every pizza on the menu—is simply whole wheat. ⊠ *Stomorica 8* ☎ *023/212–081* ▤ *AE, DC, MC, V.*

Where to Stay

There are hardly any hotels in or near Zadar's Old Town—the pension-style Venera being a distinguished exception. As you leave the center, you'll find either fairly expensive, top-end hotels or relatively simple, budget places, but not much in the middle price ranges. In mid-summer, you can step off the ferry from Pula at midnight and be reasonably assured that some relatively trustworthy person—more likely than not a pensioner who speaks more Italian than English—will offer you a room in a centrally located apartment for around 250 Kn for 2 people. You can book private rooms more formally—at a slightly higher cost—through travel agencies, which generally also offer excursions to nearby islands and national parks, including these:

Kompas (⊠ Poljana Natka Nodila 9 ☎ 023/254–304 🖷 023/254–305). **Miatrade** (⊠ Vrata sv. Krsevana ☎ 023/254–300 or 023/254–400). **Terra Travel Agency** (⊠ Matije Gupca 2a ☎ 023/337–294).

★ $$$$ 🏨 **Hotel Adriana Select.** Flanked beachside by a grove of tall pines, and encircled by a security fence (more to keep nonguests from enjoying the hotel's outdoor pool than for the sake of safety), this is an appealing place to stay even if the long, narrow lobby does resemble an airport terminal. Indeed, it is the only hotel in the Austrian-owned Falkensteiner complex here in outer Zadar's Borik resort area to look more like a villa than a package resort. Bright and modern, with warm hues, the spacious rooms (some with a sea view for only slightly more) have pine floors and large bathrooms complete with tubs. ⊠ *Majstora Radovana 7, Borik, 23000* ☎ *023/206–637* 🖷 *023/332–065* ⊕ *www.hotelborik.hr* 🛏 *48 rooms* ⚭ *Restaurant, in-room safes, in-room data ports, cable TV, minibars, 2 pools (1 indoor), gym* ☰ *AE, DC, MC, V* ❏ *MAP.*

$$$ 🏨 **Hotel President.** The name is a tad elitist and so is the place, but if you're looking for cloistered luxury, you will find it here, albeit on a bland suburban street. Though a place where an unannounced sneeze or a cough may be bad etiquette, the hotel does sparkle. The rooms have a silky look and feel, not to mention cherry-wood Biedermeier-style furniture—and it's only a 5-minute walk from Borik's public beach. The Vivaldi Restaurant, whose thick curtains are drawn even by day, offers an original variety of fish and game dishes, albeit at high prices, and a huge wine list in an atmosphere of refined elegance, its walls adorned with original oil paintings. ⊠ *Vladana Desnice 16, Borik 23000* ☎ *023/333–696* 🖷 *023/333–595* ⊕ *www.hotel-president.hr* 🛏 *27 rooms* ⚭ *Restaurant, in-room safes, in-room data ports, cable TV, minibars, bar* ☰ *AE, DC, MC, V* ❏ *BP.*

¢ 🏨 **Hotel Venera.** Formerly the Javič Guest House, this small, friendly hotel is tucked away in a quiet side street a few minutes' walk from Narodni trg. As of this writing, it's the only hotel in the Old Town. What you get is a modest-size room that's a tad more sparkling (with a private, shower-equipped bathroom) than most private rooms in town while being only a bit pricier. With soothing blue tones and carpeting, the rooms—there are four on each of three floors—have closets of varying size. Though there's no breakfast, filling up at one of the many nearby cafés is no problem. ⊠ *Ul Šima Ljubića 4A, 23000* ☎ *023/214–098 or 098/330–958* 🛏 *12 rooms* ⚭ *In-room safes, cable TV, minibars; no A/C* ☰ *No credit cards.*

¢ 🏨 **Pension Albin.** On the narrow, busy but tree-lined road that leads from the city center to the Borik resort area, the Pension Albin is one of Zadar's best places to stay and even eat. The jovial owner, Albin Jurin, is a cel-

Fodor'sChoice
★

ebrated local chef who opened this welcoming and elegant hotel-cum-restaurant in the mid-1980s. Despite the uninspiring, communist-era look of the main lobby, the rooms are bright and modern. Rooms in the newer building are more spacious, and have pretty, floral curtains to boot, plus an outdoor terrace. A lovely little pool is shaded by a lush wall of kiwi leaves behind the older building. You can savor some of the best cuisine in town at the hotel's restaurant. The fish in particular is superb, the olive oil is homemade, and there is a broad selection of quality wines to wash it all down. ⊠ *Put Dikla 47, 23000* ☎ *023/331–137* 🖷 *023/332–172* ⊕ *www.albin.hr* ⌨ *34 rooms* ⚐ *Restaurant, in-room safes, cable TV, minibars, pool* ▤ *AE, DC, MC, V* ⦿❙ *BP.*

Nightlife & the Arts
Summer Festivals
Keep your eyes skyward around late July, for the night of the full moon in high summer marks the **Full Moon Festival,** when Zadar's parklike seaside promenade, the Riva, is lit up by torches and candlelight, fishing boats sell their catch, and nightlong konobas pop up to provide you with drinks, figs, and cheese. This is not to mention dance and musical performances amid a generally cozy atmosphere that unfolds not only in Zadar but in many of the region's island communities.

Despite its name, **Musical Evenings in Saint Donat,** not all the monthlong series of concerts and recitals beginning in early July are held in the splendid St. Donat's Church. From late June to early August, the annual **Zadar Summer Theatre** festival sees a whole range of music, dance, and drama performed at various squares, churches, and other buildings about town. Particular years are devoted to certain themes (in 2005 it was contemporary music—from jazz to blues to flamenco—and dance). Talk about eclectic. The **Zadar snova** (Zadar of Dreams) festival, in the second week of August, welcomes everything from contemporary dance and films to comic-strip exhibits and workshops, to theatrical events, to a rich array of music, and more. ⊠ *Zadar Theater House, Široka ul 8.*

Bars & Clubs
After one heck of a makeover in 2005, what used to be Zadar's landmark café since the 1890s, **Viaz** (⊠ Široka ul 3 ☎ No phone), which was formerly the Central, is an ultramodern, hip-as-can-be café-cum-nightspot with bright yellow and orange chairs and cool ceiling lights that would fit Manhattan, San Francisco, or London like a kid glove. This is the new face of Zadar. Sip and socialize while watching the crowds stream by on bustling Široka ulica.

Cloistered in a walled garden right atop the city walls, **The Garden** (⊠ Bedemi Zadarskih Pobuna ☎ 023/254–509) used to be the coolest hangout in the former Yugoslavia. Today, it's a minimalist and exceedingly popular place to drink, soak in the sun and the views, play a game of chess, and even dance to the jazz, Latin, and downtempo elektronica. It's open all day, from 7 AM to midnight.

Adorned in futuristic Batman style, **Gotham** (⊠ Marka Oreškovića 1, next to the Nova Banka tower north of the Old Town ☎ 023/200–289) is part café (sometimes with live jazz), part cinema, and even a cool-as-can-be dance club with theme parties manned in summer by international DJs, live music from Latin to hip-hop, and go-go dancers. It's open from 11 PM Sunday through Tuesday.

Befitting its classical name, the **City Club Forum** (⊠ Marka Marulića ☎ No phone) is a smallish, colosseum-shaped space with three bars, a hedonistic, fall-of-Rome atmosphere, and music ranging from commercial pop to R&B. It's only open Friday and Saturday from 11 PM; ladies get in for free until 1 AM.

Sports & the Outdoors

Beaches
As in many another coastal city, you can feel free to take a dip even in the Old Town—the most atmospheric place to do so being the **Riva** promenade along the western side of the old town, and especially the tip of the peninsula directly over the Sea Organ, as nature's music accompanies your strokes. And then there's the **Kolovare** district, just southeast of the Old Town, with its long stretch of park-flanked beach punctuated here and there by restaurants and cafés. This is not to mention the resort complex in **Borik,** where relatively shallow waters and a sandy bottom may be more amenable to kids. Last but not least, by driving or bussing it 30 minutes north along the coast, you can reach the famously sandy beaches of **Zaton** and **Nin.** For true peace and quiet, though, your best bet is an excursion by ferry and then by foot, bicycle, or rental car out to some more isolated stretch of beach on an island of the Zadar archipelago.

Bicycling
Being relatively flat, with lots of relatively quiet thoroughfares both in the Old Town and on the outskirts of the city, Zadar is indeed a bicycle-friendly place. You can rent a bike at **Eurobike** (⊠ Obala kneza Branimira 6c ☎ 023/241–243).

Diving
Since diving on your own is possible only with two pricey permits, it is advisable to take that deep dip through a diving center (i.e., with the supervision of a licensed instructor). Just one of the many such centers in Zadar and on the surrounding coast and islands is **Zadar Sub** (⊠ Dubrovačka 20a ☎ 023/214–848).

Shopping

As hip as it otherwise seems, Zadar is bit of a dud when it comes to unique shopping opportunities; the Old Town, at least, is low on high fashion and has few outlets for quality souvenirs (as opposed to the usual kitsch, which there's plenty of). That said, those interested will be happy to know that there are a good many jewelry shops.

Galerija Morsky (⊠ Plemića Borelli 3 ☎ 091/780–6101) sells fine paintings by local artists. Music fans will want to check out **Naima** (⊠ Varoška 1 ☎ 023/315–816), which has a decent stock of Croatian folk tunes and

Dalmatian men's choral music. **Mondo Media** (✉ Široka ul, at the corner of ul Dalmatinskog Sabora across from the Konzum food store ☎ 023/315–816) focuses on Croatian as well as international popular music. **Suvenirica-Galerija More** (✉ Široka ul ☎ 023/211–624) has a quality selection of Dalmatian edibles, wine jugs, and handicrafts.

NIN

⑫ *14 km (9 mi) north of Zadar.*

On a tiny, 500-meter (1640-foot) wide island in a shallow, sandy lagoon that affords a spectacular view of the Velebit range to the northeast, Nin is connected to the mainland by two small bridges. The peaceful town of 1,700, a compact gem whose present-day size and unassuming attitude belies a stormy history, is well worth a visit, whether on the way to Zadar or as a day-trip from there, assuming that the beautiful sand beaches stretching for miles around Nin don't inspire you to stay a bit longer.

Nin was a major settlement of the Liburnians, an Illyrian people who also settled Zadar, hundreds of years before the Romans came, conquered, and named it Aenona. A vital harbor for centuries, it was the first seat of Croatia's royalty and was long the region's episcopal see, whose bishop was responsible for the conversion to Christianity of all Croatian territory. In 1382, the Venetians seized it and prospered from the trade in salt, livestock, and agriculture. However, the Venetian-Turkish wars eventually brought devastating onslaughts, including Nin's destruction in 1571; later, the Candian Wars of 1645–1669 led to the decimation of Nin and the surrounding area yet again.

Aside from its historic buildings and monuments that testify to a rich past, Nin's draw also includes the only sandy beaches on this stretch of the Adriatic, not to mention the area's medicinal, seaside mud. Since the sea here is shallow, water temperatures are warmer than in the rest of the Adriatic; moreover, the water is more saline, accounting for Nin's major export product—salt. But what would a Croatian coastal town be without the usual resort complex on its fringes? Holiday Village Zaton is a 15-minute walk from the old town.

If you're coming from Zadar, soon before you reach Nin proper, look to your left (your right if headed back toward Zadar) to see the squat, stony, 12th-century form of **St. Nicholas's Church** on a hillock out in the middle of a field, looking rather like a cake ornament, with a lone Scotch pine at the foot of the little hill keeping it company, as it were. You can enter Nin via one of two small bridges—the most likely of the two being the charming, pedestrian **Donja most** (Lower Bridge), only yards from the tourist-information office, which provides a helpful map that folds small enough to fit in your palm. If you're coming by car, you can park in a lot on the right just beyond the office and then cross the bridge, or else find a semi-legal spot along the road roughly opposite the lot, which plenty of enterprising visitors prefer.

Croatia's oldest church, the 8th-century **Crkva sv. Križa** (Church of the Holy Cross) is also known locally as the "world's smallest cathedral."

Indeed, the unadorned, three-naved whitewashed structure—which has a solid, cylindrical top and a few tall, Romanesque windows (too high to peek inside)—has an unmistakable monumental quality to it even though it's no larger than a small house. There's little to see inside, though it is sometimes open, erratically, in summer; check with the tourist office or the Archaeological Museum. ⊠ *Petra Zoranića.*

Nin's shallow coast and centuries of sand deposits preserved numerous remains from prehistory to the Middle Ages under the sea. The **Arheološki muzej** (Archaeological Museum) has a rich collection for a town of this size, including replicas of two small, late-11th-century fishing boats discovered only in 1966 and carefully removed from the sea in 1974. One of these boats has been completely reconstructed, the other only to the extent to which it had been preserved underwater. The main themes in each room are elucidated in clear English translations. ⊠ *Trg Kraljevac 8* ☎ *023/264–160* ⊡ *10 Kn* ⊙ *Tues.–Sun. 9* AM*–10* PM.

The 18th-century **Crkva sv. Anselma** (St. Anselmo's Church), dedicated to a 1st-century martyr believed to have been Nin's first bishop, was built on the site of Nin's former, 9th-century cathedral, the first cathedral of the medieval Croatian principality. To the right of the altar is a 15th-century statue of the Madonna of Zečevo, inspired by the appearance of the Virgin Mary to a woman on a nearby island. Though the church is plain—the ceiling is adorned with only a nice chandelier and a smoke detector—the foundations of the onetime cathedral are still much in evidence. Beside the church is the belfry, and next door is the treasury, which houses a stunning little collection of reliquaries containing various body parts of St. Anselmo. ⊠ *Branimirova, near Višeslavov trg* ⊡ *10 Kn* ⊙ *Treasury: May–Sept., Mon.–Sat. 10–noon and 5:30–9:30.*

Around the corner from the Archaeological Museum are the ruins of the large **Temple of Diana,** one of the few remaining testaments in Nin to the Roman era. ⊠ *Sv. Mihovila.*

Where to Stay & Eat

Though Holiday Village Zaton has its share of the usual, package-tourist accommodations, in Nin proper there's not much hotel-wise but for the **Perin Dvor** (⊠ Vl Petar Surić, 23232 ☎ 023/264–307 or 091/789–5512), a popular restaurant offering decent fare that also has five clean, comfortable kitchenette-equipped suites that can be had for €60. For a private room or apartment, check with the travel agency next door to the tourist-information office.

$$–$$$ ✕ **Konoba Branimir.** Strategically located yards away from the Church of the Holy Cross—indeed you might enter the restaurant by mistake thinking you are proceeding to the churchyard from a back entrance—this is the most pleasant place to dine in Nin. The well-prepared fare ranges from fresh seafood to meats, and desserts such as pancakes with fig marmalade. Note that the spaghetti, though listed as a children's meal, makes for a hearty "light" (and budget) meal even for an adult. ⊠ *Višeslavov trg 2* ☎ *023/264–866* ▭ *AE, DC, MC, V.*

BENKOVAC: TRULY OFF THE BEATEN PATH

IT'S A HOT AUGUST DAY, and our rickety bus is not one of those modern, air-conditioned wonders that ply the bustling coast we're about to leave. Unlike those packed coaches, however, our bus—which has just 12 passengers—leaves on time; for there is no one else waiting to get on.

We are headed to Benkovac, 37 km (23 mi) east of Zadar, away from the sea. Not far at all geographically, this town—so prominent on the map, and indeed a main transit point to points further inland—is far indeed economically and psychologically. Soon after you leave Zadar, the coastal construction boom fades away; house after house is missing its roof, a legacy of the war that ravaged the region until 1995. For a while, the Velebit range forms a striking view many miles to the left, but then the mountains vanish and the horizon is flat in all directions.

It's not that there's little tourism in Benkovac. There's none. That's how it seems, as of this writing. The only hotel in town—a concrete box called the Hotel Asseria (named after an ancient city whose ruins lie nearby)—is rented out, all of it, to a wedding party from Biograd, on the coast. The reception desk is empty. Attempts to find a private room in town are met by surprised stares. The contrast with the tourism-driven sparkle of the nearby coast is astonishing. Still, on strolling away from the bus station toward what there is of a business district, we can't help but notice that the town—though abandoned by most of its Serb population by the mid-1990s—is pleasant enough and even attractive in places, even if it is a bit worn-looking. And Benkovac is so close to Zadar, that it's easily done as a day trip anyway, so no harm done.

Among the bright spots in this region is the family-owned **Markica farm** (⌂ Jošani, near Galova ☎ 023/392–222), less than 4 km (2½ mi) from the airplane crossing. At this farm, you can sample all sorts of scrumptious homemade fare and children can play with farm animals, including a donkey and ostriches. Unless you're passing by, anyway, call before going out there; as of this writing, the English-speaking family member to ask for is Marina.

Benkovac's early-16th-century fortress, the **Kaštel** (⌂ Obitelji Benkovića 9, Benkovac ☎ 023/681–055 ⊕ www.benkovac.com), houses the local museum. This austere structure, built by the Benkovič family (after which the town probably takes its name), towers prominently on a hill a short walk above a charming town center that is home to a few pleasant if unassuming cafés and pizzerias. It's open weekdays, from 8 to 3. Admission is 10 Kn.

Near Benkovac are the massive ruins of **Asseria,** an ancient city. First settled around 6 BC by Liburnians, who built it into one of their most important towns before the Romans came, Asseria—which is nearly 500 meters (1,640 feet) long and roughly a third as wide, and is situated 6 km (3¾ mi) east of Benkovac, near the village of Podgrađe—was inhabited for more than 1,000 years before crumbling away along with the Roman empire.

For more information on the city and Asseria, contact the **Benkovac Tourist Association** (⌂ Šetalište Kneza Branimira 12, Benkovac ☎ 023/684–880).

Sports & the Outdoors

With its long sandy **beaches,** the coastline in and around Nin is widely regarded as the most beautiful—and certainly the most swimmable—in Dalmatia. The Holiday Village Zaton resort complex, a 15-minute walk from Nin, is home to **Scuba Adriatic** (✉ Holiday Village Zaton ☎ 023/280–350, 023/231–536, or 098/686–999), which offers diving excursions for advanced and beginning divers, formal diving instruction, as well as a two-hour "Discovery Diving" course.

SALI & TELAŠČICA NATURE PARK

Sali is approximately 30 km (19 mi) south of Zadar; Telaščica Nature Park is 10 km (6 mi) south of Sali.

The largest and most westerly island of the Zadar archipelago, facing the open sea, Dugi Otok culminates at its southern end with a spectacular nature preserve in and around Telaščica Bay, the town of **Sali** being the ideal access point. Situated toward the southeastern tip of the 52-km (32-mi) long island, which is no more than 4 km (2½ mi) wide, Sali is Dugi Otok's largest settlement—with around half of the island's 1,800 inhabitants, the rest of whom reside mostly in its 10 other villages—but it's an awfully peaceful little place you arrive in after the two-hour ferry ride from Zadar.

Once an out-of-the-way fishing village, Sali draws tourists these days due to its location in and near such natural splendors. It is home to several old churches, including the 1st-century **St. Mary's church,** whose baroque altar was carved in Venice. Adding to the village's appeal is its annual **Saljske užance** (Donkey Festival) during the first full weekend in August, which includes an evening ritual during which lantern-lit boats enter Sali harbor, donkey races, and *tovareća muzika* (donkey music) produced by locals blowing or braying raucously into horns. Spending at least a night or two here can provide a relatively peaceful, nature-filled respite from the rigors of tourism on the mainland or, for that matter, on more tourist-trodden reaches of the Zadar archipelago.

★ ⓮ **Telaščica Nature Park** encompasses Telaščica Bay, which cuts 7 km (4.4 mi) into the southern tip of Dugi Otok with an inner coastline so indented that it is really a series of smaller bays and a handful of islands. Flanked by high vertical cliffs facing the open sea to the west, with low, peaceful bays on the other side, it has a variety of vegetation. Relatively lush alpine forests and flower-filled fields as well as vineyards, olive groves, and onetime cultivated fields give way, as you move south, to bare rocky ground of the sort that predominates on the Kornati islands, whose northern boundary begins where Telaščica Nature Park ends.

Aside from Telaščica's other attractions, most of which are accessible only by boat, one of the park's key highlights—accessible by land via a 20-minute drive from Sali—is the salt lake **Jezero mir,** which was formed when a karst depression was filled by the sea.

Small boats (generally with 8 to 12 passengers) bound for both Telaščica Nature Park and the northern fringes of Kornati National Park leave the east side of Sali's harbor (i.e., where the Zadar ferry arrives) at 9 or 9:30 each morning and return by 6 or 6:30 in the evening. Expect to pay 200 Kn per person, sometimes less. The best way to arrange this is in person—by going to the harborside square near the post office around 8 PM on the day before you wish to leave (which means at least a one-night stay in Sali), when boat captains gather there looking for passengers for the next day's excursion. However, the tourist-information office in Sali can put you in touch with operators by phone as well. ⊠ *Put Danijela Grbina, Sali, 23281* ☎ *023/377–096* ⊕ *www.telascica.hr.*

🄯 The **Zadar archipelago** is so close and yet so far away. Ugljan and Pašman are just two of the myriad of islands comprising the lacelike islands, and yet they are among the largest and the easiest to reach from Zadar. More than 15 ferries a day run the 5 km (3 mi) distance between Zadar and Ugljan, a 19-km (12-mi) long island whose narrow width of just a couple kilometers runs parallel to the mainland, with its midway point across from Zadar (*see* ⇨ Boat & Ferry Travel *in* Zadar & Northern Dalmatia Essentials, *below*). From the ferry landing on Ugljan, your best bet may be to head north along the seafront 10 minutes by foot to the heart of **Preko,** a fine access point to several worthwhile destinations (very) near and (not too) far. Going south will get you in roughly the same time to the unassuming fishing village of Kali. From Preko's harbor you can walk about 1 km (½ mi) further north to a shallow bay locals like to swim in; or better yet, take a taxi-boat to **Galevac,** a charming wooded islet less than 100 yards from Preko that not only has splendid swimming but also a 15th-century Franciscan monastery set in a lush green park. And then there's the **Tvrđava sv. Mihovila** (Fortress of St. Michael), a 13th-century landmark atop a hill roughly an hour's walk west of town. Though largely in ruins, the fortress offers spectacular views not only of nearby Zadar, to the west, but on a cloudless day, also of the Italian coast. Meanwhile, 10 km (6 mi) further north is the quiet village of **Ugljan,** accessible from the ferry port by a handful of buses daily. For a somewhat sleepier island experience, hop aboard one of eight buses daily from Preko to the village of **Pašman.** Continuing on, you can eventually get to Tkon, Pašman island's largest village, from where some 10 ferries daily can get you back to the mainland south of Zadar.

Where to Eat

★ **$$–$$$** ✕ **Konobe Kod Sipe.** There are plenty of tourist places harborside in Sali, but if you want to have hearty meal well above the harborside fray, you'll have to climb some steps. Start at the steps between the Suvenirica Porat store and the Gelateri Contes café, near the tip of the harbor, and walk up more than 100 of them, passing two pretty little churches on your left along the way. After the second church, follow the "Konoba" signs to this popular restaurant that serves everything from grilled calamari and pork chops to cuttlefish spaghetti and "octopus under a baking lid." The rustic decor is pleasingly punctuated by a barrel theme, with both the chairs and the tables on barrels, and the usual fishnets hanging from the ceiling's wooden beams. The outdoor terrace is shaded by grapevines (and, yes, some fishnet) plus an enticing open hearth. All this, in a villagelike atmosphere where tourists rarely tread. ⊠ *Ul sv. Marije, Sali* ☎ *023/377–137 or 098/862–704* 🚍 *No credit cards.*

Where to Stay

The tourist-information office (*see* ⇨ Visitor Information *in* Zadar & Northern Dalmatia Essentials, *below*) can put you in touch with locals who rent private rooms, at around 220 Kn per night in high season.

★ $ 🖃 **Sali Hotel.** A 10-minute walk from the harbor on the quiet waters of Saščica, the next bay north, this low-key hotel occupies a pair of two-story, concrete-boxish buildings perched on a lovely, pine-covered hill leading down to a beach on a pristine bay worlds away from the hub-bub of busier coastal resorts. The rooms are clean, comfy, and pleas-antly (*very*) blue, even if they do smell a bit of cigarette smoke. ⊠ *Adresa, Sali 23281* ☎ *023/377–049* 🖷 *023/377–078* ⊕ *www.hotel-sali.hr* 🛏 *52 rooms* ⚐ *Restaurant, in-room safes, cable TV, minibars* 🚍 *AE, DC, MC, V* ⚐ *BP.*

Sports & the Outdoors

"Diving is not about sitting around on land, sipping wine, and watch-ing the sea," says the chief instructor of Sali's **Diving Center** (⊠ Adresa, just below the Sali Hotel, Sali ☎ 098/764–274 🖷 023/377–128 ⊕ www. dive-kroatien.de), as several clients huddle nearby sipping coffee and watching the sea—true, it's cold and rainy just now. This German-owned firm, which operates out of a compact cabin on the pine-cov-ered hillside below the Sali Hotel, offers everything from a 30-minute resort course to a five-day certification course, in English if you prefer. Diving can be done both from shore or further afield from a boat, whether on Saščoca Bay itself or further out, in Teščica Nature Park or on the fringes of Kornati National Park.

MURTER & THE KORNATI ISLANDS

70 km (44 mi) south of Zadar.

Built near the ruins of the 1st-century Roman settlement of Colentum, ⑯ **Murter** has that unmistakable tourism-driven hustle and bustle in mid-summer that Sali doesn't—both because it is the key gateway to one of Croatia's chief offshore natural splendors, Kornati National Park, and because it is easily accessible by road from Zadar. However you go to Murter, you'll pass through Biograd-Na-Moru, a relatively big, bustling—but thoroughly tourist-trampled—town, where the resorts have long come to predominate in what was once a charming place; Biogrand-Na-Moru also serves as another access point for ferries to the Kornati Islands.

Murter, a town of 2,000, on the island of the same name that lies just off the mainland, is accessible by road from the main coastal route that runs south from Zadar toward Split. As important as tourism is to its present-day economy, boat building has, not surprisingly, long been vital to Murter as well. This is not to mention its olive oil, which was once so famous that it made its way to the imperial table in Vienna.

⑰
Fodor'sChoice
★

The largest archipelago in the Adriatic, **Kornati National Park** comprises more than 100 islands that are privately owned, mostly by residents of Murter, who purchased them more than a century ago from Zadar aristocrats. The new owners burned the forests to make room for sheep, which in turn ate much of the remaining vegetation. Although anything but lush today, the islands' almost mythical beauty is ironically synonymous with their barrenness: their bone-white to ochre colors represent a striking contrast to the azure sea. However, owners tend vineyards and orchards on some, and there are quite a few small buildings scattered about, mostly stone cottages—many of them on **Kornat**, which is by far the largest island, at 35 km (22 mi) long and less than a tenth as wide. Indeed, some of these cottages are available for so-called *Robinson turizm* (ask at the Murter tourist office, or enquire around town). In 1980, the archipelago became a national park. It was reportedly during a visit to Kornati in 1936 that King Edward of England decided between love for his throne and love for Wallis Simpson, the married woman who was to become his wife a year later. ✉ *Butina 2* ☎ *022/435–740* ⊕ *www.kornati.hr* ✐ *50 Kn if paid in advance, 60 Kn inside the park.*

Where to Eat

★ $$$–$$$$ ✕ **Tic-Tac.** The chef likes putting seafood in wine sauce here, always to gratifyingly delicious effect. In this elegant little restaurant near the main square, with tables lining the length of the narrow, historic alleyway where you'll also find the main entrance, you can begin with an appetizer such as mussels in wine sauce and move on to monkfish tail in wine sauce or grilled scampi in wine sauce. Whatever you get, accompany it with a glass of Graševina, the house white. ✉ *Hrokešina 5* ☎ *022/435–230 or 098/278–494* ▭ *AE, DC, MC, V.*

Where to Stay

Check with local agencies, which can find you a private room for around €30 for two: **Coronata Tourist Service** (✉ Žrtava ratova 17 ☎ 022/435–089 🖷 022/435–555 ⊕ www.coronata.hr) or **KornatTurist** (✉ Ul Hrvatskih vladara 2 ☎ 022/435–854 or 022/435–855 🖷 022/ 435–853 ⊕ www.kornatturist.hr).

$ ⊡ **Hotel Colentum.** Situated in a pine forest, the Colentum, about five minutes from the town center, offers simply furnished, bright, modern, blue-themed rooms that are a tad cramped, but whose terraces enhance your sense of space just enough. Pay 15 Kn extra per person for a sea view. Oh yes, there's a naturist beach just 1 km (.6 mi) away, if you feel like breaking free. ✉ *Put Slanica, 22243* ☎ *022/431–100* 🖷 *022/434– 255* ⊕ *www.hotel-colentum.hr* ⮑ *78 rooms* ⚭ *Restaurant, in-room safes, cable TV, tennis courts, minibars* ▭ *AE, DC, MC, V* ⦿ *BP.*

Sports & the Outdoors
Diving

Whether for exploring shipwrecks or reefs or underwater cliffs, Kornati National Park is among Croatia's most popular diving destinations. That said, you can't dive alone here, only through a qualified diving center. The permit for diving in the park is 150 Kn, which includes the park entrance fee. **Aquanaut Diving Center** (⊠ Luke, near intersection of Kornatski, across from supermarket ☎ 022/434–988 or 098/202–249 ⊕ www.divingmurter.com) offers a small menu of choice courses and excursions (to more than 100 sites), including a daylong boat trip that includes two dives and a stopover in the Kornati Islands. **Najada Diving** (⊠ Luke 57, on the jetty behind the supermarket ☎ 022/436–630 or 098/959–2415 ⊕ www.najada.com) offers supervised shore dives as well as half-day group excursions that include two dives. Among the highlights on its menu of excursions to more than 30 sites is a visit to the wreck of the World War II cargo ship *Francesca*.

Tours to Kornati National Park

All-day excursions generally include two substantial stops, one for a swim and another for a picnic, and include the park entrance fee of 50 Kn; trips usually cost around 180 Kn per person. In Murter, **Atlas** (⊠ Ul Hrvatskih vladara 8 ☎ 022/434–999) is one prominent contact to arrange such a fun-filled day.

PAKLENICA NATIONAL PARK

⑱ *50 km (31 mi) northeast of Zadar.*

For mountain scenery at its most spectacular and mountain tourism at its most advanced, you need go no further from Zadar than Paklenica National Park. The Velebit mountain range stretches along the Croatian coast for more than 100 km (62 mi), but nowhere does it pack in as much to see and do as in this relatively small, 96-square-km (60-square-mi) park, at the southern terminus of the range. Here, less than an hour from Zadar, is a wealth of extraordinary karst features from fissures, crooks, and cliffs to pits and caves. The park comprises two limestone gorges, Velika Paklenica (which ends, near the sea, at the park entrance in Starigrad), and Mala Paklenica a few kilometers to the south; trails through the former gorge are better marked (and more tourist-trodden).

All that dry rockiness visible from the seaward side of the range turns resplendently green as you cross over the mountains to the landward side. Named after the sap of the black pine, *paklina,* which was used long ago to prime boats, the park is in fact two-thirds forest, with beech and the indigenous black pine a key part of this picture; the remaining vegetation includes cliff-bound habitats featuring several types of bluebells, and rocky areas abounding in sage and heather. The park is also home to 4,000 different species of fauna, including butterflies that have long vanished elsewhere in Europe. It is also the only mainland nesting ground in Croatia for the stately Griffin vulture.

The park has more than 150 km (94 mi) of trails, from relatively easy ones leading from the **Velike Paklenica Canyon** (from the entrance in Starigrad) to the 500-meter (1,640-foot) long complex of caverns called Manita Peć cave, to mountain huts situated strategically along the way to the Velebit's highest peaks, Vaganski Vrh (1,758 meters/5,768 feet) and Sveto brdo (1,753 meters/5,751 feet). The most prominent of the park's large and spectacular caves, **Manita Peć** is accessible by foot from the park entrance in Starigrad; you can enter for a modest additional fee, but buy your ticket at the park entrance. Rock climbing is also a popular activity in the park. Meanwhile, mills and mountain villages scattered throughout Paklenica evoke the life of mountain folk from the not too distant past.

About a half-mile down the park access road in Starigrad, you pass through the mostly abandoned hamlet of **Marasovići,** from where it's a few hundreds yards more downhill to the small building where you buy your tickets and enter the park (from this point on, only by foot). From here it's 45 minutes uphill to a side path to Anića kuk, a craggy peak, and from there it's not far to Manita Peć. However, if you don't have time or inclination for a substantial hike into the mountains, you will be happy to know that even the 45-minute walk to the entrance gate and back from the main road affords spectacular, close-up views of the Velebit range's craggy ridgeline and the gorge entrance. Also, be forewarned that if you are looking to escape the crowds, you will be hard-pressed to do so here in mid-summer unless you head well into the mountains or, perhaps, opt for the park's less frequented entrance at Mala Paklenica; more likely than not, you will be sharing the sublimities of nature with thousands of other seaside revelers taking a brief respite from the coast.

Although the park headquarters is on the main coastal road in the middle of Starigrad, fees are payable where you actually enter the park on the access road. Beyond the basic park admission and the supplemental fee to enter Manita Peć cave, the park offers every imaginable service and presentation that might encourage you to part with your kunas, from half-day group tours (350 Kn) and full-day tours (700 Kn) to presentations every half-hour from 11 to noon and 4 to 7 on the park's birds of prey and on falconry. ✉ *Dr. Franje Tudmana 14a, Starigrad* ☎ *013/369–202* ⊕ *www.paklenica.hr* ✍ *30 Kn; Manita Peć cave 10 Kn* ☉ *Park: July and Aug., daily 7 AM–9 PM; Apr.–June, Sept., and Oct., daily 8 AM–noon and 4–8 PM. Cave: daily 10–1.*

Where to Eat

★ **$$** ✗ **Restaurant Miramar.** From the outside, Miramar looks much like the other restaurants along Starigrad's main thoroughfare. But here you get the added plus of hearty Dalmatian and even Bosnian specialties, not to mention huge servings. While Croatian pop music plays in the background and locals sit across the room quietly drinking beer, you can feast on Mućkalica, for example—an absolutely scrumptious if unabashedly meaty dish consisting of slices of pork with pepper and onions in a thick, peppery sauce, served on a bed of rice. The seaside building also houses 25 hotel rooms at €50 for a double. ⊠ *Sv. Jurja 23, Starigrad 23244* ☎ *023/369–017* ⊟ *AE, DC, MC, V.*

Where to Stay

For private rooms in Starigrad or nearby (around €30 high season, €20 the rest of the year), check with the tourist-information office or, better yet, the friendly travel agency **Koma-Maras** (⊠ Dr. Franje Tuđmana14, Starigrad 23244 ☎023/359–206 ☎023/359–207), where communication in English goes more smoothly. It's located in a little shopping center on your left as you go north, immediately before the INA fuel station.

$ ▦ **Hotel Alan.** Once inside this high-rise hotel, which experienced a thorough makeover in 2004, you might easily forget that you are, in fact, in a concrete box that still looks rather like a college dormitory. It's part of a complex that also includes 28 apartments in adjacent, low-rise buildings and a small campground as well as a public beach and an outdoor pool. Hotel Alan offers rooms that, though a bit cramped, are nonetheless bright and modern, with soothing pastel bedspreads. Rooms on the upper floors, at least, carry the added pleasure of stunning views of the sea on one side and mountains on the other. As an added plus, every Thursday the hotel hosts Karaoke Night. There's a 10% discount if you stay more than one night. ⊠ *Dr. Franje Tuđmana 14, Starigrad 23244* ☎ *023/209–050* ☎ *023/369–203* ⊕ *www.hotel-alan.hr* ⇨ *140 rooms* ⚿ *Restaurant, pizzeria, bar, in-room safes, cable TV, pool, minibars, gym, sauna, beach* ⊟ *AE, DC, MC, V* |○| *BP.*

★ ¢ ▦ **Hotel Rajna.** On an isolated stretch of the main road just before you enter Starigrad from the south—and close to the national park access road—this friendly little hotel is a bit concrete-boxish in appearance. However, for years now it has been offering not only a splendid view of the mountains to the east and clean, spacious (though not quite sparkling and modern) rooms but also a restaurant with carefully prepared, scrumptious seafood fare. ⊠ *Dr. Franje Tuđmana, Starigrad 23244* ☎ *023/359–121* ☎ *023/369–888* ⊕ *www.hotel-rajna.com* ⇨ *10 rooms* ⚿ *Restaurant, in-room safes, cable TV, minibars* ⊟ *AE, DC, MC, V* |○| *BP.*

Sports & the Outdoors

Tours

Koma-Maras (⊠ Dr. Franje Tuđmana14, Starigrad 23244 ☎ 023/359–206 ☎023/359–207) rents bicycles and sells tickets for various excursions in the national park as well as tickets for daylong boat trips up the lovely Zrmanja River gorge and its waterfalls, which are near Obrovac, toward the southern end of the Velebit range; the boat tours cost about 250 Kn per person. There's an ATM by the agency entrance.

ZADAR & NORTHERN DALMATIA ESSENTIALS

AIR TRAVEL

Zadar's airport is in Zemunik Donji, 9 km (5½ mi) southeast of the city. Croatia Airlines, which offers service between Zadar and Zagreb as well as Paris and other European cities, runs buses (20 Kn one-way) between the airport, the city bus station, and the harborside near the ferry port on the Old Town's peninsula.

🛈 **Croatian Airlines** ✉ Poljana Natka Nodila 7 ☎ 023/250-101 or 062/777-777.

BOAT & FERRY TRAVEL

Jadrolinija's local ferries (*trajektne linije*) and passenger boats (*brodske linije*) run daily routes that connect Zadar not only with the surrounding islands but also with Rijeka. Do check also with Miatours, which offers alternative service to the islands and also between Zadar and Ancona, Italy. Twice a day most days of the week, there is ferry service between Pula and Zadar; at 8 hours and at a cost of only 123 Kn it's a decent alternative to the bus, though a downside is that the ferry from Pula arrives in Zadar at midnight. The offices are by the Harbor Gate in the city walls, across from the ferry port.

Both Jadrolinija and Miatours run ferry routes from the port of Zadar, just outside the city walls on the western side of the old town, to Sali. The trip, which takes about two hours and costs from 30 Kn (Miatours) to 38 Kn (Jadrolinija), takes you initially south in the Zadarski kanal, then through a narrow strait between Ugljan and Pašman islands before proceeding to the island of Dugi Otok, where you stop briefly in Zaglav before heading on to Sali.

If you don't want to base yourself in Murter, you can take a cruise straight from the Borik marina just outside Zadar all the way to Kornati National Park, that almost mythical archipelago even further south. The *Blue Lagoon*, which holds 90 passengers, will take you on a full-day journey (8 AM to 6 PM) to the national park, including stops on the island of Mana and Kornat.

🛈 *Blue Lagoon* ☎ 022/334-468 or 098/875-746. **Jadrolinija** ✉ Liburnska obala 7 ☎ 023/254-800 or 023/250-555 ⊕ www.jadrolinija.hr. **Miatours** ✉ Vrata sv. Krševana 7 ☎ 023/254-300.

BUS TRAVEL

Though sometimes crowded in mid-summer, Zadar's bus station will almost certainly figure prominently in your travel plans unless you're driving or flying directly here. The trip to or from Zagreb takes about 7 hours, the ticket being around 100 Kn. Timetables are available at the station. The luggage (*garderobe*) room is open from 6 AM to 10 PM, and costs 1.20 Kn per hour.

Getting to Nin from Zadar is easy by bus. The half-hour trip follows the coastal road north; the fare is 11 Kn one-way, with buses running daily out of Zadar's station every 45 minutes or so. By bus, getting to Murter—to its tiny main square, Trg Rudina, which is where you're dropped off and get back on—from Zadar is certainly doable, if a bit complicated. You can transfer either at Šibenik or at Vodice; although the former option looks longer on the map, given the crowded confusion at Vodice's small station, Šibenik—around 12 buses daily from Zadar—may be a less trying experience (and a surer way of getting a seat) even if it might take a bit longer; about 9 buses go on from Sibenik to Murter (via Vodice). Travel time via Šibenik is 2½ hours or more (i. e., 90 minutes from Zadar to Šibenik, up to an hour of waiting time, then another 45 minutes to Murter via Vodice). The total cost: around 70 Kn via Šibenik and around 50 Kn if you go straight to Vodice (travel time is under two hours, and an even harder-to-predict wait time, since the bus from Šibenik might be contending with heavy traffic).

Numerous buses ply the one-hour route daily between Zadar and Starigrad for access to Paklenica National Park. The one way cost to or from Starigrad—via the Zadar–Rijeka bus—is between 25 Kn and 34 Kn, depending on the company. There are two stops in Starigrad; the National Park information office is between the two, and the access road to the park is near the first stop (if you're coming from Zadar).

🚌 **Zadar Bus Station** ✉ Ante Starčević 2 ☎ 023/211-555.

CAR TRAVEL
With the completion of the Mala Kapela tunnel in June 2005, the A1 motorway between Zagreb and Dalmatia has become a complete, uninterrupted whole. Zadar is the first major stop on the highway, which proceeds south toward Split. Barring traffic congestion, especially on weekends, the trip between Zagreb and Zadar is doable in 2 ½ hours. That said, you can also easily get to Zadar by bus, whether from Zagreb, Rijeka, or Split, and rent a car there if necessary. As the Zadar bus station can be a chaotic place at times, especially in mid-summer, you might want to rent a car for some excursions—to Murter, for example, which otherwise involves a somewhat complicated, time-consuming trip to or toward Šibenik with a transfer. But you'll be just fine without a car in and immediately around Zadar, as bus service is both good and affordable.

🚗 **Budget** ✉ Obala kneza Branimira 1, Zadar ☎ 023/313-681. **Hertz** ✉ Vrata sv. Krševana [downtown] and at Zadar Airport, Zadar ☎ 023/254-301 [same number for both locations]. **National** ✉ Bože Peričića 2, Zadar ☎ 091/320-0121. **Uni rent** ✉ Poljana N. Nodila 9, Zadar ☎ 023/254-162.

TRAIN TRAVEL
It's possible to travel between Zadar and Zagreb by train. Five trains run daily from Zadar to Knin (in just over 2 hours with almost 20 stops in-between), and from Knin you can transfer within an hour to a train that gets you to Zagreb in roughly 4 hours—that's around 7 hours in all from Zadar to Zagreb, for about 130 Kn one-way. Unless you want to see some relatively war-wearied parts of the interior, though, you'll do well to simply hop aboard one of the many daily Zagreb-bound buses at Zadar's bus station, which get you to the capital in less time and for less money (around 100 Kn). Trains also run between Knin and Split, and service and travel times are improving yearly on all these routes.

🚆 **Zadar Train Station** ✉ Ante Starčevica 4, Zadar ☎ 060/333-444.

EMERGENCIES
🚑 **Ambulance Ambulance** ☎ 94.
🏥 **Doctors & Dentists Main Hospital** ✉ Bože Peričića 5, Zadar ☎ 023/315-677. **Zadar Health Center** ✉ A. Medulića 1, Zadar ☎ 023/214-078 or 023/213-956.
🔥 **Fire Fire Emergencies** ☎ 93.

🔟 Pharmacies **Ljekarna Centar** Closed Sunday; ✉ Jurja Barakovića, Zadar ☎ 023/213-374 or 023/302-931. **Ljekarna Donat** Closed Sunday; ✉ Braće Vranjanina, Zadar ☎ 023/251-342.

🔟 Police **Police Emergencies** ☎ 92.

INTERNET

Zadar is Northern Dalmatia's only sizeable city and the only place you can find more than a handful of options for Internet access. If you don't mind (earphone-equipped) kids playing computer games all around you, the aptly named Internet, on the first side street to your left after you cross the pedestrian bridge into the newer part of town, will keep you close to the Old Town. Watch your step on exiting, though, as the curb is about 2 feet high. Right in the Old Town, in the atmospheric Varoš district and next door to the Trattoria Canzona Pizzeria, is the likewise well-named Internet Caffe.

🔟 **Internet** ✉ Rikarda Katalinića Jeretova 5 ☎ No phone. **Internet Caffe** ✉ Stomorica 8 ☎ 023/302-270.

VISITOR INFORMATION

If there's no English speaker at the office you happen to contact, try the Zadar County Tourist Information office or the city of Zadar's corresponding office.

🔟 **Biograd-Na-Moru Tourist Information** ✉ Trg hrvatskih velikana 2, Biograd ☎ 023/383-123 or 023/385-382 ⊕ www.tzg-biograd.hr. **Murter Tourist Information** ✉ Rudina, Murter ☎ 022/434-995 or 022/434-950 ⊕ www.tzo-murter.hr. **Nin Tourist Information** ✉ Trg braće Radića 3, Nin ☎ 023/264-280 ⊕ www.nin.hr. **Sali Tourist Information** ✉ Western side of Sali harbor, Sali ☎ 023/377-094. **Starigrad Tourist Information** ✉ Trg Tome Marašovića 1, Starigrad ☎ 023/369-245 ⊕ www.stari-grad-faros.hr. **Zadar Tourist Information** ✉ Mihe Klaića, 2 yards from Narodni trg, Zadar ☎ 023/316-166 or 023/212-412 ⊕ www.zadar.hr. **Zadar County Tourist Information** ✉ Sv. Leopolda B. Mandića 1, Zadar ☎ 023/315-107 or 023/315-316 ⊕ www.zadar.hr.

Split & Central Dalmatia

6

WORD OF MOUTH

"Trogir was beautiful: a pretty town full of ancient stone buildings with red-tiled roofs . . . The feel is similar to the Italian towns of Tuscany and Umbria, but instead of colorful plaster walls, most of the buildings are grey stone, with a few weathered green doors and shutters."

—copilot

"[By the time we got to Hvar, we were pretty tired of each day seeing something prettier than the day before. I mean we'd readjust our expectations and think to ourselves, "ok, this is what beauty is," and then Croatia would just up and slap us in the face and let us know that it wasn't done amazing us yet."

—alyssamma

By Jane Foster

CENTRAL DALMATIA IS MORE MOUNTAINOUS, wild, and unexploited than the northern coastal regions. And while tourist facilities may be less sophisticated than in Istria and Kvarner, Dalmatia's rugged limestone peaks, emerald-blue waters, countless islands, and magnificent coastal towns offer an unrefined Mediterranean charm all of their own.

The region's capital (and Croatia's second-largest city) is the busy port of Split, with its historic center protected by the sturdy walls of an imperial Roman palace. From here, you can take an overnight ferry service to Ancona, Italy, plus regular ferry and catamaran services to the outlying islands. Split is also Central Dalmatia's main base for yacht-charter companies.

A 90-minute drive up the coast, northwest of Split, lies Šibenik, home to a splendid Gothic-Renaissance cathedral. Once an important industrial center, since the war for independence Šibenik has fallen into economic decline, but it still makes a good base for visiting Krka National Park, a chain of thundering waterfalls surrounded by dense woodland, and the peaceful riverside town of Skradin.

Moving back from Šibenik toward Split, Trogir is a gem of medieval stone architecture, built on a tiny island connected to the mainland by a bridge. And a 30-minute drive down the coast from Split brings one to Omiš and the mouth of the River Cetina, forming a steep-sided valley renowned for such adventure sports as rafting and rock climbing (called free climbing in Croatia).

However, for many people what makes Central Dalmatia so special are the islands. The nearest, Brač, is home to Croatia's most photographed beach, the stunning Zlatni Rat (Golden Cape). The nearby village of Bol, backed by the soaring limestone heights of Vidova Gora, has modern hotel accommodations and excellent sports facilities.

West of Brač lies Šolta. Although there is little of cultural interest here, those lucky enough to be sailing along the south side of the island will find several idyllic bays that are accessible only by sea.

South of Brač rises the island of Hvar, home to Central Dalmatia's most exclusive destination, Hvar Town, with its 16th-century Venetian buildings ringing three sides of the harbor, its magnificent main square overlooked by a baroque cathedral, and the entire scene presided over by a proud hilltop castle.

Further out to sea still lies wild, windswept Vis, Croatia's most distant inhabited island. There are only two real settlements: Vis Town and Komiža, the latter making the best starting point for a day trip to Modra Spilja (Blue Cave) on the island of Biševo.

Back on the mainland, a two-hour drive down the coast south of Split brings you to Makarska, a popular seaside resort built around a bay filled with fishing boats and backed by the rugged silhouette of the Biokovo Mountains, with Croatia's third-highest peak, Sveti Jure (1762 meters [5,780 feet]); the peak offers stunning views over the entire region.

Lastovo, Croatia's second most distant inhabited island (after Vis), remains firmly off the beaten track, with its fertile green valleys overlooked by the crumbling stone buildings of Lastovo Town. Although it is part of Southern Dalmatia, it is not connected to the region by boat, the islanders having chosen to establish ferry and catamaran services to Split.

Exploring Central Dalmatia
About the Restaurants

Eateries fall into two main categories: you can eat in a *restoran* (restaurant) or *konoba* (tavern). Restaurants are more formal affairs, catering mainly to tourists and offering Croatian cuisine plus a choice of popular international dishes. In contrast, a konoba serves typical regional dishes; many offer a *merenda* (cut-price lunch) and at those you are likely to see locals as well as tourists.Central Dalmatian specialties are mainly seafood based. *Rižot* (risotto) reflects the region's historic ties with Venice, as does *brodet* (fish stewed in a rich tomato, onion, and wine sauce).

Fish are divided into two categories: "white" fish, including *brancin* (sea bass) and *san pjero* (John Dory) being the more expensive, while "blue" fish, including *srdele* (sardines) and *skuša* (mackerel), are cheaper but less frequently on offer. In restaurants, be aware that fresh fish is priced by the kilogram, so prices vary dramatically depending on how big your fish is.

WHAT IT COSTS in Croatian Kuna (Kn)				
$$$$	$$$	$$	$	¢
RESTAURANTS over 80	60–80	35–60	20–35	under 20

Restaurant prices are per person for a main course at dinner.

About the Hotels

Central Dalmatia's best and most expensive hotels are in Hvar Town on the island of Hvar. The region's socialist-era resort hotels are gradually being privatized and refurbished, and a number of small family-run hotels have opened as well. However, many visitors still prefer to rent a private room or apartment, a solution that offers value for money, direct contact with the locals, and (if you are lucky) an authentic stone cottage opening onto a terrace lined with potted geraniums and a blissful sea view. The season runs from Easter to late October, and peaks during July and August, when prices rise significantly and when it may be difficult to find a place to sleep if you have not booked in advance.

WHAT IT COSTS in euros (€) and Croatian kuna (Kn)				
$$$$	$$$	$$	$	¢
IN EUROS over € 225	€175–€225	€125–€175	€75–€125	under €75
IN KUNA over 1,650	1,300–1,650	925–1,300	550–925	under 550

Hotel prices are for two people in a double room in high season, excluding taxes and service charges.

Central Dalmatia warrants weeks of discovery, with many locals admitting they haven't even seen it all. However, if your time is limited, the itineraries listed below aim to give you a taste of the major attractions.

If you have 3 days

Devote day one to **Split,** exploring the historic monuments within the walls of Diocletian's Palace and attending an open-air opera performance if the Split Summer Festival is in progress. On the next day, take an early morning ferry to Supetar on the island of Brač, then a local bus to **Bol,** for an afternoon bathing on Croatia's finest beach, Zlatni Rat. Catch the late-afternoon catamaran to Jelsa on the island of Hvar, then a local bus to **Hvar Town,** the region's hippest island re-sort, where you should sleep. Next morning either check out Hvar's Venetian-style architecture or take a taxi boat to Pakleni Otoci for a swim. Catch the late-afternoon ferry back to Split for your final night.

If you have 5 days

Spend your first day in Split. On the next morning, drive or take a local bus to **Trogir,** a compact settlement of stone houses built on an island linked to the mainland by a bridge, then proceed up the coast for an afternoon in **Šibenik,** where the most visited monument is the Gothic–Renaissance Cathedral. Spend the night in either Šibenik or **Skradin.** Give day three to the waterfalls and dense woodland of **Krka National Park,** returning to Split for the night. Days four and five should be dedicated to the islands of **Brač** and **Hvar** (*see above*), re-turning to Split for the final night.

If you have 7 days

Spend your first day in Split, the second and third days in Trogir, Šibenik, Skradin, and Krka National Park, as outlined above, returning to Split on the third night. Days four and five can then be given over to the islands of Brač and Hvar (as described above) returning to Split for the fifth night. On the next morning, ei-ther drive or take a local bus down the coast to **Omiš,** from where you can set off up the **Cetina Valley** and participate in adventure sports (by prior ar-rangement). In the evening continue down the coast to **Makarska,** where you should sleep. The final day you can explore Makarska and its beaches, or ven-ture up Biokovo Mountain for spectacular views over the entire region. Return to Split for your last night.

Timing

High season runs from July through August, when the region is inun-dated with foreign tourists, predominantly Italians. During this period prices rise significantly, it's difficult to find a place to sleep if you haven't reserved in advance, restaurant staff are overworked, and beaches are crowded. On top of everything, it can be very hot. On the positive side, some museums and churches have extended opening hours, the season's open-air bars and clubs bring nightlife to the fore, and there are several cultural festivals with performances starring international musicians, dancers, and actors.

Low season runs from November through April, when many hotels and restaurants close completely, the exception being over the New Year period, when some of the more sophisticated establishments (for example in Hvar Town) open their doors for the holidays. At this time of year the weather is unreliable, but if you're lucky you could find yourself drinking morning coffee in the sunshine below a deep blue sky, albeit against a backdrop of snow-capped mountains.

However, for most people the best time to visit is mid-season, May through June and September through October. During these periods you'll miss the crowds, the weather should be sunny and dry, and the sea will be warm enough to swim; the region's hotels and restaurants will be open, but their pace slow enough to lend an air of true relaxation.

Numbers in the margins correspond to numbers on the Central Dalmatia map

SPLIT

Split is 365 km (228 mi) south of Zagreb.

Split's ancient core is so spectacular and unusual that a visit is more than worth your time. The heart of the city lies within the walls of Roman Emperor Diocletian's summer palace, which was built in the 3rd century AD. Diocletian, born in the nearby Roman settlement of Salona in AD 245, achieved a brilliant career as a soldier and became emperor at the age of 40. In 295, he ordered this vast palace to be built in his native Dalmatia, and when it was completed, he stepped down from the throne and retired to his beloved homeland. Upon his death, he was laid to rest in an octagonal mausoleum, around which Split's magnificent cathedral was built.

In 615, when Salona was sacked by barbarian tribes, those fortunate enough to escape found refuge within the stout palace walls and divided up the vast imperial apartments into more modest living quarters. Thus, the palace developed into an urban center, and by the 11th century the settlement had expanded beyond the ancient walls.

Under the rule of Venice (1420–1797), Split—as a gateway to the Balkan interior—became one of the Adriatic's main trading ports, and the city's splendid Renaissance palaces bear witness to the affluence of those times. When the Habsburgs took control during the 19th century, an overland connection to Central Europe was established by the construction of the Split–Zagreb–Vienna railway line.

After World War II, the Tito years saw a period of rapid urban expansion: industrialization accelerated and the suburbs extended to accommodate high-rise apartment blocks. Today the historic center of Split is included on UNESCO's list of World Heritage Sites.

Exploring Split

The old town (often referred to as Grad), where most of the architectural monuments are found, lies within the walls of Diocletian's Palace,

Historic Monuments

The shores of Central Dalmatia abound with spectacular architecture, bearing witness to its rich and complex history. There are three UNESCO World Heritage Sites in the region: Diocletian's Roman Palace in Split; the old town of Trogir with its 13th-century Romanesque Cathedral; and in Šibenik the 16th-century Gothic–Renaissance Cathedral. Fortunately, many historic centers have been listed and protected, saving them from the ravages of modern development.

Island Retreats

Everyone loves the romantic image of escaping to an island, and in Central Dalmatia there are plenty to choose from. The two that stand out are Hvar and Vis. Hvar is probably Croatia's hippest island, pulling gossip column–worthy celebrities, would-be artists, politicians, and nudists. The main resort, Hvar Town, seems to have it all: beautifully preserved Venetian-style architecture, stylish modern hotels, classy seafood restaurants, and a sophisticated nightlife. In contrast, distant Vis remains free of commercial development. Closed to foreigners until 1989 (during the Tito years it was a Yugoslav naval base) it is now very "in" with the yachting crowd, who appreciate its unspoiled nature, tumble-down stone cottages, and rustic eateries.

6

Beaches

The best beaches and the cleanest water for swimming are on the islands. Croatia's most stunning beach has to be Zlatni Rat, a cape made up of fine shingle, close to the village of Bol on the island of Brač. If you want to enjoy it at its best, try to avoid peak season, when it becomes very crowded. Close to Hvar Town lie the Pakleni Otoci (Pakleni islands), a group of tiny, unpopulated islets with pine woods and indented coasts offering secluded pebble beaches for bathing. Taxi boats relay visitors back and forth from Hvar Town to the most accessible spots.

Sailing

Central Dalmatia is probably Croatia's top region for sailing, thanks to the myriad islands and well-equipped marinas. Split is the main charter base, with dozens of companies keeping boats there. Other well-equipped marinas in the region can be found in Trogir, Skradin, and Vodice on the mainland, and Palmižana, Vrboska, and Milna on the islands.

Adventure Sports

In the Cetina Valley, near Omiš, the River Cetina has cut a high-sided canyon between the mountains of Mosor and Biokovo, with a series of rapids sided by sheer-faced cliffs, making this one of the country's major spots for rafting and rock climbing. A short distance further down the coast, Biokovo Mountain, behind Makarska, is a nature park and home to rare animals such as chamois goats and mouflon sheep, which thrive on the scanty pastures and bare limestone rocks. On the island of Brač, Zlatni Rat offers good conditions for windsurfing, whereas the mountain of Vidova Gora is popular for hiking and mountain biking.

Central
Dalmatia

which gives onto the seafront promenade, known to locals as the Riva. West of the center, Varoš is a conglomeration of stone fishermen's cottages built into a hillside, behind which rises Marjan, a 3½-km (2-mi) long peninsula covered with pinewoods. Southeast of the center, the ferry port, bus station, and train station are grouped close together on Obala Kneza Domagoja.

Numbers in the text correspond to numbers in the margin and on the Split map.

What to See

★ ❶ **Dioklecijanova Palača** (Diocletian's Palace). The original palace was a combination of a luxurious villa and a Roman garrison, based on the ground plan of an irregular rectangle. Each of the four walls bore a main gate, the largest and most important being the northern *Zlatna Vrata* (Golden Gate), opening onto the road to the Roman settlement of Salona. The entrance from the western wall was the *Željezna Vrata* (Iron Gate), and the entrance through the east wall was the *Srebrena Vrata* (Silver Gate). The *Mjedna Vrata* (Bronze Gate) in the south wall faced directly onto the sea, and during Roman times boats would have docked here. The city celebrated the palace's 1700th birthday in 2005. ⊠ *Obala Hrvatskog Narodnog Preporoda, Grad.*

★ ⑩ **Galerija Meštrović** (Mesßtrović Gallery). A modern villa surrounded by extensive gardens, this building designed by Ivan Meštrovic was his summer residence during the 1920s and '30s. Some 200 of his sculptural works in wood, marble, stone, and bronze are on display, both indoors and out. Entrance to the Galerija Meštrovića is also valid for the nearby **Kaštelet** (✉ Šetalište Ivana Meštrovića 39), housing a chapel containing a cycle of New Testament bas-relief wood carvings that many consider Meštrović's finest work. ✉ *Šetalište Ivana Meštrovića 46, Meje* ☎ *021/340–800* ⊕ *www.mdc.hr* 🖭 *20 Kn* ☉ *May–Sept., Tues.–Sun. 9–9; Oct.–Apr., Tues.–Sat. 10–4, Sun. 10–2.*

❻ **Gradski Muzej** (City Museum). Split's city museum is worth a quick look both to witness the collection of medieval weaponry and to see the interior of this splendid 15th-century town house. The dining room, on the first floor, is furnished just as it would have been when the Papalić family owned the house, giving some idea of how the aristocracy of that time lived. ✉ *Papaličeva 1, Grad* ☎ *021/344–917* ⊕ *www.mdc.hr* 🖭 *10 Kn* ☉ *Nov.–May, Tues.–Fri. 9–4, weekends 10–noon; June–Oct., daily 9–noon and 6–9.*

❺ **Jupiterov Hram** (Jupiter's Temple). This Roman temple was converted into a baptistery during the Middle Ages. The entrance is guarded by the mate (unfortunately damaged) of the black-granite sphinx that stands in front of the cathedral. Inside, beneath the coffered barrel vault and ornamented cornice, the 11th-century baptismal font is adorned with a stone relief showing a medieval Croatian king on his throne. Directly behind it, the bronze statue of St. John the Baptist is the work of Meštrović. ✉ *Kraj Sv Ivana, Grad* 🖭 *5 Kn* ☉ *May–Oct., daily 8–6.*

❹ **Katedrala Sveti Dujam** (Cathedral of St. Dominius). The main body of the cathedral is the 3rd-century octagonal mausoleum designed as a shrine to Emperor Diocletian. During the 7th century, refugees from Salona converted it into an early Christian church, ironically dedicating it to Sv Duje (St. Domnius), after Bishop Domnius of Salona, one of the many Christians martyred during the late emperor's persecution campaign. The cathedral's monumental main door is ornamented with magnificent carved wooden reliefs, the work of Andrija Buvina of Split, portraying 28 scenes from the life of Christ and dated 1214. Inside, the hexagonal Romanesque stone pulpit, with richly carved decoration, is from the 13th century. The high altar, surmounted by a late-Gothic canopy, was executed by Bonino of Milan in 1427. Nearby is the 15th-century canopied Gothic altar of Anastasius by Juraj Dalmatinac. The elegant 200-foot Romanesque-Gothic bell tower was constructed in stages between the 12th and 16th centuries. ✉ *Peristil, Grad* 🖭 *Cathedral free, bell tower 5 Kn* ☉ *Sept.–June, daily 8–noon and 4:30–7; July–Aug., daily 8–8.*

⑪ **Marjan** (Marjan Hill). Situated on a hilly peninsula, this much-loved park is planted with pine trees and Mediterranean shrubs and has been a protected nature reserve since 1964. A network of paths crisscrosses the grounds, offering stunning views over the sea and islands. ✉ *Marjan.*

Split

0 — 1/4 mile
0 — 1/4 kilometer

① Omladinska

②

Trg.
Republike

① Sredmanuška
⑨

Strosmajerov
Park

⑦

Dominisova

⑧ Željezna
vrata

⑥ Papa
liceva

Kresimirova

⑤

⑥ Iliske Akad **⑦** **②**

Poljana Kraljice
Jelene

Trg
Brace
Radica

⑤

③

④

Srebrna
vrata

⑨–**⑪** **③** **④**

Obala Hrvatskog Narodnog Preporoda

③
⑧

Mjedena
Vrata **①** Severova

Obala Lazareta

Kralja Zvonimira

Obala Lazareta

⑩–**⑫**

KEY

① *Exploring Sights*

① *Hotels & Restaurants*

IMPERIAL QUIRKS

MANY POWERFUL STATE LEADERS *tend toward eccentricity, and Roman Emperor Diocletian was no exception. Born to a humble family in Dalmatia, he went on to govern the empire for 20 years, proving to be an astute and innovative leader. However, he was also something of a megalomaniac. Believing himself to be Jupiter's representative on Earth, he set about persecuting Christians, ordering religious scriptures to be burnt, churches destroyed, and thousands of believers executed. He dressed in robes of satin and gold, sporting a crown embedded with pearls and shoes studded with precious stones. His imperial apartments were guarded by eunuchs, and anyone who came into his presence was obliged to fall prostrate on the ground out of respect. The best known of his many massive building schemes is Diocletians' Baths in Rome, a vast complex of marble and mosaics, constructed by 10,000 Christian prisoners for the pleasure of some 3000 bathers.*

need a break? Having reached this point you're undoubtedly in need of refreshment. Sit on a sofa at **Vidilica** (⊠ Nazorov Prilaz, Marjan), a lounge-style café terrace, and order a long, cold drink. Then sit back and enjoy the breathtaking view.

❾ Muzej Hrvatskih Arheološki Spomenika (Museum of Croatian Archaeological Monuments). This modern building displays early Croatian religious art from the 7th through the 12th centuries. The most interesting exhibits are fine stone carvings decorated with plaitwork design, surprisingly similar to the geometric patterns typical of Celtic art. In the garden you can see several stećci, monolithic stone tombs dating back to the cult of the Bogomils (an anti-imperial sect that developed in the Balkans during the 10th century). ⊠ Šetalište Ivana Meštrovića, Meje ☎ 021/358–420 ⊕ www.mhas-split.hr ⊠ Free ☉ June–Oct., Tues.–Sat 10–1 and 5–8; Nov–May, Tues.–Sat. 9–4.

❽ Narodni Trg (People's Square). A pedestrianized expanse paved with gleaming white marble, this is contemporary Split's main square. Although religious activity has to this day centered on Peristil, Narodni trg became the focus of civic life during the 14th century. In the 15th century, the Venetians constructed several important public buildings here: the Town Hall (housing a small Ethnographic Museum, with erratic opening hours), plus the Rector's Palace and a theater, the latter two sadly demolished by the Habsburgs in the 19th century. The Austrians, for their part, added a secessionist building at the west end of the square. ⊠ Grad.

❷ Peristil (Peristyle). From Roman times up to the present day the main public meeting place within the palace walls, this spacious central courtyard is flanked by marble columns topped with Corinthian capitals and richly ornamented cornices linked by arches. There are six columns on both the east and west sides, and four more at the south end, which mark the monumental entrance to the Vestibul. During the Split Summer Fes-

tival, Peristil becomes an open-air stage hosting evening opera performances. ⊠ *Grad.*

The summer terrace at the **Luxor Café** (⊠ Peristil, Grad) makes a
perfect place to sit over coffee or a glass of local wine and absorb the
2,000 years of magnificent architecture that surround you.

❸ Vestibul. The cupola of this domed space would once have been decorated with marble and mosaics. Today there's only a round hole in the
top of the dome, but it produces a stunning effect: the dark interior, the
blue sky above, and the tip of the cathedral's bell tower framed in the
opening. ⊠ *Peristil, Grad.*

❼ Zlatna Vrata (Golden Gate). Formerly the main land entrance into the
palace, Zlatna Vrata, on the north side of the palace, is the most monumental of the four gates. Just outside the Zlatna Vrata stands Meštrović's gigantic bronze **statue of Grgur Ninski** (Bishop Gregory of Nin).
During the 9th century, the bishop campaigned for the use of the Slav
language in the Croatian Church, as opposed to Latin, thus infuriating
Rome. This statue was created in 1929 and placed on Peristil to mark
the 1,000th anniversary of the Split Synod, then moved here in 1957.
Note the big toe on the left foot, which is considered by locals to be a
good luck charm and has been worn gold through constant touching.
⊠ *Dioklecijanova, Grad.*

Where to Eat

Split does have some good restaurants, though they're not always easy
to find. As in any city of fishermen and sailors, seafood predominates
here. In most restaurants, fresh fish is normally prepared over a char-
coal fire and served with *blitva sa krumpirom* (Swiss chard and potato
with garlic and olive oil). For a cheaper option, bear in mind that the
pizza in Split is almost as good as (and sometimes even better than) that
in Italy. Last but not least, complement your meal with a bottle of Dalmatian wine.

$$$–$$$$ ✕ **Adriatic Grašo.** Inside the ACI marina, close to the gardens of Sveti
Stipan, this seafood restaurant has a light and airy minimalist interior
with a glazed frontage, and a summer terrace where you can watch the
yachts sail in and out of port. In the vein of "slow food" (a reaction
against fast food that started in Italy in the late 1980s), the kitchen gives
great care to seasonal ingredients and presentation. The owner, Zoran
Grašo, is a retired basketball player, so you may spot some well-known
sporting stars from time to time among the diners. ⊠ *Uvala Baluni,
Zvončac* ☎ *021/398–560* ▤ *AE, DC, MC, V.*

$$$–$$$$ ✕ **Šumica.** The first thing you'll notice upon arrival at Šumica, which is
set in the shade of pine trees overlooking Bačvice Bay, is the number of
black BMWs in the parking lot. The atmosphere in the dining room,
which tends to be overly formal, is more than compensated for by the
fresh sea breezes on the summer terrace. The house specialty is tagli-
atelle with salmon and scampi. ⊠ *Put Firula 6, Bačvice* ☎ *021/389–
895* ▤ *AE, DC, MC, V.*

$$–$$$$ ✗**Konoba Varoš.** The dining-room walls are hung with seascapes and fishing nets and the waiters wear traditional Dalmatian waistcoats. The place can seem a little dour at lunchtime but mellows when the candles are lit during the evening. The fresh fish and *pržene lignje* (fried squid) are excellent, and there's also a reasonable choice of Croatian meat dishes. It's a five-minute walk west of the center, at the bottom of Varoš. ⊠ *Ban Mladenova 7, Varoš* ☎ *021/396–138* ▭ *AE, DC, MC, V.*

$$–$$$ ✗**Kod Jose.** This typical Dalmatian *konoba* is relaxed and romantic, with exposed stone walls and heavy wooden furniture set off by candlelight. The waiters are wonderfully discreet and the *rižot frutta di mare* (seafood risotto) delicious. You'll find it just outside the palace walls, a five-minute walk from Zlatna Vrata (Golden Gate). ⊠ *Sredmanuška 4, Manuš* ☎ *021/347–397* ▭ *AE, DC, MC, V.*

$–$$$ ✗**Adriana.** Overlooking the seafront promenade, Adriana is a perfect spot for people-watching day and night. It can get a little rowdy, with loud music and large groups, but the food is remarkably good, with good grilled meat dishes such as *čevapčići* (kebabs), *pohani sir* (fried cheese), salads, and pizzas. ⊠ *Obala Hrvatskog Narodnog preporoda 6, Grad* ☎ *021/344–079* ▭ *AE, DC, MC, V.*

$–$$ ✗**Pizzeria Galija.** The best pizzas in town, as well as delicious pasta dishes and a range of colorful salads, are to be found in this centrally located pizzeria, which is close to the fish market. A favorite with locals, its dining room is bustling and informal, with heavy wooden tables and benches, and a large brick oven; draft beer and wine are sold by the glass. The owner, Željko Jerkov, is a retired Olympic gold medal–winning basketball player. ⊠ *Tončićeva 12, Grad* ☎ *021/347–932* ▭ *No credit cards.*

Where to Stay

Split has often been overlooked as a sightseeing destination and considered a mere transit point to the islands. As a result, it suffers from a shortage of good places to stay. What's more, during the 1990s many hotels were used to house refugees, and some still need to be refurbished. However, several establishments are pleasant, fairly central, and reasonably priced.

$$$
Fodor'sChoice
★
▥**Hotel Vestibul Palace.** Split's first boutique hotel opened in June 2005. Within the palace walls and accessed through the ancient vestibule, the interior of this building has been carefully renovated to expose Roman stone and brickwork, which have been cleverly combined with more modern, minimalist designer details. A bar and restaurant can be found on the ground floor, and seven rooms are upstairs, complete with subtle lighting and plasma TVs. ⊠ *Iza Vestibula 4, Grad, 21000* ☎ *021/329–329* 🖷 *020/329–333* ⊕ *www.vestibulpalace.com* ⟿ *5 rooms, 2 suites* ⚴ *Restaurant, room service, in-room safes, minibars, cable TV, in-room data ports, bar, laundry service* ▭ *AE, DC, MC, V* ⊶ *BP.*

$$ ▥**Hotel Park.** Smart and reliable, Hotel Park reopened in 2001 after extensive renovation work. The building dates back to 1921 and lies 10 minutes east of the city walls, overlooking Bačvice Bay. The rooms are modern and neatly furnished, and a pleasant terrace with palms offers views over the sea. ⊠ *Hatzeov Perivoj 3, Bačvice, 21000* ☎ *021/406–*

400 🏠 *021/406–401* ⊕ *www.hotelpark-split.hr* ⤳ *54 rooms, 3 suites* ⛄ *Restaurant, room service, minibars, cable TV, in-room data ports, fitness classes, massage, sauna, bar, laundry service, meeting rooms* ▭ *AE, DC, MC, V* ⏏ *BP.*

$$ ⊞ **Hotel Split.** A 25-minute trek east of the center, Hotel Split is a white contemporary building overlooking the sea. The rooms have modern furnishings, comfortable work desks, and decorated in blues and whites. A small beach has sunbeds and parasols, and an outdoor pool. The hotel also has decent business facilities. ✉ *Put Trstenika 19, Trstenik, 21000* ☎ *021/303–111* 🏠 *021/303–011* ⊕ *www.hotelsplit.hr* ⤳ *135 rooms, 8 suites* ⛄ *2 restaurants, room service, minibars, cable TV, Internet room, pool, beach, 3 bars, laundry service, business services, meeting rooms, car rental* ▭ *AE, DC, MC, V* ⏏ *BP.*

$ ⊞ **Hotel Jadran.** This small 1970s-style hotel lies close to the ACI marina and the gardens of Sveti Stipan, overlooking Zvončac Bay. A pleasant 15-minute walk along the seafront brings you to the city center. All the rooms are decorated in blue-and-white and have balconies with either a sea view or a park view. There are decent sports facilities: The Croatian national water-polo team trained here for the 2004 Olympics. ✉ *Sustipanjska put 23, Zvončac, 21000* ☎ *021/398–622* 🏠 *021/398–586* ⊕ *www.hoteljadran.hr* ⤳ *31 rooms, 2 suites* ⛄ *Restaurant, café, cable TV, pool, gym, massage, sauna, bar, meeting room* ▭ *AE, DC, MC, V* ⏏ *BP.*

$ ⊞ **Hotel Peristil.** Offering one of only three chances to wake up within the palace walls, Hotel Peristil lies behind the cathedral, just inside Srebrena Vrata, the city gate leading to the open-air market. The 12 rooms are comfortable and well-equipped, and most have wooden floors. The small ground floor restaurant is functional but hardly romantic. ✉ *Poljana Kraljice Jelena 5, Grad, 21000* ☎ *021/329–070* 🏠 *021/329–088* ⊕ *www.hotelperistil.com* ⤳ *12 rooms* ⛄ *Restaurant, cable TV, in-room safes, minibars, in-room data ports* ▭ *AE, DC, MC, V* ⏏ *BP.*

$ ⊞ **Hotel Slavija.** Split's first hotel when it opened in 1900, Slavija occupies an 18th-century building within the palace walls. Fully renovated in 2004, the 25 rooms are basic but comfortable, and the ones at the top have terraces affording views over the city's terra-cotta roofs. Some travelers may find the noise from the surrounding open-air bars excessive. Breakfast is served in the bar area, but there is no restaurant as such. ✉ *Buvinina 2, Grad, 21000* ☎ *021/323–840* 🏠 *021/323–868* ⊕ *www.hotelslavija.com* ⤳ *25 rooms* ⛄ *Cable TV, in-room data ports, bar* ▭ *AE, DC, MC, V* ⏏ *BP.*

Nightlife & the Arts

Split is much more lively at night during the summer season, when bars stay open late, discos hold open-air parties by the sea, and the Split Summer Festival offers a respectable program of opera and classical music concerts.

Nightlife

Through summer, many bars have extended licenses and stay open until 2 AM. The clubbing scene is rather tame, but the local twenty-some-things frequent the discos listed below. In August, rock musicians from Croatia and the other countries of the former Yugoslavia perform open-air concerts. There's no particular source of information about what's on, but you'll see posters around town if anything special is planned.

BARS   With a colorful bohemian interior and a courtyard garden lit with flaming torches, **Ghetto Klub** (✉ Dosud 10, Grad ☎ No phone) pulls in the cool, young artsy crowd and hosts occasional exhibitions and concerts. Hidden away on a small piazza in the Old Town, **Jazz** (✉ Poljana Grgur Ninski, Grad ☎ No phone) offers outdoor tables and an artsy, intellectual clientele. Close to Zlatna Vrata, **Teak** (✉ Majstora Jurja 11, Grad ☎ No phone) is a small café with an exposed stonework and wood interior plus tables outside through summer. It's popular with high-brow locals, who come here to leaf through the piles of international newspapers and magazines. One of several amusing but vaguely pretentious bars overlooking Bačvice Bay, **Tropic Club Equador** (✉ Kupalište Bačvice, Bačvice ☎ 021/323–574) serves pricey cocktails to a background of Caribbean music and fake palms.

DISCOS   In an underground space below the bars overlooking Bačvice Bay, **Discovery** (✉ Kupalište Bačvice, Bačvice ☎ 021/488–556) plays a mix of mainstream, techno, disco, and rock. At **Metropolis** (✉ Matice Hrvatska 1, Trstenik ☎ 021/305–110) a program of theme nights and special performances attracts a mixed crowd of all ages. Commercial techno music predominates, with a smattering of rock and pop. Croatian singers perform at **Shakespeare** (✉ Cvjetna 1, Trstenik ☎ 021/519–492) on weekends, backed up by a selection of commercial techno and disco dance music played by DJs.

The Arts

Kino Bačvice (✉ Put Firula, Bačvice) is an open-air summer cinema in the pine woods above Bačvice Bay. Predominantly English-language films are shown in original version with subtitles. Running from mid-July to mid-August, the **Split Summer Festival** (✉ Trg Gaje Bulata 1, Grad ☎021/363–014 ⊕ www.splitsko-ljeto.hr) includes a variety of open-air opera, classical-music concerts, and theatrical performances, the highlight being *Aïda* on Peristil.

Sports & the Outdoors

Beaches

The best beach is **Uvala Bačvica** (Bačvice Bay), a 10-minute walk east of the Old Town, where you will find showers, beach chairs, and umbrellas to rent, plus numerous cafés and bars offering refreshments.

Sailing

Well connected to the rest of Europe by plane and ferry—and within just a few hours sailing of several of the Adriatic's most beautiful islands—Split is the center of the yacht-charter business in Dalmatia. For a listing of Split-based charter companies, see ⇨ Sailing & Cruising the Croatian Coast *in* Understanding Croatia. The 364-berth **ACI marina**

(✉ Uvala Baluni, Zvončac ☎ 021/398–548) is southwest of the city center. It stays open all year and is a base for dozens of charter companies organizing sailing on the Adriatic.

White-Water Rafting

Atlas Travel Agency (✉ Trg Brace Radića 6 ☎ 021/343–055 ⊕ www.atlascroatia.com) organizes one-day guided rafting expeditions on the River Cetina, with the transfer from Split and back included in the deal.

Shopping

Dalmatian women—and those from Split in particular—are renowned for their elegant sense of style. Despite a poor local economy, you'll find countless exclusive little boutiques selling women's clothes and shoes imported from Italy. However, the city's most memorable shopping venue remains the *pazar,* the colorful open-air market held each morning just outside the palace walls. When looking for gifts, bear in mind that Dalmatia produces some excellent wines, which you can buy either in Split or while visiting the islands.

Croata (✉ Mihovilova Širina 7, Grad ☎ 021/346–336), overlooking Trg Brace Radića, close to the seafront, specializes in "original Croatian ties" in presentation boxes. **Vinoteka Bouquet** (✉ Obala Hrvatskog Narodnog Preporoda 3, Grad ☎ 021/348–031) is a small shop selling a select choice of Croatian regional wines, plus some truffle products and olive oils.

ŠIBENIK

⑫ *75 km (47 mi) northwest of Split.*

Šibenik's main monument, its Gothic-Renaissance cathedral, built of pale grey Dalmatian stone and designated a UNESCO World Heritage Site, stands on a raised piazza close to the seafront promenade. From here, a network of narrow cobbled streets leads through the medieval quarter of tightly-packed, terra cotta–roof houses, and up to the ruins of a 16th-century hilltop fortress.

The city has never been considered a real tourist destination. Before the Croatian war for independence, it was a relatively prosperous industrial center, but when the factories closed, Šibenik sunk into an economic depression. However, the cathedral more than warrants a look, and it makes a decent base for visiting the waterfalls of Krka National Park.

★ Šibenik's finest piece of architecture, the **Katedrala Sv Jakova** (Cathedral of St. Jacob), was built in several distinct stages and styles between 1431 and 1536. The lower level is the work of Venetian architects who contributed the finely-carved Venetian-Gothic portals, whereas the rest of the building follows plans drawn up by local architect Juraj Dalmatinac, who proposed the Renaissance cupola. Note the frieze running around the outer wall with 74 faces carved in stone, depicting the locals from that time. The cathedral's best-loved feature, the tiny baptistery with minutely chiseled stone decorations, was designed by Dalmatinac but executed by Andrija Aleši. As you leave, take a look at the bronze statue just outside the main door: that's Dalmatinac himself, by Croatia's greatest 20th-century sculptor, Ivan Meštrović. ⊠ *Trg Republike Hrvatske* ▦ *Free* ⊙ *Daily 9–7.*

Where to Eat

$$–$$$ ✕**Gradska Vijećnica.** On the main square, this 16th-century Venetian building was originally the town hall. Croatian dishes top the menu, with several Italian and vegetarian options, and the house specialty is *paprika punjena sirom* (peppers stuffed with cheese). The best tables are under the arched portico out front, overlooking the cathedral. There's occasional live jazz in the evenings. ⊠ *Trg Republike Hrvatske 1* ☎ 022/213–605 ▭ *AE, DC, MC, V.*

$$–$$$ ✕**Uzorita.** Since 1898, customers have frequented tables in Uzorita's wooden-beamed dining room and vine-covered courtyard garden. The emphasis is on seafood, notably shellfish. The signature dish is *arambasici od plodova mora u morskim algama* (seaweed rolls stuffed with seafood), a creative take on traditional Croatian *sarma* (cabbage leaves filled with rice and mince). Uzorita is a 20-minute walk northeast of the town center. ⊠ *Bana Josipa Jelačića 50* ☎ 022/213–660 ▭ *AE, DC, MC, V.*

Where to Stay

$ ▦ **Hotel Jadran.** On the seafront promenade, just a 2-minute walk from the cathedral, the Jadran is a white, 1970s-era, five-story hotel that was fully renovated in spring 2005. The furnishings are simple but smart, and the café terrace looks onto the sailboats moored up along the quay. ⊠ *Obala dr Franje Tudjmana 54, 22000* ☎ 022/212–644 ▭ 022/212–480 ⊕ *www.rivijera.hr* ⇆ *57 rooms* ⚭ *Restaurant, café, minibars, cable TV* ▭ *AE, DC, MC, V* ⚭ *BP.*

KRKA NATIONAL PARK

★ ⑬ *Skradin is 16 km (10 mi) north of Šibenik.*

The Krka River cuts its way through a gorge shaded by limestone cliffs and dense woodland, tumbling down toward the Adriatic in a series of spectacular pools and waterfalls. The most beautiful stretch of its course has been designated as **Nacionalni Park Krka** (Krka National Park). There are several entrances into the park, but the easiest and most impressive route of arrival is to drive from Šibenik to the town of Skradin, then take a 25-minute boat ride up the Krka River on a national-park ferry (price included in entrance fee). This will bring you to the park entrance close to Skradinski Buk.

Within the park there are a couple of snack bars, plus wooden tables and benches for picnics. However, for a full-blown meal your best bet is to return to riverside Skradin, which is itself also well worth a look. The town dates back to Roman times, though its recent history is also significant. During the Croatian war for independence it was on the front line, being on the edge of the Serb-held Krajina. Serbs and Croats had lived together peacefully for centuries, as can be seen from Skradin's two church spires, one Catholic the other Orthodox. But in August 1995, most of the Serbs fled when the Croatian army sprung the surprise *Oluja* (Operation Storm), and they are only now beginning to return. On a happier note, Skradin is popular with sailors, thanks to its marina, and is also home to several good seafood restaurants, where you can order the highly esteemed local shellfish.

A series of seven waterfalls are the main draw here, the most spectacular being Skradinski Buk, where 17 cascades fall 40 meters into an emerald-green pool, perfect for bathing. Moving up river, a trail of wooden walkways and bridges crisscrosses its way through the woods and along the waterside to the next falls, Roški Slap, passing the tiny island of Visovac, home to a Franciscan Monastery, en route. It's possible to visit the monastery by boat. The national-park office is in Šibenik. ⌂ *Trg Ivana Pavla II 5 Šibenik* ☎ *022/217–720* ⊕ *www. npkrka.hr* ⊠ *60 Kn* ☉ *May–Oct., daily 8–8; Nov.–Apr., daily 9–5.*

Where to Eat

$$–$$$ ✕ **Zlatne Školjke.** A favorite among the yachting crowd, due in part to its location close to ACI marina, Zlatne Školjke occupies a natural stone building with a terrace overlooking the water. Popular dishes include *crni rižot* (black risotto made with cuttlefish), *špageti s plodovima mora* (seafood pasta), and *riba na žaru* (barbecued fresh fish). ⊠ *Grgura Ninskog 9, Skradin* ☎ *021/771–022* ⊟ *AE, DC, MC, V.*

Where to Stay

$ 🏨 **Hotel Skradinski Buk.** A friendly, family-run hotel in a refurbished stone town house in the center of Skradin is also the only hotel in town. It has comfortable rooms and a restaurant with a pleasant terrace out front. The hotel stays open year-round. ⊠ *Burinovac, Skradin 22222* ☎ *022/ 771–771* 🖶 *022/771–770* ⊕ *www.skradinskibuk.hr* ⇔ *26 rooms* ⌂ *Restaurant, minibars, cable TV, in-room data ports, bar* ⊟ *AE, DC, MC, V* ⦿ *BP.*

Sports & the Outdoors

Skradin, approached by boat through the Šibenik Channel, is a favorite retreat for those **sailing** on the Adriatic. It's also a popular place to leave boats (especially wooden ones) for the winter as the water is less saline here, thanks to the fresh water running down from the Krka River. The 153-berth **ACI Marina** (⊠ Skradin ☎ 022/771–365 ⊕ www.aci-club. hr) stays open year-round.

Shopping

While in Skradin, pay a visit to **Vinarija Bedrica** (⊠ Fra Luje Maruna 14, Skradin ☎ 022/771–095), an old-fashioned family-run wine cellar where you can taste and buy bottles of locally produced wine and rakija.

TROGIR

⑭ *27 km (17 mi) west of Split.*

On a small island no more than a few city blocks in length, the beautifully preserved medieval town of Trogir is connected to the mainland by one bridge and tied to the outlying island of Čiovo by a second. The settlement dates back to the 3rd century BC when it was colonized by the Greeks, who named it Tragurion. It later flourished as a Roman port. With the fall of the Western Roman Empire, it became part of Byzantium and then followed the shifting allegiances of the Adriatic. In 1420, the Venetians moved in and stayed until 1797.

Today it is a UNESCO World Heritage Site and survives principally from tourism. You can explore the city in about an hour. A labyrinth of narrow, cobbled streets centers on Narodni trg, the main square, where the most notable buildings are located: the 15th-century loggia and clock tower, the Venetian-Gothic Čipko Palace, and the splendid *katedrala* (cathedral), with its elegant bell tower. The south-facing seafront promenade is lined with cafés, ice-cream parlors, and restaurants, and there are also several small hotels that offer a reasonable alternative to accommodations in Split.

Fodor's Choice The remarkable **Katedrala Sveti Lovrijenac** (Cathedral of St. Lawrence),
★ completed in 1250, is a perfect example of the massiveness and power of Romanesque architecture. The most striking detail is the main (west) portal, adorned with superb Romanesque sculpture by the Croatian master Radovan. The great door, flanked by a pair of imperious lions that form pedestals for figures of Adam and Eve, is framed by a fascinating series illustrating the daily life of peasants in a kind of Middle Ages–comic strip. In the dimly lit Romanesque interior, the 15th-century chapel of Sveti Ivan Orsini (St. John Orsini) of Trogir features statues of saints and apostles in niches facing the sarcophagus, on which lies the figure of St. John. The bell tower, built in successive stages—the first two stories Gothic, the third Renaissance—offers stunning views across the ancient rooftops. ⊠ *Trg Ivana Pavla II* 🖾 *Free* 🕙 *June–Oct., daily 8–7; Nov.–May, daily 8–noon and 4:30–7.*

Where to Eat

$$–$$$ ✕ **Čelica.** An old wooden car ferry, anchored next to Čiovo bridge, is the venue for this unusual eatery. The owner is a fisherman who catches what is on offer. The former captain's bridge is now a bar, and the car platform and cargo hold have been converted to serve as the dining space. The house specialty is *riblja juha* (fish soup). The bridge is a 5-minute walk from the Old Town. ⊠ *Čiovo Bridge* 🕾 *021/882–344* 🖃 *AE, DC, MC, V* 🕙 *No lunch Nov.–Mar.*

$–$$$ ✕ **Restaurant Fontana.** On the seafront overlooking the Trogir Channel, this highly esteemed restaurant and pizzeria has a vast waterside terrace. Fresh fish and seafood top the menu but can be pricey, whereas pizza makes a cheap alternative. ⊠ *Obrov 1* 🕾 *021/884–811* 🖃 *AE, DC, MC, V.*

Where to Stay

$ ▦ **Hotel Fontana.** In the old town overlooking the Trogir Channel, this old building has been tastefully refurbished to form a small hotel above a popular restaurant. Most of the rooms have Jacuzzi. It's possible to have breakfast outside on the seafront terrace. ✉ *Obrov 1, 21220* ☎ *021/885–744* 📠 *021/885–755* ⊕ *www.fontana-commerce.htnet.hr* 🛏 *13 rooms, 1 suite* ♨ *Restaurant, pizzeria, room service, some kitchenettes, minibars, cable TV, bar, meeting room* ▤ *AE, DC, MC, V* ⍩ *BP.*

$ ▦ **Villa Sikaa Hotel.** This 18th-century villa has been converted into a small, family-run hotel overlooking the Trogir Channel with a view back to the Old Town. All the rooms have wooden floors and shiny, newly tiled bathrooms. Two computers with Internet access are available in the bar, and it is possible to rent bicycles. ✉ *Obala kralja Zvonimira 13, 21220* ☎ *021/881–223* 📠 *021/885–149* ⊕ *www.vila-sikaa-r.com* 🛏 *8 rooms, 2 suites* ♨ *Restaurant, minibars, cable TV, Internet room, bicycles, bar, meeting room* ▤ *AE, DC, MC, V* ⍩ *BP.*

Sports & the Outdoors

Several charter companies have their boats based in Trogir, making the town a key destination for those sailing on the Adriatic. The 180-berth **ACI Marina** (✉ Trogir ☎ 021/881–544 ⊕ www.aci-club.hr) is open year-round.

OMIŠ & THE CETINA VALLEY

⑮ *28 km (17½ mi) southeast of Split.*

A easy day trip from Split, Omiš is a pleasant seaside town with a colorful open-air market and a conglomeration of old stone houses backed by a small hilltop fortress. What makes it special is its location at the mouth of a dramatic gorge, where the Cetina River meets the sea. It is also the venue of the Dalmatian Klapa Festival, which attracts singers from all over Croatia.

The Cetina River carves a spectacular gorge with the fertile, green **Cetina Valley** at the bottom, surrounded by sheer limestone cliffs. As the river tumbles its way down toward the sea over a series of rapids, it has become a popular and challenging venue for rafting and rock-climbing. An asphalt road follows the course of the river upstream from Omiš, leading to a couple of pleasant waterside restaurants.

Where to Eat

$$–$$$ ✕ **Radmanove Mlinice.** This renovated water mill is well known for miles around for its fresh *pastrva* (trout) and *janjetina* (roast lamb) served at tables under the trees in a picturesque riverside garden. It lies 6 km (4 mi) from Omiš, up the Cetina Valley. ✉ *Cetina Valley regional road, direction Zadvarje* ☎ *021/862–073* ▤ *AE, DC, MC, V* ☺ *Closed Nov.–Mar.*

$$–$$$ ✕ **Restoran Kaštil Slanica.** With a large riverside terrace and an indoor dining space, Kaštil Slanica serves freshwater specialties such as frogs' legs and trout, plus freshly baked bread. The signature dish is *brudet od jegulja* (eel stewed in tomato and white wine, served with polenta). It lies 4 km (2½ mi) upstream from Omiš. ⊠ *Slanica* ☎ *021/861–783* ▭ *AE, DC, MC, V.*

Where to Stay

¢ ⊞ **Hotel Settlement Brzet.** Totally refurbished in 2004, Brzet overlooks a pebble beach and is backed by a pine forest. The hotel offers basic accommodation within a 15-minute walk from the Omiš town center. All the rooms have balconies and a sea view. ⊠ *Brzet 13, Omiš 21310* ☎ *021/756–880* 🖷 *021/756–900* ⊕ *www.hotels-omis.com* ⇨ *87 rooms* ⚲ *Restaurant, cable TV, beach* ▭ *AE, DC, MC, V* ♥ *Closed Dec.–Mar.* ⦿⧛ *BP.*

The Arts

The **Dalmatian Klapa Festival** (⊠ Ivana Katušića 5, Omiš ☎ 021/861–015) features traditional Croatian harmony singing from various regions along the coast. It lasts three weeks each summer, usually starting in late June, during which performances are staged in the parish church and on the main square.

Sports & the Outdoors

The Cetina Valley has become a destination for both white-water rafters and rock climbers, who appreciate the sheer limestone cliffs of the canyon. Several small adventure-tour companies can arrange Cetina Valley trips. There's also a company in Split that organizes one-day rafting trips on the Cestina (*see* ⇨ White-Water Rafting *in* Sports & the Outdoors *in* Split, *above*).

Active Holidays (⊠ Knezova Kačić, Omiš ☎ 021/863–015 ⊕ www. activeholidays-croatia.com) offers rafting and rock climbing in the Cetina Valley, as well as windsurfing at nearby Ruskamen beach.

BRAČ

⑯ *9 nautical mi south of Split by ferry.*

Close at hand and well-connected to Split by ferry and catamaran services, the island of Brač can be visited in an easy day trip, though you may want to stay a night or two. With extensive tourist development along the coast and a stark wild interior, the island's top resort, **Bol**, is best known for its stunning beach and is also a prime windsurfing spot.

To get there, either catch an early morning Jadrolinija ferry from Split to Supetar (9 nautical mi) and then take a bus across the island to the south coast, or catch the mid-afternoon Jadrolinija catamaran from Split to Bol (24 nautical mi), which then continues to Jelsa on the island of Hvar.

★ ☯ A spectacular beach, **Zlatni Rat** (Golden Cape), in the south-coast fishing village of Bol, is the main attraction on Brač. A tree-lined coastal promenade leads from the village to an extraordinary geographical cape composed of tiny pebbles, which juts out ¾ km (⅓ mi) to sea, moving and changing shape slightly from season to season depending on the winds. This is Croatia's prime site for windsurfing and an ideal beach for kids, as the water is shallow and the seabed is easy on their feet. ⊠ *Bol, 1 km (2 mi) west of town center.*

The village of Bol is backed by the highest peak on all the Croatian islands, **Vidova Gora.** From here, at a height of 778 meters (2,552 feet) above sea level, the Adriatic sea and the islands of Hvar and Vis spread out before you like a map. It's possible to reach the top following a clearly-marked footpath from Bol, but be sure to wear good hiking boots, take plenty of water, and expect to walk at least two and a half hours to reach the summit. Alternatively, Big Blue (*see* ⇨ Sports & the Outdoors, *below*) organizes mountain-biking trips (for experienced mountain bikers) on Vidova Gora, with the option of a minibus ride part way. ⊠ *Bol, 4 km (2½ mi) north of the town center.*

Where to Eat

$$–$$$ ✗ **Gušt.** Possibly the most authentic eatery in Bol, Gušt serves traditional Dalmatian dishes and homemade rakija at heavy wooden tables and benches in a whitewashed dining room decorated with an eccentric array of old local paintings and fishing tools. Ceiling fans keep the interior cool and airy, and there are several tables out on the terrace. ⊠ *Frane Radić 14, Bol* ☎ *021/635–911* ▤ *AE, DC, MC, V* ☉ *Closed Nov.–Mar.*

$$–$$$ ✗ **Konoba Mlin.** This old stone mill, which originally used to make flour for the town's bread and is now a cultural monument, has been refurbished to form a summer restaurant. There's a wide choice of barbecued meat and fish dishes. A terrace with tables overlooks the sea. ⊠ *Ante Starčević 11* ☎ *021/635–376* ▤ *No credit cards* ☉ *Closed Oct.–May.*

Where to Stay

$$ 🏨 **Hotel Ivan.** Built of Dalmatian stone with traditional green wooden window shutters, and set in a walled garden with a pool, Hotel Ivan opened in 2002. The suites (which are called apartments) have kitchenettes and are suitable for families. The hotel offers special programs to help you slim down and stop smoking, if you want to add a healthy component to your Croatia vacation. It's open year-round. ⊠ *David cesta 11a, Bol 21420* ☎ *021/640–888* 🖶 *021/640–846* ⊕ *www.hotel-ivan. com* ➷ *16 rooms, 32 suites* ⚴ *Restaurant, café, minibars, cable TV, in-room data ports, pool, massage, meeting rooms* ▤ *AE, DC, MC, V* ⊚ *BP.*

$ 🏨 **Hotel Kaštil.** This harborside stone building has been tastefully refurbished without becoming overly design-conscious. Interior walls are predominantly white with occasional splashes of vivid yellow or red, and the furnishings are minimalist. There's a street-level pizzeria and cocktail bar with wicker sofas, plus an upper-level restaurant with a romantic terrace looking down onto the water. ⊠ *Frane Radića 1, 21420* ☎ *021/635–995* 🖷 *021/635–997* ⊕ *www.kastil.hr* ⇆ *32 rooms* ⌂ *Restaurant, pizzeria, cable TV, bar* ⊟ *AE, DC, MC, V* ⊙ *Closed Nov.–Feb.* ⵊⵔⵊ *BP.*

Sports & the Outdoors

The obvious spot for bathing is the glorious **Zlatni Rat** beach, complete with a café and snack bar, plus paddle boats and jet skis for rent through peak season. Be aware that to the west of Zlatni Rat lies a small beach reserved for nudists.

For windsurfing and scuba-diving training and equipment rentals, the best established local company is **Big Blue** (⊠ Podan Glavice 2, Bol ☎ 021/635–614 ⊕ www.big-blue-sport.hr), which also rents mountain bikes and organizes cycling trips on Vidova Gora.

HVAR

⓱
Fodor'sChoice
★

Hvar Town is 23 nautical mi south of Split by ferry.

The island of Hvar bills itself as the "sunniest island in the Adriatic." Not only does it have the figures to back up this claim—an annual average of 2,724 hours of sunshine with a maximum of two foggy days a year—but it also makes visitors a sporting proposition, offering them a money-back guarantee if there is ever a foggy day (which has been known to happen).

Hvar is also the name of the capital, near the island's western tip. The little town rises like an amphitheater from its harbor, backed by a hilltop fortress and protected from the open sea by a scattering of small islands known as Pakleni Otoci. Along the palm-lined quay, a string of cafés and restaurants is shaded by colorful awnings and umbrellas. A few steps away, the magnificent main square, **Trg Sveti Stjepan,** the largest piazza in Dalmatia, is backed by the 16th-century Katedrala Sveti Stjepan (Cathedral of St. Stephen). Other notable sights include the kazalište (a theater) and the Franjevački Samostan (Franciscan Monastery).

Hvar Town is currently a very "in" spot, so expect it to be crowded and expensive through peak season. Visitors have included King Abdullah of Jordan and his wife, Queen Rania, Italian clothing entrepreneur Luciano Benetton, and local tennis champion Goran Ivanišević.

The easiest way to reach Hvar Town is to catch a mid-afternoon Jadrolinija catamaran from Split, which stops at Hvar Town (23 nautical mi) before continuing to the South Dalmatian islands of Korčula and Lastovo. Alternatively, take an early morning Jadrolinija ferry from Split to Stari Grad (23 nautical mi) and then catch a local bus across the island.

On the upper floor of the Arsenal, the **Kazalište** (Theater) opened in 1612, making it the oldest institution of its kind in Croatia and one of the first in Europe. The Arsenal building, where Venetian ships en route to the Orient once docked for repairs, dates back to the 13th century but was reconstructed after damage during a Turkish invasion in 1571. ⊠ *Trg*

Sv Stjepana, Hvar Town ✉ *15 Kn* ☉ *May–Oct., daily 9–1 and 5–9; Nov.–Apr., daily 10–noon.*

East of town, along the quay past the Arsenal, lies the **Franjevački Samostan** (Franciscan Monastery). Within its walls, a pretty 15th-century Renaissance cloister leads to the former refectory, now housing a small museum with several notable artworks. ☒ *Obala Ivana Lučića Lavčevića, Hvar Town* ✉ *15 Kn* ☉ *May–Oct., daily 10–noon and 5–7.*

Where to Eat

$$–$$$$ ✗ **Macondo.** This superb fish restaurant lies hidden away on a narrow, **Fodor'sChoice** cobbled street between the main square and the fortress—to find it, fol-
★ low the signs from Trg Sv Stjepana. The dining room is simply furnished with wooden tables, discreet modern art, and a large open fire. The food and service are practically faultless. Begin with the delicate scampi pâté, followed by a mixed seafood platter, and round off with a glass of homemade *orahovica* (walnut rakija). ☒ *2 blocks north of trg Sv Stjepana, Hvar Town* ☎ *021/742–850* ▭ *AE, DC, MC, V* ☉ *Closed Dec.–Mar.*

$$–$$$$ ✗ **Palazzo Paladini.** In a beautiful Renaissance-courtyard garden planted with orange trees, this long-standing, family-run restaurant serves up Dalmatian specialties with an emphasis on seafood. The signature dish is *hvarska gregada* (local fish stew with aromatic herbs and potatoes), and the chef also does a highly praised vegetarian platter. ☒ *1 block north of trg Sv Stjepana, Hvar Town* ☎ *021/742–104* ▭ *AE, DC, MC, V* ☉ *Closed Jan.–Apr.*

$$–$$$$ ✗ **Restoran Palmižana.** On the tiny island of Sveti Klement, a 20-minute taxi boat ride from Hvar Town, this restaurant is backed by a romantic wilderness of Mediterranean flora and offers stunning views over the open sea. The interior is decorated with modern Croatian art, and there are classical-music recitals on Sunday morning. Besides fresh seafood, goodies include *kozji sir sa rukolom* (goat cheese with arugula), and *pašticada* (beef stewed in sweet wine and prunes). Recent customers have included retired Croatian soccer player Davor Šuker and Formula One multimillionaire Bernie Ecclestone. ☒ *Vinogradišće Uvala, Sveti Klement* ☎ *021/717–270* ▭ *AE, DC, MC, V* ☉ *Closed Nov.–Mar.*

$$–$$$ ✗ **Bacchus.** With outdoor tables on the main square, this small and sometimes chaotic eatery is popular with locals for its *merenda* (inexpensive prix-fixe lunch), and is reputed to prepare the best *ramsteak* (rump steak) in town. It stays open year-round. ☒ *Trg Sv Stjepana, Hvar Town* ☎ *021/742–698* ▭ *AE, DC, MC, V.*

Where to Stay

♻ $$ 🏨 **Hotel Amfora.** A colossal white, modern structure overlooking its own bay with a pebble beach, the Amfora is backed by pine woods and lies a pleasant 10-minute walk along the coastal path from the center of town. All rooms have balconies, and there are excellent sports and recreation facilities, making this an ideal choice for families on longer stays. ☒ *Hvar Town 21450* ☎ *021/741–202* 🖷 *021/741–711* ⊕ *www. suncanihvar.hr* ↩ *305 rooms, 20 suites* ♨ *Restaurant, café, room ser-*

vice, minibars, cable TV, in-room data ports, 6 tennis courts, indoor pool, gym, hair salon, massage, sauna, beach, dive shop, windsurfing, boccie, bowling, bar, convention center ▤ AE, DC, MC, V ⊙ Closed Nov.–Mar. ⦶ BP.

$$ ⌸ **Hotel Palace.** Commanding a prime site on the edge of the main square and overlooking the harbor, the Palace remains open most of the year, offering much lower prices during the off-season. A former Venetian loggia is incorporated into the hotel and used as an elegant salon. The indoor pool has heated seawater, and the upper-level restaurant terrace affords splendid views out to sea. Closed through winter, it opens briefly for New Year celebrations. ⊠ *Trg Sv Stjepana, Hvar Town 21450* ☎ *021/741–966* 🖷 *021/742–420* ⊕ *www.suncanihvar.hr* ⇱ *73 rooms, 5 suites* ⌕ *Restaurant, café, room service, minibars, cable TV, Internet room, indoor pool, massage, sauna, bar* ▤ AE, DC, MC, V ⊙ *Closed Dec.–Mar.* ⦶ *BP.*

$$ ⌸ **Pod Stine.** This peaceful, family-run hotel lies on the coast, a 15-minute walk west of the town center. There's a pebble beach backed by palms and pine woods, complete with sunbeds, parasols, a shower, and even a berth for a yacht, if you are coming in by sea. All the rooms have sea views, and most have balconies. Breakfast is served on a glorious terrace overlooking the water. ⊠ *Hvar Town 21450* ☎ *021/740–400* 🖷 *021/740–499* ⊕ *www.podstine.com* ⇱ *40 rooms* ⌕ *Restaurant, café, room service, minibars, cable TV, in-room data ports, Internet room, beach, bar* ▤ AE, DC, MC, V ⊙ *Closed Dec.–Apr.* ⦶ *BP.*

$ ⌸ **Hotel Croatia.** A family-run hotel surrounded by a pine-scented garden overlooks the sea and is a 10-minute walk southeast of the main square. The building dates back to 1936, and the furnishings are basic but comfortable. Several of the rooms have four beds, making them convenient for families. The hotel offers one-day sailing trips to the island of Vis, and also runs one-week yoga-and-sailing programs. Closed through winter, it opens briefly for New Year celebrations. ⊠ *Majerovica, Hvar Town 21450* ☎ *021/742–400* 🖷 *021/741–707* ⊕ *www. hotelcroatia.net* ⇱ *28 rooms* ⌕ *Restaurant, beach, bar, meeting room* ▤ AE, DC, MC, V ⊙ *Closed Oct.–Mar.* ⦶ *BP.*

Nightlife & the Arts

Croatia is generally not a hot spot for nightlife, but the island of Hvar may be starting a renaissance on the party front. Several stylish cocktail bars and clubs have opened in the past few years to cater to the annual influx of summer visitors.

Classical-music recitals in the cloisters of the Franciscan Monastery have long been the highlight of the **Hvar Summer Festival.** Also look out for theater, folklore, and jazz at various open-air locations around town. The annual festival runs from mid-June to late September.

Carpe Diem (⊠ Riva, Hvar Town ☎ 021/717–234 ⊕ www.carpe-diem-hvar.com), a harborside cocktail bar with a summer terrace decked out with oriental furniture and potted plants and two burly bouncers at the gate, is where Hvar's richest and most glamorous visitors come to see and be seen. Stop in to see why Hvar has been labeled the next Ibiza.

It's open late. **Enigma** (⌂2 blocks west of the seafront, Jelsa ☎No phone), formerly Mlin, reopened in June 2005, bringing the British-style club scene to Jelsa (the owners previously worked for London's Ministry of Sound). Locals have always claimed that Jelsa (22 km[14 mi] east of Hvar Town) has the best nightlife on the island; this club may prove them right. Tiny but stylish, it combines a white lounge and cocktail garden serving champagne and cocktails with a late-night club attracting international guest DJs. **Veneranda** (⌂ Sv Veneranda, Hvar Town ☎ No phone) has no pretensions, just open-air drinking and dancing on the grounds of a former Greek Orthodox Monastery. Most evenings begin with a film projection after dusk: the crowds arrive after midnight. It is a 10-minute walk west of town. Follow the seafront promenade, then head for the lights in the pine woods.

Sports & the Outdoors

Beaches
Although there are several decent beaches within walking distance of town—the best-equipped being the Hotel Amfora's pebble beach, 10 minutes west of the main square—sun-worshippers in-the-know head for the nearby Pakleni Otoci (Pakleni Islands), which can be reached by taxi boats that depart regularly (in peak season, every hour, from 8 to 8) from in front of the Arsenal in the town harbor. The best known and best served are **Sveti Jerolim** (on the island of the same name, predominantly a nudist beach), **Stipanska** (on the island of Marinkovac, a clothing-optional beach), and **Palmižana** (on the island of Sveti Klement, also clothing-optional).

Diving
Those with a taste for underwater adventure might have a go at scuba diving. The seabed is scattered with pieces of broken Greek amphorae, while the area's biggest underwater attraction is the Stambedar sea wall, home to red and violet gorgonians (a type of coral), which is close to the Pakleni Islands. For courses at all levels, try **Diving Center Viking** (⌂ Podstine, Hvar Town ☎ 021/742–529 ⊕ www.viking-diving.com).

Sailing
Hvar Town is a popular port of call for those sailing on the Adriatic; the town harbor is packed out with flashy yachts through peak season. **ACI Marina** (⌂ Palmižana Bay, Sveti Klement ☎ 021/744–995 ⊕ www. aci-club.hr) in Palmižana Bay on the island of Sveti Klement, one of the Pakleni Otoci, lies just 2.4 nautical mi from Hvar Town. This 160-berth marina is open from April through October and is served by regular taxi boats from Hvar Town through peak season.

VIS

🔞 *34 nautical mi southwest of Split by ferry.*

Closed to foreigners until 1989, the distant island of Vis is relatively wild and unexploited. To get here from Split, you can either take the SEM Marina fast catamaran service, or a 2½-hour Jadrolinija ferry ride to arrive in Vis Town. Built around a wide harbor, the town is popular with yachters, who appreciate its rugged nature, unpretentious fish restaurants, and excellent locally produced wine. The pretty fishing village of Komiža is 11 km (7 mi) from Vis Town. From here, you're just a 40-minute boat ride away from the Modra Spilja (Blue Cave), often compared to the Blue Grotto on Italy's Capri.

Throughout the summer, local fishermen will take tourists from both Vis Town and Komiža into the **Modra Spilja** (Blue Cave) by boat. Some of these trips are done on a regular basis. Hidden away on the small island of Biševo (5 nautical mi southwest of Komiža), the cave is 78 feet long and 39 feet wide. Sunlight enters through the water, reflects off the seabed, and casts the interior in a fantastic shade of blue. If you're lucky, you'll have time for a quick swim. Ask at the marina or at the tourist-information office to see who is offering trips. ⊠ *Boševo.*

Where to Eat

$$–$$$$ ✕ **Jastožera.** The former lobster house, built in 1883, was cleverly converted to make an impressive restaurant in 2002. Tables are set on wooden platforms above the water, and it's even possible to enter the central dining area in a small boat. The house specialty is *jastog sa spagetima* (lobster with spaghetti). ⊠ *Gunduličeva 6, Komiža* ☎ *021/713–859* ▭ *AE, DC, MC, V* ⊘ *Closed Oct.–Apr.*

$$–$$$$ ✕ **Villa Kaliopa.** With tables set under the trees in the romantic walled
Fodor'sChoice garden of a 16th-century villa, dinner at this restaurant in Vis Town is
★ an unforgettable experience. The menu changes daily depending on what fresh fish and shellfish have come in. Your server will bring a platter to the table so you can choose your own fish before it's cooked. ⊠ *V Nazora 32, Vis Town* ☎ *021/711–755* ▭ *AE, DC, MC, V* ⊘ *Closed Nov.–Mar.*

$$–$$$ ✕ **Konoba Bako.** Popular with locals and visitors alike, this excellent fish restaurant overlooks a tiny bay in Komiža. Outdoors, tables are set right up to the water's edge, and inside there's a small pool with lobsters and amphoras. The *salata od hobotnice* (octopus salad), *škampi rižot* (scampi risotto), and barbecued fish are all delicious. ⊠ *Gunduličeva 1, Komiža* ☎ *021/713–742* ▭ *AE, DC, MC, V* ⊘ *Closed mid-Nov.–mid-Feb.*

$$–$$$ ✕ **Pojoda.** A modern glass-and-wood conservatory looks onto a courtyard garden planted with orange and lemon trees, accessed through an archway off a narrow side street. Dishes are named in local dialect: check out the *manistra na brudet* (bean and pasta soup) and *luc u verudi* (tuna stewed with vegetables). ⊠ *Don Cvjetka Marasovića 8, Vis Town* ☎ *021/711–575* ▭ *AE, DC, MC, V* ⊘ *Closed Nov.–Mar.*

Where to Stay

$ 🏠 **Hotel Paula.** In Vis Town, east of the ferry quay, this friendly, family-run hotel is hidden away between stone cottages in a quiet, cobbled side street. All the rooms are smartly furnished and modern; downstairs, there's a good fish restaurant with tables on a walled summer terrace. It stays open all year. ⊠ *Petra Hektorovića 2, Vis Town 21480* ☎ *021/711–362* ⌑ *12 rooms* ⚑ *Restaurant, cable TV, bar* ▭ *AE, DC, MC, V* ⎮⊙⎮ *BP.*

$ ⌐ **Tamaris.** Overlooking the harbor and seafront promenade in Vis Town, Tamaris occupies a late-19th-century building. The location is perfect, the rooms basic but comfortable, and it stays open all year. ⊠ *Šetalište Apolonija Zanelle 5, Vis Town 21480* ☎☎ *021/711–350* ⮧ *27 rooms* ☖ *Restaurant, cable TV, bar* ☰ *AE, DC, MC, V* ⦿I *BP.*

MARKARSKA

⑲ *67 km (42 mi) southeast of Split.*

The seafront promenade, lined with palms and cheerful open-air cafés, looks onto a protected bay dotted with wooden fishing boats. From here, one enters the Old Town, a warren of stone buildings and cobbled streets surrounding the main square, which is backed by the parish church and a small open-air market off to one side. The atmosphere is relaxed and easygoing. The only drama you'll likely see is created by the limestone heights of Biokovo Mountain, which seems to alternate between protecting and threatening the town, depending on the color of the sky and the cloud formations that ride over its rugged peaks.

Makarska has developed an unpretentious, relatively cheap brand of tourism, popular with East Europeans. It does get very busy through peak season; the ideal time to visit is either late spring or early autumn, when the weather is perfect for hiking on Biokovo.

Behind Makarska, a large area of the rocky heights that form Biokovo Mountain have been designated as **Park Prirode Biokovo** (Biokovo Nature Park; ⊠ Trg Tina Ujevića 1/I, Makarska ☎ 021/616–924). Part of the Dinaric Alps, which run from Slovenia down to Montenegro, Biokovo abounds in rare indigenous plant species. It's possible to reach the highest peak, Sveti Jure (1,762 meters/5,781 feet) in five and a half hours from Makarska. However, this is a strenuous hike, for which you will need good boots and plenty of water. Few staff in the park's office speak English; it's usually much easier to organize an excursion through Biokovo Active Holidays (*see* ⇨ Sports & Activities, *below*), a company that offers organized trips up the mountain, traveling part of the way by jeep.

Where to Eat

★ **$$–$$$$** ✗ **Stari Mlin.** Ethnic music, incense, and colorful canvases set the mood inside this old stone building, and the internal garden is draped with vines and decorated with pots of herbs and cherry tomatoes. Barbecued seafood tops the menu, but there is an extra surprise here, a select choice of authentic Thai dishes. The owner worked for several years aboard a cruise ship before returning home to run the family restaurant. ⊠ *Prvosvibanska 43* ☎ *021/611–509* ☰ *AE, DC, MC, V* ⊘ *Closed Nov.–Mar.*

$$–$$$ ✗ **Hrpina.** This long-standing, family-run restaurant overlooks a small piazza just off the main square. Dalmatian seafood dishes such as *školjke na buzaru* (shellfish in garlic, white wine, and parsley) and *crni rižot* (black risotto made from cuttlefish) are served at heavy wooden tables on a terrace lined with potted geraniums. During the winter season (Nov.–Mar.) only the bar is open. ✉ *Trg Hrpina 2* ☎ *021/611–619* ▭ *No credit cards* ☉ *Closed Nov.–Mar.*

Where to Stay

$ 🏨 **Hotel Biokovo.** In the center of Makarska, on the palm-lined seafront promenade, this old-fashioned hotel was renovated in 2004. All the rooms have pine floors; fabrics are either royal blue or bordeaux red. The ground-floor terrace café is popular with locals all year long. ✉ *Obala Kralja Tomislava, 21300* ☎ *021/615–244* 🖶 *021/615–081* ⊕ *www. hotelbiokovo.hr* ⇨ *55 rooms, 5 suites* ⌂ *Restaurants, pizzeria, café, minibars, cable TV, in-room data ports, Internet room, massage, meeting room* ▭ *AE, DC, MC, V* ◉ *BP.*

$ 🏨 **Hotel Porin.** This 19th-century building stands on the seafront promenade and was refurbished to form a small hotel in 2002. There's a small roof terrace for hotel guests, a restaurant overlooking the sea that caters weddings and seminars, and a café accessed from the cobbled street one block back from the seafront. ✉ *Marineta 2, 21300* ☎ *021/613–744* 🖶 *021/613–688* ⊕ *www.hotel-porin.hr* ⇨ *7 rooms, 1 suite* ⌂ *Restaurant, café, minibar, cable TV* ▭ *AE, DC, MC, V* ◉ *BP.*

Sports & the Outdoors

Beaches

The main town beach, a 1½-km (1-mi) stretch of pebble backed by pine woods, lies northwest of the center and close to a string of big modern hotels. Alternatively, walk along the narrow coastal path southeast of town to find rocks and a series of secluded coves. Further afield, the so-called Makarska Rivjera is a 40-km (25-mi) stretch of coast running from Brela to Gradac, dotted with fishing villages that have developed into seaside resorts, each with their own shingle beach or concrete bathing area.

Hiking

For sound information about hiking, your best bet is to contact **Biokovo Active Holidays** (✉ Gundulićeva 4 ☎ 021/679–655 ⊕ www.biokovo.net). This agency started out by specializing in one-day guided hiking trips up Biokovo Mountain, but has now expanded its program to include a range of one-week hiking-and-boating options throughout the region. You can also make unusual "sunrise" and "sunset" visits to Biokovo, entailing a jeep ride, a short walk, and a stop for food and drinks while you enjoy the mountain-top views. Tours are available April through October.

Diving

Local underwater attractions include a nearby reef, known as Kraljev Gaj, which is populated by sponges, coral, octopi, and scorpion fish, while further out from the coast you can visit the *Dubrovnik,* an old steam boat that sunk in 1917. Scuba-diving enthusiasts, as well as complete beginners, can try **More Sub** (✉ Krešimira 43, Makarska ☎ 021/ 611–727 ⊕ www.more-sub-makarska.hr) for organized diving trips and training at all levels.

LASTOVO

㉑ *Lastovo island is 80 km (50 nautical mi) west of Dubrovnik (no direct ferry) and 80 km (50 nautical mi) southeast of Split (daily direct ferry connection).*

Very few Croatians have visited Lastovo, though they will all tell you that it's beautiful. Like Vis, Lastovo was a Yugoslav military naval base during the Tito years and was, therefore, closed to foreigners, so commercial tourism never developed. Today there is still just one hotel.

Lying far out to sea, Lastovo is an island of green fertile valleys and is practically self-sufficient: locally caught seafood, not least the delicious lobster, and homegrown vegetables are the staple diet. The main settlement, Lastovo Town, is made up of stone houses built amphitheater-style into a hillside, criss-crossed by cobbled alleys and flights of steps; they're renowned for tall chimneys resembling minarets. The only other settlement on the island is the small port of Ubli, which lies 10 km (6 mi) from Lastovo Town.

Although it is officially in Southern Dalmatia, locals chose to have direct transport links with Split in Central Dalmatia rather than Dubrovnik. To get there, take the Jadrolinija daily ferry service from Split to Ubli, stopping at Hvar Town and Vela Luka en route. Jadrolinija also runs a daily catamaran from Split covering the same route; it's faster but a little more expensive.

Where to Eat

$$–$$$$ ✕ **Konoba Triton.** Triton is widely-acknowledged to be the best restaurant on island, and it's particularly popular with those traveling by sailboat, who can moor up on a small quay out front. The owner catches and cooks the fish himself; he also produces the wine, olive oil, and vegetables. You'll find it in Zaklopatica, a north-facing bay 3 km (2 mi) west of Lastovo Town. There are several apartments to rent upstairs. ✉ *Zaklopatica* ☎ *020/801–161* ▤ *No credit cards* ۞ *Closed Nov.–Mar.*

$$–$$$ ✕ **Konoba Bačvara.** Traditional home-cooked Dalmatian fare is served at this family-run eatery in an old stone building in Lastovo Town. Barbecued seafood predominates, and you'll also have the chance to try homegrown vegetables and local wine. ✉ *Počival, Lastovo Town* ☎ *020/801–131* ▤ *No credit cards* ۞ *Closed Nov.–May.*

Where to Stay

$ ▦ **Hotel Solitudo** The only hotel on the island, Hotel Solitudo (confusingly sometimes referred to as Hotel Ladesta) is a modern white building, in a peaceful bay backed by pines, 3 km (2 mi) north of Ubli. All the rooms have a balcony and sea view, and sports facilities include a beach, diving club, and 50-berth marina. The hotel rents out bicycles, boats, and surfboards. Renovation work began in 2001 and has yet to be completed. It stays open all year. ✉ *Pasadur, 3 km (2 mi) from Ubli, 20290* ☎ *020/802–100* ▤ *020/802–444* ⇝ *68 rooms* ⌂ *2 restaurants, cable TV, bar, beach, dive shop, marina* ▤ *AE, DC, MC, V* ⑩ *BP.*

Sports & the Outdoors

Beaches

The best beaches lie on **Saplun**, one of the tiny, unpopulated **Lastovnjaci islands**, which are a short distance northeast of Lastovo and are served by taxi-boats through high season.

Diving

Paradise Diving Center (✉ Pasadur, 3 km [2 mi] from Ubli ☎ 020/805–179 ⊕ www.diving-paradise.net) is a scuba-diving center based in Hotel Solitudo. Just a 5-minute boat ride from the diving center and at a depth of 15 meters (49 feet), lies a reef of red, yellow, and violet gorgonias. Farther afield, experienced divers can expect to explore sea caves and sunken ships.

Sailing

Hotel Solitudo Marina (✉ Pasadur, 3 km [2 mi] from Ubli ☎ 020/802–100) is a 50-berth marina attached to Hotel Solitudo.

SPLIT & CENTRAL DALMATIA ESSENTIALS

AIR TRAVEL

The national carrier, Croatia Airlines, operates domestic flights from Split to Zagreb, Dubrovnik, Pula, and Osijek. During the summer high season, you can fly directly to Split from Amsterdam, Brussels, Frankfurt, Istanbul, London, Lyon, Manchester, Milan, Munich, Paris, Prague, Rome, Skopje, Tel Aviv, Vienna, Warsaw, and Zurich. Also through summer, it flies nonstop from the island of Brač to Zagreb, Munich, and Frankfurt. Adria, British Airways, ČSA and Malev also fly to Split.

✈ Adria Airways ✉ Obala kneza Domagoja, Gradska Luka, Split ☎ 021/338–445. **British Airways** ✉ Split Airport, Kaštela ☎ 021/797–303. **Croatia Airlines** ✉ Obala Hrvatskog Narodnog Preporoda 9, Grad, Split ☎ 021/362–997. **ČSA** ✉ Dominisova 10, Grad, Split ☎ 021/343–422. **Malev** ✉ Split Airport, Kaštela ☎ 021/895–274.

AIRPORTS & TRANSFERS

Split is served by Split Airport (SPU) at Kaštela, 25 km (16 mi) northwest of the city center. The island of Brač is served by Brač Airport at Veško Polje, 14 km (8¾ mi) northeast of Bol.

✈ Split Airport ✉ Kaštela ☎ 021/203–171 general information, 021/203–218 lost and found ⊕ www.split-airport.hr. **Brač Airport** ✉ Veško Polje ☎ 021/559–711 general information ⊕ www.airport-brac.hr.

AIRPORT You can take an airport bus to obala Lazereta, near the Split Bus Sta-
TRANSFERS tion. For your return, the airport bus leaves Split 90 minutes before each flight. A one-way ticket costs 30 Kn, and the travel time is 40 minutes. Brač airport is not served bus but taxis are available.

✈ Split airport bus ☎ 021/203–171.

BOAT & FERRY TRAVEL

From June through September, Blue Line, Jadrolinija, and Tirrenia Navigazione all run regular services to Ancona (Italy), departing 9 PM from Split and arriving in Ancona at 7 AM the following day. The same vessels depart at 9 PM from Ancona to arrive in Split at 7 AM. Journey time is approximately 10 hours either direction. Through winter these services are reduced slightly.

From June to September, the Italian company SNAV runs Croazia Jet, a daily catamaran service between Ancona (Italy) and Split, departing at 5 PM from Split and arriving in Ancona at 9 PM. The same vessel departs at 11 AM from Ancona to arrive in Split at 3 PM. The journey time is four hours either direction. The same company runs Pescara Jet, a daily catamaran service between Pescara (Italy) and Split, stopping at Stari Grad (island of Hvar) en-route. The vessel departs at 8 AM from Split and arrives in Pescara at 12:45 PM, then leaves Pescara at 2:45 PM arriving back in Split at 7:30 PM.

Jadrolinija operates coastal ferries that run from Rijeka to Dubrovnik during high season (July and August). Ferries depart from Rijeka most evenings and arrive in Split in the early morning on the following day (journey time is approximately 10 hours) and then continue down the coast to Dubrovnik (journey time is approximately 9 hours), stopping at Stari Grad (island of Hvar) and Korčula en route. During the rest of the year, the service is less frequent and slower, as on some days the ferry also stops at Zadar and Sobra (island of Mljet).

Jadrolinija runs daily ferries to Supetar (island of Brač), Stari Grad (island of Hvar), and Vis from Split.

Jadrolinija runs a daily catamaran from Split to Hvar Town (island of Hvar), which then continues to Vela Luka (island of Korčula) and Ubli (island of Lastovo). A separate service runs to Bol (island of Brač) and then continues to Jelsa (island of Hvar).

🚢 **Jadrolinija** ☎ 021/338-333 ⊕ www.jadrolinija.hr. **Blue Line** ☎ 021/352-533 ⊕ www.bli-ferry.com. **SNAV** ☎ 021/322-252 ⊕ www.snav.it. **Tirrenia Navigazione** ☎ 021/338-335 ⊕ www.tirrenia.it.

BUS TRAVEL
International buses arrive daily from Trieste (Italy), Ljubljana (Slovenia), Munich, and Stuttgart (Germany). There are buses once a week from Vienna (Austria), and London (UK) via Paris (France).

There are good bus connections to destinations all over Croatia. There are approximately 30 buses per day to Zagreb, 12 to Dubrovnik (in Southern Dalmatia), 14 to Zadar (in Northern Dalmatia) and 12 to Rijeka (in Kvarner). Buses traveling south to Dubrovnik stop at Makarska en route, while those going north to Zadar stop at Šibenik. In addition, regular local buses run every 30 minutes up the coast to Trogir and down the coast to Omiš. Timetable information is available from the Split Bus Station.

🚌 **Split Bus Station** ✉ Obala Kneza Domogoja 12, Split ☎ 060/327-327.

CAR TRAVEL
While visiting Split and the nearby islands of Brač, Hvar, and Vis, you are certainly better off without a car. However, you may wish to rent a vehicle to drive up the coast to Šibenik and Krka National Park, or down

the coast to Omiš and Makarska, although these destinations are also well served by buses.

🚹 **Budget** ✉ Hotel Marjan, Obala K Branimira, Kaštela ☎ 021/399-214 ✉ Split Airport, Kaštela ☎ 021/203-151. **Dollar Thrifty** ✉ Hotel Marjan, Obala K Branimira, Split ☎ 021/399-000 ✉ Split Airport, Kaštela ☎ 021/895-329. **Hertz** ✉ Tomića Stine 9, Split ☎ 021/360-455 ✉ Split Airport, Kaštela ☎ 021/895-230. **Mack** ✉ Hotel Split, Put Trstenik 19, Split ☎ 021/303-008 ⊕ www.mack-concord.hr.

EMERGENCIES
🚹 Ambulance **Ambulance** ☎ 94.
🚹 Doctors & Dentists **Hitno Ponoč** (Casualty) ✉ Spinčićeva 1, Split ☎ 021/556-111.
🚹 Fire **Fire Emergencies** ☎ 93.
🚹 Pharmacies **Dobri** ✉ Gundulićeva 52, Split ☎ 021/348-074. **Lučac** ✉ Pupačićeva 4, Split ☎ 021/533-188.
🚹 Police **Police Emergencies** ☎ 92.

INTERNET
During the summer, small temporary Internet cafés spring up in the main resorts; some may be nothing more than a regular café with a PC in the corner. Even on the islands, you will find somewhere to check e-mail. However, very few well-established, fully-equipped Internet cafés exist in the region.

MAIL & SHIPPING
🚹 **Split Main Post Office** ✉ Obala Kneza Domagoja, Split lies on the road leading along the seafront from the center of town to the ferry port. It is open daily 7 AM–8 PM.

MONEY MATTERS
There are banks in all the destinations mentioned in this chapter. ATMs are now widespread, and you will find at least one even in small towns on the islands. It is possible to exchange currency in banks and also in most local travel agencies.

TAXIS
In Split, the main taxi ranks lie at each end of the *Riva* (Obala Hrvatskog Preporoda): in front of the *pazar* (open-air market) and in front of Hotel Bellevue. You will also find taxis waiting outside the train station (Obala Kneza Domagoja). Or you can call for a taxi in Split.
🚹 **Radio Taxi** ☎ 970 in Split.

TOURS
In Split, Šibenik and Trogir, the respective tourist-information centers organize informative and amusing guided tours of their cities. In addition, Atlas organizes one-day excursions departing from Split (by bus or hydrofoil) to various destinations in the region, including rafting in the Cetina Valley. The company also offers a one-day trip to the pilgrimage site of Medjugorje where the Virgin Mary is said to have appeared in 1981 (in Bosnia Herzegovina, passports required).
🚹 **Atlas** ✉ Trg Brace Radića 6, Split ☎ 021/343-055 ⊕ www.atlas-croatia.com. **Split Tourist Information Center** ✉ Peristil, Split ☎ 021/345-606. **Šibenik Tourist Information Center** ✉ Fausta Vrančića 18, Šibenik ☎ 022/212-075. **Trogir Tourist Information Center** ✉ Trg Ivana Pavla II 1, Trogir ☎ 021/881-412.

TRAIN TRAVEL

There are three day trains and two night trains (with sleeping cars) daily between Split and Zagreb (journey time 5½ hours daytime; 8½ hours nighttime). In addition, there are three day trains daily between Split and Šibenik (journey time approximately 3½ hours, with a change at Perković).

🚆 **Split Train Station** ✉ Obala Kneza Domogoja 9, Split ☎ 060/333-444 ⊕ www. hznet.hr.

VISITOR INFORMATION

🚆 **Split & Dalmatia County Tourist Board** ✉ Prilaz brace Kaliterna 10/I, Split ☎ 021/ 490-032 ⊕ www.dalmatia-cen.com. **Bol Tourist Information Center** ✉ Porat Bolskih Pomoraca, Bol ☎ 021/635-638 ⊕ www.bol.hr. **Hvar Town Tourist Information Center** ✉ Trg Sv Stjepana 16, Hvar Town ☎ 021/741-059 ⊕ www.hvar.hr. **Lastovo Tourist Office** ✉ Lastovo, Lastovo ☎ 020/801-018 ⊕ www.lastovo-tz.net. **Makarska Tourist Information Centre** ✉ Obala Kralja Tomislava 16, Makarska ☎ 021/616-288 ⊕ www. makarska.hr. **Omiš Tourist Information Centre** ✉ Trg Kneza Miroslava, Omiš ☎ 021/ 861-350. **Skradin Tourist Information Center** ✉ Obala Bana Šubića 1, Skradin ☎ 022/ 771-306 ⊕ www.skradin.hr. **Split Tourist Information Center** ✉ Peristil, Split ☎ 021/ 345-606 ⊕ www.visitsplit.com. **Šibenik Tourist Information Center** ✉ Fausta Vrančića 18, Šibenik ☎ 022/212-075. **Trogir Tourist Information Center** ✉ Trg Ivana Pavla II 1, Trogir ☎ 021/881-412. **Vis Tourist Information Center** ✉ Šetalište Stare Isse 5, Vis Town ☎ 021/717-017 ⊕ www.tz-vis.hr.

Dubrovnik & Southern Dalmatia

7

By Jane Foster The highlight of Southern Dalmatia is undoubtedly the majestic walled city of Dubrovnik, from 1358 to 1808 a rich and powerful independent republic, which exerted its economic and cultural influence over almost the entire region. Jutting out to sea and backed by rugged mountains, it's an unforgettable sight and now Croatia's most upmarket and glamorous destination.

From Dubrovnik a ferry runs all the way up the coast to Rijeka in the Kvarner region, making several stops along the way, and occasionally extending its itinerary to include an overnight lap from Dubrovnik to Bari, Italy. There are also regular local ferry and catamaran services from Dubrovnik to outlying islands. The nearest and most accessible of these are the tiny car-free Elefitis, ideal as a day trip for someone on a short stay who still wants a brief taste of island life.

Moving down the mainland coast, Cavtat was founded by the ancient Greeks. Today a sleepy fishing town through winter, it turns into a cheerful holiday resort come summer, with a palm-lined seaside promenade, several sights of cultural note, and a handful of reasonably priced hotels.

Back up the coast, northwest of Dubrovnik, lies the village of Trsteno, with its delightful Renaissance arboretum stepping down toward the sea in a series of terraces. Proceeding northwest one arrives at Ston, known for its oysters and mussels, and its 14th-century walls forming the gateway to Pelješac Peninsula. Pelješac is of particular note for its excellent red wines: several families open their vineyards and cellars to the public for wine tastings. The main destination here is Orebić, a low-key resort with a good beach and water-sports facilities, backed by a majestic hillside monastery.

From Orebić there are regular ferry crossings to Korčula Town, on the island of Korčula, one of the most sophisticated settlements on the Croatian islands, with its fine Gothic and Renaissance stone buildings bearing witness to almost 800 years of Venetian rule. Nearby Lumbarda provides a good stretch of sand beach, plus a delicate white wine known as Grk.

In contrast to Korčula, the sparsely-populated island of Mljet offers little in the way of architectural beauty but has preserved its indigenous coniferous forests, which rim the shores of two emerald-green saltwater lakes. They are contained within the borders of Mljet National Park, a haven for hiking, mountain biking, swimming, and kayaking.

If you're traveling from Central to Southern Dalmatia by road, you'll pass through a narrow coastal strip given over to Bosnia-Herzegovina, so have your passport at hand for the border checkpoint. Most Croatian buses have a 20-minute stop here so people can jump off and shop, since many things—notably cigarettes—are much cheaper in Bosnia.

Exploring Southern Dalmatia

About the Restaurants

Seafood predominates throughout the region. Restaurants in Dubrovnik are the most expensive, and tend to cater for up-market international tastes, with expensive "white" fish topping most menus and multilin-

Southern Dalmatia is more than just Dubrovnik. The itineraries below aim to give you some idea of what to see in a limited time.

If you have
3 days

Devote day one to **Dubrovnik,** walking a full circuit of the city walls, exploring the historic monuments in the Old Town, and attending an open-air concert or theatrical performance if the Dubrovnik Summer Festival is in course. On Day 2, make an early start to visit the arboretum at **Trsteno,** a green wilderness of exotic planting in the grounds of a Renaissance villa. Return to Dubrovnik to take the midday ferry to **Lopud,** one of the car-free Elafiti islands, and walk across the island for an afternoon Swimming on the Šunj sand beach. If Lopud's romantic escapism appeals, stay overnight; otherwise, return to Dubrovnik for the bright lights. Next morning splash out on a taxi-boat ride along the coast from Dubrovnik's old harbor to **Cavtat.** Return either by taxi-boat or local bus to Dubrovnik for your final night.

If you have
5 days

Spend your first day in Dubrovnik, as outlined above. Next morning, take a taxi boat to Cavtat as outlined in the previous itinerary, returning to Dubrovnik in time for the early evening bus to **Korčula Town,** where you should sleep. Next day check out Korčula's Venetian-style architecture in the morning, then spend the afternoon either on the beach at Lumbarda, or rent a motor boat and visit the tiny scattered islets of the Korčula archipelago. Stay a second night in Korčula; if you're lucky you might catch an evening performance of the Moreška sword dance. On the next morning take a ferry to **Orebić** on the Pelješac Peninsula. First walk up to the Franciscan Monastery, then devote the afternoon to exploring the local vineyards and wine cellars, either independently by car or as part of an organized tour group. Stay the night in Orebić. The following day catch the early morning bus for Dubrovnik. En route you could jump off at **Ston** to explore the 15th-century defensive walls and walk over to Mali Ston to sample the local oysters. **Trsteno** is another possible stop en route. Return to Dubrovnik in the afternoon to prepare for your final night.

If you have
7 days

Spend your first four days as on the itinerary above. On day five, wake up in Orebić then travel southeast along the Pelješac Peninsula to Trstenik to catch the morning ferry to Polače on the island of **Mljet.** Proceed to Pomena, where you will stay the night. Now you are already within the confines of **Mljet National Park,** a paradise of dense pine woods, centering on two interconnected saltwater lakes. Here you can either hike or rent a mountain bike to cycle the perimeter of the lakes, or take time out to swim. Alternatively, Odissej Hotel in Pomena can arrange a half-day sailing or diving trip. In the evening take a national park boat to St. Mary's Islet on Veliko Jezero, occupied by a former monastery, which now hosts a restaurant, making a romantic venue for dinner. On the next morning drive the length of Mljet to spend a few hours on the sand beach of Saplunara. Leave the island via the port of Sobra aboard the mid-afternoon ferry for Dubrovnik, where you should spend your final evening.

7

gual waiters pampering diners. The region's top venue for shellfish is the village of Mali Ston on the Pelješac Peninsula, where locally grown *ostrige* (oysters, at their best from February through May) and *dagnje* (mussels, at their best from May through September) attract diners from far and wide. Similarly, the island of Mljet is noted for its *jastog* (lobster), a culinary luxury that is highly appreciated by the sailing crowd.

If you are lucky enough to find food prepared *ispod peke,* be sure to try it. A terra-cotta casserole dish, usually containing either lamb or octopus, is buried in white embers over which the *peka* (a metal dome) is placed to ensure a long, slow cooking process. Such dishes often need to be ordered one day in advance. Regarding desserts, the region's specialty is *rožata,* an egg-based pudding similar to French crème caramel.

WHAT IT COSTS in Croatian Kuna (Kn)				
$$$$	**$$$**	**$$**	**$**	**¢**
RESTAURANTS over 80	60–80	35–60	20–35	under 20

Restaurant prices are per person for a main course at dinner.

About the Hotels

Southern Dalmatia's (and indeed Croatia's) best and most expensive hotels are in Dubrovnik. The top-notch establishments lie in and near the Old Town, whereas in nearby Lapad you'll find around 20 large, modern Socialist-era hotels, which are rapidly being bought by foreign investors and renovated to include 21st-century luxuries such as wellness centers. Outside Dubrovnik standards drop, with some hotels still without air-conditioning or Internet service. Many visitors prefer to rent a private room or apartment: it's cheaper, more homey, and gives you a chance to live as the locals do.

Many hotels in Dubrovnik stay open all year. For the rest of the region, the season runs from Easter through late October, peaking during July and August, when prices rise significantly and it may be difficult to find a place to sleep if you have not booked in advance.

WHAT IT COSTS in euros (€) and Croatian kuna (Kn)				
$$$$	**$$$**	**$$**	**$**	**¢**
IN EUROS over € 225	€175–€225	€125–€175	€75–€125	under €75
IN KUNA over 1,650	1,300–1,650	925–1,300	550–925	under 550

Hotel prices are for two people in a double room in high season, excluding taxes and service charges.

Timing

Dubrovnik receives visitors all year. Although some stay in town for several nights, many others arrive by cruise ship (en route from Venice to the Greek islands), flooding the streets during daylight hours but disappearing come sunset. The city is exceptionally crowded during the Summer Festival (mid-July to mid-August), with everyone from international

History

The region's best-known and most magnificent historic monument has to be Dubrovnik's Old Town, which has been declared a UNESCO World Heritage Site. Northwest along the coast, tiny Ston is noteworthy for its 14th-century walls, which formed a unique defense system, effectively controlling land access onto Pelješac Peninsula. Korčula Town, a compact settlement of medieval stone buildings on a small peninsula, owes its ingenious "herring-bone" urban plan and elegant Gothic and Renaissance architecture to Dubrovnik's arch rival, Venice. Fortunately, each of these historic centers has been protected from the threat of careless modern development.

7

Islands

The region's islands offer the perfect opportunity to escape the chaos of modern-day life. The tiny, car-free Elafiti islands, which can be visited as a day trip from Dubrovnik, make a fine introduction to Dalmatia as it once was. Further out to sea, Mljet remains wild and relatively free of commercial development. One-third of Mljet has been declared a National Park to protect its indigenous pine woods and two saltwater lakes.

Wine

Southern Dalmatia produces some excellent wines, most notably the reds from the Pelješac Peninsula and the whites from the island of Korčula. On Pelješac, just one grape variety, Plavac Mali (closely related to the California favorite, Zinfandel) produces three different sorts of red—Dingač, Postup, and Plavac—depending on the soil and topography of the vineyards it grows in. Here, several family-run wine cellars offer wine-tasting sessions, the best-known being Grgić in Trstenik, Bartulović in Prizdrina, and Matuško in Potomje. On Korčula, the grape variety Pošip produces a crisp dry white wine, with the best coming from the interior villages of Čara and Smokvica. And near Lumbarda, the golden-colored Grk is highly-esteemed and said to date back to the ancient Greeks. The Dubrovnik-based travel agency Atlas runs wine-tasting trips to both Pelješac and Korčula.

Beaches

The best beaches and the cleanest water for swimming are on the islands. Sand is rare in Croatia, but in Southern Dalmatia you'll find blissful, non-commercial, back-to-nature, sandy beaches at Lumbarda (on Korčula), Saplunara (on Mljet), and Šunj (on Lopud). Trstenica in Orebić is a 1-km- (½-mi-) long stretch of mixed sand and pebble. Nudism is popular, and official nudist beaches are marked FKK (from the German *Freikorperkultur,* meaning "free body culture"). Eastwest in Dubrovnik is a fully-equipped, see-and-be-seen beach club just outside the city walls, where you'll spot international celebrities and would-be's sporting designer swimwear.

Sailing

Southern Dalmatia is a paradise for yachting enthusiasts, thanks to its myriad islands and well-equipped marinas. Dubrovnik ACI marina is the region's main charter base, with around a dozen companies keeping boats there. Other marinas in the region include the Korčula ACI marina on Korčula, and the Hotel Odisej marina on Mljet. The latter hosts the highly-regarded ANA Sailing School, offering one-week sailing courses at various levels through summer. If you take a typical one-week charter departing from Dubrovnik, you can expect to visit the Elafiti, Mljet, and Korčula and to really get off the beaten path.

performers to backpackers scrambling to find a room in the Old Town. Some hotels offer Easter and New Year packages, so you can expect Dubrovnik to be surprisingly busy at these times, too.

The rest of the region is more easygoing, with seasonal fluctuations similar to the rest of the Croatian coast. The July and August high season brings an influx of foreign visitors, the majority of whom are from Europe. Prices rise significantly during this period, as do temperatures, and accommodation can be difficult to find: as compensation, the long summer evenings offer cultural performances and late-night drinking below the stars.

Low season runs from November through April, a period when many hotels and restaurants close completely. That said, through winter you may be lucky enough to find bargain-priced accommodation and blissful days of sunshine and deep blue sky, albeit with a bracing chill in the air. For most people the best time to visit is the shoulder season, May through June and September through October. You'll find no crowds, decent weather, and a chance to tune into the local way of life.

Numbers in the margins correspond to numbers on the Southern Dalmatia and Dubrovnik maps.

DUBROVNIK

Lying 216 km (135 mi) southeast of Split and commanding a splendid coastal location, Dubrovnik is one of the world's most beautiful fortified cities. Its massive stone ramparts and splendid fortress towers curve around a tiny harbor, enclosing graduated ridges of sun-bleached orange-tiled roofs, copper domes, and elegant bell towers.

In the 7th century AD, residents of the Roman city Epidaurum (now Cavtat) fled the Avars and Slavs of the north and founded a new settlement on a small rocky island, which they named Laus, and later Ragusa. On the mainland hillside opposite the island, the Slav settlement called Dubrovnik grew up. In the 12th century, the narrow channel separating the two settlements was filled in, and Ragusa and Dubrovnik became one. The city was surrounded by defensive walls during the 13th century, and these were reinforced with towers and bastions during the late 15th century.

From 1358 to 1808, the city existed as a powerful and remarkably sophisticated independent republic, reaching its Golden Age during the 16th century. In 1667, many of its splendid Gothic and Renaissance buildings were destroyed by an earthquake. The defensive walls survived the disaster, and the city was rebuilt in baroque style.

Dubrovnik lost its independence to Napoleon in 1808, and in 1815 passed to Austro-Hungary. During the 20th century, as part of Yugoslavia, the city became a popular tourist destination, and in 1979 it was listed as a UNESCO World Heritage Site. During the war for independence, it came under heavy siege, though thanks to careful restoration work, few traces of damage remain. Today, Dubrovnik is once again a fashionable, high-class destination, with recent visitors including Tom Cruise, Sharon Stone, John Malkovich, and Sir Roger Moore.

Exploring Dubrovnik

All of the main sites lie in Stari Grad (Old Town) within the city walls, an area which is compact and car-free.

What to See

⓬ **Akvarij** (Aquarium). This dark, cavernous space houses several small pools and 27 well-lit tanks containing a variety of fish from rays to small sharks, as well as other underwater denizens such as sponges and sea urchins. Children will find the octopus, in his glass tank, either very amusing or horribly scary. ⊠ *Damjana Jude 2, Stari Grad* ☎ *020/323–978* 💳 *25 Kn* ☉ *June–Sept., daily 9–8; Apr., May, Oct., and Nov., daily 9–6; Dec.–Mar., daily 9–1.*

❽ **Crkva Svetog Vlaha** (Church of St. Blaise). This 18th-century baroque church replaced an earlier one destroyed by fire. Of particular note is the silver statue on the high altar of St. Blaise holding a model of Dubrovnik, which is paraded around town each year on February 3, the Day of St. Blaise. ⊠ *Luža, Stari Grad* 💳 *Free* ☉ *Daily 8–noon and 4:30–7.*

need a break?

Gradska Kavarna (⊠ Placa, Stari Grad) occupies the old Arsenal building and remains Dubrovnik's favorite meeting place for morning coffee with cakes or an evening aperitif. It has an ample summer terrace for when the weather is nice.

6 **Dominikanski Samostan** (Dominican Monastery). With a splendid, late-15th-century floral Gothic cloister as its centerpiece, the monastery is best known for its museum, which houses a rich collection of religious paintings by the so-called Dubrovnik School from the 15th and 16th centuries. Look out for works by Božidarević, Hamzić, and Dobričević, as well as gold and silver ecclesiastical artifacts crafted by local goldsmiths. ⊠ *Sv Domina 4, Stari Grad* ☎ *020/321–423* ⊠ *10 Kn* ☼ *May–Oct., daily 9–6; Nov.–Apr., daily 9–5.*

4 **Franjevačka Samostan** (Franciscan Monastery). The monastery's chief claim to fame is its pharmacy, which was founded in 1318 and is still in existence today; it's said to be the oldest in Europe. There's also a delightful cloistered garden, framed by Romanesque arcades supported by double columns, each crowned with a set of grotesque figures. In the Treasury a painting shows what Dubrovnik looked like before the disastrous earthquake of 1667. ⊠ *Placa 2, Stari Grad* ☎ *020/321–410* ⊠ *15 Kn* ☼ *May–Oct., daily 9–6; Nov.–Apr., daily 9–5.*

★ **3** **Gradske Zidine** (City Walls). Most of the original construction took place during the 13th century, though the walls were further reinforced with towers and bastions during the following 400 years. On average they are 80 feet high and up to 10 feet thick on the seaward side, 20 feet on the inland side. ⊠ *Placa, Stari Grad* ☎ *020/324–641* ⊠ *30 Kn* ☼ *May–Sept., daily 8–7; Oct.–Apr., daily 9–3.*

13 **Muzej Pravoslavne Crkve** (Orthodox Church Museum). Next door to the Orthodox Church, this small museum displays religious icons from the Balkan region and Russia, as well as several portraits of eminent early-20th-century Dubrovnik personalities by local artist Vlaho Bukovac. ⊠ *Od Puca 8, Stari Grad* ☎ *020/323–823* ⊠ *10 Kn* ☼ *May–Oct., daily 9–2; Nov.–Apr., Mon.–Sat. 9–2.*

10 **Katedrala Velika Gospa** (Cathedral of Our Lady). The present structure was built in baroque style after the original was destroyed in the 1667 earthquake. The interior contains a number of notable paintings, including a large polyptych above the main altar depicting the *Assumption of Our Lady,* attributed to Titian. The Treasury displays 138 gold and silver reliquaries, including the skull of St. Blaise in the form of a bejeweled Byzantine crown and also an arm and a leg of the saint, likewise encased in decorated golden plating. ⊠ *Bunićeva Poljana, Stari Grad* ☎ *020/323–459* ⊠ *Cathedral free, Treasury 7 Kn* ☼ *Daily 8–7.*

9 **Knežev Dvor** (Bishop's Palace). Originally created in the 15th century but reconstructed several times through the following years, this exquisite building with an arcaded loggia and an internal courtyard shows a combination of late-Gothic and early Renaissance styles. On the ground floor there are large rooms where, in the days of the Republic, the Great Council and Senate held their meetings. Over the entrance to the meet-

DUBROVNIK UNDER SIEGE

FROM NOVEMBER 1991 TO MAY 1992, *Dubrovnik was intermittently shelled by the Yugoslav army and Serb and Montenegrin irregulars, who were stationed on the rugged hills behind the city. Electricity and water supplies were cut off, and the local population took refuge in basements, surviving on a slowly diminishing quantity of foodstuffs, fuel, and medical supplies. The city's massive medieval fortifications stood up well to the assault, though none of Dubrovnik's main monuments was targeted—apparently the Yugoslav army wanted to capture the city intact. Extensive media coverage whipped up a storm of international criticism over the wanton bombing of this historic city, which effectively turned world opinion against Belgrade and in favor of granting Croatia diplomatic recognition. Once hostilities ceased, the clean-up and rebuilding began. During the second half of the 1990s, money poured in from all over the world for the restoration of the shrapnel-scarred facades and the shattered terra-cotta rooftops. Today, thanks to the work of highly skilled craftsmen, barely any traces of war damage remain.*

ing halls a plaque reads: OBLITI PRIVATORUM PUBLICA CURATE (Forget private affairs, and get on with public matters). Upstairs, the rector's living quarters now accommodate the Gradski Muzej (City Museum), containing exhibits that give a picture of life in Dubrovnik from early days until the fall of the Republic. ⊠ *Pred Dvorom 3, Stari Grad* ☎ *020/321–497* 🖼 *20 Kn* ☉ *May–Oct., daily 9–6; Nov.–Apr., daily 9–2.*

❷ Placa. This was once the shallow sea channel separating the island of Laus from the mainland. Although it was filled in during the 12th century, it continued to divide the city socially for several centuries, with the nobility living in the area south of Placa and the commoners living on the hillside to the north. Today it forms the venue for the *korzo,* an evening promenade where locals meet to chat, maybe have a drink, and generally size one another up. ⊠ *Stari Grad.*

⓫ Pomorski Muzej (Maritime Museum). Above the Aquarium, on the first floor of St. John's Fortress, this museum's exhibits illustrate how rich and powerful Dubrovnik became as one of the world's most important seafaring nations. On display are intricately detailed models of ships as well as engine-room equipment, sailors' uniforms, paintings, and maps. ⊠ *Damjana Jude 2, Stari Grad* ☎ *020/323–904* 🖼 *15 Kn* ☉ *May–Oct., daily 9–6; Nov.–Apr., Tues.–Sun. 9–2.*

❺ Sinagoga (Synagogue). This tiny 15th-century synagogue, the second-oldest in Europe (after Prague's) bears testament to Dubrovnik's once thriving Jewish community, made up largely of Jews who were expelled from Spain and Italy during the medieval period. ⊠ *Žudioska 5, Stari Grad* ☎ *020/321–028* 🖼 *10 Kn* ☉ *Weekdays 10–8.*

❶ Vrata od Pila (Pile Gate). Built in 1537 and combining a Renaissance arch with a wooden drawbridge on chains, this has always been the main entrance to the city walls. A niche above the portal contains a statue of Sveti

Vlah (St. Blaise), the city's patron saint, holding a replica of Dubrovnik in his left hand. From May to October, guards in deep-red period-costume uniforms stand vigilant by the gate through daylight hours, just as they would have done when the city was a republic. ⊠ *Pile, Stari Grad.*

❼ Vrata od Ploča (Ploče Gate). One of two entrances into the town walls, Ploče comprises a stone bridge and wooden drawbridge plus a 15th-century stone arch bearing a statue of Sveti Vlah (St. Blaise). As at Pile Gate, guards in period costume stand vigilant here through the summer season. ⊠ *Ploče, Stari Grad.*

⓮ War Photo Limited. Shocking but impressive, this modern gallery devotes
FodorśChoice two entire floors to war photojournalism. Past exhibitions include im-
★ ages from conflicts in Afghanistan, Iraq, former-Yugoslavia, Israel, and Palestine. Refreshingly impartial by Croatian standards, the message—that war is physically and emotionally destructive whichever side you are on—comes through loudly and clearly. You'll find it in a narrow side street running between Placa and Prijeko. ⊠ *Antuninska 6, Stari Grad* ☎ *020/322–166* ⊕ *www.warphotoltd.com* ✆ *25 Kn* ☉ *May–Oct., daily 9–9; Nov.–Apr., Tues.–Sat. 10–4, Sun. 10–2.*

Where to Eat

As elsewhere along the coast, seafood dominates restaurant menus. The narrow, cobbled street Prijeko, which runs parallel to Placa, is packed with touristy restaurants and waiters touting for customers. Less commercial and infinitely more agreeable eateries are scattered throughout the town.

$$$–$$$$ ✕ **Restaurant Atlas Club Nautika.** Probably Dubrovnik's most exclusive restaurant, Nautika lies close to Pile Gate, just outside the city walls. It occupies the former Nautical Academy building, dating from 1881, and has two terraces overlooking the sea. A sound choice for business lunches and formal celebrations, the restaurant serves shellfish, lobster, and fresh fish, as well as meat dishes and has an excellent wine list. ⊠ *Brsalje 3, Pile* ☎ *020/442–526* ☰ *AE, DC, MC, V.*

$$–$$$ ✕ **Marco Polo.** This favorite haunt of actors and musicians during the Summer Festival is in the Old Town, close to Crkva Sv Vlaha. The minuscule dining room is only big enough for four tables, but there's a summer terrace in the courtyard. Choose from a range of excellent seafood dishes, including shellfish, risottos, and fresh fish. ⊠ *Lučarica 6, Stari Grad* ☎ *020/323–719* ☰ *AE, DC, MC, V* ☉ *Closed Nov.–Mar.*

★ $$–$$$ ✕ **Orhan.** With tables on a small quay close to the water's edge, this highly-regarded but friendly and easygoing restaurant specializes in seafood, while also offering a range of typical Dalmatian meat dishes. You'll find it just outside Pile Gate, at the foot of Lovrijenac fortress. ⊠ *Od Tabakarije 1, Pile* ☎ *020/414–183* ☰ *AE, DC, MC, V.*

$$–$$$ ✕ **Tovjerna Sesame.** Just outside the city walls and close to Pile Gate, this romantic eatery occupies a vaulted, candlelit space with bohemian decor. It's popular with locals, and the menu is adventurous by Dalmatian standards: beef carpaccio with Parmesan, rocket (arugula), and capers; pasta truffle dishes, and a range of beautifully presented, creative salads. It's ideal for a light supper accompanied by a good bottle of wine. ⊠ *Dante Alighieria, Pile* ☏ *020/412–910* ▭ *AE, DC, MC, V.*

$$ ✕ **Lokanda Peškarija.** Just outside the town walls, overlooking the old
Fodor'sChoice harbor and next to the covered fish market, this seafood restaurant is
★ a particularly good value. It has a split-level interior with exposed stone walls and wooden beams, plus outdoor candlelit tables by the water. Locals love it, so reservations are recommended, especially for dinner. ⊠ *Na Ponti, Stari Grad* ☏ *020/324–750* ▭ *AE, DC, MC, V* ☺ *Closed Jan. and Feb.*

★ **$–$$** ✕ **Kamenica.** Overlooking the morning market in the Old Town, Kamenica remains popular for its fresh oysters and generous platters of *girice* (small fried fish) and *pržene ligne* (fried squid). It's cheap and cheerful, and if you don't like seafood, you can always get a cheese omelet. ⊠ *Gundulićeva Poljana 8, Stari Grad* ☏ *No phone* ▭ *No credit cards* ☺ *No dinner Nov.–Mar.*

$–$$ ✕ **Mea Culpa.** Within the city walls and open until midnight year-round, Mea Culpa is said to make the best pizza in town. The dining room is a bit cramped, and you may find the music unreasonably loud, but from spring to autumn there are large wooden tables outside on the cobbled street. ⊠ *Za Rokom 3, Stari Grad* ☏ *020/323–430* ▭ *No credit cards.*

$ ✕ **Lapad.** Opened in summer 2005, Lapad is part of Srdela Snack, a chain of eateries specializing in "blue" fish such as sardines, mackerel, and tuna, all essential to the traditional Dalmatian diet. Informal, fun, and healthy, it also offers seasonal salads and locally produced wine. You'll find it in the grounds of the Grand Hotel Park on Lapad Peninsula. ⊠ *Šetalište Kralja Zvonimira 39, Lapad* ☏ *020/434–852* ▭ *AE, DC, MC, V.*

Where to Stay

There are only two small but extremely desirable hotels within the city walls. The most exclusive establishments line the coastal road east of the center, offering stunning views of the Old Town and the sea, whereas modern hotels with cheaper rooms and decent sports facilities can be found in Lapad, 3 km (2 mi) west of the center. The only way to save money in Dubrovnik is to rent a private room, but, like the hotels, even these can be up to double the price of those elsewhere in Croatia.

$$$$ ▥ **Hotel Excelsior.** On the coastal road east of the center, this prestigious modern hotel offers well-furnished rooms with balconies overlooking the sea and Old Town. Each of the luxury suites has a jetted tub. It's slightly lacking in charm, but there are excellent sports, health and beauty, and business facilities. Of special note is the Taverna Rustica, a highly-regarded restaurant with romantic nighttime views across the water to the city walls; it's popular with residents and non-residents alike. ⊠ *Put Frane Supila 12, Ploče 20000* ☏ *020/353–300* 🖷 *020/414–214* ⊕ *www. hotel-excelsior.hr* 🛏 *146 rooms, 18 suites* ⚴ *2 restaurants, café, room service, in-room fax, some in-room hot tubs, minibars, cable TV, in-room data ports, indoor pool, gym, massage, sauna, hair salon, bar, laundry service, Internet room, convention center, meeting rooms* ▭ *AE, DC, MC, V* ⊚ *BP.*

$$$$ ⌑ **Pučić Palace.** In the heart of the Old Town, occupying a beautifully re-
Fodor'sChoice stored 18th-century baroque palace, this small luxury boutique hotel of-
★ fers the sort of aristocratic delights that its location suggests: rooms with
dark oak parquet floors and wood-beam ceilings, antique furnishings,
and Italian mosaic-tile bathrooms supplied with Bulgari toiletries. Fine
wining and dining are also possible here, with the Defne restaurant serving eastern Mediterranean cuisine on a romantic upper-level terrace lined
with potted lemon trees. The ground-floor Café Royal is a popular meeting point for morning coffee and pastries, with tables outside on the piazza on warm days. In the evening, head for the adjoining Razonoda wine
bar, where you can sample some of Croatia's most sought-after wines
and spirits. ⌧ *Ul od Puča 1, Stari Grad 20000* ☎ *020/326–200* 🖷 *020/*
326–223 ⊕ *www.thepucicpalace.com* ⌦ *19 rooms* ⌑ *Restaurant, café,*
room service, minibars, cable TV, in-room safes, in-room data ports, bar,
laundry service ⊟ *AE, DC, MC, V* ⍾*BP.*

$$$$ ⌑ **Villa Dubrovnik.** This romantic retreat lies a 20-minute walk east of
the center and comprises a white modernist structure built into the
rocks, as well as a series of terraces and a garden coming down to a hide-
away cove with a small beach. The rooms are light and airy, and all have
balconies and views across the water to Lokrum island and the Old Town.
There's a complimentary boat service to and from the Old Town; airport transfers by private car are available on request. From mid-July to
mid-September you must take half-board; outside of the peak season
bed and breakfast rates are also available. ⌧ *V Bukovaca 6, Ploče*
20000 ☎ *020/422–933* 🖷 *020/423–465* ⊕ *www.villa-dubrovnik.hr*
⌦ *40 rooms* ⌑ *Restaurant, café, room service, minibars, cable TV, in-*
room data ports, gym, beach, Internet room ⊟ *AE, DC, MC, V*
⊘ *Closed Dec.–Mar.* ⍾*MAP.*

$$$ ⌑ **Hotel Stari Grad.** One of only two hotels in the Old Town, this re-
fined and intimate establishment occupies a renovated palace that once
belonged to the Drašković family, giving you some idea of how the local
aristocracy once lived. The rooms are furnished with reproduction an-
tiques, and in summer breakfast is served on a lovely roof terrace with
views over the surrounding buildings. You'll find it in a quiet side
street close to Pile Gate. ⌧ *Od Sigurate 4, Stari Grad 20000* ☎ *020/*
322–244 🖷 *020/321–256* ⊕ *www.hotelstarigrad.com* ⌦ *8 rooms*
⌑ *Minibars, cable TV, in-room data ports, laundry service* ⊟ *AE,*
DC, MC, V ⍾*BP.*

$$–$$$ ⌑ **Hotel Bellevue.** Built into a spectacular rocky cliff overlooking the sea,
with its own beach below (accessible by elevator), the Bellevue lies be-
tween the Old Town and Gruž harbor. Most of the rooms have a bal-
cony and sea view. Closed for renovation through winter 2005, it will
reopen in summer 2006, after which it will operate year-round. ⌧ *Pera*
Čingrije 7, 20000 ☎ *020/413–306* 🖷 *020/414–058* ⊕ *www.hotel-*
bellevue.hr ⌦ *49 rooms* ⌑ *2 restaurants, room service, minibars, cable*
TV, beach, bar ⊟ *AE, DC, MC, V* ⍾*BP.*

$$ ⌑ **Grand Hotel Park.** This modern hotel in Lapad is surrounded by a green,
leafy park and is close to the sea. Rooms are simple, modern, and com-
fortable, with views of either the sea or gardens; 71 rooms in an annex
are more basic but have the plus of being in a renovated, though older,

THE REPUBLIC OF DUBROVNIK

AS AN INDEPENDENT REPUBLIC *from 1358 to 1808, Dubrovnik kept its freedom not through military power, but thanks to diplomatic cunning. Would-be aggressors, including Hungary and the Ottoman Turks, were paid an annual fee in return for peaceful relations, and Dubrovnik avoided involvement in international conflicts between Christians and Muslims, preferring to remain neutral.*

The republic's economy was based on shipping and trading goods between Europe and the Middle East, and by the 16th century the republic had consulates in some 50 foreign ports, along with a merchant fleet of 200 ships on the Mediterranean. By this time, its territory had also extended to include 120 km (75 mi) of mainland coast (from Neum to the Bay of Kotor) plus the islands of Lastovo and Mljet.

The chief citizen was the Rector, who had to be over 50; he was elected for only a

month at a time to share management of the republic's business with the Grand Council (composed of members of the local nobility) and the Senate (a consultative body made up of 45 "wise men," all over the age of 40). Most of the military and naval commands were held by members of the nobility, while lower-ranking soldiers were mercenaries from the regions that are now Germany and the Czech Republic. The increasingly prosperous middle class carried on trade. The Archbishop of Dubrovnik had to be a foreigner (usually an Italian), a law intended to keep politics and religion apart.

Outstandingly sophisticated for its time, Dubrovnik was very conscious of social values: the first pharmacy opened in 1317; the first nursing home was founded in 1347; slave trading was abolished in 1418, and the first orphanage opened in 1432.

---

building. The main restaurant offers live music on an open-air terrace through summer, and there's a good range of sports and business facilities. Maybe a little far from the Old Town for sightseeing enthusiasts (it's 4½ km [3 mi] to the city walls) this hotel is recommended for those on longer stays who want to take things slowly and relax. ⊠ *Šetalište Kralja Zvonimira 39, Lapad 20000* ☎ *020/434–444* 🖷 *020/437–433* ⊕ *www.grandhotel-park.hr* 💤 *156 rooms, 71 annex rooms, 6 suites* ⅄ *2 restaurants, café, room service, minibars, cable TV, in-room data ports, 2 pools (1 indoor), massage, sauna, bar, convention center, meeting rooms, Internet room* 🖃 *AE, DC, MC, V* ⌾ *BP.*

$$ 🏨 **Hotel Lapad.** Occupying a 19th-century building with a garden and an outdoor pool, Hotel Lapad overlooks Gruž harbor, just a 15-minute walk west of the Old Town, making it a good mid-range option. A boat service to nearby beaches is at your disposal. It offers good discounts off season. Only rooms in the renovated wing have air-conditioning. ⊠ *Lapadska obala 37, Lapad 20000* ☎ *020/432–922* 🖷 *020/417–230* ⊕ *www.hotel-lapad.hr* 💤 *193 rooms* ⅄ *Restaurant, café, room service, minibars, cable TV, pool, hair salon, bar; no a/c in some rooms* 🖃 *AE, DC, MC, V* ⊙ *Closed Nov.–Mar.* ⌾ *BP.*

$ ▦ **Hotel Zagreb.** Set in a small garden with palms, close to a pleasant pebble beach, this red 19th-century building is right on the seafront promenade in Lapad. One of the best low-cost options in Dubrovnik, it offers a restaurant with a terrace, and comfortable air-conditioned rooms with en-suite bathrooms, but no extras. There's not even a pool, which is a consideration if you're not into pebbly beaches. A convenient bus stop is nearby if you don't fancy the 4-km (2½-mi) walk to the Old Town. ⊠ *Šetalište Kralja Zvonimira 27, Lapad 20000* ☎ *020/438–930* 🖷 *020/ 436–006* ☞ *24 rooms* ⅃ *Restaurant, room service, cable TV, bar* ▤ *AE, DC, MC, V* ⊙ *Closed Nov.–Mar.* ⑩ *BP.*

Nightlife & the Arts

Restrained through winter, aristocratic Dubrovnik wakes up with a vengeance come summer. Most nightlife takes place under the stars, as bars set up outdoor seating, discos take place by the sea, and even the cinema is open-air. The world-renowned Dubrovnik Summer Festival offers quality theatrical performances and classical-music concerts with international performers. An after-dinner drink at an outdoor table in the Old Town makes a romantic way to round of the evening. Those in search of more lively pursuits should visit one of several chic night clubs with music and open-air bars, which cater to the city's tanned and glamorous summer visitors.

Nightlife

BARS **Hard Jazz Cafe Troubadour** (⊠ Bunićeva Poljana 2, Stari Grad ☎ 020/ 323–476) is a long-standing Dubrovnik institution with occasional impromptu jazz concerts. Well-worn antiques and memorabilia fill the cozy, candlelit interior, and through summer tables spill outside onto the piazza. **Hemingway** (⊠ Pred Dvoram, Stari Grad) is a see-and-be-seen cocktail bar with outdoor tables and cushioned wicker chairs, perfect for people-watching.

DANCE CLUBS **Eastwest Beach Club** (⊠ Frana Supila, Banje Beach ☎ 020/412–220) One of several chic new establishments where you might spot well-known actors and sports people, Eastwest combines a daytime café overlooking a well-equipped pebble beach, and a nighttime restaurant with an Italian-inspired menu and a cocktail bar and rooftop VIP open-air lounge open until 5 AM. You'll find it a 5-minute walk east of the Old Town. **Labarint** (⊠ Dominika 2, Stari Grad ☎ 020/322–222) opened in 2003 and is still attracting a moneyed, 40-something clientele. The club combines a late-night terrace bar with live music and views over the old harbor, a black-and-red nightclub with live cabaret and jazz, and a smart restaurant in a cozy, ancient-walled dining space.

The Arts

Dubrovnik's cultural highlight is the annual **Dubrovnik Summer Festival** (🗐 Poljana P Miličevića 1 ☎ 020/323–400 ⊕ www.dubrovnik-festival. hr), which runs from early July to late August. The world-renowned festival includes a variety of open-air classical concerts and theatrical performances, notably Shakespeare's *Hamlet,* at various venues within the city walls. **Kino Slavica** (⊠ Dr. A. Starčevića 42, Pile) is an open-air summer cinema in a walled garden between the Old Town and Lapad. Predominantly English-language films are shown in their original versions with subtitles.

Sports & the Outdoors

Beaches

The more up-market hotels, such as the Excelsior and Villa Dubrovnik, have their own beaches that are exclusively for the use of hotel guests. The most natural and peaceful beaches lie on the tiny island of **Lokrum**, a short distance south of the Old Town. Through high season boats leave from the Old Harbor, ferrying visitors back and forth from morning to early evening. Ferries run every half hour from 9 AM to 7:30 PM. Tickets cost 25 Kn.

The **Eastwest Beach Club** (⊠ Frana Supila, Banje Beach ☎ 020/412–220), just a short distance from Ploče Gate, is a fashionable spot with a small pebble beach complete with chaise-longue and parasols, water-skiing and jet-skiing facilities, and a chic café.

Sailing

The 450-berth **ACI marina** (⊠ Mokošica ☎ 020/455–020) is 2 nautical mi from Gruž harbor and 6 km (3½ mi) from the city walls. The marina is open year-round, and a number of charter companies are based there.

Shopping

Despite its role as an important tourist destination, Dubrovnik offers little in the way of shopping or souvenir hunting. If you're in search of gifts, your best bet is a bottle of good Dalmatian wine or *rakija*.

Croata (⊠ Put Frane Supila 12, Ploče ☎ 020/353–279), a small boutique in the Hotel Excelsior, specializes in "original Croatian ties" in presentation boxes. **Djardin** (⊠ Miha Pracata 8, Stari Grad ☎ No phone) sells beautiful, funky modern jewelry made from colored stones: chunky necklaces, bracelets, and dangling earrings. Sophisticated and tasteful, with a touch of eccentricity, pieces are displayed in an old building with a courtyard garden. You'll find it in the Old Town, close to the Orthodox Church Museum. **Dubrovačka Kuća** (⊠ Svetog Dominika, Stari Grad ☎ 020/322–092), a tastefully decorated wine shop, stocks a fine selection of regional Croatian wines, *rakija*, olive oil, and truffle products, plus works of art by contemporary artists on the upper two levels; it's close to Ploče Gate.

Tours

Atlas Travel Agency (⊠ Čira Čarića 3, Dubrovnik ☎ 020/422–222 ⊕ www.atlas-croatia.com) organizes one-day tours of the Pelješac vineyards by bus, combining wine tasting and lunch in a typical Dalmatian konoba, with the transfer to and from Dubrovnik included.

LOPUD

⑮ *Lopud lies 7 nautical mi northwest of Dubrovnik by ferry.*

Thirteen tiny islets make up the Elafiti Islands, which are less than a one-hour ferry ride from Dubrovnik. Historically, they have always been under Dubrovnik's control, first when monks from the Franciscan Monastery used to visit the islands to gather herbs for use in their pharmacy; later, when local aristocracy kept summer villas here. Today there are still no cars on the islands, and only the three larger ones—Koločep, Lopud and Šipan—are inhabited, with a total population of less than 900.

There are regular ferry services between Dubrovnik and Koločep, Lopud, and Šipan. Any of the three can be comfortably visited as a day-trip, but if you intend to stay a night, Lopud is the best equipped to deal with visitors.

With a year-round population of approximately 300, tiny Lopud has just one settlement, Lopud Town, made up of old stone houses built around a sheltered bay, plus a handful of seasonal eateries, a large 1970s hotel, a couple of small family-run hotels occupying restored villas, and a tourist office, which is open only from May through October. From town, a concrete footpath leads through pinewoods and herb-scented olive groves: follow the signs, and in 15 minutes you will have crossed the island to arrive at Šunj, a glorious 1 km- (½-mi-) long sand beach curving around a southeast-facing cove.

Where to Eat

$$–$$$ ✕ **Restoran Obala.** This friendly eatery offers fine dining on the seafront promenade, with idyllic sunset views across the bay. The house specialty is *školjke na buzaru* (mixed shellfish cooked in wine and garlic), and if you're lucky you'll also be treated to live music. ⊠ *Obala Iva Kuljevana* ☎ *020/759–170* ▭ *AE, DC, MC, V* ⊗ *Closed Nov.–Mar.*

Where to Stay

$$–$$$ 🏨 **Hotel Villa Vilina.** This old stone villa, with palms out front overlooking the sea, has been carefully restored as a boutique hotel with a small pool. The restaurant serves dishes made from homegrown produce. Rooms with a sea view are slightly more expensive, but worth it. ⊠ *Obala Iva Kuljevana 5, 20222* ☎ *020/759–333* 🖨 *020/759–060* ⊕ *www.villa-vilina.hr* ⤴ *14 rooms, 3 suites* ♿ *Restaurant, room service, minibars, cable TV, outdoor pool, meeting room* ▭ *AE, DC, MC, V* ⊗ *Closed Nov.–Apr.* ⦿ *BP.*

$–$$ 🏨 **Hotel Glavović.** Lopud's first hotel when it opened in 1927, Hotel Glavovic was renovated in 2004. The rooms are very basic and rather lacking in character, but the restaurant has a lovely seaside terrace. It's recommended for those wishing to escape the hustle and bustle of modern-day life, not for those looking for full resort comforts. ⊠ *Obala Iva Kuljevana, 20222* ☎ *020/759–359* 🖨 *020/759–358* ⊕ *www.hotel-glavovic.hr* ⤴ *12 rooms, 2 suites* ♿ *Restaurant, room service, cable TV, in-room data ports, beach* ▭ *No credit cards* ⊗ *Closed Nov.–Apr.* ⦿ *BP.*

CAVTAT

⓰ *17 km (10½ mi) southeast of Dubrovnik.*

Founded by the ancient Greeks as Epidauros, then taken by the Romans and renamed Epidaurum, the original settlement on the site of Cavtat was subsequently destroyed by tribes of Avars and Slavs in the early 7th century. It was those Romans who fled Epidaurum that founded Dubrovnik.

Today's Cavtat, which developed during the 15th century under the Republic of Dubrovnik, is an easygoing fishing town and small-scale seaside resort. The medieval stone buildings of the Old Town occupy a small peninsula with a natural bay to each side. A palm-lined seaside promenade with open-air cafés and restaurants curves around the main bay, while the second bay is overlooked by a beach backed by several Socialist-era hotels.

Cavtat can be visited as a half-day trip from Dubrovnik. The easiest way to get there is by bus. Much more fun, but also more expensive, is a taxi-boat ride along the coast from Dubrovnik's Old Harbor (7 nautical mi); the journey time is approximately one hour.

Mauzolej Obitelji Račić (Račić Mausoleum). In the cemetery, on the highest point of a pine-scented peninsula, this mausoleum was created by Croatian sculptor Ivan Meštrović for the Račić family in 1921. Made from white marble and capped with a cupola, it is octangular in plan, and the main entrance is guarded by two art-nouveau caryatids. It was closed for restoration in summer 2005, but can still be visited upon request. ⊠ *Rat* ☎ *020/478–646* 🖾 *5 Kn* ☉ *By appointment only.*

Galerija Vlaho Bukovac (Vlaho Bukovac Gallery). The former home of local artist Vlaho Bukovac (1855–1922) has been renovated to provide a gallery for contemporary exhibitions on the ground floor. Upstairs, around 30 of Bukovac's oil paintings, tracing the periods he spent in Paris, Prague, and Cavtat, are on display in his former studio, along with pieces of period furniture. ⊠ *Bukovćeva* ☎ *020/478–646* 🖾 *20 Kn* ☉ *Tues.–Sat. 10–1 and 4–8; Sun. 4–8.*

Where to Eat

$$-$$$ ✕ **Leut.** Considered by many to be the best restaurant in Cavtat, Leut has an open-air terrace on the seafront promenade, with outdoor heaters so you can still eat out in winter. Favorite dishes include a delicious *rižot od škampi* (scampi cream risotto) and the local sweet specialty, *dubrovačka rožata* (Dubrovnik crème caramel). ⊠ *Trumbićev put 11* ☎ *020/478–477* 🖃 *AE, DC, MC, V.*

$$-$$$ ✕ **Taverna Galija.** Barbecued fish tops the bill here, along with seafood risotto and pasta dishes, colorful salads and a welcome but limited choice of vegetarian platters. You'll find it in a narrow alleyway leading uphill from the harbor, close to Hotel Supetar. ⊠ *Vuličevićeva 1* ☎ *020/478–566* 🖃 *AE, DC, MC, V* ☉ *Closed Nov.–Mar.*

Where to Stay

$$$ ⌂ **Hotel Croatia.** Occupying its own rocky, pine-studded peninsula, just a 10-minute walk west of the center, this vast 1970s hotel offers modern, luxurious rooms decorated in pastel shades, plus excellent sports facilities including three seawater pools and two beaches equipped with sunbeds and umbrellas. ⊠ *Frankopanska 10, 20210* ☎ *020/475–555* 🖷 *020/478–213* ⊕ *www.hoteli-croatia.hr* 📞 *480 rooms, 7 suites* ♨ *3 Restaurants, café, room service, minibars, cable TV, in-room safes, in-room data ports, indoor pool, outdoor pool, gym, massage, hair salon, 2 bars, 2 beaches, convention center, meeting rooms, Internet room* ▭ *AE, DC, MC, V* ☉ *Closed mid-Nov–mid-Mar* ⏅ *BP.*

$ ⌂ **Hotel Supetar.** On the seafront promenade overlooking the harbor, this old stone building has been renovated to provide basic but comfortable rooms, and an upper-level restaurant with a terrace where breakfast is served through summer. ⊠ *Dr Ante Starčević 27, 20210* ☎ *020/479–833* 🖷 *020/479–858* 📞 *28 rooms* ♨ *Restaurant, cable TV* ▭ *AE, DC, MC, V* ☉ *Closed Nov.–Mar.* ⏅ *BP.*

Sports & the Outdoors

The best beaches lie east of the center, overlooking **Uvala Tiha** (Tiha Bay) where most of the large modern hotels are located.

If you are interested in scuba diving, **Ronilački Klub Konavle** (⊠ Trumbićev Put 25, Cavtat ☎ 020/478–774) organizes cerficiation and diving trips.

TRSTENO

⑰ *24 km (15 mi) northwest of Dubrovnik.*

A small village on the coastal road between Split and Dubrovnik (E65), Trsteno, an otherwise insignificant place, has been put on the map by its arboretum. There's nowhere particularly memorable to eat in the village, but the small Trsteno café, which lies to the right of the arboretum's main entrance, has tables in the garden making a pleasant setting for coffee or a cold drink.

Within the grounds of a small Renaissance villa, **Trsteno Arboretum** was set up during the 16th century by the Gucetić family. Laid out on a geometric plan, it is filled with exotic trees and shrubs grown from seeds and saplings collected by local sailors on distant voyages. The site itself is breathtaking, with the grounds running down toward a cliff overlooking the sea. The baroque fountain of Neptune and two nymphs dates from 1736. The best time to visit is spring or fall, when the leaves are changing color. ⊠ *Magistrala Trsteno* ☎ *020/751–019* 🎟 *15 Kn* ☉ *May–Oct., daily 8–8; Nov.–Apr., daily 8–3.*

STON

⑱ *54 km (34 mi) northwest of Dubrovnik; 67 km (42 mi) plus 2 nautical mi from Korčula.*

Today Ston is best known for its fresh oysters and mussels, grown in Mali Ston Channel and served in a handful of year-round waterside restaurants in Mali Ston. Historically, the town dates back to 1333, when it was founded by the Republic of Dubrovnik. It's made up of two separate settlements, Ston (on the main Dubrovnik–Orebić road) and Mali Ston (just off the main road), which were each individually fortified; a system of defensive walls was then built to connect the two, effectively controlling land access onto the peninsula. Dubrovnik's chief interest in Ston was its salt pans, out of which the republic made a considerable profit. Of the original 5½ km (3 mi) of walls, 3 km (2 mi) remain intact. Begin your visit in Ston, then follow the walls on foot to arrive in Mali Ston, about 15 minutes away by foot.

Where to Eat

$$–$$$$ ✗ **Bota.** Occupying a 14th-century salt warehouse, Bota is known for its menu of outstanding, locally caught seafood. If raw oysters make you squeamish, try the *pohane oštrige* (oysters deep-fried in breadcrumbs). Also look out for the extraordinary *stonski makaruli,* a pudding made from pasta, nuts, sugar, and cinnamon, unique to Ston but said to originate from Spain. ✉ *Mali Ston* ☎ *020/754–482* ☐ *AE, DC, MC, V.*

★ **$$–$$$$** ✗ **Kapitanova Kuća.** Known throughout Croatia, the name of this restaurant is synonymous with Ston and fresh oysters. Most people come here exclusively to eat shellfish grown in Mali Ston Channel, but you'll also find a limited choice of meat dishes. The owner and cook, Lidija Kralj, has been presented a cooking award by Croatian national television. The Kralj family also run the nearby Hotel Ostrea. ✉ *Mali Ston* ☎ *020/754–264* ☐ *AE, DC, MC, V.*

Where to Stay

$$ ⊞ **Hotel Ostrea.** A former mill, this old stone building has been renovated to make a small upscale hotel complete with wood floors and antique furniture. There's a ground-floor restaurant with a terrace shaded by awnings, where breakfast is served through summer. It stays open all year. ✉ *Mali Ston, 20230* ☎ *020/754–555* 🖷 *020/754–575* ⊕ *www.ostrea.hr* ⇒ *9 rooms, 1 suite* ⚒ *Restaurant, room service, minibars, cable TV, meeting room* ☐ *AE, DC, MC, V* ⧖ *BP.*

Sports & the Outdoors

The best beach for swimming lies in Prapratna Uvala (Prapratna Bay), 3 km (2 mi) south of Ston.

OREBIĆ

⑲ *Orebić is 110 km (69 mi) northwest of Dubrovnik and 2 nautical mi northeast of Korčula.*

Backed by the rocky heights of Sveti Ilija (961 meters [3153 feet]), Orebić straggles along the coast, facing across a narrow sea channel to the island of Korčula. Historically, the town spent several centuries under the Republic of Dubrovnik, supplying many able seamen to the republic's merchant navy. From 1865 to 1887, the town even had its own shipping company: today you can see a string of villas, set in gardens overlooking the coastal promenade, built by wealthy local sea captains.

Today tourism is the chief source of income. Attractions include a decent sand beach, a delightful hillside monastery, and the proximity of the Pelješac Peninsula's vineyards, which produce highly esteemed red wines. A regular ferry service links Orebić to Korčula, with approximately 10 crossings per day through peak season; journey time is 20 minutes. Visitors on a tight budget often opt to stay in Orebić and visit Korčula, rather than vice versa, as the former is notably cheaper.

A 20-minute walk along a pleasant country road that winds its way up through pine woods brings you to the delightful 15th-century hillside **Franjevački Samostan** (Franciscan Monastery), perched 152 meters (492 feet) above sea level. The view across the sea channel to the island of Korčula is most impressive, and the view, in fact, explains the monastery's prime location. During the days of the Republic of Dubrovnik, Pelješac was under Dubrovnik's control while Korčula was ruled by her arch rival, Venice. From this privileged vantage point, the Franciscan monks would spy upon their island neighbors, under strict orders to send a messenger to Dubrovnik if trouble looked likely.

In its heyday, the monastery was home to twenty-some monks; now only two remain. However, it is a most welcoming retreat, with a lovely cloister and a fascinating museum, displaying scale models of the ships that local sea captains sailed across the oceans, and an array of votive pictures dedicated to the Virgin, commissioned and donated by sailors who had been saved from trouble on the high seas. Before leaving, check out the cemetery, where gray marble tombstones shaded by cypress trees mark the final resting places of many a local seafarer. ✉ *Orebić* ☎ *020/713–075* 💷 *10 Kn* ⊙ *Mon.–Sat. 9–noon and 4–7, Sun. 4–7.*

Where to Eat

$$–$$$ ✗ **Mlinica.** Set in a garden, with a footpath running down to the seafront, this old stone building was formerly an olive mill. The flagstone floor and a wooden beamed ceiling have been kept, and wooden tables and benches have also been added to create a rustic eatery serving delicious octopus and lamb dishes prepared under a *peka* (a metal dome used for slow cooking over embers). It's open from May through October for dinner only. ✉ *Štalište Kneza Domagoja* ☎ *020/713–886* 🖃 *AE, DC, MC, V* ⊙ *Closed Nov.–Apr. No lunch.*

$$–$$$ ✕ **Pelješki Dvor.** Heavy wooden furniture fills a series of small, inter-connected dining rooms at this informal restaurant, recommended for barbecued meat and fish dishes. There's also a sunny, walled garden with outdoor tables. ⊠ *Obala Pomoraca 28* ☎ *020/713–329* ▤ *AE, DC, MC, V* ☺ *Closed Nov.–Mar.*

Where to Stay

$ ▦ **Hotel Orsan.** A pleasant 15-minute walk along the coastal path from the center of town brings you to this 1970s building, set in a terraced garden with palms, cypresses, and a pool, which also fronts a pebble beach. All the rooms have balconies, looking onto either the sea or the park. ⊠ *Kralja Petra Krešimira IV 119, 20250* ☎ *020/713–026* ▦ *020/713–267* ⊕ *www.orebic-htp.hr* ⮎ *94 rooms, 3 suites* ⌂ *Restaurant, café, room service, minibars, cable TV, pool, bar, beach* ▤ *AE, DC, MC, V* ☺ *Closed Nov.–Mar.* ⫤ *BP.*

$ ▦ **Hotel Rathaneum.** Overlooking the sea and backed by pine woods, this 1970s Socialist-era building lies a 10-minute walk along the coastal path from town. Most rooms have balconies and a sea view. Sports facilities include bicycles, canoes, and surf boards for rent, and a small beach out front. ⊠ *Kralja Petra Krešimira IV 107, 20250* ☎ *020/713–022* ▦ *020/714–310* ⊕ *www.orebic-htp.hr* ⮎ *145 rooms, 30 suites* ⌂ *Restaurant, café, room service, cable TV, pool, gym, sauna, bar* ▤ *AE, DC, MC, V* ☺ *Closed Nov.–Mar.* ⫤ *BP.*

Sports & the Outdoors

Beaches
The best beach, **Trstenica** is a 1½-km (1-mi) stretch of sand and pebble, lying on the east side of Orebić. Through summer it is equipped with showers, sunbeds, and umbrellas for hire, and a snack bar.

Diving
Diving instruction and trips are available from **Orebeach Club Hotel** (⊠ 1 km [½ mi] west of Orebić, on the local road to Kućište ☎ 020/713–985 ⊕ www.orebeachclubhotel.com) from early May through late October.

Windsurfing
The Korčula Channel, between Pelješac and the island of Korčula, offers perfect conditions for windsurfing. You can receive instruction and rent boards from **Orebeach Club Hotel** (⊠ 1 km [½ mi] west of Orebić, on the local road to Kućište ☎ 020/713–985 ⊕ www.orebeachclubhotel.com) from early May through late October.

Wine Tasting
Several family-run vineyards and wine cellars are open to the public for wine tasting and purchases. Tasting sessions usually include a selection of three or four different wines and maybe some rakija, and are accompanied by bread and cheese. Sessions last between 30 minutes and 1 hour. You need private transport to reach the vineyards, and it is best to call one day in advance, as vineyards are often busy with large tour groups.

Bartulović Vina (✉ Prizdrina, 13 km [8 mi] southeast of Orebić ☎ 020/742–346) is a friendly, family-run vineyard especially popular with visitors thanks to its authentic Dalmatian konoba with exposed stone walls and rustic wooden tables and benches. It's the best choice if you want to combine wine tasting with a full-blown meal, as they will prepare lunch or dinner if you call one day in advance. If you do not opt for a full meal, your wine-tasting session will be accompanied by homemade bread, *pršut,* sheeps' cheese, and olives. The Bartulović family have been making wine on Pelješac for some 470 years, and they now produce around 25,000 bottles per year. As everywhere on Pelješac, red predominates, but this vineyard is unique in that it also produces small quantities of rosé.

Matuško Vina (✉ Potomje, 15 km [9 mi] southeast of Orebić ☎ 020/742–393) has a recently built shop where visitors can taste and buy wines. On the shelves you will find Dingač (top-quality red wine), Plavac Mali (quality red wine), Rukatac (quality dry white wine from Korčula) and Stolno Vino (red and white table wines). The shop is open daily (summer 7 AM–8 PM; winter 7 AM–5 PM). A typical tasting session consists of two red wines (Plavac and Dingać), plus prošek (a sweet wine similar to sherry), loza (rakija made from grapes), and višnjevača (rakija made from cherries), accompanied by bread and cheese.

KORČULA

Korčula island is 49 nautical mi northwest of Dubrovnik and 57 nautical mi southeast of Split by ferry.

Southern Dalmatia's largest, most sophisticated, and most visited island, Korčula was known to the ancient Greeks, who named it *Kerkyra Melaina,* or "Black Corfu." Between the 10th and 18th centuries it spent several periods under Venetian rule, much to the frustration of Dubrovnik, which considered the Italian city-state its arch rival. Today, most Croatians know it for its traditional sword dances and its excellent white wines.

Korčula is also the name of the capital, which is near the island's eastern tip. At first view, it seems like a much smaller version of Dubrovnik: the same high walls, the circular corner fortresses, and the church tower projecting from within an expanse of red roofs. The main difference lies in the town plan, as narrow side streets run off the main thoroughfare at odd angles to form a herring-bone pattern, preventing cold winter winds from whistling unimpeded through town. The eight centuries under Venetian rule bequeathed the town a treasure trove of Gothic and Renaissance churches, palaces, and piazzas, all built from fine local stone, upon which the island's early wealth was based. Korčula's main claim to fame, though one still disputed by historians, is that it was the birthplace of Marco Polo (1254–1324). The center is small and compact and can be explored in an hour.

The most impressive way to arrive in Korčula Town is by Jadrolinija coastal ferry from Dubrovnik, which stops here en route to Rijeka. Less pleasurable but faster is the daily bus service connecting Dubrovnik and

Korčula Town, which follows the regional road along Pelješac Peninsula, then boards a ferry at Orebić for a short crossing to Korčula. Alternatively, the island is also served by the port of Vela Luka, close to its western tip, with daily ferry and catamaran services running between Split (Central Dalmatia) and the island of Lastovo, stopping at Vela Luka en route. From Vela Luka, a bus runs the length of the island to Korčula Town.

What to See

⑳ Katedrala (Cathedral). On the main square, the splendid Gothic-Renaissance cathedral is built from a wheat-colored stone that turns pale gold in sunlight, amber at sunset. Enter through the beautifully carved Romanesque main portal, which is guarded by Adam and Eve standing upon twin lions. Inside, check out the elegant 15th-century ciborium; within, two paintings are attributed to the Venetian master Tintoretto. ⌧ *Trg Sv Marka* 🎟 *10 Kn* ⊘ *May–Oct., daily 9–2 and 5–8; Nov.–Apr., by appointment.*

㉑ Kopnena Vrata (Land Gate). The main entrance into the Old Town is topped by the 15th-century Revelin Tower, housing an exhibition connected with the *Moreška* sword dance, and offering panoramic views over the Old

Town. ⊠ *Kopnena Vrata* 🏛 *10 Kn* ⊗ *July and Aug., daily 9–9; May, June, Sept., and Oct., daily 9–7; Nov.–Apr., by appointment only.*

㉒ Kuća Marca Pola (Marco Polo House). A couple of blocks east of the main square is the place where the legendary 13th-century discoverer is said to have been born, when Korčula was part of the Venetian Empire. At present only the tower is open, with a modest exhibition about Polo's life on the first floor, and a belvedere up top offering panoramic views. There are plans to restore the entire house and garden to form an educational museum, though this project is unlikely to be completed before summer 2007. ⊠ *Ul Marka Pola* 🏛 *10 Kn* ⊗ *July and Aug., daily 9–9; May, June, Sept., and Oct., daily 9–7; Nov.–Apr., by appointment only.*

㉓ Opatska Riznica (Abbot's Treasury). Next to the cathedral, the treasury museum occupies the 17th-century Renaissance Bishop's palace. This collection of sacral art includes Italian and Croatian Renaissance paintings, the most precious being a 15th-centruy triptych, *Our Lady with Saints,* by the Dalmatian master Blaž Jurjev Trogiranin, plus gold and silver ecclesiastical artifacts and ceremonial vestments. ⊠ *Trg Sv Marka* 🏛 *10 Kn* ⊗ *May–Oct., daily 9–2 and 5–8; Nov.–Apr., by appointment only.*

Where to Eat

$$–$$$$ ✕ **Adio Mare.** A long-standing favorite with locals and visitors alike, Adio
Fodor'sChoice Mare occupies a Gothic-Renaissance building in the Old Town, close
★ to Kuća Marca Pola. There's a high-ceiling dining room as well as an open-plan kitchen so you can watch the cooks while they work. The menu has not changed since the restaurant opened in 1974: expect Dalmatian classics such as *pašta-fažol* (beans with pasta) and *pašticada* (beef stewed in wine and prunes), as well as fresh fish and seafood. The local wine, *pošip,* is excellent. ⊠ *Ul Marka Pola* ☎ *020/711–253* 🖃 *AE, DC, MC, V* ⊗ *Closed Nov.–Mar. No lunch.*

$$ ✕ **Planjak.** This down-to-earth eatery harks back to the former Socialist era. Expect hearty Balkan home cooking such as *sarma* (cabbage leaves stuffed with rice and meat) and *gulaš* (goulash). Locals tend to sit inside, while visitors eat out on the terrace. You'll find it on a small piazza, one block back from the ferry landing station. It's open year-round. ⊠ *Plokata 19 Travanja 1914* ☎ *020/711–015* 🖃 *AE, DC, MC, V.*

Where to Stay

$$ 🏨 **Hotel Liburnija** On a small peninsula just a 10-minute walk east of the center, with views across the water back to the Old Town, this modern low-rise hotel has basic but comfortable rooms and good sports facilities. Rooms with a sea view have a small surcharge. ⊠ *Obala Hrvatskih Mornara, 20260* ☎ *020/726–280* 🖷 *020/726–272* 🖃 *83 rooms ⚭ 2 restaurants, room service, minibar, cable TV, outdoor pool, meeting room, beach; no a/c* 🖃 *AE, DC, MC, V* ⊗ *Closed Nov.–Feb.* 🍽 *BP.*

$–$$ 🏨 **Hotel Korčula.** Built in 1871, when the area was a part of Austria-Hungary, the building was converted to become the island's first hotel in 1912. Exuding old-fashioned charm, it offers discreet service and a delightful seafront café terrace, ideal for watching the sunset over the water. It's the only hotel in the Old Town; all the others are a short distance east of the center. ⊠ *Obala Dr Franje Tudmana, 20260* ☎ *020/711–078* 🖷 *020/711–746* 📠 *20 rooms* 🍴 *Restaurant, café, room service, cable TV; no a/c* 🗖 *AE, DC, MC, V* 🍴❘ *BP.*

Nightlife & the Arts

On the tip of the peninsula, inside the Tiepolo Tower, part of the town fortification system, **Cocktail Bar Massimo** (⊠ Šetalište Petra Kanavelića ☎ 020/715–073) offers wonderful sunset views. It's open from May through October. The **Moreška** (⊠ Kopnena Vrata 🎫 80 Kn) is a colorful sword dance originally performed each year on July 29 (the feast day of the town's protector, St Theodore), but now it's performed at 9 PM each Monday and Thursday evening from May to October just outside the city walls, next to the Kopnena Vrata (Land Gate). Tickets are available for 80 Kn at hotel receptions and travel agencies throughout town.

Sports & the Outdoors

Beaches

The closest spot for a quick swim is Banje, a small pebble beach about 10 minutes by foot east of the town walls, close to Hotel Liburnija. For more leisurely bathing, the best beaches lie near the village of **Lumbarda**, which is 6 km (4 mi) southeast of Korčula Town. The most popular of these is the sandy south-facing Przina, 2 km (1 mi) south of Lumbarda, while the smooth-white-stoned Bili Žal lies a short distance east of Lumbarda.

If you don't like the local beach options, rent a speed boat from **Rent-a-Djir** (⊠ Obala Hrvatskih Mornara ☎ 020/715–120 ⊕ www.korcula-rent.com) and take to the open sea to explore the tiny scattered islets of the nearby Korčula archipelago, which has many secluded bays for swimming.

Diving

MM Sub (⊠ Lumbarda ☎ 020/712–288 ⊕ www.mm-sub.hr) is a diving center based in Lumbarda offering diving instruction and trips for those with some experience. Nearby diving destinations include an underwater archaeological site, as well as several sea caves and shipwrecks.

Sailing

The 159-berth **ACI marina** (⊠ Korčula ☎ 020/711–661) remains open all year.

Wine Tasting

Atlas Travel Agency (⊠ Trg 19 Travanja ☎ 020/711–060 ⊕ www.atlas-croatia.com) organizes one-day wine tours of either Korčula island or the Pelješac Peninsula, combining visits to the vineyards, wine tasting, and lunch in a typical Dalmatian konoba. Transfers to and from Korčula Town by bus is included.

Shopping

Cukarin (✉ Hrvatska Bratske Zajednice ☎ 020/711–055), is a family-run store renowned for its four different types of delicious handmade biscuits, as well as homemade *rakija* flavored with local herbs.

MLJET

㉔ *Polače is 18 nautical mi west of Dubrovnik by ferry.*

Mljet is a long, thin island of steep, rocky slopes and dense pine forests, more than a third of which is contained within Mljet National Park. The Kings of Bosnia, who ruled the island during medieval times, gave it to Benedictine monks from Puglia in Italy during the 12th century, who in turn passed it on to the Republic of Dubrovnik in 1410. No great towns ever grew up here, and today it is home to half a dozen small villages, with a total population of about 1,100 people. Lovers of ancient Greek literature will be interested to know that Mljet has been identified as Homer's lost island Ogygia, where Ulysses met the nymph Calypso.

The most convenient and speedy ferry service is the high-speed catamaran *Nona Ana,* operated by the Rijeka-based company, Alpex. The service runs daily, leaving Dubrovnik at 9 AM, and departing from Polače at 7 PM to return to the city. Tickets are available through the Dubrovnik-based agency **Atlantagent** (✉ Stjepana Radića 26, Dubrovnik ☎ 020/419–044).

Nacionalni Park Mljeta (Mljet National Park). A local bus runs from the port of Sobra to the National Park at the west end of the island. If you arrive on Mljet through Polače, you are within walking distance of the park. Upon arrival, pay the entrance fee at one of several wooden kiosks (if you stay overnight, this fee is included in the price of your accommodation). Within the densely forested park lie two interconnected saltwater lakes, Malo Jezero (Little Lake) and Veliko Jezero (Big Lake), ideal for swimming from spring to autumn. Boats run to the charming 12th-century Benedictine Monastery on Otočić Svete Marije (St. Mary's Islet), in the middle of Veliko Jezero, and a series of footpaths and bike paths traverse the park. Mountain bikes and kayaks are available for hire at Mali Most, the bridge between the two lakes, and at Hotel Odisej in Pomena. ✉ *Pristanište 2, Govedjari* ☎ *020/744–086* ⊕ *www.np-mljet.hr* ▣ *65 Kn.*

★ One of Croatia's few sandy beaches, **Saplunara,** lies at the southeastern tip of the island, outside the confines of the national park. Happily, it remains relatively wild and untended, so there are no facilities as such, but you will find several seasonal eateries in the tiny nearby settlement of the same name. ✉ *Saplunara, 15 km (10 mi) southeast of Sobra.*

Where to Eat

$$$–$$$$ ✕ **Taverna Melita.** On St. Mary's Islet, on Veliko Jezero, dining tables are arranged on the waterside terrace in front of the monastery. The menu includes a good range of meat and fish dishes, with lobster, the local

specialty, taking pride of place. The restaurant runs a boat to and from Pristanište after 8:30 PM, when the national park's ferry service stops. ⊠ *Otočić Svete Marije* ☎ *020/744–145* ▤ *AE, DC, MC, V* ⊘ *Closed Oct.–Mar.*

$$–$$$$ ✕ **Nine.** Overlooking the seafront in Pomena, with several mooring spaces on the quay out front, Nine is popular with the yachting crowd. Seafood predominates: the owner keeps live *jastog* (lobster) in a well outside and fishes them out to cook upon request. ⊠ *Pomena* ☎ *020/ 744–037* ▤ *AE, DC, MC, V* ⊘ *Closed Oct.–Mar.*

Where to Stay

$–$$ ▥ **Hotel Odisej.** The only hotel on the island, Odisej is a large, white modern structure overlooking the sea in the village of Pomena, a 15-minute walk from Malo Jezero. The rooms are basic but comfortable, and there are excellent sports facilities, including a scuba diving school, a small marina and sailing school, as well as bicycles, surf boards, kayaks, and canoes to rent. The hotel lies 30 km (20 mi) from Sobra and 5 km (3 mi) from Polače, and can arrange transfers to and from these ports. ⊠*Pomena, 20226* ☎*020/362–111* ▤*020/744–042* ⊕*www.hotelodisej. hr* ⇝*157 rooms, 2 suites* ⚒ *2 Restaurants, room service, minibars, cable TV, bar* ▤ *AE, DC, MC, V* ⊘ *Closed Nov.–Mar.* ⊯ *BP.*

Sports & the Outdoors

Beaches

The best beach, **Saplunara,** is sandy and backed by pine woods. It lies on the southeastern tip of the island, outside of the National Park. Within the park, the water in Malo Jezero (Little Lake) and Veliko Jezero (Big Lake) tends to be several degrees warmer than that in the sea, so the swimming season is somewhat extended.

Diving

For scuba diving, try the **Freaky Diving Center** (⊠ Hotel Odisej, Pomena ☎ 020/362–111 ⊕ www.freaky-diving.com) at Hotel Odisej. Advanced divers can ask to explore the *S57,* a well-preserved German torpedo boat that sank in 1944, and now lies just 6 nautical mi from the dive center.

Sailing

In summer, the highly-regarded **Ana Sailing School** (⊠ Hotel Odisej, Pomena ⊕ www.sailing-ana.hr) opens a seasonal base at the Hotel Odisej, offering one-week sailing courses. The hotel can also arrange half-day sailing trips for those who want a few hours at sea without being committed to the ropes.

DUBROVNIK & SOUTHERN DALMATIA ESSENTIALS

AIR TRAVEL

The national carrier, Croatia Airlines, operates year-round internal flights between Dubrovnik, Zagreb, and Split, plus summer flights to Pula and Osijek. Through summer, it also flies regularly between

Dubrovnik and Amsterdam, Brussels, Frankfurt, Glasgow, Istanbul, London, Manchester, Nottingham, Milan, Munich, Paris, Prague, Rome, Skopje, Tel Aviv, Vienna, Warsaw, and Zurich. British Airways, ČSA, and Malev all fly to Dubrovnik. ČSA has no local office, but the travel agency Atlas sells tickets.

7 **British Airways** ✉ Dubrovnik Airport, Pile, Dubrovnik ☎ 020/773-212. **ČSA** ✉ Atlas, Čira Čarića 3 Dubrovnik ☎ 020/422-222. **Croatia Airways** ✉ Brsalje 9, Pile, Dubrovnik ☎ 020/413-777 **Malev** ✉ Dubrovnik Airport, Pile, Dubrovnik ☎ 020/773-208 May–Oct. only.

AIRPORTS & TRANSFERS

Dubrovnik is served by Dubrovnik Airport (DBV) at Čilipi, 18 km (11 mi) southeast of the city.

7 **Dubrovnik Airport** ☎ 020/773-377 general information, 020/773-328 lost and found ⊕ www.airport-dubrovnik.hr.

AIRPORT
TRANSFERS
The airport bus leaves the Dubrovnik Bus Station 90 minutes before each flight and meets all incoming flights. A one-way ticket costs 25 Kn. Journey time is approximately 20 minutes.

7 **Airport bus** ☎ 020/773-232. **Dubrovnik Bus Station** ✉ Put Republike 19, Pile, Dubrovnik ☎ 020/357-088.

BOAT & FERRY TRAVEL

From June to September, Jadrolinija run a regular ferry service between Dubrovnik and Bari (Italy). Ferries depart from Bari late in the evening (every day except Wednesday), arriving in Dubrovnik early the next morning, with a similar schedule from Dubrovnik (every day except Thursday) to Bari (journey time approximately eight hours either direction). After September, the service is reduced to two crossings a week. The Italian company Azzurra Lines runs a similar service, also from June to September.

During high season (July to August), Jadrolinija coastal ferries depart Rijeka most evenings, arriving in Dubrovnik early the following afternoon. From Dubrovnik, the ferries depart mid-morning to arrive in Rijeka early the following morning (journey time approximately 20 hours in either direction). Coming and going, these ferries stop at Sobra (island of Mljet), Korčula, Stari Grad (island of Hvar), and Split. During the rest of the year, the service is less frequent, and the ferry puts in an extra port of call at Zadar.

From Dubrovnik, Jadrolinija runs daily car ferries to the Elafiti islands (Koločep, Lopud, and Šipan) and Sobra (island of Mljet). If you are traveling as a foot passenger, a faster (but more expensive) way to reach Mljet is to take *Nona Ana*, a high-speed catamaran running daily from Dubrovnik to Sobra and Polače (island of Mljet); the catamaran service is operated by the Rijeka-based Alpex, and tickets are available through the Dubrovnik-based agency, Atlantagent. And from mid-June to mid-September, SEM operates a daily car ferry from Trstenik (Pelješac Peninsula) to Polače (island of Mljet). It is also possible to visit Mljet as part of an organized day trip by catamaran from Dubrovnik or Korčula Town, operated by the Atlas travel agency.

Last but not least, the island of Korčula is connected to the Pelješac Peninsula by a Jadrolinija car-ferry service operating several times a day between Orebić and Dominče (2 km [1 mi] from Korčula Town). A Mediteranska Plovidba ferry runs a frequent passenger service between Orebić and Korcula Town (foot passengers only).

🚹 **Alpex** 🕿 051/325-460 ⊕ www.alpex.hr. **Atlantagent** ⊠ Stjepana Radića 26, Dubrovnik 🕿 020/419-044. **Azzurra Lines** 🕿 020/313-178 ⊕ www.azzurraline.com. **Jadrolinija** 🕿 020/418-000 ⊕ www.jadrolinija.hr. **Mediteranska Plovidba** 🕿 020/711-156. **SEM** 🕿 021/352-533 ⊕ www.sem-marina.hr.

BUS TRAVEL

There are daily bus services from Dubrovnik to Ljubljana (Slovenia); Medjugorje, Mostar, and Sarajevo (Bosnia-Herzegovina); and Trieste (Italy); plus a twice-weekly service to Frankfurt (Germany) and a once-weekly service to Zurich (Switzerland). There are regular bus routes between Dubrovnik and destinations all over mainland Croatia, with approximately 12 buses per day to Split (Central Dalmatia), eight to Zagreb and three to Rijeka (Kvarner). Within the Southern Dalmatia region, there are four buses daily to Ston and two to Orebić on Peljesac Peninsula, one of which continues to Korčula. Regular local buses run every hour up the coast to Trstenik, and every 30 minutes down the coast to Cavtat. Timetable information is available from Dubrovnik Bus Station.

🚹 **Dubrovnik Bus Station** ⊠ Put Republike 19, Pile, Dubrovnik 🕿 020/357-088.

CAR TRAVEL

While visiting Dubrovnik and the nearby islands of Mljet and Korčula, you are certainly better off without a car. However, as the city is not linked to the rest of Croatia by train, you may wish to rent a car if you are traveling on to Split or Zagreb, rather than taking the plane or bus.

🚹 **Car Rental Agencies Best Buy Rent** ⊠ V Nazora 9, Pile, Dubrovnik 🕿 020/422-043 ⊠ Dubrovnik Airport, Čilipi 🕿 020/773-373. **Milenium Rent** ⊠ Put Iva Vojnovića 5, Lapad, Dubrovnik 🕿 020/333-176 ⊕ www.milenium-rent.com. **Budget** ⊠ Obala Stjepana Radića 24, Gruž, Dubrovnik 🕿 020/418-998 ⊠ Dubrovnik Airport, Čilipi 🕿 020/773-290. **Hertz** ⊠ F Supila 9, Ploče, Dubrovnik 🕿 020/425-000 ⊠ Dubrovnik Airport, Čilipi 🕿 020/771-568. **Mack** ⊠ F Supila 3, Ploče, Dubrovnik 🕿 020/423-747 ⊕ www.mack-concord.hr.

EMERGENCIES

🚹 **Ambulance Ambulance** 🕿 94.

🚹 **Doctors & Dentists Hitno Ponoč** (Casualty,) ⊠ Roka Mišetića, Lapad, Dubrovnik 🕿 020/431-777.

🚹 **Fire Fire Emergencies** 🕿 93.

🚹 **Pharmacies Gruž** ⊠ Gruška obala, Gruž, Dubrovnik 🕿 020/418-990. **Kod Zvonika** ⊠ Placa, Stari Grad, Dubrovnik 🕿 020/321-133.

🚹 **Police Police Emergencies** 🕿 92.

INTERNET

During the summer, small temporary Internet cafés spring up in the seaside resort towns, so even on the islands you will find somewhere to check e-mail. However, many are nothing more than a regular café with a PC in the corner. The one well-established, fully-equipped Internet café of note in the region is Netcafe, in Dubrovnik.

🛈 **Netcafe** ✉ Prijeko 21, Stari Grad, Dubrovnik ☎ 020/321-025.

MAIL & SHIPPING

The Dubrovnik main post office is close to the bus station, a 15-minute walk northwest of the Old Town. It is open Monday to Friday, from 7 AM to 8 PM, Saturday from 8 to 4.

🛈 **Dubrovnik Main Post Office** ✉ Put republike 32, Dubrovnik.

MONEY MATTERS

You'll find banks in all the destinations in the region (including the island of Lopud) mentioned in this chapter. ATMs are now widespread and you will find at least one even in small towns on the islands. It is possible to exchange currency in banks and also in most local travel agencies.

TAXIS

In Dubrovnik, there are taxi ranks just outside the city walls at Pile Gate and Ploče Gate, and in front of Gruž harbor.

🛈 **Taxi Station Gruž** ☎ 020/418-112. **Taxi Station Pile** ☎ 020/424-343. **Taxi Station Ploče** ☎ 020/416-158.

TOURS

The Dubrovnik and Korčula Tourist Offices organize informative and amusing guided tours of their respective cities. In addition, Atlas organize one-day excursions departing from Dubrovnik (by bus or hydrofoil) to various destinations in the region, including wine tasting in the Pelješac vineyards. One-day tours to neighboring countries (passports required) include the pilgrimage site of Medjugorje, Bosnia-Herzegovina, where the Virgin Mary is said to have appeared in 1981; to Mostar, Bosnia-Herzegovina, with its Turkish-inspired old town and reconstructed bridge, and the Bay of Kotor, Budva, and the jet-setters' retreat of Sveti Stefan, Montenegro.

🛈 **Atlas** ✉ Čira Čarića 3, Dubrovnik ☎ 020/422-222 ⊕ www.atlas-croatia.com. **Dubrovnik Tourist Office** ✉ Stradun, Stari Grad, Dubrovnik ☎ 020/321-561 ⊕ www.tzdubrovnik.hr. **Korčula Tourist Office** ✉ Obala Dr Franje Tudjmana, Korčula ☎ 020/715-701 ⊕ www.korcula.net.

VISITOR INFORMATION

🛈 **Dubrovnik & Nertva County Tourist Board** ✉ ul. Cvijete Zuzorić 1/1, Stari Grad, Dubrovnik ☎ 020/324-999 ⊕ www.visitdubrovnik.hr. **Cavtat Tourist Office** ✉ Tiha 3, Cavtat ☎ 020/478-025 ⊕ www.tzcavtat-konavle.hr. **Dubrovnik Tourist Office** ✉ Stradun, Stari Grad, Dubrovnik ☎ 020/321-561 ⊕ www.tzdubrovnik.hr. **Korčula Tourist Office** ✉ Obala Dr Franje Tudjmana, Korčula ☎ 020/715-701 ⊕ www.korcula.net. **Lopud Tourist Office** ✉ Lopud, Lopud ☎ 020/759-086. **Mljet Tourist Office** ✉ Polače ☎ 020/744-086. **Orebić Tourist Office** ✉ Trg Mimbeli, Orebić ☎ 020/713-718 ⊕ www.tz-orebic.com. **Ston Tourist Office** ✉ Ston ☎ 020/754-452.

Slovenia

WORD OF MOUTH

"When in Ljublijana go to the castle and check out the gift shop/gallery . . . the director/curator has assembled a terrific collection of Slovenian art/craft. It was a terrific way to 'tour' the country and get a glimpse of the Slovenian artworld."

—Bailey

"Lake Bled is fantastically scenic so even if you stay in Ljubljana instead, it's worth the drive to see it on a day trip."

—JulieVikmanis

"Slovenia is great for adrenalin sports and is beautiful with lots of different types of landscapes."

—SloJan

By Mark Baker **SLOVENIA MAY BE THE BEST-KEPT SECRET IN EUROPE.** Just half the size of Switzerland, the country is often treated as fly-over—or drive-through—territory by travelers heading to better-known places in Croatia or Italy. That's good news for anyone choosing Slovenia as a destination in its own right. It means fewer crowds—even in the peak summer touring months—fewer hassles, and in many ways a more authentic travel experience.

And Slovenia's sights are no less outstanding than those of its neighbors. Admittedly, Slovenia's small Adriatic coastline—not even 30 miles end to end—can't match Croatia for sheer natural beauty. But the coastal towns, especially the intact Venetian jewel of Piran, are lovely in their own right. The Julian Alps northwest of the capital are every bit as spectacular as their sister alpine ranges in Austria and Switzerland. The electric-blue-turquoise waters of the Soča River, rushing out of the mountains, must be seen—or better, rafted—to be believed. And that's just a start. The extensive cave systems, unspoiled countryside, and even the funky charm of Ljubljana await those with the imagination to choose a destination that is more off the beaten path.

Slovenia's relative obscurity owes much to its history. From Roman times to nearly the present day, Slovenian territory was incorporated into far-larger empires, relegating Slovenia through the ages to the role of rustic, if charming, hinterland.

The territory of Slovenia has been inhabited for tens of thousands of years, but the country's modern history begins with the arrival of the Romans in the 1st century BC. They built villas along the coast and founded the inland urban centers of Emona (Ljubljana) and Poetovio (Ptuj), which today still retain traces of their Roman past. The 6th century AD saw the first influx of Slav migrants, the ancestors of present-day Slovenes, who set up an early Slav state. During the 8th century, the region came under the control of the Franks, and in the 9th century it was passed to the dukes of Bavaria.

In 1335 the Habsburgs took control of inland Slovenia, dividing it into the Austrian crown lands of Carinthia, Carniola, and Styria. Meanwhile, the coastal towns had requested Venetian protection, and they remained under *la serenissima* until 1797, after which they, too, were taken by Austria. During the 15th and 16th centuries, the Turks, eager to extend the Ottoman Empire across the Balkans and north to Vienna, made repeated attacks on the region. However, Slovenia remained under the Habsburgs until 1918, with the exception of a brief period from 1809 to 1813, when it became part of Napoléon's Illyrian Provinces.

In the aftermath of World War I, Italy seized control of the coastal towns, whereas inland Slovenia became part of the Kingdom of Serbs, Croats, and Slovenes; in 1929, the name of the kingdom was changed to Yugoslavia (Land of the Southern Slavs).

Hitler declared war on Yugoslavia in 1941, and shortly afterward Axis forces occupied the country. Slovenia was divided between Germany,

Slovenia's small size can be an advantage. From the centrally located capital, Ljubljana, you can drive to any point in the country in three or four hours.

If you have 3 days

If you have limited time, take one day to discover the Old Town of **Ljubljana.** For the next two days, choose between the mountains or the coast. If you're looking for natural beauty and/or adventure, head for the mountains and lakes of Triglav National Park. Base yourself in **Bled** or **Bohinj.** For the third day, get an early start and head for **Bovec,** via **Kranjska Gora,** for hiking or white-water rafting on the Soča River. If you seek sun and sea instead, go southwest toward the Karst and coast. Stop off at the Škocjan Caves enroute, and spend your nights in the beautiful Venetian port of ▣ **Piran.**

8

If you have 5 days

For a longer stay, combine the two optional itineraries listed above. Spend the first day and night exploring Ljubljana's Old Town before making your way northwest to the mountains. After nights in Bled and/or Bohinj and exploring the Soča River valley, continue southwest to the coast. Use Piran as your base for visiting the coastal towns of **Izola** and **Portorož.**

If you have 7 days

If you have a full week, spend a day and night in Ljubljana and then make your way east for a night to the wine-making area around **Maribor** and **Ptuj.** Return to the capital, and then head north for the beauty of the Alps, as outlined in the five-day itinerary. Wrap up the week with a couple of days relaxing on the coast. In hot weather, you can go for a swim at the beaches around Portorož.

Italy, and Hungary. Josip Broz, better known as Tito, set up the anti-Fascist Partisan movement, and many Slovenes took part in resistance activities. When the war ended in 1945, Slovenia became one of the six constituent republics of Yugoslavia, with Tito as president. Slovenes today are proud of their Partisan past, and traveling through the country you see monuments and wall plaques bearing the red star, a symbol of the Partisans and of Communist ideology; many squares and roads are still named after Tito.

Half Slovene and half Croat, Tito was undeniably an astute leader. He governed Yugoslavia under Communist ideology, but the system was far more liberal than that of the Soviet-bloc countries: Yugoslavs enjoyed freedom of movement, and foreigners could enter the country without visas. During the Cold War, Tito never took sides but dealt cleverly with both East and West, thus procuring massive loans from both.

However, when Tito died in 1980, the system he left behind began to crumble. The false nature of the economy, based on borrowing, became apparent. During the 1980s, an economic crisis set in and inflation soared. Slovenia, accounting for only 8% of Yugoslavia's population, was producing almost a third of the nation's exports. This hard-earned foreign currency ended up in Belgrade and was used in part to subsidize the poorer republics. It was time for change.

In early 1990, buoyed by the recent revolutions across Eastern Europe, Slovenia introduced a multiparty system and elected a non-Communist government. Demands for increased autonomy from Yugoslavia were stepped up, with the threat of secession. A referendum was held, and nearly 90% of the electorate voted for independence. Unlike the other Yugoslav republics, Slovenia was made up almost exclusively of a single ethnic group: Slovenes. Thus, the potential status of ethnic minorities, should the republic secede, was never an issue. Slovenia proclaimed independence on June 25, 1991, and the so-called 10-Day War followed. Yugoslav federal troops moved in, but there was little violence to compare with the heavy fighting in nearby Croatia and Bosnia. Belgrade had already agreed to let Slovenia go.

In 1992, Slovenia gained international recognition as an independent state and began the painstaking process of legal, political, and economic reform needed to join the European Union. That effort bore fruit in May 2004, when Slovenia, along with seven other central and eastern European countries, was admitted into the EU. Today, Slovenia's future looks bright. It's simply a matter of time before the country's charms are fully discovered.

Exploring Slovenia

The principal areas of interest to tourists include the lively and very likable capital Ljubljana, the Julian Alps and Triglav National Park to the northwest, the alpine lakes of Bled and Bohinj, and the Adriatic coast and the Karst region to the southwest. The region to the east, centering on Maribor, Ptuj, and the Haloze Hills, has several vineyards and excellent wine cellars.

About the Restaurants

Slovenia's prime contribution to dining has got to be the *gostilna,* essentially an inn or tavern but cleaner, warmer, and more inviting than the English translation suggests. These are frequently family-run, especially in the smaller towns and villages, with mom in the kitchen and pop out front pouring beers and taking orders. The staff is usually happy to suggest local or regional specialties. Some of the better ones are situated alongside vineyards or farms.

Meal times follow the Continental norm for lunch and dinner. Even if a restaurant posts earlier opening times, the kitchen won't normally start operating until noon. Dinners typically start around 7 PM. It can be tough finding a breakfast place, so it's best to take the standard hotel or pension offering of sliced meats and cheeses when available.

Restaurants usually close one day a week. In larger towns like Ljubljana that's likely to be Sunday. In resort areas that cater to a weekend crowd, Monday is the usual day off. If in doubt, phone ahead.

8

Bicycling
Biking is becoming more and more popular every year. In Ljubljana, you'll see bikes everywhere. Several shops and many hotels rent bikes; in truth, the easiest way to negotiate the capital is on two wheels. Other biking centers include Maribor, the areas around Lake Bohinj, Kranjska Gora, and Bovec, and the Karst. The country roads to the north of Ribčev Laz, near Bohinj, are relatively flat and easy for bikers of all sorts. Bovec, in the mountains, is more of a challenge. The Karst, with its many wine roads, is ideal, though it's often difficult there to find places that rent bikes. Local tourist agencies can advise on trails and rental options. Local hiking maps usually also identify trails suited to cycling. A brochure, *Slovenia by Bicycle,* is available from the Slovenian Tourist Board.

Hiking
Slovenes love their mountains, and when you reach the northwest of the country you will understand why. The most popular alpine hiking route runs from Maribor, near the Austrian border, to Ankaran on the Adriatic coast. It crosses Triglav National Park and can be walked in 30 days. For less devoted walkers, a day or two of backpacking from one of the alpine resorts is an invigorating way to explore the landscape. Bovec, Bohinj, and Krajnska Gora are all excellent hiking bases. Mountain paths are usually well-marked, and mountain lodges have dormitory-style accommodations. Detailed maps are available at local tourist-information centers.

Horseback Riding
The country's most famous equestrian center is the Lipica Stud Farm, home of the splendid Lipizzaner white stallions. Riding lessons are available, though the farm is geared more toward experienced riders than beginners. It also offers summer riding sessions lasting several days to several weeks. For beginners, a better option might be the Mrcina Ranč at Studor, near Lake Bohinj. Visitors to the Krka Valley can ride at the Struga Equestrian Center at a 12th-century medieval manor near Otočec Castle. The brochure *Riding in Slovenia, Home of the Lipizzaner,* is available from the Slovenian Tourist Board.

Kayaking, Canoeing & Rafting
The Soča River has ideal conditions for white-water rafting, kayaking, hydrospeeding (a small board for bodysurfing waves), and canyoning. The season lasts from April to October. The best rapids lie between Bovec and Kobarid. Numerous outfitters in Bovec rent boats and equipment and also offer instruction and guided rafting and kayaking trips. Less exhilarating—though still very fun—river rafting is available near Bled and Bohinj.

Wine & Spirits
Slovenes enjoy drinking and produce some excellent wines, but very little of the total output is exported. You can tour the three main wine regions following a series of established "wine roads" (*vinska cesta*). These routes pass through rolling hills, woodlands, and villages and lead directly to vineyards and wine stores. The best white wines, *sivi pinot* (pinot grigio) and *beli pinot* (pinot blanc), are produced in the Podravje region in northeast Slovenia. A notable red is Teran, a varietal made from the refosk grape

and produced in the Karst region to the southwest. There has been a recent drive to introduce more sparkling wines: look for the excellent Penina, made using the classic Champagne method from chardonnay and pinot blanc grapes. The favorite national spirit is the potent *rakija*. The base is alcohol distilled from fruit; a variety of wild herbs are added later to give it a more distinct flavor.

WHAT IT COSTS in Slovenian Tolar (SIT)				
	$$$$	$$$	$$	$	¢
RESTAURANTS	over 4000	3000–4000	2000–3000	1000–2000	under 1000

Restaurant prices are per person for a main course at dinner.

About the Hotels

Don't expect Slovenia to be a cheap option; lodging prices are similar to what you see in Western Europe. During peak season (July and August), many hotels—particularly those on the coast—are fully booked. Hotels are generally clean, smartly furnished, and well run. Establishments built under Communism are often equipped with extras such as saunas and sports facilities but tend to be gargantuan structures lacking in soul. Hotels dating from the turn of the 20th century are more romantic, as are the castle hotels. Over the last decade many hotels have been refurbished and upgraded.

Private lodgings are a cheaper alternative to hotels, and standards are generally excellent. Prices vary depending on region and season. Look for signs proclaiming *sobe* (room to let) or *apartma* (apartments), alongside roads or in towns. Local tourist information centers, or in resorts like Bled or Piran private travel agencies, will often maintain lists of local rooms for rent.

Many hotels will offer better rates for stays of more than three days. Hotel rates frequently include breakfast—usually a mix of breads, cheeses and cold cuts served buffet style. Pensions and private rooms may include lunch or dinner—be sure to ask what's included in the price and whether you can opt out if you choose. Room rates are typically billed interchangeably in tolars or euros.

Between April and October camping is a reasonable alternative. Most campgrounds are small but well-equipped. On the coast, campsites are found at Izola and Ankaran. In Triglav National Park and the Soča Valley there are sites at Bled, Bohinj, Bovec, Kobarid, Soča, and Trenta. Camping outside of organized campsites is not permitted.

To really experience day-to-day life in the countryside you should stay on a working farm. Agrotourism is rapidly growing in popularity, and at most farms you can experience an idyllic rural setting, delicious home cooking, plus a warm family welcome. A brochure, *Tourist Farms in Slovenia,* is available from the tourist board. More information is available on the board's Web site.

SLOVENIAN CUISINE

AT FIRST GLANCE, *Slovenian cuisine looks a little like fusion food since it melds elements of Italian, Hungarian, Austrian, and Balkan cooking—often to good effect. Italy's contribution stands out most clearly in the full range of pastas and risottos you'll see on many menus. Pizza is ubiquitous and generally of high quality. From Austria come the many pork and other meat dishes and schnitzels, though they are often served with local—and sometimes unusual—sides like spinach njoki (gnocchi) or even ajda (buckwheat) dumplings. The Balkan influence is seen in the profusion of grilled meats and in one of the most common street foods: burek, an oily phyllo pastry stuffed with salty cheese or meat.*

Typical local dishes include krvavice (black pudding) served with žganci (polenta) or Kraški pršut (air-dried ham). Another favorite is jota, a filling soup of sauerkraut, beans, and smoked pork. Look too for regional specialties, such as the easier-to-eat-than-pronounce žlikrofi—tiny tortellini stuffed with minced potato, onion, and bacon that are the pride of cooks throughout the Idrija region but are nearly impossible to find anywhere else.

With the Adriatic close at hand, you can find excellent seafood. Look for mouthwatering škampi rižot (scampi risotto), followed by fresh fish prepared na žaru (grilled). Fresh trout with tržaška (garlic and parsley) sauce is a staple on any menu near the Soča river. The first-rate fish—usually priced on menus per kilogram (2.2 pounds)—are expensive, so don't be surprised when the bill comes.

For an extra boost stop at a kavarna (coffee shop) for a scrumptious, calorie-laden prekmurska gibanica, a layered cake combining curd cheese, walnuts, and poppy seeds. Another national favorite is potica, a rolled cake filled with either walnuts, chocolate, poppy seeds, or raisins.

WHAT IT COSTS in Euros (€)					
	$$$$	**$$$**	**$$**	**$**	**¢**
HOTELS	over €210	€150–€210	€100–€150	€60–€100	under €60

Hotel prices are for two people in a double room in high season, excluding taxes and service charges.

Timing

The countryside is at its most beautiful in spring and fall, though the best period to visit depends on what you plan to do during your stay. Ljubljana is vibrant the whole year through. Many visitors want to head straight for the coast. Those in search of sea, sun, and all-night parties will find what they're looking for in peak season (July and August), including cultural events, open-air dancing, busy restaurants, and crowded beaches. If you want to avoid the crowds, hit the Adriatic in June or September, when it should be warm enough to swim and easier to find a place to put your beach towel.

In the mountains there are two distinct seasons: winter is dedicated to skiing, summer to hiking and biking. Some hotels close in November

and March to mark a break between the two periods. Conditions for more strenuous walking and biking are optimal in April, May, September, and October.

Lovers of fine food and wine should visit Slovenia during fall. The grape harvest concludes with the blessing of the season's young wine on St. Martin's Day, preceded by three weeks of festivities. In rural areas autumn is the time to make provisions for the hard winter ahead: wild mushrooms are gathered, firewood chopped, and *koline* (sausages and other pork products) prepared by hand.

Numbers in the margins correspond to numbers on the Slovenia map.

LJUBLJANA

Slovenia's small but exceedingly charming capital is enjoying a tourism renaissance. The advent of low-cost flights from the United Kingdom and increased air service from other European countries has led to a dramatic influx of visitors in recent years and elevated the city's profile abroad. Tourism officials now talk of Ljubljana proudly in the same breath as Prague or Budapest as one of the top urban destinations in Central Europe. That may be wishful thinking, but there's no denying a sense of excitement as new hotels and restaurants open their doors, and each month seems to bring another admiring article in a prestigious newspaper or magazine abroad.

The tiny city center is immediately captivating. Part of the charm is doubtless the emerald green Llubljanica River that winds its way slowly through the Old Town, providing a focal point and the perfect backdrop to the cafés and restaurants that line the banks. Partly, too, it's the aesthetic tension between the stately baroque houses along the river and the white neoclassical, modern, and Secessionist set pieces that dot the streets and bridges everywhere. Meticulously designed pillars, orbs, and obelisks lend the city an element of whimsy, a feeling of good cheer that's immediately infectious. And part of the credit goes to the Ljubljaners themselves, who on a warm summer evening can be counted on to come out and party in force. It's a place that's meant to be enjoyed.

In truth, Ljubljana has always viewed itself as something special. Even when it was part of the former Yugoslavia, the city was considered a center of alternative music and arts. This was especially true during the 1980s, when it became the center of the Yugoslav punk movement. The band Laibach, noted for mocking nationalist sentiments, and the absurdist conceptual-art group Neue Slowenische Kunst (NSK) both have their roots here.

The romantic heart of the Old Town dates back centuries. The earliest settlement was founded by the Romans and called Emona. Much of it was destroyed by the Huns under Attila, though a section of the walls and a complex of foundations—complete with mosaics—can still be seen today. In the 12th century, a new settlement, Laibach, was built on the right bank of the river, below Castle Hill, by the dukes of Carniola. In

1335, the Habsburgs gained control of the region, and it was they who constructed the existing castle fortification system.

The 17th century saw a period of baroque building, strongly influenced by currents in Austria and Italy. Walk along the cobblestones of the *Mestni trg* (Town Square) and the *Stari trg* (Old Square) to see Ljubljana at its best, from the colored baroque town houses with their steeply pitched tile roofs to Francesco Robba's delightful *Fountain of the Three Carniolan Rivers.*

For a brief period, from 1809 to 1813, Ljubljana was the capital of Napoléon's Illyrian Provinces. In 1849, once again under the Habsburgs, Ljubljana was linked to Vienna and Trieste by rail. The city developed into a major center of commerce, industry, and culture, and the opera house, national theater, national museum, and the first hotels came into existence.

In 1895 much of the city was devastated by an earthquake. The reconstruction work that followed was carried out in florid Viennese Secessionist style. Many of the palatial four-story buildings that line Miklošičeva, such as the Grand Hotel Union, date from this period.

After World War I, with the birth of the Kingdom of Serbs, Croats, and Slovenes, Ljubljana became the administrative center of Slovenia. Various national cultural institutes were founded, and the University of Ljubljana opened in 1919. If you have been to Prague, you will already have seen some of the work of Jože Plečnik (1872–1957). Born in Ljubljana, Plečnik studied architecture in Vienna under Otto Wagner, then went on to lecture at the Prague School of Applied Arts and served as the chief architect for the renovation of Prague Castle. It was Plečnik who added many of the decorator touches to the city's parks, squares and bridges. Some of his finest projects include the Triple Bridge, the open-air market on Vodnik Square, and the plans for the Križanke Summer Theater.

The Tito years saw increased industrialization. The population of Ljubljana tripled, and vast factory complexes, high-rise apartments, and modern office buildings extended into the suburbs.

Exploring Ljubljana

The city center is concentrated within a small area, so you can cover all the sights on foot.

What to See

⑬ Cankarjevo nabrežje. Numerous cafés line this pretty riverside walkway. When the weather is good, tables are placed outside overlooking the water. ⊠ *Between Tromostovje and Čevljarski most.*

❶ Centromerkur. This magnificent art nouveau–style building, dating from 1903, is the oldest department store in town. Most of the structures in Ljubljana built at this time borrowed from the Viennese Secession, making this building—which draws its inspiration more from Paris—a relative rarity. The entrance, off Prešernov trg, bears a flaring iron butterfly wing and is topped by a statue of Mercury. Inside, graceful wrought-iron stairways lead to upper floors. ⊠ *Trubarjeva 1* ☎ *01/426–3170.*

Ljubljana

KEY

- ▶ Exploring sights
- ❾ Hotels & Restaurants
- 🛈 Tourist information

Exploring ▶

⑭ Čevljarski most (Cobblers' Bridge). Linking the old and new sides of town, this romantic pedestrian bridge was built in 1931 according to plans by the architect Jože Plečnik. The name is derived from a wooden structure that once stood here and was lined with shoemakers' huts.

② Franciskanska cerkev (Franciscan Church). This massive, pink high-baroque church was built between 1646 and 1660. The main altar, by Francesco Robba (1698–1757), dates from 1736. The three sets of stairs in front are a popular meeting place for students. ⊠ *Prešernov trg 4* ☉ *Daily 8–6.*

⑪ Gornji trg (Upper Square). This cobbled street, just around the corner from Stari trg, is where you'll find some of the capital's finest restaurants and a small but growing collection of design and art studios.

⑮ Križanke Poletno Gledališče (Križanke Summer Theater). In the courtyard of an 18th-century monastery, this open-air theater was constructed according to plans drawn up by Jože Plečnik. It was completed in 1976, nearly two decades after the architect's death. The theater seats 1,400, and there's a movable roof in case it rains. ⊠ *Trg Francoske Revolucije.*

off the beaten path

PLEČNIK'S HOUSE – Architecture enthusiasts will enjoy a visit to architect Jože Plečnik's house, still as he left it, to see his studio, home, and garden. The only drawback is the limited opening times: just four hours a day, two days a week. From the Križanke Summer Theater, cross Zoisova cesta, and then follow Emonska to Karunova. ⊠ *Karunova 4, Trnovo* ☎ *01/280–1600* ⌨ *SIT 1,000* ☉ *Tues. and Thurs. 10–2.*

⑫ Ljubljanski grad (Ljubljana Castle). Ljubljana's hilltop castle affords magnificent views over the river and the Old Town's terra-cotta rooftops, spires, and green cupolas. On a clear day, the distant Julian Alps are a dramatic backdrop. The castle walls date from the early 16th century, although the tower was added in the mid-19th century. The surrounding park was landscaped by Plečnik in the 1930s. ⊠ *Studentovska ul, uphill from Vodnikov trg* ☎ *01/432–7216* ⌨ *SIT 500, includes admission to top of tower* ☉ *Apr.–Oct., daily 9 AM–11 PM; Nov.–Mar., daily 10–7.*

need a break?

The castle ramparts shelter a pleasant café and summer garden. After the steep climb from the Old Town, stop in for a refreshing drink at the **Castle Terrace** (⊠ Lljubljanski grad ☎ 01/439–4140).

⑨ Magistrat (Town Hall). Guarded by an austere 18th-century facade, this building hides delightful secrets within. In the internal courtyard, for example, the walls are animated with murals depicting historic battles for the city, and a statue of Hercules keeps company with a fountain bearing a figure of Narcissus. ⊠ *Mestni trg 1* ⌨ *Free* ☉ *Weekdays 9–3, weekends as part of guided tour of city.*

⑦ Mestni trg (Town Square). This cobbled square extends into the oldest part of the city. Baroque town houses, now divided into functional apartments, present marvelously ornate facades: carved oak doors with great brass handles are framed within columns, and upper floors are decorated with balustrades, statuary, and intricate ironwork. Narrow passageways connect with inner courtyards in one direction and run to the riverfront in the other. The street-level floors contain boutiques, antiques shops, and art galleries.

need a break? If you plan to dine in the Old Town, stop first at **Movia** (⊠ Mestni trg 2 ☎ 01/425–5448) for an aperitif. This elegant little wine bar stocks a selection of first-rate Slovenian wines, for consumption both on and off the premises. It is closed Sunday.

⑱ Moderna galerija (Modern Gallery). The strikingly modern one-story structure contains a selection of paintings, sculpture, and prints by Slovenian 20th-century artists. In odd-number years it also hosts the International Biennial of Graphic Art, an exhibition of prints and installations by artists from around the world. Works by Robert Rauschenberg, Susan Rothenburg, and Max Bill have been shown. ⊠ *Cankarjeva 15* ☎ *01/241–6800* ⊕ *www.mg-lj.si* ⊠ *SIT 1,000* ☉ *Tues.–Sat. 10–6, Sun. 10–1.*

㉒ Muzej Novejše Zgodovine (Museum of Modern History). The permanent exhibition on Slovenes in the 20th century takes you from the days of Austria-Hungary, through World War II, the victory of the Partisan liberation movement and the ensuing Tito period, and up to the present day. Relics and memorabilia are combined with a dramatic sound-and-video presentation (scenes from World War II are projected on the walls and ceiling, accompanied by thundering gunfire, screams, and singing). You'll find the museum in a pink-and-white baroque villa in Tivoli Park. ⊠ *Celovška 23* ☎ *01/300–9610* ⊕ *www.muzej-nz.si* ⊠ *SIT 800* ☉ *Tues.–Sun. 10–6.*

㉑ Narodna galerija (National Gallery). This imposing turn-of-the-20th-century building houses the greatest collection of Slovenian art from the 13th through the early 20th century, and a smaller but impressive collection of European paintings. ⊠ *Cankarjeva 20* ☎ *01/241–5418* ⊕ *www.ng-slo.si* ⊠ *SIT 800* ☉ *Tues.–Sun. 10–6.*

⑳ Narodni muzej (National Museum). The centerpiece here is a bronze urn from the 5th century BC known as the Vace Situle. Discovered in Vace, Slovenia, it is a striking example of Illyrian workmanship. ⊠ *Muzejska 1* ☎ *01/241–4400* ⊕ *www.narmuz-lj.si* ⊠ *SIT 1,000* ☉ *Tues., Wed., and Fri.–Sun. 10–6, Thurs. 10–8.*

❽ Robbov Vodnjak (Robba's Fountain). When the Slovene sculptor Francesco Robba saw Bernini's *Fountain of the Four Rivers* on Piazza Navona during a visit to Rome, he was inspired to create this allegorical representation of the three main Kranjska rivers—the Sava, the Krka, and the Ljubljanica—that flow through Slovenia. ⊠ *Mestni trg.*

⑰ Slovenska Filharmonija (Slovenian Philharmonic Hall). This hall was built in 1891 for one of the oldest music societies in the world, established in 1701. Haydn, Brahms, Beethoven, and Paganini were honorary members of the orchestra, and Mahler was resident conductor for the 1881–82 season. ⊠ *Kongresni trg 10* ☎ *01/241–0800.*

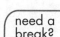

From the Philharmonic Hall, head to the other side of Kongresni trg to find **Zvezda** (✉ Kongresni trg 4 ☎ 01/421–9090). This popular café has comfortable chairs and minimalist lighting, making it a perfect spot for an afternoon *kava smetana* (coffee with whipped cream). The ice cream and cakes are made on the premises and the staff never hurries you.

⑲ **SNG Opera in Balet** (Slovenian National Opera and Ballet Theater). This neo-Renaissance palace, with an ornate facade topped by an allegorical sculpture group, was erected in 1892. When visiting ballet and opera companies come to Ljubljana, they perform here. ✉ *Župančičeva 1* ☎ *01/241–1764* ⊕ *www.operainbalet-lj.si* ☉ *Weekdays 11–1 and one hour before performances.*

⑩ **Stari trg** (Old Square). More a narrow street than a square, the Old Square is lined with cafés and small restaurants. In agreeable weather, tables are set out on the cobblestones.

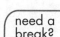

The best cup of tea in Ljubljana—as well as great coffees—and one of the few breakfast places in town can be found at **Čajna Hiša** (✉ Stari trg 3 ☎ 01/439–4140).

⑤ **Stolnica sveti Nikolaja** (Cathedral of St. Nicholas). This proud baroque cathedral overshadows the daily market on Vodnikov trg. Building took place between 1701 and 1708, and in 1836 the cupola was erected. In 1996, in honor of the pope's visit, new bronze doors were added. The main door tells the story of Christianity in Slovenia, whereas the side door shows the history of the Ljubljana diocese. ✉ *Dolničarjeva 1* ☎ *01/234–2690* ⊕ *http://lj-stolnica.rkc.si* ⊠ *Free* ☉ *Daily 7–noon and 3–7.*

⑯ **Trg Francoske Revolucije** (French Revolution Square). When Napoléon took Slovenia, he made Ljubljana the capital of his Illyrian Provinces. This square is dominated by Plečnik's **Ilirski Steber** (Illyrian Column), which was erected in 1929 to commemorate that time.

③ **Tromostovje** (Triple Bridge). This striking structure spans the River Ljubljanica from Prešernov trg to the Old Town. The three bridges started as a single span, and in 1931 the two graceful outer arched bridges, designed by Plečnik, were added.

④ **Vodnikov trg** (Vodnik Square). This square hosts a big and bustling flower, fruit, and vegetable market. An elegant riverside colonnade designed by Plečnik runs the length of the market, and a bronze statue of the Slovene poet Valentin Vodnik, after whom the square is named, overlooks the scene. ☉ *Market Mon.–Sat. 7–3.*

⑥ **Zmajski most** (Dragon's Bridge). Four fire-breathing winged dragons crown the corners of this locally cherished concrete-and-iron structure.

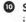

ŽALE – To see one of Plečnik's most dramatic structures, ride bus No. 2, 7, or 22 from the post office out to Žale, a cemetery and memorial designed by the architect in the 1930s. The entrance colonnade and adjoining promenades reflect the Secessionist influence, creating a tranquil resting place inside. ✉ *Tomačevska cesta, Novo Jarse.*

Where to Eat

Central European food is often considered bland and stodgy, but in Ljubljana you can eat exceptionally well. Fresh fish arrives daily from the Adriatic, and the surrounding hills supply the capital with first-class meat and game, dairy produce, and fruit and vegetables. Ljubljana's relative diversity also affords an opportunity to dabble in international cuisines like Mexican, Japanese, and Chinese if you've already spent some time in the countryside and are looking for a change of pace. At some of the better restaurants the menus may verge on nouvelle cuisine, featuring imaginative and beautifully presented dishes. Complement your meal with a bottle of good Slovenian wine; the waiter can help you choose an appropriate one. For a lunchtime snack visit the market in Vodnik Square. Choose from tasty fried squid and whitebait in the riverside arcade or freshly baked pies and *kròf* (jelly-filled doughnuts) at the square's bakeries.

★ **$$$$** ✕ **Gostilna As.** This refined restaurant—not to be confused with the on-premises beer garden and after-hours club of the same name—is tucked away in a courtyard just off Wolfova ul. As—or "Ace"—is *the* place to try innovative fish dishes (priced by the dekagram) and pasta specialties, all complemented by a first-rate wine list. The ambience is old-fashioned, but the dishes are creative and modern. ⊠ *Knafljev prehod 5a* ☎ *01/425–8822* ⚭ *Reservations essential* ▤ *AE, DC, MC, V.*

$$$–$$$$ ✕ **Chez Eric.** A happy marriage of French and Slovenian cooking. The small number of entrées—four meat and four fish—ensure that each item gets the attention it deserves. Eat on the terrace in warmer months. The restaurant occupies the former site of the Rotovž, next to the town hall on Mestni trg. ⊠ *Mestni trg 3* ☎ *01/251–2839* ▤ *AE, DC, MC, V* ⊘ *Closed Sun.*

$$$–$$$$ ✕ **Pri sv. Florijanu.** On Gornji trg, on the way to the castle, this upscale eatery serves up a new generation of Slovenian cuisine with an international touch, borrowing from French and Asian influences. In every season the chef seems to have the right touch with Slovenia's bounty; porcini mushroom risotto and pumpkin ravioli in the fall, asparagus soup and *motovílec* (lamb's lettuce) salad in the spring. The service is both inviting and discreet. ⊠ *Gornji trg 20* ☎ *01/251–2214* ▤ *AE, DC, MC, V.*

$$$–$$$$ ✕ **Sushimama.** A light sushi dinner paired with a crisp white wine can be a welcome antidote to the heavy meat and starch offered on most Slovenian menus. This new arrival boasts a Japanese chef, fresh fish, and a spare, minimalist decor that focuses your attention on the food. ⊠ *Wolfova 12* ☎ *070/727–272* ▤ *AE, DC, MC, V* ⊘ *Closed Sun.*

$$$ ✕ **Zlata Ribica.** Although there is a good range of Slovenian and Italian specialties, it's not the food that's the main draw here—it's the riverside location near the Triple Bridge. On a warm, summer evening, there's not a better table in town. Despite the name, which translates as "goldfish," there's not much in the way of seafood here—instead the focus is on salads, grilled meats, and game. ⊠ *Cankarjevo nab 5* ☎ *01/241–2680* ▤ *AE, DC, MC, V.*

$$ ✕ **Ljubljanski Dvor.** Situated close to Čevljarski most, overlooking the river, this restaurant doubles as a pizzeria (which remains open on Sunday, when the restaurant is closed). The summer terrace makes it an ideal stopping point for lunch. ⊠ *Dvorni trg 1* ☎ *01/251–6555* ⊟ *AE, DC, MC, V* ⊘ *Closed Sun.*

$$ ✕ **Špajza.** A few doors away from Pri sv. Florijanu, you'll find a restaurant with a series of romantic candlelit rooms and bohemian decor. The menu has local specialties like *Kraši pršut* (Karst air-dried ham) and scampi tails, as well as an inspired selection of salads. They do a great tiramisu. ⊠ *Gornji trg 28* ☎ *01/425–3094* ⊟ *AE, DC, MC, V* ⊘ *Closed Sun.*

$–$$ ✕ **Lunch Cafe.** As the name implies, the perfect spot for a quick and easy soup-and-salad lunch, or a light pasta dinner. The focus here is simple food done well. The affable staff is knowledgeable about wines, and the low prices make it a good place to sample a couple of glasses. ⊠ *Stari trg 9* ☎ *01/425–0118* ⊟ *AE, DC, MC, V.*

$–$$ ✕ **Při Skofu.** This tiny, eclectic neighborhood place serves as a kind of temple for foodies in the suburb of Trnovo. The emphasis is on traditional Slovenian cooking, but not the sort that makes it on to many standard menus. The gnocchi, risotto, and buckwheat dumplings come highly recommended. Most ingredients are purchased daily at Ljubljana's open-air market. The menu changes daily, so ask the server what looks good that day. ⊠ *Rečna 8, Trnovo* ☎ *01/426–4508* ⊟ *AE, DC, MC, V.*

★ $–$$ ✕ **Trta.** In a country filled with pizza joints, this may be Slovenia's best. It offers super-sized pies, fresh and inventive ingredients, and a small garden for warm evenings. Walk south along the river (on the same side as the Old Town), cross over busy Zoisova cesta, and continue along Grudnovo nabrežje. ⊠ *Grudnovo nab 23* ☎ *01/426–5066* ⊟ *AE, DC, MC, V* ⊘ *Closed Sun.*

Where to Stay

Most of the listed hotels are clustered conveniently around Miklošičeva cesta, the main axis running from the train station down to Tromostovje (Triple Bridge). Ljubljana is expensive by Central and Eastern European standards (comparable to those in Western Europe), but hotel standards are high. In summer you can get better deals through private accommodations or university dorms. Ask about these options at the tourist-information center kiosk in the train station.

$$$$ ▦ **Hotel Lev.** A series of renovations since 1997 have transformed a nondescript modern building into the country's leading hotel. The Lev makes up for its location—about a 10-minute walk from the city center—with stunning views of Tivoli Park and the Julian Alps outside of Ljubljana. Parking is free, and you'll find easy access to all major highways; soundproof windows keep traffic from spoiling the comfort. Rooms are decorated in soothing pastel tones. Check the Web site for occasional summer discounts. ⊠ *Vošnjakova 1, 1000* ☎ *01/433–2155* 🖷 *01/433–2003* ⊕ *www.hotel-lev.si* 🛏 *170 rooms* ♤ *Restaurant, café, room service, minibars, some in-room safes, cable TV, in-room data ports, Internet room, gym, hair salon, bar, casino, dry cleaning, laundry service, business services, meeting rooms, car rental, free parking, no-smoking rooms* ⊟ *AE, DC, MC, V* ❤ *BP.*

★ **$$$** 🏨 **Grand Hotel Union.** The pricier "Executive" section of this bustling hotel complex in central Ljubljana occupies a magnificent Secessionist-style building; the interior and furnishings remain typically turn-of-the-20th-century Vienna. The "Business" section is in an attached modern building overlooking a pleasant courtyard with a fountain; all the rooms in this section have broadband Internet connections. All hotel facilities are shared by both sections of the hotel and have been modernized with great care. ⊠ *Miklošičeva 1–3, 1000* ☎ *01/308–1270* 🖷 *01/308–1015* ⊕ *www.gh-union.si* ✒ *297 rooms, 12 suites* △ *2 restaurants, café, some in-room data ports, some kitchens, in-room safes, minibars, cable TV with movies, indoor pool, gym, massage, sauna, shops, some in-room broadband, Internet room, business services, no-smoking rooms* ⊟ *AE, DC, MC, V* 🍽 *BP.*

$$–$$$ 🏨 **Domina Grand Media Ljubljana.** It's the hotel of the future. At least that's what the owners of this—the city's newest addition to the four-star lodging class—would have us believe. Some of the high-concept amenities include plasma screens in all the rooms, total Internet connectivity, a fully-equipped wellness center, and retro-modern furniture straight out of the Jetsons. The location is a bit out of the way, but the hotel offers free shuttle service to the center. ⊠ *Dunajska cesta 154* ☎ *01/588–2500* 🖷 *01/588–2599* ⊕ *www.dominagmljubljana.com* ✒ *160 rooms, 57 suites* △ *2 restaurants, café, in-room safes, minibars, cable TV with movies, in-room broadband, in-room data ports, WiFi, wellness center, sauna, business services, no-smoking rooms* ⊟ *AE, DC, MC, V* 🍽 *BP.*

$$ 🏨 **Best Western Slon Hotel.** Close to the river, this high-rise hotel stands on the site of a famous 16th-century inn and maintains an atmosphere of traditional hospitality. The breakfast is among the finest in the city. The run-of-the-mill rooms are comfortable, and the wood floors are a nice alternative to wall-to-wall carpeting. ⊠ *Slovenska 34, 1000* ☎ *01/470–1131* 🖷 *01/251–7164* ⊕ *www.hotelslon.com* ✒ *185 rooms* △ *2 restaurants, café, room service, in-room broadband, WiFi, in-room safes, minibars, cable TV with movies, hot tub, sauna, shops, Internet, meeting rooms, parking, no-smoking rooms; no a/c in some rooms* ⊟ *AE, DC, MC, V* 🍽 *BP.*

$$ 🏨 **City Hotel.** The former Turist Hotel has undergone a makeover. The result has been enhanced services, such as wider Internet access for guests, but at a higher price. The basic rooms are clean and the location is excellent. ⊠ *Dalmatinova 15, 1000* ☎ *01/234–9130* 🖷 *01/234–9140* ⊕ *www.cityhotel.si* ✒ *123 rooms* △ *2 restaurants, some kitchenettes, minibars, cable TV, WiFi, Internet room, bicycles, meeting rooms* ⊟ *AE, DC, MC, V.*

★ **$** 🏨 **Emonec.** Billing itself as the city's newest two-star hotel, Emonec fills a long time gap in the market for a clean, affordable hotel in the center. Don't expect much in the way of frills or services, but the simple modern rooms are tastefully furnished, the breakfast is fine, and the staff is helpful. At this price level in Ljubljana, that's a considerable bargain. ⊠ *Wolfova 12* ☎ *01/200–1520* 🖷 *01/200–1521* ⊕ *www.hotel-emonec.com* ✒ *26 rooms* △ *Cable TV, in-room broadband, Internet room, bicycles, meeting rooms, parking (free); no a/c* ⊟ *AE, DC, MC, V* 🍽 *BP.*

$ ⚏ **Pension Mrak.** This friendly pension offers good value with simple but comfortable rooms and a decent restaurant. It is situated on a quiet side street, close to the Križanke Summer Theater. ✉ *Rimska 4, 1000* 📠 *01/421–9600* 🖨 *01/421–9655* ⊕ *www.daj-dam.si* ⇴ *30 rooms* ⚒ *Restaurant, in-room safes, cable TV, Internet room; no A/C in some rooms* ▤ *AE, DC, MC, V.*

Nightlife & the Arts

Although they were considered the workaholics of Yugoslavia, Slovenes do know how to enjoy themselves. One in 10 of the capital's inhabitants is a student, hence the proliferation of trendy cafés and small art galleries. Each year the International Summer Festival breathes new life into the Ljubljana cultural scene, sparking off a lively program of concerts and experimental theater. For information about forthcoming cultural events, check *Events in Ljubljana,* a monthly pamphlet published by the Ljubljana Promotion Center, and the English-language magazine *Ljubljana Life,* both available in major hotels and tourist offices.

Nightlife

The listed bars and clubs are all situated within walking distance of the center. However, during summer the all-night party scene moves to the Adriatic coast, where open-air dancing and rave parties abound.

CAFÉS   The most idyllic way to close a summer evening is with a nightcap on the terrace of one of the riverside cafés in the Old Town.

Hip **Cafe Galerija** (✉ Mestni trg 5 📠 01/426–0327) serves stylish cocktails by candlelight in a North Africa–inspired hideout. With a large terrace and glamorous clientele, **Cafe Maček** (✉ Krojaška 5 📠 01/425–3791) is the place to be seen down by the river. **Caffe Boheme** (✉ Mestni trg 19 📠 01/548–1342) in the heart of the Old Town is spacious inside and has a terrace with tables and umbrellas outside.

MUSIC   For Latino music or a pick-me-up breakfast in the early hours, visit **Casa del Papa** (✉ Celovška 54A 📠 01/434–3158): three floors of exotic food, drinks, and entertainment in tribute to Ernest Hemingway. For live jazz visit **Jazz Club Gajo** (✉ Beethovnova 8 📠 01/425–3206), which attracts stars from home and abroad. Clark Terry, Sheila Jordan, and Woody Shaw have all performed here. The student-run club **K4** (✉ Kersnikova 4 📠 01/431–7010) hosts visiting DJs and plays a mix of musical styles—house, hip hop, surf—throughout the week. It attracts a young and alternative crowd; Sunday is gay night.

BARS & CLUBS   If it's rowdy beer-drinking and shot-downing you're looking for, the epicenter for this is the courtyard just off of Wolfova ulica 6, or in nice weather just follow the crowds—and the noise—to **As Lounge** (✉ Knafljev prehod 📠 01/425–8822) and **Cutty Sark** (✉ Knafijev prehod 📠 01/425–1477).

Bar Minimal (✉ Mestni trg 4 📠 01/426–0138), as the name suggests, is a spare, all-white space for Ljubljana's beautiful people. One place that is definitely not chic is the shabby former squat **Metelkova** (✉ Metelkova, Tabor 📠 01/432–3378). At one time this was an army barracks that was occupied by students and transformed into a multipurpose venue for shows and happenings. It's constantly under threat of demolition by city authorities. If you get hunger pangs after a night in the bars in the Old Town, head to **Romeo** (✉ Stari trg 6 ☎ No phone) for great sandwiches and quesadillas. It's open until midnight. For great cocktails, head over to **Salon** (✉ Trubarjeva 23 ☎ 01/433–2006) on a funky street just north of the main Old Town cluster. The gold lamé and leopard-skin interior lends a cool, East Village–like vibe.

The Arts

ANNUAL EVENTS Each year in June, the International Jazz Festival and the Druga Godba (a festival of alternative and ethnic music) are staged at the Križanke Summer Theater. For schedules and tickets contact the box office at Cankarjev dom. Ljubljana's **International Summer Festival** (✉ Trg Francoske Revolucije 1–2 ☎ 01/241–6026 ⊕ www.festival-lj.si) is held each July and August in the open-air Križanke Summer Theater. Musical, theatrical, and dance performances attract acclaimed artists from all over the world.

PERFORMANCE **Cankarjev dom** (Cankar House; ✉ Prešernova 10 ☎ 01/241–7100
HALLS ⊕ www.cd-cc.si), opened in 1980 as a modern, rather characterless venue. As a cultural center, however, it is the driving force behind the city's artistic activities, offering up-to-date general information and tickets. A progressive film festival takes place here every November.

CLASSICAL MUSIC Ljubljana has plenty of events for classical-music lovers. The season, which runs from September through June, includes weekly concerts by the Slovenian Philharmonic Orchestra and the RTV Slovenia Orchestra, as well as performances by guest soloists, chamber musicians, and foreign symphony orchestras. The 19th-century performance hall housing concerts by the **Slovenska Filharmonija** (Slovenian Philharmonic; ✉ Kongresni trg 10 ☎ 01/241–0800 ⊕ www.filharmonija.si) is a traditional classical-music venue. The orchestra dates to 1908, but its predecessors have roots in the early 18th century.

FILM Cinemas generally screen the original versions of films, with Slovenian subtitles. **Kinoteka** (✉ Miklošičeva 28 ☎ 01/434–2520 ⊕ www.kinoteka. si) runs some great retrospectives.

THEATER, DANCE Ljubljana has a long tradition of experimental and alternative theater,
& OPERA with dance often thrown into the mix. Contemporary dance plays by the internationally recognized choreographers Matjaz Faric and Iztok Kovac and performances by the dance troupes Betontanc and En Knap are ideal for English speakers.

From September through June the **SNG Opera in Balet** (Slovene National Opera & Ballet Theater; ✉ Župančičeva 1 ☎ 01/241–1764 ⊕ www.operainbalet-lj.si) stages everything from classical to modern and alternative productions.

Shopping

While you wouldn't come to Slovenia to do much serious shopping, fashionable shoe stores abound in Ljubljana; for the latest selection head to shops on Stari trg in the Old Town. If you want to do some hiking but have come unprepared, **Anappurna** (⌧ Krakovski Nasip 10 ☎ 01/426–3428) has a good selection of mountaineering equipment. You can pick up antiques and memorabilia at the **Ljubljana Flea Market** (⌧ Cankarjevo nab), held near Tromostovje (Triple Bridge) each Sunday morning. The most interesting shopping experience is undoubtedly a visit to the **open-air market** (⌧ Vodnikov trg), where besides fresh fruit and vegetables you can find dried herbs and locally produced honey. **Skrina** (⌧ Breg 8 ☎ 01/425–5161) has some unusual local crafts.

Side Trip to the Krka Valley

Numbers in the margins correspond to the Krka Valley map.

A drive through the Krka Valley makes a perfect day-trip from Ljubljana. The monasteries of Stična and Pleterje offer insight into contemporary monastic life, and there are two castles, Otočec and Mokrice, where you can stop for lunch—or a romantic overnight stay in exquisite surroundings.

Take the E70 highway east out of Ljubljana, and then turn right at Ivančna Gorica to follow a secondary road along the Krka Valley. For a more direct journey home, return to the E70 just north of Šentjernej. There are also buses from Ljubljana to Ivančna Gorica and Šentjernej, but these are only practical if you don't mind walking the final stretch to the monasteries.

★ ㉓ The **Stična Samostan** (Stična Monastery) lies 2 km (1 mi) north of Ivančna Gorica. Founded by the Cistercians in 1135, the monastery was fortified in the 15th century to protect against Turkish invasion. Today there are only 10 monks, plus 3 nuns who attend to the cooking. The monks produce excellent herbal teas that work (allegedly) against cellulite, insomnia, poor memory, and practically every other problem you can think of, on sale in the monastery shop. The early Gothic cloisters, the baroque church, and the adjoining **Slovenian Religious Museum** are open to the public. The museum's collections include archives dedicated to the work of Bishop Friderik Baraga, a 19th-century missionary to the United States who compiled the first dictionary of the Native American Otchipwe language. Call first to arrange a visit. ⌧ *Stična 17, Ivančna Gorica* ☎ *01/787–7100* ⌧ *SIT 700* ☉ *Tues.–Sat. 8–11 and 2–5, Sun. 2–5.*

★ ㉔ The Carthusian monks of **Pleterje Samostan** (Pleterje Monastery) aim "to find God in silence and solitude." Therefore you can't enter the monastery proper, but you are welcome to view the magnificent 15th-century Gothic church and to watch a fascinating audiovisual presentation (in English) about the way the monks live. The walled monastery is nestled in a lonely valley surrounded by woods. Once a week the monks take a 45-minute walk around the perimeter of the complex. The route is marked with a blue circle and yellow cross, so you can follow the trail independently. A small shop sells rakija, honey, wine, and cheese made by the monks. To reach the monastery from Stična Monastery follow the Krka River through Zagradec, Žužemberk, and Novo Mesto. At Šen-

The Krka Valley

tjernej, turn south and travel for 6 km (4 mi) to reach Pleterje. ⊠ *Drča 1, Šentjernej* ☎ *07/308–1225* ▭ *Free* ⊙ *Daily 8–5.*

Where to Stay & Eat

\$\$\$–\$\$\$\$ ✕▣ **Hotel Grad Otočec.** About 8 km (5 mi) west of Šentjernej, on the road to Novo Mesto, you will find the entrance to the medieval Otočec castle, dating from the 13th century. Now a luxury hotel, complete with period furniture, Otočec sits on an island in the Krka River and is accessible by a wooden bridge. You can also camp on the castle grounds. Nonguests are welcome to dine in the restaurant, where the house specialty is locally caught game. Or just stop by for a drink in the courtyard café. Equestrian and tennis centers are close by. ⊠ *Grajska 1, Otočec ob Krki, 8222* ☎ *07/307–5700* ▤ *07/307–5420* ⊕ *www.krka-terme. com* ⇋ *16 rooms* ⅍ *Restaurant, cable TV, meeting rooms* ▤ *AE, DC, MC, V* ⅋ *BP.*

✋ **\$–\$\$** ✕▣ **Hotel Toplice.** With 11 springs supplying thermal water, Terme Čatež is the largest natural spa in Slovenia. Hotel Toplice—the newest of the four hotels connected to the spa—is the ultimate destination for recharging your batteries. It houses expansive indoor thermal baths as well as a fully loaded sports center. ⊠ *Topliska 35, Čatež ob Savi, 8251* ☎ *07/ 493–5023* ▤ *07/493–5025* ⊕ *www.terme-catez.si* ⇋ *110 rooms*

⬧ *Restaurant, minibars, in-room safes, Internet room, golf privileges, 7 tennis courts, indoor pool, health club, spa, bowling, squash, Ping-Pong, business services, meeting rooms* ▭ *AE, DC, MC, V* ⦿ *BP.*

Sports & the Outdoors

For horse lovers the **Struga Equestrian Center** (✉ Otočec ☎ 07/307–5627), at a 12th-century medieval manor, is a 20-minute walk from Otočec Castle. The center offers riding lessons and rents horses.

MARIBOR, PTUJ & HALOZE HILLS

During the 1st century AD, Poetovio, now known as Ptuj, was the largest Roman settlement in the area that is now Slovenia. Much later, in the 13th century, Maribor was founded. Originally given the German name Marchburg, the city took its Slavic name in 1836. For centuries the two towns competed for economic and cultural prominence within the region, and Maribor finally gained the upper hand in 1846, when a new railway line connected the city to Vienna and Trieste. The area between Maribor and Ptuj is a flat, fertile flood plain formed by the Drava River. South of Ptuj lie the hills of Haloze, famous for quality white wines.

Numbers in the margin correspond to numbers on the Maribor, Ptuj, and the Haloze Hills map.

Maribor

❷❺ *128 km (79 mi) northeast of Ljubljana on the E57.*

The presence of thousands of university students gives Maribor—Slovenia's second-largest city—a youthful vibe. You'll find plenty of pubs and cafés, especially in the Lent district along the Drava River. The Old Town has retained a core of ornate 18th- and 19th-century town houses, typical of imperial Austria, and much of it is off-limits to cars.

The heart of the Old Town is **Rotovški trg** with the **Kužno Znamenje** (Plague Memorial) at its center and overlooked by the proud 16th-century Renaissance **Rotovž** (town hall).

From Rotovški trg, a number of traffic-free streets lead down to a riverside promenade, known as **Lent.** It is lined with bars, terrace cafés, restaurants, and boutiques.

Below the streets of Maribor lies one of Europe's largest wine cellars. The **Vinag wine cellar** has some 3½ km (2 mi) of underground tunnels, holding almost 6 million liters of wine. Tours and tastings can be arranged in advance by phone. ✉ *Trg Svobode 3* ☎ *02/220–8111* ⦿ *www.vinag.si.*

The Vodni Stolp (Water Tower), a former defense tower, houses the **Vinoteka Slovenskih Vin** (Slovenian Wine Shop). Here you can sample and purchase more than 500 different Slovenian vintage wines. ✉ *Usnjarska 10* ☎ *02/251–7743.*

Where to Eat

$$$ ✕ **Toti Rotovž.** Close to the town hall, this building has been carefully restored to reveal vaulted brick ceilings and terra-cotta floors. The

Maribor, Ptuj, and the Haloze Hills

restaurant serves an eclectic mix of Slovene and international dishes, whereas the *klet* (wine cellar) in the basement cooks up barbecued steaks. ✉ *Glavni trg 14* ☎ *02/228–7650* ▭ *AE, DC, MC, V.*

Where to Stay

In summer, Maribor University dorms are open to visitors, providing a cheap alternative to hotels. For details ask at the Maribor tourist information center.

$ 🏨 **Hotel Orel.** The modern Orel offers the best accommodations in the city center—an easy stroll down the pedestrian zone to the river. There is a pleasant restaurant at street level, the rooms are comfortable, and the service is friendly. ✉ *Grajski trg 3A, 2000* ☎ *02/250–6700* 🖷 *02/251–8497* ⊕ *www.termemb.si* 🛏 *80 rooms* ⚒ *Restaurant, minibars, cable TV, parking* ▭ *AE, DC, MC, V* ⦿ *BP.*

Sports & the Outdoors

In winter in the Pohorje Mountains, just 6 km (4 mi) southwest of Maribor, you'll find alpine ski runs and cross-country trails. A cable car takes you from the south side of town up to the winter resort.

Two well-established biking paths pass though the region. The 95-km (59-mi) Drava Trail follows the course of the Drava River through the

Kozjak Hills to Maribor and then proceeds to Ptuj. The 56-km (35-mi) Jantara Trail runs from Šentilj on the Austrian border to Maribor and continues to Slovenska Bistrica. However, finding a place to rent a bike can be somewhat problematic. Inquire at the Maribor tourist-information center for assistance and information.

Ptuj

26 *25 km (15 mi) southeast of Maribor, 130 km (78 mi) from Ljubljana.*

Ptuj, built beside the Drava River and crowned by a hilltop castle, hits the national news each year in February with its extraordinary Carnival celebration, known as Kurentovanje. During the 10-day festival the town's boys and men dress in the bizarre Kurent costume: a horned mask decorated with ribbons and flowers, a sheepskin cloak, and a set of heavy bells around the waist. The task of the Kurent is to drive away the winter and welcome in the spring. You can see Kurent figures on 18th-century building facades in the center of Ptuj, on Jadranska ulica No. 4 and No. 6. It's a charming place and worth an overnight stay.

Ptujski Grad (Ptuj Castle) stands at the top of a steep hill in the center of town. Planned around a baroque courtyard, the castle houses a museum that exhibits musical instruments, an armory, 15th-century church paintings, and period furniture. ⊠ *Grajska Raven* ☎ *02/787–9230* ⊕ *www.pok-muzej-ptuj.si* ✉ *SIT 600* ☉ *Mid-Apr.–mid-Oct., daily 9–6; mid-Oct.–mid-Apr., daily 9–4.*

The **Ptuj Regional Museum,** in a former Dominican monastery, has an outstanding collection of ancient artifacts and coins, as well as Roman statuary and tombstones. The museum offers guided tours in English. ⊠ *Muzejski trg 1* ☎ *02/787–9230* ✉ *SIT 1,000* ☉ *Sept.–June, daily 9–6; July and Aug, weekdays 9–6, weekends 9–8.*

Vinska Klet (Ptuj Wine Cellars) offers a tasting session with five different wines, bread, and cheese, plus a bottle to take home. You are also given a tour of the underground cellars. A sound-and-video presentation takes you through the seasons of winemaking at the vineyards. The wines stocked here come predominantly from the Haloze Hills. One of the best wines is *Šipon,* a dry white that pairs nicely with pork dishes and rich sauces. ⊠ *Vinarski trg 1* ☎ *02/787–9810* ✉ *SIT 1,300–SIT 1,700* ☉ *Weekdays 7–7, Sat. 7–noon.*

Where to Eat

★ **$$$** ✕ **Ribič.** This lovely riverside restaurant is arguably the city's best. Though the menu offers seafood such as crab and lobster, the real treats here are the river fish, such as trout. The interior is simple, and the walls are hung with fishing nets. In warmer months, sit on the terrace with a view over the Drava. ⊠ *Dravska 9* ☎ *02/749–0653* ▭ *AE, DC, MC, V.*

Where to Stay

★ **$** ▦ **Garni Hotel Mitra.** If you stay overnight in Ptuj, you'll do fine in this popular, three-story, old-fashioned inn. The 19th-century facade suits the street just perfectly. Note that the rooms can get hot in summer—

it's best to request a room on the cooler second floor, away from the roof. ✉ *Prešernovo 6* ☎ *02/787–7455* 📠 *02/787–8889* 🌐 *www. hotelptuj.com* 🛏 *21 rooms, 2 apts.* ⚐ *Restaurant, minibars, cable TV, meeting room; no a/c* ▤ *AE, DC, MC, V* ⦿ *BP.*

Sports & the Outdoors

If you have access to a bike, you'll find a great run to the east of Ptuj along the 20-km (12 mi) Jeruzalem-Ljutomer *Vinska cesta* wine road. Ask at the Ptuj tourist-information center for more information.

🕘 **Terme Ptuj** (✉ Pot v Toplice 9 ☎ 02/782–7821 📠 02/783–7771 🌐 www. terme-ptuj.si) is more a family fun center than a serious spa, with a big pool and water park. You can also rent bikes here.

The Haloze Hills

㉗ *Borl Castle is 11 km (7 mi) southeast of Ptuj, 140 km (84 mi) from Ljubljana.*

The Haloze Hills lie south of Ptuj, close to the Croatian border. Grapes are generally planted on the steeper, south-facing slopes, to take full advantage of the sunshine, whereas the cooler, north-facing slopes are covered with trees and pastures. The best way to explore the region is to pick up the Haloze wine route near **Borl Castle,** through an undulating landscape of vineyards and woodlands. For a map of the route plus a comprehensive list of vineyards and wine stores open to the public, inquire at the Ptuj tourist-information center.

On the road between Podlehnik and Poljčane, keep an eye out for the sign for Štatenberg Castle; you can't stay there, but it has a good restaurant. Built between 1720 and 1740, Štatenberg is a typical example of the baroque style favored by the local aristocracy during the 18th century.

Where to Eat

$$ ✕ **Štatenberg Castle.** This restaurant serves traditional dishes, such as roast meats, accompanied by excellent local wines. Throughout summer you can sit at tables outside in the courtyard. ✉ *Štatenberg 86, Makole, 8222* ☎ 02/803–0216 ▤ No *credit cards* ☽ *Closed Mon.*

Maribor, Ptuj & Haloze Hills Essentials

BUS TRAVEL

Regular buses link Maribor and Ptuj to Ljubljana. However, the train is cheaper and more comfortable. An hourly bus service connects Maribor and Ptuj; the 45-minute journey costs around SIT 900.

🚺 **Maribor Bus Station** ✉ Mlinska 1, Maribor ☎ 02/235-0212.

CAR TRAVEL

To reach Maribor from Ljubljana take the E57; for Ptuj turn off at Slovenska Bistrica. A car is almost essential for exploring the Haloze Hills wine route. Some of the country roads are narrow and winding. Although there is snow in winter, it is extremely rare to find roads closed.

TRAIN TRAVEL

Regular train service links Ljubljana and Maribor; several international trains continue to Graz and Vienna. It is also possible to reach Ptuj by train from Ljubljana, though you may have to change at Pragersko. For information contact Ljubljana's train station (⇨ Train Travel *in* Ljubljana Essentials). Several trains daily connect Maribor and Ptuj, with a change at Pragersko; the 45-minute journey costs around SIT 800.

🚆 **Maribor Train Station** ⊠ Partizanska 50, Maribor ☎ 02/292-2100.

VISITOR INFORMATION

🚆 **Maribor Tourist Information** ⊠ Partizanska 47, Maribor ☎ 02/234-6611 ⊕ www.maribor-tourism.si. **Ptuj Tourist Information** ⊠ Slovenski trg 3, Ptuj ☎ 02/771-0173 ⊕ www.ptuj-tourism.si.

THE ALPS & THE SOČA VALLEY

Northwest of Ljubljana lies an unspoiled region of breathtakingly beautiful mountains, alpine lakes, and fast-running rivers. Much of the region is part of the protected Triglavski Narodni Park (Triglav National Park), and it's the perfect jumping-off spot for adventure pursuits of all sorts. Superior skiing, hiking, rafting, biking, and fly-fishing draw people here from around the world.

Each of the major towns and resorts in the region—Bled, Bohinj, Kranjska Gora, and Bovec—offers something a little different. At Bled the focus is on comfort and excellent facilities, poised against a fairy-tale backdrop of an island church in a green-blue lake. Bohinj's charms are more rustic—a pristine deep-green alpine sea, bordered by mountains on three sides. Kranjska Gora and Bovec offer more immediate access to high-octane adventure. The former is Slovenia's leading ski resort. In summer it opens its lifts to mountain bikers and free-riders seeking the adrenaline rush of a dash down the slopes. Bovec, on the Soča river, offers world-class rafting and canyoning—or gentler floats—down what must be one of the world's most beautiful mountain streams.

These regional centers can be approached individually or, in summer, by car or bus as part of a large loop running northwest from Ljubljana. Proceed first to Bled and on to Bohinj, then push on further north to Kranjska Gora, over the impossibly high Vršic pass, and down to Bovec. The return to Ljubljana is via the World War I battle town of Kobarid and Idrija.

en route

On the road to Bled from Ljubljana you pass a junction for Radovljica. Turn off here to see the lovingly preserved 17th-century town center and visit the intriguing **Čebelarski muzej** (Beekeeping Museum) (⊠ Linhartov trg 1, Radovljica ☎ 04/532-0520 ⊡ SIT 500 ⊙ May–Aug., Tues.–Sun. 10–1 and 4–6; Sept. and Oct., Tues.–Sun. 10–noon and 3–5; Mar., Apr., Nov., and Dec., Wed. and weekends 10–noon and 3–5)

Numbers in the margin correspond to numbers on the Triglav National Park and the Soča Valley map.

Bled

28 *50 km (31 mi) northwest of Ljubljana on the E61.*

Bled is among the most magnificently situated mountain resorts in Europe. The healing powers of its thermal springs were known during the 17th century. In the early 19th century the aristocracy arrived to bask in Bled's tranquil alpine setting. Even today—when Bled can swell to overflowing in the high season of July and August—it retains something of the refined feel of a *fin-de-siècle* spa town.

Recent years have brought a string of improvements to Bled's tourist facilities. New resorts and wellness centers, arguably the country's best golf course, and a clutch of new adventure-oriented travel agencies mean there is now much more to do than simply stroll the banks of the lake. Bled is also an excellent base for hikes into the eastern half of Triglav National Park.

Blejsko Jezero (Lake Bled) is nestled within a rim of mountains and surrounded by forests, with a castle on one side and a promenade beneath stately chestnut trees on the other. Horse-drawn carriages clip-clop along the promenade while swans glide on the water. On a minuscule island in the middle of the lake the lovely **Cerkov svetega Martina** (St. Martin's Pilgrimage Church) stands within a circle of trees. Take a ride over to the island on a *pletna,* an old-fashioned canopied wooden boat similar to a Venetian gondola.

The stately 16th-century **grad** (castle) perches above the lake on the summit of a steep cliff, against a backdrop of the Julian Alps and Triglav Peak. You can climb up to the castle for fine views of the lake, the resort, and the surrounding countryside. An exhibition traces the development of the castle through the centuries, with objects from archaeological finds to period furniture on display. ⊠ *Bled* ☎ *04/578–0525* ☜ *SIT 1,200* ⊙ *May.–Sept., daily 8–8; Oct.–Apr., daily 9–5.*

> **need a break?**
>
> Even if you're not staying at the illustrious **Grand Hotel Toplice** (⊠ C. Svobode 20 ☎ 04/579–1000), you're welcome to use its sauna and soak in the thermal waters (28°C [83°F]) of the indoor swimming pool. A small admission fee includes a towel and locker. Or try the Toplice's wellness center for various massage treatments, facials, and the tantalizingly labeled "citrus body sensation" (a full-body massage with orange and lemon balm).

The **Soteska Vintgar** (Vintgar Gorge) was cut between precipitous cliffs by the clear Radovna River, which flows down numerous waterfalls and through pools and rapids. The marked trail through the gorge leads over bridges and along wooden walkways and galleries. ⊠ *Zgornje Gorje Rd., 5 km (3 mi) northwest of Bled.*

Where to Eat

★ **$$$** ✕ **Gostilna Lectar.** This warm country-style inn serves an impressive selection of traditional dishes. For a cross-section of the local cuisine, try the pumpkin soup, the Peasant's Plate (buckwheat dumplings, mixed smoked meats, potatoes, and fresh steamed vegetables), and the apple strudel. The restaurant is 10 km (5½ mi) south of Bled on the E61 highway. ⊠ *Linhartov trg 2, Radovljica* ☎ *04/537–4800* ▭ *AE, DC, MC, V.*

$$ ✕ **Gostilna pri Planincu.** This friendly place is busy year-round. Locals meet here for morning coffee or a bargain prix-fixe lunch—or just to drink the cheapest beer in town. While rowdy farmers occupy the front bar, lovers share a candlelit supper in the dining room. Portions are "for people who work all day": roast chicken and fries, steak and mushrooms, black pudding, and turnips. For dessert, walnut *štrukli* (dumplings) are served with cream. ⊠ *Grajska 8* ☎ *04/574–1613* ▭ *AE, DC, MC, V.*

$$ ✕ **Mlino.** Follow the footpath along the south side of the lake 20 minutes from the center of Bled to reach this informal family restaurant with a lovely garden terrace. Try the Mlino Plate, a mixed platter of barbecued meats served with *djevec* (rice cooked with vegetables). There is a special menu for children, and boats are for hire on the lake. ⊠ *C. Svobode 45* ☎ *04/574–1404* ▭ *AE, DC, MC, V.*

$–$$ ✕ **Pletna.** An informal pizzeria not far from Mlino has excellent pizzas, very good grilled meats, and a second-story terrace with a lovely view over the lake. Follow the footpath along the south side of the lake about 15 minutes from the center of Bled. ⊠ *C. Svobode 37* ☎ *04/576–7211* ⊟ *AE, DC, MC, V.*

Where to Stay

$$$–$$$$ ⌂ **Vila Bled.** Late Yugoslav president Tito was the gracious host to numerous 20th-century statesmen at this former royal residence, amid 13 acres of gardens overlooking the lake. It was converted into a luxurious hotel in 1984 and became part of the Relais & Châteaux group in 1987. After a renovation in 2004, the managers wisely chose to retain many of the original furnishings from the 1950s—giving the rooms and public areas a formal but still retro-chic feel. It's unique. ⊠ *C. Svobode 26, 4260* ☎ *04/579–1500* ⊟ *04/574–1320* ⊕ *www.vila-bled.com* ⟿ *10 rooms, 20 suites* ⌂ *Restaurant, golf privileges, tennis court, lake, hair salon, boating, spa, bar, shop, meeting rooms* ⊟ *AE, DC, MC, V* ⦿ *BP.*

★ **$$$**   ⌂ **Grand Hotel Toplice.** This old-fashioned, ivy-covered resort hotel has been favored by British travelers since the 1920s. Directly on the lake, the main building has balconies and big windows from which you can take in dramatic views of the castle and the Julian Alps. The rooms, lounges, and bar are all furnished with antiques and heirloom rugs. It's worth the splurge for a lakeside room. ⊠ *C. Svobode 20, 4260* ☎ *04/579–1000* ⊟ *04/574–1841* ⊕ *www.hotel-toplice.com* ⟿ *206 rooms* ⌂ *3 restaurants, cable TV, indoor pool, gym, hot tub, massage, sauna, bar, meeting room* ⊟ *AE, DC, MC, V* ⦿ *BP.*

$ ⌂ **Bledec Youth Hostel.** Just 5 minutes from the lake and 10 minutes from the castle, Bledec is one of the cleanest and most comfortable youth hostels in Europe. Rooms have mostly three or four beds; there are no private double rooms or private baths. ⊠ *Grajska 17, 4260* ☎ *04/574–5250* ⊟ *04/574–5251* ⊕ *www.mlino.si* ⟿ *13 rooms with shared bath* ⌂ *Restaurant, bar, Internet room; no a/c* ⊟ *MC* ⊗ *Closed Nov.* ⦿ *BP.*

Sports & the Outdoors

During summer, the lake turns into a family playground, with swimming, rowing, sailing, and windsurfing. The main swimming area lies below the castle along the northern shore. In winter on Straža Hill, immediately above town, you can ski day and night, thanks to floodlighting. Just 10 km (6 mi) west of Bled, a larger ski area, Zatrnik, has 7 km (4 mi) of alpine trails. The area's two golf courses—the 18-hole "Kings" course and the 9-hole "Lake" course—are located 4 km (2 mi) outside of town at the Golf & Country Club Bled. For information on winter and summer sports, contact Bled's tourist-information center or one of the many private travel and activity agencies around town.

Bled Rafting (⊠ Hrastova 2, Bled ☎ 041/678–008 ⊕ www.bled-rafting. si) specializes in rafting, kayaking, and canyoning trips on area rivers. **Golf & Country Club Bled** (⊠ Kidričeva 10c, Bled ☎ 04/537–7711 ⊕ www. golf.bled.si) runs the area's two golf courses; rents clubs, caddies and carts; provides instruction, and sanctions golf events. **3glav Adventures** (⊠ Ljubljanska 1, Bohinj ☎ 041/683–184 ⊕ www.explore-more.com) is a great young outfit that can put together hiking and rafting outings, or organize more extreme activities like parachuting and paragliding.

Bohinjsko Jezero

29 *25 km (17 mi) southwest of Bled, 75 km (45 mi) from Ljubljana.*

Bohinjsko Jezero (Lake Bohinj) lies to the south and west of Bled along a crowded two-lane highway that thins out the further you travel from Bled. If you're driving, follow the signs to "jezero" (lake). The lake area proper begins in the small lakeside village of Ribčev Laz.

Lake Bohinj is quieter, wilder and in many ways prettier than Bled, its sister lake to the east. Unlike Bled, Bohinj lies entirely within the Triglav National Park. This has greatly inhibited development of the shore and surrounding areas. The entire length of the north shore is wild and accessible only by foot. The lake, at an altitude of 1,715 feet, is surrounded on three sides by the steep walls of the Julian Alps. The altitude means the temperature of the water—even in August—rarely rises above a brisk but still swimmable 74 degrees.

There is no town called "Bohinj" as such. The small village of Ribčev Laz, on the eastern end of the lake functions as the de facto town center, where you'll find a grocery store, post office, currency exchange, an ATM, and the tourist-information center. On the western shore lies the remote village of Ukanc, anchored by the Hotel Zlatorog, a campsite, and a few small shops. Just to the north and east of Ribčev Laz are the tiny hamlets of Stara Fužina, Studor, and Srednja Vas. Addresses are simple enough when you figure out what they mean: the name of the village is first, followed by the house or building number; administratively, "Bohinjsko Jezero" is treated as the "town."

On the eastern bank of Lake Bohinj in Ribčev Laz, you'll find the 15th-century Gothic church of **Sveti Janez** (St. John). The small church has a fine bell tower and contains a number of notable 15th- and 16th-century frescoes. The church was closed for repairs at the time of this writing, but it was expected to reopen sometime in 2006. ⊠ *Ribčev Laz.*

At the west end of Lake Bohinj near Ukanc a cable car leads up **Mt. Vogel** to a height of 5,035 feet. From here, you have spectacular views of the Julian Alps massif and the Bohinj valley and lake. From the cable-car base, the road continues 5 km (3 mi) beyond the lake to the point where the Savica River makes a tremendous leap over a 59-meter (195-foot) waterfall. The cable car runs year-round from 8 AM until 6 PM (until 7 PM in July and August). A round-trip ticket costs SIT 1,600.

Gasoline-powered engines are not allowed on Lake Bohinj because of the danger of pollution. The super quiet **Turistična Ladja** (Tourist Boat) runs on electrical power. The boat makes hourly runs during daylight hours from June to mid-September from the boat dock just below Ribčev Laz to Camp Zlatorog on the western side of the lake and back. A ticket costs SIT 1,000 each way.

Where to Eat

Most of the hotels and pensions in the area offer full or least half-board, reducing the number of independent restaurants. That's not to say there aren't places worth searching out. And pension food can sometimes become monotonous, so there may be afternoons or evenings when you want to strike out on your own anyway.

★ $$ ✕ **Gostilna Rupa.** Excellent home-cooked meals and a breathtaking view off the terrace toward the valley and the mountains beyond are your reward for an easy 5-km (3-mi) drive or bike ride from Ribičev Laz to the tiny hamlet of Srednja Vas. If you're really hungry, order the house specialty *mavželj* (essentially spiced ground beef and pork, breaded and fried); it comes served with buckwheat dumplings, sauerkraut, and potatoes. You won't need dessert. On Thursday in warm weather there's a pig roast. ✉ *Srednja Vas 87* ☎ *04/572–3401* ▬ *AE, DC, MC, V.*

$$ ✕ **Pizzerija Center.** About the only option in the main commercial center, Ribčev Laz, for a quick lunch or dinner, this place serves agreeable enough pizzas, but try the grilled lake fish (*charr*) if you see it on the menu—it's a local treat. ✉ *Ribčev Laz 50* ☎ *04/572–3170* ▬ *AE, DC, MC, V.*

$ ✕ **Planšar.** This tiny, informal eatery in the tiny village of Stara Fužina— just down from Ribčev Laz—is something of a local institution and one of the few places to sample the area's cheeses—hard and soft. Mix and match cheese and dumpling plates, or go for a hot, filling soup. For dessert, it's *štrukli* (dumplings) served with cream. ✉ *Stara Fužina 179* ☎ *04/ 572–3095* ▬ *AE, DC, MC, V.*

Where to Stay

The Bohinj area is the perfect place to bypass the hotels and stay in a private home or pension. The tourist-information center in Ribčev Laz maintains an extensive list. Pensions are usually priced per person and often include lunch or dinner. Some of the nicest properties are in the outlying villages of Ukanc, Stara Fužina, and Srednja Vas—though you'll need your own transportation (bike or car) to get there.

$$ ▦ **Villa Park.** A luxurious little A-frame pension sits astride an impossibly gorgeous Alpine meadow and just beside the bright-green Savica stream that feeds Lake Bohinj. Hardwood floors, tasteful furnishings, and full modern conveniences put this head and shoulders above the typical offerings. The entrance is down a tiny road just beyond the Zlatorog Hotel in Ukanc. ✉ *Ukanc 129, 4265* ☎ *04/572–3300* ⊕ *www. vila-park.com* ⇥ *10 rooms* ⌂ *Restaurant, in-room safes, cable TV, in-room data ports, sauna, bar, meeting room* ▬ *AE, DC, MC, V* ⦿ *BP.*

↻ $ ▦ **Hotel Zlatorog.** A very likable, guest-friendly alpine-style hotel stands on the far western edge of the lake. The facilities—including an indoor pool, sauna, and proximity to the ski lifts—make it a great winter choice. The large lawn and on-site playground are perfect for families with young children. Even if you're not staying here, you can rent bikes or use the hotel's two tennis courts (SIT 1,100 an hour). Rooms are divided between the main hotel and an adjoining villa. ✉ *Ukanc 65, 4265* ☎ *04/572–3381* ⊕ *www.alpinum.net* ⇥ *43 rooms, 31 villa rooms* ⌂ *Restaurant, minibars, cable TV, 2 tennis courts, indoor pool, sauna, bicycles, bar, playground, meeting room* ▬*AE, DC, MC, V* ⦿ *BP.*

$ ▦ **Pension Stare.** This delightful family-run pension is on the far western end of the lake in the tiny hamlet of Ukanc. To find it, continue beyond the Hotel Zlatorog, down a tiny lane and over a plank bridge. The young couple who own it will greet you with a glass of wine or beer on the terrace. It's very popular, so book in advance. ⊠ *Ukanc 128, 4265* ☎ *04/574–6400* ⊕ *www.national-park-hotel.com* ⬎ *10 rooms* ♿ *Restaurant; no a/c, no room TVs* ☰ *AE, DC, MC, V* ◉| *BP.*

¢ ⊡ **Hotel Bellevue.** Off the beaten track, high above Ribčev Laz, this 1930s-era alpine lodge nevertheless affords wonderful views of the lake. Be sure to request a lake-side room. Agatha Christie apparently fell in love with the hotel and stayed here for a month in 1967 on a working holiday. The hotel has set up an Agatha Christie reading room, complete with mini-library and typewriter. ⊠ *Ribčev Laz 65, 4265* ☎ *04/572–3331* 🖷 *04/572–3684* ⊕ *www.alpinum.net* ⬎ *76 rooms* ♿ *Restaurant, cable TV, tennis court, volleyball, bar, meeting room* ☰ *AE, DC, MC, V* ◉| *BP.*

Sports & the Outdoors

Bohinj is a natural base for exploring the trails of the Triglav National Park. Before heading out, pick up a good trail map from the tourist-information center. The cable car to Vogel is an excellent starting point for many of the walks. Just remember to get an early start, wear proper hiking boots, take plenty of water, and protect yourself against the sun. Other popular warm-weather pursuits include swimming, biking, rafting, canyoning, and horseback riding. In winter you can ski at the ski areas of Vogel and Kobla.

Alpinsport (⊠ Ribčev Laz 53 ☎ 04/572–3486 ⊕ www.alpinsport.si), in the village of Studor, rents mountain bikes and organizes raft, kayak, hydrospeed (a small board for bodysurfing rapids), and canyoning trips. **Perfect Adventure Choice/PAC Sports** (⊠ Ribčev Laz 50 ☎ 04/574–6511 ⊕ www.pac-sports.com) is another local outfitter offering river trips and ♻ rafting, as well as bike rental and caving expeditions. **Mrcina Ranč** (⊠ Studor, Bohinj ☎ 041/790–297 ⊕ www.bombagroup.com) organizes horseback rides in and around Bohinj and the Triglav National Park to suit all skill levels. It's open year-round.

Kranjska Gora

③⓪ *39 km (24 mi) northwest of Bled, 85 km (51 mi) from Ljubljana.*

Kranjska Gora, amid Slovenia's highest and most dramatic peaks, is the country's largest ski resort. In summer, the area attracts hiking and mountaineering enthusiasts. It's a pleasant town in any season. The resorts spread out along the perimeter, leaving the surprisingly charming core intact.

Where to Eat

★ $$ ✗ **Gostilna pri Martinu.** This beautifully appointed traditional gostilna has excellent home-cooking. Try the homemade sausages or a local favorite, *telecja obara* (veal stew). ⊠ *Borovška 61* ☎ *04/582–0300* ☰ *AE, DC, MC, V.*

$$ ✗ **Papa Joe.** *The* place to party during ski season serves excellent drinks and decent pizzas and sandwiches. The real draw is the late-night closing time; in season, Papa Joe doesn't close its doors until 5 AM. ⊠ *Borovška 86* ☎ *04/588–1526* ☰ *AE, DC, MC, V.*

$ ✗ **Bar Planet.** The cute, laid-back place is just off the main square, and it's perfect for a morning coffee and a light roll or sandwich. ⊠ *Borovška 77* ☎ *No phone* ▭ *No credit cards.*

Where to Stay

Most of Kranskja Gora's hotels are relatively large and were built during the 1970s and '80s to accommodate ski groups. The tourist-information center can help you find smaller properties, pensions, and private rooms if you are looking for something simpler and cheaper.

$–$$ ▥ **Hotel Larix.** A large, modern hotel, similar in price and appearance to the Hotel Kompass across the street, the Larix is cheerier and offers better facilities. These include a large indoor pool, sauna, and wellness center. The location is right next to the main ski lifts on the slopes. Even if you're not staying here, you can pay to use the pool and sauna. ⊠ *Borovška 99* ☎ *04/588–4100* 🖷 *04/588–4479* ⊕ *www.htp-gorenjka. si* ➬ *120 rooms* ♨ *3 restaurants, cable TV, indoor pool, gym, sauna, spa, bar, casino, meeting rooms* ▭ *AE, DC, MC, V* ⦿ *BP.*

★ **$** ▥ **Hotel Kotnik.** This charming little pastel yellow inn is just a few minutes' stroll from the central square and has a well-informed reception desk. Traditionally furnished rooms are simple but fine for a short stay. Oven-fired pizzas are served in the adjoining restaurant. ⊠ *Borovška 75, Kranjska Gora* ☎ *04/588–1564* 🖷 *04/588–1859* ⬧ *kotnik@siol. net* ➬ *15 rooms* ♨ *Restaurant, room service, cable TV, meeting room* ▭ *AE, DC, MC, V* ⦿ *BP.*

Sports & the Outdoors

Skiing is the number-one sport in Kranjska Gora. There are more than 30 km (20 mi) of downhill runs, 20 ski lifts, and 40 km (25 mi) of groomed cross-country trails open during the winter ski season, which typically runs from mid-December through mid-March. During summer, from late May through mid-September, mountain biking is big, and you'll find plenty of places to rent bikes, as well as 12 marked trails covering 150 km (93 mi) to take you through scented pine forests and spectacular alpine scenery. An unused railway track, tracing the south edge of the Karavanke Alps, brings hikers and bikers all the way to the village of Jesenice, about 20 km (12 mi) away. The Kranjska Gora Bike Park is oriented more toward experienced free-riders and thrill-seekers—those who like to take their bikes to the top of the hill and careen back down. There are also numerous hiking trails; you can pick up a good local trail map from the tourist-information center or at kiosks around town.

Fun Bike Park Kranjska Gora (⊠ Borovška 103, Kranjska Gora ☎ 031/ 499–499 ⊕ www.kranjskagora.mtbpark.si) rents full- and front-suspension mountain bikes for use along downhill mountain and forest trails. The emphasis here is on fast, adrenaline-filled rides. Lifts are open from May through the third week of September.

Kranjska Gora Recreational Ski Center (⊠ Borovška 103, Kranjska Gora ☎ 04/588–1414 ⊕ www.rtc-zicnice-kranjskagora.si) runs the lifts and is the main center for skiing information. The Web site—though mostly in Slovenian—lists prices in English and has a live Web cam so that you can see the conditions.

Sport Bernik (✉ Borovška 88a, Kranjska Gora ☎ 04/588–1470) is a full-service sports-equipment rental center, with both skis and mountain bikes in their respective seasons. It's located close to the ski center.

en route

From Kranjska Gora, head south over the breathtaking **Vršič Pass,** some 1,601 meters (5,252 feet) above sea level. You'll then descend into the beautiful Soča Valley, winding through the foothills to the west of Triglav Peak and occasionally plunging through tunnels. From Trenta, continue west for about 20 km (13 mi) to reach the mountain adventure resort of Bovec.

In Trenta, you'll find the Triglav National Park Information Center at **Dom Trenta** (✉ Na Logu v Trenti, Trenta ☎ 05/388–9330). Here, you can watch a presentation about the history and geography of the region and tour the small museum. It's a also a good access point to the 20-km (12-mi) Soča Trail that winds its way along the river's banks. The center is open from April through October, daily from 10 to 6.

Bovec

③ *35 km (22 mi) south of Kranjska Gora, 124 km (74 mi) from Ljubljana.*

Bovec is a friendly, relaxed, youth-oriented town that owes its modern existence largely to the adventure tourism possibilities afforded by the Soča River. The center is filled with private travel agencies, all offering a similar array of white-water rafting, kayaking, canoeing, hydrospeeding, and canyoning trips. The Soča—by the time it reaches Bovec—is a world-class river that regularly plays host to international rafting events. The main tour operators are experienced, and the rafting trips are aimed at all levels of experience. The river is at its best in spring, swelled by the melting snow caps. But it is raftable throughout the summer. Even if you don't decide to ride, plan a walk along the Soča's banks—the emerald green or electric blue (depending on the glint of the sun) color of the water must be seen to be believed.

Where to Eat

With its emphasis on sport, Bovec is not exactly teeming with great places to eat. Nevertheless there are a couple of central gostilnas that serve basic food, and the hotel restaurants are decent as well.

$$ ✕ **Gostilna Sovdat.** A clean and family-run inn serves basic pork and other meat dishes, Wiener schnitzel, and several pasta entrées. Open-air seating is in the back. ✉ *Trg Golobarskih Žrtev 24* ☎ *05/388–6027* ⊟ *AE, DC, MC, V.*

$ ✕ **Gostišče Vančar.** This charmingly rustic guest house about 3 km (2 mi) outside of Bovec is in the small village of Čezsoča. The restaurant is very popular with locals from the neighborhood, and the portions are huge. The house also has six very clean and comfortable rooms to let. ✉ *Čezsoča 43, Čezsoča* ☎ *05/389–6076* ⊟ *No credit cards.*

Where to Stay

$ ⊡ **Alp.** This1970s-era hotel has been modernized and remains in good shape. The rooms are clean and functional. The location is central, just a couple steps away from the main activities agencies and tourist office. Guests can use the Hotel Kanin swimming pool. ⊠ *Trg Golobarskih Žrtev 48* ☎ *05/388–4000* 🖷 *05/388–4002* 🛏 *103 rooms* ⌂ *Restaurant, pool, cable TV, bar* ⊟ *AE, DC, MC, V* ⦿⧚ *BP.*

$ ⊡ **Hotel Dobra Vila.** A welcome high-end addition to the local lodging scene is a lovingly restored, early-20th-century telephone exchange building. The owners added a wine cellar, a top-class restaurant, a reading room, and lovely public areas. The rooms and bath facilities have period fittings. ⊠ *Mala vas 112* ☎ *05/389–6400* 🖷 *05/389–6404* ⊕ *www.dobra-vila-bovec.com* 🛏 *12 rooms* ⌂ *Restaurant, minibars, cable TV, Internet room, wine bar, cinema, library, laundry service* ⊟ *AE, DC, MC, V* ⦿⧚ *BP.*

Sports & the Outdoors

White-water rafting is not the only game in town. Bovec is a great base for leisurely cycling trips or more aggressive mountain-bike climbs. Private bike outfitters or the tourist-information center can provide maps and advice. It's also a great base for hiking the western regions of the Triglav National Park. The map *Bovec z Okolico* is available at the tourist-information center and kiosks around town; it marks out several good walks and bike trips of varying degrees of difficulty.

Alpe Šport Vančar (⊠ Trg Golobarskih Žrtev 28 ☎ 05/389–6350 ⊕ www.bovecsport.com) arranges rafting, kayaking, and canyoning trips of all types as well as paragliding. It is well-regarded locally. **Outdoor Freaks** (⊠ Klanc 9a ☎ 041/553–675 ⊕ www.freakoutdoor.com) rents high-quality Cult mountain bikes and is a good source for local riding and trail information. **Soča Rafting** (⊠ Trg Golobarskih Žrtev 48 ☎ 05/389–6200 ⊕ www.socarafting.si) is one of the better-known rafting and kayaking outfitters.

Kobarid

32 *21 km (13 mi) from Bovec, 115 km (71 mi) from Ljubljana.*

From Bovec the road follows the Soča River south, running parallel with the Italian border, to pass through the pretty market town of Kobarid.

It's hard to believe now that this idyllic scene was home to some of the bloodiest mountain battles ever fought. In 1917—toward the end of World War I—the combined forces of the Austrian and German armies launched a surprise offensive to try to dislodge Italian forces holding Kobarid and the surrounding Soča Valley. The battle raged on as hundreds of thousands were killed under appalling conditions on both sides. In the end, the Italians retreated and were almost knocked out of the war. "Caporetto"—Kobarid's Italian name—became synonymous throughout Italy with shame and defeat.

Fodor'sChoice In the center of Kobarid, the **Kobariški muzej** (Kobarid Museum) has a ★ fascinating exhibition of the fighting, including diaries of the soldiers

CloseUp
SLOVENIA AND HEMINGWAY?

THE AMERICAN WRITER ERNEST HEMINGWAY
is not someone you normally associate
with Slovenia. His terrain usually runs
more to bullfights and elephant hunts and
the intellectual circles of Paris in the
1920s. Yet Hemingway spent some of the
most impressionable months of his life in
the town of Kobarid during World War I.
At the time, he was a volunteer ambulance
driver for the Italian army. Kobarid—or
Caporetto in Italian—was an eastern
garrison town for the Italians, who were
trying to push their way north and east
into Austria-Hungary. The battles—pitting
the Italians on one side against the
combined forces of the Austrian and
German armies—were some of the
bloodiest of the war. The great offensive of
October 1917, when the Austrians and

Germans finally knocked Italy out of the
region and out of the war, cost both sides
hundreds of thousands of lives.
Hemingway later drew on his experiences
here for the novel A Farewell to Arms, and
the book is worth re-reading for its moving
depictions of the region and the war. The
excellent Kobarid museum includes an
emotional tape-recording of some of
Hemingway's observations—alongside
diary notations from ordinary soldiers—of
the unimaginable horrors of those days.
The title of Hemingway's book could serve
as the region's motto today. The Soča
River valley draws thousands of Italian,
German, and Austrian tourists each year,
showing that within just two generations
the hatreds that unleashed such horrific
fighting have been buried.

involved. The museum also gives a 20-minute video presentation—with projections, sound effects, and narration in English.

The **Kobarid Historical Walk** takes you on a 5-km (3-mi) hike through lovely countryside, over a hair-raising bridge, and past a spectacular waterfall. You'll follow the former front line and visit various sites related to World War I along the way. The path is clearly marked, and a self-guiding pamphlet and map are available at the Kobarid Museum. ⊠ *Gregorčičeva 10* ☎ *05/389–0000* ⊕ *www.kobariski-muzej.si* ⊠ *SIT 900* ☉ *Daily 9–7.*

Where to Stay & Eat

$–$$$ ✕🏠 **Hotel Hvala.** This delightful family-run hotel is possibly one of the
Fodor'sChoice   most welcoming places you'll ever stay. The excellent hotel restaurant,
★   Restauracija Topli Val—easily the best in the area—serves local trout and freshwater crayfish, as well as mushrooms and truffles in season. Italians drive over the border just to eat here. ⊠ *Trg Svobode 1, 5222* ☎ *05/389–9300* 🖷 *05/388–5322* ⊕ *www.topli-val-sp.si* ▭ *28 rooms, 4 suites* ⟁ *Restaurant* ▭ *AE, DC, MC, V* �ㅣⓄⅠ *BP.*

Sports & the Outdoors

The Soča is a prime fishing spot. The river is well stocked with marble trout, rainbow trout, and grayling. However, if you want to fish, bring your own equipment—or be prepared to buy it here—as it is almost impossible to rent. You also need to buy a day permit; for details inquire at Hotel Hvala. The season runs from April through October.

X Point (⊠ Stresova 1 ☎ 05/388–5308) organizes kayaking, rafting, and canyoning trips and also rents out mountain bikes. In Srpenica, 13 km (8 mi) northwest of Kobarid, **Alpine Action** (⊠ Trnovo ob Soči, Srpenica ☎ 05/388–5022) arranges river trips and rents bikes.

Idrija

③③ *50 km (31 mi) from Kobarid, 60 km (37 mi) from Ljubljana.*

Proceed south from Kobarid, passing through the town of Tolmin and on to Idrija, a former mercury-mining town with some interesting sites, excellent food, and one of the country's most beautiful old hotels. Idrija is also known for its handmade lace.

Head to **Anthony's Shaft** to see the oldest part of the mercury mine, the miners' chapel dating back to the 18th century, and a video about the way the miners once lived. ⊠ *Kosovelova 3* ☎ *05/377–1142* ⊙ *Tours weekdays at 10 and 4; weekends at 10, 3, and 4.*

Where to Eat

★ **\$\$** ✕ **Gostilna Kos.** This old-fashioned inn reputedly serves some of the best *Idrijski žlikrofi* (tortellini filled with potato, onion, and smoked pork) around. You can have yours served as a side with roast pork or goulash, or as a main course served plain or topped with sauce. ⊠ *Tomšičeva 4* ☎ *05/372–2030* ⊟ *AE, DC, MC, V.*

Where to Stay

\$\$ 🏠 **Kendov Dvorec.** This exclusive 14th-century manor house is in Spod-
Fodor's Choice nje Idrija, 4 km (2½ mi) from Idrija. Each bedroom is individually dec-
★ orated with 19th-century antiques and details such as bed linens edged with local handmade lace. Reserve a room well in advance because the reputation of this hotel keeps it full. The restaurant is not open to the public, but the owners will prepare a special meal if you phone ahead. ⊠ *Spodnje Idrija, 5280* ☎ *05/372–5100* 🖷 *05/375–6475* ⊕ *www.kendov-dvorec.com* 🛏 *11 rooms* ᗡ *Restaurant, minibars, cable TV, in-room data ports, meeting rooms* ⊟ *AE, DC, MC, V* ᝍ❘ *BP.*

Shopping

Numerous boutiques sell *Idrijska čipka* (Idrija lace). For the most original designs try **Studio Irma Vončina** (⊠ Mestni trg 17 ☎ 05/377–1584). It's open weekdays 10 to noon and 1 to 4, Saturday 10 to noon.

Alps & the Soča Valley Essentials

BUS TRAVEL

Hourly buses link Ljubljana to Bled, Bohinj, and Kranjska Gora. There are also several buses daily from Ljubljana through Idrija to Kobarid and on to Bovec. The resorts are linked by local buses; their frequency depends on the season. For schedule and fare information ask at a local tourist-information center.

CAR TRAVEL

From Ljubljana a four-lane highway (E61) runs northwest past Kranj and continues—occasionally reverting to a two-lane highway on some

CloseUp

THERE'S MORE TO ŽLIKROFI THAN MEETS THE EYE

SLOVENIAN COOKING MAY SEEM FAIRLY SIMPLE *at first, but there's often a lot more work that goes on behind the scenes than you might think. If you travel near the town of Idrija, look out especially for the delicious žlikrofi on many local menus. The pasta dish has been a regional specialty since the mid-1800s, when it was a favorite of hungry miners working the local mercury shafts. But don't be deceived by the relatively simple stuffed tortellini that arrive on your plate; rest assured a lot of effort went on in the kitchen beforehand. In fact, the process is so involved that a couple of years ago the Ministry of Tourism decided to set up a special certification process. Only inns and restaurants that abide by the rules can call their product authentic Idrija žlikrofi.*

So how to tell the echt from the fake? The ministry sets out the following: the filling must be a mix of potatoes, smoked bacon, onions, spice, and herbs. The filling is then formed into balls the size of a hazelnut and placed on a sheet of thin dough. The dough is folded over and pressed together between the balls so that, to quote, "a sort of ear shape is gained." The ministry also advises not to push the dough down too hard so as to leave the žlikrofi looking like they're wearing a little hat. The ministry doesn't say what the penalty is for the hapless gostilna that breaks the rules. Rest assured, however, that whatever shape your žlikrofi arrive in, they're likely to be delicious—served as a side or a main course with cheese or mushroom sauce.

stretches—to the resorts of Bled and Kranjska Gora. Lake Bohinj lies 25 km (15 mi) southwest of Bled along local highway 209. The Vrsic Pass, which connects Kranjska Gora and Bovec, is closed during the winter. If you want to go to Idrija, Kobarid, or Bovec from November to April you will have to approach them via the south.

TRAIN TRAVEL

In theory it is possible to reach the area from Ljubljana by train, but because Bled Jezero station lies some distance from Lake Bled, and Bohinjska Bistrica station lies even further from Lake Bohinj, it is simpler and quicker to take the bus.

From mid-June to mid-September ABC Rent-a-Car in Ljubljana arranges trips on an old-fashioned steam locomotive, following the Bohinj line, through the Soča Valley. The trip begins from Jesenice, stops in Bled and Bohinjska Bistrica, and finally brings you to Most na Soči. This is a very family-friendly excursion.

🚉 **ABC Rent-a-Car** ✉ Ulica Jožeta Jame 16, Ljubljana ☎ 01/510-4320.

VISITOR INFORMATION

🚉 **Bled Tourist Information** ✉ C. Svobode 15, Bled ☎ 04/574-1122 ⊕ www.bled.si. **Bohinj Tourist Information** ✉ Ribčev Laz 48, Bohinj ☎ 04/574-6010 ⊕ www.bohinj. si. **Idrija Tourist Information** ✉ Lapajnetova 7, Idrija ☎ 05/377-3898 ⊕ www.rzsidrija.si. **Kobarid Tourist Information** ✉ Gregorčičeva 10, Kobarid ☎ 05/389–9200 ⊕ www.kobarid.si. **Kranjska Gora Tourist Information** ✉ Tičarjeva 2, Kranjska Gora ☎ 04/588–1768 ⊕ www.kranjska-gora.si.

THE KARST & ADRIATIC COAST

As you move south and west from Ljubljana toward the Adriatic, the breeze feels warmer, the air smells fresher, and the landscape looks less and less like Austria and more and more like Italy.

The word "Karst," or in Slovenian *Kras,* is both a geological and geographic term referring to the large limestone plateau stretching roughly from Nova Gorica in the north to well beyond Divača in the south. It is bordered on the west by the Italian frontier and on the east by the fertile, wine-growing Vipava valley. The Karst is typified by sinkholes, underground caves, and streams. The region is dotted by caves, including two—Postojna and especially Škocjan—of jaw-dropping beauty and size.

To most Slovenians, the word "Karst," conjures up two things: *pršut* (air-dried ham) and blood-red Teran wine. The two pair beautifully, especially with a plate of cheese and a basket of homemade bread, taken at a traditional *osmica,* a small farmhouse restaurant. Teran is a strong wine made from the refosk grape that you will either love or loathe from the first sip. It takes its name from the *terra rossa,* or red soil, that typifies the Karst.

For visitors, the Karst is ideal for low-key exploration. The gentle terrain and the many wine roads (look for the sign that reads *vinska cesta*) are perfect for leisurely walks or bike rides. Several wine roads can be found in the area around the town of Komen and along the main road from Komen to Dutovlje. The pretty towns—with their old stone churches and red-tiled roofs—are a delight. If you have wheels, visit Stanjel to the east of Komen. It's a nearly abandoned hilltop village that's found new life as a haven for artists. The Lipica stud farm—the original breeding ground of the famed Lipizzaner horses of Vienna's Spanish Riding School—is an excellent base.

A little further on, Slovenia's tiny piece of the Adriatic coast gives tourists a welcome chance to swim and sunbathe. Backed by hills planted with olive groves and vineyards, the small strip is only 47 km (26 mi) long and dominated by the towns of Koper, Izola, Piran, and Portorož.

Following centuries of Venetian rule, the coast remains culturally and spiritually connected to Italy, and Italian is still widely spoken. The medieval port of Piran is a gem and a must-see. Its Venetian core is nearly perfectly preserved. Portorož is a classic fun-and-sun resort. Koper, Slovenia's largest port, and Izola, its biggest fishery, are workaday towns that nevertheless retain a lot of historical charm. For beachgoers the best-equipped beach is at Bernadin, between Piran and Portorož. The most unspoiled stretch of coast is at the Strunjan Nature Reserve—which also has an area reserved for nudists—between Piran and Izola.

Piran and Portorož are very different in character, but either can serve as an excellent base depending on what you plan to do. Choose Portorož if your primary interest is swimming and sunbathing, or if you're seeking a modern hotel with all of the amenities. Pick Piran if you're looking for something quainter, quieter and more starkly beautiful. Whatever you choose, you can travel easily between the two. Buses make the 10-minute trip at least once an hour in season.

Both Piran and Portorož fill to capacity in July and August, so try to arrange accommodation in advance. If you show up without a room, enquire at one of the privately run travel agencies. Along the coast, these are likely to be more helpful than the local tourist-information centers.

Numbers in the margin correspond to numbers on the Karst Region and the Adriatic Coast map.

Postojnska Jama

㉞ *44 km (27 mi) from Ljubljana.*

Postojnska Jama (Postojna Cave) conceals one of the largest networks of caves in the world, with 23 km (14 mi) of underground passageways. A miniature train takes you through the first 7 km (4 mi), to reveal a succession of well-lit rock formations. This strange underground world is home of the snakelike "human fish" on view in an aquarium in the Great Hall. Eyeless and colorless because of countless millennia of life in total darkness, these amphibians can live for up to 60 years. Temperatures average 8°C (46°F) year-round, so bring a sweater, even in summer. Tours leave every hour on the hour throughout the year. ⊠ *Jamska 30, Postojna* ☎ *05/700–0100* ⊕ *www.postojna-cave.com* ✉ *SIT 3,100* ⊙ *May–Sept., daily 8:30–6; Apr. and Oct., daily 8:30–5; Nov.–Mar., weekdays 9:30–1:30, weekends 9:30–3.*

Škocjanske Jame

⊛ *26 km (16 mi) from Postojna, 76 km (46 mi) from Ljubljana.*

C̆ The 11 interconnected chambers that make up the **Škocjan Jama** (Škocjanske Caves) stretch for almost 6 km (about 4 mi) through a dramatic, **Fodor's**Choice janske Caves) stretch for almost 6 km (about 4 mi) through a dramatic,
★ subterranean landscape so unique that UNESCO has named them a World Heritage Site. The 90-minute walking tour of the two chilly main chambers—the Silent Cave and the Murmuring Cave—winds past otherworldly dripstone sculptures, massive sinkholes, and stalactites and stalagmites that resemble the horns of some mythic creature. The highlight is Europe's largest cave hall, a gorge 146 meters (438 feet) high, 123 meters (369 feet) wide, and 300 meters (900 feet) long, spanned by a narrow bridge lit with footlights. Far below, the brilliant jade waters of the Reka River rush by on their underground journey. The view is nothing short of mesmerizing. ⊠ *Škocjan 2, Divača* ☎ *05/763–2840* ⊕ *www.gov.si/parkskj* ✉ *SIT 2,000* ⊙ *June–Sept., daily at 10, 11:30, and 1–5 (tours leave hrly); Apr., May, and Oct., tours daily at 10, 1, and 3:30; Nov.–Mar., tours at 10 and 1.*

Štanjel

⊛ *25 km (15 mi) from Divača (Škocjan Caves), 100 km (60 mi) from Ljubljana.*

Many consider this to be Slovenia's prettiest village. Certainly the setting is dramatic. **Štanjel Grad,** a rugged stone castle, and the gleaming white tower of the **Church of St. Daniel** pitched atop a steep rocky rise, are the major attractions. The village has been inhabited since medieval times, and its walled fortifications helped repel invasions by marauding Turks in the 15th century. But Štanjel was badly damaged in World War II, and much of the old village today stands empty.

There are strong signs Štanjel may be on the road to recovery. Artists have adopted part of the village and have converted some of the abandoned houses to studios. The castle terrace hosts regular musical events in warm weather. The adjoining gallery holds a permanent collection of the modern painter and graphic artist Lojze Spacal—a fascinating find for fans of the abstract and geometric art of the 1950s and '60s.

Aside from a small café on the castle terrace, the village itself has few facilities.

The major focus of tourism in the small village is **Štanjel Grad** (Štanjel Castle). The **Tourist Information Centre Štanjel** (☎ 05/769–0056) can advise on events and places to stay and eat, as well as help you arrange a guided walking tour through the village or the castle. The center is open when the castle is open for visitors. **Galerija L. Spacala** (☎ 05/769–0197) showcases the work of Lojze Spacal, one of Italy's leading graphic artists of the late 1950s and 60s, who adopted the Karst as his spiritual home. This small gallery includes some of his best work from the period as well as later designs. During the season, the gallery is open Tuesday and Friday through Sunday from 10 to 6. Admission is SIT 400. ☎ *05/769–0056 for Castle* ⊕ *www.komen.si* ☒ *Free* ☉ *May–Sept., Mon. and Wed.–Sat. 11–5, Sun. 2–6.*

Where to Eat

$$–$$$ ✗ **Pelicon.** This wonderful farm, now set up as an agrotourism center, serves homemade regional specialties such as *pršut* (cured ham) and salami, roast meats, gnocchi, and štrukli, all served with Teran wine. You'll find it near Komen, midway between Sežana and Nova Gorica (from Sežana, take the road north toward Štanjel, then at Dutovlje turn left and follow a narrow country road to Komen). ☒ *Coljava 5, Coljava* ☎ *05/766–8061* ☖ *Reservations essential* ☰ *No credit cards* ☉ *Closed weekdays.*

$ ✗ **Osmica Kmetija Kosmina.** One of a number of local *osmicas* in the area. These informal, farmer-run restaurants are perfect for a casual open-air lunch or dinner. Huge plates of *pršut,* sausage, salami, and cheese can be washed down with a jug of Teran wine. To find it, follow the road out of Komen to Gorjensko, and then follow the signs along a tiny road to Brje. It's open daily, from early to late (9 AM to 1 AM). ☒ *Brje pri Komnu* ☎ *05/766–7240* ☰ *No credit cards.*

Lipica

③⑦ *5 km (3 mi) west of Divača, 30 km (18 mi) south of Stanjel, 80 km (50 mi) from Ljubljana.*

Lipica is best known as the home of the *Kobilarna Lipica,* the Lipica Stud farm, where the fabled white Lipizzaner horses were first bred. The horse farm is still the primary reason most people come here, though the area has developed into a modern sports complex, with two hotels, a popular casino, an indoor pool, tennis courts, and an excellent 9-hole golf course. It makes a pleasant, hassle-free base for exploring the nearby Škocjan caves and Karst region. The horses, the large areas of green, and the facilities of the Hotel Maestoso—including a pool—are all great for families with children.

☾ The **Kobilarna Lipica** (Lipica Stud Farm) was founded in 1580 by the Austrian archduke Karl II. It's where the white Lipizzaners—the majestic horses of the famed Spanish Riding School in Vienna—originated. Today the farm no longer sends its horses to Vienna, but breeds them for its own performances and riding instruction. The impressive stables and grounds are open to the public. Riding classes are available, but lessons are geared toward experienced riders and must be booked in advance. ☒ *Lipica 5, Sežana, 6210* ☎ *05/739–1708* ⊕ *www.lipica.org* ☉ *Dres-*

sage performances June–Oct., Tues., Fri., and Sun. at 3. Stable tours July and Aug., daily 9–6; Apr.–June and Sept. and Oct., daily 10–5; Nov.–Mar., daily 11–3.

Where to Eat

$$$ ✕ **Gostilna Gombač.** Just down the street from the similar Muha, the only obvious difference between these two gostlinas is a pleasant terrace here for dining outdoors on a warm evening. The kitchen is most proud of its game—try the roast hare *zajec* served with a plate of *njoki* (gnocchi) and a glass of Union beer. ⊠ *Lokev 165, Lokev* ☎ *05/767–0466* ▤ *No credit cards.*

$$$ ✕ **Gostilna Muha.** A friendly, family-run tavern in the village of Lokev is about 4 km (2 mi) from the Lipica stud farm. Sit back and allow the proprietor to suggest the day's specialties. A good starter is *jota*, a thick soup of smoked pork, sauerkraut, and beans, followed by slow-roasted pork and a green salad topped with a spoonful of beans. ⊠ *Lokev 138, Lokev* ☎ *05/767–0055* ▤ *No credit cards.*

Where to Stay

$ ▤ **Hotel Maestoso.** The modern building dates from the 1970s, but nevertheless it's well-maintained and comfortable. The rooms are clean, all with modern bath facilities; some even have a terrace. The friendly reception desk can help you get your bearings. The equipment room on the side of the hotel will rent golf clubs and carts. The Hotel Klub—behind the Maestoso—rents bikes. ⊠ *Lipica 5* ☎ *05/739–1790* ▤ *05/734–6370* ⊕ *www.lipica.org* ⇆ *65 rooms* ♨ *Restaurant, minibars, cable TV, Internet room, tennis courts, indoor pool, 9-hole golf course, miniature golf, hair salon, casino, sauna, bar, meeting rooms* ▤ *AE, DC, MC, V* ❘◉❘ *BP.*

Koper

❸❽ *50 km (30 mi) southwest of Divača (Lipica), 105 km (63 mi) to Ljubljana.*

Today a port town surrounded by industrial suburbs, Koper nevertheless warrants a visit. The Republic of Venice made Koper the regional capital during the 15th and 16th centuries, and the magnificent architecture of the Old Town bears witness to the spirit of those times.

The most important buildings are clustered around **Titov trg,** the central town square. Here stands the **Cathedral,** which can be visited daily from 7 to noon and 3 to 7, with its fine Venetian Gothic facade and bell tower dating back to 1664. Across the square the splendid **Praetor's Palace,** formerly the seat of the Venetian Grand Council, combines Gothic and Renaissance styles. From the west side of Titov trg, the narrow, cobbled **Kidriceva ulica** brings you down to the seafront.

need a break? Stop for coffee or a glass of wine at **Loggia Cafe,** housed within the 15th-century Venetian Gothic loggia. In summer there are tables out on the terrace overlooking the town square. ⊠ *Titov trg 1* ☎ *05/621–3213.*

HRASTOVLJE – Hidden behind the 16th-century defensive walls of this small town is the tiny Romanesque **Cerkev sveti Trojice** (Church of the Holy Trinity). The interior is decorated with a remarkable series of frescoes, including the bizarre *Dance Macabre,* completed in 1490. The church is locked, but if you ask in the village the locals will be glad to open it for you. From Koper take the main road toward Ljubljana; then follow the signs for Hrastovlje (22 km [14 mi] from Koper).

Where to Eat

$$$ ✕ **Skipper.** Noted for its vast summer terrace overlooking the marina, Skipper is popular with the yachting fraternity. The menu includes pasta dishes, risottos, grilled meats, and fish. ⊠ *Kopališko nab 3* ☎ *05/627–1750* ▤ *AE, DC, MC, V.*

$–$$ ✕ **Marina.** This popular pizza place is just across from the Skipper on the port. Try the house specialty, pizza "Koper," a salty but irresistible mix of goat cheese, capers, and *pršut* ham. ⊠ *Kopališko nab 2* ☎ *05/627–1982* ▤ *No credit cards.*

Izola

39 *6 km (4 mi) from Koper, 112 km (67 mi) from Ljubljana.*

Izola is a normally placid fishing town that lets its hair down in summer. DJs decamp from Ljubljana for parties on the coast, artists set up their studios, and the city adopts the relaxed persona of a shaggy beach town. Less industrial than Koper and less self-consciously pretty than Piran, Izola makes a perfect day outing.

It's also a great place to eat. Unlike Piran, where the seafront restaurants cater almost exclusively to tourists, Izola's harbor restaurants are the real deal. The fish is fresh and the customers—many of them local Slovenes—are demanding.

Like that of its immediate neighbor, Koper, the city's history goes back hundreds of years. Izola rose to prominence in the Middle Ages and then declined in the 16th and 17th centuries with the rise of the port of Trieste in present-day Italy. The name Izola comes from the Italian word for "island" and describes a time when the walled city in fact was an island. The city walls were knocked down by the French occupation at the start of the 19th century. The bricks were then used to connect the city to the mainland.

There are few, if any, "must-sees" in Izola. Instead, take some time to stroll the pretty lanes of the old town and port.

Where to Eat

The best restaurants are situated along the marina. The restaurants fill quickly in the evenings, so go early to be assured of a table.

$$$ ✕ **Ribič.** This is the local favorite. The day's catch and prices are listed on a chalkboard out front. If in doubt, ask the server what looks good that day. You can be sure the fish is fresh, but watch the prices. The fish

are sold by weight, and you may end up paying more than you intended. ✉ *Veliki trg 3* ☎ *05/641–8313* ☰ *AE, DC, MC, V.*

Nightlife

During summer, the Adriatic coast becomes a haven for all-night parties. **Ambasada Gavioli** (✉ Izola ☎ 05/641–8212 ⊕ www.ambasada-gavioli.com) remains one of the coast's—and the country's—best dance clubs. Gavioli regularly brings in DJs from around the world to play techno, trance, funk, and fusion. You'll find it southwest of the port in the city's industrial area.

Sports & the Outdoors

You can rent yachts at the Izola marina from **Jonathon d.o.o.** (✉ Izola ☎ 05/677–8930). Prices vary depending on the season and the size of the yacht.

Portorož

🔟 *7 km (4 mi) from Izola, 124 km (75 mi) from Ljubljana.*

Portorož is the most popular of Slovenia's seaside resorts. The name—Port of Roses—recalls the time, a hundred years ago, when it was an exclusive haunt for Austro-Hungarian aristocrats. Those days, however, are long gone. Portorož today definitely caters to the the everyman. Here you'll find chock-a-block hotels, restaurants, bars, casinos and nightclubs—all of the things you associate with a modern package-holiday destination.

Portorož is difficult to grasp at first. The central area is small, while hotels and resorts spread out in all directions along the coast and the surrounding hills. Most of the action takes place along a small stretch of seacoast. Here you'll find the public beaches (which charge a small fee to swim), a pool, and a string of shops and low-priced eateries.

Where to Eat

$$–$$$ ✕ **Ribič.** Enjoy good fresh fish in a relaxed garden setting, 2 km (1 mi) down the coast from Portorož at Seča. ✉ *Seča 143, Seča* ☎ *05/677–0790* ☰ *AE, DC, MC, V* �)} *Closed Tues.*

Where to Stay

Staying in Portorož is expensive, but the hotel standards are high. Many hotels offer cheaper package deals when booked in advance. If you are looking for a cheaper option on accommodations, book a room through **Maona** (✉ Obala 14b, Portorož ☎ 05/674–0363 ⊕ www.maona.si), a local travel agency.

$$$ 🏨 **Grand Hotel Bernardin.** In a complex of three large, modern hotels, the Bernardin occupies a pretty and secluded bluff above the seashore. All modern amenities are here, including the area's only on-site convention center. The affiliated Hotel Histrion has a full-service wellness center and offers special packages. There's an attached water park. ✉ *Obala 2, 6320* ☎ *05/695–0000* ☒ *05/674–6410* ⊕ *www.h-bernardin.si* ➷*230 rooms, 19 suites* ♿ *2 restaurants, café, room service, minibars, cable TV, Internet room, indoor pool, gym, hair salon, spa, beach, bar, convention center, parking* ☰ *AE, DC, MC, V* ⭐◎⭐ *BP.*

$-$$ 🏨 **Grand Hotel Palace.** This modern seaside hotel is connected to the thermal-spa recreation center, which offers massages and medicinal treatments. Rooms are comfortable, and the service is professional. Three other hotels are adjacent in the same complex and interconnected, offering a similar level of service. This is the most expensive of the four. ✉ *Obala 43, 6320* ☎ *05/696–1025* 📠 *05/696–9003* ⊕ *www.hoteli-palace.si* ⤺ *189 rooms, 7 suites* ⚘ *2 restaurants, minibars, cable TV, 2 pools (1 indoor), spa, bar, parking (fee)* ▭ *AE, DC, MC, V* ⦿ *BP.*

Sports & the Outdoors
You can rent bikes at **Atlas Express** (✉ Obala 55 ☎ 05/674–8821).

Piran

41 *3 km (2 mi) from Portorož, 126 km (76 mi) from Ljubljana.*

The jewel of the Slovenian coast, the medieval walled Venetian town of Piran stands compact on a small peninsula, capped by a neo-Gothic lighthouse and presided over by a hilltop Romanesque cathedral. Narrow, winding, cobbled streets lead to the main square, Trg Tartini, which in turn opens out onto a charming harbor. Historically, Piran's wealth was based on salt-making. Culturally, the town is known as the birthplace of the 17th-century violinist and composer Giuseppe Tartini.

If you are arriving by car, don't even try to negotiate the tiny lanes around the harbor. Instead leave the car in the lot outside of town; the lot furthest out has the cheapest long-term rates. A shuttle bus will then take you into town.

☽ The **Sergej Mašera Pomorski muzej** (Sergej Mašera Maritime Museum) tells the story of Piran's connections with the sea. There is a beautiful collection of model ships, sailors' uniforms, and shipping instruments, and a fascinating historical section on the town's changing affiliations over the centuries. ✉ *Cankarjevo nab 3* ☎ *05/671–0040* ⊕ *www.portoroz.si* 🎟 *SIT 500* ⊙ *Maritime Museum Apr.–June and Nov.–Mar., Tues.–Sun. 9–noon and 3–6; July and Aug., Tues.–Sun. 9–noon and 6–9.*

Where to Eat
Piran's waterfront is filled with romantic, open-air restaurants. The quality of the food and the relatively high prices are pretty much uniform. The best advice is to stroll the walk and see which one appeals. Better food at better prices can be found away from the shore, though then you sacrifice the view.

$$$$ ✗ **Gostilnica.** The most intimate of the seafront restaurants is situated toward the end of the promenade. It's a good place to try the *rižota s škampi* (scampi risotto), or another favorite, *njoki s skampi in gorgonzola* (shrimp gnocchi with gorgonzola sauce). ✉ *Prešernovo nab* ☎ *05/673–2226* ▭ *AE, DC, MC, V.*

★ **$$$** ✗ **Neptun.** Highly regarded by the locals, this tiny, family-run place focuses on all manner of fish, grilled or fried. Try the grilled shrimp or calamari. In summer you can dine at tables along the quiet street. ✉ *Župančičeva 7* ☎ *05/673–4111* ▭ *No credit cards.*

Where to Stay

Piran only has a small number of hotels, and most visitors opt to stay in private rooms or pensions. In season, it's easiest and cheapest to book through the centrally located private travel agency **Maona** (✉ Cankarjevo nab 7, Piran ☎ 05/673–4520 🖷 05/673–4519 ⊕ www.maona.si), which offers doubles in private homes starting at around €50–€60 a night. The rate will be higher for stays of less than three nights. Ask for something central and look at the room before accepting; some rooms can be charming, others are just basic.

$–$$ 🏨 **Hotel Piran.** A modern building on a quiet patch of coastline close to the seaside restaurants, Hotel Piran is the best place to stay if a sea view is what you're after. Breakfast is served on a rooftop terrace, where you can enjoy stunning views of the Adriatic. ✉ *Kidričevo nab 4, 6330* ☎ *05/ 676–2502* 🖷 *05/676–2520* ⊕ *www.hoteli-piran.si* 🛏 *80 rooms, 10 suites* ♿ *Café, some minibars, cable TV, bar, Internet room, some pets allowed; no a/c* ☰ *AE, MC, V* ❙❂❙ *BP.*

★ $ 🏨 **Hotel Tartini.** An old facade hides a modern interior with a spacious central atrium. Most rooms have terraces that open out to views of the surrounding red-tiled roofs or the harbor. The location, overlooking Trg Tartini, is out of this world. If you can live without being on the seafront, this is your best option in town. ✉ *Trg Tartini 15, 6330* ☎ *05/671– 1000* 🖷 *05/671–1665* ⊕ *www.hotel-tartini-piran.com* 🛏 *43 rooms, 2 suites* ♿ *Restaurant, minibars* ☰ *AE, DC, MC, V* ❙❂❙ *BP.*

The Arts

Piran Musical Evenings are held in the cloisters of the Minorite Monastery every Friday in July and August. The **Primorski Summer Festival** of open-air theater and dance is staged in Piran, Koper, Portorož, and Izola.

The Karst & Adriatic Coast Essentials

BOAT TRAVEL

During summer, it is possible to reach the Slovenian coast by regularly scheduled ferry service from Italy.

BUS TRAVEL

Several buses a day connect Ljubljana to Koper, Piran, and Portorož, passing through Postojna and Divača on the way. There is also a daily service connecting the coastal towns to Trieste, Italy.

A network of local buses connects all listed sights, with the exception of those in Štanjel and Lipica. Schedules vary depending on the time of year, so contact a local bus station for information.

CAR TRAVEL

A car is advisable for touring the Karst region. However, parking can be a problem along the coast during summer, when town centers are closed to traffic. The E63 highway connects Ljubljana to the coast, passing through the Karst region en route.

TOURS

Adriatic Safari arranges boat trips along the coast from the Piran marina. 🛈 **Adriatic Safari** ✉ Kosovelova 8, Piran ☎ 05/677–1282.

TRAIN TRAVEL

Four trains daily link Ljubljana and Koper, passing through Postojna and Divača en route.

VISITOR INFORMATION

⊞ Štanjel Tourist Information ⊠ Štanjel Grad, Štanjel ☎ 05/769-0056 ⊕ www.komen. si. **Koper Tourist Information** ⊠ Ukmarjev trg 7, Koper ☎ 05/663-2010 ⊕ www. koper.si. **Izola Tourist Information** ⊠ Sončno nab. 4, Izola ☎ 05/640-1050 ⊕ www. izola.si. **Lipica Tourist Information** ⊠ Lipica 5, Lipica ☎ 05/739-1580 ⊕ www.lipica. org. **Piran Tourist Information** ⊠ Trg Tartini 2, Piran ☎ 05/673-0220 ⊕ www.piran. com. **Portorož Tourist Information** ⊠ Obala 16, Portorož ☎ 05/674-0231 ⊕ www. portoroz.si. **Postojna Tourist Information** ⊠ Jamska 9, Jamska ☎ 05/720-1610 ⊕ www. postojna-cave.com.

SLOVENIA ESSENTIALS

AIR TRAVEL

There are no direct flights between the U.S. and Slovenia. The Slovenian national carrier, Adria Airways, flies from many Western European cities to Ljubljana Airport. Adria also has flights to the capitals of other ex-Yugoslav republics from Ljubljana. Adria is a regional carrier of the Star Alliance, linking it with the extensive networks of Austrian Airways, United Airlines, Lufthansa, Air Canada, and LOT, among others. In Slovenia, tickets can be purchased by phone and delivered anywhere in the country in 24 hours.

The U.K.-based airline EasyJet, a low-cost carrier, now flies regularly to Ljubljana from London's Stansted airport and from Berlin. Aeroflot, Air France, Austrian Airways, Hungary's Malev, and Czech Airlines all now offer regular connections to Ljubljana from their respective capital cities.

⊞ Adria Airways ⊠ Gosposvetska 6, Ljubljana ☎ 01/239-1910 ⊕ www.adria-airways. com. **Aeroflot** ⊠ Dunajska cesta 21, Ljubljana ☎ 01/230-7560 ⊕ www.aeroflot.com. **Air France** ⊠ Kuzmičeva 5, Ljubljana ☎ 01/436-4068 ⊕ www.airfrance.com. **Austrian Airlines** ⊠ Gosposvetska 6, Ljubljana ☎ 01/280-1920 ⊕ www.aua.com. **Czech Airlines/CSA** ⊠ Brnik Airport Terminal, Brnik ☎ 04/206-1750 ⊕ www.czechairlines.cz. **EasyJet** ⊕ www.easyjet.com. **Lufthansa** ⊠ Gosposvetska 6, Ljubljana ☎ 01/239-1900 ⊕ www.lufthansa.com. **Malev** ⊠ Brnik airport terminal, Brnik ☎ 04/206-1676 ⊕ www. malev.hu.

AIRPORTS & TRANSFERS

The Ljubljana Airport is at Brnik, 25 km (15 mi) north of the city.

⊞ Ljubljana Airport ⊠ Brnik ☎ 04/206-1981 ⊕ www.lju-airport.si.

TRANSFERS Public bus service runs regularly between the airport and Ljubljana's main bus station in the city center. Buses depart from the airport every hour on the hour weekdays and slightly less frequently on weekends. Tickets cost around SIT 700. A private airport shuttle makes the same run in slightly less time. Departures average every 90 minutes or so and the cost is SIT 1,000. A taxi costs approximately SIT 7,000. The ride takes about 30 minutes.

⊞ Ljubljana Airport Shuttle ☎ 040/887-766.

BIKING

There's no better way to see the city than by bike. Special bikeways cross the city in all directions, and the pedaling is pretty easy for the most part—just remember to yield to pedestrians and be mindful of other cyclists. Many hotels offer bikes to guests and the private outfitters listed below will rent bikes. Rates range from SIT 500 an hour to SIT 2500 for the day. In addition, the Ljubljana Bike Project—in conjunction with city government—has made 150 cycles available for rent at reduced prices at various points around the city. For more information, ask at Ljubljana's Turistično Informacijski Center (⇨ Visitor Information, *below*).

🚲 **Maček** ✉ Krojaška 5, Ljubljana ☎ 01/425-3791. **Tir bar** ✉ Trg OF 7, Ljubljana ☎ 031/888-086.

BOAT & FERRY TRAVEL

From early March to late October the *Prince of Venice* high-speed catamaran makes regularly scheduled trips between Venice and Izola, with connecting bus service to Piran and Potorož. Kompas Travel in Potorož can make the booking. The trip takes 2½ hours.

Venezia Lines offers similar runs between Venice and Piran in season, and offers overnight hotel packages in Venice. Maona Travel in Piran can arrange this.

🚲 **Kompas** ✉ Obala 41, Portorož ☎ 05/617-8000 🖷 05/617-8014 ⊕ www.kompas-online.net. **Maona** ✉ Cankarjevo nab 7, Piran ☎ 05/673-4520 🖷 05/673-4519 ⊕ www.maona.si.

BUS TRAVEL

International and domestic bus lines and the Ljubljana municipal bus service all operate conveniently from the city's main bus terminal, not far from the center.

Private coach companies operate to and from Trieste in Italy and Zagreb in Croatia, as well as other European destinations further afield. Domestic bus service is frequent from the capital to most Slovenian cities and towns (including most of the destinations in this guide). Outside of a car, the bus remains the only practical option to Bled and Bohinj and mountain destinations west and north of the capital. Except during peak travel periods, you can simply buy your ticket on the bus when you board. Otherwise, purchase tickets a day in advance with a reserved seat. Many buses do not run on Sunday.

Within Ljubljana, the municipal bus network is extensive, and service is frequent during weekdays. Service continues but is less frequent on Saturday, Sunday, and holidays. Buses on most lines stop running around 11 PM. To ride the bus, buy plastic bus tokens (*žetoni*) at kiosks and post offices, or simply pay the fare (SIT 300) in exact change to the driver.

🚲 **Llubljana Bus Station** ✉ Trg OF 5, Ljubljana ☎ 01/090-4230 ⊕ www.ap-ljubljana.si.

BUSINESS HOURS

Most banks are open weekdays 9 to noon and 2 to 4:30, Saturday 9 to 11. You can also change money at exchange desks in hotels, gas stations, tourist agencies, supermarkets, and small exchange offices. The main museums are open Tuesday through Sunday from 10 to 6. Larger shops are open Monday through Saturday from 10 to 6, while smaller ones may open mornings only from 10 to 2. Most stores are closed Sunday. Restaurants typically close one day a week—usually Sunday, but sometimes Monday.

CAR RENTALS

To rent a car you must have a license that is valid in the issuing country. A midsize car costs about $110 (SIT 22,000) for 24 hours, with unlimited mileage—but much better rates are available for longer periods or if the car is booked in advance over the Internet. You'll also need a valid credit card. Rental agencies can be found in all major towns and at the Ljubljana Airport, *see* Car Rentals *in* Llubljana Essentials.

🔃 **AMZS-Hertz** ✉ Dunajska 122, Ljubljana ☎ 01/530-5380 ⊕ www.hertz.si. **Avis** ✉ Čufarjeva 2, Ljubljana ☎ 01/430-8010 ⊕ www.avis.si. **Budget** ✉ Miklošičeva 3, Ljubljana ☎ 01/421-7340 ⊕ www.budget-slovenia.com. **Dollar/Thrifty Car Rental** ✉ Brnik air terminal, Brnik ☎ 04/236-5750 ⊕ www.subrosa.hr. **Kompas Rent-a-Car** ✉ Zaloška 171, Ljubljana ☎ 01/548-4700 ⊕ www.kompas-rac.si. **National Rent a Car** ✉ Baragova 5, Ljubljana ☎ 01/588-4450 ⊕ www.nationalcar-slovenia.com.

CAR TRAVEL

From Budapest and Vienna the Slovenian border is no more than a two-hour drive; from Prague it's eight hours. A tunnel speeds traffic through the Karavanke Alps between Slovenia and Austria. From Vienna the passage is by way of Maribor to Ljubljana, with a four-lane highway most of the way. Slovenia's roads also connect with Italy's *autostrada*.

You don't need a car if you are not planning to leave Ljubljana; however, traveling by car undoubtedly gives you the chance to reach remote areas of the country when and as you wish. Main roads between large towns are comparable to those in Western Europe. Toll plazas are frequent, so have small bills and change handy.

Gas stations on border crossings and main roads leading to larger towns are open 24 hours a day, while others are open Monday through Saturday from 7 AM to 8 PM.

PARKING In major towns parking spaces are marked with a blue line and a sign denoting time restrictions. Buy a ticket, obtainable from gas stations and newsstands; write down the time you parked, and attach it to your windshield. Parking is a major headache in Ljubljana and along the coast. The best advice is to find a parking lot and leave the car there for the duration.

RULES OF THE ROAD Slovenes drive on the right and are obliged to keep their headlights on at all times. Speed limits are 60 kph (37 mph) in urban areas and 120 kph (74 mph) on highways. Local drivers are courteous by European standards. The permitted blood alcohol level is 0.05%; drivers caught exceeding this level can expect penalties similar to those of other European countries.

CUSTOMS & DUTIES

ON ARRIVAL Slovenia is now a part of the EU. As with most European countries, you can import duty-free 200 cigarettes, 1 liter of spirits, and 2 liters of wine.

Foreign citizens can bring personal items into the country without paying customs taxes.

ON DEPARTURE Any visitor who buys goods worth more than SIT 15,000 (about $75) at any one store on a single day is entitled to a refund of taxes. When you make a purchase, ask for a Request for VAT Refund form, *Zahtevek za vracilo DDV*. A customs officer will certify the form when you leave the country. To obtain the refund, go to the Kompas MTS office at the border crossing point or the airport. Exporting historic artifacts is forbidden.

EMBASSIES & CONSULATES
🛈 **Australian Consulate** ✉ Trg republike 3/XII, Ljubljana ☎ 01/425-4252 🖷 01/426-4721. **Canadian Consulate** ✉ Miklošičeva 19, Ljubljana ☎ 01/430-3570 🖷 01/430-3575. **U.K. Embassy** ✉ Trg republike 3/IV, Ljubljana ☎ 01/200-3910 🖷 01/425-0174. **U.S. Embassy** ✉ Prešernova 31, Ljubljana ☎ 01/200-5500 🖷 01/200-5555.

EMERGENCIES
🛈 **Ambulance & Fire** ☎ 112. **Emergency Road Assistance** ☎ 987. **Police** ☎ 113. **Lekarna Miklošič Pharmacy** ✉ Miklošičeva 24, Ljubljana ☎ 01/231-4558. **Ljubljana Emergency Medical Services** ☎ 01/232-3060.

ENGLISH-LANGUAGE BOOKSTORES
Kod in Kam specializes in maps and travel books. MK Knjigarna Konzorcij has a good selection of English books and magazines on the upper floor.
🛈 **Kod in Kam** ✉ Trg Francoske Revolucije 7, Ljubljana ☎ 01/200-2732. **MK Knjigarna Konzorcij** ✉ Slovenska 29, Ljubljana ☎ 01/241-0655.

HOLIDAYS
January 1–2; February 8 (Prešeren Day, Slovene cultural day); Easter Sunday and Monday (in March or April); April 27 (National Resistance Day); May 1 and 2 (Labor Day); June 25 (Slovenia National Day); August 15 (Assumption); October 31 (Reformation Day); November 1 (All Saints' Day); December 25; December 26 (Independence Day).

INTERNET
Many hotels now set aside at least one terminal for guests to access the Internet—and some of the better places are now adding wireless Wi-Fi networks. Ljubljana has several Internet cafés (known locally as cyber cafés), though these are harder to find in outlying cities and towns. Frequently cafés and bars will maintain a computer terminal or two and allow access for a fee—usually around SIT 500 to SIT 600 an hour.
🛈 **Xplorer CyberCafe** ✉ Petkovškovo nab 23, Ljubljana ☎ 01/430-1991 is the best in town, centrally located and has long opening hours. **Val Hostel** ✉ Gregorčičeva 38a, Piran ☎ 05/673-2555, a charming hostel in the center of Piran, offers Internet access to nonguests for a nominal fee.

LANGUAGE
Slovene is the country's chief language. In the east, signs are posted in Slovene and Hungarian; on the Adriatic coast both Slovene and Italian are officially used. English, German, and Italian are spoken in many places.

In Slovene the words for street (*ulica*) and drive (*cesta*) are abbreviated to ul and c. *Nabrežje* (abbreviated to nab) means "embankment." The word for square is *trg*.

MAIL & SHIPPING

POSTAL RATES Postage is assessed according to weight. The standard international letter rate, including airmail, is SIT 167 for very light letters, and SIT 281 for standard size. Postcards sent abroad cost SIT 143. Post offices are open weekdays from 8 to 6 and Saturday from 8 to noon. Stamps are also sold at hotels, newsstands, and kiosks.

MONEY MATTERS

Costs for goods and services are on a par with those of Western Europe. Notable exceptions are public transportation, alcohol, and cigarettes, all of which are cheaper here.

CURRENCY Though Slovenia is a member of the European Union, it has retained its national currency, the tolar (SIT). There are notes of SIT 10,000, SIT 5,000, SIT 1,000, SIT 500, SIT 200, SIT 100, SIT 50, SIT 20, and SIT 10, and coins of SIT 500, SIT 50, SIT 20, SIT 10, SIT 5, and SIT 1. Euros are widely accepted and are frequently the billing currency for items like hotel rooms and rental cars.

At this writing the exchange rate was about SIT 240 to the euro, SIT 190 to the U.S. dollar, SIT 160 to the Canadian dollar, SIT 150 to the Australian dollar and SIT 350 to the pound sterling.

PASSPORTS & VISAS

Valid passport holders from the United States, Canada, the EU, many European countries outside of the EU, Australia, and New Zealand do not need visas for stays of 30 days or less. Citizens of other countries must apply in advance for a 90-day visa from a Slovenian embassy or consulate.

TAXIS

Private taxis operate 24 hours a day. Phone from your hotel or hail one in the street. Drivers are bound by law to display and run a meter.

TELEPHONES

COUNTRY CODE The country code for Slovenia is 386. When dialing from outside the country, drop any initial "0" from the area code.

INTERNATIONAL CALLS To make international calls, dial "00" and then the appropriate country code (calls to the United States and Canada, for example, are preceded by "001"). International calls can be made from local telephones or post offices. For collect calls dial the operator. For international inquiries, dial international directory assistance.

🛈 International Directory Assistance ☎ 1180. Operator ☎ 115.

LOCAL CALLS Pay phones take magnetic telephone cards, available from post offices and kiosks. Lower rates apply from 10 PM to 7 AM and all day Sunday.

🛈 Local Directory Assistance ☎ 1188.

TIPPING

Tax is already included in listed prices. Tips are not included in restaurant bills, and a 10% tip is considered customary. If the service is especially good, tip 15%.

TOURS

Informative and amusing sightseeing walks, organized by the Ljubljana Promotion Center, depart from the Magistrat on Mestni trg daily, June through September. From October through May tours are on Sunday and can be booked through Ljubljana's Turistično Informacijski Center (⇨ Visitor Information, *below*).

TRAIN TRAVEL

There are several trains daily to Venice (5 hours), Vienna (6 hours), and Budapest (8 hours). There is an overnight service to Prague (12 hours) and a rapid daytime EuroCity connection to Berlin (15 hours). The train station is just north of the city center.

⑦ **Ljubljana Train station** ✉ Trg OF 6, Ljubljana ☎ 01/291-3332 ⊕ www.slo-zeleznice. si.

TRAVEL AGENCIES

Local travel agencies often supplement the work of the official tourist information centers and can frequently help in booking excursions and finding rooms. In Bled and on the Adriatic coast, the local private agencies are the main source for finding private accommodation.

⑦ **Cmona Globtour** ✉ Baragova 5, Llubljana ☏ 01/588-4400 🖶 01/588-4455. **Kompas Turizem Ljubljana** ✉ Pražakova 4, Llubljana ☎ 01/200-6100 🖶 01/200-6434 ⊕ www.kompas.si. **Promet T & T** ✉ Celovška 23, Llubljana ☎ 01/519-3511 🖶 01/519-5345. **Tirtur Ljubljana** ✉ Majorja Lavriča 12, Llubljana ☎ 01/519-8802 🖶 01/519-8809.

VISITOR INFORMATION

Ljubljana's Turistično Informacijski Center (Tourist Information Center) is next to the Triple Bridge on the Old Town side. It's an excellent resource for maps, brochures, advice, and small souvenirs like postcards and T-shirts. It's open weekdays from 8 to 7, Saturday 9 to 5, and Sunday 10 to 6. If you are arriving by train, the TIC kiosk in the train station can help you find accommodations. It's open daily from 8 AM to 9 PM from June through September and 10 to 6 from October through May.

The Slovenian Tourist Board provides information and produces excellent publications on all kinds of tourist activities throughout the country. Each region also has its own tourist-information center. For individual centers, *see* Visitor Information *in* regional Essentials sections.

⑦ **Slovenian Tourist Information Center** ✉ Krekov trg 10, Ljubljana, 1000 ☎ 01/306-4575 ⊕ www.slovenia-tourism.si **Turistično Informacijski Center** (Tourist Information Center [TIC]) ✉ Stritarjeva, Ljubljana ☎ 01/306-1215 ⊕ www.ljubljana.si. **TIC kiosk** ✉ Trg OF 6, Ljubljana ☎ 01/433-9475.

UNDERSTANDING CROATIA & SLOVENIA

A SHORT HISTORY OF CROATIA

CROATIA SITS ASTRIDE THE GEOGRAPHICAL BOUNDARY between the Balkans and Central Europe. Croats, who speak a Slavic language, are related—linguistically and ethnically—to many of the other Slavic peoples of Europe, including their neighbors the Serbs, Slovenes, and Bosnians. Croatia and its peoples have also been heavily influenced over the centuries by the Romans, Turks, Italians, and Austrians. An essay such as this can provide only a brief overview of developments, but it is worth mentioning three themes that will assist travelers in understanding a great deal of Croatia's past. The first theme is that history has left an important physical legacy in architecture from Roman times to the wars of the 1990s. The second theme pertains to Croatia's human landscape, which evinces considerable diversity in ethnicity, culture, and language. The third theme is the strained political scene in 20th-century Croatia, hotly contested by radical political movements on both the right and the left.

The Early History of the Croatian Lands

The three main regions that form Croatia today are known as Slavonia, Dalmatia, and Croatia proper (the inland region also known as Civil Croatia). These have also been called the "Triune Kingdom." In addition, the ethnically mixed Istrian peninsula is now considered Croatian territory. Bosnia-Herzegovina has a mixed population and once had a pronounced regional identity, but some Croat nationalists consider it their territory.

Even before the influx of the Slavs between 500 and 800 AD, the region of Croatia had a long history. The Illyrians and Thracians were originally at home there, and traces of Hellenistic and Celtic influences can also be seen. From the 3rd century BC to the 1st century AD, Rome controlled the Balkans; indeed, at times

Croatian history was closely tied to Roman politics, even though it was hardly a central province of the far-flung empire. For instance, the well-known Emperor Diocletian (284–305 AD) was from Dalmatia, as were four other emperors. After his reign, Diocletian returned to his native Split, where he built a large palace. The city of Pula also contains many important Roman sites dating from this time.

Rome's influence on the Croatian lands has been far-reaching. The Romans developed the region's basic infrastructure and industries related to mining and metallurgy. The Croatian coast was established as an outpost of European high culture; this connection was soon strengthened by the Croats' conversion to Christianity and later by ties to the Renaissance city-states of Italy, especially Venice. The Italian influence can be felt even today, particularly in the Istrian peninsula and on some of the islands.

As the Empire was divided into its Eastern and Western halves, the internal frontier came to symbolize for many the "fault line" between Latin culture and Roman Catholicism, on the one hand, and Greek culture and Orthodox Christianity, on the other. The division was actually always quite porous and inexact, but its nature changed during the Ottoman Turkish invasions starting in the 14th century. Islam again became one of the major religions of Europe, and new ethnic groups arrived or were created in the former Byzantine lands.

Despite the fact that the Croatian lands clearly belonged to Rome's sphere of influence, the Croatian culture went through some complicated developments after the fall of the western portion of the Roman Empire in 476 AD. First, many Croats—like their neighbors, the Slovenes—had been converted to Christianity by Frankish (or "German") missionaries from Charlemagne's Holy Roman Empire. Second, Croatian monks working in Dalmatia developed a unique alphabet, known as Glagolitic, from contact with Orthodox missionaries. Croatia remained Catholic after the official religious break between Rome and Constantinople in 1054, but the Glagolitic alphabet was used in some places into the 19th century, serving to reinforce Croatian identity amidst various political and ethnic rivalries. Finally, the Ottoman occupation of the Balkans made much of Croatia into a contested region of population flux and the new cultural norms associated with being a "bulwark of Christendom."

The first independent Croatian state was formed by the leader Tomislav. In 924 he was crowned king of Croatia and recognized by the pope. Although historians disagree over the exact extent of his territory, Tomislav did set another important precedent as well: he united many regions of the former Roman provinces of Dalmatia and Pannonia (central Croatia and Slavonia). The national symbols of the kuna (currency denomination) and šahovnica (red-and-white checkerboard coat of arms) originated at this time.

Croatia in the High Middle Ages

By 1102 the royal line had died out, and the Sabor (assembly of nobles) accepted Hungarian rule. Croatia preserved its own laws and customs through the Pacta Conventa, which seems to have been essentially a personal union between the countries, not an annexation. Medieval Croatia also achieved considerable cultural heights. The first known writing in Croatian dates from around 1100, on a stone tablet from the island of Krk, known as the Bašćanska Ploča. In the 16th century, Dubrovnik dramatist and poet Ivan Gundulić (1555–1638) wrote *Osman* in the Croatian language to inspire resistance to the Turks. Croatia's unique literary history had begun. Dubrovnik also boasted major scientists and composers.

Soon there were three major outside forces contending for Croatian territory: the Ottoman Empire, the Kingdom of Hungary, and the Venetian Republic. The Venetians quickly displaced rivals such as the Byzantine Empire and the kingdoms of Serbia and Bosnia. A major blow came in 1202, when Venice directed the Fourth Crusade to sack the important port of Zadar.

The Ottoman expansion into Europe reached Hungary in 1526; Sultan Suleiman defeated Hungary's King Lajos at Mohacs. The Croatian nobles had already been defeated at Udbina in 1493. Ottoman rule would last for 150 years, but the Hungarian and Croatian nobility quickly opted for personal union with the royal Habsburg family in Vienna. In 1593 the Croats stemmed the tide of Turkish invasion by the successful defense of the fortress-city of Sisak, but intense fighting in the area continued until the Treaty of Karlowitz in 1699. That momentous agreement removed most of Croatia and Hungary from Ottoman sovereignty, and Habsburg rule continued.

The wealthy city-state of Dubrovnik retained its independence until Napoléon's invasion of 1797. Bosnia-Herzegovina, home to many Croats and other groups, would remain under Ottoman rule until 1878. As central Croatia was liberated by the crusading Habsburgs, they created a military frontier zone that is often known by its Croatian (and Serbian) name of Vojna Krajina. The frontier included the Lika region south of Zagreb and stretched all along the southern periphery of the Empire from Italy to Romania. The Austrians recruited Serbs and other groups into the area, adding new minority groups to the Croatian lands.

The nobility, or landowning class, of Croatia played the key role in developments over the next several centuries. Croatia's basic feudal structure was preserved by the Habsburgs, although some nobles from the Zrinski and Frankapan families were executed for plotting against Vienna. The country also remained overwhelmingly

Catholic; Catholic scholars working in Venice and Rome also produced the earliest dictionaries and grammars of the Croatian language.These trends stand in sharp contrast to the neighboring Serb lands, where Ottoman rule removed nearly all traces of the traditional elites. The Croat nobles resented Vienna for its attempts at centralization and its territorial compromises with the Ottomans. At times the Croats gravitated, culturally and politically, toward outside powers that could provide leverage in their struggle against Vienna: Russia, France, and even at times their own erstwhile foes the Venetians and the Ottomans.

The Croatian National Revival

The remaining Croatian nobility was revived as a political "nation" by the enlightened despotism of one of the most iconoclastic of the Habsburg emperors, Joseph II (r. 1780–1790). Joseph's modernizing vision involved centralization of power in Vienna and, to some extent, Germanization. Both of these processes elicited strong negative reactions around the Empire, where traditional autonomy existed in many areas. In Croatia it was the nobility who responded with alarm both to Joseph and to the excesses of the French Revolution. Many in the Croatian elite chose to strengthen ties with Hungary, forming a political party known as the Unionists, or Magyarones, a term corresponding basically to "Hungarophiles."

In 1809 the invading Napoléon created a short-lived satellite state out of conquered Habsburg lands called the Illyrian Provinces. This state abolished feudalism and turned local administration, including language policy, over to the Croats and Slovenes. These actions increased popular awareness of Croatian nationality. It was from these two starting points—both of them reactions to external events—that the tortured development of modern, mass nationalism in Croatia began.

The Magyarone solution soon became problematic as Hungary gradually increased its control over the Croatian lands decade by decade. Croats, now alienated from both Vienna and Budapest, began to react in various new ways. Of considerable importance was the Illyrian Movement, which was at once a Croatian national movement and a kind of supranational forerunner of Yugoslavism. Its chief exponent was the writer and editor Ljudevit Gaj, who helped establish the basis for the modern Croatian language. The Illyrians espoused political cooperation among the Slovenes, Serbs, and Croats within the framework of the Habsburg Empire; they were basically federalists and did not seek an independent nation-state just for Croats. The National Party, led by Bishop Josip Strossmayer, revived Illyrianism in the form of Yugoslavism and also greatly enriched Croatian cultural life by founding the Yugoslav Academy of Sciences and the modern University of Zagreb.

Croatia, like many other societies, was part of a multiethnic empire when the ideas of Romantic nationalism reached it; it also lacked a strong middle class that understood liberal government. Croatian nationalism is complex, involving both political (or civic) and ethnic considerations. As in other Balkan states, the necessity for Croats to distinguish themselves from their closely related neighbors, and to compete with them for shared territory, sometimes fostered the growth of exclusionist mindsets.

In 1848, nationalism and liberalism brought major insurrections across Europe. Although Hungary rebelled, the Croats remained loyal to Vienna. In the middle of the 19th century, the Croatian political scene was dominated by an important figure named Josip Jelačić (1801–1859), an Austrian military officer and a convinced Illyrianist. In 1848 the Habsburgs turned to him to help defeat the nationalist uprising in Hungary. He succeeded and managed to unite nearly all Croatian territory under Austrian rule.

He also abolished feudalism and promoted Croatian interests on major cultural issues. Although Jelačić is a Croatian hero today, he also propounded a progressive version of nationality based on regional rather than ethnic identity.

The long-reigning Emperor Franz Josef tried to placate the Hungarians by issuing the Ausgleich (Compromise) in 1867, breaking the empire in two and renaming it "Austria-Hungary." The Croats wisely negotiated their own version of the Ausgleich, known as the Nagodba, in 1868.

Into the Great War: From Habsburgs to Yugoslavs

This arrangement gave the Croats, at last, a considerable degree of internal autonomy, and Croatia even had representatives in the Hungarian parliament and cabinet and also in Vienna. But it also provided for the Croatian territories to be split up again, with control over Dalmatia and Istria going to Vienna while Slavonia and central Croatia were under the Hungarian crown. In addition, the major port of Rijeka was run as a separate entity by Budapest.

These final Habsburg decades were turbulent. Territorial divisions wounded Croatian pride and hindered economic development. Hungarian manipulation of the political scene and attempts at Magyarization continued. Count Károly Khuen-Héderváry ruled from 1883 to 1903 and became notorious for setting Croatia's Serbian and ethnic Croatian populations against each other. Despite his tactics and the turmoil of World War I, the Serbs and Croats of Croatia actually achieved a considerable level of political cooperation. They succeeded in forming coalitions to push for reunification of the Croatian lands and to oppose misrule from both Budapest and Vienna.

In 1918, with the Habsburg Empire vanquished, a combination of factors resulted in Croatian politicians leading their country into the new Kingdom of Serbs, Croats, and Slovenes (called Yugoslavia after 1929). By 1921 many Croats grew suspicious of the new state, run from Belgrade by the Serbian king. Many political parties, as well as the ban (viceroys) and the Sabor, were suppressed. Royal legitimacy was shaky: Serbs dominated the police, military, and economy; agriculture, the mainstay of the economy, languished; and Italy retained possession of large amounts of Croatian territory in Istria and Dalmatia. Stjepan Radić, the leader of the powerful Croatian Peasant Party, alternately boycotted and negotiated with the central government; his murder in 1928 fueled radicalism in Croatia.

As World War II approached, Belgrade grew more willing to compromise with Croatia. A 1939 arrangement known as the Sporazum restored the ban and Sabor and combined many Croatian lands into one autonomous unit. But war broke out just weeks later.

World War II & the Second Yugoslavia

The darkest chapter in Croatian history took place amidst the chaos of World War II. An interwar political agitator on the fascist right, Ante Pavelić (1889–1959) rose to power and ruled the "Independent State of Croatia" for 49 bloody months.

Pavelić, who founded the Ustaša (insurrectionist) movement in 1929, originally developed his ideas within the tradition of the Croatian Party of Right. This group, founded by Ante Starčević (1823–1896) in 1861, advocated the creation of a greater Croatia, including Bosnia-Herzegovina. They believed that Bosnian Muslims (today's Bosniaks) and Serbs were ethnic Croats who had been forced to adopt other faiths. Pavelić developed ties with similar movements in Nazi Germany, Bulgaria, Hungary, and especially Mussolini's Italy. The Ustaša helped assassinate King Aleksandar in 1934. The most revolutionary aspects of the Ustaša movement were their willingness to use terror and genocide against minorities in order to form an ethnically "pure" Croatian state and their desire to create a mass political movement that displaced the established elites in the country.

Mussolini's army installed Pavelić's government in Zagreb after the Axis invasion of 1941, and the Nazis agreed to let Pavelić rule. Croatia was immediately split into two spheres of influence. The Ustăa were unpopular, but they ruled by terror over a population that included vast numbers of non-Croatians, especially Serbs. The Germans were increasingly disconcerted by the Ustaša's murderous policies, which spawned significant resistance movements. The main German goal in the region was simply the extraction of mineral and agricultural wealth. In all, the Ustaša government killed over 300,000 Serbs, along with tens of thousands of Jews and Roma (Gypsies). In addition to a number of concentration camps like the notorious Jasenovac east of Zagreb—where about 85,000 people, mostly Serbs, were killed—many horrific rural massacres occurred. Pavelić's state was a failure; the Communist Partisans and the Chetniks (Serbian royalists) actually controlled much of its territory.

Yugoslavia was reconstituted after World War II, this time under the rule of Josip Broz Tito (1892–1980), a Communist born in Croatia. The trauma of World War II was the main reason for decades of "Croatian silence" in Yugoslavia. In 1967, leading cultural and academic figures broke ranks with the party and publicly asserted the distinctiveness and legitimacy of the Croatian language. This was divisive because it ran counter to the official embrace of a common "Croato-Serbian" or "Serbo-Croatian" language and culture.

A period of dissent and crackdown known as the "Croatian Spring" followed. There were demonstrations, strikes, and many debates in print about Yugoslavia's political discrimination and economic exploitation. This lasted until 1972 and resulted in Tito sidelining numerous prominent Croatian Communists, including many who could have provided cosmopolitan, intelligent alternatives to both Communism and what came after. The repression belies the fact that Tito's regime became, after 1952, the most liberal socialist state in Eastern Europe; in addition, the LCY (League of Communists of Yugoslavia) was not averse to using the nationalism of some Yugoslav peoples (such as the Bosnians, the Macedonians, and the Albanians of Kosovo) to further its agenda—just not Croatian nationalism.

Famous political figures in Croatia in the postwar period included Tito, of course, but also his close ally Vladimir Bakarić, who held a number of important governmental posts. Franjo Tuđman, a Communist Partisan officer during World War II and then a historian, was jailed several times for questioning centralist orthodoxy on national issues. The poet Vlado Gotovac, who again became a pro-democracy dissident under President Tuđman in the 1990s, was purged in the Croatian Spring, and the philosophers Milan Kangrga and Rudi Supek of the countrywide Praxis movement attracted attention and official disfavor with their alternative analyses of Marx.

Despite significant grievances, Croatia underwent considerable modernization under Communist rule. There were increases in industrialization, urbanization, life expectancy, standard of living, and literacy. New universities were founded in Split, Rijeka, and Osijek. Croatia's beaches became famous across Europe. The economy was also helped by the large numbers of Croats who worked abroad as *Gastarbeiter* (guest workers), but heavy immigration and low birth rates left many worried about the country's demographic future.

Both Serbia and Croatia felt the heavy hand of Tito's rule; as the most powerful traditional nations in Yugoslavia, Tito neutralized their ability to rock the federal boat. The LCY encouraged nation-building, however, in Bosnia, Macedonia, Montenegro, and among the Albanians of

Kosovo both as a counterweight to Croatian and Serbian ambitions and as a developmental strategy.

From Tito to Tuđman & Beyond: Sovereign Croatia

Historians disagree over when Yugoslavia passed the point of no return. At some point in the decade between Tito's death in 1980 and the momentous political changes in Slovenia and Croatia by 1991, the breakup actually began. In 1990, Slovenia and Croatia held free, multiparty elections, declared their sovereignty, and held referenda in which they overwhelmingly approved the idea of independence. But even then the eventual violence was not inevitable. Two highly regarded Croatian reformist politicians, Ante Marković and Stjepan Mesić, were stymied in their efforts to place the Yugoslav federation on a new foundation. What soon exploded were not the so-called "ancient ethnic hatreds" but rather the aggressive and conflicting aims of various political factions competing in a superheated environment. This violence was furthered by the egoism of conniving politicians, sensationalism in the media, and mixed signals from Western Europe and the United States.

The 1980s had been extremely tense across the country. Serbs and Albanians clashed in Kosovo; hyperinflation, unemployment, public debt, and strikes characterized a ruined economy; and the fall of the Berlin Wall marked the end of other European socialist states. The rise of the dictator Slobodan Milošević in Serbia brought new levels of confrontation to politics and revealed gross Serbian manipulation of the economy. Croats and Slovenes gradually realized that Yugoslavia was unworkable as a country.

The Serbian population, incited by ambitious politicians, lashed out at Croat police in the spring of 1991. Thus, even before Croatia's declaration of independence on June 25, 1991, the villages of Pakrac and Borovo Selo became scenes of bitter bloodshed, as did the famed Plitvice Lakes National Park and other areas in central Croatia. There were about 600,000 Serbs living in Croatia, comprising over 12% of the population. The new Croatian government, led by the now-nationalist Tuđman, was brash in its treatment of minorities and irresponsible in its handling of the legacy of World War II, and these approaches greatly increased Serbs' anxiety.

After secession, full-scale fighting broke out. The autumn of 1991 saw two shocking sieges: the bloody street-fighting and massacres at Vukovar in Slavonia and the weeks-long shelling of venerable Dubrovnik for no legitimate military purpose. The contemporary Croatian poet Slavko Mihalić described this era as one in which the Serbian leader—"the one who sends the bombs"—grimly and accurately promised to turn Croatia into a "national park of death." In fact Milošević was willing to let Croatia secede but without its Serb-inhabited regions; later, he and Tuđman agreed on how to partition Bosnia-Herzegovina as well.

In May 1992, the war spread to independence-minded Bosnia, where 200,000 people died, many of them civilians, and two million were made homeless. In Croatia, 10,000 people were killed and over a fourth of the country fell to the Serbs. Large numbers of Croats and Bosnians were driven from their homes with terror campaigns of "ethnic cleansing." With American aid, Croatian forces rallied in the summer of 1995 and recaptured Slavonia and the Krajina region. Many thousands of Serbs fled and property issues remain unresolved. Croatian forces also committed atrocities in Bosnia-Herzegovina, but most of the international community finally recognized that the lion's share of guilt for the wars themselves belonged to the Serbian government. The Dayton peace accords of late 1995, backed by NATO's military might, paved the way for Serbian withdrawal from Croatia and Bosnia.

President Tuđman was roundly criticized internationally for his authoritarian tendencies and over-zealous nationalism. Internal opposition grew as well, especially over his censorship and policies in Bosnia. Tuđman allowed political parties other than the HDZ (Croatian Democratic Union), but they were weak until his death in December 1999. Since then, Mesić has been president, and the prime ministership has been held by both the Social Democrats of Ivica Račan and the revived HDZ of Ivo Šanader. Since Tuđman's death, Croatia has begun serious cooperation with the Hague war-crimes tribunal. Many other reforms have also succeeded, but open questions include the quest for autonomy by the ethnically and historically distinct region of Istria and Croatia's ability to cooperate on a variety of issues with its neighbors. Most Croats still look forward to joining the European Union in the next several years.

— *John K. Cox, Associate Professor of History,*
Wheeling Jesuit University

WINE IN CROATIA

THE CROATS, THE FIRST OF THE INVADING SLAVS to take up the cult of the vine, arrived in their viticulturally blessed homeland as recently as the 7th century BC and can today lay claim to some of the world's richest winemaking resources. A wine renaissance is occurring in Croatia today. The early 20th century was bad for the wine business—phylloxera, war, crippling economic policies, all of which ravaged wineries here and led to the mass emigration of many vintners who fled to the United States, New Zealand, Australia, South Africa, and South American countries. Bringing their knowledge of vine cultivation and wine production with them, they left Croatia's vineyards virtually deserted.

More recently, the 1990–1995 war for Croatian independence, which cast a global spotlight on the tiny country, nearly wiped out a viticulture two millennia in the making. It appears, however, that the land itself cannot forget its heritage. Blessed with unique geography, so crucially ideal for wine, Croatia currently hosts more than 100 indigenous grapes—second only to Italy. As Croatian vintners are rushing to expand before the country enters the European Union, the country's wines are once again finding a special place in the hearts of oenophiles everywhere. Perhaps it's a pleasant coincidence that Zinfandel, the backbone and darling of California's wine industry, has been traced back recently to its reputed place of origin—Kaštel Novi, near Split, on the Dalmatian coast.

Millions of years ago during the Eucene period, plate tectonics created the distinctive coastal landscapes of Dalmatia and Istria, the most important wine-producing regions. In the steep limestone bluffs of the Dalmatian Karst, several indigenous varieties have proven themselves exceptionally suited to the environment. To the casual observer, prominent layers of limestone belie the existence of buried layers of rich, ancient soil and ample moisture from underground drainage systems. Steep, rocky cliffs, hills, valleys, caves, and 1,185 islands that were created during the shifting of the Earth's plates created an area known as the "golden corridor" of the Adriatic. This Mediterranean landscape is particularly suited to Vitus vinifera L (the cultivated grapevine), a hearty and prolific, yet temperamental plant that requires precise combinations of climate, geography, and soil to flourish. In Croatia, with her numerous, diverse microclimates, the grape has had the necessary conditions to proliferate and adapt to isolated environments.

Winemaking & Its Deep Roots

The Delmati, an Illyrian tribe, were the first to cultivate the vine in modern-day Croatia, as early as the 11th century BC. When the Romans invaded the Dalmatian Coast in the 3rd century BC, they discovered that wine production had preceded them; they found, in fact, an entire wine industry. The Greeks, who'd been sharing the region with the Illyrians, had not failed to exploit *Vitus sylvestris* (the wild grapevine), which was plentiful there, merging it with the strains of the cultivated vines they brought from their own country. The conquering Roman soldiers also brought new varietals with them as a way of expanding their culture; the vine itself was a symbol of their power.

By the 9th century, Croatian princes had a cup bearer as part of their court staff, whose duties involved wine-cellar maintenance and the selection and serving of wines within the court. When Venice subjugated much of Dalmatia in the 14th century, the planting of new vineyards was restricted to the areas around Split. It was in this period that noble families, after building their vineyards, built fortresses in the middle of their estates for protection, perhaps anticipating the destruction of the coming Venetian-Turkish wars. In Slavonia and Dalmatia, a large number of the vineyards, then documented at more than 7,000, were destroyed during these wars. By the time the Habsburgs had ousted the Ottomans, the Austrians were already well on their way to introducing new varietals to the area, capitalizing on the superior wine-producing capacity of their newly acquired resources.

Modern developments in cloning techniques and the use of industrial machinery brought winemaking in Croatia to the economic position it occupies today, where 10% of the population derives income from the industry. By the end of Marshall Tito's reign, however, only a tenth of Croatia's then-extant 180,000 hectares survived the farm mechanization of Communism, and many of those fields were burned in the war of the early 1990s. The government plans to free up state-owned land to plant 13,000 hectares of new vineyards by 2007. Nevertheless, things are moving slowly.

The Napa Valley Connection

Croatia has had some world-class help in reestablishing its winemaking industry. Miljenko "Mike" Grgič of Napa Valley fame is at the forefront of the race to expand and realize the potential of Croatia's indigenous varietals. Grgič left Croatia in 1954, feeling stifled by the Communist government. In California, he became renowned as a winemaker when his 1973 Chateau Montelena Chardonnay won a blind tasting in Paris. Afterwards, the top-quality wine market opened its mind and wallet to wines from the world over. Mr. Grgič then established Grgich Hills Cellar in Napa Valley, and it is now one of California's most respected producers.

When Croatia won its independence in 1995, Mike Grgič went back to establish **Grgič Vina** (✉ Trstenik 78, Trstenik ☎ 020/748–090) in a tiny town of some 100 residents on the Peljesac peninsula in Central Dalmatia. Croatia's first international winery surprised everyone by turning a profit

within two years (5 to 10 years is typical). The winery produces high-end boutique wines: a flavorful, fruity white from the indigenous pošip; and a ruby-red, from the hearty plavac mali, the "little blue" grape that is widely considered the highest-quality Croatian varietal. These bottles range between $20 and $50 a bottle. Grgič hopes to support the local wine communes by using their grapes as well.

Labels, Regions & Wineries

A bit of wine label terminology is sure to enhance your sampling experience: red wine is called either *crno vino* or *crveno vino,* whereas white wine is *bijelo vino*; *ruzica* may label a rosé. Dessert wine (*desertno vino*) is an easy one. *Jenusavo vino* (sparkling wine) is a bit more difficult to remember. As for descriptive terminology, *suho vino* indicates a dry wine, and *polosuh vino* means medium-dry. *Slatko vino* is sweet; *prirodno* is organic. The highest-quality wines are labeled *vrhunsko* (literally, top quality). *Geografsko porijelko* (geographical origin) precedes the name of the grape: *Primoštenski Babić* means Babić grown in Primošten.

Croatia is split into two main winegrowing regions: the arid continental part and the coastal region, much of which shares the same latitude as Bordeaux, Provence, Tuscany, and Oregon. The continental region produces 90% of the country's whites, whereas the coastal almost 70% of the reds. There are 12 sub-regions in Croatia, the most important of which are: **Central and Southern Dalmatia** (*Sjeverna* and *Južna Dalmacija*), where the hearty plavac mali flourishes on the Pelejesic Peninsula, and the Dubrovačka malvasia (served as a delicacy in the 14th century) was once produced; **Middle Dalmatia** (*Sredja Dalmacija*), where the famous babič grape is grown near Primošten; and the **Northern Coastal Belt** (*Hrvatsko Primorje*), which includes the islands of Cres, Lošinj, Rab, Pag, and Krk—famous for the *Žlatina* varietal, which is produced by the Katunar winery. These are breathtaking regions, as is **Istria**

(*Istra*), known for its *malvasia Istriana* (white) and *teran* (red). The region of **Medđjimurje,** situated in continental Croatia along the Slovenian and Hungarian border, also has some fine wineries specializing in white wines made from *graševina* grapes, better known as Welschriesling, as well as tramina, chardonnay, and sauvignon blanc.

Although a work in progress at this writing, a general **Web site** (⊕ www.hrvatska-vina.com) on Croatian wines and winemakers is being set up to facilitate vineyard visitations and schedule wine tastings.

Istrian Wineries

At **AgroLaguna Winery** (⊠ Vukovarska 19, Poreč ☎ 052/432–203 or 052/432–111) it is possible to taste a number of high-quality Istrian wines. One varietal, malvazija, is well-known throughout the Adriatic, dating back to the days of the Venetian city-states. Muškat ottonal is another high-quality native variety. Small, lovingly produced batches of barrique provide high-quality (red) wine. Gran teran, from **Moreno Coronica** (⊠ Koreniki 86, Koreniki ☎☎ 052/730–196), in the north-east corner of the peninsula, has been a gold-medal winner at international wine competitions.

Northern Coastal Belt Wineries

At **Katunar winery** (⊠ Sv. Nedilija, Vrbnik, Krk ☎051/857–393 ⊕www.katunar.com), in the Kvarner Gulf, you can sample the žlahtina varietal, which is indigenous to the island. Individual visits and group tours can be arranged to sample the dry white *žhlatina Katunar* or the *černo Katunar* (a dry red), or the "pearl wine" *biser mora,* a dessert wine produced from 100% zlahtina grapes. This dry white wine is famous among Croatians around the world.

Central & Southern Dalmatian Wineries

The rich bouquet of the ruby-red *Dingač,* the current darling of Croatia's export market, goes perfectly with a traditional meal of roast *janjetina* (lamb) or a plate of grilled *lignje* (baby squid). The *plavac mali* grapes grown on the steep hillsides of Dingač produce a full-bodied, slightly dry wine. These particular 168 acres, along with some areas of Hvar, have the highest average temperatures in Croatia, the reason why Dingač's alcohol content may reach as high as 17.6%, the highest of Croatian wines. The seaside slopes upon which the grapes are grown are so steep that donkeys are the only possible helpmates (machine-harvesting is impossible). The donkey found on some bottles of Dingač is a symbol of the hearty, stubborn vine that reaches its full-potential in this very limited region.

At one of Croatia's best-known wineries, **Vinarija Dingač Cooperative** (Dingač Co-operative; ⊠ Potomje ☎ 020/742–010) it is possible to sample several excellent wines. Each year, Vinarija Dingač produces 12,500 cases of a deep-red wine that is fruity without being sweet. In a market flooded with low-priced good-quality wines from South Africa and Australia, many in the Croatian wine industry believe that the future of Croatian wine depends on these superior products. This boutique-style varietal is widely available abroad. In Southern Dalmatia's Pelješac Peninsula, visitors are welcome at **Vinarija Ivo Skaramucha** (⊠Rijavichno, Kina Peljeshka ☎ 020/742–211) to sample the indigenous plavac mali varietals.

Frano Miloš Winery (⊠ Ponikve 15, Ston ☎ 020/753–098) is north of Dubrovnik. Visitors may have the opportunity to sample obscure small-batch wines of unique geographic origins. Be ready to try such wines as plavac ponikve, nadhanuche, and stagnum. The stagnum here is of a particularly high quality. **Villa Coruna** (⊠ Ston ☎ 020/833–126 or 020/833–146) is a small, country restaurant perched over a bay where you can sample delicious white wines made in small batches from pošip grape by the owner Andres Vuković, who delights in pairing his lovingly crafted wine with oysters freshly plucked from the sea.

On the beautiful lavender-scented island of Hvar you can visit **Plančić Winery** (✉ 21462 Vrbanj Svirče, Stari Grad, Hvar ☎☎ 21/768–030 ⊕ www.plancic.com), where Antun Plančić has been producing a variety of top-quality wines, including rosé and dessert wines, as well as some local rakija since 1919. Look out for *bogdanuša* (dry white wine) or *Ivan Dolac* (A SELECT RED). **The Plenkovic Winery** (✉ Sveta Nedilja, Hvar ☎ 021/745–725), along with its restaurant and hotel, are also well-worth a visit. In fact, in the past few years the *zlatan plavac* (a dry red) made by Zlatan Plenković has continually won prestigious awards at local and international wine fairs. Plenković may soon become the largest single-family producer in Croatia.

Northern Dalmatia Wineries
The vineyards that surround Primošten Bay have been compared to a honeycomb and are an impressive sight to behold. A photograph of the region even hangs in the lobby of the United Nations building in New York. The stone walls, so carefully built by human hands centuries ago, have the UN-administered status of a monument to human effort. The fields of babicć grapes surrounding Primošten Bay were built upon layers of rock—an unlikely success story—but the vines adapted to the karst landscape, their roots going deep into the soil. Since replanting from American rootstock, babić has spread throughout Dalmatia, but the best babić wines are still produced on Primošten, in the town of Šibenik. The **Bibič Winery** (✉ Plastovo ☎ 023/329–260), which operates a wine boutique in Zadar, produces wine both from native Dalmatian varieties, including babić, plavina, lašina, and debit, and non-native grapes, including grenache and shiraz. The winery is just outside of Skradin. **Vinoplod-Vinarija** (✉ Velimira Škorpika 2, Šibenik ☎ 022/333–671 or 022/334–011), the award-winning makers of primoštenski babić, can be contacted for tours and tastings.

Continental Wineries
Jakopič Winery (✉ Železna Gora 92, Orehovčak Štrigova ☎☎ 040/851–300), near the spa town of Sveti Martin in the Varaždin region, is operated by brothers Martin and Branimir Jakopič, who offer superb dining as well as scenic tours of the lush vineyards situated on the borders of Slovenia, Hungary, and Austria. A 20-minute drive northwest of the town of Čakovec brings you close to the Slovenian border in the heart of lush, green vineyard country. Here, at the **Lovreč Winery** (✉ Sveti Urban ☎ 40/830–171) four generations have been cultivating the vines; the winery is known for high-quality, award-winning wines made from chardonnay, sauvignon blanc, pinot gris, Johannesberg riesling, white riesling, and gewürztraminer. Wine-tasting sessions are available in English. If you call ahead, you may also arrange to attend seminars and lectures about vine cultivation.

The Zinquest: Finding Zinfandel in Croatia
Much excitement has been generated in recent years around California's ubiquitous zinfandel grape, whose origin had long been guessed at, but which remained shrouded in mystery. Until recently, that is. In 1998, Professor Carole Meredith of the University of California at Davis, a renowned grapevine geneticist who had previously uncovered the origins of chardonnay, cabernet sauvignon, and petit syrah, began a similar search for zinfandel's origin. The exciting four-year project, which entailed the collection of leaf samples from indigenous varieties of southern Dalmatian, DNA fingerprinting analyses of samples cultivars, and comparisons with zinfandel cuttings from California, shed new light on the origins of the state's most popular grape.

In the spring of 1998, assisted by Jasenka Piljač, a former student at the University of California at Davis, and two Croatian scientists, Ivan Pejić and Edi Maletić, Professor Meredith collected leaf samples from 148 individual plavac mali vines in Southern Dalmatia. Thirty-one samples were collected on the island of Hvar, and 105 from the Peljesac Peninsula. Twelve samples were also taken on the island of Korčula. Although the initial search in 1998 gave no positive matches with zinfandel, the expeditions that followed led the team of scientists to an old vineyard in Kaštel Novi, where a few additional "suspects" were discovered. The DNA analyses performed at Davis confirmed that a wine locally known as crljenak kaštelanski—completely forgotten and virtually eradicated from Dalmatian vineyards—is the long-sought Croatian corollary of zinfandel.

The small vineyard where crljenak kaštelanski was found belongs to a local firefighter, Ivica Radunić, who owns **Radunić Winery** (✉ Narodnog Preporoda 46-Brce, Kaštel Novi ☎ 021/231–138 ✍ ivicaradunic@vip.hr web). His family's winegrowing tradition goes back several generations, and the winery is conveniently located near the Split Airport. Ivica is happy to accommodate visitors.

Jasenka Piljač's book, *Zinfandel: A Croatian-American Wine Story* (⊕ www.crozinfandel.com) chronicles her work as a part of the Meredith Zinquest team and includes in-depth information about Croatia's viticultural past, present, and future. Hers is the only serious book on Croatian viticulture available in English.

— *Marijana Oroz*

SAILING & CRUISING THE CROATIAN COAST

THE CROATIAN ADRIATIC has over 2000 km (1242 mi) of mainland coast, with more than 1000 islands and islets (67 of which are inhabited). Unlike Greece, where the islands are dispersed, the Croatian islands run parallel to and close to the mainland coast, which, for the most part, means easy island-hopping in protected waters.

Besides the picturesque coastal towns, Croatia has three national parks on the sea: Brijuni National Park (a cluster of 14 small green islands just off Istria), Kornati National Park (an archipelago of 89 arid rocky islands, islets, and reefs off North Dalmatia), and Mljet National Park (a large fertile island, one-third of which is covered with coniferous forest, in South Dalmatia). In addition, Krka National Park (a spectacular series of waterfalls in a canyon in Central Dalmatia), can even be approached by sailboat, if you sail up the Šibenik Channel as far as Skradin.

Sailing

Often considered a glamorous and expensive way to travel, a holiday aboard a sailboat is now an affordable alternative to a land-bound vacation. In fact, it is the ultimate way of exploring Croatia's stunningly beautiful mainland coast and islands. No other form of transport gives you such flexibility and such close contact with the sea: Aboard a yacht you can sunbathe on the deck, put down anchor and swim wherever you choose, and discover isolated coves accessible only from the water, some of which have idyllic beaches and informal restaurants serving the very freshest seafood. And, surprisingly, a week aboard a sailing boat can work out cheaper than staying in a mid-range hotel.

If you are already an experienced sailor, you can charter a so-called bareboat yacht, meaning that you rent just the boat and sail independently. By Croatian law, at least one of the crew needs to have an internationally recognized sailing license, plus a radio certificate (available from all Port Authorities).

If you have never sailed before, or have little experience, then you will need a skipper. Generally skippers do more than just guide the boat: most are from the region and, therefore, know the local waters and weather conditions, the history and culture, the protected coves for putting down anchor, the local gastronomic hideouts, and the best diving spots. Most charter companies have their own skippers (who generally speak at least two foreign languages, including English).

The third option is sailing in a flotilla. A flotilla is a group of yachts (typically between 5 and 10), with people of mixed levels of sailing experience, led by a qualified expert. You gain the privacy of your own sailboat but also the security of knowing that help is always close at hand should you need it. Of course, you also get to meet new people.

A typical one-week sailing itinerary in Central Dalmatia could run as follows. Day 1: Set sail from Split to Maslinica on the island of Šolta. Day 2: Maslinica to Vis Town of the island of Vis. Day 3: Sail round the island, from Vis Town to Komiža, calling at Biševo en-route. Day 4: Komiža to Hvar Town on the island of Hvar. Day 5: Hvar Town to Bol on the island of Brač. Day 6: Bol to Milna on the island of Brač. Day 7: Early morning departure from Milna to Split.

The Croatian Adriatic has 50 well-equipped marinas providing 13,500 sea berths and 4,500 dry berths. All berths are equipped with water and power supplies, and most marinas also have at least one restaurant, a grocery store, a nautical-gear store, a repair shop, a gas station, and toilets and showers. Some, but not all, have laundry facilities. The leading nautical-tourism company, Adriatic Croatian International (known as ACI, pronounced "Atsi"), runs 21 marinas. Nineteen Croatian marinas have been awarded the European "Blue Flag" for safety, cleanliness, and respect for the environment. Most marinas stay open all year.

Last but not least, remember that Croatia recently introduced a law declaring zero-alcohol tolerance for those in charge of a boat. If you are caught sailing in a state of inebriation you could face steep fines.

Charter Companies

On the Croatian Adriatic, there are over 140 charter companies operating tens of thousands of boats of all sizes, making this one of the busiest charter areas in Europe. As a rough guide to prices, in summer 2005, Sail Croatia offered a six-berth yacht from €3,050 per week, working out to €508 per person per week, though this price does not include food, fuel, or mooring fees.

The most popular way to research and book charter yachts is via the Internet. Most sites include photos and layout schemes of the boats, lists of onboard equipment, and even sample itineraries. Once you have selected your boat, all you need to do is confirm the availability of the date with the charter company and pay a nonrefundable deposit equal to 30% to 50% of the charter price. The remaining 50% to 70% of the charter fee is usually paid four weeks before the commencement of the charter.

The season runs from May through October, with the best winds for sailing in May and June. Demand and prices peak in July and August, when you can expect calmer sea and less wind, making conditions ideal for motor boats but less fun for true sailors. During peak season, charter rentals generally begin at 5 PM Saturday and end at 9 AM the following Saturday.

Some companies offer extra activities, which can be combined with sailing, such as scuba diving, kayaking, surfing, hiking, mountain biking, or vineyard tours. Another popular option is "sail and stay," which gives you a week aboard a yacht followed by a week in a hotel or villa. There are even special sailing packages for weddings and honeymoons. As tourism is developing rapidly in Croatia, you should check with individual companies to see what the new season has to offer.

International Companies

Most of the international companies are headquartered in the U.K., but there are a couple of worldwide operations that have offices in the U.S. as well.

Activity Yachting (Formerly Activity Holidays: ✑ South View, Boxham La., Sidlesham, West Sussex, U.K. PO20 7QF ☎ [44] 1243/641–304 ⊕ www.activityyachting.com) offers sailing programs that operate along the 161 km (100-mi) stretch of coastline between Split and Zadar. Flotilla holidays (with or without tuition) are available, sharing a five-berth boat. Bareboat rental can also be arranged, or you can take a tailor-made program combining a week's sailing with a week in a villa or hotel.

LateSail (✑ Lombard House, 12–17 Upper Bridge St., Canterbury, West Sussex, U.K. CT1 2NF ☎ [44] 1227/479–900 ⊕ www.latesail.com) acts as a clearing house for the world's leading charter operators and offers a wide range of yachts at cut prices in over 50 destinations, including Croatia.

Nautilus (✑ 56 High St., Edenbridge, Kent, U.K. TN8 5AJ ☎ [44]1732/867–445 ⊕ www.nautilus-yachting.com) keeps yachts, catamarans, and motorboats at bases in Pula, Zadar, Biograd, Murter (close to Kornati National Park), Split, and Dubrovnik. Flotilla sailing is also available.

Neilson (✑ Locksview, Brighton Marina, Brighton, U.K. BN2 5HA ☎ [44] 870/333–3356 ⊕ www.neilson.co.uk) is based in Lumbarda on Korčula. It offers one-week flotilla sailing (generally from Lumbarda to Dubrovnik and back), and a two-week villa-and-flotilla combination, with the first week ashore learning sailing basics, and the second week aboard a boat. It is also possible to combine surfing, cycling, and scuba diving with sailing.

Sail Croatia (𝄐 963 Fulham Rd., London, U.K. SW6 5JJ ☎ [44] 8717/338–686 ⊕ www.sailcroatia.net) offers a fleet of 15 yachts of various sizes up to 56 feet, sleeping between two and 10 people; or you can book one of a couple of larger crewed yachts measuring up to 100 feet with 12 berths. Boats can be chartered on a bareboat basis or with a skipper who will provide guidance and tuition. Itineraries are flexible, but departures are generally from Split. It's also possible to opt for sail-and-stay, including time on land.

Sailing Holidays (𝄐 Mount Pleasant Rd., London, U.K. NW10 3EH ☎ [44] 20/8459–8787 ⊕ www.sailingholidays.com) is a flotilla specialist, offering both informal flotillas and bareboat sailing, or a combination of the two (a couple of days with a flotilla then the rest of the week alone). If you set off from their base in Kremik (Primošten, near Šibenik) you will visit Kornati National Park, and if you start from Tučepi (near Makarska) you will sail down to Dubrovnik.

Sunsail (𝄐 21 Jacques-Grosselin, Carouge, Geneva, Switzerland CH-1227 ☎ [41] 22/827–3040, [44] 2392/222–300 in the U.K., 410/280–2553 or 888/350–3568 in the U.S. ⊕ www.sunsail.com) is one of the world's leading sailing specialists. The company offers both flotilla and bareboat holidays, from bases in Pula, Kornati (near Zadar), Kremik (Primošten, near Šibenik) and Dubrovnik.

The Moorings (𝄐 19345 U.S. 19 N 4, Clearwater, FL 33764-3147 ☎ 888/952–8420 or 727/535–1446 ⊕ www.moorings.com) is an international sailing specialist with bases in Dubrovnik and Trogir in Croatia. The company offers bareboat, skippered, and flotilla sailing in yachts

and catamarans with anything from two to five double-cabins.

Croatian Companies

If you want to simply rent a boat and chose your own skipper, you can contact the **Adriatic Skipper Association** (⊕ www.usj.hr). Expect to pay €100 per day for his or her services, and remember that you are also responsible for the skipper's food. For a full list of charter companies, the **Croatian National Tourist Board** (⊕ www.croatia.hr) publishes a list on its Web site. Go to "Tourism Plus" then "Nautics," where you will find region-by-region listings.

Club Adriatic (☎ [385] 1/466–8220 ⊕ www.charter.hr) is an online charter service with over 1,300 bareboat, crewed, and luxury yachts along the coast. The site is particularly recommended when you are searching for special low-season offers and last-minute discounts.

ACI (𝄐 M. Tita 151, Opatija, Croatia 51410 ☎ [385] 51/271–288 ⊕ www.aci-club.hr) is Croatia's largest marine management company. It runs charters from its bases in Trogir and Vodice (both Central Dalmatia), either bareboat or with a skipper.

Croatia Yacht Charter (𝄐 Trg Hrvatske Bratske Zajednice 8, Split, Croatia 21000 ☎ [385] 21/339–587 ⊕ www.croatia-yacht-charter.com) has 350 sailing boats, motor yachts, luxury mega-yachts, and old-fashioned wooden gullets (sleeping up to 48 people). It is possible to hire bareboat, with a skipper, or in the case of the larger boats, with a full crew including a captain, cook, sailor, and waiter. The company can also organize weddings, honeymoons, and other celebrations aboard. Starting bases are in Poreč, Pula, Krk, Zadar, Sukošan, Biograd, Primošten, Rogoznica, Trogir, Split, and Dubrovnik.

Pivatus (𝄐 Pješčana uvala IV/19, Matina Veruda, Pula, Croatia 52100 ☎ [385] 52/215–155 ⊕ www.pivatus.hr) has bases in Pula, Zadar, and Split, chartering sailing boats and motorboats of various sizes, both bareboat or with a skipper.

Sailing Schools

Adriatic Nautical Academy (ANA; ⊕ www. sailing-ana.hr) is an annual sailing school held at Jezera on the island of Murter (in Central Dalmatia), offering intensive one-week courses (March through October). The school also has a smaller summer base at the Hotel Odisej in Pomena on the island of Mljet (in Southern Dalmatia) through the high season (July to August). In 2005, a one-week course at Jezera cost €540.

Ultra Sailing (⌂ Uvala B aluni, Split, Croatia 21000 ☎ [385] 21/398–980 ⊕ www.ultra-sailing.hr) was founded by several former members of the Croatian Olympic Team, who now work as instructors, offering one-week courses (March through October) in Milna on the island of Brač (in Central Dalmatia). In 2005, a one-week course cost €510 (March to June and September to October) or €600 (July to August).

Cruising

A visitor with limited time in Croatia will find that traveling down the Adriatic aboard a cruiser is an ideal way to see the country's mainland ports and islands. Although it is tempting to try using the Jadrolinija coastal ferry, which runs from Rijeka to Dubrovnik with several stops en route, it's not really an ideal solution. The timetable is complicated and inconsistent, with different arrival and departure times each day, and some days there's no boat at all. At best, the ferry makes a fine way to travel overnight from Rijeka to Split, or through the day from Split to Korčula or Dubrovnik.

Many of the well-known international cruise lines (notably Carnival, Celebrity, Costa, Crystal, Cunard, Holland America, Norwegian, Oceania, Orient Lines, Princess, Seabourn, Silversea, Star Clippers, and Windstar) now include Croatia on their regular Mediterranean itineraries, mainly en route from Venice to the Greek islands.

Croatia is also included in some so-called "Eastern Mediterranean" cruises, which might include Greece, Turkey, and ports in North Africa and the Middle East. The favorite port of call is undoubtedly Dubrovnik, but Korčula Town, Hvar Town, Split, Šibenik, Rab Town, Opatija, Pula, and Rovinj also show up on some itineraries.

An alternative to cruising on a large ship is traveling aboard a medium-sized old-timer. Several Croatian companies now offer informal one-week cruises on beautifully restored wooden gullets, generally taking between 12 to 40 passengers.

Cruise Adriatic (⌂ Uljanik Plovidba, Carrarina 6, Pula, Croatia 52100 ☎ [385] 52/212–955 or 52/211–544 ⊕ www.cruisecroatia.com) runs just one ship, the MS *Dalmacija*, whose main claim to fame is having been used in the film *The Talented Mr. Ripley*. The *Dalmacija* has been carefully renovated to preserve her old-fashioned charm, retaining the teakwood promenade and sun-deck, and details such as brass handrails. Each year from late April to early November, she runs one-week cruises along the Adriatic, departing from Venice (Italy) and visiting Korčula, Dubrovnik, Corfu (Greece), Kotor (Montenegro), Split, and Pula, before returning to Venice. The crew is Croatian, and there are 140 cabins accommodating a total of 300 passengers.

Dubrovnik Travel (⌂ Metohijska 2, Dubrovnik, Croatia 20000 ☎ [385] 20/313–555 ⊕ www.dubrovniktravel.hr) operates eight boats with capacities ranging from 20 to 300 passengers. Its largest boat, the MS *Arion*, runs one-week cruises from Rijeka, calling at Zadar, Split, Dubrovnik, Kotor (Montenegro), Korčula, and Pula. One of the company's most interesting ships is the *Karaka*, a new, three-masted vessel built to the plans of a 15th-century Dubrovnik cargo ship, with room for 215 passengers.

Elite Travel (⌂ Vukovarska 17, Dubrovnik, Croatia 20000 ☎ [385] 20/358–200

⊕ www.elite.hr) offers one-week motor-sail cruises aboard old-timers running Saturday to Saturday. The "Dalmatian Highlights Cruise," for up to 26 passengers, starts and ends in Dubrovnik, visiting the Elafiti, Mljet, Korčula, and Hvar islands. Alternatively, the "Adriatic Paradise Cruise" has a capacity of 40 passengers, beginning and ending in Split, taking in Trogir, Vodice, the scattered islands of Kornati National Park, Zadar, plus an inland excursion to the waterfalls of Krka National Park.

Katarina Line (⊕ Box 87, M Tita 75/I, Opatija, Croatia 51410 ☎ [385] 51/272–110 or 51/272–972 ⊕ www.katarina-line.hr) offers one-week cruises aboard vintage sailing ships from mid-May to mid-October, for groups of between 20 and 38 passengers. Departures are from Opatija and Split (Saturday 1 PM) and Dubrovnik (Sunday 1 PM). Itineraries are variable but include visits to the islands and plenty of time for swimming.

— Jane Foster

CROATIAN VOCABULARY

English	Croatian	Pronunciation

Basics

Yes/no	Da/ne	dah/neh
Please	Molim (vas)	**moh**-leem (vahs)
Thank you (very much)	Hvala (lijepo)	**hvah**-lah (lyeh-poh)
Excuse me	Oprostite	oh-proh-stee-teh
Hello	Zdravo	**zdrah**-voh
I'm sorry.	Žao mi je.	**zhah**-oh mee yeh
Do you speak English?	Da li govorite engleski?	Dah lee **goh**-voh-ree-teh **ehn**-glehs-kee
I don't understand.	Ne razumijem.	neh rah-**zoo**-myehm
Please show me . . .	Molim vas, pokažite mi . . .	moh-leem vahs, **poh**-kah-zhee-teh mee
I am American (m/f).	Ja sam Amerikanac (Amerikanka).	yah sahm **ah**-meh-ree-kah-nahts **ah**-meh-ree-kahn-kah
My name is . . .	Zovem se . . .	**zoh**-vehm seh
Right/left	Desno/Lijevo	**dehs**-noh/**lyeh**-voh
Open/closed	Otvoreno/zatvoreno	**oh**-tvoh-reh-noh/ **zah**-tvoh-reh-noh
Where is . . . ?	Gdje je . . . ?	gdyeh yeh
. . . the train station?	. . . željeznička? stanica/kolodvor	**zheh**-lehz-neech-kah **stah**-neet-sah/**koh**-loh-dvohr
. . . the bus stop?	. . . autobusna stanica?	**ahoo**-toh-boos-nah **stah**-nee-tsah
. . . the airport?	. . . aerodrom?	**ah**-eh-roh-drohm
. . . the post office?	. . . pošta?	**posh**-tah
. . . the bank?	. . . banka?	**bahn**-kah
Here/there	Ovdje/tamo	**ohv**-dyeh/**tah**-moh
I would like. . .	Molim (vas). . . /	**moh**-leem (vahs)/
	Htio/htjela bih. . . (m/f)	hteeoh/htyeh-lah beeh
How much does it cost?	Koliko košta?	**koh**-lee-koh **kosh**-tah
Postcard	Razglednica	**rahz**-gleh-dnee-tsah
Help!	Upomoć!	**oo**-poh-moch

Numbers

One	Jedan	**yeh**-dahn
Two	Dva	dvah

Three	Tri	tree
Four	Četiri	**cheh**-tee-ree
Five	Pet	peht
Six	Šest	shest
Seven	Sedam	**seh**-dahm
Eight	Osam	**oh**-sahm
Nine	Devet	**deh**-veht
Ten	Deset	**deh**-seht
One hundred	Sto	stoh
One thousand	Tisuća	**tee**-soo-chah

Days of the Week

Sunday	Nedjelja	**neh**-dyeh-lyah
Monday	Ponedjeljak	**poh**-neh-dyeh-lyahk
Tuesday	Utorak	**oo**-toh-rahk
Wednesday	Srijeda	**sryeh**-dah
Thursday	Četvrtak	**cheht**-vruh-tahk
Friday	Petak	**peh**-tahk
Saturday	Subota	**soo**-boh-tah

Where to Sleep

A room	Soba	**soh**-bah
The key	Ključ	klyooch
With bath/shower	S kupaonicom/	suh koo-pah-**oh**-nee-tsohm/
	tušem	**too**-shehm

Food

A restaurant	Restoran	rehs-**toh**-rahn
The menu	Jelovnik	yeh-**lohv**-neek
The check, please.	Molim, račun.	**moh**-leem, **rah**-choon
Can I order, please?	Mogu li naručiti, molim vas?	**moh**-goo lee nah-**roo**-chee-tee, moh-leem vahs
Breakfast	Doručak	**doh**-roo-chahk
Lunch	Ručak	**roo**-chahk
Dinner	Večera	**veh**-cheh-rah
Bread	Kruh	krooh
Butter	Putar/maslac	**poo**-tahr/mahs-lahts
Salt/pepper	Sol/papar	sohl/**pah**-pahr

Wine	Vino	**vee**-noh
Beer	Pivo	**pee**-voh
Water/mineral water	Voda/ mineralna voda	**voh**-dah/ **mee**-neh-rahl-nah **voh**-dah
Milk	Mlijeko	**mlyeh**-koh
Coffee	Kava	**kah**-vah
Tea	Čaj	chay

SLOVENIAN VOCABULARY

English	Slovenian	Pronunciation

Basics

English	Slovenian	Pronunciation
Yes/no	Da/ne	dah/nay
Please	Prosim	**proh**-seem
Thank you (very much)	Hvala (lepa)	**hvah**-lah (**lay**-pah)
Excuse me	Oprostite	oh-pros-**tee**-tay
I'm sorry	Žal mi je	zh-**ow** mee yay
Hello/how do you do	Dober dan	**doh**-boo dan
Do you speak English?	Govorite angleško?	goh-vor-**ee**-tay ang-**lay**-shkoh
I don't speak Slovenian.	Ne govorim slovensko.	nay goh-vor-**eem** sloh-**ven**-skoh
I don't understand.	Ne razumem.	nay raz-**oom**-em
Please speak slowly.	Prosim, govorite počasi.	**proh**-seem, goh-vor-ee-tay poh-**chah**-see
Please write it down.	Prosim, napišite.	**proh**-seem, nah-**pee**-shee-tay
Please show me.	Prosim, pokažite.	**proh**-seem, poh-**kah**-zhee-tay
I am American	Jaz sem američan	yoo sum ah-mer-ee-**chan**
I am English	Jaz sem anglež	yoo sum ang-**lezh**
My name is . . .	Ime mi je . . .	ee-**may** mee yay . . .
Right/left	Desno/levo	**des**-noh/ **lee**-voh
Open/closed	Odprt/zaprt	**od**-prt/ **za**-prt
Arrival/departure	Prihod/odhod	pree-**hod**/ od-**hod**
Where is . . . ?	Kje je . . . ?	k-**yay** yay . . . ?
. . . the train station?	. . . železniška postaja?	zheh-**lay**-zneesh-kah post-**ay**-ah
. . . the bus stop?	. . . avtobusna postaja?	aw-toh-**boos**-nah post-**ay**-ah
. . . the airport?	. . . letališče?	let-al-**ee**-shuh-cheh
. . . the post office?	. . . pošta?	**poh**-shtah
. . . the bank?	. . . banka?	**ban**-kah
Stop here	Vstavi tukaj	uh-**stah**-vee **took**-aj
I would like . . .	Hotel bi . . .	hot-**ay**-oo bee . . .
How much does it cost?	Koliko stane?	**koh**-lee-koh **stah**-nay
Letter/postcard	Pismo/dopisnica	**pee**-smoh/doh-**pee**-

		snee-tsah
By airmail	Zračna pošta	**zrah**-chnah **poh**-shtah
Help!	Na pomoč!	nah poh-**moch**

Numbers

One	Ena	enah
Two	Dva	dvah
Three	Tri	tree
Four	Štiri	**shtee**-ree
Five	Pet	pit
Six	Šest	shest
Seven	Sedem	**sed**-em
Eight	Osem	**oh**-sem
Nine	Devet	deh-**vit**
Ten	Deset	deh-**sit**
One hundred	Sto	stoh
Two hundred	Dve sto	dvee stoh

Days of the Week

Monday	Ponedeljek	poh-neh-**dee**-lyek
Tuesday	Torek	**tor**-ek
Wednesday	Sreda	**sree**-dah
Thursday	Četrtek	**chet**-rtek
Friday	Petek	**pee**-tek
Saturday	Sobota	soh-**boh**-tah
Sunday	Nedelja	nay-**dee**-lyah

Where to Sleep

A room	Soba	**soh**-bah
The key	Ključ	kluh-**yooch**
With bath/a shower	s kopanicu/s prho	skoh-pan-**ee**-tsoo/ **spruh**-hoh

Food

Restaurant	Restavracija	rest-aw-**rats**-ee-yah
The menu	Jedilnik	yed-**eel**-nik
The check, please.	Prosim, račun.	**proh**-seem, rach-**oon**
Breakfast	Zajtrk	**zay**-trik
Lunch	Kosilo	kos-**eel**-oh
Dinner	Obed	oh-**bed**

Bread	Kruh	kroo
Butter	Maslo	**mas**-loh
Salt/pepper	Sol/poper	sol/**poh**-per
Bottle	Steklenica	stek-len-**ee**-tsah
Red/white wine	Črno/belo vino	chur-noh/bel-oh **vee**-noh
Beer	Pivo	**pee**-voh
Water/mineral water	Voda/mineralna voda	**voh**-dah/min-er-**al**-nah **voh**-dah
Milk	Mleko	**mlih**-koh
Coffee (with milk)	Kava z mlekom	**kah**-vah **zmlih**-kom
Tea (with lemon)	Čaj z limono	chay zleem-**on**-oh

INDEX

PHOTO CREDITS

NOTES

NOTES

NOTES

NOTES

ABOUT OUR AUTHORS

Although there's no substitute for travel advice from a good friend who knows your style, our contributors are the next best thing—the kind of people you would poll for travel advice if you knew them.

Mark Baker is a journalist and freelance correspondent, based in Prague. He is one of the original editors of the English language weekly newspaper, *The Prague Post,* and a long-time correspondent for Radio Free Europe/Radio Liberty. His assignments have taken him throughout Eastern Europe. Mark was the editor of the first Fodor's guide to the Czech and Slovak Republics published after the 1989 Velvet Revolution, and has been a past contributor to Fodor's guides to Eastern and Central Europe.

John K. Cox is associate professor and chair of history at Wheeling Jesuit University. His other publications include *The History of Serbia* (Greenwood, 2002) and *Slovenia: Evolving Loyalties* (Routledge, 2005). He specializes in 20th-century Balkan intellectual history and is currently writing a study of the works of Ismail Kadare.

Jane Foster is a freelance writer who hails from the Yorkshire Dales in the U.K. She studied for a degree in architecture before moving to Rome in 1990, where travel, art, and culture became her main interests. In 1996, she made a brief visit to Croatia and was immediately capitvated by the countries of the former Yugoslavia. She lived in Split for six years, where she learned to speak Croatian and cook Dalmatian-style, and also fell prey to the pleasures of sailing and nudism. Although she is now based in Athens, she makes frequent trips back to Croatia for both work and pleasure.

Tim Gosling pole-vaulted over the English Channel and sprinted to Central Europe in 1997. He's written guidebooks to Prague, Albania, Croatia, and Slovakia. He currently works as a freelance journalist and editor in Prague. A keen amateur sportsman—when his aging knees allow— he fantasizes about world championship medals from his Letná home.

Betsy Maury, a former senior editor at Bantam, Doubleday, Dell, lived in Slovenia for four years, traveling widely in that country and in neighboring Croatia. Since 1999, she has made her home in Budapest. Her enthusiasm for Hungarian cuisine—as well as a love of Hungarian wine—keeps her busy exploring the cosmopolitan city in search of interesting restaurants, and her love of wine has brought her to Croatia on several occasions. She travels widely throughout Central Europe, working as a freelance writer.

A contributor to previous Fodor's guides to Eastern & Central Europe and Budapest, **Paul Olchváry** lived in Hungary from 1990 to 2000 and has thoroughly explored not only that country but also neighboring Croatia over the years. Translator of nine books from the Hungarian and a writer of short stories and novels, he was a copywriter at Princeton University Press from 2000 to 2005, when he absconded with his wife Dorottya to a cabin in the woods of Kismaros, Hungary, to pursue his own writing.

Marijana Oroz graduated with a degree in English from the Ohio State University and still contributes to *Columbus Alive,* a major weekly publication in the area. Her parents hail from Croatia, and her visits to the country and exposure to her sister's wine-importing business have familiarized her with the beauty of the Croatian landscape and its viticultural treasures. Because of her family's roots, Croatian wine is as close to her heart as it is to her palate.